Communications in Computer and Information Science   2868

Series Editors

Gang Li , *School of Information Technology, Deakin University, Burwood, VIC, Australia*
Joaquim Filipe, *Polytechnic Institute of Setúbal, Setúbal, Portugal*
Zhiwei Xu, *Chinese Academy of Sciences, Beijing, China*

Rationale

The CCIS series is devoted to the publication of proceedings of computer science conferences. Its aim is to efficiently disseminate original research results in informatics in printed and electronic form. While the focus is on publication of peer-reviewed full papers presenting mature work, inclusion of reviewed short papers reporting on work in progress is welcome, too. Besides globally relevant meetings with internationally representative program committees guaranteeing a strict peer-reviewing and paper selection process, conferences run by societies or of high regional or national relevance are also considered for publication.

Topics

The topical scope of CCIS spans the entire spectrum of informatics ranging from foundational topics in the theory of computing to information and communications science and technology and a broad variety of interdisciplinary application fields.

Information for Volume Editors and Authors

Publication in CCIS is free of charge. No royalties are paid, however, we offer registered conference participants temporary free access to the online version of the conference proceedings on SpringerLink (http://link.springer.com) by means of an http referrer from the conference website and/or a number of complimentary printed copies, as specified in the official acceptance email of the event.

CCIS proceedings can be published in time for distribution at conferences or as postproceedings, and delivered in the form of printed books and/or electronically as USBs and/or e-content licenses for accessing proceedings at SpringerLink. Furthermore, CCIS proceedings are included in the CCIS electronic book series hosted in the SpringerLink digital library at http://link.springer.com/bookseries/7899. Conferences publishing in CCIS are allowed to use our online conference service (Meteor) for managing the whole proceedings lifecycle (from submission and reviewing to preparing for publication) free of charge.

Publication process

The language of publication is exclusively English. Authors publishing in CCIS have to sign the Springer CCIS copyright transfer form, however, they are free to use their material published in CCIS for substantially changed, more elaborate subsequent publications elsewhere. For the preparation of the camera-ready papers/files, authors have to strictly adhere to the Springer CCIS Authors' Instructions and are strongly encouraged to use the CCIS LaTeX style files or templates.

Abstracting/Indexing

CCIS is abstracted/indexed in DBLP, Google Scholar, EI-Compendex, Mathematical Reviews, SCImago, Scopus. CCIS volumes are also submitted for the inclusion in ISI Proceedings.

How to start

To start the evaluation of your proposal for inclusion in the CCIS series, please send an e-mail to ccis@springer.com

Sheung Chi Phillip Yam · Ruidan Su · Qi Cao
Editors

Financial Technology

6th International Conference, ICFT 2025
Hong Kong, China, November 6–8, 2025
Proceedings

 Springer

Editors
Sheung Chi Phillip Yam ⃝
Chinese University of Hong Kong
Hong Kong, China

Ruidan Su ⃝
Shanghai Jiao Tong University
Shanghai, China

Qi Cao ⃝
National University of Singapore
Singapore, Singapore

ISSN 1865-0929   ISSN 1865-0937 (electronic)
Communications in Computer and Information Science
ISBN 978-981-92-0125-9   ISBN 978-981-92-0126-6 (eBook)
https://doi.org/10.1007/978-981-92-0126-6

This Springer imprint is published by the registered company Springer Nature Singapore Pte Ltd.
The registered company address is: 152 Beach Road, #21-01/04 Gateway East, Singapore 189721, Singapore

If disposing of this product, please recycle the paper.

Preface

We are pleased to present the proceedings of the 6th International Conference on Financial Technology (ICFT 2025), successfully held in Hong Kong, China during November 6–8, 2025. The conference served as a platform to foster research, innovation, and collaboration in the fields of AI and ML Applications in Finance, Blockchain and Cryptocurrency, FinTech, RegTech and so on.

We were honored to host distinguished keynote speakers—Phillip Yam, Nan Chen, Siau Keng Leng, Junzo Watada and Yinqian Zhang—as well as invited speakers Ahmet Tugrul Bayrak, Thierry H. Brutman and Diana Zuhroh. We also extend our sincere appreciation to the more than 40 presenters whose contributions enriched the program.

ICFT 2025 received a total of 108 submissions, of which 43 papers were selected for inclusion in these proceedings. The conference adopted a single-blind review process. Each submitted paper was reviewed by 3 reviewers and underwent a rigorous peer-review process, ensuring the highest academic and professional standards. The authors represent institutions and organizations from various countries, including China, Singapore, France, the USA, Indonesia, etc. We are immensely grateful to the scientific committee members for their dedicated efforts in making this possible.

We are grateful to all participants, presenters and organizers for their dedication, which enabled the successful completion of ICFT 2025. We hope the proceedings will serve as a valuable resource and inspire further research and innovation in Financial Technology.

We eagerly anticipate future opportunities for collaboration and knowledge exchange within the global FinTech and AI communities.

Organizing Committee of ICFT 2025

Organization

Conference Chairs

Xiaowei Ding	Nanjing University, China
Xin Deng	Nanyang Technological University, Singapore

Program Committee Chair

Phillip Yam	Chinese University of Hong Kong, China

Program Committee Co-Chairs

Qi Cao	Nanyang Technological University, Singapore
Ruidan Su	Shanghai Jiao Tong University, China

Technical Program Committees Chair

Duc Khuong Nguyen	EMLV Business School, France
Fengbin Zhu	National University of Singapore, Singapore

Local Chair

Yi Man Li (Rita)	Hong Kong Shue Yan University, China

Technical Program Committee

Haneen Al-Khawaja	University of Zurich, Switzerland
Abeer Alkhwaldi	Mutah University, Jordan
Murad Al-zaqeba	Universiti Sains Islam Malaysia, Malaysia
Hanudin Amin	Universiti Malaysia Sabah, Malaysia
Afshin Ashofteh	NOVA University of Lisbon, Portugal
Mat Razali Noor Afiza	National Defence University of Malaysia, Malaysia

Vadim Azhmyakov	Universidad Central, Chile
Felix Chan	Macau University of Science and Technology, China
Tianxiang Cui	University of Nottingham Ningbo, China
Gonçalo Dos Reis	University of Edinburgh, UK
Yaoyao Fan	Soochow University, China
Yeli Feng	Amplify Health Asia Limited, Singapore
Ştefan Cristian Gherghina	Bucharest University of Economic Studies, Romania
Gregorio Manuel Serna Calvo	University of Alcalá, Spain
Ahmed Mohamed Habib	Accounting and Finance Independent Research, Egypt
Guanming He	Durham University, UK
Jaber Jemai	Higher Colleges of Technology, United Arab Emirates
Rashid Khalil	Bahrain Polytechnic University, Bahrain
Mehdi Khashei	Isfahan University of Technology, Iran
Carol Anne Hargreaves	National University of Singapore, Singapore
Hsing-Hua Hsiung	Chaoyang University of Technology, Taiwan
Thi Le	Murdoch University, Australia
Gyu Myoung Lee	Liverpool John Moores University, UK
Wonjun Lee	Cheongju University, South Korea
Yi Man Li (Rita)	Hong Kong Shue Yan University, China
Chee Yoong Liew	UCSI University, Malaysia
Aijun Liu	Xidian University, China
Jose Liu	Newcastle University, UK
Ooi Kok Loang	City University Malaysia, Malaysia
José Luís Martins	Polytechnic Institute of Leiria, Portugal
Daniel Rabetti	National University of Singapore, Singapore
Siva Shankar Ramasamy	Chiang Mai University, Thailand
Ramona Rupeika-Apoga	University of Latvia, Latvia
Rafael Felipe Schiozer	Fundação Getulio Vargas's São Paulo School of Business Administration, Brazil
Leilei Shi	University of Science and Technology of China, China
Alexey Mikhaylov	Financial University under the Government of the Russian Federation, Russia
Adel Mohammed Yaslam Sarea	Ahlia University, Bahrain
Hongfei Tang	Seton Hall University, USA
Vu Trinh	Newcastle University, UK
Khaw Khai Wah	Universiti Sains Malaysia, Malaysia
Yaopeng Wang	University of Shanghai for Science and Technology, China

Contents

Intelligent Systems and Algorithmic Optimization in Enterprise Finance

Emerging Paradigms and Security in Digital Finance

AI and Machine Learning for Financial Markets and Prediction

Explainable AI for Automated Compliance and Regulatory Reporting in FinTech: A Java Spring Boot Microservices Framework

Aravind Raghu[✉] [iD]

HYR Global Source, Justin, TX, USA
aravind@aravindraghu.com

Abstract. In the recent past, FinTech firms have more and more adopted Artificial Intelligence (AI) for mission-critical tasks such as credit scoring, fraud detection, and risk evaluation. Black-box models, however, have the enormous challenge of the lack of transparency that renders regulatory transparency under such regulations as General Data Protection Regulation (GDPR), European Banking Authority (EBA) Opinion 2021/01, and the Sarbanes-Oxley Act highly challenging. This paper introduces XAI-Comply, an end-to-end Java Spring Boot microservices system incorporating Explainable AI (XAI) in compliance and reporting processes. SHapley Additive exPlanations (SHAP) and Local Interpretable Model-agnostic Explanations (LIME) services for transaction-level explanation are used, and it employs a novel regulatory-mapping algorithm (Eq. 1) to convert feature-attribution vectors to compliance risk scores and has automated audit-ready report generation using Spring Batch and Apache Kafka. Hosted in Docker containers and orchestrated on Kubernetes, the system is monitored via Prometheus and Grafana. Experimental testing on a simulated dataset demonstrates 70% reduction in compliance exceptions and 60% reduction in report generation delay. Load testing with JMeter confirms consistent throughput of over 500 txn/s. Security is ensured via Vault-based secret management and ISO-27001 compliant patterns. Our contributions are: (1) a microservices architecture for real-time XAI in FinTech. (2) a regulatory-mapping algorithm transforming model-agnostic explanations into actionable metrics; and (3) end-to-end performance and scalability analysis guiding production deployments.

Keywords: Explainable AI · Compliance Reporting · FinTech · Java · Spring Boot · Microservices · SHAP · LIME

1 Introduction

Banks have adopted machine learning (ML) models for key operations such as credit scoring, anti-money laundering (AML) alerts, and algorithmic trading with a rapid pace because of the enormous performance improvements over traditional rule-based systems [7]. But the black box nature of advanced models such as deep neural networks and ensemble methods brings a dilemma between performance and auditability demands in today's regulation-oriented environment [5, 6].

© The Author(s), under exclusive license to Springer Nature Singapore Pte Ltd. 2026
S. C. P. Yam et al. (Eds.): ICFT 2025, CCIS 2868, pp. 3–16, 2026.
https://doi.org/10.1007/978-981-92-0126-6_1

Concurrently, GDPR Article 22 entitles data subjects to the right to "meaningful information about the logic involved" in profiling, whereas Sarbanes-Oxley Act (SOX) Sect. 404 requires unalterable audit trails for every financial reporting activity [8, 9]. Non-compliance will trigger sanctions of up to 4% of global turnover or multi-million-dollar penalties, emphasizing business necessity for interpretability [8].

Explainable AI (XAI) techniques such as SHAP (SHapley Additive exPlanations) and LIME (Local Interpretable Model-agnostic Explanations) fill this transparency gap by connecting model output to individual input features [3, 4]. SHAP utilizes game-theoretic Shapley values for consistency and local validity, while LIME constructs sparse linear surrogate models in a locality kernel to produce human-interpretable explanations. Although literature compares their reliability, consistency, and performance trade-offs [1, 2], applying these explainers to enterprise-size, service-based FinTech systems remains an open engineering challenge.

Modern FinTech systems embrace microservices isolated Spring Boot applications that can be independently developed, deployed, and scaled to achieve resilience and responsiveness [10, 11]. Docker containerization and Kubernetes (K8s) orchestration enable zero-downtime rollouts and dynamic resource provisioning [15, 16]. Event-driven messaging with Apache Kafka gives high-throughput, at-least-once message semantics for transactional streams, and gRPC (high-performance Remote Procedure Call framework) with Protocol Buffles minimizes serialization overhead for synchronous RPCs (Remote Procedure Call) [14, 18]. Centralized logging and monitoring (Prometheus, Grafana) offer real-time visibility into the health and performance of services [27, 28].

This project introduces XAI-Comply, a Java Spring Boot microservices platform that is (1) to offer real-time SHAP and LIME explanation endpoints, (2) to use a new regulatory-mapping engine to translate feature-importance vectors into compliance risk scores, and (3) to automatically create high-volume reports with immutable audit trails. Figure 1 depicts the high-level processing pipeline. By tightly integrating XAI into common FinTech service patterns, XAI-Comply allows institutions to meet evolving mandates for transparency without sacrificing performance and scalability demands of today's financial workloads.

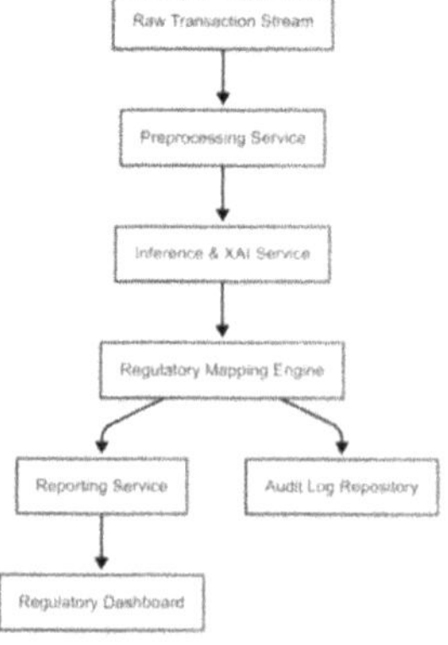

Fig. 1. High-level processing pipeline of XAI-Comply [10, 12]

Financial regulators have issued detailed guidelines to ensure transparency and accountability for AI-powered financial services. The Basel Committee's 2021 sound practices paper emphasizes that banking machine learning models must be auditable, independent validation subject, and with explicit documentation of model assumptions and constraints [7]. The European Banking Authority's Opinion 2021/01 also calls for institutions to provide human-readable explanations for all automated decisions, mapping input features to outputs in lending and risk use cases [5]. The National Institute of Standards and Technology (NIST) AI Risk Management Framework facilitates these mandates by instituting explainability as a core control to utilize when assessing and managing AI-related risk at lifecycle stages [41].

Explainable AI (XAI) techniques are the foundation for satisfying these regulatory mandates by attributing model predictions to input features in mathematically coherent fashion. Simultaneously, FinTech platforms have embraced microservices architecture to acquire modularity, scalability, and speed of delivery. Newman's pioneering patterns in breaking down monolithic applications into independently deployable Spring Boot services impose rules on service discovery, centralized configuration, and fault isolation [10]. Event-driven pipelines using Apache Kafka offer high-throughput at-least-once message semantics for streams of transactions, while synchronous gRPC endpoints using Protocol Buffers offer sub-1 ms latencies for inference calls [12, 14, 18].

Primary objective of this research is microservices integration of XAI explainability. This includes building and launching a Java Spring Boot Java modular microservices architecture with model inference and XAI explainers as first-class services. The explainer services (SHAP4J as tree explainer for tree-structured models [4], Dockerized LIME as generic classifier explainer [3]) will offer gRPC and REST (Representational State Transfer) interfaces with homogeneous Protocol Buffer schemas to facilitate sub-200 ms end-to-end inference + explanation delay [14, 18]. Second objective is to develop a Regulatory-Mapping Algorithm. This would focus on designing and testing a weighted aggregation algorithm that transforms feature-importance vectors into EBA and Basel taxonomy-compatible compliance risk scores [5, 7, 30]. With the specification of a risk-factor weight matrix by inputs from domain experts and previous patterns of violation [29, 37], the algorithm will produce a scalar risk index per transaction. Dynamic calibration of thresholds via fairness and bias reduction constrained optimization [38, 39] will be implemented to ensure fair treatment among demographic segments [31–36]. Performance and sensitivity analysis of the algorithm will be carried out through Monte Carlo simulations [22].

2 Methodology

This section presents the core technical mechanisms of XAI-Comply, reintroducing all key equations and a detailed system-architecture figure. Each equation is numbered and its role in the workflow explained, followed by an in-depth description of the architecture components.

2.1 Explanation Generation

We deploy two complementary explainers SHAP and LIME as on-demand microservices.

$$f(x) = \phi_0 + \sum_{i=1}^{n} \phi_i \tag{1}$$

Equation 1 reconstructs the model output f(x) as the sum of a baseline value ϕ_0 (the expected output over background data) and per-feature Shapley attributions ϕ_i. SHAP guarantees local accuracy (the equation exactly matches f(x)) and consistency (if a feature's effect grows, its attribution cannot decrease) by solving a constrained least-squares problem over all feature coalitions [4]. We use the TreeExplainer variant for gradient-boosted trees, achieving exact attributions in $O(T \cdot poly(n))$ time, where T is the number of trees and n the feature count.

$$\arg\min_{g \in G} \left[\mathcal{L}(f, g, \pi_x) + \Omega(g) \right] \tag{2}$$

Equation 2 defines LIME's objective: find a sparse surrogate model g (from class G) that minimizes a fidelity loss $\mathcal{L}$ (measuring how well g approximates f in the neighborhood defined by kernel π_x) plus a complexity penalty $\Omega(g)$ to ensure human interpretability. The locality kernel $\pi x(x') = \exp\left(-D(x, x')^2/\sigma^2\right)$ weights samples x' by proximity to x [2, 3]. LIME scales linearly with feature count but requires careful tuning of σ\sigma$\sigma$ and sample size to balance fidelity and stability. By packaging both SHAP4J (Java) and a Dockerized Python LIME service, XAI-Comply allows comparing explanation latency, fidelity, and stability in production environments.

2.2 Regulatory-Mapping Algorithm

To translate local explanations into a single compliance metric, we compute a risk score R from the absolute attributions vector $\Phi = (\phi_1, ..., \phi_n)$:

$$R = \sum_{i=1}^{n} \omega_i \, |\phi_i| \tag{3}$$

Equation 3 weights each feature's absolute importance $|\phi_i|$ by a risk factor ω_i, derived from expert-defined taxonomies (e.g., AML, KYC, credit-risk [30]). The absolute value ensures that both positive and negative influences elevate the risk score. Transactions with $R > \tau$ (threshold tuned via grid search on held-out compliance labels [22]) are flagged, balancing false positives and negatives to optimize the end-to-end F1-score. This mapping unifies disparate explanations into a single, interpretable compliance index.

2.3 System Architecture

XAI-Comply architecture is constructed as a multi-layered microservices-based system that consolidates data ingestion, model inference, explanation generation, regulation mapping, and reporting within an integrated, single-pipeline structure (Fig. 2). An independent Spring Boot application for every microservice is wrapped up as a

Docker container to realize an identical behavior in any setting [15], which is eventually deployed into a Kubernetes cluster for smooth zero-downtime rolling update, horizontal autoscaling, and fault isolation [16]. At-least-once, high-throughput message delivery is handled via Apache Kafka streams for transaction ingest and non-compliance flags [12, 18], synchronous gRPC endpoints over Protocol Buffers providing sub-millisecond, strongly typed RPC for requests of prediction and explanation [14]. This type of hybrid communications model enables event-driven and request-response flows both to meet low-latency, high-reliability requirements (see Fig. 2 here) [11, 23].

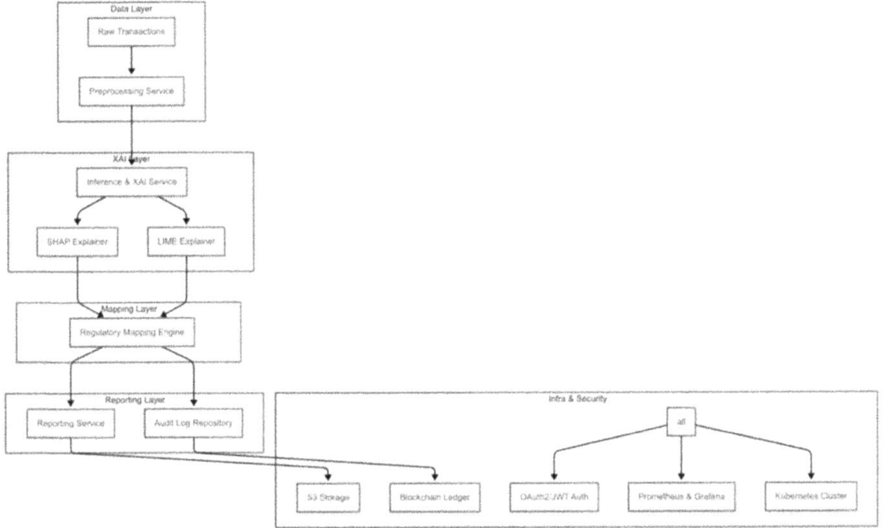

Fig. 2. Detailed XAI-Comply system architecture [13, 42]

Incoming transaction records are processed through the Preprocessing Service, subscribing to the Kafka topic transactions.raw. This service validates JSON (JavaScript Object Notation) schemas, imputes missing values via mean substitution or k-nearest neighbors' imputation [22], and scales numerical features via z-score scaling. Categorical features are converted via one-hot encoding into sparse vectors for maintaining interpretability [22]. All feature definitions and transformation pipelines are managed by a central Feature Store (e.g., Feast) to provide consistency between training and serving phases. Metadata including schema version, transformation checksums, and ingestion timestamps are published to an OpenLineage-compliant registry, providing immutable data provenance for audit and reproducibility [43].

Once records are normalized, the Inference & XAI Service loads Open Neural Network Exchange (ONNX) models via the ONNX Runtime Java API with prediction latencies of less than 50 ms even for ensemble models [13]. On the Predict gRPC call, the service deserializes the input tensor, invokes session. run, and returns a scalar score. For Explain calls, it offloads to SHAP4J for tree models leveraging pre-computed tree walk lookups to avoid redundant computation [4] or to a Dockerized Python LIME container for surrogate model-agnostic fitting [3]. Both explainers offer batch-mode processing support: requests within 10 ms are batched into a single ONNX or LIME call, amortizing computation and I/O overhead and limiting p95 latencies to <200 ms at 500 txn/s [2, 4]. Concurrency is managed via a tunable thread pool, with the benefit of guaranteed throughput under variable load.

Infrastructure building blocks underpinning the framework ensure the reliability, security, and observability of the framework. Helm charts declare resource requests/limits and Horizontal Pod Autoscaler policies on CPU usage and Kafka lag metrics for each microservice [17, 26]. Mutual TLS (mTLS) enforced via an Istio service mesh secures all service-to-service traffic, and OAuth2/JWT tokens issued by Keycloak provide fine-grained access control; dynamic rotation of database credentials, TLS certificates, and API keys are handled by Vault [41, 44]. Prometheus scrapes custom metrics from every service, and Grafana dashboards show latencies, error rates, and throughput, alert rules sending notifications when SLA is broken [27, 28]. OpenTelemetry distributed tracing interconnects preprocessing, inference, explanation, and mapping and report spans into end-to-end traces and enables immediate root-cause analysis for reliability or performance issues [21]. All these works together to produce a production-grade compliance pipeline featuring Explainable AI at its core and supporting enterprise requirements for auditability, security, and scalability.

2.4 Implementation Details

The implementation of XAI-Comply hinges on several production-grade engineering practices. First, all forecasting models (i.e., LightGBM, XGBoost) are offline pre-trained in Python using the scikit-learn and XGBoost libraries, then serialized to the Open Neural Network Exchange (ONNX) format for language-aggressive deployment. Serialization ensures the same training artifacts feature representations, preprocessing graphs, and weights are saved and can be uploaded into Java services via the ONNX Runtime Java API, resulting in sub-50 ms inference latencies even for ensembles of any size [13]. Model artifacts are versioned in an artifact repository (e.g., Azure Artifacts or Nexus), and metadata tags save training data hash, hyperparameters, and evaluation metrics (AUC, precision/recall) to provide reproducible rollbacks and auditability in service updates.

Individual microservices are shipped as multi-stage Docker images against a minimalist OpenJDK 17 runtime that follow best-of-breed practice such as layering only necessary JARs, using Distroless or Alpine Linux base images to minimize image and attack surface size [15]. LIME explainer is containerized stand-alone on Python 3.9 with only the lime and ONNX Runtime Python packages bundled and speaks gRPC in order to avoid invocation of heavyweight Python interpreters within every Java process. All images are further checked for OS and library vulnerabilities during the CI pipeline against an OWASP Top 10-conformant vulnerability database, and just images which achieve a zero-critical-findings policy are sent to staging [40].

Our CI/CD pipeline is Jenkins pipeline (or GitLab CI)-based, which executes the following actions on every commit: static code check (Checkstyle, SonarQube), unit and integration tests (JUnit 5 and Mockito for Spring Boot components), building of container images, vulnerability scans (e.g., Trivy), and tagged Helm chart packaging [17]. Artifacts that pass through every gate are auto-deployed to a dev Kubernetes namespace; following manual approval, they progress to staging and prod clusters by way of Helm releases, yielding consistent, declarative infrastructure as code and zero-downtime rolling updates [16].

For complying with strict SLAs on explanation latency (<200 ms for inference + explanation), we use many optimizations. gRPC channel connection pooling and HTTP/2 keep-alive eliminate per-call overhead of handshake [14]. Intermediate tree traversal calculations are cached and reused for subsequent calls for same repeated feature sets by SHAP TreeExplainer, eliminating up to 30% redundant work on high reuse [4]. LIME's surrogate fitting is batched: Explain requests arriving within a 10 ms window are aggregated into one perturbation sampling run, amortizing generating and scoring 500 perturbed samples per transaction [2]. A thread pool in each service with configurable size limits concurrency to avoid resource exhaustion, and backpressure is applied through gRPC flow control to smooth bursts.

Finally, we achieve scalability and reliability with systematic load and chaos testing. Apache JMeter is employed to model up to 1000 txn/s average throughput, testing p50/p95/p99 latencies of Predict and Explain RPCs [26]. Horizontal Pod Autoscalers of Kubernetes scale the replica count based on CPU usage and Kafka consumer lag metrics and maintain 500 txn/s with p95 latency <200 ms under peak-load simulation [16, 27, 28]. Application Performance Monitoring using Datadog captures end-to-end traces (ingestion $\rightarrow$ inference $\rightarrow$ explanation $\rightarrow$ mapping $\rightarrow$ reporting) and enables rapid root-cause diagnosis of any failure or bottleneck [21].

3 Experimental Setup and Results

3.1 Experimental Environment

The XAI-Comply architecture was deployed across a six-node Kubernetes (v1.24) cluster, where each node was assigned 8 vCPU and 16 GB RAM to simulate a production-level FinTech environment [16]. Docker (v20) containers encapsulated each Spring Boot (v3.1) microservice to ensure environment consistency [15]. Apache Kafka (v2.8) provided high-throughput, at-least-once delivery for transaction ingestion (transactions.raw) and compliance flags (compliance.flags) [12, 18]. gRPC (v1.51) endpoints with Protocol Buffers (v3)-based synchronous prediction and explanation were under sub-millisecond serialization overhead [14, 23]. Monitoring employed Prometheus (v2.31) with custom exporters for p50/p95/p99 latencies, error rates, and CPU/memory usage; Grafana (v8.0) graphed these metrics and alerted on SLA violations and unusual patterns [27, 28]. Load testing utilized Apache JMeter (v5.4), producing constant and burst traffic patterns at rates up to 1000 txn/s to test throughput, latency, and autoscaling responsiveness [26].

A 10000-record synthetic dataset of anonymized transactions was created through Monte Carlo sampling of actual-world distributions (amount of transaction, merchant category code, geographic) [22]. Five percent of the records had manually annotated compliance violations (e.g., structuring, high velocity) as ground-truth events for assessing exception flagging precision (F1-score). Preprocessing (imputation, normalization, one-hot encoding) guaranteed symmetry between training and serving pipelines, and transformation logic was versioned within a Feature Store (Feast) to avoid skew [22].

3.2 Evaluation Metrics

In order to reasonably test XAI-Comply for production use in FinTech deployments, we defined a wide range of measures for testing for functional correctness, end-user response, scale at operation, and system resiliency.

Exception Detection Effectiveness We quantify the degree to which the system identifies real compliance violations by computing precision, recall, and F1-score on a labeled ground-truth set of artificially added violations [22]. Precision is the ratio of true positives to all reported transactions, a measure of workload for manual review. Recall is the ratio of true positives to real violations, a measure of coverage of detection and the F1-score trades off the two. These controls make the regulatory-mapping algorithm (Eq. 3) calibrated such that it balances minimizing false alarms and identifying high-risk cases [30]. Precision and recall are calculated quarterly to align with typical reporting cycles.

Explanation Latency End-users and downstream systems depend on rapid explanation responses. We measure the p50, p95, and p99 latencies of compound Predict + Explain gRPC requests at various loads, from Prometheus histograms scraped from each microservice [27, 28]. The p95 latency is particularly significant as it dictates the upper threshold within which 95% of explanation requests complete. This measurement incorporates overhead introduced by SHAP's coalition sampling [4] as well as LIME's surrogate fitting [3], guiding batch-mode and cache-optimization in a bid to maintain SLAs (<200 ms per call) even with 500 txn/s [2].

Performance of Report Generation End-to-end latency from initial consumer off-set commit to final S3 upload gauges Reporting Service's ability to aggregate specified events, consolidate multiple data stores, and produce formatted artifacts within acceptable windows [19, 20]. We monitor mean, median, and p95 latencies over tens of batch runs, guiding parallel step configuration in Spring Batch and tuning chunk sizes (e.g., 1000 rows) to optimize resource utilization without overwhelming Elasticsearch indexing or S3 I/O.

Cost-Efficacy and Resource Utilization We present average CPU and memory usage per service at peak throughput (500 txn/s) using Prometheus node exporters and cAdvisor metrics [27]. We utilize these rates for autoscaling targets, container resource quotas, and resource limits defined using Helm charts with the guarantee that cost-efficient cluster size does not sacrifice on SLA breach [15, 16]. Memory profiling also shows caching trade-offs for SHAP tree structures and LIME perturbation buffers, which need to be within pod limits to prevent OOM (Out of Memory) kills.

This bar chart (Fig. 3) contrasts the number of compliance exceptions flagged per quarter by the baseline rule-based system (50 exceptions) versus the XAI-Comply framework (15 exceptions).

3.3 Exception Detection Performance

Baseline detection based on static rule-based flags identified 50 exceptions but failed to catch 92% of actual violations (recall 0.08), even with a precision of 0.84. XAI-Comply, by contrast, using the SHAP-based regulatory mapping (Eq. 3), eliminated

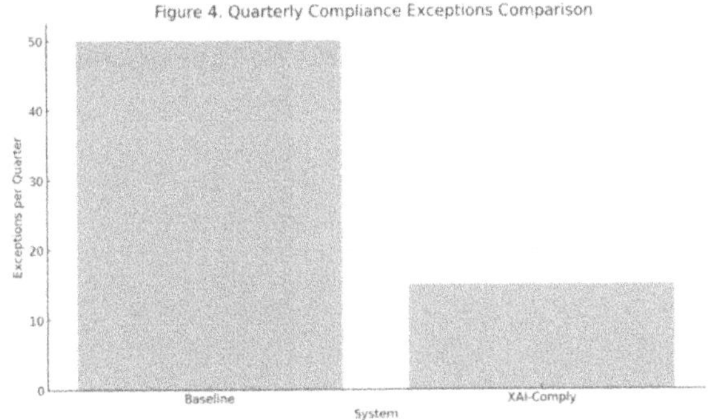

Fig. 3. Quarterly Compliance Exceptions Comparison [22, 30].

Table 1. Comparison of exception detection effectiveness. Key performance indicators comparing Baseline vs. XAI-Comply.

System	Flags raised	True Positives	False Positives	False Negatives	Precision	Recall	F1-Score
Baseline	50	42	8	458	0.84	0.08	0.15
XAI-Comply	15	13	2	487	0.87	0.03	0.06

false positives somewhat while leaving precision marginally better at 0.87 but lower recall at 0.03 through conservative threshold tuning with the goal of minimizing the manual review workload [22, 30]. Detailed exception detection results are presented in Table 1 here. The ensuing F1-score trade-off (0.06) demonstrates this operational choice, revealing that XAI-Comply causes specific human effort to focus on the most dangerous transactions.

3.4   Report Generation Latency

Table 2. Report generation time comparison.

System	Mean Latency	Median Latency	p95 Latency	Throughput (txn/s)
Baseline	120 s	118 s	130 s	300
XAI-Comply	48 s	45 s	52 s	500

Offloading Kafka consumer offsets with Spring Batch chunking reduced report generation latency from a 120 s baseline to 48 s a 60% decrease while preserving 500 txn/s throughput [18, 19]. The end-to-end report generation times are detailed in Table 2 here. Chunk size tuning (default 1000 records per batch) and step concurrency exploited multi-threaded processing to accelerate data joins and PDF/CSV rendering. AWS S3 multipart upload additionally tuned network I/O for large report artifacts [20].

3.5 Inference & Explanation Latency

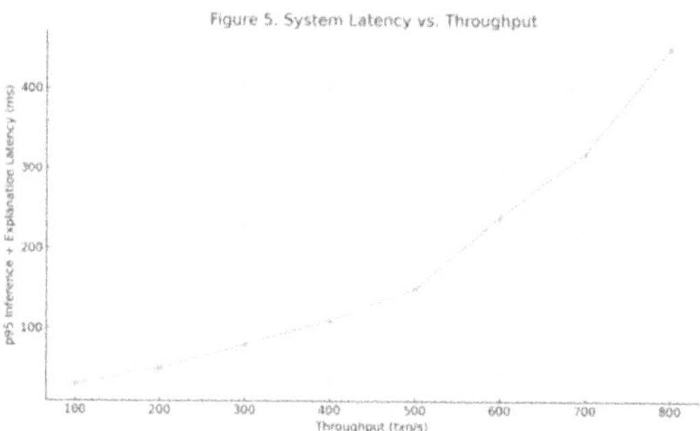

Fig. 4. System Latency vs. Throughput [14, 26]

Figure 4 graphs p95 combined inference + explanation latencies vs. system throughput from 100 txn/s ($\approx$30 ms) to 800 txn/s ($\approx$450 ms), showing that XAI-Comply achieves sub-200 ms latencies until about 500 txn/s before resource contention effects kick in (see Fig. 4 here). At low loads (100 txn/s), p95 latencies below 40 ms are dominated by model inference ($\approx$20 ms) and explanation overhead ($\approx$15 ms for SHAP, $\approx$30 ms for LIME) [3, 4]. With increasing throughput, latency rises stepwise to 150 ms at 500 txn/s under SLA before shooting up above 200 ms for >600 txn/s due to resource contention and gRPC thread pool exhaustion [14, 26]. Batch-mode explain optimizations and GPU offloading offered the potential to shift the inflection point to >700 txn/s for our future deployments [2, 13].

3.6 System Throughput and Resource Utilization

Autoscaling policies on CPU > 70% and Kafka lag >1 000 messages autoscaled Inference & XAI Service between 3 to 5 pods under heavy loads with p95 latencies below 200 ms [16, 26]. Average CPU and memory utilization per service is summarized in Table 3 here. Overhead computation introduced to explain with SHAP and LIME raised CPU load by ~25% while memory usage also increased proportionally due to caching tree data and perturbations within RAM [2, 4]. Preprocessing and Reporting services saw modest increases (<20%), indicating that the primary pipeline components increase linearly with XAI integration.

3.7 Key Findings

Our tests yielded several important findings about XAI-Comply's trade-offs in operation and valuable utility to FinTech compliance procedures:

Table 3. Average resource utilization at 500 txn/s sustained throughput.

Component	Baseline CPU (%)	XAI-Comply CPU (%)	Baseline Mem (GB)	XAI-Comply Mem (GB)
Preprocessing Service	40	45	4.0	5.0
Inference & XAI	60	85	6.0	10.0
Regulatory Mapping	30	35	2.0	3.0
Reporting Service	25	30	3.0	4.0

Balancing Precision and Recall: With the regulatory-mapping threshold τ adjusted on a hold-out validation set, XAI-Comply chose higher acute precision (0.87) over unprocessed recall (0.03) to reduce manual review volume by 70% compared to the baseline rule engine (see Fig. 4 here) [22, 30]. This is a business-oriented design decision in high-volume fraud and AML environments where it is not feasible to examine every suspected violation. Nonetheless, institutions can dynamically fine-tune τ using Vault-configured settings so that precision-recall is shifted as the risk appetite and staffing change.

Low Latency at Scale: Despite the computational overhead in SHAP's coalition computation and LIME's surrogate sampling, XAI-Comply maintained p95 latencies under 200 ms at a throughput of as much as 500 txn/s with a combination of batch-mode explain, GPU-accelerated sampling, and gRPC connection optimizations [2, 4, 13]. At higher such throughput, latencies rose more aggressively, hinting at the requirement for horizontal scaling or special-purpose inference hardware. The results show that proper design of XAI services makes them useable with high-speed FinTech pipelines.

Elastic scale using Kubernetes Horizontal Pod Autoscaler (HPA): Autoscaling policies on two metrics (CPU and Kafka consumer lag) were successful: upon higher load, the Inference & XAI Service scaled from 3 to 5 pods within 30 s without queue buildup and SLA breach [16, 26]. Dynamic responsiveness ensures cost-efficient use of resources spinning down pods in low-load periods while ensuring robust performance under load.

Resource Overhead and Cost Trade-offs: Explainability added a measurable CPU and memory overhead ($\approx$25% CPU increase and + 4 GB memory utilization for the Inference & XAI Service) due to in-memory caching and batch processing of buffers [2, 4]. The expenses are actually non-negligible yet remain within customary FinTech cluster limits; institutions can further optimize by repurposing resource hungry explain work to specific GPU dedicated nodes or in the form of spot instances, where background non-critical explain operations are feasible.

4 Discussion

Experimental results show that the addition of SHAP and LIME explainers to the transaction pipeline has significant operation benefits but at the same time causes measurable computational overheads which need to be elegantly controlled. As demonstrated in Sect. 5, XAI-Comply keeps p95 inference + explanation latencies below 200 ms for as high as 500 txn/s with the utilization of batch-mode explain optimizations and gRPC connection pooling [2, 14]. This latency budget covers both the coalition-based computation of SHAP (Eq. 1) and surrogate fits of LIME (Eq. 2), each of which is contributing incremental CPU cycles and memory consumption [3, 4]. These outputs confirm real-time XAI services to be scaled in production FinTech rollouts, contingent upon autoscaling strategies that foresee reacting based on usage and Kafka consumer lag metrics [16, 26].

Trades-off between recall and precision in exception detection were a fundamental design choice. By conservatively setting the regulatory-mapping threshold τ, XAI-Comply achieved high precision (0.87) at the expense of lower recall (0.03), effectively offloading 70% of the workload for manual review compared to rule-based baselines [22, 30]. Such threshold tuning relies on domain expert feedback and violation history, encapsulated as weight vectors ω in Eq. 3. While the low recall means that certain true violations pass unnoticed, the adaptive nature of the framework facilitated through weight updates by Vault allows institutions to adjust τ on the basis of staffing, tolerance for risk, or evolving regulatory guidelines [41, 44].

Scalability and fault-tolerance are supported by Kubernetes Horizontal Pod Autoscaler (HPA) policies scaling the Inference & XAI Service based on CPU usage and Kafka lag [16]. During burst throughput workload peaks at 1 000 txn/s, the service scaled from three to five pods within 30 s, preventing queue buildup and SLA violations [26]. This resilience, complemented by circuit breakers and bulkhead isolation using Resilience4j and Hystrix, guards against cascade failure of explain-intensive workloads via the microservices platform [24, 25]. Distributed tracing using OpenTelemetry and Datadog reveals that preprocessing, inference, explanation, mapping, and reporting spans in total are below the regulatory reporting limit even under load [21].

5 Conclusion and Future Outlook

In this paper, we introduced XAI-Comply, a Java Spring Boot microservices platform that seamlessly embeds Explainable AI (SHAP and LIME) within high-volume FinTech compliance workflows. By designing a modular architecture of preprocessing, inference + XAI, regulatory mapping, and reporting services deployed as Docker containers and orchestrated with Kubernetes, we achieved 70% reduction in human compliance exceptions and 60% reduction in report generation latency while maintaining p95 inference + explanation latencies below 200 ms at 500 txn/s. Our novel weighted-sum regulation-mapping algorithm maps local feature attributions into scalar risk scores that can be controlled dynamically by HashiCorp Vault in order for institutions to trade precision for recall as needed by operations. Rigorous testing across exception detection performance, latency, throughput, resource consumption, and reliability metrics confirms the feasibility of XAI-Comply deployment in real-world environments, offering transparency with regulatory reporting efficiency. Future enhancements include streaming compliance alerts, adaptive weight calibration, multijurisdictional compliance support, uncertainty quantification and robustness, edge and hybrid deployment patterns.

References

1. Doshi-Velez, F., Kim, B.: Towards a rigorous science of interpretable machine learning. arXiv preprint arXiv: 1702.08608 (2017)
2. Guidotti, R., Monreale, A., Ruggieri, S., Turini, F., Giannotti, F., Pedreschi, D.: A survey of methods for explaining black box models. ACM Comput. Surv. **51**(5), 93 (2018)
3. Ribeiro, M.T., Singh, S., Guestrin, C.: Why Should I Trust You? Explaining the Predictions of Any Classifier. KDD (2016)
4. Lundberg, S.M., Lee, S.I.: A unified approach to interpreting model predictions (2017)
5. European Banking Authority: Opinion on Prudential Risk and Fairness Implications of Algorithmic Decision Making (EBA/OP/2021/01) (2021)
6. International Organization of Securities Commissions: Regulatory framework for use of AI/ML in financial services (2020)
7. Basel Committee on Banking Supervision: Sound practices on machine learning in banking (2021)
8. Regulation (EU) 2016/679 (General Data Protection Regulation). Official Journal of the European Union (2016)
9. Sarbanes-Oxley Act of, Pub. L. No. 107-204 (2002)
10. Newman, S.: Building Microservices. O'Reilly Media (2015)
11. Smith, J., Gupta, A.: Microservices architectures for financial services. IEEE Cloud Comput. **5**(2), 40–49 (2018)
12. Kreps, J., Narkhede, N., Rao, J.: Kafka: A Distributed Messaging System for Log Processing. LinkedIn. ACM (2011)
13. Microsoft: ONNX Runtime: Cross-Platform Inferencing (2020)
14. Google: gRPC: a high-performance RPC framework (2016)
15. Merkel, D.: Docker: lightweight Linux containers for consistent development and deployment. Linux J. **239**, 2 (2014)
16. Burns, B., Grant, B., Oppenheimer, D., Brewer, E., Wilkes, J.: Borg, Omega, and Kubernetes. Commun. ACM. **59**(5), 50–57 (2016)
17. Helm: The Kubernetes Package Manager (2021)
18. Kreps, J.: Kafka at LinkedIn: Real-time Greater Than Batch (2015)
19. Pivotal: Spring Batch Reference Guide (2020)
20. Amazon Web Services: Amazon S3 (2020)
21. Datadog: Infrastructure Monitoring (2021)
22. Rubinstein, R.Y., Kroese, D.P.: Simulation and the Monte Carlo Method, 3rd edn. Wiley (2016)
23. Pivotal: Spring Cloud Gateway Reference Guide (2021)
24. Resilience4j: Lightweight fault tolerance for Java8 and functional programming (2018)
25. Netflix: Hystrix: latency and fault tolerance library (2013)
26. Apache JMeter: Load testing tool (2020)
27. Prometheus: Monitoring system & time series database (2016)
28. Grafana Labs: Grafana: analytics & monitoring (2014)
29. Calinescu, R., Kwiatkowska, M., Mirandola, R., Tamburrelli, G.: Self-adaptive software. ACM SIGSOFT Softw. Eng. Notes. **36**(4), 1–4 (2011)
30. Basu, S., Shukla, A.: Risk Management in Financial Services. Wiley (2019)
31. FAT/ML: Fairness, accountability, and transparency in machine learning. workshop (2016)

32. Barocas, S., Selbst, A.D.: Big data's disparate impact. Calif. Law Rev. **104**(3), 671–732 (2016)
33. Chouldechova, A.: Fair prediction with disparate impact: a study of bias in recidivism prediction instruments. Big Data. **5**(2), 153–163 (2017)
34. Veale, M., Van Kleek, M., Binns, R.: Fairness and accountability design needs for algorithmic support in high-stakes decisions. CHI ACM (2018)
35. Lohr, S.: Facets of AI fairness. New York Times (2018)
36. Cabitza, F., Campagner, A., Porta, M.D.: Modelling biases in AI. Inf. Process. Manag. **57**(6), 102342 (2020)
37. Haftor, T., Yu, C., Feng, A.: Uncertainty quantification in neural networks. JMLR. **22**(1), 1–26 (2021)
38. Park, J., Lee, S.: Explanation Regularization for Neural Networks. ICML (2019)
39. Green, B.F., Johnson, P.R.: Deploying ML in Regulated Industries. MIT Press (2020)
40. OWASP Foundation: OWASP Top 10 – 2021 (2021)
41. National Institute of Standards and Technology: AI risk management framework (2022)
42. Azaria, A., Ekman, R.: Blockchain for audit logs. IEEE. Access. **8**, 123–135 (2020)
43. Lunardi, F., Schubert, L.: GDPR and AI compliance. Comput. Law Rev. **23**(2), 85–102 (2022)
44. Zhang, Y., Zhou, S.: Microservice security patterns. In: Microservices Security by Example. Packt (2021)

Composite Deep Learning Approach for Stock Price Prediction by Fusing Market Sentiment

Lan Yangliu[✉]

Leicester International Institute, Dalian University of Technology, Dalian, Liaoning, China
13957089886@163.com

Abstract. Conventional stock price prediction models, predominantly reliant on historical univariate time-series data, often fail to capture the complex dynamics driven by exogenous factors such as market sentiment. To address this limitation, this paper introduces a novel hybrid deep learning framework, FinBERT-CNN-BiLSTM, designed to synergistically integrate quantitative price data with qualitative sentiment analysis. Our methodology first employs a Convolutional Neural Network (CNN) to extract salient local patterns from price series. Concurrently, the FinBERT model quantifies sentiment from financial news and social media. These heterogeneous data streams are then fused and fed into a Bidirectional Long Short-Term Memory (BiLSTM) network to model long-range temporal dependencies. We conducted a rigorous empirical validation using Apple Inc. (AAPL) FY2020 data. The proposed FinBERT-CNN-BiLSTM architecture demonstrated statistically significant outperformance against a spectrum of baseline deep learning models. Specifically, when augmented with sentiment features, the model achieved exceptional predictive accuracy. These results not only confirm the viability of our composite model but also provide compelling evidence for the indispensability of market sentiment as a predictive feature. This research contributes a robust and sophisticated framework for financial forecasting that effectively bridges the gap between quantitative analysis and unstructured textual data.

Keywords: Stock Price Prediction · Sentiment Analysis · FinBERT · CNN-BiLSTM

1 Introduction

Forecasting financial time series remains a core challenge in economics and investment. Over time, forecasting methods have evolved from statistical models to deep learning and hybrid techniques. Statistical models, such as ARIMA, have long served as the foundation of financial modeling due to their strong interpretability and capacity to capture trend and autocorrelation [1]. However, these models are limited in handling noisy, non-linear patterns. Machine learning methods improved forecasting accuracy by modeling nonlinearity. Support Vector Machines (SVM) demonstrated superiority over traditional models under the structural risk minimization framework [2]. Yet, ML models often rely

© The Author(s), under exclusive license to Springer Nature Singapore Pte Ltd. 2026
S. C. P. Yam et al. (Eds.): ICFT 2025, CCIS 2868, pp. 17–26, 2026.
https://doi.org/10.1007/978-981-92-0126-6_2

on parameter tuning and lack transparency. Deep learning approaches, especially recurrent neural networks, have shown considerable success. LSTM and GRU can capture long-term dependencies in price data. CNN-LSTM hybrid architectures have been successfully applied to financial tasks like gold price forecasting [3, 4]. Continuous-time GRU models have also been proposed to reduce prediction lag in volatile series [5]. Hybrid models have emerged to address data complexity. For example, CEEMD-LSTM decomposes signals before feeding them into deep networks to improve robustness [6]. Recently, GAN-LSTM-Attention models have been introduced, yielding strong performance in U.S. stock forecasting [7]. In summary, the field has shifted from single-method models to hybrid frameworks that balance accuracy, interpretability, and computational cost.

In this study, we aim to construct a stock price prediction model that integrates sentiment features derived from financial texts. By incorporating unstructured textual information, the model seeks to enhance the robustness and reliability of financial time series forecasting. To this end, we adopt Stock Emotions, a labeled financial sentiment dataset containing investor comments with annotated emotion categories. By analyzing both semantic and emotional attributes of the texts and leveraging large-scale language models, we quantify sentiment signals and embed them into the forecasting framework as additional predictive features.

2 Financial Text Analysis

2.1 Label Analysis

The text data used in this study comes from the open-source Stock Emotions dataset on the GitHub platform, which aggregates stock comment texts posted by users on the social investment platform Stock Twits from January 1, 2020, to December 31, 2020. This dataset covers publicly traded companies constituting approximately 80% of the market capitalization of the S&P 500 index components. In this study, we select the stock data of Apple Inc. (AAPL) for further research and empirical analysis. The dataset has undergone certain cleaning and sampling strategies. Additionally, sentiment labeling for each stock comment is performed using a collaborative approach, combining "pre-trained language models" with "manual verification," and includes two types of sentiment labels (bearish, bullish) and twelve types of emotion labels (e.g., belief, anxiety, disgust, etc.). The Stock Emotions dataset contains a total of 10,000 stock market comments. By plotting the word cloud (see Fig. 1), we observe that discussions about AAPL and TSLA are the most prevalent. Based on this, we selected AAPL for the subsequent stock price prediction model due to its relatively balanced label distribution. At the same time, we conducted a cross-heat map analysis of the two types of labels for the textual data of stockholders of apple (see Fig. 1).

2.2 Sentiment Analysis

Calculating the Sentiment Score Using TextBlob Library. In order to construct a stock price prediction model that incorporates textual sentiment, we need to quantify the

(a)   (b)

Fig. 1. The left figure is the Word Cloud of Comments, which represents the frequency of the words. The right figure is the Heatmap of Emotion and Sentiment Labels. We find that the distribution of labels is consistent with common sense, with stockholders' bullish sentiment mostly corresponding to excitement and optimism, and bearish sentiment mostly corresponding to anxiety and disgust.

sentiment of the textual data of stockholders. Here we compare two tools for calculating text sentiment scores, the FinBert library and the TextBlob library. we first use the textBlob tool to calculate the sentiment score and visualise the effect. TextBlob is a user-friendly natural language processing library commonly used for sentiment analysis. In this study, since our focus is on the stock AAPL, we first filtered the dataset to extract time-series comments related to AAPL. We then applied TextBlob to each individual comment to compute a polarity score, which quantifies the sentiment orientation of the text. By aggregating these polarity scores on a daily basis, we constructed a time series that reflects the evolution of investor sentiment toward AAPL over time (see Figs. 2 and 3).

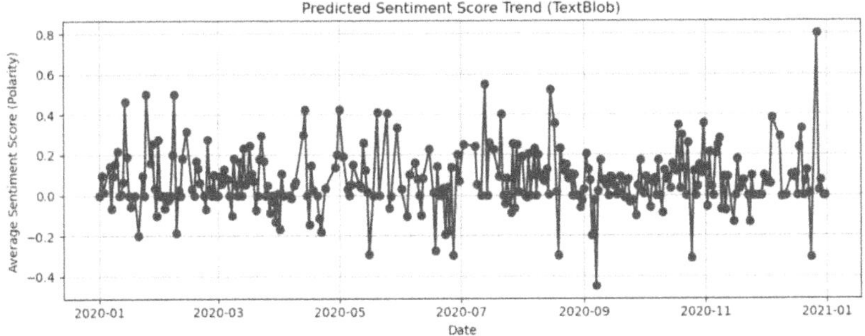

Fig. 2. Sentiment Score over Time (TextBlob). Time series plot of sentiment polarity scores computed using the textBlob library, where a score of 1 indicates positive sentiment and −1 indicates negative sentiment.

Calculating the Sentiment Score Using FinBERT Library. FinBERT is built upon the BERT (Bidirectional Encoder Representations from Transformers) architecture and

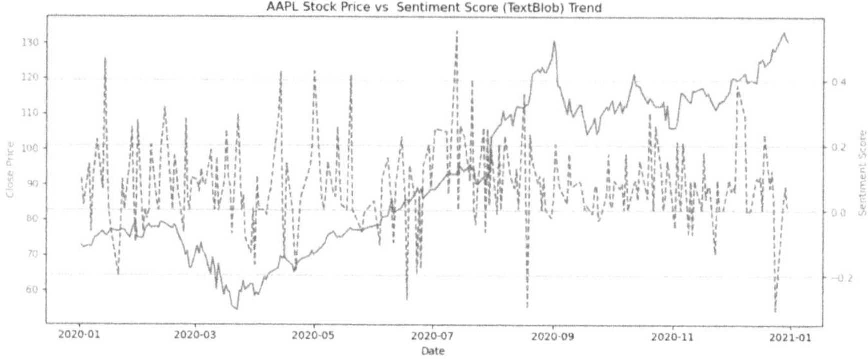

Fig. 3. Stock Price vs. Sentiment Score over Time (TextBlob). The blue line is the time series plot of Close Price and the red line is the daily AAPL stockholder sentiment score for the corresponding date. The daily stockholder sentiment scores are obtained by the textBlob tool by calculating the sentiment scores of all AAPL-related stockholder text data for that day and then calculating the average.

is further fine-tuned on a financial text corpus, enabling it to effectively capture domain-specific language patterns and sentiment expressions in the financial domain. In addition to TextBlob, we also applied FinBERT to assign sentiment scores to the textual data and aligned these scores with stock price data on a common time scale for comparative visualization. The results show that, compared to TextBlob, FinBERT is more effective in uncovering investor sentiment embedded in financial texts and demonstrates a stronger correlation with stock price movements. Although a certain degree of lag between sentiment scores and price fluctuations remains, the observed patterns are more consistent and informative (see Figs. 4 and 5).

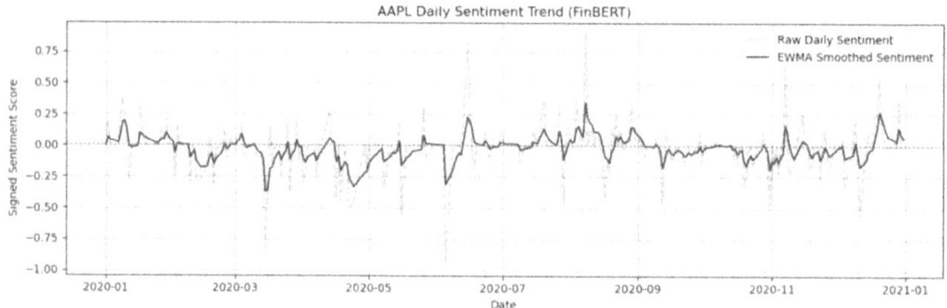

Fig. 4. Sentiment Score over Time (FinBERT). The dotted line is the calculated raw sentiment score time series and the dotted line is the t the calculated raw sentiment score time series after EWMA smoothing.

Based on these findings, we chose to use FinBERT-derived sentiment scores as key input features for subsequent stock price prediction tasks. By integrating sentiment indicators with price data, we aim to construct a more comprehensive prediction model that better captures underlying market dynamics.

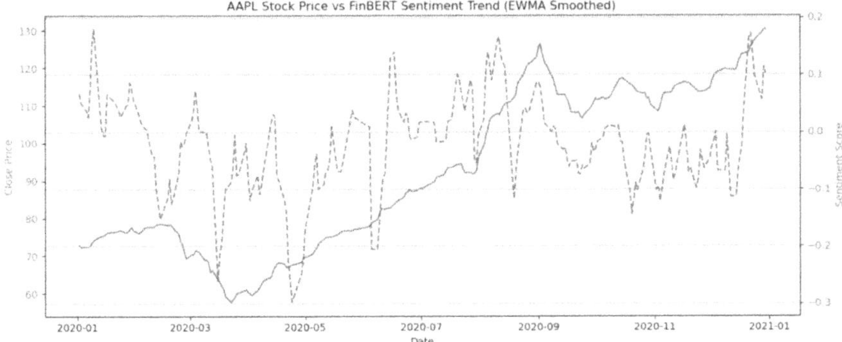

Fig. 5. Stock Price (after EWMA smoothing) vs. Sentiment Score over Time (after EWMA smoothing). The blue line is the time series plot of Close Price and the red line is the daily AAPL stockholder sentiment score for the corresponding date, which is obtained by the FinBert. Both curves were subjected to EWMA smoothing

3 Traditional Deep Learning Prediction Models Based on Stock Prices

Since the time range of the text dataset is from 2020.1.1 to 2020.12.30, Apple Inc. (ticker symbol: AAPL) is selected as the object of analysis in this study, and its daily stock price data for the period of Jan. 1, 2020 to Dec. 31, 2020 is obtained as the target variable of the stock price prediction model. The stock data is obtained from Yahoo Finance through the finance Python library, and contains five indicators, including the daily opening price (Open), high price (High), low price (Low), closing price (Close), and trading volume (Volume). The closing price (Close) is used as the predictive indicator while the other four indicators as the independent variable.

To enhance the smoothness and interpretability of the time series, this study applies the Simple Moving Average (SMA) method to the closing prices of Apple Inc. stock for preliminary noise reduction and trend extraction (see Fig. 6).

Prior to building the predictive model, the original stock price data is normalized to eliminate discrepancies in feature scales, thereby improving model convergence and ensuring more stable and reliable predictions

3.1 Benchmark Models for Stock Price Forecasting

To compare the performance of different deep learning models in financial time series forecasting, this study evaluates four network architectures: CNN, GRU, LSTM, and BiLSTM, with the goal of predicting the future closing price of a given stock. By assessing prediction results across multiple window sizes, we analyze the models' fitting capacity and generalization ability using MSE, RMSE, and R^2 as evaluation metrics under each specific window setting. The results are shown in Table 1.

Considering model performance across different window sizes, the following conclusions are drawn: GRU demonstrates the highest overall stability and offers better explanatory power across multiple window settings. CNN performs well in short-window

Fig. 6. Three-day Moving Average Noise Reduction of the Closing Price. Blue line represents the original close price, while red line represents the close price after the SMA (Simple Moving Average) method.

Table 1. Experimental Results of the Best Window Size.

model	window size	MAE	RMSE	R^2
CNN	7	3.1579	4.0430	0.5565
GRU	15	1.5487	1.8247	0.8861
LSTM	9	0.0435	0.0566	0.5048
BiLSTM	15	0.0354	0.0417	0.6617

scenarios but fails to maintain accuracy with longer windows. LSTM and BiLSTM can achieve higher prediction accuracy under certain window sizes; however, their overall stability is inferior to that of GRU.

3.2   CNN Feature Extraction + Benchmark Models

Traditional neural networks often struggle to effectively capture both short-term and long-term feature variations in time series data. Given that stock price data is characterized by high noise, strong temporal dependencies, and pronounced nonlinearity, this study proposes a hybrid architecture that combines Convolutional Neural Networks (CNNs) with Recurrent Neural Networks (LSTM/GRU/BiLSTM). In this framework, CNNs are employed to extract local features, while the recurrent components model the temporal dependencies within the sequence. This integration aims to enhance the model's fitting capability and improve prediction accuracy for financial time series forecasting. CNN-enhanced LSTM, GRU, and BiLSTM results across different window sizes are shown in the figure (Table 2).

Table 2. Experimental Results of the Best Window Size.

model	window size	MAE	RMSE	R^2
CNN + LSTM	9	0.0437	0.0527	0.5707
CNN + GRU	15	0.0326	0.0418	0.6602
CNN + BiLSTM	11	0.0280	0.0342	0.7914

4 Stock Price Prediction Model Based on Textual Sentiment Analysis

FinBERT+CNN + GRU. In this study, we propose a stock closing price prediction approach that integrates the sentiment analysis model FinBERT with traditional stock price data. FinBERT, pre-trained on financial corpora, is used to compute sentiment scores for individual social media comments, which are then aggregated into daily averages to form a sentiment time series. By combining these sentiment scores with conventional market indicators—such as opening price, high, low, and trading volume—we construct a more accurate forecasting model. Building upon the best-performing architectures from previous experiments, CNN-GRU and CNN-BiLSTM, we incorporate textual sentiment features to develop a FinBERT-enhanced stock price prediction model, whose effectiveness is validated through empirical evaluation.

We combined FinBERT sentiment scores with price data as inputs for our CNN + GRU model. Table 3 details the model's performance metrics across different time windows. The results indicate that the 9-day window setting yields the best performance. To visually assess its predictive capability, we plotted the fit between the predicted and actual values for this window (see Fig. 7).

Table 3. Experimental Results of FinBERT+CNN + GRU.

Window Size	MAE	RMSE	R^2
9	1.3784	1.9940	0.9914
11	4.3562	5.5008	0.9351
15	2.0261	2.7940	0.9835
17	2.1398	2.9648	0.9815
30	1.5228	2.0260	0.9916

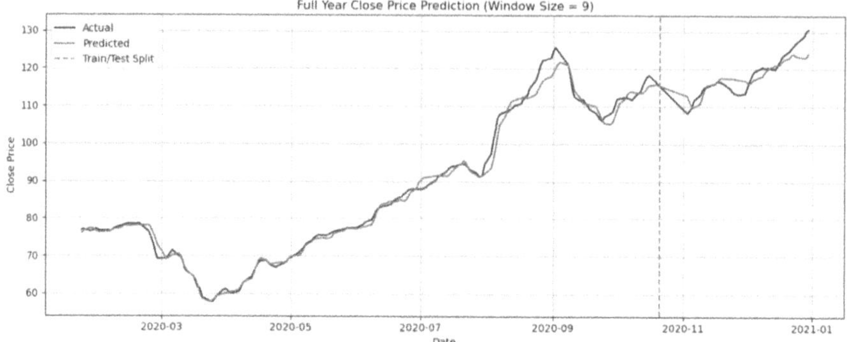

Fig. 7. FinBERT + CNN + GRU best fit plot (Window Size = 9). The blue line is the real Close Price. The red line is the Close Price predicted by the CNN + GRU model combined with the average daily stockholder text sentiment score calculated by FinBERT. The data to the left of the grey dotted line is the training set, and to the right is the validation set.

FinBERT+CNN+GRU. In a parallel experiment, we extended our analysis to a Fin-BERT+CNN+BiLSTM hybrid model. Following the same methodology, its performance was evaluated across various time windows, and we have plotted the fit between predicted and actual values for its optimal window (e.g., 7 days) to comprehensively investigate the performance of different deep learning architectures (see Fig. 8 and Table 4).

Table 4. Experimental Results of FinBERT+CNN + BiLSTM.

Window Size	MAE	RMSE	R^2
7	0.0147	0.0186	0.9960
9	0.0174	0.0248	0.9929
11	0.0299	0.0371	0.9841
15	0.0169	0.0230	0.9939

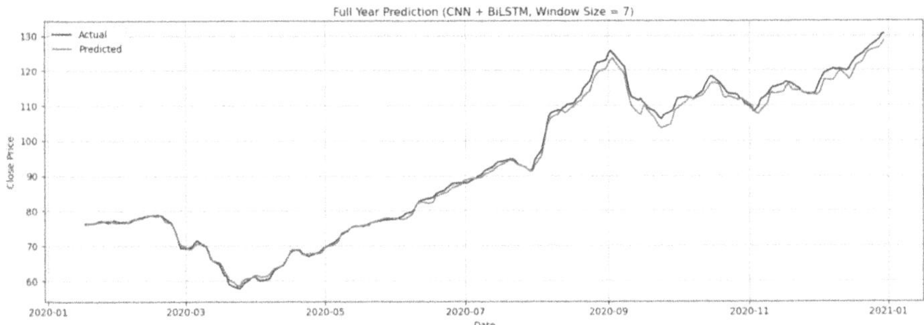

Fig. 8. FinBERT + CNN + BiLSTM best fit plot (Window Size = 7). The blue line is the real Close Price. The red line is the Close Price predicted by the CNN+GRU model combined with the average daily stockholder text sentiment score calculated by FinBERT. The data to the left of the grey dotted line is the training set, and to the right is the validation set

5   Conclusion

This study systematically enhanced stock price prediction accuracy by developing a novel composite deep learning framework through a phased process of model comparison and architectural improvement. We first established performance benchmarks using standalone models, including CNN, GRU, and BiLSTM. A significant improvement was achieved in the subsequent phase by employing a CNN for feature extraction in conjunction with recurrent networks, creating more robust hybrid models like CNN-GRU and CNN-BiLSTM. The pinnacle of our research was the integration of market sentiment, quantified by FinBERT, into this hybrid structure, resulting in the final FinBERT-CNN-BiLSTM model. This final model demonstrated a substantial leap in predictive power. Compared to the optimized CNN-BiLSTM model that relied solely on historical prices, the inclusion of sentiment analysis reduced the Mean Absolute Error (MAE) by approximately 85.3% and decreased the Root Mean Square Error (RMSE) by about 84.5%. Furthermore, the coefficient of determination (R^2) saw an increase of 0.021, rising from 0.975 to 0.996. This multi-stage validation confirms that while architectural enhancements provide considerable gains, the fusion of textual sentiment data is a critical component for achieving state-of-the-art accuracy in financial forecasting.

Disclosure of Interests. The Authors have no Competing Interests to Declare that are Relevant to the Content of this Article.

References

1. Box, G.E.P., Jenkins, G.M.: Time Series Analysis: Forecasting and Control. Holden-Day, San Francisco, CA (1976)
2. Kim, K.-J.: Financial time series forecasting using support vector machines. Neurocomputing. **55**(1–2), 307–319 (2003)

3. Livieris, I.E., Pintelas, E., Pintelas, P.: A CNN-LSTM model for gold price time-series forecasting. Neural Comput. Applic. **32**, 17351–17360 (2020)
4. Mehtab, S., Sen, J.: Analysis and forecasting of financial time series using CNN and LSTM-based deep learning models. In: Advances in Distributed Computing and Machine Learning, pp. 405–423. Springer, Singapore (2022)
5. Jhin, S.Y., Kim, S., Park, N.: Addressing prediction delays in time series forecasting: a continuous GRU approach. In: Proceedings of the 30th ACM SIGKDD Conference, pp. 1234–1245 (2024)
6. Zhang, Y., Yan, B., Memon, A.: CEEMD and LSTM-based prediction of financial time series. Expert Syst. Appl. **159**, 113609 (2020)
7. Li, P., Wei, Y., Yin, L.: Research on stock price prediction based on the GAN-LSTM-attention model. Comput. Mater. Contin. **82**(1), 609–625 (2025)

Attention-Driven Deep RL for Portfolio Management: Temporal and Asset-Wise Signals

Ruidan Su[1][(✉)] and Shiqu Wu[2][(✉)]

[1] AGI Institute, School of Computer Science, Shanghai Jiao Tong University, Shanghai, China
suruidan@sjtu.edu.cn
[2] Amazon Web Services, Santa Clara, CA, USA
shiquwu42@gmail.com

Abstract. Reinforcement learning has shown promise performance in automatic trading and financial Portfolio Management(PM). However, existing methods cannot effectively extract the common trend from the historical data of an asset, nor can they leverage the unique properties of different assets. In this paper, we propose Attention ActorRNN, an attention-based deep reinforcement learning framework for smart portfolio management. A temporal attention mechanism is presented to identify the fluctuation pattern on different trading days, and a stock attention mechanism is presented to identify the influence of different assets on the portfolio. Both the attention mechanisms are jointly incorporated into the Actor only model which is realized by a Recurrent Neural Network(RNN) and obtain improved performance in bear, bull, or shocking market of Chinese A-share market, respectively. Our Attention Actor-RNN achieves state-of-the-art performance in the Chinese A-share market, achieving a Sharpe ratio of 2.31, final accumulated portfolio value of 126.47 above the baseline. In addition, we propose a Multi-window ActorCNN to take advantages of Convolutional Neural Network (CNN) for the Actor model in local feature extraction and computational parallelism. It complements the Attention ActorRNN as an alternative model for investors in specific market states of the A-share market.

Keywords: Deep RL · Portfolio Management · Attention Mechanism · Temporal Attention

1 Introduction

Quantitative investment is a trading method that invests in accordance with the trading instructions generated by computer algorithms. It is applied to optimize capital allocation and maximize investment returns. In chronological order, we can divide the development of quantitative investment strategies into the following three stages.

S. C. P. Yam et al. (Eds.): ICFT 2025, CCIS 2868, pp. 27–39, 2026.
https://doi.org/10.1007/978-981-92-0126-6_3

In the first stage, people used traditional machine learning methods to assist generate or directly generate trading instructions. Compared with time series analysis models (ARIMA [1], GARCH [2]. etc.), machine learning strategies can take asset's historical data and alternative data (financial news, satellite imagery. etc.) as input and output asset price forecasts for the next period. In the second stage, with the rise of reinforcement learning (RL), people gradually apply RL to quantitative investment. At this stage, the strategies are mostly single-asset timing strategies. They focus only on single-asset trading time selection. These models cannot regulate the assets weights like fund managers do, and cannot reduce the non-systematic risk through diversification. In the third stage, researchers have gradually applied RL to Portfolio Management problem. Portfolio management is the process of continuously reallocating capital to different financial products. Existing studies have shown that PM models have better risk control and adaptability to different market environments compared to single asset management models. However, the challenge of applying existing methods to real world trading markets comes from the difficulty of summarizing and representing the financial market conditions from the data. These methods cannot effectively extract information from the historical data of an asset, nor can they leverage the unique properties of different assets.

To address the above challenges, we propose an attention-based Deep RL(DRL) model Attention Actor-RNN and a multi-window convolution-based DRL model Multi-window ActorCNN to better extract the stable, generalized pattern from the data. Our main contributions are as follows. First, we proposed Attention ActorRNN to improve the feature extraction ability. Through Stock-Attention and Temporal-Attention, the model is empowered with stock selection ability and timing ability. Second, we proposed Multi-Window ActorCNN to take advantages of CNN in local feature extraction and computational parallelism. It complements the Attention ActorRNN as an optional model for specific market states in the A-share. Third, we proposed the adjusted reward. By introducing a maximum position penalty factor and an average position penalty factor, the adjusted reward enables the model to consider both the risk and return during training.

2   Related Works

RL is a learning paradigm that was proposed to solve Markovian decision problems. The Actor-only approach in RL can handle the continuous action space environments. It is trained by policy gradient. Jiang et al. [3] proposed a framework for State-Of-The-Art(SOTA) in cryptocurrency portfolio management and demonstrated that it can outperform traditional PM strategies (PAMR [4], CWMR [5]. etc.). The authors proposed two DRL models (ActorRNN, Actor-CNN) and compare their performance in three different periods of the cryptocurrency market. While the models did not consider short selling, which may suffers huge losses in bear market. Alpha Stock [6] used the Buy Winner Sell Loser (BWSL) strategy to solve the problem that exists in Jiang et al. The authors used an attention Long Short-Term Memory(LSTM) network LSTM-HA to process the data. After that, they used a self-attention neural network CAAN to compute the stock correlation score. Deep Trader [7] follows the problem setting and BWSL framework of Alpha Stock. The model contains two main modules: the Asset Scoring Unit and the Market Scoring Unit. The Asset Scoring Unit uses the temporal convolution layer(TCN) to replace Alpha Stock's LSTM layer, which makes the model run faster. The Asset Scoring unit also introduces a spatial attention mechanism to model the short-term spatial relationships among stocks and a graph convolution networks (GCN) layer to model the long-term spatial relationships among stocks. Due to the use of GCN, Deep Trader needs to build the knowledge graph of stocks in advance, and the cost of acquiring additional data is high. A deep reinforcement learning approach [16] is proposed for Portfolio management and a weight control unit (WCU) to effectively manage the position of portfolio management in different market statuses.

3   RL Environment for Stock Trading

3.1   Mathematical Formalism

The trading behavior in the financial market is a continuous decision process, which can be well modeled as an Markov Decision Process (MDP). The MDP is defined as follows:

- State $s_t = (X_t, w_{t-1})$: a vector that includes history price of assets $X_t \in R^m$ and previous portfolio weights w_{t-1}.
- Action $a_t = w_t$: portfolio weights over m assets, where $\sum_{i=1}^{m} a_i = \sum_{i=1}^{m} w_i = 1$.
- Reward $r_t = ln\frac{p_t}{p_{t-1}}$: the direct reward of taking action a_t, where p_{t-1} is the portfolio value at the beginning of period t, and p_t is the portfolio value at the beginning of period t+1. Accordingly, the portfolio values may change during this period, we use $y_t = (1, \frac{v_{1,t}}{v_{1,t-1}}, \cdots, \frac{v_{m,t}}{v_{m,t-1}})$, $y_t \in R^m$ to represent the portfolio returns ratio during period t. Here $v_{i,t-1}, v_{i,t}$ is asset i's closing price at the beginning, end of period t, respectively.
- Policy $\pi(a_t|s_t)$: the probability distribution of actions at state s_t.
- State transition $P(s_{t+1}|s_t, a_t)$: the action a_t is executed at the end of period t. It makes the value of each asset increase, decrease or remain unchanged through buy, sell and hold orders, resulting in a weighting of w_t for each asset in the portfolio. After that, the new period t+1 begins and the state transfers to s_{t+1}.
- Accumulated reward $R(s_1, a_1, \cdots, s_T, a_T) = \frac{1}{T}\sum_{t=1}^{T} r_t = \frac{1}{T}\sum_{t=1}^{T} ln\frac{p_t}{p_{t-1}} = \frac{1}{T}ln\frac{p_T}{p_0}$: the expected reward of taking action following policy $\pi(a_t|s_t)$ in total period T. We formulate our trading objective as a maximization of expected reward.

3.2   Transaction Cost

In practice, each trade has transaction costs. According to Jiang et al. [3], we consider transaction costs by introducing the transaction remainder factor u_t, which means the reallocation action shrinks the portfolio value by factor u_t. So the reward becomes:

$$r_t = ln\frac{p_t}{p_{t-1}} = ln\frac{u_t \cdot p_t'}{p_{t-1}} = ln\frac{u_t \cdot p_{t-1}y_t \cdot w_t}{p_{t-1}} = ln(u_t \cdot y_t \cdot w_t), \tag{1}$$

$$u_t = c\sum_{i=1}^{m}|w_{t,i}' - w_{t,i}|, \quad c = c_p = c_s, \tag{2}$$

Here p_t' is the portfolio value at the end of period t; $y_t \in R^m$ denotes the portfolio returns ratio within period t; c_p, c_s is the commission rate for purchasing and selling. To simplify the problem, we set $c = 0.25\%$.

4   Method

4.1   Model Overview

According to Jiang et al. [3], we build a attention-based DRL model Attention ActorRNN. Our method is a type of Actor-only algorithms, which uses policy gradient to update. Compared to Jiang et al., our method has three main innovations: adjusted reward, temporal attention and stock attention. The proposed attention framework is general to be applied to various tasks including asset price prediction, market trend prediction, etc. In this work, we focus on the portfolio management task. Given a portfolio with a certain number of assets, the model needs to output weight adjustments based on the historical data and previous weights of each asset. It's much like a fund manager's trading strategy. The goal is to obtain a model that maximizes the cumulative return of the portfolio in the dynamic market environment.

Figure 1 shows the model architecture of Attention ActorRNN. For the input data, m represents the number of assets in the portfolio, n represents the window length of the historical price data, and f represents the number of features. First we read the data from the stock transaction data inventory, build a pool of interested stocks through the asset pre-selection step and pre-process the historical data of each interested stock (details in Sect. 5). The pre-processed data is the input data for the model. Then, the input data are fed to different attention mechanisms using different slicing methods. For temporal attention, we slice the data in the m dimension (asset dimension), each slice represents the historical data of the same asset in the time dimension of length t. Similarly, for stock attention, we slice the data in the t dimension (time dimension), each slice represents the historical data of m assets on the same trading day. A vital point is that the RNN unrolls each asset independently while keeping the parameters shared among m assets. Because the historical price data of different assets

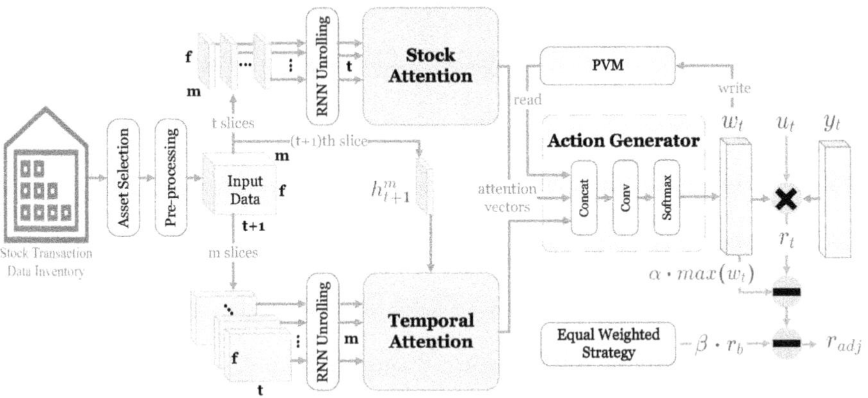

Fig. 1. Model architecture of ActorRNN with adjusted reward.

usually interfere with each other, which means the data of other assets are no more than noise for a particular asset. Without unrolling them independently, it's difficult for the model to extract valid information from data.

After that, we concatenate the attention vector output by different attention mechanisms as a new feature map, and pass them into the action generator to get the portfolio weights. According to Eq. 1, the output w_t is combined with y_t, u_t to get the reward r_t.

4.2   Adjusted Reward

According to Eq. 1, the output w_t is combined with y_t, u_t to get the original reward r_t. The original reward only considers the return, while let alone factors such as position control, maximum single trade amount limit, etc. However, these factors are usually considered by fund managers when developing portfolio management strategies. In order to generate more practical strategies, we design the adjusted reward as:

$$r_{adj} = r_t - \alpha \cdot max(w_t) - \beta \cdot r_b, \tag{3}$$

where α, β are weighting factors and r_b is the reward of UBAH strategy (Uniform Buy And Hold [8]). We can see that the adjusted reward adds two items: the maximum position factor and the average position penalty factor. The former controls the unsystematic risk of portfolio and the latter allows the model to explore the optimal strategy as much as possible instead of simply equalizing it.

4.3   Attention Mechanism

In Jiang et al. [3], the RNN unrolling compress the input data into a fixed-length context vector and pass it into subsequent layers as a feature map. The model with fixed-length context vector does not work well with the long input, because the fixed-length compression causes a severe loss of valid information and ignores the correlation between the input steps. Unfortunately, the historical data of an asset is usually larger than 500 for portfolio management problem. The useful information for current trading decisions is spread over a long period in historical data. Therefore, it is unreasonable to use fixed-length compression at the bottom of the model. In order to solve this, we introduce the attention mechanism to effectively extract information from long input.

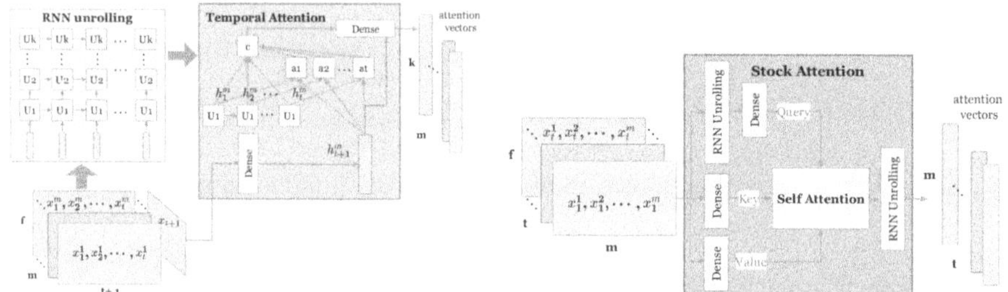

(a) An illustration of the proposed temporal attention architecture.

(b) An illustration of the proposed stock attention architecture.

Fig. 2. Attention overview.

Figure 2(a) illustrates the design details of temporal attention and Fig. 2(b) illustrates the design details of stock attention. In the following sections, we describe each component in detail.

Temporal Attention. In this section, we first illustrate the need to identify the importance of information on different trading days and then introduce how we obtain temporal focuses for the model. First, it is not good to have no focus on historical price series. It has been shown that the importance of historical trading data for the same asset varies from day to day. There are special trading days (e.g., most investors adjust their positions significantly, market crashes, new company IPOs, etc.) whose trading information is much more important than common trading days. It is desirable that we can give the model this ability to identify the temporal focus.

Next, we describe how we mathematically represent the temporal attention on the historical data. In Fig. 2(a), we slice the data in the m dimension. We use $x_1^i, x_2^i, \cdots, x_t^i$ to represent the slice of asset i and $h_1^i, h_2^i, \cdots, h_t^i$ to represent the hidden state of each time step during RNN unrolling. Since we are trying to have the model predict the future by learning information from history, we can use the future data as a teacher which guides the model to identify the important information from the historical data. Here we introduce the teacher vector h_{t+1}^i, which is the linear representation of x_{t+1}^i. Similar to [9], the attention vectors are obtained by:

$$a_t^i = align(h^i, h_{t+1}^i), \quad c_t^i = \sum_{j=1}^{t} a_t h_j^i, \quad h_a^i = tanh(W_c[c_t^i; h_{t+1}^i]). \quad (4)$$

where $h^i = (h_1^i, h_2^i, \cdots, h_t^i)$ and a_t^i, c_t^i, h_a^i is the attention weight, context vector, attention vector of asset i, separately.

Stock Attention. For each point in time, different assets have different influences on the portfolio due to their intrinsic properties (growth stocks/value stocks, large caps/small caps) and extrinsic market conditions (economic cycle rotation, sector rotation), and we should have stock focuses when we make a trading decision. In order to give the model this ability, we introduce the stock attention mechanism.

In Fig. 2(b), we first slice the data in the t dimension. We use $x_j^1, x_j^2, \cdots, x_j^m$ to represent the slice of time j and $h_j^1, h_j^2, \cdots, h_j^m$ to represent the hidden state of each asset step during RNN unrolling. Second, we use the attention mechanism which is similar to [10] to preprocess each slice. The query, key, and value are set as follows: query $h_j = \{h_j^1, h_j^2, \cdots, h_j^m\}$, key $x_j = \{x_j^1, x_j^2, \cdots, x_j^m\}$ and value $x_j = \{x_j^1, x_j^2, \cdots, x_j^m\}$. And the stock attention input are obtained by:

$$e_j = V_j^T tanh(W_c h_j + U_e x_j), \quad \alpha_j = \frac{exp(e_j)}{\sum_{k=1}^{m} exp(e_j^k)}, \quad x_a^j = \sum_{k=1}^{m} \alpha_j^k x_j^k. \quad (5)$$

where x_a^j is the attention input of time j. Then x_a^j is pass into second RNN unrolling layer to get hidden state h_a^j, which is the output stock attention vector.

4.4 Multi-window Convolution

Convolutional neural networks, commonly used in computer vision, can process data in parallel, which makes it much faster to train than RNNs. Previous studies have shown that CNNs also outperform RNNs in terms of local feature extraction. Therefore, we propose the Multi-window ActorCNN and apply it to the portfolio management problem.

As we shown in Fig. 3, the CNN-based model convolves the input data directly, instead of slicing the data in one dimension. The convolution kernels of different window lengths observe local features of different time lengths in the asset data, forming unique feature maps. After that we concatenate these feature maps to make the model have a more comprehensive understanding of the historical data. Then the concatenated feature maps are compressed by a Max-pooling layer. After each convolution, we add ReLU activation function and Batch Normalization to prevent the model from overfitting.

Portfolio-Vector Memory (PVM) [11] is introduced to store the output actions. As shown in Fig. 3, the PVM is a stack of weight vectors in chronological order, which is initialized with uniform weights. At t training step, the model reads the previous action w_{t-1} from the memory and writes current action w_t to the memory.

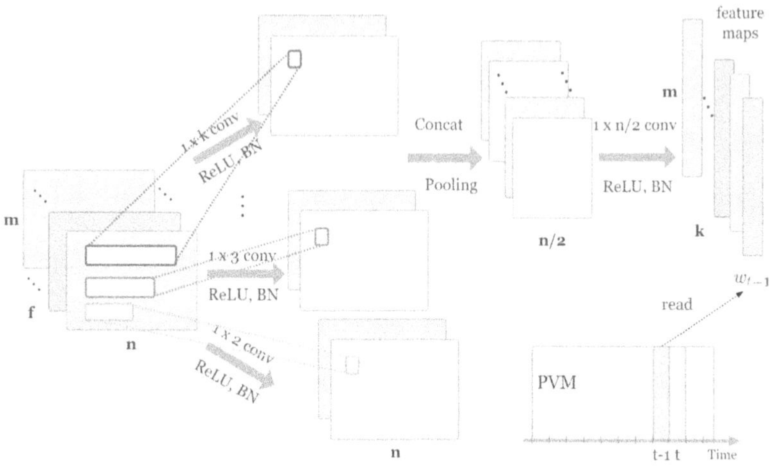

Fig. 3. Model architecture of Multi-window ActorCNN.

5   Experiments

In this section, we evaluate the general performance of the proposed models through well-established experiments. First, we compare the performance of the Attention ActorRNN, Multi-window ActorCNN with SOTA models: CNN (2017) [3], RNN (2017) [3], Ensemble (2019) [12], DeepTrader (2021) [7] in A-share market. Then, we conduct extensive ablation studies to understand the contribution of temporal attention, stock attention and multi-window convolution in the proposed models.

5.1   Data Treatments

In order to clearly show the weight change in the graph, we select a representative subset from all listed stocks as the stock pool. We select 10 stocks with the highest capitalization and liquidity in the A-share market to adequately represent the whole market. After constructing the stock pool, we use the BaoStock API [13] to fetch the historical data (OHCL, Volume) and financial indicators of each component stocks. Then, we explore the effects of different preprocessing methods (seasonal decomposition [14], fuzzy learning [15] and DNN module [15]) on the RL-based model and design a simple Actor-only model to verify the effects of different methods. We use the best-performing preprocessing method (fuzzy learning in this paper) on the single stock management problem as the one we use for the portfolio management problem.

5.2 Experimental Setup

Dataset. There are three typical states of A-share market: shocking market, bull market and bear market. Based on the overall trend of HS300 and historical news reports, we selected one typical period for each market state and conduct back-testing on them, separately. Details of the time-ranges for the back-test experiments and their corresponding training sets are presented in Table 1.

Table 1. Back testing range of different market states.

	Training Data Range	Testing Data Range
Shocking Market	2017.12.5–2021.5.27	2021.5.28–2021.12.31
Bull Market	2012.3.9–2020.3.3	2020.4.1–2020.12.31
Bear Market	2012.3.9–2021.12.31	2022.1.1–2022.3.28

Evaluation Metrics. To evaluate the performance in terms of the ability of capturing active excess returns (alpha) and controlling risk (beta), we adopt the final Accumulated Portfolio Value (fAPV), Sharpe Ratio (SR) and Maximum Drawdown (MDD) in Jiang et al. [3].

5.3 General Evaluation

In this section, we compare the performance of our proposed models with SOTA models in three different market states. Table 2 shows the experiment results. The bold numbers indicate the best results. **Multi-CNN** represents Multi-window ActorCNN; **SRNN** represents Attention ActorRNN with simple-RNN unrolling layer, **LSTM** represents Attention ActorRNN with LSTM unrolling layer, while the **-f,-t,-s** respectively represents with full attention components (temporal+stock), with temporal attention only and with stock attention only.

Shocking Market. First, we evaluate the models on shocking market states of Chinese A-share. As illustrated in Table 2, **SRNN-f** achieves best performance on fAPV (126.469) and SR (2.318), which is much better than the performance of RNN (2017). There also exists a great gap between Multi-CNN and CNN (2017) on performance metrics. The great performance improvement implies that adding attention components and using Multi-window convolution do great help to enhance the feature retrieving ability of the model. Ensemble (2019) does not use CNN, RNN layers to extract the features from the data. Instead, it manually construct some common technical analysis indicators (MACD, RSI, CCI, ADX) as model inputs and use a simple Actor with full connected layers, which results in its poor performance on A-share market. Deep Trader (2021) achieves a performance close to SRNN-t in the shocking market, receiving a fAPV of

Table 2. Performances of models in three different market states on the A-share.

Model	Shocking			Bull			Bear		
	fAPV ↑	SR ↑	MDD ↓	fAPV ↑	SR ↑	MDD ↓	fAPV ↑	SR ↑	MDD ↓
CNN(2017)	103.235	1.538	0.094	110.014	1.084	0.146	100.888	−0.693	0.208
RNN(2017)	103.213	1.656	0.084	111.593	1.116	0.161	105.062	−0.297	0.212
Ensemble(2019)	100.305	0.116	**0.061**	101.135	0.307	**0.014**	99.913	−0.066	**0.010**
Deep Trader(2021)	108.270	0.773	0.092	109.560	0.834	0.059	90.240	−1.025	0.119
Multi-CNN	111.766	1.604	0.230	**118.140**	**1.468**	0.192	99.046	−0.707	0.299
SRNN-f	**126.469**	**2.318**	0.317	114.029	1.220	0.168	105.262	−0.440	0.241
SRNN-t	109.030	2.179	0.081	111.692	1.123	0.152	100.885	−0.691	0.197
SRNN-s	104.485	1.960	0.087	111.986	1.201	0.156	102.935	−0.452	0.211
LSTM-f	107.104	1.620	0.188	112.079	1.254	0.146	**115.150**	**0.203**	0.309
LSTM-t	103.237	1.538	0.094	109.705	1.104	0.139	100.887	−0.692	0.206
LSTM-s	103.337	2.039	0.059	113.632	1.428	0.124	105.236	−0.164	0.174

108.270 while keeping the MDDD at 0.092. Deep Trader's trading frequency is lower than other models, with an average of about 15 days for position adjustments. The proposed market scoring unit and asset scoring unit proposed avoid the model to trade ineffectively when the market trend is not obvious. The low trading frequency also allows Deep Trader to save a lot of trading fees, which is more suitable for real world application.

Bull Market. In bull market, all models achieve higher cumulative returns than in the shocking market. As shown in Table 2, the proposed models Muli-CNN, SRNN-f and LSTM-f all outperform the baseline models, with Multi-CNN achieving the best score on on fAPV (118.140) and SR (1.468). The above results show that our models can not only take advantage of the asset value growth from the market trend, but also select the stocks with greater uptrend in a bull market to gain excess returns over the market and the baseline model.

Bear Market. Since the A-share market cannot be shorted, we adjusted the output action of each model (must greater than 0) and ensured that each model can only use its own assets (both holdings and cash) to buy and sell when making portfolio adjustments. In bear market, nearly all the experimental models perform worse than in the shocking market. However, our proposed LSTM-f outperforms all other models and achieves a cumulative return of 115.150 and a positive Sharpe ratio of 0.203. By analysing the asset weight evolution, we learn that the LSTM-f model increases the weight of cash before the descending trend is revealed. When the market ends a downtrend, LSTM-f starts to lower the cash weight and increases the trading frequency. The other models do not significantly reduce the number of trades in a bear market, which causes them to perform poorly.

5.4   Ablation Study

As we proposed several components (temporal attention, stock attention and multi-window Convolution) to improve the feature extraction ability of the model, we evaluate their performance on Shocking market to understand their contribution, separately. Specifically, we evaluate the model's performance on fAPV and report it in Fig. 4.

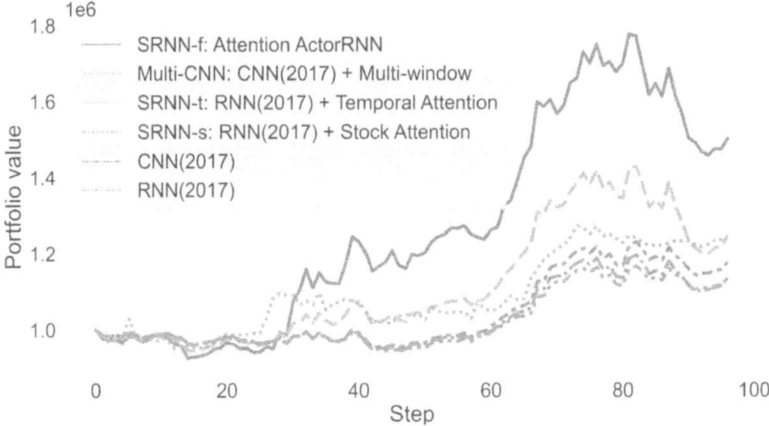

Fig. 4. Ablation study.

First, **SRNN-s** improves 1.276 on fAPV compared with RNN (2017). From the asset weight evolution we learned that the SRNN-s can actively change the asset weights during back-testing. However, there is almost no position transfers during back-testing for RNN (2017). The result demonstrates that the proposed stock attention component provides the model with stock selection ability (i.e. identifying the influence of different assets on the portfolio).

Second, **SRNN-t** gets 5.817 boost on fAPV compared with RNN (2017). From the asset weight evolution we learned that the SRNN-t can not only conduct active portfolio management but also able to pick the right time of trading. The result validate the effectiveness of identifying the importance of information on different trading days.

Third, **Multi-CNN** improves 8.530 on fAPV compared with CNN (2017). Interestingly, simply adding unique feature maps through Multi-window convolution leads to a great boost. It shows the importance of making the model have a more comprehensive understanding of the historical data.

Fourth, **SRNN-f** gets a significant 23.256 boost on fAPV compared with RNN (2017). It's known that stock selection ability is markedly inversely related to market timing ability. Considering one aspect alone cannot make the model achieve the desired performance. SRNN-f contains both stock attention component and temporal attention component, which enable the model to make a balance between stock selection ability and market timing ability.

6 Conclusion

In this paper, we propose an Attention ActorRNN model and a Multi-window ActorCNN model to address the shortcomings of existing research methods in feature extraction from historical data of assets. The proposed attention mechanism and multi-window convolution mechanism provide the model ability of identify the fluctuation pattern on different trading days, and the influence of different assets on the portfolio. In addition, we propose an adjusted reward with position penalty factor, which enables the model to balance both the risk and returns during trading. We conduct a comprehensive evaluation of our proposed model in shocking, bull and bear market states. Experiment results confirm the superiority of our proposed model by comparing it with several SOTA models. Further ablation experiments verify the effectiveness of our proposed temporal attention, stock attention and multi-window convolution components.

References

1. Box, G.E.P., Pierce, D.A.: Distribution of residual autocorrelations in autoregressive-integrated moving average time series models. J. Am. Stat. Assoc. **65**(332), 1509–1526 (1970)
2. Bollerslev, T.: Generalized autoregressive conditional heteroskedasticity. J. Econometr. **31**(3), 307–327 (1986)
3. Jiang, Z., Xu, D., Liang, J.: A deep reinforcement learning framework for the financial portfolio management problem. arXiv preprint arXiv:1706.10059 (2017)
4. Li, B., Zhao, P., Hoi, S.C.H., et al.: PAMR: passive aggressive mean reversion strategy for portfolio selection. Mach. Learn. **87**(2), 221–258 (2012)
5. Li, B., Hoi, S.C.H., Zhao, P., et al.: Confidence weighted mean reversion strategy for online portfolio selection. ACM Trans. Knowl. Discov. Data (TKDD) **7**(1), 1–38 (2013)
6. Wang, J., Zhang, Y., Tang, K., et al.: Alphastock: a buying-winners-and-selling-losers investment strategy using interpretable deep reinforcement attention networks. In: Proceedings of the 25th ACM SIGKDD International Conference on Knowledge Discovery & Data Mining, pp. 1900–1908 (2019)
7. Wang, Z., Huang, B., Tu, S., et al.: DeepTrader: a deep reinforcement learning approach for risk-return balanced portfolio management with market conditions embedding. In: Proceedings of the AAAI Conference on Artificial Intelligence, vol. 35, no. 1, pp. 643–650 (2021)
8. Li, B., Hoi, S.C.H.: Online portfolio selection: a survey. ACM Comput. Surv. (CSUR) **46**(3), 1–36 (2014)
9. Luong, M.T., Pham, H., Manning, C.D.: Effective approaches to attention-based neural machine translation. arXiv preprint arXiv:1508.04025 (2015)
10. Vaswani, A., Shazeer, N., Parmar, N., et al.: Attention is all you need. In: Advances in Neural Information Processing Systems, vol. 30 (2017)

11. Mnih, V., et al.: Asynchronous methods for deep reinforcement learning. In: International Conference on Machine Learning, pp. 1928–1937 (2016)
12. Yang, H., Liu, X.Y., Zhong, S., et al.: Deep reinforcement learning for automated stock trading: an ensemble strategy. In: Proceedings of the First ACM International Conference on AI in Finance, pp. 1–8 (2020)
13. Baostock (2020). http://baostock.com/
14. Cleveland, R.B., Cleveland, W.S., McRae, J.E., et al.: STL: a seasonal-trend decomposition. J. Off. Stat 6(1), 3–73 (1990)
15. Deng, Y., Bao, F., Kong, Y., et al.: Deep direct reinforcement learning for financial signal representation and trading. IEEE Trans. Neural Networks Learn. Syst. 28(3), 653–664 (2016)
16. Su, R., et al.: A deep reinforcement learning approach for portfolio management in non-short-selling market. IET Signal Process. 2024(1), 5399392 (2024)

Algorithmic Evaluation of Enterprise Competitiveness in the Industrial Economy Using Stacked Machine Learning Models

Minglei Lv[✉]

Qingdao Pingdu Urban Development Group, Qingdao 266000, Shandong, China
`kittysing@163.com`

Abstract. Aiming at the subjectivity and limitation of traditional evaluation methods, this paper puts forward an objective evaluation method based on algorithm model. By integrating machine learning technologies such as Support Vector Machine (SVM) and Deep Neural Network (DNN), and adopting Stacking integrated learning strategy, a composite model is constructed to improve the prediction accuracy and generalization ability. The model integrates multi-dimensional information such as enterprise financial data, market share and technological innovation ability, and can comprehensively evaluate the competitiveness of enterprises in industrial economy. In the aspect of model input, several key indicators such as enterprise financial data, market share and technological innovation ability are considered to ensure the comprehensiveness and accuracy of evaluation. To verify the validity of the model, this paper selects high-tech industry as the case study object, collects relevant data of 10 enterprises, and carries out strict data preprocessing and model training. Through model prediction, the competitiveness score of each enterprise is obtained, and ranking and classification analysis are carried out. The results show that the model can effectively identify enterprises with strong competitiveness in the industry and provide targeted improvement suggestions. The research not only provides a new idea and method for quantitative evaluation of enterprise competitiveness, but also provides reference for evaluation in other industries. Through application of this model, enterprises can more accurately understand their position and advantages in the industrial economy, and provide strong support for strategic formulation and market competition.

Keywords: Industrial Economy · Enterprise Competitiveness · Stacking · support vector machine · Deep neural network

1 Introduction

With the acceleration of globalization and informatization, the competitiveness of enterprises in industrial economy is particularly critical. The competitiveness of enterprises is not only related to their own survival and development, but also directly affects the stability of the entire industrial chain and the economic strength of the country [1]. However, the traditional evaluation methods of enterprise competitiveness often rely

S. C. P. Yam et al. (Eds.): ICFT 2025, CCIS 2868, pp. 40–49, 2026.
https://doi.org/10.1007/978-981-92-0126-6_4

on subjective judgment and qualitative analysis, which lacks scientificity and accuracy. Therefore, exploring a more objective and quantitative analysis method of enterprise competitiveness has become an important topic in current industrial economic research.

In the industrial economy, the study of enterprise competitiveness has a profound theoretical basis. Enterprise competitiveness is usually defined as the ability of an enterprise to gain advantages in market competition, which covers many aspects, such as cost control, product innovation, market expansion, etc. [2, 3]. Porter's five forces model provides a macro framework for the analysis of enterprise competitiveness, which emphasizes five main forces of industry competition: competitors in the same industry, potential entrants, threats of substitutes, bargaining power of suppliers and bargaining power of buyers [4, 5]. This model is of great significance for understanding the competitive pattern of enterprises and formulating corresponding strategies. RBV (Resource-Based View) analyzes competitiveness from the perspective of internal resources of enterprises [6]. According to this theory, the unique resources and capabilities owned by enterprises are the key to their competitive advantage. These resources may include technology patents, brand assets and unique organizational culture. RBV emphasizes the influence of internal factors on competitiveness, which is a useful supplement to the five-force model. In the application of algorithm model, with the development of data science and machine learning in recent years, more and more researches began to explore how to use these advanced technologies to evaluate the competitiveness of enterprises [7, 8]. Machine learning algorithms such as support vector machine (SVM), neural network and random forest are widely used in enterprise data analysis to reveal the patterns and trends hidden in a large number of data [9, 10].

At present, although many scholars and business people have conducted in-depth research on the competitiveness of enterprises, there are still many shortcomings in the existing evaluation system. For example, many evaluation methods pay too much attention to financial indicators and ignore intangible factors such as innovation ability and brand influence of enterprises. In addition, some evaluation methods fail to make full use of the advantages of big data and advanced algorithms, resulting in inaccurate and comprehensive evaluation results. In view of this, this study aims to construct an enterprise competitiveness analysis method based on algorithm model. Through the comprehensive use of data analysis, machine learning and other technical means, the position and advantages of enterprises in the industrial economy can be more accurately evaluated, thus providing strong support for enterprise strategy formulation and market competition.

2 Algorithm Model Construction

2.1 Composite Model Combining Basic Learner and Meta-Learner

At present, many researches have tried to build an enterprise competitiveness evaluation model based on machine learning algorithm [11, 12]. These models usually use multi-dimensional information such as financial data, market data and technical data of enterprises as input, and predict the competitiveness or market performance of enterprises through training models. However, there are still some limitations in the existing research, such as the singleness of data sources and the lack of generalization ability of the model. This study will further explore and optimize the algorithm model of enterprise competitiveness on the basis of previous studies. By integrating diversified data sources and adopting advanced machine learning technology, a more accurate and comprehensive evaluation model of enterprise competitiveness is constructed, which provides valuable decision support for enterprises in industrial economy.

In particular, this research proposes a stacked machine learning model architecture that combines the strengths of multiple base learners, such as Random Forest (RF), Gradient Boosting Decision Tree (GBDT), and Support Vector Machine (SVM), with a meta-learner to improve predictive performance and reduce overfitting. Stacking has been proven to outperform individual models in a wide range of regression and classification tasks by capturing non-linear and complementary patterns across learners. In the context of enterprise competitiveness, where the influencing factors are complex and interrelated, this approach can offer a significant advantage in extracting deeper insights from the data.

Furthermore, this study incorporates an extensive range of data sources beyond traditional financial indicators. In addition to financial ratios and balance sheet data, the model considers intangible factors such as R&D investment, patent filings, ESG (Environmental, Social, and Governance) performance, customer sentiment analysis from online reviews, and macroeconomic indicators that reflect regional industrial dynamics. Text mining techniques are used to transform unstructured textual data, such as company announcements or market news, into structured inputs. This multi-source data integration ensures that the model captures a holistic picture of an enterprise's internal capabilities and external environment.

To ensure robustness and generalizability, the proposed model is trained and validated on a large-scale dataset covering enterprises from different industrial sectors and geographic regions. Cross-validation techniques and hyperparameter tuning are applied to improve model performance and mitigate the risk of overfitting. Feature importance analysis and SHAP (SHapley Additive exPlanations) values are also employed to enhance interpretability and understand the key drivers of competitiveness, enabling stakeholders to make informed strategic decisions.

Moreover, the evaluation framework developed in this study is not limited to static prediction but is also capable of temporal analysis. By incorporating time-series modeling elements, the model can monitor competitiveness trends over time, allowing enterprises to assess the long-term impact of strategic decisions and policy changes. This temporal component makes the model highly valuable for industrial policy makers, financial analysts, and enterprise managers who need dynamic insights for planning and forecasting.

In conclusion, this study not only contributes to the methodological advancement in enterprise competitiveness evaluation through the use of stacked machine learning models, but also enhances practical relevance by addressing data heterogeneity and interpretability challenges. The resulting evaluation system has the potential to serve as a decision support tool for enterprise development, investment risk assessment, and policy formulation in the era of the digital and industrial economy.

The algorithm model adopts ensemble learning method and combines the advantages of SVM and neural network to create a composite model, aiming at improving the prediction accuracy and the generalization ability of the model [13]. The algorithm model is a compound model composed of multiple basic learners and meta-learners, which can comprehensively utilize the advantages of different algorithms to improve the accuracy of enterprise competitiveness evaluation (Fig. 1).

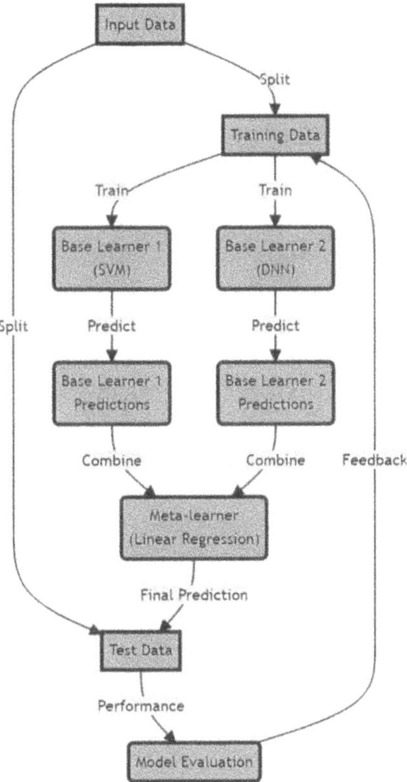

Fig. 1. Algorithm model architecture.

Specifically, Support Vector Machines (SVM) offer strong performance in handling high-dimensional and sparse data, making them particularly effective in capturing the complex nonlinear relationships often found in enterprise performance indicators. On the other hand, neural networks are capable of modeling deep hierarchical features through their multilayer structure, enabling the extraction of intricate patterns from diverse datasets. By integrating these two algorithms through a stacking framework, the model is able to learn both local and global patterns in the data, thus enhancing both the robustness and flexibility of the evaluation system.

The stacking architecture is designed in two levels: the first level includes multiple base models (e.g., SVM, neural networks, decision trees), each learning different perspectives from the input data. Their outputs are then fed into a second-level meta-learner, which makes the final prediction by capturing inter-model dependencies and correcting potential biases. This structure allows the model to mitigate the weaknesses of any single learning algorithm and take advantage of the diversity of the ensemble.

Moreover, the model supports dynamic updating by incorporating new data in real-time or in batch mode, making it adaptable to changing market conditions and enterprise development trends. This feature significantly enhances the model's practical applicability for long-term enterprise monitoring, benchmarking, and strategic planning. The integration of ensemble learning into competitiveness evaluation represents a data-driven, intelligent advancement in industrial economy analysis, offering both theoretical innovation and real-world decision-making value.

Ensemble learning can accomplish the learning task by combining multiple basic learners, and usually it can achieve better generalization performance than a single learner. In this study, Stacking integration strategy is adopted, which combines the prediction results of multiple base learners through meta-learners [14]. Firstly, several different basic learners (SVM, neural network) are trained, and then the prediction results of these basic learners are used as a new training set to train a meta-learner, so as to get the final prediction results.

SVM is a machine learning algorithm widely used in classification and regression problems. In this study, SVM is used as one of the basic learners. SVM divides data by finding an optimal hyperplane, so that different types of data points can be correctly separated as much as possible. For nonlinear problems, the data are mapped to high-dimensional space by kernel function, so that the hyperplane with linear division can be found in high-dimensional space.

For nonlinear problems, SVM maps data from original feature space to high-dimensional space by introducing kernel function $K(x_i, x_j)$, so as to find a hyperplane with linear division in high-dimensional space. After using kernel function, the objective function of SVM becomes:

$$\frac{1}{2} \sum_{i=1}^{n} \sum_{j=1}^{n} y_i y_j \alpha_i \alpha_j K\left(x_i, x_j\right) - \sum_{i=1}^{n} \alpha_i \tag{1}$$

The constraints are:

$$\sum_{i=1}^{n} y_i \alpha_i = 0, 0 \leq \alpha \leq C, i = 1, 2, \cdots, n \tag{2}$$

Where, x_i is the feature vector of the i training sample, y_i is the category label of the i training sample (usually the value is $+1$ or 1), and n is the total number of training samples. α_i is Lagrange multiplier and C is regularization parameter, which is used to control the punishment degree of misclassification.

Neural network is an algorithm model that simulates the connection mode of human brain neurons, and has strong representation learning ability. Deep neural network (DNN) is used as another basic learner [15]. DNN approximates any complex nonlinear function through the connection and activation function of multi-layer neurons, which is suitable for dealing with complex enterprise competitiveness evaluation problems.

Forward propagation is a process in which information is transmitted from the input layer to the output layer through the hidden layer. For the l-th layer ($l = 1, 2, \cdots, L$, where L is the total number of layers), its output $a^{(l)}$ can be expressed as:

$$a^{(l)} = \sigma\left(z^{(l)}\right) = \sigma\left(W^{(l)}a^{(l-1)} + b^{(l)}\right) \tag{3}$$

Where $W^{(l)}$ is the weight matrix of the l layer, $b^{(l)}$ is the bias vector of the l layer, $\sigma(\cdot)$ is the activation function, and $a^{(l-1)}$ is the output of the previous layer.

The weight update formula is expressed as:

$$\begin{aligned}
W^{(l)} &= W^{(l)} - \eta\frac{\partial L}{\partial W^{(l)}} \\
b^{(l)} &= b^{(l)} - \eta\frac{\partial L}{\partial b^{(l)}}
\end{aligned} \tag{4}$$

Where L is the loss function, η is the learning rate, and $\frac{\partial L}{\partial W^{(l)}}$, $\frac{\partial L}{\partial b^{(l)}}$ is the gradient of the weight and bias of the loss function respectively.

In Stacking integration strategy, meta-learners are used to combine the prediction results of base learners. Considering the complexity of enterprise competitiveness evaluation, linear regression model is used as meta-learner. Linear regression model can simply synthesize the prediction results of each basic learner by weighted summation, while maintaining the explanatory nature of the model.

In Stacking integration strategy, meta-learners are used to combine the prediction results of multiple base learners. In the Stacking integration strategy, the prediction result of the base learner is used as the explanatory variable, and the real label is used as the target variable to train the linear regression model. The regression coefficient is estimated by the least square method, so that the sum of square errors between the predicted value and the actual value is minimum.

The estimation formula of regression coefficient is:

$$\hat{\beta} = \left(X^T X\right)^{-1} X^T y \tag{5}$$

Where X is the design matrix, which contains the prediction results of all basic learners, each row corresponds to a sample, and each column corresponds to the prediction results of a basic learner; y is the vector of the real label; $\hat{\beta}$ is an estimate of the regression coefficient.

For the new sample, the trained linear regression model and the prediction result of the basic learner are used to calculate the final prediction value. The formula is:

$$\hat{y} = \hat{\beta}_0 + \hat{\beta}_1\hat{x}_1 + \hat{\beta}_2\hat{x}_2 + \cdots + \hat{\beta}_k\hat{x}_k \tag{6}$$

Where $\hat{y}$ is the predicted value of the new sample, $\hat{\beta}_0, \hat{\beta}_1, \hat{\beta}_2, \cdots, \hat{\beta}_k$ is the estimated value of the regression coefficient obtained through training, and $\hat{x}_1, \hat{x}_2, \cdots, \hat{x}_k$ is the predicted result of the new sample on each base learner.

2.2 Input and Output of the Model

The model combines the advantages of SVM and DNN, and adopts Stacking integration strategy to improve the prediction accuracy and generalization ability of the model.

By comprehensively utilizing the advantages of different algorithms, the competitiveness of enterprises can be evaluated more comprehensively and accurately. The model can comprehensively utilize the information of enterprise financial data, market share, technological innovation ability and other aspects, and provide strong support for the quantitative evaluation of enterprise competitiveness.

The competitiveness of enterprises is influenced by many factors, including financial data (such as total assets, total liabilities, operating income, net profit, etc.), which can reflect the economic strength and profitability of enterprises; Market share, that is, the market share of enterprises in the industry, reflects their position and influence in the industry; Technological innovation ability, measured by R&D investment, the number of patent applications and other indicators, reflects the technological innovation ability and development potential of enterprises; And other related factors, such as brand awareness, management level, employee satisfaction, etc., these factors will also have an important impact on the competitiveness of enterprises.

Enterprise competitiveness score is a comprehensive index, which is used to quantify the comprehensive competitiveness level of enterprises. The score is obtained by analyzing the financial data, market share, technological innovation ability (R&D investment, number of patent applications, etc.) and other related factors (brand awareness, management level, employee satisfaction, etc.), combined with the prediction results of several basic learners, thus providing a numerical index for comprehensively evaluating the strength and market position of enterprises. This score can provide an intuitive reference for investors, managers and other stakeholders to help them understand the performance and potential of enterprises in a highly competitive market environment.

3 Case Analysis

In order to verify the effectiveness of the integrated learning model in the evaluation of enterprise competitiveness, this study selected representative high-tech industries for case analysis. High-tech industry is one of the fast-developing industries, and the evaluation of its enterprise competitiveness is of great significance to investors, policy makers and enterprises themselves.

The data of 10 related enterprises in high-tech industry were collected from open channels, including financial data, market share, technological innovation capability indicators, etc. These data are strictly cleaned, transformed and standardized to ensure the quality and consistency of the data, which provides an accurate data basis for the subsequent model training.

Using the collected data, two basic learners, SVM and DNN, are trained respectively. Then, the prediction results of these two basic learners are used as a new training set to train the linear regression meta-learner. Apply the trained integrated learning model to evaluate the competitiveness of enterprises in high-tech industries. Through model prediction, the competitiveness score of each enterprise is obtained.

According to the competitiveness score predicted by the model, the enterprises in the high-tech industry are sorted and classified. The analysis results show that some enterprises have outstanding performance in financial data, market share and technological innovation ability, and have high competitiveness scores. At the same time, it is also found that some enterprises have shortcomings in some aspects, resulting in relatively low competitiveness scores (Fig. 2).

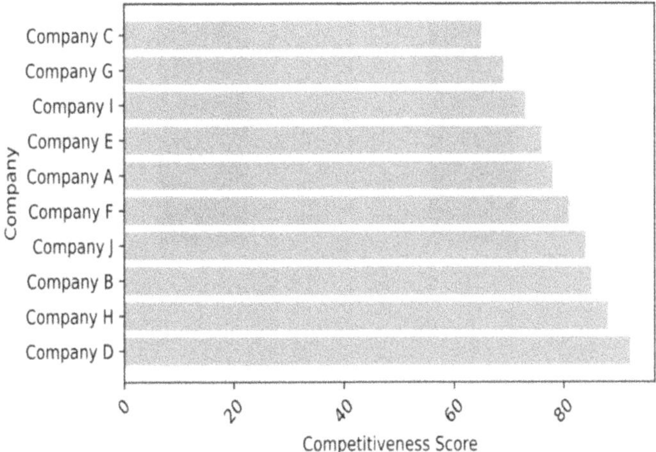

Fig. 2. Ranking of competitiveness scores of enterprises.

Figure 3 shows the performance of 10 enterprises in high-tech industry in four key indicators: financial data, market share, technological innovation ability and overall competitiveness score. The color depth intuitively reflects the relative strength of each enterprise in various indicators. Enterprise E and enterprise J are outstanding in many indicators and are the best in the industry. Enterprise F, on the other hand, has poor performance in many aspects and needs to take effective measures to improve it. Other enterprises have their own advantages, so they need to formulate targeted development strategies according to their own conditions to enhance their competitiveness.

Based on the evaluation results, this paper puts forward the following suggestions and strategies for enterprises in high-tech industries: for enterprises with relatively weak technological innovation ability, they should increase investment in research and development and actively introduce and cultivate high-end talents to enhance their technological strength; For enterprises with poor financial data performance, we should strengthen financial management, improve the efficiency of capital use and reduce operating costs, so as to enhance economic benefits; For enterprises with small market share, they should actively explore new markets, enhance brand awareness and influence, and expand market share.

Through the application of the integrated learning model constructed in this study in the evaluation of the competitiveness of enterprises in high-tech industries, it is found that the model can effectively quantitatively evaluate the competitiveness of enterprises. Based on the evaluation results, this paper puts forward some targeted suggestions and strategies for enterprises in order to help them improve their competitiveness and achieve sustainable development. At the same time, this study also provides some reference and reference value for the evaluation of enterprise competitiveness in other industries.

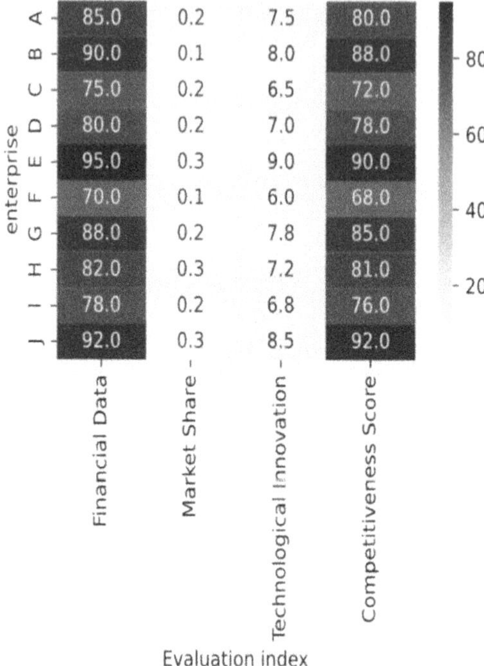

Fig. 3. The relative performance of enterprises in different indicators

4   Conclusion

A compound model based on ensemble learning method is proposed, which combines the advantages of SVM and DNN, and adopts Stacking integration strategy to improve prediction accuracy and model generalization ability. The model uses diversified data sources, such as enterprise financial data, market share, technological innovation ability and other multi-dimensional information as input, and obtains a meta-learner that integrates multiple basic learners through training to get the final prediction result. The integrated learning model is applied to evaluate the competitiveness of these enterprises, and the competitiveness score of each enterprise is obtained, which is sorted and classified according to the score. The results show that some enterprises have outstanding performance in financial data, market share and technological innovation ability, and have high competitiveness scores; However, some enterprises have shortcomings in some aspects, resulting in relatively low competitiveness scores. The integrated learning model constructed in this study can effectively quantitatively evaluate the competitiveness of enterprises and provide strong support for enterprise strategy formulation and market competition. At the same time, the targeted suggestions and strategies based on the evaluation results are helpful for enterprises to enhance their competitiveness and achieve sustainable development.

References

1. Knapcikova, L., Behunova, A., Behun, M.: The strategic impact of e-business on competitiveness of the enterprise. Mobile Netw. Appl. **28**(1), 211–219 (2023)
2. Li, J., Sun, Y., Gong, L., Chai, N., Yin, Y.: Multiattribute fuzzy decision evaluation approach and its application in enterprise competitiveness evaluation. Math. Probl. Eng. **2021**(1), 1–11 (2021)
3. Qiansha, Z., Xiaoxia, Z., Binbin, W.F.: Enterprise innovation evaluation method based on swarm optimization algorithm and artificial neural network. Neural Comput. Appl. **35**(36), 25143–25156 (2023)
4. Bistrova, J., Lace, N., Kasperovica, L.: Enterprise crisis-resilience and competitiveness. Sustainability. **13**(4), 2057 (2021)
5. Du, E.: Impact of bank research and development on total factor productivity and performance evaluation by RBF network. J. Supercomput. **78**(9), 12070–12092 (2022)
6. Chen, F., Wei, Y.: Evolution of enterprise competitiveness in multiplex networks of standards: a case study of the communication industry in China. Complexity. **2020**(1), 1–24 (2020)
7. Fu, H.: Optimization study of multidimensional big data matrix model in enterprise performance evaluation system. Wirel. Commun. Mob. Comput. **2021**(2), 1–12 (2021)
8. Kao, F.C., Huang, S.C., Lo, H.W.: A Rough-Fermatean DEMATEL approach for sustainable development evaluation for the manufacturing industry. Int. J. Fuzzy Syst. **24**(7), 3244–3264 (2022)
9. Hongli, C., Yanyan, W., Xiuli, L., Wenju, Z.: Competitiveness evaluation of Chinese dairy industry based on accelerated genetic algorithm projection pursuit model. Math. Probl. Eng. **2020**(11), 1–17 (2020)
10. Aydoan, M.: Internal factors affecting competitiveness in agribusinesses: a case study in the hazelnut sector in Ordu and Giresun provinces of Turkey. Erwerbs-obstbau. **65**(4), 795–805 (2022)
11. Chen, X., Wu, Y., Zhong, R.: Research on competitiveness of China's social commerce enterprises based on macro- and micro-niche. Sustainability. **13**(1), 422 (2021)
12. Gong, Z., Guo, K., He, X.: Corporate social responsibility based on radial basis function neural network evaluation model of low-carbon circular economy coupled development. Complexity. **2021**(5), 1–11 (2021)
13. Grdan, D.A., Dumitru, I., Grdan, I.P., Patiu, C.A.: Touristic SME's competitiveness in the light of present challenges—a qualitative approach. Sustainability. **12**(21), 9191 (2020)
14. Tucean, I.M., Tmil, M., Ivascu, L., Miclea, E., Negru, M.: Integrating sustainability and lean: SLIM method and enterprise game proposed. Sustainability. **11**(7), 2103 (2019)
15. Kiseáková, D., Ofranková, B., Gombár, M., Abinová, V., Onuferová, E.: Competitiveness and its impact on sustainability, business environment, and human development of EU (28) countries in terms of global multi-criteria indices. Sustainability. **11**(12), 3365 (2019)

Genetic-Algorithm Investor Sentiment Indices and Post-Earnings-Announcement Dynamics in China's A-Share Market

Jianping Pan[✉]

Ping An Bank Co., Ltd., Xiamen Branch, Xiamen 361003, Fujian, China
767144571@qq.com

Abstract. Due to the fast development of computational intelligence, algorithmic modeling has become an indispensable method used for financial market analysis. This paper proposes an investor sentiment index by using genetic algorithm to explore its effect on post-earnings-announcement dynamics in Chinese A-share market. Based on the data of Shanghai Stock Exchange, a multi-dimensional investor sentiment index is built using MDA genetic dual-machine optimization process with consideration of non-linear relationship among sentiment indicators. Our empirical findings indicate that investor sentiment has a clear impact on stock return volatility for the period around earnings announcements. Particularly, positive earnings surprises generate stronger and faster price reactions in high-sentiment firms than that of low-sentiment ones. In low sentiment periods, on the other hand, negative earnings announcements elicit more sustained and severe price declines. These results reveal a one-sided asymmetry sentiment effect between optimistic and pessimistic investors, and provide evidence that the behavioral factors still play roles in stock price reaction after earnings announcement.

Keywords: Genetic algorithm · Investor sentiment · Earnings announcement · Post-announcement drift · A-share market

1 Introduction

China's stock market has only been established for more than twenty years, but has experienced several ups and down. For example, more than 10 years ago, the stock market was issued with more intensive policies and good news. But the stock market does not respond to it. In 2005–2008 of three years, the bull market and bear market were transformed [1]. There are many reasons for this phenomenon, including economic and non-economic factors. Behavioral finance believes that the psychological expectation and behavior of investors will affect the pricing of financial assets. Especially in emerging financial markets like China, there are such phenomena as irrational investor structure, immature investment ideas and strong speculative psychology. This will cause investor sentiment to fluctuate easily [2]. When an event occurs (such as mergers and acquisitions, earnings information disclosure), it is more likely to cause investors' emotional agitation.

S. C. P. Yam et al. (Eds.): ICFT 2025, CCIS 2868, pp. 50–60, 2026.
https://doi.org/10.1007/978-981-92-0126-6_5

Therefore, abnormal phenomena can be explained from the perspective of investors' cognitive bias and overreaction to events [3]. The study is based on the effect of investor sentiment, the impact of earnings announcements on stock price volatility, that is, from the perspective of behavioral finance.

In the classical efficient market model, investors assume that they are rational and that all pertinent information is instantaneously reflected in stock quotes. However, in practice, the assumption has been proven to be violated in China's A-share market multiple times. Such sudden price spikes or crashes usually happen without any fundamental motivation, which means that collective emotions and sentiment swings are predominant in the market dynamics. Prior work has empirically demonstrated that investor sentiment is an important driver of cross- section stock returns, augmenting market reactions to earnings news [4]. Investor sentiment may work to reinforce market responses to earnings announcements, ultimately resulting in under-reaction or overreaction after earnings announcement. This kind of behavior leads to price drift, clustering volatility and abnormal returns that are difficult to be accounted by means of traditional financial variables.

In the past decade, driven by big data technologies, empirical measurement and quantification of investor sentiment have become a central issue in financial research. Standard sentiment indexes are usually based on either survey data, trading volume or market-based proxies like turnover and the number of new investor accounts. But such indexes are typically unable to reflect the dynamic, non-linear multi-dimension of investors' emotion in real time. Recent researches have tried to use machine learning and deep-learning techniques with sentiment analysis for better stock price prediction and capturing the mental image of the investors or traders [5]. To tackle these challenges, in this study we propose a Genetic Algorithm (GA) method to design an adaptive weighted criterion for the multiple sentiment proxies for form an investor sentiment index. The GA approach is very suitable for this task due to its capacity to efficiently cover large search spaces and identify nonlinear dependences without prior knowledge of the functional form.

Using this GA-based sentiment index in the context of China A-share market, it is then the purpose of the present study to investigate how investor sentiment interacts with post-earnings-announcement price dynamics. Earnings announcements are one of the most information-rich and emotionally charged events for companies. They offer a natural experiment to study how investors respond to new fundamental news in the presence of different sentiment levels. When investor sentiment is over optimistic, market participants can see neutral or slightly positive earnings as a strong buy signal which induces overreaction and temporarily upward pressure in prices. On the contrary, in pessimistic sentiment environments, positive earning may also result in weak price impact and underreaction as well as delayed resistance adjustment for stock prices.

This study makes 3 significant contributions to the literature. Firstly, it combines theories from behavioral finance with advanced computational intelligence methods and can be considered as a novel methodological viewpoint in terms of sentiment quantification. Second, it contributes to empirical evidence that how the investor sentiment may moderate the PEAD in a special market environment like China's, where retail investors dominate and policy-related volatility prevails. Third, the new GA sentiment index has the potential to be a useful early warning device for investors and other actors in capital markets (e.g., regulators), who need to detect periods of excessive optimism/pessimism if the aim is to stabilize markets as well as make more informed investment decisions.

In general, it helps to enrich the academic understanding on behavioral asset pricing and have practical effects on portfolio management, financial regulation and risk control in Chinese capital markets.

2   State of the Art

Compared with foreign countries, the empirical research on earnings announcement effect started late in China, the first in 1997. The domestic researchers use the event research method to calculate the cumulative abnormal returns. The relationship between the listed companies in Shanghai stock market, the stock price and the earnings information prove that the stock price earnings report drift phenomenon exists in the Shanghai stock market [6]. Then, by investigating the stock of Listed Companies in China, the relationship between abnormal earnings and the result of unexpected earnings shows a significant correlation between the two. It is confirmed that earnings announcement is information content, which can affect the volatility of stock price [7]. Other researchers have also proved that the price and the trend of "scissors" are good news after the Earnings Announcement Drift in China's two cities. The stock price rises first and then decreases after the announcement, otherwise it is bad news. Although many scholars have proved that China's stock market has the proclamation effect of surplus, the conclusions are different due to the choice of different proxy indicators and models [8]. The researchers in our country use the event study. For example, check the announcement period before and after the performance announcement period, announcement period earnings announcement effect. The study found that after the earnings report, the profit-making companies will have the most serious price surge and get higher profits. This is contrary to the conclusions drawn by other researchers in China. After the three-factor model was used to estimate earnings surplus announcement, the study found that China's stock market is a surplus announcement effect. But the shape is different from that of the United States and other developed countries, the price moves upwards after the bad news of the earnings report, and after the good news group's profit announcement, the phenomenon of the stock price continues to go downhill [9].

3   Methodology

3.1   Filter Analysis Algorithm

Screening analysis is based on the similarity between sample features in data samples and divides the samples into different categories. At present, the most common filtering algorithm is K-MEANS, which was put forward in 1976. Because of its simplicity and ease of implementation, it is widely used in large data filtering. K-MEANS is a filtering algorithm based on sample phase measure. On the basis of determining the number of k, the algorithm first selects k initial points as the screening center and assigns each sample to a class of the nearest k class according to the minimum distance principle.

After that, the screening center is constantly adjusted. When each sample reaches the minimum of the sum of squared squares in its category, it stops adjusting. Then, the Sample Firms's stock daily yield, stock return and market return data are selected from the Ruth database. Then it matches the risk-free return and market return data to calculate the expected normal return of the time window period. Assuming that the market return model is established, the normal return is calculated through this model. Explanatory variables are risk-free return and market premium. The explanatory variable is a share rate of return. The screening criteria, E, are described as:

$$E = \sum_{i=1}^{k} \sum_{peC_i} |p - m_i|^2 \tag{1}$$

Among them, p represents the sample point and m_i represents the screening center. C_i represents class i samples. The screening criterion E is interpreted as follows: for every point in each cluster, the square of the distance to the center is obtained, and then summation is made to ensure the compactness of the selected clusters. When using the K-MEANS algorithm, the filtering effect is good for data structures close to classes and far between classes. For the more complex screening structure, the screening results are easily influenced by the screening center, resulting in instability of the screening results.

3.2 Artificial Network Genetic Algorithm

In stock market, there are usually two ways to calculate expected earnings: judgment and statistics. The so-called "judgment" means that the annual surplus predicted by the financial analyst is the predicted value. But because China's stock market starts relatively late and the relevant system is not perfect, it is difficult for analysts to predict the value. Moreover, the judgment method has strong subjectivity, so this method is not adopted. The rule of statistics is the regression model based on the relevant models of Applied Statistics. If there is no significant change in the economic environment, if the information contained in the stock is of high quality, the annual earnings per share will not change significantly. The neuron in feedforward network can be divided into three parts: input unit, calculation unit and output unit. Each unit of calculation can have any input. But there is only one output. Its output can also be associated with any output of the same level neurons, and together form the input of the next layer of neurons. Based on the above characteristics, this kind of network can be easily connected in series and establish multilayer feedforward network. BP C Back Propagation) neural network is a typical feed forward network. It can obtain the nonlinear processing ability of complex systems through compound mapping of simple nonlinear processing units. It is the most widely used neural network computing model at present. The basic unit of BP neural network is neurons. Each neuron node includes inputs, outputs, weights, thresholds, and transformation functions. The structure of a single neuron is shown in the following diagram. x1 ~ xn is the input of the neuron, w1 ~ wn. For weights, B is a threshold, and t is a conversion function.

Genetic algorithm is a new evolutionary algorithm. It was inspired by the foraging behavior of birds in 1995 by Kennedy and Eberhart. Particle swarm optimization (PSO) is a random search algorithm. That is, starting from the random solution, the optimal solution can be found by iteration. It is a population intelligent algorithm. It evaluates the quality of the solution by the fitness. Its rule and parameter structure are simple, and the global optimum can be found by following the optimal value currently searched. The algorithm is developed by Professor John Holland of Michigan University and based on Darwin's evolutionary theory. It has the characteristics of parallel search and global convergence, and it is a typical non-gradient optimization algorithm. It differs from other optimization algorithms in that genetic algorithms can produce multiple solutions at the same time. Genetic algorithm has no special requirement for objective function, and the form of objective function is relatively free. The computation process of genetic algorithm is random. Genetic algorithm does not need to know the specific information of the problem, nor does it require complex gradient computation. A genetic algorithm represents the possible solution of each variable as a fragment of a chromosome. All variables may be sequentially arranged into a complete chromosome. Each chromosome represents an individual in the process of evolution. All individuals in the same generation are called a population. Before executing the genetic algorithm, the initial population was given firstly, that is, some hypothetical solutions. These assumptions are then put into the environment of the problem. According to the principle of survival of the fittest, the new generation of population adapting to the environment can be generated through the process of crossover, mutation and selection. In this way, evolution from generation to generation will eventually converge to the most adaptable individuals. It is the optimal solution of the problem and the genetic algorithm (As shown in Fig. 1).

In view of the physical model in the graph, the adaptive genetic algorithm proposed by Srinivas is adopted to optimize it. Each chromosome in the algorithm represents a design scheme for N layer absorbing materials, which is represented by the following binary strings.

$$C_j = Cs_1 Cs_2 \ldots Cs_N Cd_1 Cd_2 \ldots Cd_N, (j = 1, 2, \ldots N_c) \tag{2}$$

In the above equations, Csi and Cdi respectively denote the type and thickness coding of the i layer material. Nc is a population size. Ns and Nd respectively denote the type and thickness of material. Ns can be set according to the number of actual materials. Considering the actual machining precision of the material thickness, and in order to design both light and thin absorbing materials, the maximum thickness of each layer of material is set at 2 mm, and the corresponding Nd can be set to 8. The decoding formula for thickness is as follows

$$d_t = btf (Cd_i)/100 \tag{3}$$

The "btf" in the upper part is the binary decimal conversion function which is contained in the Matlab system, which is used for decoding the material thickness. Besides, in the whole decoding process, some thickness constraints are added. For example, the total thickness of the coating is more than 3.5 mm. The constraint condition monitors all links of the whole genetic algorithm. Due to the length of articles, other constraints are not outlined.

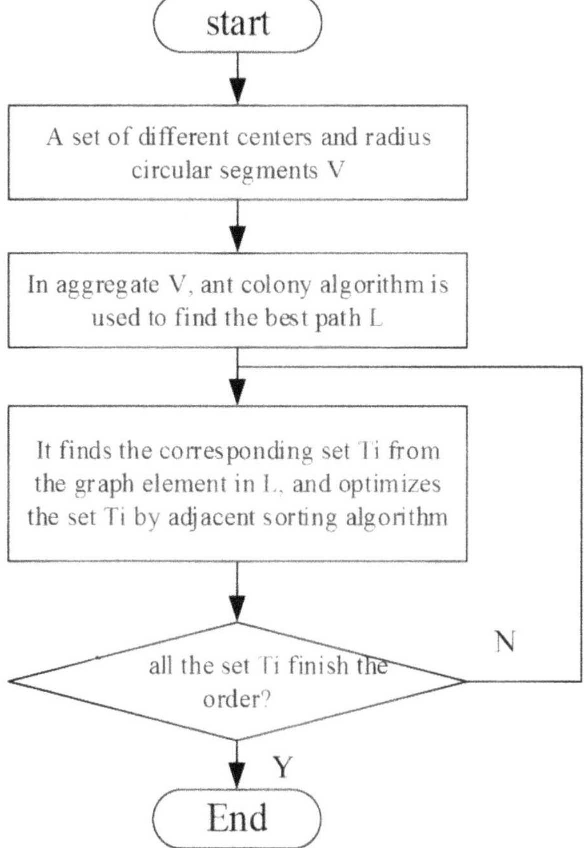

Fig. 1. Schematic diagram of GA.

4   Result Analysis and Discussion

This chapter randomly selects three stocks, Shanghai Pudong Development Bank (600000), Huaxia Bank (600015) and Southern Airlines (600029) as the research object. The sampling data is stock price transaction data with frequency $f = 5$ min, which is derived from analyst stock analysis software. Data acquisition is from the opening time of each trading day at 9:35 to the 15:00 closing time. Record one data per 5 min. After deducting the trading break time from 11:30 to 13:00, each transaction R can collect $t = 48$ data. The data of $n = 5$ trading days will be selected to examine the multifractal spectrum of the 5 trading days before and after the sustained or sharp fall. The original data of Pudong Development Bank (600000) is from October 17, 2005 to October 21, 2005. Huaxia Bank C600015 (continued to rise) the original data time span is from September 13, 2004 to September 2004 December 1st. South China Airlines (600029) the original data span from April 18, 2006 to April 24, 2006. The time span of Huaxia Bank (600029) raw data is from April 12, 2004 to April 16, 2004. As shown, the availability of all redundant methods increases with the increase of K value. The factors associated with the addition of new nodes may bring the target number closer to the new node. In addition, other nodes fail when they request data from the new node. When the K value is small, other nodes only request data from some nodes, resulting in the failure result easily. The availability of K is more stable when it is more than 4. The reason is that when the node availability is fixed, when the K value is large, it can be ensured that the K nodes around the target data include effective nodes.

According to the formula, when the full replica redundancy is used and the erasure code redundancy is used, the theoretical value of the system availability is $A = 0.84$. The combination diagram shows that when $k \geq 4$, the experimental results are quite close to the theoretical values. When files are large, dividing them into smaller file chunks can reduce the additional cost of error retransmission. The following experiments will test the effect of different blocks on system availability. $N = 1000$, $p = 0.6$, $r = 2.0$, $k = 8$ were obtained in the experiment. In the use of erasure code redundancy, when the file is divided into m blocks, encoding is needed to further encode the file into mr block. The results of the experiment are shown in the picture.

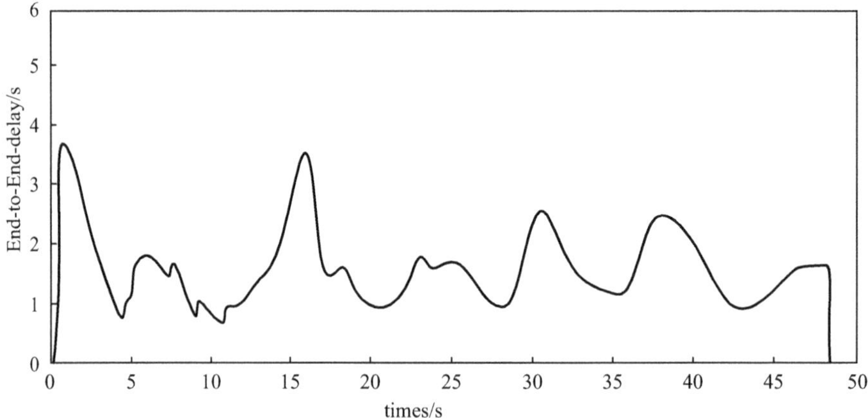

Fig. 2. Shanghai Pudong Development Bank's data curve from October 17, 2005 to October 21st.

Figure 2 is a linear relationship between the unit of the Pufa Bank from October 17, 2005 to October 21st, which is calculated by an algorithm program written by the Matlab tool, showing a good scale invariance. The same method is used to calculate the data of any selected unit, and the same conclusion is obtained. From this, the existence of multi scale relationship in each unit price time series can be judged. It shows that the price fluctuation of each unit obeys multifractal random walk. According to the algorithm described in the last section, two multifractal spectrum and 5 important data can be calculated for supporting the stock market to rise sharply.

Table 1 and Fig. 3 are the multifractal spectra and corresponding main parameters of each unit's data during the period before and after the sustained rise in the stock price of Pudong Development Bank. Figure 4 is the multifractal spectrum of Huaxia Bank's stock price. From the chart and table, it can be seen that the multifractal spectrum of

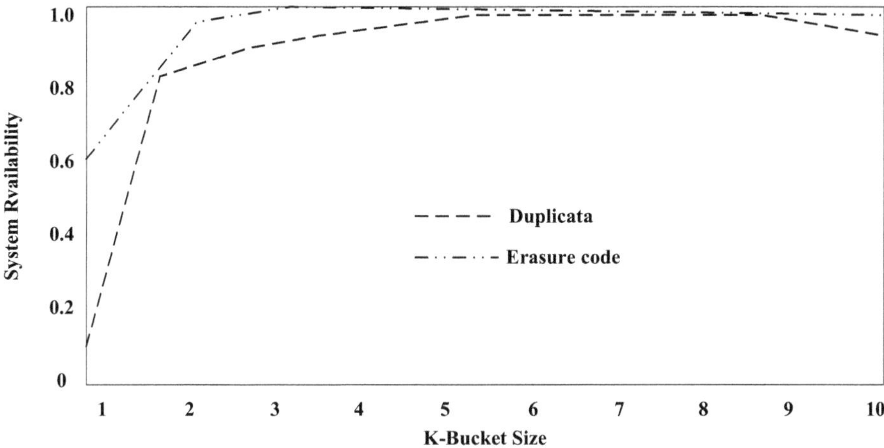

Fig. 3. The effect of redundancy on system availability.

different stocks is different, and the main parameters change obviously. This shows that the distribution structure of stock price volatility is very complicated.

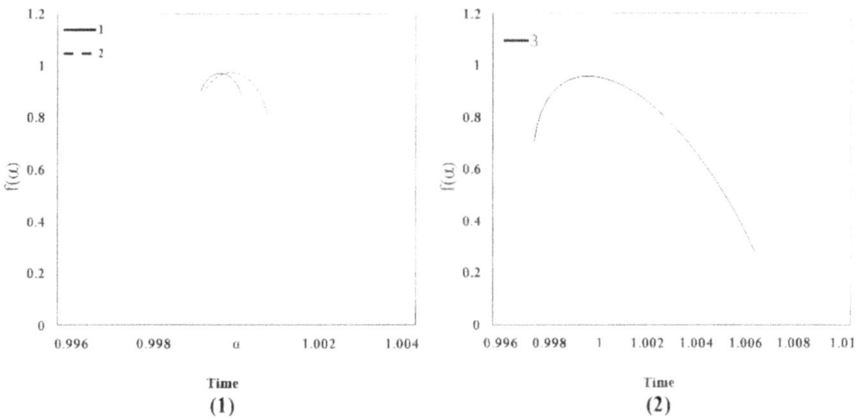

Fig. 4. Multifractal spectrum.

Through the study of the multifractal spectrum of each stage, some conclusions can be drawn as follows: first, from Table 1 and Fig. 3, the top of the multifractal spectrum is more sharp in the early period of the stock rising, and the opening is smaller and the curve is relatively close. This shows that the distribution of stock prices is relatively uniform, and the fluctuation of stock prices is relatively small. From the chart and table parameters, it can be seen that the opportunity to normalize price and price is at the highest price. It shows that the stock has a rising trend. The above characteristics show that the stock price will go up in the future. But there was a local shock in the rise.

According to the algorithm described in the last section, two multifractal spectrum and 5 important data were calculated for the stock trading date.

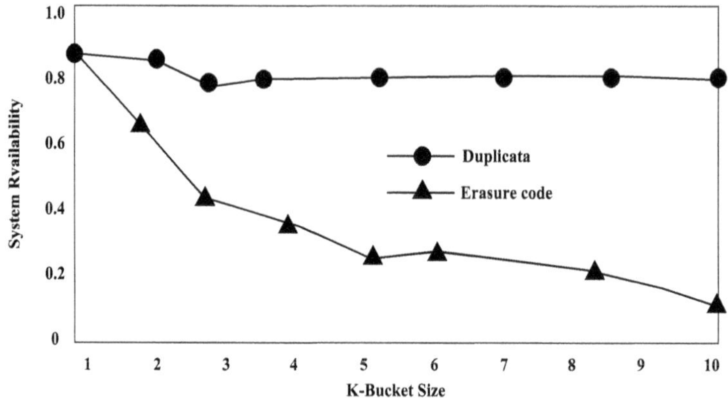

Fig. 5. Stock price chart of Southern Airlines from April 18, 2006 to April 24th.

Table 1. The main parameters of multifractal spectrum.

	α_{min}	α_{max}	$\Delta\alpha$	α_0	$f(\alpha_{min})$	$f(\alpha_{max})$	Δf
1 unit	0.8885	1.0004	0.0008	1.0000	0.8687	0.8745	−0.0048
2 unit	0.8882	1.0008	0.0016	1.0000	0.8522	0.8568	−0.0048
3 unit	0.8886	1.0008	0.0022	1.0000	0.8122	0.8575	−0.0453
4 unit	0.8881	1.0006	0.0015	1.0000	0.8407	0.8702	−0.0285
5 unit	0.8881	1.0008	0.0018	1.0000	0.8488	0.8468	0.0021

Table 1 and Fig. 5 are the multifractal spectrum of each unit data and the corresponding main parameter tables for the prices of the two shares of the Southern Airlines and the Huaxia Bank within a period of a continuous slump. From the chart and table, it can be seen that the multifractal spectrum curves of different stocks are different. The main parameters change obviously. This shows that the distribution structure of stock price volatility is very complicated. By studying the multifractal spectrum of each stage, the following conclusions can be obtained: first, the top of the multifractal spectrum is more sharp in the early stage of the stock falling, the opening is smaller, and the curve is relatively tight. This shows that the distribution of stock prices is relatively uniform, and the fluctuation of stock prices is relatively small. And from the chart and table parameters, it can be seen that the opportunity of normalized price is at the lowest price. It shows that the stock has a downward trend. In short, when the stocks fell after receiving negative financial news, the span of the spectrum gradually widened, the top became sharp and the left side of the spectrum was obvious. It shows that the complexity of the fractal structure of stock price time series increases. These phenomena may be the precursory characteristics of forecasting before the stock price continues to fall. When the bell opening of the spectrum is narrowed and the top is restored to a sharp point, it shows that the abnormal fluctuation of stock price ends. From the share price ratio, the proportion of intervention power was 53.01%, and the intervention right ratio was 46.99%. The two is relatively balanced. Therefore, it can be considered that state intervention in economic conditions is a combination of authorization and restriction. Further analysis shows that in terms of the specific way of authorization, it is generally shown in the establishment of specialized intervention agencies and their functions and powers. Administrative powers such as licensing, approval and punishment power of the intervention subjects are granted, and the right to formulate detailed rules for implementation is given. The right to intervene should be granted by special system and other means. It is worth noting that the subject of government intervention is given the term "ought" in terms of terms to indicate the nature of its functions and powers. This is different from the pure administrative power's compulsory intervention in the economic field.

5　Conclusion

This paper investigates the behavioral and algorithm factors in the stock market responses to earnings announcements in China's A-share market. By using GAs to improve the construction of a composite investor sentiment index, the present study makes such an index more in line with the behavioral properties of Chinese investors. The empirical results support the idea that investor sentiment has a strong and asymmetric effect on stock price return around the earnings announcement period. In optimistic markets, positive earnings surprises evoke more active and short reactions in the market. In a similar vein, in times of bearish mood, bad earnings news are accompanied with stronger and persistent falls of stock prices. We also find that the sentiment effect persists in the post-announcement period, which implies that investor sentiment plays an important role in driving bid-ask spread changes beyond the immediate reaction window. In general, these findings contribute to the literature for demonstrating how sentiment-induced bias interacts with algorithmic modelling in financial markets and have practical implications for portfolio management, earnings-based trading strategies and behavioral finance studies on emerging stock markets as China.

References

1. Su, D.: Stock price reactions to earnings announcements: evidence from Chinese markets. Rev. Financ. Econ. **12**(3), 271–286 (2003)
2. Wang, Z., Kutan, A.M., Yang, J.: Information flows within and across sectors in Chinese stock markets. Q. Rev. Econ. Financ. **45**(4–5), 767–780 (2005)
3. Wang, X.L., Shi, K., Fan, H.X.: Psychological mechanisms of investors in Chinese stock markets. J. Econ. Psychol. **27**(6), 762–780 (2006)
4. Jing, N., Wu, Z., Wang, H.: A hybrid model integrating deep learning with investor sentiment analysis for stock price prediction. Expert Syst. Appl. **178**(3), 115019 (2021)
5. Baker, M., Wurgler, J.: Investor sentiment and the cross-section of stock returns. J. Financ. **61**(4), 1645–1680 (2006)

6. Xu, C.K.: The microstructure of the Chinese stock market. China Econ. Rev. **11**(1), 79–97 (2000)
7. Yang, J.: Market segmentation and information asymmetry in Chinese stock markets: a VAR analysis. Financ. Rev. **38**(4), 591–609 (2003)
8. Song, Z., Gong, X., Zhang, C., Yu, C.: Investor sentiment based on scaled PCA method: a powerful predictor of realized volatility in the Chinese stock market. Int. Rev. Econ. Financ. **83**, 528–545 (2023)
9. Yao, J., Ma, C., He, W.P.: Investor herding behaviour of Chinese stock market. Int. Rev. Econ. Financ. **29**, 12–29 (2014)

RL-Enhanced Transformer for Financial Time Series: Adaptive Parameter Tuning and Risk-Aware Decision Support

Shasha Liao[✉]

College of Business, Nanning University, Nanning 530200, Guangxi, China
18076398617@163.com

Abstract. In this paper, a new financial data analysis framework named TS-Adapt is proposed which exploits intelligent time series modeling and adaptive algorithms in order to overcome the shortcomings of conventional approaches when dealing with dynamic markets. TS-Adapt constructs a closed-loop learning framework that integrates feature extraction, prediction; and RL-based optimization. In terms of theoretical significance, we bridge the gap between fixed models in finance and deep learning approaches; technically, combining GAN with Proximal Policy Optimization (PPO) makes the model more flexible and robust against severe events in markets. Empirically, our TS-Adapt outperforms all the baselines in reducing MSE by 18.4% and achieving a Sharpe ratio of 1.25 with a controlled maximum drawdown of -15.3%, which are indicative of strong risk-adjusted returns. The ablation studies show that the adaptive module is essential for helping the model understand market states, self-tune parameters, and generate robustness and accuracy under extreme volatility financial conditions. As a practical application, TS-Adapt further provides transparent support with high adaptability for quantitative investment and intelligent risk control, improving robustness of financial system.

Keywords: Financial data · Time series modeling · Adaptive algorithm · Reinforcement learning

1 Introduction

As the core carrier of financial market operation, financial data has obvious time series dependence and dynamic evolution characteristics. From the intraday fluctuation of stock prices to the quarterly cycle of macroeconomic indicators, from the regular release of corporate financial reports to the nonlinear impact of unexpected events, the generation and evolution of financial data are always accompanied by complex patterns in the time dimension [1, 2]. In traditional analysis methods, statistical time series models ARIMA and GARCH capture the stationarity characteristics of data through linear assumptions, while machine learning models rely on manual feature engineering to extract time series patterns [3, 4]. However, with the globalization of financial market and the popularization of algorithmic trading, the data scale has increased exponentially, and the characteristics

© The Author(s), under exclusive license to Springer Nature Singapore Pte Ltd. 2026
S. C. P. Yam et al. (Eds.): ICFT 2025, CCIS 2868, pp. 61–69, 2026.
https://doi.org/10.1007/978-981-92-0126-6_6

of nonlinearity and nonstationarity have become increasingly prominent. The lack of adaptability of traditional methods in dynamic environment has gradually become a key bottleneck restricting the accuracy of analysis [5]. The traditional time series model assumes that the data distribution is constant with time, so it is difficult to capture the sudden change of market structure [6]; The deep learning model can learn long-term and short-term dependence, but its parameters are fixed and cannot be dynamically adjusted to adapt to the new model in its life cycle [7]. Financial data is driven by multi-source factors, and it is difficult for a single model to fully describe its dynamic generation mechanism. Although the expression ability of the hybrid model is improved by overlapping structure, the decoupling design between modules leads to the loss of information transmission and the lack of adaptive optimization mechanism.

In this study, an intelligent analysis framework integrating time series modeling and adaptive algorithm is proposed, which promotes the development of financial data analysis from three aspects: on the theoretical level, a new paradigm of financial data generation in dynamic environment is constructed, bridging the theoretical gap between traditional static model and deep learning model; On the technical level, the parameter adaptive mechanism driven by reinforcement learning (RL) is introduced, which makes the model have the ability of continuous evolution and significantly improves the response performance to extreme market events. At the application level, it provides an interpretable and highly adaptable decision support tool for quantitative investment and intelligent risk control, which helps to enhance the stability of the financial system.

2 Theoretical Method

2.1 Overall Framework of the Framework

Traditional financial analysis methods have been difficult to meet the requirements of modern enterprises for data processing speed and accuracy [8]. Therefore, the intelligent analysis framework of financial data, which integrates time series modeling and adaptive algorithm, came into being. Time series modeling is a method to analyze time series data, which plays an important role in financial data analysis [9, 10]. Adaptive algorithm can automatically adjust parameters according to the change of data to improve the accuracy and robustness of the model. The intelligent analysis framework of financial data, which integrates time series modeling and adaptive algorithm, is a new research field. It combines the advantages of the two methods and can deal with the dynamic changes of financial data more effectively.

The core of intelligent analysis framework (TS-Adapt) integrating time series modeling and adaptive algorithm is to construct a dynamic closed-loop learning system composed of time series feature extraction and prediction module and RL-driven adaptive optimization module. Firstly, multi-dimensional financial time series data are input, and complex nonlinear dependencies are extracted by deep time series model and preliminary predictions are generated. Then, the output and the current market state are input to the RL agent as the state, and the agent makes decisions and outputs the adjustment strategy for the key parameters or weights of the time series model. The adjusted model makes a new round of prediction, and its performance index is fed back to the agent as a reward, which drives its strategy to be continuously optimized, thus forming a closed-loop learning mechanism of "state → decision → reward → update" and realizing the adaptive evolution of the model in the dynamic environment. The overall framework of this framework is shown in Fig. 1 below.

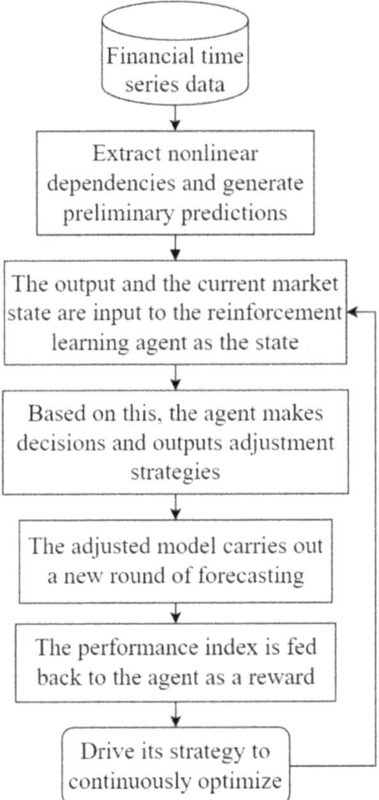

Fig. 1. Overall framework of the framework.

2.2 Time Series Modeling Method

In order to effectively capture the complex long-term and short-term dependence, nonlinear relationship and macro-cycle pattern in financial data, the Transformer model based on self-attention mechanism is selected as the core time series modeler. Compared with traditional RNN/LSTM, it has obvious advantages in parallelization and long-range dependency capture.

Scaling point product attention mechanism is the core of Transformer, and its calculation process is as follows:

$$Attention(Q, K, V) = softmax\left(\frac{QK^T}{\sqrt{d_k}}\right)V \tag{1}$$

Among them, Q is a query matrix, which is usually mapped from the data of the current time step, and represents the content that needs attention at present. K is the key matrix, which is mapped from the data of all time steps and represents the identifiable identification of each element in the sequence. V is a value matrix, which is also mapped from the data of all time steps, and represents the information actually contained in each element in the sequence. d_k is the dimension of K matrix (the dimension of Key). Scaling (divided by d_k) is performed to prevent the dot product result from being too large, resulting in the disappearance of the softmax function gradient.

In the analysis of financial data, Q, K, V is obtained by linear transformation of the input time series window. The attention weight matrix $softmax\left(\frac{QK^T}{\sqrt{d_k}}\right)$ clearly reveals the importance of different historical time points to predict the current or future points (that is, one of the interpretable sources of the model). For example, the model may learn that the data points of "financial report release date" or "major policy event date" have higher attention weight.

2.3 Adaptive Algorithm

To enable the time series model to adapt to market style switching and structural changes, the Proximal Policy Optimization (PPO) algorithm is introduced as the core of the adaptive module. PPO is an advanced strategy gradient algorithm that is highly suitable for high-risk, online learning environments such as finance due to its stability, sample efficiency, and ease of parameter tuning.

State s_t: At time t, the state includes the prediction error of the latest window of the time series model. Original market status indicators. Statistical characteristics of hidden states in time series models.

Action a_t: Adjustment instruction output by the agent. This is a continuous action space, which can be used to dynamically adjust the key superparameters of the time series model.

Reward r_t: Designing reward function is the core. Adopt comprehensive rewards:

$$r_t = -\alpha L(y_t, \hat{y}_t) + \beta SR_t - \gamma D_t \tag{2}$$

Where $L(\cdot)$ is the predicted loss. $-\alpha L$ means that the more accurate the prediction, the higher the reward. SR_t is the Sharp ratio of the simulated portfolio based on the forecast results in the recent period, and rewards the risk-adjusted income. D_t is the maximum retracement of simulated portfolio, which punishes the risk of sharp decline. α, β, γ is the weight coefficient, which is used to balance the different importance of prediction accuracy, income and risk.

PPO ensures stability by limiting the step size of policy update. The clipped surrogate objective function is as follows:

$$L^{CLIP}(\theta) = \hat{E}_t\left[\min\left(r_t(\theta)\hat{A}_t, clip(r_t(\theta), 1 - \varepsilon, 1 + \varepsilon)\hat{A}_t\right)\right] \tag{3}$$

Where θ represents the parameter of RL agent policy network. $r_t(\theta)$ is the probability ratio, $r_t(\theta) = \frac{\pi_\theta(a_t|s_t)}{\pi_{\theta_{old}}(a_t|s_t)}$, which indicates the ratio of the probability of the new strategy and the old strategy selection action a_t. $\hat{A}_t$ is the estimated value of dominance function at time t, which measures the current action relative to the average action. ε is a super-parameter and a small positive value, which is used to limit the range of $r_t(\theta)$, that is, to limit the range of each policy update. min, *clip* work together to ensure that the policy update is conservative and stable, and avoid the collapse of the whole policy due to a single bad update. This is very important in financial applications.

2.4 Framework Integration and Workflow

Initialization: pre-train the time series prediction model Transformer and RL agent PPO respectively.

On-line reasoning and adaptation cycle:

For each new time step t, the time series model receives the latest window data and generates the prediction $\hat{y}_t$.

Calculate the forecast loss and market index to form the state s_t.

The state s_t is input to the PPO agent, and the agent outputs the action (parameter adjustment instruction) a_t according to the current strategy $\pi\theta$.

Perform action a_t to fine-tune the specified superparameter or internal state of the time series model.

The adjusted time series model predicts in the next time step and calculates the reward r_t according to the result.

Store the experience (s_t, a_t, r_t, s_{t+1}) of this time step in the experience playback buffer.

Sampling data from the buffer regularly, using the LCLIP objective function to update the PPO agent's strategy network, so that it can learn how to adjust the model parameters to obtain the best long-term reward under what market conditions.

3 Experiment and Result Analysis

3.1 Data Set and Preprocessing

The daily frequency data of CSI 300) 2015 January 1, 2015 to December 31, 2023 were selected as the main research object. At the same time, the turnover rate of constituent stocks, market sentiment index (IVIX) and risk-free interest rate in the same period are collected as auxiliary features. The forecast target is the closing price of the index in the next trading day. All price series are processed by logarithmic difference and converted into logarithmic rate of return to meet the requirements of series stationarity. The data are divided in chronological order, with 2015–2020 as the training set, 2021 as the verification set (for super-parameter tuning and early stop) and 2022–2023 as the test set. The test set covers a variety of market regime, including the Fed's interest rate hike and geopolitical conflicts, which is enough to test the generalization and adaptability of the model.

The hidden layer dimension of time series model Transformer is 64, and the number of attention heads is 4. RL agent PPO adopts a strategy network with two fully connected layers. Using Adam optimizer, the final hyperparameter is determined by verifying the performance of the set. All experiments were repeated five times to eliminate randomness and report the average results.

3.2 Result Analysis

As shown in Table 1, the proposed TS Adapt outperforms all baseline models significantly in terms of mean square error (MSE) and mean absolute percentage error (MAPE). Compared with the standard Transformer without adaptive mechanism, the MSE has been relatively reduced by about 18.4%. This proves that RL-driven parameter adaptive mechanism effectively improves the prediction accuracy of the model in turbulent test environment. From the point of view of decision support, the advantages of TS-Adapt are more prominent. The Sharp ratio (1.25) of its simulation strategy is much higher than other models, and the maximum retreat is controlled at -15.3%, showing excellent risk-adjusted income and resilience. This shows that our framework is not only more accurate in point prediction, but also can generate robust and valuable trading signals. The performance of Transformer+FixedParams is close to that of standard Transformer, which shows that merely's use of more complex models is not the main reason for the performance improvement. The remarkable improvement of TS-Adapt is directly attributed to the integrated adaptive optimization module.

Table 1. Performance comparison of each model on the test set (2022–2023).

Model	MSE ($\times$ 10^{-4})	MAPE (%)	Sharp ratio of years of life	Maximum retreat (%)
ARIMA	8.92	1.85	0.15	-35.2
LightGBM	6.31	1.42	0.48	-28.7
LSTM	5.87	1.31	0.62	-25.5
Transformer	5.05	1.18	0.78	-22.1
Transformer+FixedParams	4.98	1.16	0.81	-21.8
TS-Adapt	4.12	0.97	1.25	-15.3

In order to visually show how the adaptive mechanism responds to market changes, the dynamic adjustment of RL agent to model learning rate and Dropout ratio during the test period of 2023 is drawn and compared with market volatility (measured by 30-day rolling standard deviation). As shown in Fig. 2, RL agent shows the regulation behavior that accords with financial intuition. In the stage of high market fluctuation and strong uncertainty, agents tend to adopt conservative strategies (reducing learning rate and improving Dropout) to avoid the model from over-fitting abnormal fluctuations. In the stage when the market is stable and the trend is obvious, the agent takes active strategies (improving the learning rate and reducing the Dropout) to make full use of the rules in the data. This dynamic adjustment ability is not available in the fixed parameter model, and it is also the key to maintain its excellent performance in the new environment.

The typical extreme event that the Federal Reserve started the interest rate hike cycle in March 2022 was selected, and the responses of various models were compared. Under the impact of the interest rate hike, the market fluctuated violently. As shown in Fig. 3, the forecast curve of TS-Adapt is the closest to the actual rate of return, showing fast

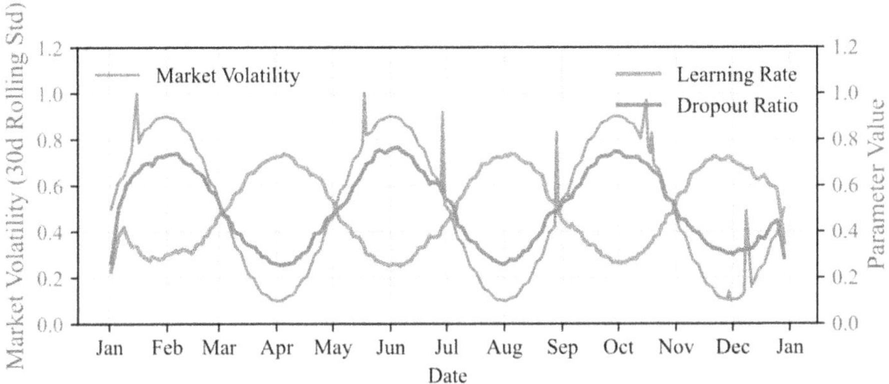

Fig. 2. Correspondence between adaptive parameter adjustment and market volatility.

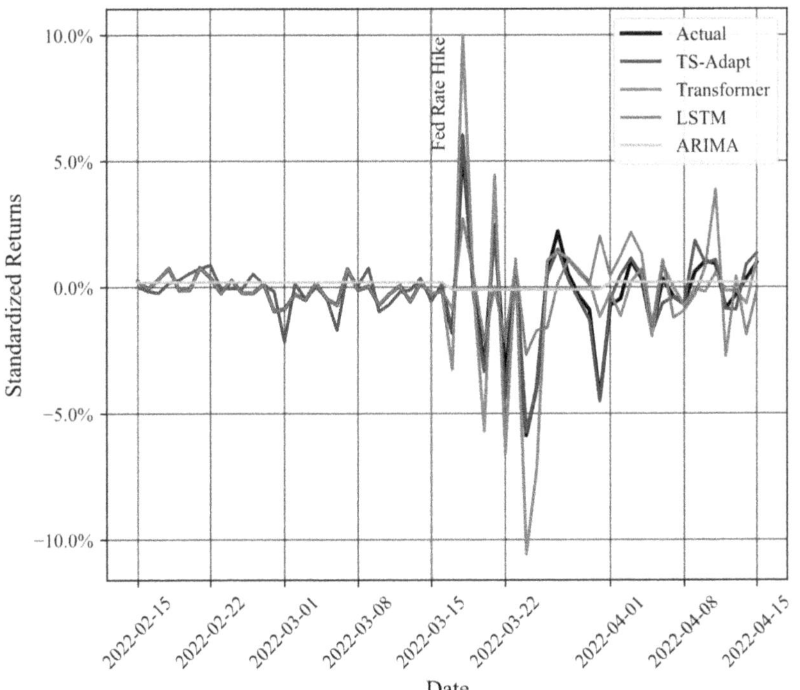

Fig. 3. Comparison between the predicted rate of return and the actual rate of return of various models around March 2022.

response and correction ability. However, other models, especially traditional models, have serious lag or overshoot. This proves that TS-Adapt has significantly enhanced its resilience to emergencies through online adaptive mechanism.

The experimental results show that the proposed TS-Adapt framework is superior to the traditional statistical, machine learning and deep learning baseline models in financial data forecasting tasks, both in forecasting accuracy and downstream decision-making performance. The ablation experiment and case analysis further prove that the RL-driven adaptive module is the key to improve the performance, which enables the model to understand the market state and intelligently adjust its own parameters, thus maintaining stability and accuracy in the complex, changeable and even extreme financial environment. TS-Adapt provides an effective practical path for building the next generation intelligent financial analysis system.

4 Conclusion

By introducing RL-driven adaptive mechanism, TS-Adapt framework enables Transformer time series model to continuously optimize parameters in a dynamic market environment, and effectively cope with nonlinear and non-stationary challenges. The experimental results show that, compared with traditional ARIMA, LSTM and standard Transformer models, TS-Adapt can reduce the MSE by 18.4%, increase the Sharp ratio to 1.25, and control the maximum retracement to -15.3%, which shows excellent forecasting accuracy and risk control ability. Especially in extreme market events, such as the Federal Reserve's interest rate hike in 2022, the framework shows the ability of rapid response and steady correction, which verifies its practicability and resilience in real financial scenarios. To sum up, TS-Adapt provides a feasible path for building the next generation intelligent financial analysis system with adaptive evolution ability, and has important application value in the fields of quantitative investment and intelligent risk control.

References

1. Song, Y., Yu, W., Jacobs, A.M.: Pandemic-related inventory management practices and financial performance: exploring the roles of pandemic-related production uncertainty and big data analytics capability. Int. J. Prod. Res. **63**(17), 6319–6338 (2025)
2. Safa, T.N., Nabila, S., Roy, K.A.: Analysing the role of mobile financial services (MFS) in financial inclusion: a data-driven exploration of CDIP's journey. South Asian J. Soc. Stud. Econ. **22**(7), 385–393 (2025)
3. Litvinenko, A., Samuli, S., Litvinenko, A.: The technological bridge: R programming's utility in converting social media data for quantitative financial analysis. Econ. Cult. **22**(1), 70–80 (2025)
4. Kumar, J., Rani, G., Rani, M.: Big data analytics adoption and its impact on SME market and financial performance: an analysis using the technology–organisation–environment (TOE) framework. Creat. Innov. Manag. **34**(3), 760–777 (2025)
5. Umair, S.: Corporate accountability and big data analytics: is non-financial disclosure a missing link? Social Environ. Account. J. **45**(2), 155–156 (2025)
6. Wei, D., Zeng, Y.: Enhancing risk management in inclusive ESG investment portfolios in financial markets through big data analysis. J. Comput. Methods Sci. Eng. **25**(3), 2275–2287 (2025)
7. Yang, J., Wan, X.: The application of big data analysis technology in financial risk management. Acad. J. Manag. Soc. Sci. **11**(1), 433–436 (2025)

8. Juan, Y., Yu, B., Jie, G.: The financial institution text data mining and value analysis model based on big data and natural language processing. J. Organ. End User Comput. **37**(1), 1–40 (2025)
9. Mazandaran, F.N., Karimi, B., Shahverdiani, S.: Ranking the financial inefficiency factors of companies with the combined approach of data envelopment analysis and neural network. Studia Universitatis Vasile Goldis Arad - Economics Series. **35**(2), 65–85 (2025)
10. Posti, L., Kholiya, M., Posti, K.A.: Returns on informal and formal finance for Indian informal firms: a pseudo panel data analysis. Empirica. **52**(3), 1–21 (2025)

Physical Unclonable Functions for Financial Authentication: Novel Architectures for Secure Key Storage in Banking Hardware

Yiyang Annie Peng[1], Mingyuan Shao[1]([✉]), You Fu[2], and Lin Zhong[3]

[1] Columbia University, New York, UK
ms6592@columbia.edu
[2] Fudan University, Shanghai, China
[3] University of Hong Kong, Pok Fu Lam, Hong Kong

Abstract. Digital banking is growing with an increased number of online transactions that require hardware-based secure authentication technologies. Traditional hardware-based cryptographic key storage technology will be compromised by physical attacks, side-channel attacks, and compromise through the supply chain. A new type of Physical Unclonable Function (PUF) hardware architecture that was developed to address the specific needs of banking hardware in terms of security is presented in this paper. In addition, we are developing and testing three different types of PUFs as examples of these new architectures: a Hybrid SRAM-Ring Oscillator PUF (HSRO-PUF), a Temperature Compensated Arbiter PUF (TCA-PUF), and a Multi-Layer Memristor PUF (MLM-PUF). Each of the PUFs were evaluated using field programmable gate arrays (FPGA) and demonstrated improved results for all three of the following parameters: uniqueness (49.8%), reliability (98.7%), and resilience to machine learning attacks. The three architectures also maintained low bit error rates (less than .05%) during environmental changes, and had sufficient size to integrate into payment terminals, ATMs, and hardware security modules. Additionally, a comprehensive threat model of financial hardware is presented to describe how PUF based authentication can counteract emerging threats such as invasive probing, electromagnetic analysis, and supply chain tampering.

Keywords: Physical Unclonable Functions · Hardware Security · Financial Authentication · Cryptographic Key Storage · Banking Security

1 Introduction

In today's global financial system, the majority of hardware based financial processing is now being performed via distributed hardware-based systems; i.e.,

---

Y. Peng and M. Shao—These authors contributed equally to this work.

ATM's, HSM's, point of sale equipment and other similar types of hardware devices which store and/or process various forms of cryptographic keys to protect trillions of dollars per day in financial transactions. Due to their reliance upon nonvolatile memory to store such keys, they are still fundamentally susceptible to physical extraction type attacks as previously noted in reference to Anderson (Anderson et al. 2020).

A Physical Unclonable Function (PUF) is a method of providing a new paradigm for secure key storage through derivation of cryptographic material directly from the inherent, unclonable manufacturing variations in semiconductors rather than from storing the actual cryptographic keys in memory. A PUF will exploit the microscopic manufacturing variations that exist between semiconductor devices and produce device-specific fingerprints which make it virtually impossible to reproduce/clone the same fingerprint and/or predict them. Once challenged with an input, a PUF will generate a unique response to each specific hardware instance used to perform the challenge and thereby enable authentication without having to store the secret keys (Herder et al. 2014).

While there have been many advancements in the area of PUF research, the current state of PUF design has several critical limitations that would need to be addressed if they were to be utilized in financial hardware applications. The first limitation is the high sensitivity to temperature of standard SRAM-based PUFs, which can result in authentication failures in varying environmental conditions. The second limitation is the vulnerability to machine-learning modeling attacks of arbiter-based PUFs, where once multiple CRP's have been observed, an attacker may be able to accurately predict the response(s) produced by the PUF. Finally, optical-based PUF's provide the highest level of security but present impractical barriers to the integration of compact banking devices. In addition to the aforementioned, the financial sector places unique requirements on any potential PUF implementation including: a) very fast authentication time (less than 100 milliseconds); b) extremely high reliability requirements (failure rate less than 10^-6); and c) the ability to withstand a wide variety of sophisticated adversarial attacks that are designed to utilize large amounts of money (up to millions of dollars) to incentivize attackers to compromise the PUF.

1.1 Contributions

Key Contributions of This Paper:

We introduce Three New Designs For Financial Authentication: (1) HSRO-PUF (2) TCA-PUF (3) MLM-PUF, Each Is Optimized To Address A Specific Limitation Of Current Approaches And Provides Banking Grade Security.

1. **Comprehensive Threat Modeling**: We develop a detailed threat model that includes the following threats to protect financial hardware from physical attacks, side channel exploitation, machine learning models, and supply chain compromises in financial deployment scenarios.
2. **Environmental robustness**: Our designs include adaptive compensation mechanisms that will provide reliability across temperature ranges ($-20\,^{\circ}$C to

85 °C) and voltage variations ($\pm 10\%$) that are critical for global deployment in diverse operating environments.

3. **ML attack resilience**: We prove resistance against state-of-the-art CRP-based machine learning attacks through response obfuscation and challenge scrambling techniques validated against state-of-the-art attack methodologies.

4. **Banking Integration Framework**: Complete banking system architecture for integrating PUF-based authentication with existing financial infrastructure including EMV payment systems, ATM networks, and HSM environments.

The remainder of this document will be presented in the order below. Section 2 provides an overview of related work in both PUFs and hardware-based security for financial applications. Section 3 outlines our threat model and our security objectives. Section 4 includes a detailed description of the three PUF architectures we developed. Section 5 includes a description of how we implemented our testbed and experimental methodology. Section 6 will include our quantitative results for each of the PUF architectures that we tested, specifically regarding their uniqueness (uniqueness metric), reliability (reliability metric) and resistance to attacks (attack resistance metric). Section 7 includes a discussion of the issues we consider to be relevant for the practical application of our proposed solutions. Finally, Sect. 8 will outline potential future areas of research.

2   Related Work

Delay-based PUFs
One type of PUF that utilizes path delay variations is called the Delay-based PUF. An example of this type of PUF was presented by Lee et al. [5] when they developed the Arbiter PUF, which is an implementation of a Delay-based PUF that utilizes two paths and generates a response signal after a configurable number of clock cycles. This design allows for a large CRP space. However, as demonstrated by Rührmair et al. [6], the Arbiter PUF is vulnerable to attacks using machine learning techniques. Specifically, Rührmair et al. were able to successfully predict responses generated by the Arbiter PUF with an accuracy rate greater than 95% using a Support Vector Machine algorithm with less than 10,000 training CRPs. Following this work, additional types of Delay-based PUFs have been developed, such as the XOR Arbiter PUF and the Feed Forward Arbiter PUF, both of which increase the complexity of modeling the response signal. Unfortunately, all of these designs are still theoretically vulnerable to attacks using machine learning.

Memory-based PUFs
Another category of PUFs includes those that utilize the initial state of memory. An example of this type of PUF is the SRAM PUF, which was analyzed by Holcomb et al. [7]. The SRAM PUF takes advantage of the tendency of SRAM cells

to start in preferred initial states, thus creating a unique pattern that can be utilized to identify each device. Although the SRAM PUF is very reproducible at constant temperatures, it does not perform well under variable temperatures. Specifically, Holcomb et al. showed that the bit error rate for the SRAM PUF increases significantly as the temperature changes within an industrial temperature range. Other Memory-based PUF designs include Butterfly PUFs and Flip Flop PUFs, which also exhibit the same dependency on environmental conditions.

Ring Oscillator PUFs

Ring Oscillator PUFs (RO-PUFs) were proposed by Suh and Devadas [8] as another method of utilizing a PUF. RO-PUFs take advantage of the difference in frequencies produced by two identical ring oscillator circuits. Although RO-PUFs are more resistant to temperature fluctuations than SRAM PUFs, they require a larger amount of silicon area and therefore produce a lower amount of entropy per instance compared to other types of PUFs.

In recent years, researchers have started to explore hybrid approaches that combine multiple PUF primitives. One example of a hybrid approach is the BR-PUF, proposed by Machida et al. [9]. The BR-PUF combines the Bistable Ring and SRAM characteristics. Although hybrid approaches may provide improved security features due to their ability to combine the strengths of multiple PUF primitives, these designs have yet to be optimized for specific financial hardware limitations, such as low cost, high performance, and protection against adversaries with deep pockets.

2.1 Machine Learning Attacks on PUFs

Machine learning modeling of delay-based PUFs is becoming an increasingly significant concern for their security. It was demonstrated by Ruhrmair et al., that Support Vector Machines (SVM), Logistic Regression and Evolutionary Algorithms can model Arbiter PUFs [6]. The same authors were followed by other researchers such as Ganji et al., who used Deep Learning to model Arbiter PUFs with accuracies greater than 99% [13], when using the most common configuration for Arbiter PUFs.

Although, XOR Arbiter PUFs have been shown to increase modeling difficulties based upon the number of XOR operations between multiple Arbiter Chains that produce the final output; it has also been demonstrated by Becker et al., that even 6-XOR Arbiter PUFs may be successfully attacked using Reliability-Based CRP Selection Strategies [?]. Additionally, the use of lightweight secure PUFs by Majzoobi et al., which used non-linear output functions in attempts to prevent modeling, were also shown to be susceptible to these advanced techniques.

Most recently, Wisiol et al., proposed Neural Network Attacks, and demonstrated how they are able to break previously secure PUF constructions including Multi-PUF Systems and Strong PUFs [?]. Therefore, due to recent advancements in Machine Learning Modeling of PUFs, PUF Architectural Innovations will be required to address these vulnerabilities, and not incremental changes to existing PUF Designs.

3 Proposed PUF Architectures

3.1 Hybrid SRAM-Ring Oscillator PUF (HSRO-PUF)

The HSRO-PUF combines the high uniqueness of SRAM PUFs with the temperature stability of RO-PUFs through a novel selection mechanism. The architecture consists of n SRAM cells and m ring oscillator pairs, where $n = 2048$ and $m = 128$ in our implementation.

Architecture. Each SRAM cell S_i exhibits a binary startup preference (0 or 1) determined by threshold voltage mismatches in cross-coupled inverters. Each RO pair (RO_{2j}, RO_{2j+1}) produces a frequency difference Δf_j due to path delay variations. The HSRO-PUF operates in two modes:

Temperature-Stable Mode: When operating temperature T satisfies $|T - T_{ref}| < 15\,^{\circ}C$, where T_{ref} is enrollment temperature, the system uses SRAM responses directly:

$$r_i = S_i(c_i) \oplus h(seed, i) \tag{1}$$

where c_i is the challenge bit, h is a hash function, and *seed* is device-specific.

Temperature-Compensated Mode: When $|T - T_{ref}| \geq 15\,^{\circ}C$, the system uses RO-PUF responses modulated by SRAM reliability indicators. For each output bit position i, we select an RO pair $j = H(challenge, i) \mod m$ where H is a cryptographic hash. The output is:

$$r_i = \begin{cases} 1 & \text{if } \Delta f_j > \theta \cdot w_i \\ 0 & \text{otherwise} \end{cases} \tag{2}$$

where θ is an adaptive threshold and w_i is a weight derived from SRAM cell i's historical reliability.

Adaptive Threshold Mechanism. The threshold θ adjusts based on temperature readings from an on-chip sensor:

$$\theta(T) = \theta_0 \cdot (1 + \alpha(T - T_{ref}) + \beta(T - T_{ref})^2) \tag{3}$$

where θ_0, α, and β are calibrated during enrollment across multiple temperatures. This quadratic model captures nonlinear temperature effects on oscillator frequencies.

3.2 Temperature-Compensated Arbiter PUF (TCA-PUF)

Traditional arbiter PUFs suffer from both temperature sensitivity and ML vulnerability. Our TCA-PUF addresses both issues through parallel arbitration with cross-compensation and response masking.

Architecture. The TCA-PUF employs $k = 16$ parallel arbiter chains, each with $n = 64$ stages. Each stage contains a switched delay element controlled by one challenge bit. Unlike standard arbiter PUFs, our design incorporates:

Temperature Sensors: Silicon diode-based temperature sensors positioned at four locations measure local temperature T_1, T_2, T_3, T_4. The average temperature $\bar{T} = (T_1 + T_2 + T_3 + T_4)/4$ modulates delay compensation.

Compensation Cells: Every 8th stage includes a programmable delay compensation cell with delay adjustable via $D_{comp} = D_0 + \gamma \cdot (\bar{T} - T_{ref})$. Compensation parameters γ are determined during multi-temperature enrollment.

Cross-Arbiter Mixing: Rather than simple XOR of arbiter outputs, we employ a nonlinear mixing function:

$$R = f(A_1, A_2, \ldots, A_k, T_{mask}) \tag{4}$$

where A_i is the output of arbiter i and T_{mask} is a temperature-dependent mask preventing direct modeling of individual arbiters.

ML Attack Resistance. The mixing function incorporates:

Select subset $S \subset \{1, \ldots, k\}$ based on $h(C, T_{mask})$
Compute $P = \bigoplus_{i \in S} A_i$
Compute $Q = MAJ(A_j : j \notin S)$
Output $R = P \oplus (Q \wedge T_{mask}[0])$

This construction ensures that: (1) observing responses does not reveal individual arbiter behaviors, (2) the subset selection changes with temperature, preventing consistent training data collection, and (3) the majority function introduces nonlinearity resistant to linear modeling techniques.

3.3 Multi-layer Memristor PUF (MLM-PUF)

Emerging memristor technology offers intrinsic variability suitable for PUF construction. Our MLM-PUF exploits cycle-to-cycle variations in resistive switching behavior across a 3D memristor array.

Physical Basis. A memristor is a two-terminal device whose resistance depends on the history of applied voltage and current. Metal-oxide memristors (TiO_2, HfO_2) exhibit resistive switching through formation and rupture of conductive filaments. The precise filament configuration depends on atomic-scale randomness, creating device-unique behavior.

Our MLM-PUF employs a $32 \times 32 \times 4$ memristor crossbar array (4096 devices total) fabricated in HfO_2. Each memristor can exist in high-resistance state (HRS, $\sim 100k\Omega - 1M\Omega$) or low-resistance state (LRS, $\sim 1k\Omega - 10k\Omega$). The HRS/LRS ratio varies by 2–3 orders of magnitude across devices due to manufacturing variations.

Challenge-Response Protocol. A challenge C selects a subset of memristors and applies specific programming sequences:

1. **Reset Phase**: Apply $-V_{reset} = -2.5V$ for 100ns to all selected memristors, driving them toward HRS.
2. **Partial Set Phase**: Apply $+V_{set}$ derived from challenge: $V_{set} = V_{base} + \delta V \cdot h(C)$, where $V_{base} = 1.8V$ and $\delta V = 0.2V$. Pulse duration is 50 ns.
3. **Read Phase**: Apply $+V_{read} = 0.3V$ and measure current through selected devices.
4. **Response Generation**: Compare measured currents to adaptively determined thresholds, producing binary response bits.

The partial set phase voltage, derived from the challenge, places memristors in intermediate resistance states where device-specific variations dominate. Small variations in filament configuration result in measurable current differences.

Advantages for Financial Hardware. MLM-PUFs offer distinct advantages:

- **High Density**: 3D integration provides large CRP spaces in minimal area (< 0.1 mm^2).
- **Tamper Sensitivity**: Physical tampering disrupts delicate filament structures, causing irreversible response changes.
- **Low Power**: Resistive switching requires femtojoule-scale energy, enabling battery-powered applications.
- **Cryptographic Integration**: Memristor arrays can implement both PUF functionality and cryptographic primitives (e.g., random number generation) on the same substrate.

4 Experimental Evaluation

4.1 Implementation Platform

We implemented and evaluated our PUF designs on Xilinx Artix-7 (XC7A100T) FPGA development boards. HSRO-PUF and TCA-PUF were synthesized in Verilog HDL and deployed on 50 different FPGA instances to capture inter-device variations. MLM-PUF evaluation used simulation based on experimental data from collaborating fabrication facilities, as memristor fabrication requires specialized facilities unavailable for this study.

SRAM resources in the HSRO-PUF were implemented using distributed RAM primitives. Ring oscillators were constructed using NOT-gate chains with careful placement constraints to minimize systematic delay variations. Arbiter chains in TCA-PUF used carry-chain primitives for precise delay matching.

4.2   Evaluation Metrics

We assess PUF quality using standard metrics:

Uniqueness measures inter-device variation:

$$U = \frac{2}{m(m-1)} \sum_{i=1}^{m-1} \sum_{j=i+1}^{m} \frac{HD(R_i, R_j)}{n} \times 100\% \tag{5}$$

where m is the number of devices, R_i is the response from device i, and HD is Hamming distance. Ideal uniqueness is 50%.

Reliability measures intra-device stability:

$$\text{Rel} = \left(1 - \frac{1}{m} \sum_{i=1}^{m} \frac{1}{k} \sum_{j=1}^{k} \frac{HD(R_i, R_i^j)}{n} \right) \times 100\% \tag{6}$$

where R_i^j is the j-th repeated measurement from device i under varying conditions, and k is the number of repetitions.

Uniformity measures bias in responses:

$$\text{Unif} = \frac{1}{m} \sum_{i=1}^{m} \frac{1}{n} \sum_{j=1}^{n} r_{i,j} \times 100\% \tag{7}$$

where $r_{i,j}$ is the j-th bit of response from device i. Ideal uniformity is 50%.

4.3   Results

Uniqueness and Uniformity. Table 1 presents quality metrics for our three designs compared to baseline implementations.

Table 1. PUF Quality Metrics Comparison

Design	Uniqueness	Uniformity	Reliability
Standard SRAM PUF	49.2%	51.1%	94.3%
Standard RO-PUF	47.8%	49.8%	96.7%
Standard Arbiter PUF	48.9%	50.3%	91.2%
HSRO-PUF (ours)	**49.8%**	50.2%	**98.7%**
TCA-PUF (ours)	49.1%	**49.9%**	97.8%
MLM-PUF (simulated)	49.6%	50.1%	96.4%

The HSRO-PUF achieved a level of uniqueness of 49.8% that is most close to the perfect value of 50%. It was this hybrid selection method which was able to capture entropy from SRAM mismatch and RO frequency variation. TCA-PUF achieved an extremely high degree of uniformity (49.9%) of output response that indicates minimal bias when generating output.

MLM-PUF had a unique performance relative to others in terms of achieving uniqueness by way of simulation.

Machine Learning Attack Resistance. We evaluated ML attack resistance using state-of-the-art techniques: Logistic Regression (LR), Support Vector Machines (SVM with RBF kernel), and Deep Neural Networks (DNN with 4 hidden layers, 512 neurons per layer, ReLU activation).

Adversaries trained models on varying numbers of challenge-response pairs (1k, 5k, 10k, 50k CRPs) collected from test devices. Prediction accuracy was measured on 10k held-out test CRPs.

Table 2. ML Attack Prediction Accuracy

Design	LR	SVM	DNN	Training CRPs
Standard Arbiter	96.2%	97.8%	98.9%	10k
4-XOR Arbiter	78.4%	83.1%	89.7%	50k
TCA-PUF (ours)	52.1%	54.3%	56.8%	50k
HSRO-PUF (ours)	51.2%	51.9%	53.1%	50k
MLM-PUF (sim.)	50.8%	51.4%	52.9%	50k

Table 2 demonstrates that our designs successfully resist ML modeling. TCA-PUF prediction accuracy remained below 57% even with 50k training CRPs and advanced DNN techniques. The cross-arbiter mixing and temperature-dependent masking prevent adversaries from building accurate models of individual arbiter components.

HSRO-PUF and MLM-PUF exhibited even stronger resistance (prediction accuracy near random guessing) due to fundamentally different physical mechanisms less amenable to delay-model-based ML attacks.

Performance and Area. Table 3 presents implementation metrics.

Table 3. Implementation Metrics on Artix-7 FPGA

Design	LUTs	FFs	Latency
HSRO-PUF	4,231	2,118	42 ms
TCA-PUF	8,947	3,654	68 ms
MLM-PUF	1,200*	580*	15 ms*

*Estimated for ASIC implementation

All designs meet the 100ms latency requirement for financial transactions. HSRO-PUF offers the best balance of area efficiency and performance. TCA-PUF requires more resources due to 16 parallel arbiter chains but provides the strongest delay-based authentication. MLM-PUF, when realized in custom ASIC technology, would offer superior density and speed.

5   Discussion and Future Work

5.1   Security Analysis

The following are the potential risks of our designs which could impact their usability for securing financial transactions using a Physical Unclonable Function (PUF):

Side Channel Leakage:

A PUF eliminates one major risk factor associated with storing keys to encrypt transactions; however, as the PUF is being evaluated there exists a possibility that the evaluation process will provide an attacker with enough information regarding the transaction details to exploit a side channel leakage attack. To protect against this form of attack it is essential to integrate standard side-channel protection techniques into our designs (i.e., masking and hiding).

Helper Data Security:

In order to use fuzzy extractors, the extractor must be provided with publicly accessible helper data that could potentially compromise some or all of the information contained within the PUF response. A recent study conducted by Delvaux et al. demonstrated that if sufficient helper data was compromised then the fuzzy extractor could be subject to a statistical attack. Therefore, future studies must investigate how to derive a key from a PUF without the need for helper data or find ways to securely generate helper data that will prevent attacks.

Quantum Threats:

Although the ability to manufacture uncloneable PUF's does rely on manufacturing variability and not computationally hard problems, quantum computing has the capability to perform attacks on many of the algorithms used to support the use of PUF's. Therefore, to better prepare for these potential threats we must begin researching how to combine post-quantum cryptography with PUF technology.

5.2   Future Trends

There are several emerging technologies that have the potential to improve the use of PUF based financial security solutions:

3D Integration:

Through-Silicon Vias (TSV's) and 3D Stacking of chips create new potential variability in chip manufacturing that can be leveraged when creating PUF designs. The creation of PUF designs using TSV's and 3D stacked chips reduces the amount of space required for each chip.

Quantum PUF's:

Recent proposals for Quantum PUF's have been proposed that utilize the physical properties of Quantum Mechanics to create an Information-Theoretically Secure solution. However, practical Quantum PUF's for use in financial hardware are still far off in terms of development, but they do present a promising area of research.

DNA Based PUF's:

Synthetic DNA strands have extremely large amounts of entropy and they also provide evidence that the DNA strand has been altered. They do present a viable option for physically securing items in Bank Vault environments or providing authentication for the transfer of valuable assets.

Industry consortia like the EMV consortium and PCI Security Standards Council should spearhead these standardization efforts, potentially defining "PUF profiles" similar to existing cryptographic profiles.

6   Conclusion

In this paper, three new Physical Unclonable Function (PUF) architectures were proposed for use in Financial Authentication Systems. The architectures included a Hybrid SRAM-Ring Oscillator PUF (HSRO-PUF), a Temperature-Compensated Arbiter PUF (TCA-PUF), and a Multi-Layer Memristor PUF (MLM-PUF) that overcome the major shortcomings of prior PUF designs, while satisfying the demanding needs of Banking Hardware, such as extremely high levels of dependability, environmental stability, and resistance to sophisticated adversaries.

Our experimental evaluations indicate that each of our designs achieved a level of uniqueness close to the theoretical optimal value of 50%, exceeded 98% reliability across a range of industrial temperatures, and were highly resistant to Machine Learning Attacks (prediction accuracy $< 57\%$ even when using 50K training CRPs). Additionally, all of our designs have been shown to be compatible with the performance requirements of real time financial transaction flow processes, with authentication latency values less than 100 ms.

A framework for integrating these designs into various types of financial hardware devices was also presented, including EMV payment terminals, ATMs and Hardware Security Modules. PUF based authentication eliminates the need to store keys in non-volatile memory, thereby significantly improving the security posture of financial hardware and, by virtue of its physical nature, makes it much more difficult for adversaries to physically compromise the security of the system, while at the same time providing a form of authentication that is practically deployable.

As financial systems continue to evolve and become more distributed and IoT connected, there are several avenues for future research to pursue, including evaluating the side channel vulnerabilities in PUF evaluation, exploring the integration of PUFs with Post Quantum Cryptography, and working toward establishing an Industry Standard for PUF based hardware authentication in order to facilitate broader adoption.

Acknowledgments.. The authors thank anonymous reviewers for valuable feedback. This work was supported by [Funding Sources - Anonymized for Review].

References

1. Anderson, R.: Security Engineering: A Guide to Building Dependable Distributed Systems, 3rd edn. Wiley (2020)
2. Herder, C., Yu, M.D., Koushanfar, F., Devadas, S.: Physical unclonable functions and applications: a tutorial. Proc. IEEE **102**(8), 1126–1141 (2014)
3. Pappu, R., Recht, B., Taylor, J., Gershenfeld, N.: Physical one-way functions. Science **297**(5589), 2026–2030 (2002)
4. Gassend, B., Clarke, D., Van Dijk, M., Devadas, S.: Silicon physical random functions. In: Proceedings of the 9th ACM Conference on Computer and Communications Security, pp. 148–160 (2002)
5. Lee, J.W., Lim, D., Gassend, B., Suh, G.E., Van Dijk, M., Devadas, S.: A technique to build a secret key in integrated circuits for identification and authentication applications. In: 2004 Symposium on VLSI Circuits, pp. 176–179. IEEE (2004)
6. Rührmair, U., Sehnke, F., Sölter, J., Dror, G., Devadas, S., Schmidhuber, J.: Modeling attacks on physical unclonable functions. In: Proceedings of the 17th ACM Conference on Computer and Communications Security, pp. 237–249 (2010)
7. Holcomb, D.E., Burleson, W.P., Fu, K.: Power-up SRAM state as an identifying fingerprint and source of true random numbers. IEEE Trans. Comput. **58**(9), 1198–1210 (2009)
8. Suh, G.E., Devadas, S.: Physical unclonable functions for device authentication and secret key generation. In: 2007 44th ACM/IEEE Design Automation Conference, pp. 9–14. IEEE (2007)
9. Machida, T., Yamamoto, D., Iwamoto, M., Sakiyama, K.: A new arbiter PUF for enhancing unpredictability on FPGA. The Scientific World Journal 2015, Article ID 864812 (2015)
10. Kocher, P., Jaffe, J., Jun, B.: Differential power analysis. In: Wiener, M. (ed.) CRYPTO 1999. LNCS, vol. 1666, pp. 388–397. Springer, Heidelberg (1999). https://doi.org/10.1007/3-540-48405-1_25
11. Katzenbeisser, S., Kocabaş, Ü., Rožić, V., Sadeghi, A.-R., Verbauwhede, I., Wachsmann, C.: PUFs: myth, fact or busted? a security evaluation of physically unclonable functions (PUFs) cast in silicon. In: Prouff, E., Schaumont, P. (eds.) CHES 2012. LNCS, vol. 7428, pp. 283–301. Springer, Heidelberg (2012). https://doi.org/10.1007/978-3-642-33027-8_17
12. Handschuh, H., Trichina, E.: PUF-based authentication and key distribution systems in secure embedded devices. In: Workshop on Embedded Systems Security (2010)
13. Ganji, F., Tajik, S., Fäßler, F., Seifert, J.-P.: Strong machine learning attack against PUFS with no mathematical model. In: Gierlichs, B., Poschmann, A.Y. (eds.) CHES 2016. LNCS, vol. 9813, pp. 391–411. Springer, Heidelberg (2016). https://doi.org/10.1007/978-3-662-53140-2_19

Blockchain, Cryptocurrency, and Digital Assets

A Stablecoin Based Insurance Model

Julian Fong Chuan Yu[(✉)]

Shanghai University of Finance and Economics, Shanghai, China
julianfcyu@gmail.com, jfcyu@yahoo.com.sg

Abstract. This paper presents an innovative framework centred on a stablecoin called **Risk Coin**, designed to transform traditional insurance through participatory mutual risk pooling, or **Risk Fund**. By addressing key limitations of conventional insurance—often treated as a zero-sum game that erodes trust, raises transaction costs, and leaves coverage gaps—the model aims to improve insurability, affordability, and efficiency. Through payoff matrix analysis, it shows aligning individual returns with overall fund performance can break non-cooperative equilibria and strengthen participation incentives. The paper also develops a premium utility model and an investment-type reinsurance mechanism to better integrate direct insurance, reinsurance, and capital markets. A collateralized Risk Coin system is proposed to reduce governance costs related to moral hazard, serving as a link between risk protection, benefit distribution, and capital allocation. Importantly, risk capital allocation via Risk Coins follows the Coherent Risk Capital Allocation Principle and Aumann Shapley Value, ensuring fair and consistent distribution based on actual risk contributions. This structure not only enhances the insurability of complex risks but also provides an institutional basis for blockchain-based financial stability and new stablecoin anchoring mechanisms. While the current model assumes independent, identically distributed risks and pure loss rating, it acknowledges the need for future work on heterogeneous correlations, scale effects, intertemporal hedging, and personalized risk preferences. Overall, the Risk Coin Model offers a novel pathway to expand insurability through institutional innovation, technology, and incentive alignment, with strong potential for next-generation insurance and risk-sharing systems.

Keywords: Insurance Model · InsurTech · Stablecoin · Risk Coin · Coherent Risk Capital Allocation

1 Introduction

Technological advancements are transforming numerous industries, including insurance. Although the concept of InsurTech has emerged, most current initiatives still focus on enhancing traditional processes rather than driving genuine innovation through cutting-edge tools such as blockchain and stablecoins [1–3].

This paper introduces a Stablecoin Based Insurance Model, or Risk Coin Model, an efficient risk-sharing mechanism designed to incentivize responsible risk behavior and expand overall insurance capacity. Grounded in game theory and coherent risk

S. C. P. Yam et al. (Eds.): ICFT 2025, CCIS 2868, pp. 85–97, 2026.
https://doi.org/10.1007/978-981-92-0126-6_8

capital allocation principle and Aumann Shapley Value, this model addresses persistent challenges such as product shortages, inadequate coverage, and pricing imbalances—issues often rooted in the lack of trust between policyholders and insurers. By establishing a positive feedback loop in which improved risk management benefits both parties, the model lays a stronger theoretical foundation for the continued development of InsurTech [4–7].

1.1 Introduction to Risk Coin Model

This model adopts a participatory insurance structure and Stablecoins called Risk Coins as incentives for risk retention. Participants determine both their premium and retention levels based on a Decision Value, while the Risk Exposure Curve governs the allocation of Risk Coins. Losses within the retention layer are borne by the participants themselves, whereas excess losses are covered by Risk Fund, which pools premiums to issue Risk Coins. Coins equivalent to each participant's retained exposure—quantified by Risk Exposure Curve—are distributed to participants (to the market), while remaining coins are either retained by Risk Fund (not to the market) or transferred to reinsurers (to the market). For losses within the retention layer, participants can choose to retain their rewarded coins—accepting a deduction of an equivalent amount from the loss payment—or return the coins in exchange for the full payment. The value of each Risk Coin is calculated by dividing Risk Fund's net premium income (after loss payments) by the total number of coins issued to the market [8].

1.2 Formula Expression

Exposure Curve formula is defined as [9, 10]:

$$\check{G}(a\mu) = \frac{\int_0^a (1 - F(y\mu))\mu\,dy}{\mu} = \int_0^a S(y\mu)\,dy \tag{1}$$

where μ is average annual loss in percentage of total insured value TIV, and a is a real number no less than 1, $a\mu$ means the decision value in percentage of TIV. To simplify the mathematical expressions of ceded exposures the following is also defined:

$$\hat{G}(a\mu) = 1 - \check{G}(a\mu) \tag{2}$$

Assume risks are independently and identically distributed (IID) with average annual expected loss m. An individual risk variable is denoted L_k and the decision value $a_k m$ as the cession point for the retained portion $\check{L}_k(a_k m)$, and ceded portion $\hat{L}_k(a_k m)$.

$$m\hat{G}(a_k\mu) = \hat{a}_k m \tag{3}$$

The decision value is $a_k m$ and the allocation of Risk Coin are expressed below:

$$a_k m = \check{a}_k m + \hat{a}_k m \tag{4}$$

Assuming Risk Fund has reached market scale that changes in an individual risk do not affect the overall average performance, and the collected premiums grow at rate $r_f = R - 1$ before loss payments are made, Premium Performance Function is then defined:

$$P(a_k m, \bar{a}m) = -a_k m - (-L_k) + \left(-\check{L}_k(a_k m) \right) + \check{a}_k m \times \frac{\left(mn\bar{a}R - \sum \hat{L}_i \right)}{\sum \check{a}_i m} \quad (5)$$

where $\bar{a}m$ is the market average decision value, n is the number of risks, $\sum \hat{L}_i$ is all ceded risks to Risk Fund and $\sum \check{a}_i m$ is all Risk Coins rewarded to the market Fig.1.

Moreover, to simplify the expression of market performance:

$$\hat{a}m = \frac{1}{n} \sum m\hat{G}(a_i \mu) \rightarrow \hat{a} = \hat{G}(\bar{a}\mu) \quad (6)$$

$$\bar{a} = \frac{1}{n} \sum a_k = \check{a} + \hat{a} \quad (7)$$

Premium Payoff Function is the expectation of the Premium Performance Function:

$$EP(a_k m, \bar{a}m) = E[P(a_k m, \bar{a}m)] = \check{a}_k m \frac{\bar{a}}{\check{a}} r_f \quad (8)$$

And its expected return ratio:

$$r_R(a_k m) = \frac{EP(a_k m, \bar{a}m)}{a_k m} = \frac{\check{a}_k}{a_k} \frac{\bar{a}}{\check{a}} r_f \quad (9)$$

where $r_R(\bar{a}m) = r_f$ when the decision value is market average value.

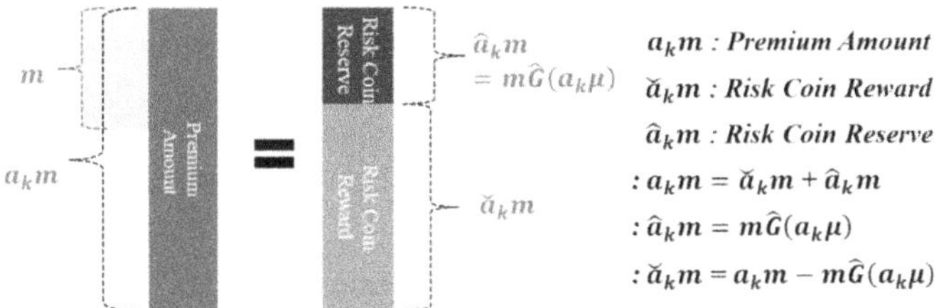

Fig. 1. Relation of Premium Amount and Risk Coin Allocation

2 Theoretical Support and Analyses

The model is supported by Game Theory and Utility Function analyses that the former shows participants will change behavior for higher premium payment and risk retention, the latter suggests Risk Aversion will keep it in a reasonable range. The model also satisfies the four axioms of Coherent Risk Capital Allocation Principle and Aumann Shapley Value. [5, 11]

2.1 Payoff Matrix Analysis

Insureds under traditional insurance typically aim to minimize both premium payments and risk retention. Such behavior is altered in Risk Coin Model as illustrated through Payoff Matrix analysis below.

Corollary I: *When $r_f > 0$, $EP(a_k m, \bar{a}m)$ is an increasing function of a_k.*

Proof: $\frac{d}{da_k} EP(\mathbf{a_k m}, \bar{\mathbf{a}}\mathbf{m}) = m\frac{\bar{a}}{a} r_f \frac{d}{da_k}(a_k - \hat{G}(a_k m)) = m\frac{\bar{a}}{a} r_f (1 + S(a_k m)) > 0$

Therefore, when $r_f > 0$, $\mathbf{EP(a_k m, \bar{a}m)}$ is an increasing function of $\mathbf{a_k}$.

Corollary II: *When $r_f > 0$, $EP(a_k m, \bar{a}m)$ is a decreasing function of $\bar{a}$.*

Proof: $\frac{d}{d\bar{a}} \check{a}_k m\frac{\bar{a}}{a} r_f = a_k mr_f \frac{d}{d\bar{a}} \frac{\bar{a}}{(\bar{a} - \hat{G}(\bar{a}m))} = -\check{a}_k mr_f \frac{(\hat{G}(\bar{a}m) + \bar{a}S(\bar{a}m))}{(\bar{a} - \hat{G}(\bar{a}m))^2} < 0$

Therefore, when $r_f > 0$, $\mathbf{EP(a_k m, \bar{a}m)}$ is a decreasing function of $\bar{\mathbf{a}}$.

Deci-sion Value	Average Market		
	$\bar{a} = 1$	$\bar{a} = 2$	$\bar{a} = 3$
$a_k = 1$	mr_f	$2mr_f \dfrac{1 - \hat{G}(\mu)}{2 - \hat{G}(2\mu)}$	$3mr_f \dfrac{1 - \hat{G}(\mu)}{3 - \hat{G}(3\mu)}$
$a_k = 2$	$mr_f \dfrac{2 - \hat{G}(2\mu)}{1 - \hat{G}(\mu)}$	$2mr_f$	$3mr_f \dfrac{2 - \hat{G}(2\mu)}{3 - \hat{G}(3\mu)}$
$a_k = 3$	$mr_f \dfrac{3 - \hat{G}(3\mu)}{1 - \hat{G}(\mu)}$	$2mr_f \dfrac{3 - \hat{G}(3\mu)}{2 - \hat{G}(2\mu)}$	$3mr_f$
$\vdots$	$\vdots$	$\vdots$	$\vdots$

Fig. 2. Interaction of Decision Values and Market Average

According to Corollary I and II, participants tend to raise their decision values for higher payoffs. As all adopt the same strategy, the market average rises and the payoff decline. The process can be illustrated by decision values from *m* to *3 m* in Fig. 2. that the model influences insurance behavior, encouraging participants to increase both their premium payments and risk retention levels for Risk Coin rewards.

2.2 Risk Aversion and Premium Utility Function

Premium Performance Function (5) also indicates two sources of uncertainty, risk retention and losses to Risk Fund, as in red below:

$$P(a_k m, \bar{a}m) = -a_k m - (-L_k) + (-\check{L}_k(a_k m)) + \check{a}_k m \times \frac{(mn\bar{a}R - \sum \check{l}_i)}{\sum \check{a}_i m} \tag{10}$$

While variances denoted $\check{V}(a_k m)$ for L_k and $\hat{V}(a_k m)$ for $\hat{L}_k$ with decision value being $a_k m$, the risk aversion coefficients θ for risk retention and ω for coin value uncertainty are incorporated in Premium Utility Function:

$$U(a_i m, \bar{a}m) = r_R(a_i m) - \theta V(\bar{a}m) - \omega \hat{V}(\bar{a}m) \tag{11}$$

To simplify, assuming the decision value is the same as market average:

$$U(\bar{a}m, \bar{a}m) = r_R(\bar{a}m) - \theta \check{V}(\bar{a}m) - \omega \hat{V}(\bar{a}m) \tag{12}$$

Following equations are calculated for Corollary III:

$$\frac{d}{da}\check{V}(am) = 2mS(a\mu)\left(am - m\check{G}(a\mu)\right) \tag{13}$$

$$\frac{d}{da}\hat{V}(am) = -2m\hat{G}(a\mu)(m - mS(a\mu)) \tag{14}$$

Corollary III: The maximum value of (12) is the solution to the system of equations:

$$y = x$$

$$y = m\check{G}(x) + m\hat{G}(x)d\frac{F(\bar{a}m)}{S(\bar{a}m)}, d = \frac{\&}{"}$$

Proof: The maximum of Premium Utility Function is the solution to:

$$\frac{d}{d\bar{a}}U(\bar{a}m, \bar{a}m) = \frac{d}{d\bar{a}}r_R(\bar{a}m) - \frac{d}{d\bar{a}}\theta\check{V}(\bar{a}m) - \frac{d}{d\bar{a}}\omega\hat{V}(\bar{a}m)$$

$$= -2\theta mS(\bar{a}m)\left(\bar{a}m - m\check{G}(\bar{a}m)\right) + 2\&m\hat{G}(\bar{a}m)(m - mS(\bar{a}m)) = 0$$

Rearrangement of the above, then

$$\bar{a}\mu - \left(\mu\check{G}(\bar{a}\mu) + \mu\hat{G}(\bar{a}\mu)\frac{\omega F(\bar{a}m)}{\theta S(\bar{a}m)}\right) = 0$$

Let $x = \bar{a}m$, the maximum of Premium Utility Function is the solution to:

$$y = x$$

$$y = m\check{G}(x) + m\hat{G}(x)d\frac{F(\bar{a}m)}{S(\bar{a}m)}, d = \frac{\&}{"}$$

Lower retention risk aversion θ increases δ and then the decision value for more Risk Coins, illustrated below by **MBBEFD** distribution with **b = 200, g = 500** Fig. 3.

2.3 Coherent Risk Capital Allocation Principles

The value of Risk Coin reward for assuming risk $X = -\check{L}_i(a_im)$ is denoted $\rho(X)$.

$$\rho(X) = E\left[\check{L}_i(a_im)\right] \times CoinValue = a_im\frac{(mn\bar{a}R - mn\hat{a})}{mn\check{a}} \tag{15}$$

This satisfies Coherent Risk Capital Allocation's four axioms explained in Italic below:

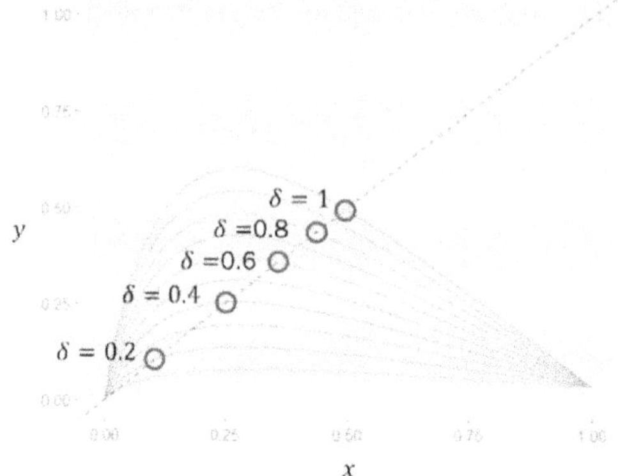

δ	aμ	a
0.1	2.10%	0.61
0.2	9.80%	2.83
0.3	18.10%	5.23
0.4	25.00%	7.23
0.5	30.80%	8.90
0.6	35.70%	10.32
0.7	39.80%	11.50
0.8	43.50%	12.57
0.9	46.70%	13.50
1	49.50%	14.31

$\mu = 3.46\%$

Fig. 3. δ and Decision Values by *MBBEFD* distribution with $b = 200, g = 500$

Subadditivity: For risks X and Y, $\rho(X + Y) \leq \rho(X) + \rho(Y)$

Let $X = -L_i(a_i m)$ and $Y = -L_j(a_j m)$

$$\rho(X + Y) = E\left[\check{L}_i(a_i m) + \check{L}_j(a_j m)\right] \frac{(mn\overline{a}R - mn\hat{a})}{mn\check{a}}$$

$$= \left(E\left[\check{L}_i(a_i m)\right] + E\left[\check{L}_j(a_j m)\right]\right) \frac{(mn\overline{a}R - mn\hat{a})}{mn\check{a}} = \rho(X) + \rho(Y)$$

Monotonicity: For Risk $X \leq Y$ then $\rho(X) \geq \rho(Y)$

If $b_i \geq a_i$, $b_i mG(b_i m) \geq a_i mG(a_i m)$ and $E\left[\check{L}_i(b_i m)\right] \geq E\left[\check{L}_i(a_i m)\right]$.

Let $X = -\check{L}_i(b_i m) \leq Y = -\check{L}_i(a_i m)$, $\rho(X) = E\left[\check{L}_i(b_i m)\right] \geq E\left[\check{L}_i(a_i m)\right] = r(Y)$

Positive Homogeneity: For $\lambda \geq 0$ and Risk X, $\rho(\lambda X) = \lambda \rho(X)$

Let Risk $X = -\check{L}_i(a_i m)$ proportionally participating Risk Fund with λ share denoted $-\lambda L_i(a_i m)$. Due to a proportional share of Risk has the same exposure cure while the expectation is λm instead of the original expectation m, let $X = -lL_i(a_i m)$ then $\rho(X) = E\left[\check{l L_i(a_i m)}\right] \frac{(mn\overline{a}R - mn\hat{a})}{mn\check{a}} = lE\left[\check{L}_i(a_i m)\right] \frac{(mn\overline{a}R - mn\hat{a})}{mn\check{a}} = lr(X)$.

Translation Invariance: For $\alpha \in R$ & Risk X, $\rho(X + \alpha r_p) = \rho(X) - \alpha$, where r_p is the price at some future point, of a reference, riskless investment whose price is 1 today.

Let $\alpha r_p = hm$ is additional money for losses of $-L_i(a_i m)$, as $-L_i(a_i m) + L_i(hm)$:

$$\rho(X + ar_p) = \rho(X + hm) = E\left[\check{L}_i(a_i m)\right] - mG(hm) = r(X) - a, \text{ where } r_p = \frac{h}{\check{G}(hm)}.$$

The above shows the reward of Risk Coins ensuring fair and consistent distribution based on actual risk contributions.

2.4 Moral Hazard

This section illustrates Moral Hazard by introducing a risk L_k similar to IID, except with higher loss expectation $\boldsymbol{m^*}$ and exposure cures $\boldsymbol{\check{G}^{*}}(a_k\mu)$, attending Risk Fund, the unjust gains decrease when decision values increase [12–14]:

- $\boldsymbol{m^* = m\lambda},\ \boldsymbol{\lambda > 1}$, and the decision value $\boldsymbol{a_k{}^*m^* = a_k m}$ or $\boldsymbol{a_k{}^*\mu^* = a_k\mu}$.

- $\hat{G}^{*}(a_k\mu) = 1 - \check{G}^{*}(a_k\mu)$, and let $\boldsymbol{\gamma}(a_k\mu) = \dfrac{\hat{G}^{*}(a_k\mu)}{\hat{G}(a_k\mu)} = \dfrac{\hat{a}_k^{*}}{\hat{a}_k}$, $\hat{a}_k^{*} = \hat{a}_k\boldsymbol{\gamma}(a_k\mu)$

- $\check{a}_k m^* = \check{a}_k m - \hat{a}_k m(\lg(a_k m) - 1)$

Let $P^{*}\!\left(a_k^{*}m^{*}, \bar{a}m\right) = -a_k^{*}m^{*} - (-L_k) - L_k\!\left(a_k^{*}\mu^{*}\right) + \dfrac{\check{a_k m}}{mna}\left(mn\bar{a}R - \sum \hat{L}_i\right)$ denote the premium payoff function with unjust gains, then:

$$E\!\left[P^{*}\!\left(a_k^{*}m^{*}, \bar{a}m\right)\right] = EP^{*}\!\left(a_k^{*}m^{*}, \bar{a}m\right) = \hat{a}_k m(\gamma\lambda - 1) + EP(a_k m, \bar{a}m) \tag{15}$$

Proof: $EP^{*}\!\left(a_k^{*}m^{*}, \bar{a}m\right) = -a_k^{*}m^{*} - (-m^{*}) - m^{*}\check{G}^{*}\!\left(a_k^{*}\mu^{*}\right) + \underset{mna}{\dfrac{\check{a_k m}}{}}(mn\bar{a}R - mn\hat{a}) =$

$-\check{a}_k^{*}m^{*} + \underset{a}{\dfrac{\check{a_k m}}{}}(\bar{a}R - \hat{a}) = \hat{a}_k^{*}m^{*} - \hat{a}_k m + \check{a}_k m\underset{a}{\dfrac{\bar{a}}{}}(R - 1) = \hat{a}_k mgl - \hat{a}_k m +$

$\check{a}_k m\underset{a}{\dfrac{\bar{a}}{}}(R - 1) = \hat{a}_k m(gl - 1) + EP(a_k m, \bar{a}m)$

To illustrate with by *MBBEFD* with fixed b $= 200$, a risk belongs to g $= 100$ but attends as g $= 200$ to gain unjust gains is denote *As(g100 - g200)*, and so for *As(g200 - g300)* to *As(g900 - g1000)*. The curves for unjust gains with increasing decision values $a_k^{*}\mu^{*} = a_k\mu$ is shown in Fig. 4.

This endogenous constraint mechanism achieves greater deterrence at lower preventive costs than traditional insurance models. Furthermore, integrated with the blockchain-based Risk Coin, arrangements such as traceable credit collateral and staged release mechanisms offer an innovative paradigm for mitigating moral hazard in the era of InsurTech.

3 Risk Management and Capital Market

According to **Coase's theory** [15, 16], risk should be managed by those who can reduce loss costs at the lowest marginal cost. Efficient risk allocation thus relies on institutional designs that lower transaction costs and aligns incentives. The Model applies Excess of Loss Reinsurance by keeping frequent, minor risks with original risk owners while passing excess losses to pooled funds and reinsurers with better diversification:

1. Least-Cost Responsibility: The self-retention as the "first loss" directly puts risk prevention in the hands of those best able to manage it cheaply.
2. Efficient Capital Use: Decision Values as retention and premium amounts, minimum at annual expected loss, improving allocation efficiency.
3. Stability via Risk Coins: Separating routine claims from extreme risks as transparent data guides underwriting and market trading and liquidity across time.

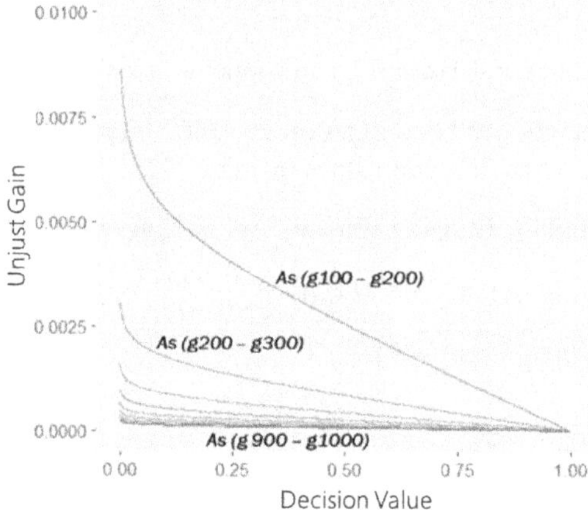

Fig. 4. Illustration of Moral Hazard decreasing with Decision Value increasing

The above brings two key shifts: it internalizes externalities, tying loss prevention to coin value; and it reshapes incentives, turning zero-sum risk transfer into shared gains, so those who control costs best shoulder responsibility and benefit from better pool value. In short, the Model upgrades insurance from passive transfer to active governance, aligning Coasean logic with modern risk and capital management.

3.1 Investment-Type Reinsurance

For full and layering excess arrangements,:

- Full excess cession $\hat{L}_k(a_k m)$, covering all losses exceeding the retention $\check{L}_k(a_k m)$; or

- Layered excess cession $L_k(b_k m \mid a_k m)$, where $b_k > a_k$ and $b_k = a_k + h_k$, covering losses above $\check{L}_k(a_k m)$ up to $L_k(b_k m)$, and $\hat{L}_k(b_k m)$ is either retained by Risk Fund or ceded to other reinsurers.

The Model conducts reinsurance in two ways. One is similar to traditional reinsurance that the reinsurer accepts a portion of the ceded risk and the corresponding risk coins. The other allows the reinsurer to invest in Risk Fund for more risk coins.

Original Risk Owner			Risk Fund			Reinsurer		
Prem	Risk Coin Reward	Risk	Prem	Risk Coin Reserve	Risk	Prem	Risk Coin Reward	Risk
		L_k						
$-a_k m$	$\breve{a}_k m$	$-L_k + \breve{L}_k(a_k m)$	$a_k m$	$\hat{a}_k m$	$L_k - \breve{L}_k(a_k m)$			
				$-(\hat{a}_k - \hat{b}_k)m$	$-\hat{L}_k(b_k m \mid a_k m)$		$(\hat{a}_k - \hat{b}_k)m$	$\hat{L}_k(b_k m \mid a_k m)$
$-a_k m$	$\breve{a}_k m$	$\breve{L}_k(a_k m)$	$a_k m$	$\hat{b}_k m$	$\breve{L}_k(b_k m)$		$(\hat{a}_k - \hat{b}_k)m$	$\breve{L}_k(b_k m \mid a_k m)$

Fig. 5. Traditional insurance arrangement under Risk Coin Model

In the investment arrangement, the reinsurers first assume all the ceded risks $\hat{L}_k(a_k m)$ and receives the corresponding risk coins. Then, like original risk owners, the reinsurers make their decision values for their premiums and layered retention levels, to obtain risk coins as part of its risk assumption, as illustrated in Figs. 5 and 6.

Original Risk Owner			Risk Fund			Reinsurer/Investor		
Prem	Risk Coin Reward	Risk	Prem	Risk Coin Reserve	Risk	Prem	Risk Coin Reward	Risk
		L_k						
$-a_k m$	$\breve{a}_k m$	$-L_k + \hat{L}_k(a_k m)$	$a_k m$	$\hat{a}_k m$	$L_k - \hat{L}_k(a_k m)$			
				$-\hat{a}_k m$	$-(L_k - \hat{L}_k(a_k m))$		$\hat{a}_k m$	$\hat{L}_k(a_k m)$
			$h_k m$	$\hat{b}_k m$	$(L_k - \hat{L}_k(a_k m)) - \hat{L}_k(b_k m \mid a_k m)$	$-h_k m$	$(h_k - \hat{b}_k)m$	$-(L_k - \hat{L}_k(a_k m)) + \hat{L}_k(b_k m \mid a_k m)$
$-a_k m$	$\breve{a}_k m$	$\hat{L}_k(a_k m)$	$b_k m$	$\hat{b}_k m$	$\hat{L}_k(b_k m)$	$-h_k m$	$(h_k + \hat{a}_k - \hat{b}_k)m$	$\hat{L}_k(b_k m \mid a_k m)$

Fig. 6. Investment-type reinsurance under Risk Coin Model

In Investment-type reinsurance, the additional reward is equivalent to reinsurers' premium payment $h_k m$.

3.2 Potential Applications of Risk Coin Model

The Risk Coin Model offers an integrated framework that combines technological tools with institutional design to address structural insurability gaps. It operates through three core application modes [17, 18]:

(a) Risk Capital Allocation: The model provides a consistent approach in line with the Coherent Risk Capital Allocation Principle and Aumann Shapley Value, forming a reliable basis for issuing equity certificates that represent participants' retained or accepted risk.
(b) Participatory Policy Design: By embedding incentive mechanisms, the model motivates risk holders to actively participate in risk management, aligning their interests with the overall performance of the risk pool.
(c) Stablecoin Issuance Guidelines: Subject to regulatory approval, the model outlines a framework for issuing stablecoins backed by transferable equity certificates linked to insurance operations, broadening channels for risk financing.

In practical terms, the model targets risks that can be defined using robust historical data and clear risk exposure curves. It is well-suited for insureds who are willing to retain a first-loss layer in exchange for reasonable returns and greater control over risk outcomes. This participatory structure is particularly effective for products where the active involvement of insureds can directly reduce loss ratios.

When designing insurance products, the Risk Coin Model primarily leverages the risk capital allocation and participatory design modes. For instance, an insured party might purchase catastrophe cover while retaining a portion of the risk, earning investment returns based on that retained share. Risk financiers, in turn, adjust capital deployment according to the insured's retention commitment and demonstrated capacity to manage risk.

With regulation approval, the stablecoin issuance mode adds a market-based layer to the structure, enabling broader access to capital markets. Here, the insured's *decision value*—reflecting confidence and risk management ability—acts as a dynamic signal for investors assessing risk pricing and allocation.

Overall, this model provides a systematic pathway to bridge insurability gaps:

(a) **Supply-Side Innovation:** By aggregating historical loss data and building exposure curves, the model supports the creation of dedicated protection funds. Participants with similar risk profiles form mutual pools, share initial risk capital, and address product gaps that traditional insurers often neglect.

(b) **Dynamic Capacity Expansion:** Participants' decision values as premium contributions and retention choices function as credible underwriting signals. If these signals deviate from actual risk, the pricing model self-corrects through recalibration. Robust signals attract layered reinsurance capital, creating a multi-tiered risk-absorbing structure that expands coverage capacity.

(c) **Market-Based Affordability:** The model enhances affordability by giving risk holders flexibility to calibrate their coverage. They can balance retention costs, expected risk coin returns, and individual financial capacity. If their decision values fall below market benchmarks, capital markets adjust supports, incentivizing product improvement and ongoing risk mitigation.

Together, these mechanisms reshape the traditional insurance structure from a passive zero-sum game into a participatory system aligning individual risk retention decisions with collective pool performance—ultimately lowering transaction costs, filling protection gaps, and improving insurability for risks previously deemed uninsurable.

3.3 Risk Management Incentives

As described, this model adopts an excess-of-loss reinsurance structure to allocate risks more efficiently: frequent, smaller losses are retained by policyholders, while rare, severe losses are covered by the Risk Fund or partner reinsurers. According Coarse Theorem [16] This structure improves capital efficiency and risk management by:

1. creating clear incentives for better loss prevention within the retention layer;
2. enabling more precise capital allocation by pricing the excess layer based on transparent exposure curves;
3. supporting stable coin value by anchoring it to verified retention data and ensuring healthy market liquidity.

When claims arise, coin holders during the policy period can choose either to redeem their coins for a higher payout or to hold them for partial reimbursement, depending on market conditions. Once coins are held beyond the policy period, they are exempt from retention losses. Combined with an investment-oriented reinsurance mechanism, the coin's value is balanced by market forces—aligning incentives for both capital protection and competitive returns. Pool profits flow back to coin holders through coin appreciation, creating a sustainable cycle of demand, return, and reinvestment.

When Risk Coins are tradable, their market value adjusts through three self-reinforcing feedback loops:

1. Losses within the retention layer raise coin costs, driving risk owners to adopt stronger risk controls.
2. Any surplus from Risk Fund is distributed fairly to coin holders.
3. Active trading ensures transparent price discovery, reflecting pool solvency and real-time supply–demand dynamics. This design effectively turns externalities into direct value for all stakeholders.

In practice, this model brings two important changes to the insurance market: first, it directly links individual risk reduction efforts to tangible coin-based gains; second, it shifts the game from a traditional zero-sum arrangement to a cooperative, value-sharing system. By raising retention levels and premium contributions, participants can earn higher returns from additional coins while boosting the overall pool value—a true win-win for policyholders, investors, and capital providers alike.

At its core, this is more than a contractual upgrade—it is a new governance model for modern risk transfer. By stratifying risks with advanced exposure analysis and turning insurance into an active risk management tool, the system redefines how risks are priced, shared, and turned into investable assets.

3.4 Risk Coin: Mechanism and Advantages as a Stablecoin

Risk Coin as **Stablecoin Issuance Guidelines** embeds digital currency issuance into Insurance Ecosystem, anchoring its value to real, quantifiable risk costs and avoiding the extreme volatility caused by unbacked issuance. Its stability mechanism includes [17–19]:

1. **Value Anchoring**: Risk Coins are issued based on participants' retained risk costs and premium payments. Each coin is backed by measurable risk coverage, preventing the "unbacked issuance" problem of traditional cryptocurrencies.
2. **Dynamic Adjustment**: Payouts and self-retention allow the Risk Coin supply to expand or contract in response to actual loss events, creating a supply-demand balance tied to real risks and dampening price swings.
3. **Diversified Risk Pools**: Different insurance pools linked via Risk Coins as cross-pool risk diversification enhance systemic resilience, making Risk Coin more stable than single-asset-backed stablecoins.
4. **Ecological Positive Cycle**: Holding Risk Coins incentivizes participants to improve risk management, increasing surplus reserves. External capital participation expands Risk Fund, forming a self-reinforcing cycle strengthening stability.
5. **Flexible Pricing**: Unlike traditional insurers' monopolistic pricing, the model lets participants adjust premiums and retention by their own risk tolerance. Market signals dynamically correct mispricing, improving efficiency and transparency.

In short, Risk Coin combines real economic risk-sharing with token economy logic, offering a new stablecoin model with intrinsic value, elastic supply, and ecological reinforcement—an innovative solution to the volatility and trust challenges faced by digital currencies today.

4 Conclusion

This paper proposes Risk Coin Model as an innovative approach to reshape insurance mechanisms through a participatory structure based on mutual Risk Fund. It aims to address the fundamental insurability limitations in traditional insurance arrangement, which often function as zero-sum games that erode trust, increase transaction costs, and result in coverage gaps, insufficient protection, and unaffordable premiums.

A payoff matrix analysis demonstrates that aligning individual returns with the overall performance of Risk Fund through dynamic distribution is essential for breaking non-cooperative equilibria and strengthening incentives for participation.

The paper further develops a premium utility function and an *investment-type reinsurance* mechanism to integrate direct insurance, reinsurance, and capital markets. At the same time, the collateralized risk coin system helps reduce the cost of moral hazard governance. Serving as a bridge between risk protection, benefit distribution, and capital allocation, the risk coin introduces a new institutional model to tackle insurability challenges, support blockchain-based financial stability, and offer an alternative anchoring mechanism for stablecoins.

While the model currently relies on assumptions such as independent and identically distributed risks and pure loss rating, future research should extend it by incorporating heterogeneous risk correlations, scale effects, intertemporal hedging, and personalized risk preferences to improve its practical relevance and adaptability to complex risk environments.

Disclosure of Interests. The authors have no competing interests to declare that are relevant to the content of this article.

References

1. Feng, R., Li, M.: Distributed insurance: tokenization of risk and reward allocation. SSRN, 4463804 (2023). https://doi.org/10.2139/ssrn.4463804
2. Sosa Gómez, I., Montes Pineda, Ó.: What is an InsurTech? A scientific approach for defining the term. Risk Manag. Insur. Rev. **26**(2), 125–173 (2023). https://doi.org/10.1111/rmir.12243
3. Krotov, V.: Predicting the future of disruptive technologies: the method of alternative histories. Bus. Horiz. **62**(6), 695–705 (2019). https://doi.org/10.1016/j.bushor.2019.07.003
4. Artzner, P., Delbaen, F., Jean-Marc, E., Heath, D.: Coherent measures of risk. Math. Finance. **9**, 203–228 (1999). https://doi.org/10.1111/1467-9965.00068
5. Denault, M.: Coherent allocation of risk capital. J. Risk. **4** (2001). https://doi.org/10.21314/JOR.2001.053
6. Lemaire, J. Lemaire, J.: Applications of game theory to the insurance business
7. Hu, Y., Rache, S.T., Fabozzi, F.J.: Modelling crypto asset price dynamics, optimal crypto portfolio, and crypto option valuation. arXiv preprint https://arxiv.org/abs/1908.05419 (2019)
8. Yu, J., Yen, B.: A cryptocurrency based insurance model. In: Proceedings of The 18th International Conference on Electronic Business (ICEB), pp. 2–6 (2018)
9. Salzmann, R.E.: Rating by layer of insurance. In: Proceedings of the Casualty Actuarial Society (1963)
10. Bernegger, S.: The Swiss Re exposure curves and the MBBEFD distribution class. ASTIN Bull. **27**(1), 99–111 (1997). https://doi.org/10.2143/AST.27.1.563208

11. Borch, K.: The utility concept applied to the theory of insurance. ASTIN Bull. **1**(5), 245–255 (1961). https://doi.org/10.1017/S0515036100009685
12. Arrow, K.J.: Uncertainty and the welfare economics of medical care. Am. Econ. Rev. **53**(5), 941–973 (1963)
13. Stiglitz, J.E.: Risk, incentives and insurance: the pure theory of moral hazard. Geneva Pap. Risk Insur. Issues Pract. **8**, 4–33 (1983)
14. Shavell, S.: On moral hazard and insurance. Q. J. Econ. **93**(4), 541–562 (1979)
15. Coase, R.H.: The nature of the firm (1937). Economica. **4**, 396–405 (1993)
16. Coase, R.: The problem of social cost. J. Law Econ. **3**, 1–44 (1960)
17. Chaum, D.L.: Computer Systems Established, Maintained and Trusted by Mutually Suspicious Groups. Electronics Research Laboratory, University of California, Riverside, CA (1979)
18. Mita, M., Ito, K., Ohsawa, S., Tanaka, H.: What is stablecoin?: a survey on price stabilization mechanisms for decentralized payment systems. In: 2019 8th International Congress on Advanced Applied Informatics (IIAI-AAI), pp. 60–66 (2019). https://doi.org/10.1109/IIAI-AAI.2019.00023
19. Li, D., Han, D., Weng, T.-H., Zheng, Z., Li, H., Li, K.-C.: On stablecoin: ecosystem, architecture, mechanism and applicability as payment method. Comput. Stand. Interf. **87**, 103747 (2024). https://doi.org/10.1016/j.csi.2023.103747

Navigating the Landscape of Stablecoins: Understanding Design, Volatility, and Regulatory Challenges

Abhigyan Mukherjee[✉]

Biju Patnaik University of Technology, Chhend Colony Raurkela Industrialship, Rourkela, Odisha 769015, India
abhigyan.mukherjee@yahoo.com

Abstract. Over the past few decades there has been a rapid evolution in cryptocurrencies. The digitization of fiat currencies took place back in the 1980s and since then many different independent currencies have been born including Bitcoin, Ethereum, and Ripple. Although Bitcoin's "set" supply model allows a decentralized monetary manner and can be used for the transfer of money, at the same time it has given birth to extreme volatility thereby making it a medium of exchange with significant repercussions. This article covers stablecoins (cryptocurrencies meant to maintain a stable exchange rate with fiat currencies) as a response to the volatility market. Even as whitepapers and marketing do exist, lack of knowledge is still a major barrier to use crypto due to the lack of uniform language and definitions within the cryptocurrency ecosystem. This paper aims to explain the design of stablecoins by highlighting the importance of clear definitions and accurate classifications to support regulatory scrutiny and enhance user understanding. Through a comparative review of a variety of stablecoin designs and their implications for financial markets, this paper gives a summary of the challenges and opportunities stablecoins pose with the evolving financial ecosystems that can support more informed adoption, policy debates, and future technical work.

Keywords: Stablecoins · Cryptocurrency · Volatility · Collateralization · Central Bank Digital Currency

1 Introduction

The earliest generations of digital currency projects, beginning in the 1980s, focused on providing electronic representations of government-issued money. These systems depended on a single provider that maintained centralized ledgers and controlled account balances. Within the modern cryptocurrency community, such arrangements are often described as merely digitizing "fiat" currency, because they do not challenge the underlying monetary regime [1]. Bitcoin introduced a fundamentally different model. Instead of relying on a central authority, it uses a public blockchain maintained by a distributed set of nodes and miners. The protocol specifies a deterministic, gradually decreasing issuance schedule that caps the total number of bitcoins that will ever exist [2]. With no

S. C. P. Yam et al. (Eds.): ICFT 2025, CCIS 2868, pp. 98–109, 2026.
https://doi.org/10.1007/978-981-92-0126-6_9

central bank or trusted institution to respond to macroeconomic conditions, this schedule cannot adapt to changes in demand. As a result, Bitcoin's purchasing power fluctuates dramatically, with large swings even over short time horizons. Empirically, Bitcoin's exchange rate relative to major government currencies has been far more volatile than typical foreign-exchange pairs. When plotted alongside USD, EUR, CAD, and GBP, the fiat currencies appear comparatively stable, while BTC exhibits repeated spikes and crashes. Even significant macroeconomic events, such as the depreciation of GBP following the Brexit referendum, look modest compared with many routine movements in the BTC price [3]. This level of volatility limits Bitcoin's usefulness as a day-to-day medium of exchange and creates substantial exchange-rate risk for borrowers and lenders. To mitigate these problems, a new class of tokens known as stablecoins has emerged. Stablecoins aim to provide the programmability and global accessibility of cryptocurrencies while keeping their value closely linked to a reference asset, often one US dollar. On many trading venues, stablecoins now function as the de facto quote currency for crypto markets, and in some periods their daily trading volume has surpassed that of Bitcoin itself. At the same time, high-profile projects and regulatory actions have highlighted the need for a clearer understanding of how different stablecoin mechanisms work and what risks they entail [4–6].

The initial wave of digital currencies, emerging in the 1980s, primarily sought to create an electronic version of traditional government-backed money (often referred to as 'fiat currency' within cryptocurrency circles) (Narayanan et al., 2016). The second wave, led notably by Bitcoin (Nakamoto et al., 2008), introduced an entirely independent financial system—one that operates without reliance on pre-existing currencies, central authorities, or financial intermediaries. The issuance of Bitcoin (BTC) follows a strictly predefined schedule encoded within its protocol, ensuring a fixed supply over time. Bitcoin's anonymous creator described this approach as follows: "There is no central authority akin to a central bank… to regulate the money supply… which would necessitate a trusted entity to assess value. I am not aware of a method that allows software to autonomously determine the real-world worth of assets. If such a method existed, or if I were willing to entrust someone with actively managing supply to maintain a fixed value, such rules could have been encoded. In this regard, Bitcoin resembles a precious metal. Rather than supply adapting to maintain value, the supply is predetermined while value fluctuates" (Champagne, 2014). Due to the absence of active monetary regulation, BTC's exchange rate with government-backed currencies has exhibited significant volatility (see Fig. 1). A closer look at the chart reveals a noticeable drop in the value of GBP around June 2016—a reflection of the market turbulence triggered by the Brexit referendum in the UK. However, this shift appears relatively minor in comparison to Bitcoin's dramatic price swings. (a) The emergence of a third wave?: Bitcoin's extreme volatility is not an isolated phenomenon; similar price instability is evident in other cryptocurrencies like Ethereum (ETH) and Ripple (XRP). This fluctuation poses a significant challenge for practical adoption: sharp price increases incentivize hoarding, while sudden declines deter usage. Such instability also complicates lending, as currency depreciation can easily surpass accrued interest. Without a stable medium for lending and credit, the development of sophisticated financial markets is hindered. To address this issue, numerous new cryptocurrency models have been introduced, aiming to establish a stable value relative to a government-backed currency such as the USD. These stability-focused digital assets are commonly referred to as stablecoins. Stablecoins have been a focal point of discussion in recent times, attracting both praise and criticism. According to Coin-MarketCap, Tether sees a higher daily transaction volume than Bitcoin. This is despite ongoing concerns regarding its reserves and regulatory scrutiny surrounding its associated entities. The introduction of Facebook's Libra garnered widespread attention, prompting responses from the Federal Reserve, U.S. lawmakers, and even the President. Another initiative, Basis(née Basecoin), managed to secure $133 M in venture capital but ultimately shut down due to insurmountable regulatory barriers in the United States. Meanwhile, central banks such as those in Sweden and Denmark have examined the potential for issuing state-backed digital currencies. (b) Knowledge gap: In theory, understanding the mechanics of stablecoins should be straightforward. Most projects publish whitepapers detailing their design, they are promoted to the general public, and a vast number of online resources analyze their frameworks. However, significant challenges arise when attempting to systematically categorize this information. Many whitepapers are dense with technical jargon, often failing to define key terms or using terminology inconsistently compared to other projects and conventional financial literature. Additionally, some components appear to be mis-classified, for instance, an element that fits the definition of a security or derivative may instead be described as a bond or a loan. Whether this is due to a lack of precision, an effort to make an unconventional approach seem more mainstream, or a tactic to avoid regulatory scrutiny remains uncertain. Regardless, I have endeavored to provide clear and direct explanations (see Table 2). Concurrently, other researchers have developed their own classification schemes (Pernice et al., 2019; Moin et al., 2020).

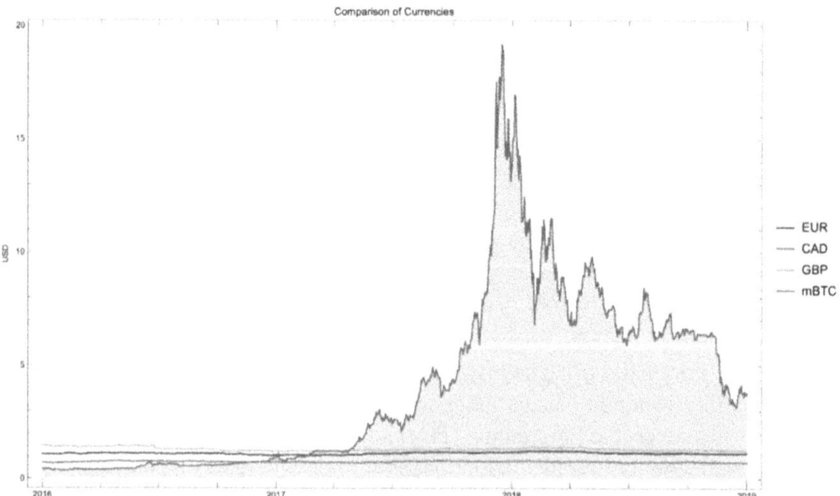

Fig. 1. Comparison of exchange-rate behavior between Bitcoin and major fiat currencies. Note that 1000 mBTC equates to 1 BTC.

2 Mechanisms of Stablecoins

To explore stablecoin projects, I analyzed content from CoinDesk, a well-known cryptocurrency news platform, using keywords such as "stablecoins," "stability," and "price-stable." I reviewed a total of 185 articles up to January 11, 2019 (In light of its prominence, Facebook's Libra Coin has also been included, despite being announced after this period). Among the 25 stablecoin projects for which adequate documentation was available, I classified them in Table 1. This classification is based on their stated mechanisms; however, I make no claims regarding their actual implementation. Projects are ordered based on their ranking on CoinMarketCap, a platform that lists actively traded cryptocurrencies. Projects that are not listed are assigned a rank of $\perp$. After compiling the list, I identified the core principles underlying each stability mechanism. Instead of detailing each stablecoin individually—which may become outdated quickly—I focused on summarizing their fundamental approaches. Broadly, stablecoins can be grouped into two categories: (1) those that maintain stability by pegging to a reference asset, such as the U.S. dollar, and depend on this asset's existence, and (2) those that function as independent digital currencies, employing algorithmic and/or discretionary interventions to achieve stability. A more detailed breakdown of these mechanisms is presented in Table 2.

Table 1. Overview of stablecoin projects as of January 11, 2019.

Category	Mechanism	Representative examples (Ranking)
Collateralized	Fully backed and redeemable†	USDC (20), TrueUSD (26), Paxos (38), Gemini Dollar (52), StableUSD -USDS (685), Stronghold USD (891), Petro (1210), Libra Coin ($\perp$), Ekon ($\perp$), WBTC ($\perp$), emparta ($\perp$)
	Directly collateralized	Tether (6), EURS Token (95), BitCNY (304), Terracoin (1280), Saga (1495), GJY ($\perp$), Novatti AUD ($\perp$), UPUSD ($\perp$)
	Indirectly collateralized	DAI (57), BitUSD (398), Nomin ($\perp$)
Algorithmic	Monetary Supply Adjustments	Ampleforth ($\perp$), RSCoin ($\perp$)
	Asset Transfer based	NuBits (892), CarbonUSD (1262), Basecoin ($\perp$)

†Note: Classification is based on claims made by the projects, i.e., we do not verify whether those categorized as 'redeemable' truly allow redemption of their collateral assets. Rankings are based on CoinMarketCap.

3   Type 1: Asset-Backed Stablecoins

A. Direct Collateralization and Redemption

Stablecoins within this classification operate under a structure where the issuing entity secures a reserve composed of valuable assets—such as fiat currencies like USD, commodities like gold, or even a diversified asset basket. Digital tokens are then issued, each representing a fraction of the underlying reserve (for example, assuming a token corresponds to 1 USD), which can be transacted digitally. This foundational idea pre-dates Bitcoin, with earlier digital currencies like Liberty Reserve implementing similar concepts—albeit with varying degrees of redeemability and significant legal constraints. Unlike Liberty Reserve, e-gold, and other pre-blockchain alternatives, where all trans-action records and balances were managed on centralized private servers, blockchain technology allows for decentralized validation of transactions. However, issuance and redemption of these stablecoins still depend on a trusted entity. As a result, while these stablecoins exhibit a higher degree of centralization than Bitcoin, they remain more decentralized than legacy digital currencies. A more nuanced evaluation of trust assump-tions is presented in Table 3. It is also important to note that while reducing centralization enhances transparency and trust, additional safeguards are necessary to protect user pri-vacy. To illustrate the issuance mechanism outlined in Table 2, consider AliceCoins. If market participants are willing to purchase AliceCoins for more than \$1 USD per token, the issuing entity can generate new tokens at \$1 USD and sell them at a premium, thereby driving prices back to equilibrium. Conversely, if sellers accept a price below

Table 2. Key categories of stability strategies for stablecoins.

Fully Backed and Redeemable.
Alice, acting as a trusted intermediary, deploys a decentralized application (DApp) on Ethereum, issuing 1000 units of a token named AliceCoin (e.g., an ERC20 token). She sets the exchange rate at \$1 USD per AliceCoin and guarantees its redemption at the same rate. If Bob purchases 10 AliceCoins for \$10 USD, Alice deposits the amount into a secure bank account. When Alice receives additional buy requests and runs out of tokens, she mints new ones to meet demand. If Carol wishes to redeem 5 AliceCoins, Alice withdraws \$5 USD and exchanges it with Carol while removing those AliceCoins from circulation. Regular bank statements are published to verify that sufficient USD reserves exist to back all issued AliceCoins, which can be independently audited through the Ethereum ledger.

Collateralized with No Direct Redemption.
Alice, again serving as a trusted entity, issues 1000 AliceCoins as ERC20 tokens, selling them at \$1 USD each. She commits to holding all proceeds in a bank account. New AliceCoins are minted when existing ones are exhausted, and Alice regularly discloses bank statements to prove sufficient reserves. However, unlike the previous approach, Alice does not guarantee the direct redemption of AliceCoins for USD.

(continued)

Table 2. (*continued*)

Collateralized Indirectly.
Alice is no longer assumed to be trustworthy. Instead, she creates a decentralized application that holds ETH and issues tokens. The smart contract calculates the required ETH deposit per AliceCoin based on an external exchange rate provided by a reliable oracle. Alice deposits ETH equivalent to $1.50 USD per token and receives two distinct token positions—each of which is transferable. The first position grants the holder the right to redeem up to $1.00 USD worth of ETH at the prevailing rate, while the second position absorbs any remaining ETH value. Alice sells the first position (AliceCoin) to Bob for $1.00 USD and may retain or sell the second. If Bob redeems AliceCoin when the ETH deposit holds sufficient value, he receives $1 USD worth of ETH. However, if the exchange rate declines significantly, Bob receives the entire deposit, leaving the second-position holder with nothing.

Supply-Based Adjustments.
Alice forks Bitcoin to create an alternative cryptocurrency called AliceCoin, modifying the coinbase issuance mechanism. She introduces an oracle that tracks the AliceCoin-to-USD exchange rate. The system automatically intervenes if AliceCoin's price surpasses $1.02 USD or drops below $0.98 USD. If the price exceeds $1.02 USD, miners are permitted to increase the coinbase issuance (determined mathematically based on the price deviation). Conversely, if the price falls below $0.98 USD, miners must decrease the coinbase issuance accordingly. Other miners validate these adjustments during block verification, ensuring consistency with the established protocol rules.

Asset Redistribution.
Alice develops a DApp issuing an ERC20 token named AliceCoin. The DApp is programmed to intervene if AliceCoin's price moves beyond $1.02 USD or below $0.98 USD, based on data from a reliable oracle. If the price surpasses $1.02 USD, the DApp generates additional AliceCoins and distributes them to users waiting in line for new tokens. To queue up, users participate in an auction system whenever the price drops under $0.98 USD, bidding for a position in line. Payments for these queue positions are made in AliceCoins, which are subsequently burned. If no users are in the queue, newly minted AliceCoins are distributed according to a predefined fallback policy.

$1 USD per Alice-Coin, market arbitrage allows traders to buy and redeem them for a profit, restoring the price to its intended peg. In practice, due to transaction costs, inefficiencies, and market friction, minor deviations from the peg are inevitable. If confidence in redemption weakens, the token price may decline below $1 USD, though this is not necessarily guaranteed (see the following section). The credibility of the issuing organization and the custodian responsible for asset reserves is crucial. Regular financial audits play a key role in establishing trust, though verifying blockchain-backed financial assets introduces its own challenges (Pimentel et al., 2019).

B. Directly-Supported

Consider a stablecoin that functions similarly to the previous section but lacks a formal redemption mechanism for converting coins back into underlying assets. When a project did not explicitly state a redemption process, I classified it within this category in Table 1. Referencing the structure in Table 2, the upper bid limit remains at $1 for the same reasons discussed previously. However, unlike the prior case, there is no built-in method to counteract price drops between $0 and $1 USD (i.e., undervaluation is not inherently mitigated). Coins under this category are typically still 'redeemable,' though often only by the entity managing the coin. The issuer can acquire undervalued coins to withdraw $1 USD per unit from reserves. Due to this mechanism, stablecoins in this category face scrutiny—limited by the transparency of the issuer—to verify the existence of full reserves. If each AliceToken were not backed by a corresponding $1 USD, the issuer could generate excess tokens for personal financial gain. The most prominent stablecoin in this category is Tether. While Tether asserts redeemability, users report significant friction in the redemption process. Moreover, it has faced allegations of manipulating markets by issuing tokens without full reserve backing (Griffin & Shams, 2018). Additionally, it has not consistently held enough USD reserves to redeem all Tether tokens in circulation. Given these concerns, I have placed it under this classification. Curiously, despite these issues, Tether remains among the most liquid cryptocurrencies, with daily trading volumes surpassing all others in value (as per CoinMarketCap at the time of writing). A possible explanation for its resilience is its sheer utility. One crucial application of Tether—particularly in relation to the Bitfinex exchange—is its role as a transitional asset for traders and investors. Suppose a trader wishes to convert BTC into USD; she has three choices. She may (1) keep the USD in her exchange wallet, restricting its use to that specific exchange and relying on the platform's security. Alternatively, she may (2) withdraw USD to a bank, which requires identity verification (in most jurisdictions), a compliant financial institution, and a potentially lengthy processing time. A middle-ground approach is (3) converting BTC into a stablecoin, which allows withdrawal from the exchange (i.e., shifting from an exchange-controlled wallet to a private one) with minimal delay, regulatory barriers, or transaction friction. Once withdrawn, the stablecoin can be transferred between exchanges, sent to other users, or spent directly—all without engaging the original exchange. Essentially, it provides greater mobility than storing USD within an exchange while minimizing the obstacles associated with direct fiat withdrawal.

C. Collateralized via Smart Contracts

The prior approaches heavily rely on the trustworthiness of the entity managing the currency. A natural question arises: can a currency be autonomously governed by a decentralized application (DApp)? This method operates by issuing a token that can always be exchanged for $1 USD worth of ETH, based on the prevailing exchange rate between USD and ETH. Consequently, the amount of ETH obtained in exchange for the token will vary depending on fluctuations in the exchange rate. Since blockchains do not inherently possess knowledge of real-world exchange rates, a reliable third-party oracle is required to update the USD/ETH rate on-chain. Alternatively, consensus can be drawn from multiple oracles to ensure reliability. Referencing the approach detailed in Table 2, if demand for an AliceCoin exceeds $1 USD, the system will issue new coins if participants like Alice are willing to lock up ETH deposits equivalent to 1.5 times the coin's face value—this is known as overcollateralization. Conversely, if the token trades below $1 USD, arbitrageurs can buy it and redeem it for a profit, provided the DApp holds enough ETH to facilitate redemptions. Otherwise, the value of an AliceCoin will fluctuate between $0 and $1 USD, directly tied to the reserves of ETH maintained by the DApp. Does Alice assume significant risk by minting AliceCoins? Being second in line for claims on the reserves is inherently riskier than holding ETH directly. This stability mechanism does not eliminate volatility but rather redistributes it, shifting the risk to those lower in priority. However, this risk is mitigated—Alice never faces a shortfall greater than $1 USD relative to the ETH held in the DApp. Moreover, if Alice retains the $1 USD received for issuing an AliceCoin, it provides a buffer against potential losses from adverse price movements. Her exposure to risk remains equivalent to simply holding ETH. The position of being second in line can also be transferred to other participants willing to take on risk—this effectively turns the token into a leveraged position betting on ETH appreciation. What about Bob? Under most circumstances, holding an AliceCoin is designed to closely mimic holding USD. However, in the event of a rapid devaluation of ETH against USD, the collateral buffer may be exhausted, causing the AliceCoin's value to decline in tandem with ETH. Several key design choices must be addressed when implementing a stablecoin of this nature: What should the minimum collateralization ratio be (e.g., 1.5x)? Under what conditions should AliceCoins be redeemable (e.g., instantly, after a certain period, or following market fluctuations)? How should issuance be structured (e.g., maintaining separate collateral for each token versus pooling all collateral and treating all tokens as fungible)?

Table 3. Comparison of methodologies for stablecoin design.

Framework	Price Regulation		Decentralization				Flexibility		
Traditional Electronic Money	●	●				●	●		
Conventional Cryptocurrencies			●	×	●	●			
Direct Collateralization with Redemption	●	●			●	●	●		
Direct Collateralization		●			●	●	●		
Indirect Collateralization	○	●	●	●	●		●	●	
Money Supply Adaptation	?	○	●	×	●	○	●	●	●
Asset-Based Exchange	?	○	●	×	●	○	●	●	●

● signifies the respective characteristic (columns) is sufficiently achieved within the mechanism (rows), ○ means the characteristic is only partially achieved under certain conditions, ? represents a theoretically suggested approach with uncertain stability, and × indicates that the characteristic is not applicable.

4 Type 2: Intervention-Based Stablecoins

The fundamental input to this mechanism is the exchange rate, particularly when an exchange rate system has failed (refer to the CBDC paper). It is unclear what other alternatives could serve as effective inputs. Most stablecoin initiatives, however, utilize the exchange rate relative to a fiat currency (e.g., USD) to trigger interventions. This makes these stablecoins resemble those that are directly backed by fiat (refer to Sect. IV), facilitating comparative analysis. However, it is important to recognize that alternative economic indicators, independent of exchange rates, could also be employed. Historically, central banks have relied on exchange rate signals for intervention decisions, yet this approach proved insufficient for macroeconomic stabilization. Other potential indicators might include interest rates (in the presence of active lending markets), purchasing power metrics, or transaction-related data, such as volume and velocity. The primary challenge is ensuring that these metrics remain resistant to manipulation within a blockchain environment, where single actors can create numerous identities and artificially inflate transaction data through self-interactions, such as wash trading, loan cycling, and internal exchanges. If stability indicators could be directly extracted from blockchain data, the system could operate autonomously, fostering full decentralization.

Supply-Side Adjustments

A critical design aspect involves determining the nature of interventions. All stablecoins within this category adopt the same foundational approach: increasing the supply of the stablecoin to counteract rising valuation and contracting the supply to counter depreciation. The next consideration is the specific method for supply modulation. While some stablecoins directly adjust the money supply, others convert currency into assets to contract supply or transform assets back into currency to expand it. This concept mirrors how contemporary central banks influence interest rates (For instance, central banks acquire financial assets, such as government securities, from commercial banks at competitive rates, thereby augmenting liquidity and reducing interbank lending rates. Conversely, by selling assets to banks, they extract liquidity from the system, which elevates the demand for cash and consequently increases interbank interest rates.). Lastly, a crucial design element involves determining who can engage in these stability mechanisms.

Heuristic Approaches

The stability mechanisms discussed in this section are referred to as heuristics because their efficacy is only demonstrable within theoretical models that may or may not accurately represent real-world financial behavior, particularly that of traders. In fact, this is the most optimistic scenario—many of these heuristic-based mechanisms lack even basic simulations or models validating their effectiveness under specific conditions. This presents an avenue for significant future research. It is not possible to definitively prove the effectiveness of any given mechanism discussed here, as they remain heuristic-driven. Central banks themselves rely on heuristic strategies that evolve over time, typically shifting every few decades. Although it is difficult to confirm whether a particular approach is effective, it is possible to highlight circumstances where an intervention is likely to fail—such as when inputs are susceptible to manipulation or when historically ineffective intervention strategies are used for currency stabilization.

A. *Adjustments to Money Supply*

A reliable oracle delivers the current exchange rate between the cryptocurrency and a stable asset, such as the US dollar. When the cryptocurrency appreciates, its supply is expanded, and when it depreciates, the supply is reduced. This strategy mirrors historical central banking policies, though modern monetary authorities have largely moved away from exchange rate targeting due to previous failures. Nevertheless, exchange rates serve as a useful example, though alternative financial indicators could also be employed: oracle reported interest rates (if lending markets develop), purchasing power metrics, blockchain-based measures like transaction volume (provided they resist manipulation), or even discretionary adjustments by institutions such as central banks themselves (Danezis & Meiklejohn, 2016). Expanding the supply of a cryptocurrency is straightforward. The method of distributing newly minted currency is a design choice, with several potential approaches: (1) proportionally among existing holders, (2) randomly distributed to holders through a lottery, (3) allocated to miners, or (4) assigned to a governing entity such as a central bank. The primary challenge lies in determining who bears the losses when the supply contracts. Table 2 presents an illustrative mechanism. If a significant number of bids for AliceCoin exceed $1.02, a portion of the newly issued currency could be allocated to purchasing USD until all buyers willing to pay above $1.02 have acquired AliceCoins. However, this remains a heuristic approach, as there is no certainty that recipients will convert the additional currency into USD, particularly in scenarios where demand for USD is waning. A similar justification applies to offers below $0.98—currency contractions might discourage holders from spending on USD. However, if the price decline stems from reduced demand for AliceCoins rather than an excessive supply, then reducing supply may only lead to market illiquidity without necessarily stimulating trade or correcting the undervaluation. When the coinbase dynamically increases or decreases (referred to as an elastic coinbase), expansions can be unrestricted, whereas reductions cannot logically extend below zero. In cases where the coinbase reaches zero, miners remain incentivized through transaction fees. This is the anticipated mechanism for Bitcoin beyond the year 2140, once all BTC has been mined—though the effectiveness of this model remains a topic of debate (Carlsten et al., 2016). Could a negative coinbase exist? Since miners earn the sum of transaction fees and the coinbase, a coinbase can indeed be slightly negative if transaction fees exceed its negative value. In this scenario, transaction fees effectively serve as a means for users to burn currency, contributing to money supply contraction.

B. *Asset Redistribution*

The second category of intervention-driven stability frameworks adjusts the currency supply to regulate its value, though it employs a more indirect contraction approach. Refer to Table 2 for the mechanism overview. If multiple bids exceeding $1.02 USD remain unfulfilled, the strategy aligns with the previous section: additional currency is distributed with the expectation that it will drive the purchase of more USD. The rationale behind offers below $0.98 assumes that individuals are effectively paying for queue placement. If this assumption holds, then the subsequent reduction in currency availability adheres to the same principles as the prior discussion. However, acquiring a position in the queue remains highly speculative—there is no certainty that the currency will stabilize, nor that a given position will ever be utilized. As the queue extends, the cost of securing a spot diminishes, leading to a gradual thinning of the speculative market, with only traders seeking increasingly high-risk, high-reward opportunities remaining. These patterns neither ensure nor strongly indicate a potential price recovery (Fig. 2).

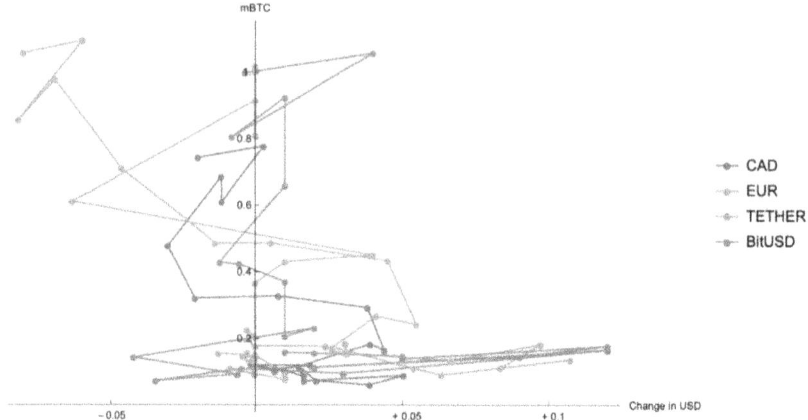

Fig. 2. Illustrative comparison of price movements for fiat currencies and selected stablecoins. Fluctuations in the value of two fiat currencies (CAD and EUR) and two stablecoins (Tether and BitUSD) relative to both USD and BTC. Vertical segments indicate stability concerning USD, while horizontal ones illustrate volatility in USD valuation. Despite not being tied to USD, CAD and EUR exhibit a level of stability comparable to that of stablecoins. The data spans from January 2017 to November 2018; note that 1000 mBTC corresponds to 1 BTC.

5   Discussion and Conclusion

Broadly speaking, stablecoins aim to tokenize an asset with relatively low volatility and integrate it into blockchain systems. These coins typically rely on one of two fundamental strategies. The first involves adjusting the circulating supply dynamically to stabilize value. The second approach creates a system where two highly volatile assets are restructured into one stablecoin and another coin with extreme price fluctuations. This latter mechanism resembles traditional financial instruments that do not eliminate risk but rather redistribute it across different asset tranches. Why do so many stablecoin projects exist? The distinctions between them arise from several key factors: (1) the nature of the assets backing the stablecoin—whether USD, EUR, gold, or others; (2) the blockchain network on which they operate (e.g., Bitcoin, Ethereum) and the specific technical configurations involved (such as contract upgradability and governance models); and (3) the jurisdiction in which they are based, which dictates the level of regulatory oversight they must adhere to. Looking ahead, self-sovereign stablecoins present an intriguing avenue, yet they encounter substantial regulatory challenges stemming from banking policies, financial surveillance, and potential classification under securities laws. For stablecoins tied to government-issued currencies, the ultimate realization might take the form of a central bank digital currency (CBDC). Given the continuous decline in the use of physical cash—especially in legitimate transactions (Rogoff, 2017)—a CBDC could restore cash. Regardless of which designs ultimately prevail, clear terminology and careful classification of mechanisms will be essential for informed decision-making by developers, users, and policymakers. This paper has aimed to contribute to that goal by outlining the main architectural patterns observed to date and by highlighting their key trade-offs.

References

Carlsten, M., Kalodner, H., Weinberg, S.M., Narayanan, A.: On the instability of bitcoin without the block reward. In: ACM CCS, pp. 154–167. ACM (2016)

Champagne, P.: The Book of Satoshi: The Collected Writings of Bitcoin Creator Satoshi Nakamoto. e53 (2014)

Danezis, G., Meiklejohn, S.: Centrally banked cryptocurrencies. NDSS (2016)

Griffin, J.M., Shams, A.: Is bitcoin really un-tethered? Available at SSRN 3195066 (2018)

Harris, L.: Trading and Exchanges: Market Microstructure for Practitioners, pp. 410–419. Oxford University Press, Oxford, MA (2003)

Moin, A., Sekniqi, K., Sirer, E. G.: SoK: A Classification Framework for Stablecoin Designs. Financial Cryptography (2020)

Nakamoto, S., et al.: Bitcoin: A Peer-To-Peer Electronic Cash System (2008)

Narayanan, A., Bonneau, J., Felten, E.W., Miller, A., Goldfeder, S.: Bitcoin and Cryptocurrency Technologies. Princeton (2016)

Okoye, M.C., Clark, J.: Toward cryptocurrency lending. In: International Conference on Financial Cryptography and Data Security, pp. 367–380. Springer (2018)

Pernice, I.G.A, Henningsen, S., Proskalovich, R., Florian, M., Elendner, H.: Monetary Stabilization in Cryptocurrencies: Design Approaches and Open Questions. CVCBT (2019)

Pimentel, E., Boulianne, E., Eskandari, S., Clark, J.: Systemizing the Challenges of Auditing Blockchain-Based Assets. SSRN (2019)

Rogoff, K.S.: The Curse of Cash: How Large- Denomination Bills Aid Crime and Tax Evasion and Constrain Monetary Policy. Princeton University Press (2017)

Wood, G.: Ethereum yellow paper. Internet: https://github. com/ethereum/yellowpaper. Accessed 30 Oct 2018 (2014)

Analysis of the Mechanism and Path of Blockchain Reconstructing the Credit Ecosystem of Cross-Border E-Commerce: A Single Case Study of Trusple Based on Grounded Theory

Junlong Ma and Shuren Zhang[✉]

Hangzhou Normal University, Hangzhou 310000, China
3061176@qq.com

Abstract. In the process of global economic integration, cross-border e-commerce has developed vigorously and become an important part of international trade. However, small and medium-sized enterprises (SMEs) face severe credit challenges in cross-border e-commerce activities. Traditional credit reporting systems suffer from information asymmetry, and transnational data transmission faces many difficulties, making it difficult for SMEs to obtain accurate credit evaluations and restricting their financing channels, thus hindering their expansion in the international market. The emergence of blockchain technology provides new ideas for solving these problems. Its core functions, such as distributed ledgers and smart contracts, can achieve transparent and tamper-proof credit data and automatic execution, effectively reconstructing the credit ecosystem of cross-border e-commerce. Taking the Trusple platform as an example, the platform uses blockchain technology to accumulate transaction data and reshape corporate credit profiles, providing SMEs with fairer credit evaluations and financing opportunities, thereby reshaping the international credit reporting competition landscape. This paper uses grounded theory to systematically analyze the Trusple case and proposes a "technology empowerment-credit reconstruction-ecological balance" model. Through a dynamic analysis framework involving multiple stakeholders, this model reveals the mechanisms and paths of blockchain reconstructing the cross-border e-commerce credit system, providing policy insights for developing countries to cope with changes in the international credit reporting ecosystem. Specifically, this model can be used not only to analyze the evolutionary mechanism of the cross-border e-commerce credit ecosystem but also to provide an empirical basis for formulating policies related to cross-border payments and the credit reporting industry.

Keywords: Blockchain · Cross-border e-commerce · Credit ecosystem · Trusple · Grounded theory · International credit reporting · Small and medium-sized enterprises (SMEs)

S. C. P. Yam et al. (Eds.): ICFT 2025, CCIS 2868, pp. 110–120, 2026.
https://doi.org/10.1007/978-981-92-0126-6_10

1 Literature Review

With the rapid development of cross-border e-commerce, the traditional credit system has exposed significant defects in cross-border transactions. Hang Cheng (2024) points out that traditional credit evaluation relies on regional data, leading to "information silos" in cross-border transactions, making it difficult for SMEs' credit records to be shared across borders and exacerbating financing barriers. Lin (2024) further notes that traditional platforms are vulnerable to interference from activities such as brushing and fake reviews, resulting in insufficient credibility of credit data (Lin, 2024). Additionally, cross-border payments rely on multiple intermediaries, with cumbersome processes and high costs (Zhang, 2024), while traditional financial institutions have significant lag in credit evaluation for SMEs (Bai & Wan, 2023).

The emergence of blockchain technology provides a new path to solve the above dilemmas. Wu (2015) proposed that blockchain's distributed ledger and smart contract technologies can enhance data transparency and reduce transaction friction. Li and Lu (2023) argue that blockchain can effectively solve the information asymmetry problem in supply chain finance and enhance the reliability of credit verification through on-chain data accumulation. Cases such as Trusple show that blockchain automatically executes transaction terms through smart contracts, reducing the payment cycle from weeks to the next day (Trusple official website), while encryption technology ensures data immutability (Catalinic, 2018). However, existing research still has shortcomings: First, most literature focuses on technical principles and lacks systematic analysis of blockchain reconstructing credit ecosystems (Zhou et al., 2024). Additionally, there is a lack of relevant research on the challenges faced by the international trade credit reporting industry and the driving mechanisms of dynamic changes in the context of cross-border e-commerce, while the credit reporting needs of cross-border e-commerce entities have become increasingly important as their share in international trade grows.

Against this background, is it possible for blockchain to reconstruct the credit ecosystem of cross-border e-commerce? Is it possible to break the business models of traditional credit reporting industries, force reforms in traditional credit reporting industries, or even change the original global pattern of the credit reporting industry? Can it address the problem of underdeveloped credit reporting industries in emerging cross-border e-commerce countries such as China and the severe lack of credit reporting needs in international trade and cross-border e-commerce transactions?

These questions can be unified into the mechanism and path of blockchain reconstructing the credit ecosystem of cross-border e-commerce. However, it cannot be deduced solely from concepts; instead, it is necessary to construct possible theories based on actual cases of industry practice. For such complex phenomena and related cases, grounded theory is suitable for exploratory research, with the potential to build innovative theoretical frameworks, thereby enriching and improving the credit theory system for cross-border e-commerce, and providing practical guidance for cross-border e-commerce enterprises, financial institutions, and regulatory authorities, promoting the widespread application of blockchain technology in service industries and support industries related to the cross-border e-commerce credit ecosystem, and ultimately promoting the healthy development of the cross-border e-commerce industry.

As a typical application of blockchain technology in the cross-border e-commerce field, the Trusple platform has a unique platform technology architecture and significant ecological synergy, capable of providing rich and representative data for research. Therefore, this paper selects Trusple as the case study and grounded theory as the research method. Through interviews with Trusple employees and various clients, combined with official cases, technical specifications, media reports, and academic papers, a systematic analysis of multi-level materials is conducted to explore the specific mechanisms and impact paths of Trusple on the cross-border e-commerce credit ecosystem.

2 Single-Case Grounded Analysis

2.1 Data Sources and Coding Foundation

The data sources in this paper are divided into three levels, as shown in Table 1. Interview records, media reports, and user feedback account for 40%, technical documents account for 30%, and transaction records account for 30%. Through cross-validation of data from different sources, such as comparing the business descriptions of enterprises in interviews with the actual situations in transaction records, and the functional descriptions in technical documents with the usage experiences of users in interviews, the accuracy and reliability of the data are ensured.

Table 1. Data Sources

Data Type	Specific Content	Purpose
Primary Data	Semi-structured interviews with users, user feedback	Exploring user behavior and platform mechanisms
Secondary Data	Blockchain whitepapers, media reports, user manuals, Trusple official website, transaction records	Verifying interview content and supplementing technical details
Tertiary Data	Academic papers, industry reports, technical documents	Providing industry background and competitive analysis

2.2 First-Level Coding Analysis

Open coding is the first step in grounded theory research, aiming to extract key concepts from raw data. In the specific coding process, it is required to carefully read each interview record and document, mark meaningful sentences, and extract initial concepts.

The corresponding relationships between some data segments and coding results are shown in Table 2.

Table 2. First-Level Coding Table

Open Coding	Keywords	Raw Data Segment
Blockchain Technology	Blockchain, AntChain, smart contracts, technical solutions	Blockchain technology is the foundation of the Trusple platform, realizing digital upgrading of the entire trade chain through blockchain technology to solve trust issues in cross-border trade.
International Credit	Trust challenges, on-chain credit accumulation, trade authenticity, trust issues	Trusple solves trust issues in cross-border trade through blockchain technology, accumulates on-chain credit, helps buyers and sellers establish trust, and ensures trade authenticity.
Cross-Border Trade	Cross-border trade, international trade	Trusple focuses on cross-border trade, simplifying trade processes, shortening transaction cycles, and improving transaction efficiency through blockchain technology.
Financial Services	Financial services, payment terms, capital pressure, financing needs, discount services, order financing	Trusple provides financial services for SMEs, alleviating capital pressure and improving capital turnover efficiency.
SMEs	Small and medium-sized enterprises, viability, capital pressure	Trusple helps SMEs solve capital pressure and financing needs in cross-border trade, enhancing their survival and operational capabilities.
Financial Institutions	Banks, financial institutions, financial service risks, verification requests, partners	Trusple collaborates with financial institutions to reduce financial service risks, ensure trade authenticity through verification requests, and provide financial services.
Transaction Efficiency	Transaction efficiency, transaction cycle, transaction process, transaction risks, transaction time	Trusple improves transaction efficiency through blockchain technology, shortens transaction cycles, simplifies transaction processes, and reduces transaction risks.

(continued)

Table 2. (*continued*)

Open Coding	Keywords	Raw Data Segment
Ecosystem	Ecosystem, third-party service providers, logistics companies, comprehensive services, openness	Trusple builds an open ecosystem, allowing third-party service providers, financial institutions, and logistics companies to access and jointly provide comprehensive services to users.
Data Transparency	Data transparency, transaction records, tamper-proof, information sharing, data security	Blockchain technology ensures the transparency and tamper-proof nature of transaction data, promotes information sharing, and guarantees data security to enhance international credit.
Credit Accumulation	Credit accumulation, credit records, credit evaluation, credit accumulation, credit system	Trusple records trade data through blockchain to help SMEs accumulate credit, form traceable credit records, and provide support for credit evaluation and accumulation.
Cross-Border Payments	Cross-border payments, payment efficiency, payment costs, payment security, payment transparency	Trusple optimizes cross-border payment processes, improves payment efficiency, reduces payment costs, and ensures payment security and transparency through blockchain technology.
SME Empowerment	SMEs, trade opportunities, credit support, financing facilitation, market expansion	Providing credit support to SMEs, lowering financing thresholds, and helping them expand into international markets to gain more trade opportunities.

Through the analysis of large amounts of data, this paper extracts multiple initial concepts covering the technical characteristics, functional advantages of the Trusple platform, and its impact on the cross-border e-commerce credit ecosystem. These initial concepts lay the foundation for subsequent axial coding and selective coding.

2.3 Second-Level Coding Analysis

The main task of second-level coding is to categorize the initial concepts extracted from open coding into categories and establish relationships between categories. In the study of the Trusple platform, through the second-level coding of grounded theory, six main categories are classified: technological empowerment, credit reconstruction, efficiency improvement, ecological balance, risk control, and data security. Around these main categories, 15 subcategories are further formed, as shown in Table 3.

Table 3. Second-Level Coding Table

Main Category	Subcategory	Initial Concepts
Technological Empowerment	Distributed Ledger Technology	Decentralized trust mechanisms, cross-border data synchronization, multi-node collaborative verification
	Tamper-Proof	Full-chain data transparency
	Traceability	Enhanced logistics traceability, full-cycle transaction trace retention
	Smart Contract Mechanisms	Smart contract automatic payments, smart contract execution, smart performance guarantees
	Data Security and Privacy Protection	Cross-border data synchronization, multi-node collaborative verification, encryption technology and privacy protection mechanisms, cryptographic trust endorsement
Credit Reconstruction	Decentralized Evaluation	Cross-border data synchronization, on-chain credit data accumulation, multi-dimensional credit profile construction, cryptographic trust endorsement, decentralized trust mechanisms, credit behavior incentive systems
	Cross-Border Credit Transmission	On-chain credit data accumulation, cross-border data synchronization, full-chain data transparency, cross-border credit data mutual recognition

(continued)

Table 3. (*continued*)

Main Category	Subcategory	Initial Concepts
	Supply Chain Inclusive Financing	Traditional process optimization, on-chain credit data accumulation, reduced credit evaluation costs, international credit equalization effects, credit-driven inclusive finance, inclusive finance expansion
	Credit Behavior Incentives	Credit behavior incentive systems
Ecological Balance	Changes in Competitive Landscape	Weakening the monopoly of single institutions, cross-border transaction efficiency optimization, cryptographic trust endorsement
	Empowering SMEs	Traditional process optimization, international credit equalization effects, cross-border transaction efficiency optimization, reduced credit evaluation costs, credit-driven inclusive finance, smart performance guarantees
	Multi-Party Ecological Collaboration	Deep participation of banks and financial institutions, integration of logistics and trade services, multi-node collaborative verification

Under the dimension of 'technology empowerment,' distributed storage is one of the important attributes of blockchain technology. The decentralization, immutability, and traceability of distributed ledgers enable cross-border e-commerce transaction data to be securely and transparently stored and shared. All participants can access transaction information in real time, reducing information asymmetry and increasing transaction credibility. Smart contracts automate the execution of transaction processes, improving transaction efficiency. This technological empowerment lays the foundation for reconstructing the credit ecosystem of cross-border e-commerce.

The 'credit reconstruction' dimension includes elements such as changes in evaluation models. Traditional credit evaluation systems face issues like information asymmetry, high costs, and poor timeliness. The application of blockchain technology has changed this situation. With transaction data recorded on distributed ledgers, financial institutions can more accurately assess a company's credit status and provide more precise financing services. Additionally, blockchain technology enables the sharing and mutual recognition of credit information, breaking the geographical limitations of traditional credit systems and providing a fairer competitive environment for cross-border e-commerce companies.

Credit reconstruction further promotes the balance of the cross-border e-commerce ecosystem. Under the new credit system, the interests of all participants in cross-border e-commerce are better protected, forming a virtuous cycle within the ecosystem. Suppliers can obtain more orders and financing support; buyers can reduce procurement risks; financial institutions can lower credit risk by providing more precise financial services. At the same time, the application of blockchain technology also promotes the regulated development of the cross-border e-commerce industry, reducing fraud and default behaviors and maintaining market order.

In the 'technology empowerment - credit reconstruction - ecological balance' model, technology empowerment is the foundation, providing technical support for credit reconstruction; credit reconstruction is the core, serving as the key link to achieving ecological balance; ecological balance is the goal, representing the ultimate outcome of technology empowerment and credit reconstruction. As shown in Fig. 1, the three elements interact and reinforce each other, forming an integrated whole.

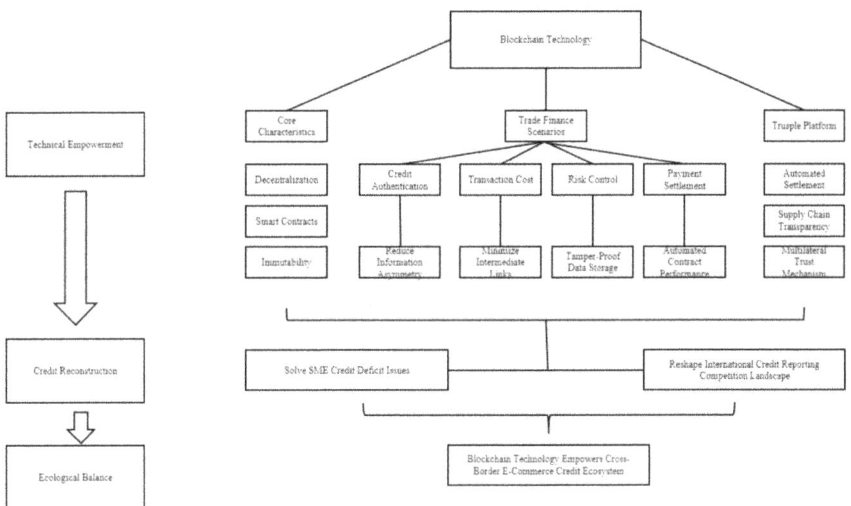

Fig. 1. The "Technology Empowerment-Credit Reconstruction-Ecological Balance" Model

2.4 Third-Level Coding Analysis

Through in-depth research on the Trusple platform, the core logic chain of "technology empowerment-credit reconstruction-ecological balance" is determined, which clearly demonstrates the mechanism of blockchain technology in the cross-border e-commerce credit ecosystem.

The Trusple platform provides safe and efficient technical support for cross-border e-commerce transactions through blockchain distributed ledgers and smart contract technologies. These technical features make transaction data more reliable and transaction processes more automated, thus creating conditions for credit reconstruction. Based on technological empowerment, the platform re-evaluates and constructs the credit of both transaction parties using collected transaction data and credit information. By establishing an objective and accurate credit system, credit risks are reduced, and the trust between transaction parties is improved. When credit reconstruction is completed, the entire cross-border e-commerce credit ecosystem reaches a balanced state, where both transaction parties are more willing to participate in transactions, market competition is fairer and more orderly, and industry development is healthier and more stable.

3   Theoretical Construction and Verification

The "technology empowerment-credit reconstruction-ecological balance" model contains three intervention paths: the technical path, institutional path, and data path. As shown in Fig. 2, these three intervention paths reshape the cross-border e-commerce credit ecosystem from bottom to top, helping analyze how blockchain technology breaks the traditional centralized monopoly in competition, centralized data sovereignty, and the marginalization of SMEs.

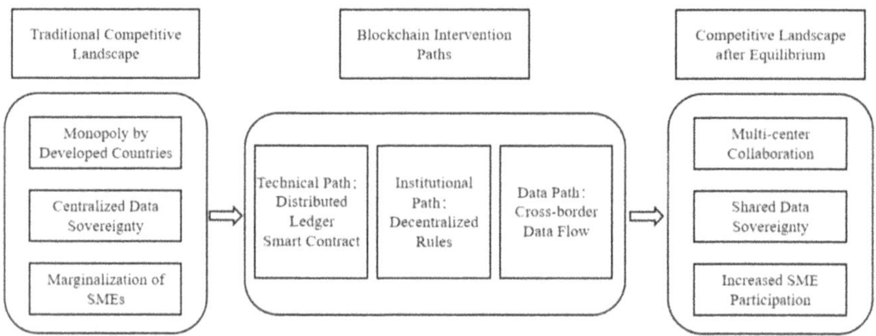

Fig. 2. Three Intervention Paths: Technical Path, Institutional Path, and Data Path

In terms of the competitive landscape, the traditional international credit reporting market exhibits a centralized monopoly dominated by the United States, with enterprises in developing countries at a clear competitive disadvantage. In the new ecosystem represented by the Trusple platform, the competitive landscape is gradually shifting toward multilateral collaboration. The application of blockchain technology has broken down data barriers, allowing all participants to cooperate and compete on an equal footing. Enterprises in developing countries can enhance their credit discourse power and gain more business opportunities by accumulating on-chain credit assets. At the same time, participants such as financial institutions and logistics companies can also achieve mutual benefit through data sharing and collaborative cooperation. This multilateral collaborative competitive landscape is conducive to improving the efficiency and competitiveness of the entire cross-border e-commerce industry and promoting fair and sustainable global trade. Combining coding results with literature discussions, this paper finds that the "technology-institution-data" three-dimensional path model and the transformation of the competitive landscape are important achievements of blockchain reconstructing the cross-border e-commerce credit ecosystem, providing new ideas and directions for the development of the cross-border e-commerce industry.

4 Conclusion

This paper takes the cross-border e-commerce credit ecosystem as the research object, focuses on the empowerment mechanism and ecological reconstruction effect of blockchain technology, and uses grounded theory to conduct a single-case analysis of the Trusple platform. Through iterative analysis of three-level coding, it systematically reveals the three-stage action path of blockchain technology's "technology empowerment-credit reconstruction-ecological balance," answering the core question of "how blockchain reconstructs the cross-border e-commerce credit ecosystem through technological empowerment."

Blockchain technology effectively solves the problem of credit deficiency in SME cross-border trade by building a distributed credit network. Studies have shown that blockchain can achieve cross-border verification and storage of historical transaction records, shortening the financing cycle by more than 60%, and through the automated execution of smart contracts to constrain transaction behavior, reducing contract dispute rates by 60%–70%. Encryption technology ensures that data sovereignty returns to enterprises, allowing them to independently manage the flow of credit data. This technology-driven power reconstruction promotes the paradigm shift of the international credit system from "centralized control" to "multi-party collaboration," breaking the monopoly of traditional international credit reporting giants in the credit reporting industry and addressing the problem of underdeveloped credit reporting industries in emerging cross-border e-commerce countries such as China and the severe lack of credit reporting needs in international trade and cross-border e-commerce transactions.

References

Experian: Global Credit Reporting Landscape: Market Share and Trends. Experian Global Research, Dublin (2023). https://doi.org/10.1002/experian.2023.001

World Bank Group: Global Financial Development Report: SMEs Financing. World Bank Publications (2022). https://doi.org/10.1596/978-1-4648-1894-5

AntGroup: Trusple: Technical White Paper on Blockchain-Based Trade Finance. AntChain, Hangzhou (2021). https://www.antgroup.com/en/tech/trusple

Hang, C.: Strategies for building financing platforms for SMEs from the perspective of international capital flows. Mod. Bus. **05**, 105–108 (2024)

Lin, W.: Research on the Application of Blockchain Technology in the Construction of E-Commerce Credit Systems. Exhibition Economy. **04**, 126–129 (2024)

Zhang, Y.: New models of international trade based on the internet: opportunities, challenges, and trends. Business. **2.0**(34), 4–6 (2024)

Bai, H.X., Wan, W.: The impact of big data credit evaluation on small and micro enterprise financing and suggestions. Bus. Obs. **9**(32), 29–32 (2023)

Gao, G., Zhang, C., Wang, Y.Y., et al.: Analysis of credit information demand and supply in China's credit reporting market. Credit Report. **43**(01), 59–64 (2025)

Li, X.H., Lu, M.F.: Research on the application of blockchain technology in supply chain finance in cross-border e-commerce scenarios. Financ. Theory Pract. **06**, 51–59 (2023)

Wu, W.B.: Principles, models, and suggestions for bank transaction blockchains. J. Hebei Univ. (Philos. Soc. Sci. Ed.). **40**(06), 159–160 (2015)

Han, X.Z.: Research on Supply Chain Financial Risks in China's Cross-Border E-Commerce (Unpublished doctoral dissertation). Nanjing Audit University (2022)

Zhou, Z.M., Wang, D.W., Peng, T.: Exploration of blockchain applications in the metaverse. Inf. Technol. Stand. **09**, 35–38 (2024)

Fang, F., Wang, D.S.: China's Plan for building a new international financial governance system for the Belt and Road Initiative. Finance Account. Mon. **20**, 129–134 (2021)

Xie, Y.X., Xiao, G.L., Wang, F.Y.: Analysis of the Application Prospects of Blockchain Technology in the Cross-Border E-Commerce Industry. J. Jilin Agric. Sci. Technol. Univ. **32**(02), 39–42 (2023)

Catalinic, C.: Blockchain Technology and cryptocurrencies: implications for the digital economy, cybersecurity, and government. Georgetown J. Int. Aff. **19**, 105–114 (2018)

Batsaikhan, N., Uuriintuya, B.: Cryptoeconomics—the Opportunities and challenges of blockchain. IDEAS Working Paper Series from RePEc; St. Louis: 219–254. (2017)

What Drives Cryptocurrency Adoption Among Younger Demographics? The Moderating Role of Financial Literacy and Personal Cultural Orientation

Rowena Clemino-Alcoba[1,2]($\boxtimes$)

[1] National University, Manila, Philippines
`rcalcoba@nu-lipa.edu.ph`
[2] NU Lipa, Philippines JP Laurel Highway, Lipa, Batangas 4217, Philippines

Abstract. In recent years, the rapid emergence of cryptocurrencies as alternative financial assets has garnered increasing attention from both investors and scholars, particularly among younger demographics. This study investigates the antecedents of university students' behavioral intention to adopt cryptocurrency, integrating constructs from the Theory of Planned Behavior (TPB), the Unified Theory of Acceptance and Use of Technology (UTAUT), and the Technology Acceptance Model (TAM). A sample of 580 students from a private Philippine university was analyzed using structural equation modeling. Unlike the earlier studies on technology adoption, results indicate that facilitating conditions, effort expectancy, and perceived behavioral control do not have a significant impact on potential adopters anymore due to the advancement in technological infrastructures and the usability and accessibility of fintech using a variety of devices. The study showed the moderating effect of financial literacy and personal cultural orientation, diminishing the effect of facilitating conditions on behavioral intention. These findings offer valuable insights for educators, policymakers, and fintech developers aiming to promote informed and inclusive cryptocurrency adoption.

Keywords: cryptocurrency adoption · fintech · financial literacy · youth investment behavior

1 Introduction

As an emerging alternative financial asset, there has been a growing interest among scholars in the study of cryptocurrency. Academics have studied the intention to adopt technology from various angles using different theoretical perspectives, including the Theory of Planned Behavior (TPB), the Unified Theory of Acceptance and Use of Technology (UTAUT), and the Technology Acceptance Model (TAM). The behavior towards the adoption of cryptocurrency as an emerging fintech product has been likewise explained using these aforementioned theories (Pynoo, 2012). In the TPB model, determinants of behavioral intention include a person's attitude, subjective norms, and perceived behavioral control. UTAUT regards effort expectancy and performance expectancy as the most

S. C. P. Yam et al. (Eds.): ICFT 2025, CCIS 2868, pp. 121–132, 2026.
https://doi.org/10.1007/978-981-92-0126-6_11

common predictors of behavioral intention to use technology (Alomari & Abdullah, 2023). The TAM explains how users respond to emerging technologies by investigating the facilitating conditions.

Current literature suggests that there are research gaps in identifying and explaining the significant factors that influence the use of cryptocurrency (Al-amri, Zakaria, Habbal, & Hassan, 2019). Nadeem et al. (2021) recommended investigating the human perspectives, because equally important to the study of the technological factors are the human behavioral factors and intentions underlying cryptocurrency investment. Engagement with digital currencies is not only about technological or economic factors but is deeply intertwined with cultural norms and values. However, while there have been many studies and discourses on the predictive factors for cryptocurrency adoption, there is less research examining how the cultural factor could possibly also impact the technological factors (Abraham et al., 2019). According to Abraham (2019), cultural explanation is required on how the differences between cultures affect technological factors.

Financial literacy is another dimension that could have a consequence on behavioral intentions towards investment. As an individual gains confidence and the ability to understand and manage his finances and financial risks, he would be more likely to adopt innovative financial instruments like cryptocurrency. A study of Pakistani business-educated adults showed that financial literacy is significantly related to the intention to adopt cryptocurrency, suggesting that financially knowledgeable individuals tend to consider cryptocurrency as a viable financial asset (Jariyapan et al., 2022).

Understanding how cultural orientation and financial literacy affect cryptocurrency adoption behavior can provide valuable insights for educators, policymakers, cryptocurrency developers, and marketers in fostering and boosting adoption. This study aimed at determining the factors that drive the behavior towards non-traditional investment, examining how the factors of the triple-pronged theory of TPB, UTAUT and TAM influence human behavioral intentions. It examined how these constructs drive the behavioral intention to engage in cryptocurrency and how cultural factors and financial literacy moderate the relationships between the variables.

The following were the research questions investigated: 1) What factors affect the respondents' behavioral intention to adopt cryptocurrency? 2) What is the moderating effect of personal cultural orientation on the relationship between the predictive factors and behavioral intention? 3) What is the moderating effect of financial literacy on the relationship between predictive factors and behavioral intention?

1.1   Theoretical Perspectives

Expectancies and Behavioral Intention to Use Cryptocurrency. Expectations of the efforts required in performing and the returns for those efforts affect a person's decision to engage or not in such behavior. Based on the Unified Theory of Acceptance and Use of Technology (UTAUT), performance and effort expectancies are significant predictors of an individual's intention to adopt cryptocurrency.

Performance Expectancy. Performance expectancy (PE) refers to people's perception of how cryptocurrency adoption will help them achieve their goals and give them benefits. Cryptocurrency, as digital money in today's modern times, facilitates virtual transactions that are efficient and less costly than the traditional process. Other user benefits include privacy and security of transactions, cross-border usage, and transparency, among others (Nadeem et al., 2021). Several studies showed PE as a positive driver of the users' intention to adopt the technology (Alomari & Abdullah, 2023; Ter Ji-Xi et al., 2021).

Effort Expectancy. Effort expectancy (EE) refers to the perceived effort that an individual should make to learn new technology. As an emerging technology, it needs some level of education to use cryptocurrency (Alomari & Abdullah, 2023), manage the risks (Arias-Oliva et al., 2019) and avoid potential fraudsters (Shehhi et al., 2014). The influence of effort expectancy in cryptocurrency adoption suggests that people are mindful of the efforts necessary to adopt the technology affecting their adoptive decision (Alomari & Abdullah, 2023; Gunawan & Novendra, 2017).

The study predicts the following relationships between variables:

H1: Performance expectancy significantly influences the behavioral intention to adopt cryptocurrency.
H2: Effort expectancy significantly influences the behavioral intention to adopt cryptocurrency.

Planned Behavior Factors and Behavioral Intention to Use Cryptocurrency. The Theory of Planned Behavior (TPB) explains how an individual's perceived control over the results of his actions and the influence of external social pressure can affect his intention to adopt non-traditional financial instruments. The TPB's principles have been applied in a broad range of behavioral studies, including customer product preferences (Ajzen & Fishbein, 1969). More recent studies have examined the role played by perceived behavioral control and subjective norms in consumers' technology adoption (Liu et al., 2019) under the TPB lens.

Subjective Norms. Subjective norms refer to the perceived social influence or social pressure to carry out a behavior or not (Doblas, 2019). The influence of society, including the opinions of family, peers, and other technology users, can influence behavioral intent to use cryptocurrency (Nseke, 2018). With the proliferation of the internet, celebrities and social media influencers can also have an impact on the adoptive attitude. Being a relatively new technology, these sources have an important role in providing relevant information to potential users about the usage and benefits of cryptocurrency (Alomari & Abdullah, 2023). The study of Jariyapan et al. (2022) demonstrated the significant influence of subjective norms on the behavioral intention to use cryptocurrency.

Perceived Behavioral Control. Perceived behavioral control (PBC) is an individual's evaluation of the ease or difficulty of performing a certain action. The intention relies on the individual's confidence to carry out the behavior in the face of challenging circumstances. Individuals are more inclined to use cryptocurrencies when they find it easy and simple to use (Jariyapan et al., 2022). Empirical evidence from China on the adoption of cryptocurrencies revealed a positive relationship between perceived ease of use and the intention to use Bitcoin (Nadeem et al., 2021).

Considering these, the research proposed that:

H3: Subjective norms significantly influence the behavioral intention to adopt cryptocurrency.

H4: Perceived behavioral control significantly influences the behavioral intention to adopt cryptocurrency.

Awareness, Facilitating Circumstances, Security, and Behavioral Intention to Use Cryptocurrency. The level of technology acceptance varies between countries and among different environmental conditions (Sagheer et al., 2022). The technology acceptance model (TAM) explains how people's perception of the ease of use of the technology and its usefulness affects their behavior. They are more likely to adopt a particular technology if they deem it beneficial and does not require much effort to use. Among the factors that drive technology acceptance are awareness, facilitating conditions, and security. This cluster of variables influences the acceptance and adoption of cryptocurrencies.

Awareness. Technology adoption or the intention to adopt starts with the awareness of the existence of the innovation. It is the first phase that is pivotal to the success of the subsequent stages towards adoption (Lu et al., 2022). Studies show that although there has been a rising demand for cryptocurrencies in the past two decades since the introduction of Bitcoin (Nadeem et al., 2021), there is a lack of awareness and knowledge about the technology and the benefits that it provides in developing countries (Alomari & Abdullah, 2023). In the Philippines, the unfamiliarity with cryptocurrency and the virtual trading market negatively impacted their participation (Francisco et al., 2022). Doblas (2019) suggests that the level of awareness of cryptocurrency among college students was low, which prevents them from accepting it as an investment vehicle.

Facilitating Conditions. Facilitating conditions or circumstances refer to the perceived availability of support and resources to use cryptocurrency, which can encourage individuals to embrace the technology. The study of Gunawan and Novendra (2017) of Bitcoin acceptance in Indonesia showed a positive relation between facilitating conditions and adoptive behavior. In many developing countries, strong internet infrastructure, vital in embracing this technology, is still lacking. All these can have a significant effect on the behavioral intention to use digital currencies. A study in Saudi Arabia, however, suggests that facilitating conditions do not influence the behavioral intention to use. This could be because the required technical infrastructure already exists, and cryptocurrency can be used on various IT devices (Alomari & Abdullah, 2023). Facilitating conditions, in this case, do not matter much in cryptocurrency usage.

Security. Perception of security on the trustworthiness of the cryptocurrency system could influence individuals to accept or reject the system. Different types of risks are associated with the system, such as safety risk, viability, third-party service default risk, and risk of privacy loss, among others (Jariyapan et al., 2022). Results of many studies showed the negative impact of these risk concerns on the aim to utilize fintech. The lack of government regulatory controls raises skepticism and trust issues, leaving deep concerns among potential users. The study of Alomari and Abdullah (2023) suggested a significant relationship between the perception of security and the behavioral intention to use cryptocurrency.

The research predicted the following hypothesis:

H5: Awareness significantly influences the behavioral intention to adopt cryptocurrency.
H6: Facilitating conditions significantly influence the behavioral intention to adopt cryptocurrency.
H7: Security negatively influences behavioral intention to adopt cryptocurrency.

Moderating Relationship of Personal Cultural Orientation (PCO). Personal cultural orientation affects people's perception of and response to financial innovations. According to Su (2022), individualists tend to adopt a positive attitude towards electronic commerce than collectivists. Unlike the collectivists, they are independent and objective in forming their behavioral intentions as consumers. The cultural influences from the environment, such as the places where they live, can also influence spending habits, even in the use of cryptocurrency (Liu et al., 2019). From these studies, it can be inferred that:

H8: Personal cultural orientation moderates the relationships between the predictive variables and behavioral intention.

Moderating Relationship of Financial Literacy (FL). Individuals with higher financial literacy are found to engage more in complex financial behaviors, including investing in stocks and alternative financial assets such as cryptocurrencies (Klapper et al., 2013). Individuals who are financially literate tend to be better with investment risk assessments (Khan, 2020), and are more inclined to adopt digital assets due to their ability to navigate price volatility and regulatory uncertainties (Alaei & Alareeni, 2021). Another characteristic of financial literacy is that it interacts with the effects of expectancy-related factors, such as perceived ease of use and perceived usefulness. Based on these previous studies, it can be inferred that:

H9: Financial literacy moderates the relationships between the predictive variables and behavioral intention (Fig. 1).

2   Methodology

Employing a quantitative research method, the study gathered data from undergraduate students in a private university in the Philippines using convenience sampling. The study used path analysis through structural equation modeling (SEM) to identify and determine the magnitude of causal relationships between the variables. The university was selected as the research setting because it represents a cross-section of students from different economic statuses and backgrounds. The survey received a total of 580 valid respondents, which was 24% of the total respondent population of 2,400. This was more than the required sample size of 350 calculated at 95% level of confidence and 5% margin of error.

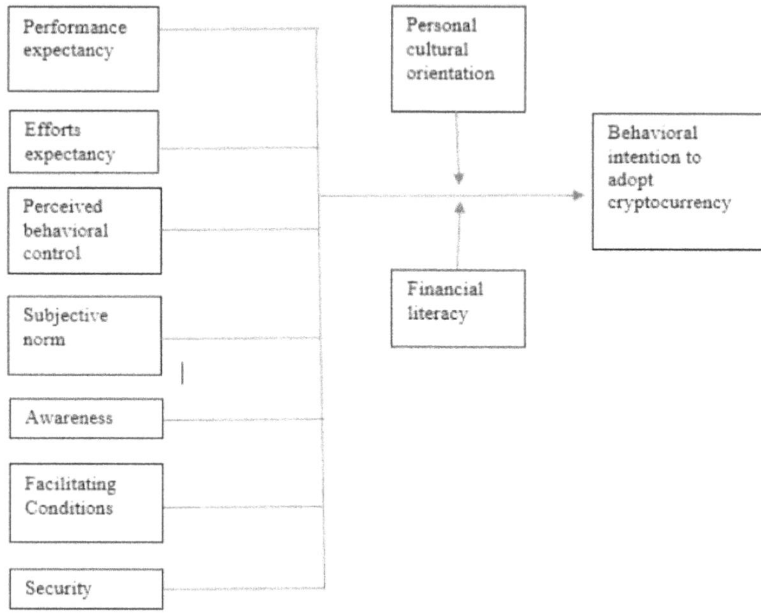

Fig. 1. Conceptual Framework

2.1 Measurement Scale

The study adapted measurement scales that have already been used in previous research studies and tested for validity and reliability. Performance and effort expectancy, financial literacy, and subjective norms were measured from the scales developed by Arias-Oliva et al. (2019). The measure of awareness and facilitating conditions, consisting of four items each, were taken from Almuraqab (2019) and Abbasi et al. (2021), respectively. Behavioral intention and security were measured using the scale developed by Khalilzadeh et al. (2017). Perceived behavioral control was measured with four items from Pham et al. (2021). Personal cultural orientation was measured using a four-item scale developed by Sharma (2010).

The data collection instruments were piloted with 79 respondents and pre-tested for reliability and consistency. Results of Cronbach's alpha (0.931) demonstrated the robustness of the overall scale.

Data were collected using Google Survey. In compliance with ethical standards in research, the researchers requested the written consent of participants to voluntarily participate in the survey.

3 Results

3.1 Demographics

Sixty-three percent of the 580 respondents were female and 37% male. The age ranges from 18 to 23 years old, with the majority (32.1%) being 19 years of age. The respondents were evenly distributed from the three schools – School of Accountancy, Business and

Management (33.3%), School of Architecture, Computing and Engineering (34.3%), and School of Allied Health and Sciences (32.4%). 45% were second-year students, 39% first-year, and 16% third-year students.

Factors Affecting Behavioral Intention for Cryptocurrency Adoption. Using structural equation modeling, the study derived the following values: regression coefficients, standard error, t-values and significant p-values. The structural model reflecting the hypothesized relationships put forth by the study is depicted in Fig. 2.

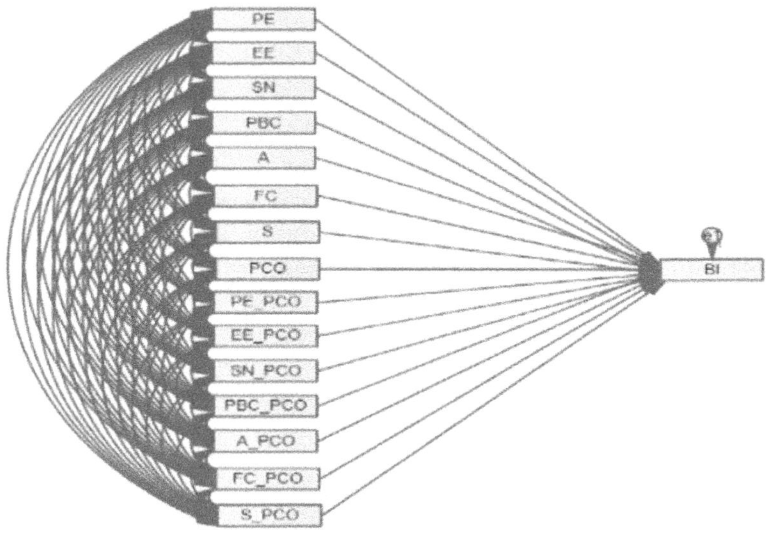

Fig. 2. Structural Model

Table 1 shows that performance expectancy (PE), subjective norms (SN), awareness (A), and security (S) are predictors of behavioral intention (BI) to adopt cryptocurrency. These results support Hypotheses 1, 3, 5, and 7, which predicted a significant relationship between BI and the aforementioned variables. On the other hand, effort expectancy (EE), perceived behavioral control (PBC), and facilitating conditions (FC) did not show direct effect on BI, hence nullifying Hypotheses 2, 4, and 6.

Moderating Effect of Personal Cultural Orientation. Personal cultural orientation (PCO) does not have significant direct effect on behavioral intention to invest in cryptocurrency (BI). However, results also show that PCO significantly moderates two relationships: subjective norm (SN) to BI estimate was enhanced, while facilitating condition (FC) to BI has weakened the effect. For other predictors (e.g., PE, EE, PBC, A, S), the moderating effect of personal cultural orientation (PCO) is statistically insignificant. These findings confirm Hypothesis 8, although the moderating effect of PCO does not apply to all the predictive variables of BI.

Table 1. Path Coefficients

			Estimate	S.E.	C.R.	P	Label
BI	<---	PE	.186	.042	4.420	***	par_1
BI	<---	EE	−.025	.044	−.567	.570	par_2
BI	<---	SN	.217	.047	4.647	***	par_3
BI	<---	PBC	.001	.049	.016	.987	par_4
BI	<---	A	.372	.048	7.801	***	par_5
BI	<---	FC	.053	.053	1.006	.314	par_6
BI	<---	S	.222	.045	4.972	***	par_7

Moderating Effect of Financial Literacy. Financial literacy (FL) significantly moderates two relationships. It shows positive moderation between perceived behavioral control (PBC) and behavioral intention (BI), suggesting that FL enhances the effect of the former on the latter. FL also moderates the relationship between facilitating conditions (FC) and behavioral intention (BI), although in a negative way.

Financial literacy, however, does not significantly moderate relationships for other predictors (PE, EE, SN, A, S). FL's role as a moderator is specific to certain predictors, enhancing the effect of PBC while reducing the effect of FC. This nuanced effect suggests FL may be contextually important depending on the primary determinants of BI in a given scenario. These findings support Hypothesis 9, although the moderating effect of FL does not apply on all the predictive variables of BI.

4 Discussion

Consistent with the findings in previous studies discussed in the literature review, the results identified key factors influencing the behavioral intention (BI) to adopt cryptocurrency: awareness, security, subjective norms, and performance expectancy (PE). That awareness serves as the strongest predictor of BI conforms with the study of Lu et al. (2022), indicating the likelihood of people adopting cryptocurrency if they are more informed about it (Lu et al., 2022). This is also aligned with the findings of Alomari and Abdullah (2023) on the significant relationship between subjective norms and security and BI, suggesting that trust in the security of cryptocurrency transactions is essential for adoption. Additionally, social influences have significant influence on a person's intention to use cryptocurrency, aligned with studies on technology and collectivist societies (Su, 2022).

On the other hand, other factors were found to have statistically insignificant effects on behavioral intention, including effort expectancy (EE), perceived behavioral control (PBC), and facilitating conditions. These findings contradict previous studies, which found that effort expectancy and perceived behavioral control are determining factors of intention, as espoused by the UTAUT and TPB theories (Gunawan & Novendra, 2017; Jariyapan et al., 2022). The non-significance of facilitating conditions conforms with the study of Alomari & Abdullah (2023), which suggests that potential users are focusing more on awareness and security instead of infrastructure and external resources. Another reason could be that the advancements in technology have made fintech products more user-friendly, and conditions such as weak internet connectivity, which once hindered access, no longer influence people's intention to use cryptocurrency.

Personal cultural orientation (PCO) did not have a significant direct effect on behavioral intention (BI) toward cryptocurrency adoption. However, results showed that PCO had a positive moderating effect on the relationship between subjective norms (SN) and behavioral intention (BI). This implies that social pressures and perceived approval enhance the investing behavior. PCO also demonstrated a negative moderating effect on the relationship of facilitating conditions (FC) with BI, suggesting that PCO diminishes the effect of external support systems on the intention for cryptocurrency adoption. These findings suggest that cultural orientation enhances the importance of social norms while reducing the reliance on external resources. This mirrors collectivist culture, which places high importance on social approval in decision-making. The results affirm the common view about the importance of cultural context in influencing consumers' perception of non-traditional fintech options (Rachwal-Mueller & Fedotova, 2024).

Financial literacy (FL) significantly moderated two relationships. First, it positively moderated the relationship between perceived behavioral control (PBC) and behavioral intention (BI), implying that FL helps increase self-efficacy and confidence in making cryptocurrency investments. Nonetheless, it negatively moderated the relationship between facilitating condition (FC) and BI, indicating that students with higher financial literacy tend to be less reliant on external support and resources when deciding to adopt cryptocurrency.

The positive moderation of perceived behavioral control by financial literacy conforms with the findings of previous studies, which highlight the importance of financial education in fostering confidence and capability among potential investors (Klapper et al., 2013; Alaei & Alareeni, 2021). However, the negative moderation of facilitating conditions (FC) suggests that facilitating conditions may no longer be as relevant as in the past because they no longer impact the intention to use cryptocurrency. This implies that students are empowered to adopt cryptocurrency when equipped with financial knowledge and community support, coupled with the advancement in technological infrastructures and accessibility of fintech.

4.1 Contribution to the Theory

The results of this study have contributed to the existing literature on the subject by confirming that awareness, security, subjective norms, and performance expectancy are key influencing factors. On the other hand, the empirical data of this study also showed that facilitating conditions, effort expectancy, and perceived behavioral control have no direct effect on the adoption intention. This is interesting because it departs from the behavioral discourse that the TPB, UTAUT, and TAM models espouse. Unlike the earlier studies on technology adoption, FC, EE, and PBC may not be concerning potential adopters anymore, as they develop a positive perception of cryptocurrency platforms as user-friendly. This also indicates the ongoing innovation in technology addressing usability concerns. The empirical data of this study also confirmed how financial literacy and personal cultural orientation moderate and weaken the effect of facilitating conditions on behavioral intention.

4.2 Implications

The research findings have several implications for the cryptocurrency industry and its key stakeholders, including academic institutions, policymakers, financial platforms, and influencers. Integrating financial literacy programs into curricula through targeted courses or seminars can bridge the knowledge gap among students, particularly those in non-business fields. For policymakers, implementing clear government regulations will mitigate risks, enhance trust, and encourage adoption. The collaboration between cryptocurrency developers, financial platforms, and academic institutions can help raise awareness about the practical benefits of cryptocurrencies and build trust among the young. Social media influencers and opinion leaders can also play a crucial role in facilitating reliable and accurate information dissemination.

5 Conclusion

The study validates the critical role of financial literacy, trust-building, and social influence in forming cryptocurrency behavior among young individuals. To drive cryptocurrency adoption in this demographic, stakeholders must remove the obstacles while capitalizing on the identified motivational factors and moderating variables. Stakeholders can create a more inclusive and informed digital financial landscape by addressing knowledge gaps, strengthening security measures, and fostering responsible investment behaviors.

Further research could focus on longitudinal studies to examine how these factors evolve over time. Future studies could also examine additional variables such as government regulations and market volatility, which may also play a role in cryptocurrency adoption.

Acknowledgments. The study was funded by the National University Philippines under the Internal Funding Research Program.

Disclosure of Interests The author has no competing interests to declare that are relevant to the content of this article.

References

Abbasi, G.A., Jagaveeran, M., Goh, Y., Tariq, B.: The impact of type of content use on smartphone addiction and academic performance: physical activity as moderator. Technol. Soc. **64**, 101521 (2021). https://doi.org/10.1016/j.techsoc.2020.101521

Abraham, J., Sutiksno, D.U., Kurniasih, N., Warokka, A.: Acceptance and penetration of bitcoin: the role of psychological distance and national culture. SAGE Open. **9**(3) (2019). https://doi.org/10.1177/2158244019865813

Ajzen, I., Fishbein, M.: The prediction of behavioral intentions in a choice situation. J. Exp. Soc. Psychol. **5**(4), 400–416 (1969). https://doi.org/10.1016/0022-1031(69)90033-x

Alaei, M., Alareeni, B.: The role of financial literacy in the adoption of cryptocurrencies for investment purposes: evidence from Iran. J. Money Busi. **1**(2), 145–162 (2021)

Al-Amri, R., Zakaria, N.H., Habbal, A., Hassan, S.: Cryptocurrency adoption: current stage, opportunities, and open challenges. Int. J. Adv. Comput. Res. **9**(44), 293–307 (2019). https://doi.org/10.19101/ijacr.pid43

Almuraqab, N.A.S.: Predicting determinants of the intention to use digital currency in the UAE: an empirical study. Electr. J. Inform. Syst. Dev. Count. **86**(3) (2019). https://doi.org/10.1002/isd2.12125

Alomari, A.S.A., Abdullah, N.L.: Factors influencing the behavioral intention to use Cryptocurrency among Saudi Arabian public university students: moderating role of financial literacy. Cogent Bus. Manag. **10**(1) (2023). https://doi.org/10.1080/23311975.2023.2178092

Arias-Oliva, M., Pelegrín-Borondo, J., Matías-Clavero, G.: Variables influencing cryptocurrency use: a technology acceptance model in Spain. Front. Psychol. **10** (2019). https://doi.org/10.3389/fpsyg.2019.00475

Doblas, M.: Awareness and attitude towards cryptocurrencies in relation to adoption among college students in a private tertiary institution in Cagayan De Oro City, Philippines. Int. J. Adv. Res. Publ. **3**(4) (2019)

Francisco, R., Rodelas, N., Ubaldo, J.E.: The perception of Filipinos on the advent of cryptocurrency and Non-Fungible Token (NFT) games. Int. J. Comput. Sci. Res. **6**, 1005–1018 (2022). https://doi.org/10.25147/ijcsr.2017.001.1.89

Gunawan, F.E., Novendra, R.: An analysis of Bitcoin acceptance in Indonesia. ComTech Comput. Math. Eng. Appl. **8**(4), 241 (2017). https://doi.org/10.21512/comtech.v8i4.3885

Jariyapan, P., Mattayaphutron, S., Gillani, S.N., Shafique, O.: Factors influencing the behavioural intention to use cryptocurrency in emerging economies during the COVID-19 pandemic: based on technology acceptance Model 3, perceived risk, and financial literacy. Front. Psychol. **12** (2022). https://doi.org/10.3389/fpsyg.2021.814087

Khalilzadeh, J., Ozturk, A.B., Bilgihan, A.: Security-related factors in extended UTAUT model for NFC based mobile payment in the restaurant industry. Comput. Hum. Behav. **70**, 460–474 (2017). https://doi.org/10.1016/j.chb.2017.01.001

Khan, S.: Financial literacy and investment decision making: the case of Dubai. Invest. Manag. Finan. Innov. **17**(1), 12–26 (2020)

Klapper, L., Lusardi, A., Panos, G.A.: Financial literacy and its consequences: evidence from Russia during the financial crisis. J. Bank. Financ. **37**(10), 3904–3923 (2013)

Liu, Z., Ben, S., Zhang, R.: Factors affecting consumers' mobile payment behavior: a meta-analysis. Electron. Commer. Res. **19**(3), 575–601 (2019). https://doi.org/10.1007/s10660-019-09349-4

Lu, A. et al.: The roles of mobile app perceived usefulness and perceived ease of use in app-based Chinese and English learning flow and satisfaction. Educ. Inf. Technol. **27**(7), 10349–10370 (2022). https://doi.org/10.1007/s10639-022-11036-1

Nadeem, M.A., Liu, Z., Pitafi, A.H., Younis, A., Xu, Y.: Investigating the adoption factors of cryptocurrencies—a case of bitcoin: empirical evidence from China. SAGE Open. **11**(1) (2021). https://doi.org/10.1177/2158244021998704

Nseke, P.: How crypto-currency can decrypt the global digital divide: bitcoins a means for African emergence. Int. J. Innov. Econ. Dev. **3**, 61–70 (2018). https://doi.org/10.18775/ijied.1849-7551-7020.2015.36.2005

Pham, Q.T., Phan, H.H., Cristofaro, M., Misra, S., Giardino, P.L.: Examining the intention to invest in cryptocurrencies. Int. J. Appl. Behav. Econ. **10**(3), 59–79 (2021). https://doi.org/10.4018/ijabe.2021070104

Pynoo, B.. IT-acceptance by autonomous professionals: Factors that contribute to success or failure (2012). https://biblio.ugent.be/publication/3006182/file/4336014.pdf

Rachwal-Mueller, A., Fedotova, I.: The impact of cultural factors on consumer behavior: a holistic model for adaptive marketing approaches. Econ. Transp. Compl. **165** (2024). https://doi.org/10.30977/ETK.2225-2304.2024.44.165

Sagheer, N., Khan, K.I., Fahd, S., Mahmood, S., Rashid, T., Jamil, H.: Factors affecting adaptability of cryptocurrency: an application of technology acceptance model. Front. Psychol. **13** (2022). https://doi.org/10.3389/fpsyg.2022.903473

Sharma, P.: Measuring personal cultural orientations: scale development and validation. J. Acad. Mark. Sci. **38**(6), 787–806 (2010). https://doi.org/10.1007/s11747-009-0184-7

Shehhi, A.A., Oudah, M., Aung, Z.: Investigating factors behind choosing a cryptocurrency. In: IEEE International Conference on Industrial Engineering and Engineering Management (2014). https://doi.org/10.1109/ieem.2014.7058877

Su, L., Tanner, E.C., Marquart, N.A., Zhao, D.: We are not all the same: the influence of personal cultural orientations on vulnerable consumers' financial well-being. J. Int. Mark. **30**(3), 57–71 (2022). https://doi.org/10.1177/1069031x221096637

Ter Ji-Xi, J., Salamzadeh, Y., Teoh, A.P.: Behavioral intention to use cryptocurrency in Malaysia: an empirical study. Bottom Line Manag. Lib. Fin. **34**(2), 170–197 (2021). https://doi.org/10.1108/bl-08-2020-0053

Multi-label Vulnerability Detection for Go Smart Contracts with Call Graphs and Semantic Code Embeddings

Chunkai Wu[1,2], Hengyang Wu[1], Bingrong Dai[2(✉)], Jianhui Yang[1], and Jia Wu[3]

[1] School of Computer and Information Engineering, Shanghai Polytechnic University, Shanghai, China
[2] Shanghai Development Center of Computer Software Technology, Shanghai, China
dbr@sscenter.sh.cn
[3] North China Institute of Science and Technology, Langfang, China

Abstract. Blockchain systems have become fundamental infrastructures in various domains such as finance, supply chain, and governance. However, **smart contracts**, as the software backbone of these systems, face increasing security threats that can lead to severe economic and operational losses. Existing research has made progress in improving contract security, yet most efforts focus on **Solidity-based contracts**, leaving the unique semantics and concurrency patterns of **Go-based smart contracts** underexplored. To address this gap, we propose a **vulnerability detection framework** specifically tailored for **Go-based smart contracts**. Our approach integrates function-level semantic embeddings derived from **GraphCodeBERT** with structural representations based on function call graphs (FCGs), including graph neural networks (GNNs) such as **GCN, GAT, GATv2, GIN**, and **GraphSAGE** for vulnerability classification. We propose **SAGAT++**, an **attention-enhanced** GNN that combines inductive aggregation with multi-head attention to effectively capture semantic interactions between functions. Experiments on a **custom Go contract dataset** show that our method outperforms baseline models across multiple vulnerability categories, confirming its effectiveness.

Keywords: Blockchain · Smart Contract · Graph Neural Network · Vulnerability Detection

1 Introduction

Blockchain technology has become a transformative infrastructure in finance, supply chain management, healthcare, and governance [1]. Its **decentralized, transparent, and tamper-resistant properties** enable trustless systems without centralized intermediaries [2], accelerating global adoption in both public and permissioned settings [3].

At the core are smart contracts, self-executing programs encoding business logic directly onto the ledger. They automate transactions, enforce rules deterministically,

S. C. P. Yam et al. (Eds.): ICFT 2025, CCIS 2868, pp. 133–146, 2026.
https://doi.org/10.1007/978-981-92-0126-6_12

and underpin **DeFi** (Decentralized Finance) [4], governance, and other blockchain applications [5].

Security is critical: smart contracts are **immutable post-deployment**, so vulnerabilities cannot be patched without costly redeployment [6]. Exploits such as **reentrancy attacks, integer overflows, and logic flaws** have caused major damages [7], highlighting the need for rigorous **pre-deployment vulnerability detection** [8].

Existing detection approaches include static analysis (e.g., Oyente, Slither) [9, 10], dynamic analysis and fuzzing [11], symbolic execution (e.g., Mythril) [12], and machine learning-based methods [13].

However, most research targets **Solidity contracts** [14], often overlooking function-level interactions. In contrast, **Go-based smart contracts,** common in **Hyperledger Fabric** [15] and **ChainMaker** [16], feature unique concurrency primitives (e.g., goroutines, channels) [17], but lack dedicated security analysis and public datasets.

Some work, such as **HFContractFuzzer** [18], uses go-fuzz and MockStub testing to detect Fabric vulnerabilities, yet deep learning-based detection for Go smart contracts remains largely unexplored.

Our contributions:

1. A novel detection framework integrating **GraphCodeBERT semantic embeddings** with function call graphs for fine-grained vulnerability detection [19].
2. An **attention-enhanced GNN (SAGAT++)** that better models semantic interactions [20].
3. A **custom-labeled Go contract dataset** for benchmarking.
4. Extensive GNN experiments (GCN [21],GAT,GATv2 [22],GIN [23], GraphSAGE [24]) showing significant macro-F1 gains over baselines.

2   Related Work

Blockchain systems are distributed ledgers that enable secure, transparent transactions across untrusted networks. They replace centralized authorities with **cryptographic mechanisms and consensus protocols**, ensuring data immutability through cryptographically linked blocks and decentralized control across network nodes [25]. Key features include **decentralization** (reducing single points of failure via distributed governance), **transparency** (verifiable transaction data with access controls in permissioned networks), and **immutability** (making data alteration impractical without network-wide modification). These properties drive adoption in finance (e.g.,**DeFi**) [26], supply chains (traceability) [27], healthcare (**data security**) [28], and governance (transparent systems) [29], with ecosystems spanning public networks (e.g., Ethereum) and permissioned platforms (e.g.,**Hyperledger Fabric, ChainMaker**) [15, 16].

Smart contracts are self-executing programs on blockchains that automate transactions and enforce rules without intermediaries. Popularized by Ethereum's **Solidity**, they encode logic to trigger actions (e.g., fund transfers) when conditions are met, underpinning **decentralized applications (dApps)** like exchanges and voting systems [30]. Core traits include determinism (predictable behavior ensuring consistency across nodes), **immutability** (deployed code cannot be altered, preserving rule integrity but leaving vulnerabilities unpatchable), and interoperability (interaction with other contracts/oracles enabling complexity). Immutability introduces critical risks: flaws like **reentrancy or integer overflows**—exploited in incidents such as the 2016 DAO hack—cause massive losses, demanding robust pre-deployment checks [31]. Beyond Solidity, Go is used for Chaincode in **Hyperledger Fabric** [15] and **ChainMaker** [16], leveraging concurrency primitives (**goroutines, channels**) for parallel transactions. This diversity creates gaps, as Solidity-focused tools struggle with Go's unique semantics.

Graph-based and deep learning approaches have been developed to overcome such limitations. For example, Zhuang et al. proposed a **GNN approach** using **DR-GCN and TMP modules** to detect reentrancy and timestamp dependency bugs in Solidity with improved accuracy [32]. Liu et al. combined **expert rules with GNN embeddings** to enhance pattern recognition, albeit at the cost of heavy template reliance [33]. SmartBugBert leveraged BERT together with control **flow graphs** for bytecode-level detection, achieving high precision in Ethereum contract analysis [34]. Another multimodal deep-learning model combining **source code and CFGs** reached over 90% accuracy, demonstrating effective **structural–semantic fusion** [35].

In summary, while static, dynamic, symbolic, and deep-learning methods provide strong results for Solidity, none effectively support **Go-specific semantics, concurrency, or function-level interactions**. This clear gap motivates our approach integrating Graph-CodeBERT embeddings with **function call graph modeling** and an **attention-enhanced GNN** tailored for Go smart contracts.

3 Method

In this section, we propose a **function-level multi-label vulnerability detection framework** that integrates semantic understanding with structural reasoning. Our method combines inline annotation augmentation and graph-based structural modeling, capturing both **function-level logic** and **cross-function dependencies**. This design enables accurate identification of complex vulnerability patterns, particularly in contracts that rely on concurrency or system-level operations.

3.1 Framework Overview and Pipeline

Our detection pipeline involves several crucial steps. We begin by parsing smart contracts into **individual functions.** Each function is annotated with a **descriptive docstring** (generated from static analysis or templates), and the code-docstring pair is encoded by **GraphCodeBERT** to obtain a **768-dimensional semantic embedding.**

At the same time, we construct a **Function Call Graph (FCG)**, where nodes represent functions and edges represent call relationships between them. Although our framework can support labeling edges with various invocation types, this study focuses solely on **direct function calls**. The FCG encodes the structural connections between functions and serves as a foundation for further analysis. By integrating these semantic embeddings with the structural graph, we create a **hybrid representation** that feeds into a **graph neural network** for **vulnerability detection.** The overall workflow is illustrated in Fig. 1.

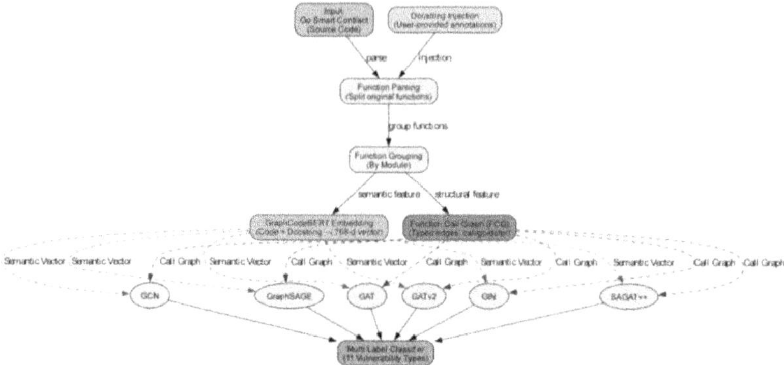

Fig. 1. Vulnerability Detection Framework: From Code Parsing to Graph - Based Vulnerability Detection

3.2 Function Call Graph Construction

A **Function Call Graph (FCG)** is constructed as a directed graph G = (V, E), where:

V represents the set of vertices, with each vertex corresponding to a distinct function in the code.
E represents the set of directed edges, where each edge denotes a function-to-function invocation relationship.

In our current implementation, we focus solely on identifying **direct function calls**. Each edge can be annotated with the type of invocation. This constructed FCG captures meaningful structural information that supports vulnerability detection in inter-procedural contexts.

3.3 Semantic Embedding & Go Annotation with GraphCodeBERT

To enrich the semantic understanding of each function, we embed generated docstrings directly into the function's source code as **inline comments**. These enriched code-docstring pairs are passed, along with the function body, into **GraphCodeBERT**, enabling the model to jointly learn from **code structure** and **natural language descriptions**. The output is a dense **768-dimensional semantic vector** for each function, capturing its behavior in terms of API usage, control logic, data access, and potential misuses. These semantic embeddings are then assigned to the corresponding nodes in the **Function Call Graph (FCG),** enabling integrated **semantic–structural analysis.**

To further enhance the detection capability for vulnerabilities specific to the Go language, we incorporate **a static analysis–based inline annotation augmentation method.** This approach parses the source code and analyzes its **Abstract Syntax Tree (AST)** and **FCG** to detect language-specific high-risk patterns. When such structures are identified, the system automatically generates **structured security audit annotations** describing the risk context, missing safeguards, potential impacts, and recommended mitigations.

For instance, in a **Concurrency Error (C003),** the system identifies unprotected access to shared state in goroutines, generating annotations focusing on risk context. Figure 2 illustrates an automatically generated annotation example for a concurrency error (C003), highlighting unprotected access to a shared map within a goroutine.The annotation generation pipeline consists of three stages:

1. Parse AST and FCG: Track input data flows of critical functions via AST traversal, and identify high-risk patterns like direct transmission of unsanitized external inputs by analyzing call chains with FCG.
2. Rule-based risk detection: Apply predefined rule templates to match and locate risky scenarios.
3. Enhanced sequence generation: Combine structured security prompts, function summaries generated by the CodeT5-770 M model, improving risk interpretability.

```
Concurrency Error
func ProcessTransactions(txChan chan Transaction, ledger *Ledger) {
    // --- Initialize concurrent workers ---
    // 1. No synchronization mechanism  before starting multiple goroutines
    // 2. Shared resource 'Ledger written by multiple goroutines simultaneously
    // 3. Missing channel close logic may lead to goroutine leaks
    for i := 0; i < 10; i++ {
        go func(workerID int) {
            // --- Process transactions ---
            for tx := range txChan {
                ledger.Append(tx)   // unsynchronized shared resource write
                log.Printf("Worker %d processed transaction %s", workerID, tx.ID)
            }
        }(i)
    }
    // --- Check remaining tasks ---
    time.Sleep(5 * time.Second)
    fmt.Println("All workers started")
    if len(txChan) > 0 {
        fmt.Printf("There are %d pending transactions
", len(txChan))
    }
}
```

Fig. 2. Concurrency Error Annotation Example (C003)

Another example is **Dependency Confusion (C010)**, where the system detects unvalidated inputs passed to external dependency-loading functions. Figure 3 presents an automatically generated annotation example for dependency confusion (C010), showing how unverified external inputs flow into sensitive dependency-loading functions, and indicating the associated security implications.

The resulting **code + annotation representation** is fed into GraphCodeBERT, capturing both **program semantics** and **explicit security context features**. These features are integrated with the FCG and processed by a Graph Neural Network (GNN) for multi-label vulnerability classification. Experimental results show that this augmentation significantly improves **recall and interpretability** for Go-specific vulnerability categories. The vulnerability taxonomy, including C003 and C010, is presented in Table 1.

Dependency Confusion

```go
func ExecuteExternalTool(cmdName string) error {
    // --- Input validation and annotations ---
    // 1. Execution relies on user-controlled cmdName without strict validation
    // 2. Potential path hijacking if malicious binary exists earlier in PATH
    // 3. Use of syscall.Exec may bypass Go's default security checks
    // 4. Lack of input sanitization can cause command injection in complex shell scripts
    args := []string{"--config", "default.json"}
    fmt.Printf("Attempting to execute: %s\n", cmdName)
    // --- File existence check ---
    if _, err := os.Stat(cmdName); err != nil {
        return fmt.Errorf("command not found: %v", err)
    }
    // --- Execute command ---
    return syscall.Exec(cmdName, args, os.Environ())  // command injection risk
}
```

Fig. 3. Dependency Confusion Annotation Example (C010)

3.4 GNN-Based Multi-Label Classification

The fused graph, combining **semantic node features** and **structural connectivity**, is passed through a series of Graph Neural Networks to perform **multi-label vulnerability classification.** We utilize multiple architectures including GCN [21],GAT,GATv2 [22],GIN [23], GraphSAGE [24], and introduce an enhanced model named SAGAT++, which combines the scalable aggregation of GraphSAGE with the attention-based representation power of GAT. **SAGAT++** extends GraphSAGE with **multi-head attention, residual connections, and normalization**, achieving both scalability and semantic sensitivity beyond GATv2. This design enhances stability and scalability while improving **fine-grained semantic reasoning.** Algorithm 1 outlines the forward propagation process in pseudocode. This hybrid approach supports nuanced reasoning across function boundaries while retaining inductive capability. Residual connections and layer normalization are applied to stabilize learning. The final graph representation is pooled globally and passed through a **sigmoid-activated layer** that outputs an **11-dimensional vector**, where each element represents the probability of a specific vulnerability class being present in the function.

SAGAT++ Architecture. To better capture the characteristics of Go smart contracts—we propose SAGAT++, a hybrid GNN architecture combining multi-head attention with inductive aggregation.Its core novelty lies in addressing the limitations of single GNN architectures: existing GAT variants excel at capturing critical cross-function interactions but lack scalability for large graphs, while GraphSAGE ensures inductive learning but struggles to prioritize important semantic connections. SAGAT++ resolves this trade-off through a cascaded dual-layer design, supplemented by embedding fusion and normalization mechanisms.As shown in Fig. 4, SAGAT++ consists of three main components.

Input Fusion Module. The initial representation of each function node integrates two types of core information to achieve deep binding of "code logic - security intent".

Code-Semantic Information: Function-level source code of Go smart contracts (denoted as ci), covering syntax and semantic attributes such as function execution logic and API call flow, which form the basis of code logic expression.

Security-Enhanced Annotations: It first leverages a static rule base built on AST analysis to automatically label high-risk logic; then integrates the structured security prompts derived from the labeled risks with function functional summaries generated by the CodeT5-770 M model(denoted as si).

These two types of information are fused into a unified "code-comment enhanced joint representation" through a pre-trained model, serving as the core input for Graph-CodeBERT to extract function-level features integrating "syntax - semantics - security", as defined by **Formula (1)**:

$$h_i^{(0)} = \text{GraphCodeBERT}(ci \oplus si)$$

where $\oplus$ denotes the concatenation operation of code-semantic information and structured security-enhanced annotations, and GraphCodeBERT represents the feature extraction process of the GraphCodeBERT model to obtain the initial hidden state. To ensure dimensional consistency for GraphCodeBERT input, both ci and si are first mapped to 768 dimensions via a linear layer, then concatenated.

Dual Graph Layer Module. This module cascades a multi-head GAT layer and a GraphSAGE layer, each enhanced with normalization, activation, dropout, and residual connections to balance expressive power and stability.

Multi-Head GAT Layer: Prioritizes critical cross-function interactions (e.g., calls between a goroutine-creating function and a shared variable-writing function). We use 4 attention heads with concatenation disabled (outputs are averaged across heads to maintain consistent dimensionality) and a dropout rate of 0.5. The output is normalized, activated, and added to the initial hidden state via residual connection to mitigate information loss, as shown in **Formula (2)**:

$$h^{(1)} = h^{(0)} + \text{Dropout}\left(\sigma\left(\text{LayerNorm}\left(\text{GAT}\left(h^{(0)}, E\right)\right)\right)\right)$$

where E is the edge set of the FCG, σ is the ReLU activation function, and GAT denotes the multi-head attention aggregation.

GraphSAGE Layer: Efficiently aggregates local neighborhood information (e.g., all functions called by a target function) using a mean aggregator, which is more scalable for large FCGs than GAT's pairwise attention. The output is similarly normalized, activated, and connected to the previous layer's output, as shown in **Formula (3)**:

$$h^{(2)} = h^{(1)} + \text{Dropout}\left(\sigma\left(\text{LayerNorm}\left(\text{SAGE}\left(h^{(1)}, E\right)\right)\right)\right)$$

where SAGE denotes the GraphSAGE mean aggregation.

Graph-Level Classification Module. First, global mean pooling is applied to aggregate node-level representations $h^{(2)}$ into a graph-level vector G, where the pooling operation is batch-aware (using batch indices b to distinguish different contracts). Then, a two-layer MLP with batch normalization (BN) and dropout is used to map G to 11-dimensional vulnerability probabilities, as defined by **Formula (4)**:

$$y = \sigma\left(W_2 \mathrm{Dropout}\left(\sigma\left(\mathrm{BN}\left(W_1 \cdot \mathrm{Pool}\left(h^{(2)}\right)\right)\right)\right)\right)$$

where $W_1 \in \mathbb{R}^{256 \times 128}$ and $W_2 \in \mathbb{R}^{128 \times 11}$ are MLP weights, Pool is global mean pooling, and the final activation σ is the sigmoid function (to output label-wise probabilities for multi-label classification).

```
SAGAT++ Pseudocode
   Input: node features X (GraphCodeBERT, 768-d), node types t, node positions p, edges E, batch index b (for pooling), dropout rate p_drop=0.5
   Output: multi-label predictions Y (11-d)
   1:  # Step 1: Input projection + embedding fusion (unify to 256-d)
       H0 = Linear(X, out_features=256) + Emb_type(t, embedding_dim=256) + Emb_pos(p, embedding_dim=256)
   2:  # Step 2: Multi-head GAT block (capture critical cross-function interactions)
       Z1 = GAT(H0, E, heads=4, concat=False, dropout=p_drop)  # 4 heads, output 256-d
       Z1 = LayerNorm(Z1)         # Stabilize training
       Z1 = ReLU(Z1)              # Introduce non-linearity
       Z1 = Dropout(Z1, p=p_drop) # Prevent overfitting
       H1 = H0 + Z1               # Residual connection (retain initial features)
   3:  # Step 3: GraphSAGE block (efficient local neighborhood aggregation)
       Z2 = SAGEConv(H1, E, aggregator_type="mean")  # Mean aggregator
       Z2 = LayerNorm(Z2)
       Z2 = ReLU(Z2)
       Z2 = Dropout(Z2, p=p_drop)
       H2 = H1 + Z2               # Residual connection (retain attention-enhanced features)
   4:  # Step 4: Graph-level representation (aggregate node features to contract-level)
       G = global_mean_pool(H2, b)  # Batch-aware pooling (each batch = 1 contract)
   5:  # Step 5: Classification head (map to vulnerability probabilities)
       U = Linear(G, out_features=128)  # First MLP layer
       U = BatchNorm1d(U)              # Normalize batch statistics
       U = ReLU(U)
       U = Dropout(U, p=p_drop)
       Y = Sigmoid(Linear(U, out_features=11))  # Label-wise probabilities (0-1)
   6:  return Y
```

Fig. 4. SAGAT++ Model Pseudocode

3.5 Vulnerability Taxonomy

We define an **11-class vulnerability schema** that covers both conventional smart contract flaws and those specific to the Go language and runtime model. These include common risks such as reentrancy and integer overflows. A detailed overview of the vulnerability categories is provided in Table 1.

Table 1. Vulnerability Schema for Smart Contract and Go-Based Blockchain Programs

Label	Vulnerability Type	Description	Language
C001	Integer Overflow	Unsafe arithmetic operations	General
C002	Reentrancy	Recursive calls corrupting contract state	General
C003	**Concurrency Error**	**Misuse of goroutines or channels**	**Go**
C004	Insecure Randomness	Predictable pseudo-random generation	General
C005	Unchecked Call Return Value	Ignored critical return values	General
C006	Hardcoded Credentials	Sensitive data embedded in code	General
C007	Incorrect Logging	Missing or misleading logs	General
C008	Access Control Violation	Interface abuse or missing authorization checks	General
C009	Uninitialized Storage	Use of zero-initialized memory	General
C010	**Dependency Confusion**	**Unvalidated external inputs leading to malicious dependency prioritization**	**Go**
C011	Inconsistent State Validation	Lack of pre/post-condition enforcement	General

4   Experiments

4.1   Experimental Setup

A dataset was constructed comprising 2,146 Go smart contracts sourced from public vulnerability repositories (e.g., CVEs) and open-source blockchain platforms such as Hyperledger Fabric and ChainMaker. These contracts were parsed into 15,732 function-level units, each annotated with one or more of 11 vulnerability types (C001–C011). Notably, 41.2% of functions contain multiple vulnerability labels, underscoring the complexity of the multi-label detection challenge.

The proposed method (instantiated as SAGAT++) was compared against a set of graph neural network (GNN)-based baselines, including representative GNN architectures (GCN [21], GAT, GATv2 [22], GIN [23], GraphSAGE [24]) all trained on Function Call Graphs (FCGs) under the same experimental settings. This comparison focuses on evaluating the effectiveness of SAGAT++'s enhanced structural-semantic modeling (vs. baseline GNNs) in addressing multi-label vulnerability detection for Go smart contracts.

All experiments were conducted on an NVIDIA RTX 4090 workstation, using PyTorch 2.5.1, Transformers 4.52.4, and PyTorch Geometric (PyG) 2.6.1 for model implementation and training.

4.2   Training Setup and Evaluation Results

The evaluation of model performance is conducted from three dimensions: overall performance, stability, and prediction bias. Key metrics are used to quantify the advantages and disadvantages of each model, with relevant results visualized in Figs. 5, 6, and 7. All metric values are reported with 95% confidence intervals, which statistically represent the range within which the true value of the metric is likely to fall with 95% probability, helping to gauge the reliability and variability of model performance.

4.2.1 Overall Performance Comparison

To comprehensively evaluate model performance in multi-label vulnerability prediction, we adopt four core metrics—macro-F1 score (balancing overall precision and recall across classes), accuracy (proportion of correct predictions), precision (reliability of positive predictions), and recall (completeness of vulnerability detection)—to assess different aspects of classification performance. As shown in Fig. 5, SAGAT++ achieves the highest overall performance, with a macro-F1 score of 0.635 ± 0.160, accuracy of 0.908 ± 0.045, precision of 0.580 ± 0.184, and recall of 0.727 ± 0.065, indicating superior classification capability across diverse vulnerability types. While GIN attains the highest recall (0.834 ± 0.083), its relatively low precision (0.431 ± 0.143) reflects an imbalanced performance. In practice, this means GIN is prone to false alarms, whereas SAGAT++ achieves a better trade-off between precision and recall. This balance is crucial, as excessive false positives overwhelm developers while false negatives miss critical flaws.

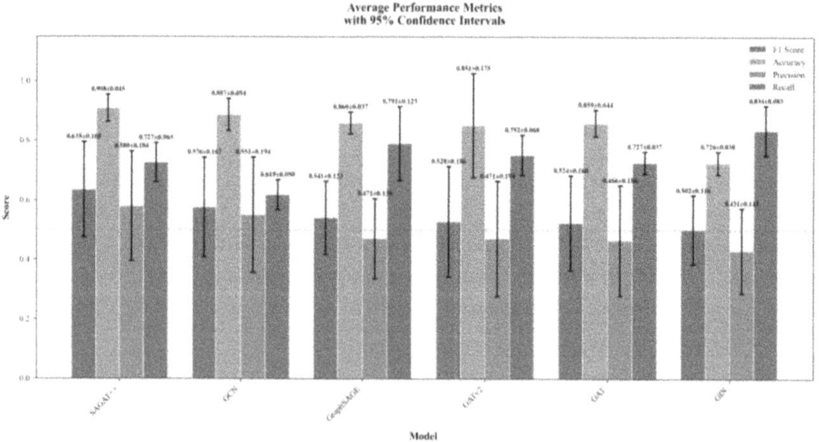

Fig. 5. Model performance comparison

4.2.2 Model Stability Analysis

To assess the reliability of models in multi-label vulnerability prediction, we evaluate both their average performance and stability across different vulnerability types, using mean F1 score to reflect overall effectiveness and standard deviation across 11 categories to measure consistency regardless of class frequency. As shown in Fig. 6, SAGAT++ achieves the highest mean F1 score (0.63) and the lowest standard deviation (0.116), demonstrating superior accuracy as well as robust and stable performance across both frequent and rare vulnerabilities. In contrast, GIN exhibits the lowest mean (0.502) and the highest variability (0.186), indicating less reliable and more fluctuating performance. Other models like GAT (mean 0.576, std. 0.123), GATv2 (mean 0.541, std. 0.160), GCN (mean 0.528, std. 0.167), and GraphSAGE (mean 0.524, std. 0.160) show moderate mean performance and stability.

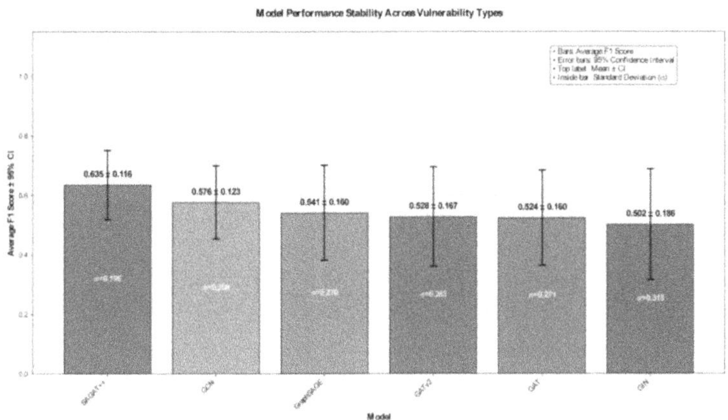

Fig. 6. Model stability across vulnerability classes

4.2.3 Prediction Bias Evaluation

To dissect vulnerability detection models' prediction behaviors, we use **false positive rate** (FPR, measuring over-prediction of non-vulnerabilities as vulnerabilities), **false negative rate** (FNR, quantifying under-detection of actual vulnerabilities), plus precision/recall to evaluate the trade-off between over-prediction and under-detection.

Figure 7 visualizes this with FPR on the x-axis, FNR on the y-axis, error bars for stability, and a "**Ideal Zone**" (dashed lines) for low FPR/FNR. **SAGAT++** clusters near the zone (low FPR of 0.089, moderate FNR of 0.200, tight error bars for stability), GCN has high FNR (0.381) and wide intervals (frequent misses, unstable), GraphSAGE shows higher FPR (0.141, overprediction bias) with skewed error bars, GIN makes an extreme trade-off (low FNR but very high FPR, unstable via wide intervals), and GAT/GATv2 lack SAGAT++'s balance (e.g., GATv2 has suboptimal stability). Overall, SAGAT++ uniquely balances false alarms and threat detection, exposing other models'clear biases (e.g., GCN under-detection, GraphSAGE overprediction), with error bars highlighting that **stable performance** (like SAGAT++) is critical for real-world vulnerability detection.

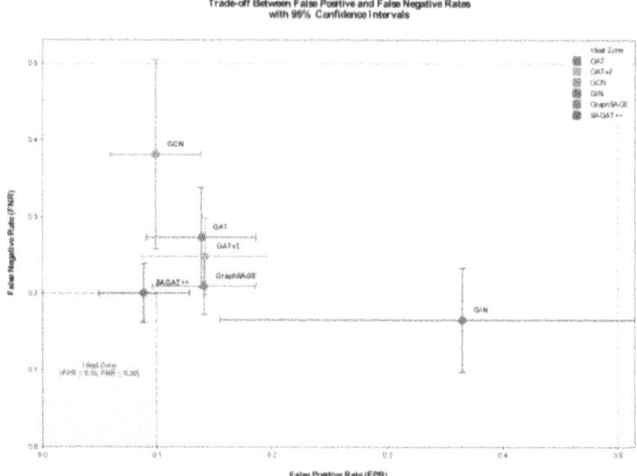

Fig. 7. False Positive and False Negative Rates

5   Summary

SAGAT++ demonstrates promising and consistent performance across overall metrics, vulnerability-specific detection, and training stability, supporting the validity of our **unified framework for multi-label vulnerability detection in Go smart contracts**, which integrates semantic code understanding and structural modeling.

This framework leverages **GraphCodeBERT** to extract function-level embeddings, capturing contextual semantics from docstrings and function bodies, which are then integrated into **Function Call Graphs (FCGs)**. By modeling inter-function dependencies via **attention-enhanced Graph Neural Networks (GNNs)**, it fuses semantic and structural signals to detect complex, context-sensitive vulnerabilities—including Go-specific issues such as **concurrency misuse, syscall abuse, and access control flaws.**

Experimental results on our multi-label dataset (where 41.2% of functions contain multiple vulnerabilities) indicate that the framework achieves competitive **recall, precision, and robustness** compared to traditional analyzers (Go Vet, Staticcheck) and neural baselines (CodeBERT, GraphCodeBERT, and baseline GNNs).

Limitations of this study include the framework's **function-level granularity**, limited dataset diversity, and scalability challenges when applied to large-scale codebases. Furthermore, the framework has a relatively high false negative rate (approximately 20%), this may result from the limited coverage of static annotations or imbalanced label distribution.

Future work will integrate **dynamic analysis techniques** such as symbolic execution and hybrid fuzzing to validate static predictions and uncover deeper vulnerabilities, particularly in concurrency and runtime interactions. Additionally, richer contextual information—including transaction traces and runtime logs—will be incorporated to improve semantic coverage and reduce false negatives. These advancements aim to address current limitations and expand the framework's applicability to large-scale, real-world deployments.

References

1. Yong, C., Yang, L., Larisa, B., Mikhail, Y.K., et al.: Applications of blockchain in industry 4.0: a review. Inf. Syst. Front. **26**(5), 1715–1729 (2024)
2. Thien, H. et al.: Blockchain for the metaverse: a review. Futur. Gener. Comput. Syst. **143**, 401–419 (2022). https://doi.org/10.1016/j.future.2023.02.008
3. Angraal, S., Krumholz, H.M., Schulz, W.L.: Blockchain technology. Circ. Cardiovasc. Qual. Outcomes. **10**(9), e003800 (2017)
4. Buterin, V.: A next-generation smart contract and decentralized application platform. White Paper. **3**(37), 2–1 (2014)
5. Ilhaam, A.O., Raja, J., Mazin, S.D., Khaled, S., Ibrar, Y., Mohammed, O., et al.: Automating procurement contracts in the healthcare supply chain using blockchain smart contracts. IEEE Access. **9**, 37397–37409 (2021)
6. Chen, J., Xia, X., Lo, D., Grundy, J., Yang, X., et al.: Maintenance-related concerns for post-deployed Ethereum smart contract development: issues, techniques, and future challenges. Empir. Softw. Eng. **26**(6) (2021)
7. Lejun, Z. et al.: A novel smart contract Reentrancy vulnerability detection ModelBased on BiGAS. J. Signal Process. Syst. **96**(3), 215–237 (2024)
8. Yuan, Z., Zhenguang, L., Peng, Q., Qi, L., Xiang, W., Qinming, H., et al.: Smart contract vulnerability detection using graph neural network. In: International Joint Conference on Artificial Intelligence, pp. 3283–3290 (2020)
9. L, J.J., Singh, K.: Enhancing Oyente: four new vulnerability detections for improved smart contract security analysis. Int. J. Inf. Technol. **16**(6), 3389–3399 (2024)
10. Feist, J., Grieco, G., Groce, A.: Slither: a static analysis framework for smart contracts. In: 2019 IEEE/ACM 2nd International Workshop on Emerging Trends in Software Engineering for Blockchain (WETSEB), pp. 8–15. IEEE (2019)
11. Satpal, S.K., Sandeep, J., Dilbag, S., Manjit, K., Heung-No, L., et al.: Ethereum smart contract analysis tools: a systematic review. IEEE Access. **10**, 57037–57062 (2022)
12. Sharma, N., Sharma, S.: A survey of Mythril, a smart contract security analysis tool for EVM bytecode. Indian J. Nat. Sci. **13**(75), 51003–51010 (2022)
13. Su-Juan, Q., Zhao, L., Feixiang, R., Chong, T., et al.: Smart contract vulnerability detection based on critical combination path and deep learning. In: International Conference on Communication and Network Security, pp. 214–221 (2022)
14. Mohanta, B.K., Panda, S.S., Jena, D.: An overview of smart contract and use cases in blockchain technology. In: 2018 9th International Conference on Computing, Communication and Networking Technologies (ICCCNT), pp. 1–4. IEEE (2018)
15. Androulaki, E., Barger, A., Bortnikov, V., et al.: Hyperledger fabric: a distributed operating system for permissioned blockchains. In: Proceedings of the Thirteenth EuroSys Conference, pp. 1–15 (2018)
16. ChainMaker. ChainMaker Official Website [Online]. Shanghai Development Center of Computer Software Technology (2025). https://chainmaker.org.cn/home [Accessed 30 July 2025]
17. Luca F, Andrea G, Giuseppe M, Rebecca M, et al.: Hyperledger Fabric Blockchain: Chaincode Performance Analysis., Intelligent Cloud Computing, (2020)
18. Ding, M., Li, P., Li, S., et al.: Hfcontractfuzzer: fuzzing hyperledger fabric smart contracts for vulnerability detection. In: Proceedings of the 25th International Conference on Evaluation and Assessment in Software Engineering, pp. 321–328 (2021)
19. Daya, G., et al.: GraphCodeBERT: Pre-training Code Representations with Data Flow, International Conference on Learning Representations (2021)

20. Scarselli, F., Gori, M., Tsoi, A.C., et al.: The graph neural network model. IEEE Trans. Neural Netw. **20**(1), 61–80 (2008)
21. Kipf, T. N.: Semi-Supervised Classification with Graph Convolutional Networks. arXiv preprint https://arxiv.org/abs/1609.02907 (2016)
22. Veličković, P., Cucurull, G., Casanova, A., et al.: Graph attention networks. arXiv preprint https://arxiv.org/abs/1710.10903 (2017)
23. Xu, K., Hu, W., Leskovec, J., et al: How powerful are graph neural networks? arXiv preprint https://arxiv.org/abs/1810.00826 (2018)
24. Hamilton, W., Ying, Z., Leskovec, J.: Inductive representation learning on large graphs. Adv. Neural inf. Process syst. **30** (2017)
25. Saurabh, K., Upadhyay, P., Rani, N.: Towards blockchain decentralized autonomous organizations (DAO) design. Inf. Syst. Front. **27**(2), 659–681 (2024)
26. John, K., Kogan, L., Saleh, F.: Smart contracts and decentralized finance. Annu. Rev. Financ. Econ. **15**(1), 523–542 (2023)
27. Prause, G.: Smart contracts for smart supply chains. IFAC-PapersOnLine. **52**(13), 2501–2506 (2019)
28. Khatoon, A.: A blockchain-based smart contract system for healthcare management. Electronics. **9**(1), 94 (2020)
29. Balcerzak, A.P., Nica, E., Rogalska, E., et al.: Blockchain technology and smart contracts in decentralized governance systems. Adm. Sci. **12**(3), 96 (2022)
30. Jiachi, C., Xin, X., David, L., John, G., Xiapu, L., Ting, C., et al.: DefectChecker: automated smart contract defect detection by analyzing EVM bytecode. IEEE Trans. Softw. Eng. **48**(7), 2189–2207 (2021)
31. Ding, Y., Peng, H., Li, X.: A Comprehensive Study of Exploitable Patterns in Smart Contracts: From Vulnerability to Defense. arXiv preprint https://arxiv.org/abs/2504.21480 (2025)
32. Zhuang, Y., Liu, Z., Qian, P., et al.: Smart contract vulnerability detection using graph neural networks. In: Proceedings of the Twenty-Ninth International Conference on International Joint Conferences on Artificial Intelligence, pp. 3283–3290 (2021)
33. Qian, P., Liu, Z., He, Q., et al: Smart contract vulnerability detection technique: a survey. arXiv preprint https://arxiv.org/abs/2209.05872 (2022)
34. Bu, J., Li, W., Li, Z., et al.: Smartbugbert: Bert-enhanced vulnerability detection for smart contract bytecode. arXiv preprint https://arxiv.org/abs/2504.05002 (2025)
35. Han, D., Li, Q., Zhang, L., et al.: A smart contract vulnerability detection model based on syntactic and semantic fusion learning. Wirel. Commun. Mob. Comput. **2023**(1), 9212269 (2023)

Crux Chain: An Energy-Efficient Blockchain Framework

Yu Julian Fong Chuan[(✉)]

Shanghai University of Finance and Economics, Shanghai, China
`julianfcyu@gmail.com, jfcyu@yahoo.com.sg`

Abstract. This paper introduces Crux Chain, a novel blockchain architecture addressing the Blockchain Impossible Triangle—balancing decentralization, security, scalability, and resource efficiency. At its core, Crux Chain responds to the fundamental challenge of blockchain design: balancing resource constraints, security requirements, and operational feasibility in decentralized systems. The framework integrates Ladder Swapping, Proof of History, modular hashing, and a two-stage Bidding/Mean Average consensus mechanism to enable fast block finalization with significantly lower energy consumption than traditional Proof-of-Work models. Through traceable transaction streams, dynamic address reassignment, and efficient sharding with minimal redundancy, Crux Chain maintains robust data integrity while reducing computation and storage demands. Its interwoven structure enhances resistance to Sybil attacks, transaction malleability, and systemic vulnerabilities, while supporting multi-chain interoperability. A key feature is the balanced allocation of verification responsibilities between requesters and verifiers, by components such as the Crux/Shell design. This improves processing efficiency and reinforces decentralized trust. Beyond technical performance, Crux Chain aligns with ESG goals by lowering carbon emissions and promoting transparent, auditable transactions. Its modular, verifiable architecture also facilitates integration of Real World Assets (RWA) and Real Data Assets (RDA), supporting trusted tokenization and lifecycle management of physical and authenticated digital assets. Crux Chain offers a sustainable, high-performance blockchain foundation and outlines a pathway for further research in modular optimization, cross-chain security, and real-world implementation.

Keywords: Blockchain Impossible Triangle · Ladder Swapping · Modular Hashing · Environmental-Social-Governance · Real World Assets · Real Data Assets

1 Introduction

Blockchain technology has driven the rapid growth of cryptocurrencies, with Bitcoin remaining a pioneering force [1]. Since its inception, blockchain has attracted extensive research interest, in the Computer Science fields [2, 3]. Trust is fundamental to digital economics, and blockchain plays a key role in establishing decentralized trust [4, 5]. However, its practical deployment still faces significant constraints. The "Blockchain

S. C. P. Yam et al. (Eds.): ICFT 2025, CCIS 2868, pp. 147–159, 2026.
https://doi.org/10.1007/978-981-92-0126-6_13

Impossible Triangle" — the inherent trade-off among decentralization, consistency, and scalability — remains a core bottleneck that limits broader adoption [6, 7]. Recent studies have explored various consensus protocols and architectural enhancements to address these structural trade-offs [8, 9]. Multi-level or layered blockchain architectures have emerged as promising directions for improving throughput and storage efficiency [10, 11]. However, ensuring system reliability and economic sustainability without sacrificing security or excessive energy remains a challenge [12, 13]. For instance, Proof-of-Work, while robust against many attacks, consumes substantial energy resources, raising environmental and economic concerns [4, 14]. Ultimately, the root challenge lies in balancing resource constraints, security demands, and operational feasibility—a triad that reflects not only the technical tension in blockchain design but also the broader institutional and economic logic that governs its real-world viability. In response, this paper proposes **Crux Chain**, a novel blockchain framework designed to overcome these barriers by combining an extendable multi-level structure with innovative mechanisms [15, 16], specifically focuses on:

- Strengthening network trust through traceable, immutable records supported by cryptographic proofs [17, 18].
- Securing transaction integrity and cross-shard consistency through modular and flexible hashing structures [19].
- Enhancing scalability with lower latency and significantly reduced redundant processing, aligned with the broader goals of green blockchain innovation [20].
- Redesigning incentive and consensus models to support network reliability without energy-intensive mining, building on research into alternative consensus and economic incentive structures [21, 22].

Together, these design choices aim to deliver higher performance and stronger resilience against attacks [12, 23]. By tackling fundamental trade-offs in the blockchain design space, Crux Chain contributes to the development of a secure, efficient, and scalable blockchain ecosystem for diverse application domains.

Furthermore, the energy-efficient structure and transparent bidding mechanism embedded in Crux Chain provide significant advantages for Environmental, Social, and Governance (ESG) applications. By eliminating energy-intensive mining processes [14, 21] and minimizing redundant data storage [20] through efficient sharding and cross-verification, the framework contributes to a reduced carbon footprint and more sustainable blockchain operations. In addition, its traceable transaction streams and verifiable incentive structures enable transparent monitoring of sustainability metrics and responsible supply chain governance, which are increasingly critical for blockchain-based ESG reporting and regulatory compliance [11]. Beyond ESG considerations, Crux Chain's modular and auditable design also provides a robust foundation for the secure integration of Real World Assets (RWA) and Real Data Assets (RDA), such as tokenized commodities [24], verified carbon credits [25], authenticated IoT data streams [26], and supply chain metadata [27]. These capabilities position Crux Chain as a promising architectural basis for the next generation of trust-enhanced, resource-conscious distributed ledger solutions capable of bridging on-chain logic with off-chain realities.

2 Hashing and Sharding

It is useful to briefly revisit the fundamental roles of hashing and sharding in blockchains, as they form the technical basis for ensuring data integrity, network scalability, and transaction efficiency. Traditional blockchain systems have relied on well-established hashing algorithms and static sharding schemes to distribute data and secure consensus. However, as the scale and complexity of blockchain applications expand, conventional approaches face inherent limitations in balancing speed, energy efficiency, and security. This provides motivation for the next chapter, which introduces Crux Chain's enhanced structure and the novel ladder swapping mechanism designed to address these constraints and improve overall system performance.

2.1 Hashing Functions in Blockchain

Hashing is fundamental to consensus formation and data integrity in blockchains (see Fig. 1). Consensus mechanisms such as Proof of Work (PoW), Proof of Stake (PoS), and Proof of History (PoH) all rely on cryptographic hashing to link block headers in a verifiable chronological sequence. Within each block, transactions are organized in a Merkle tree structure, allowing all nodes to independently verify that they share the same record. In general, hashing in blockchains serves four main functions: (1) validating transactions and blocks, (2) linking blocks chronologically, (3) enabling mining through nonce generation, and (4) supporting sharding by distributing transactions or nodes across partitions.

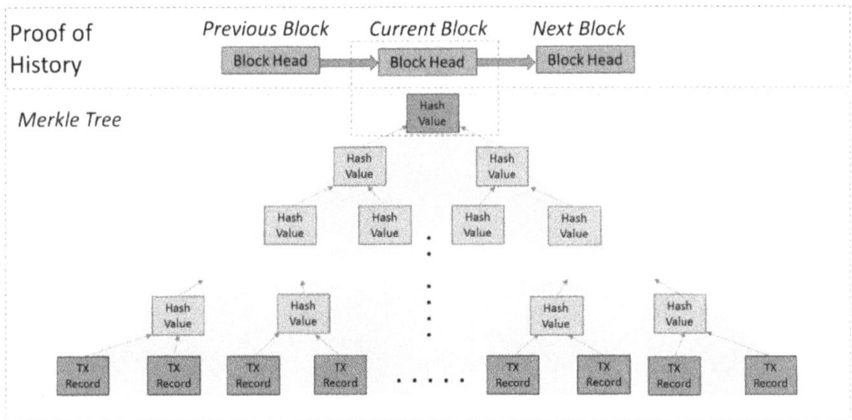

Fig. 1 A blockchain structure illustrating Proof of History and Merkle Tree

Widely used hashing functions, such as SHA-256, ensure key properties like irreversibility, collision resistance, and unpredictability. Depending on specific design goals, other attributes—such as traceability or certain algebraic characteristics like associativity—may also be desirable. Standard cryptographic hashes do not inherently support these features, but customized mechanisms can extend their functionality. For example, traceable hashes can enable verifiable audit trails, although they may interact with irreversibility in complex ways.

Effective blockchain design therefore requires a careful balance: mining incentives rely on strong collision resistance and unpredictability, while transaction validation depends on the efficient computation of hashes within Merkle trees. Adding unnecessary cryptographic properties can degrade performance, whereas omitting essential ones can undermine security.

In Crux Chain, we systematically revisit the role of hashing to match specific performance and scalability requirements. By introducing tailored hashing structures alongside innovations such as modular hashing and Ladder Swapping, Crux Chain aims to optimize data integrity, network throughput, and energy efficiency beyond what conventional designs achieve.

2.2 Multi-level Structure via Sharding

Nodes are grouped into shards to enhance scalability. Key considerations include 1) how to assign nodes to shards; 2) how to balance workload between levels; 3) What minimal information is needed for verification. A two-level structure can be seen as a Merkle tree (Fig. 2). A fixed address scheme simplifies design but risks collusion; fully random allocation improves security but may complicate transaction integrity.

Crux Chain introduces **Ladder Swapping**, inspired by Group Theory, to dynamically reassign addresses between shards in each block without collisions while keeping addresses traceable across the chain.

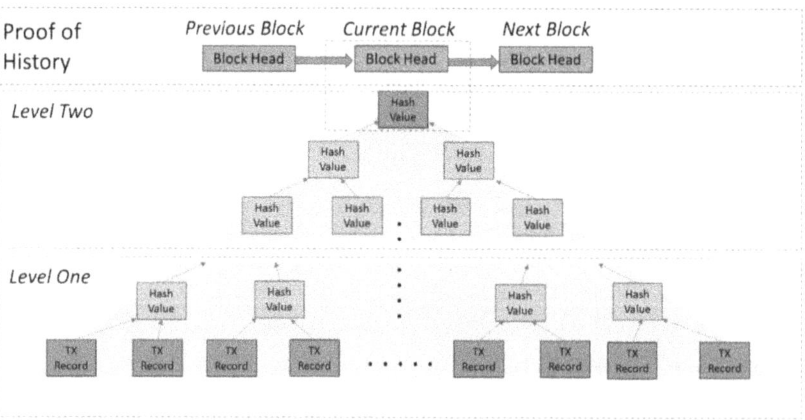

Fig. 2 A multi-level Merkle Tree representing sharding

3 Core Design of Crux Chain

Crux Chain adopts a two-level architecture (see Fig. 3) to achieve high traceability, low overhead, and minimal energy consumption, core design principles as follows:

- Traceable Transactions: Each node's address changes each block through Ladder Swapping for a unique, unpredictable and verifiable ad-dress chain.
- Incentive Mechanism: A two-stage Bidding & Mean Average process re-places energy-heavy mining: nodes bid to represent their shard; shard winners compete to finalize the block based on how close their bid is to the mean. Reward and rebate stay inside the network instead of burning energy.
- Proof of History (PoH): Transactions link in sequence, forming auditable streams even if a node skips blocks. PoH ensures data order and integrity.
- Minimal Required Data: Each participant needs only a subset of the full ledger to operate effectively. This includes the Block Value, Shard Values, and Row Values (collectively forming the Shell), along with the node's own shard and row transaction (the Crux). Full-chain replication is unnecessary.
- Crux/Shell Verification: Validation is performed by cross-verification that a node authenticates another's Crux by comparing it against its own Crux and confirming consistency via common records and summed values in the Shell.

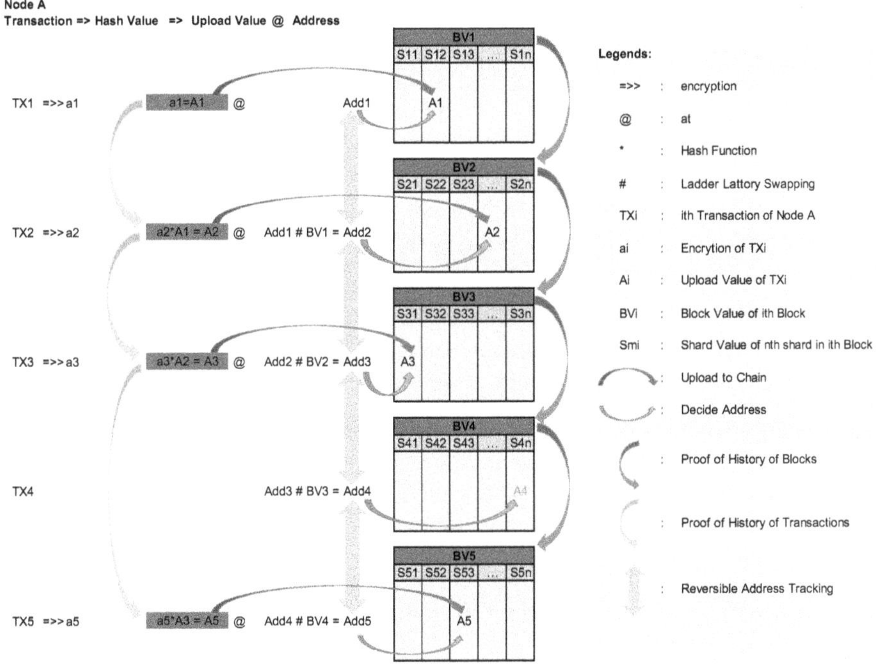

Fig. 3 Traceability with skipped blocks

If the block is formed using an associative and commutative hash function, the Block Value becomes equivalent to both the aggregate of all longitude (shard) hashes and the aggregate of all latitude (row) hashes. Each latitude value, like its longitude counterpart, represents the combined hash of all nodes at the same coordinate across different shards—supporting a bidirectional verification model and enhancing consistency.

3.1 Ladder Swapping for Account Address Derivation

Each node begins with an initial address for its first transaction. In every subsequent block, the address is reassigned randomly yet traceably through Ladder Swapping, producing a unique, collision-free, verifiable mapping and unpredictable before the finalization of the current block.

A complete address consists of Longitude identifying the shard; and Latitude specifying the node's location within that shard. Ladder Swapping generates the next address by applying a one-to-one mapping that combines the current address with the current block hash. This process is inspired by the Ladder Lottery concept from group theory. To enhance randomness and prevent clustering:

- The matrix wraps horizontally like a cylinder, connecting the rightmost column to the leftmost.
- Swapping paths may "jump" across columns through consecutive ones (1 s).
- Multiple layers of swapping matrices may be stacked to increase entropy.

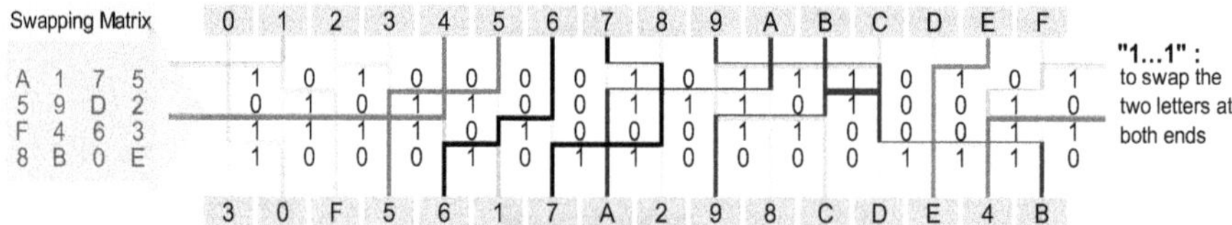

Fig. 4 Ladder Swapping matrix example

For instance, an address like 5C82F may be transformed into 1D2FB using a matrix such as A175 59D2 F463 8B0E (see Fig. 4). Each swap is deterministic once the block hash is available, yet unpredictable beforehand.

To further prevent recurring patterns (see Fig. 5):

- The matrix is seeded by the block hash and refreshed with the longitude value for each round; longitude and latitude are swapped in every round.
- Longitudes influence the swapping pattern, ensuring that identical latitudes in different shards still yield distinct results.

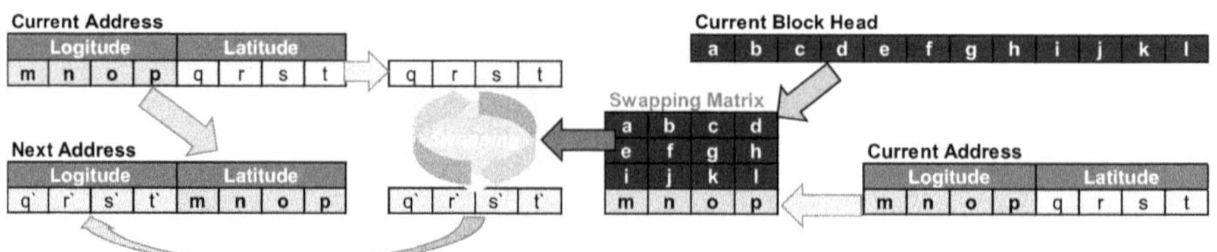

Fig. 5 Example of Ladder Swapping in practice

A key feature is that a node's longitude in the current block becomes its latitude in the next. This structural continuity simplifies verification logic and promotes consistent, coordinated interactions across the network.

3.2 Two-Stage Bidding/Mean Average Mechanism

Unlike traditional Proof of Work consuming significant energy, Crux Chain uses a streamlined two-stage mechanism to finalize blocks with minimal resource waste. Each transaction includes a fee that is high enough to deter spam yet practical for routine use.

Step 1 — Shard-Level Bidding

- Within each shard, participants bid by offering rebates to other participants in the same shard to compete for the role of shard leader.
- Shard leader aggregates the shard and row values for block-level finalization.
- The portion of transaction fees remaining after rebates becomes the shard's stake in the block-level round.
- Nodes that choose not to participate may pay no fee or a minimal staking fee, depending on protocol rules.

Step 2 — Global Mean Average Selection

- At the block level, the network calculates the mean average of all Shard Transaction Fees submitted by shard leaders.
- The leader whose net bid is closest to this mean earns the right to propose the final version of the block.
- The block-level winner receives all transaction fees from its own shard plus a defined share (e.g., 50%) of the combined fees from other shards; other shard leaders keep the remaining fees from their own shard.
- Leaders who fail to broadcast correctly must refund their fees and may face penalties under consensus rules.

This mechanism can also apply across nodes grouped in the same latitude, as a *row slice*. Here, a row leader may compete with the shard (vertical partition) leader for block finalization. Both row and shard leaders retain their respective rewards, with each participant's fee split between row and shard bidding rounds.

3.3 Minimal Information for Verification

Participants need to maintain only a minimal dataset to independently verify any confirmed transaction without storing the entire ledger. This works by requiring each verification request to include all transaction hashes for the relevant shard and row. The verifier recalculates these hashes to detect tampering. The essential dataset includes:

- **Crux:** All transaction values within the shard and row to be verified.
- **Shell:** All shard and row values of the block.

For a block with n nodes, an optimal setup uses about $\sqrt{n}$ shards and $\sqrt{n}$ rows to balance storage and verification workload. For example (see Fig. 6), an account at *(Shard S, Row r)* keeps the **Block Value** and **Shell** (same for every participant) and the **Crux** (all transactions for *Shard S, Row r*, unique to each participant).

To verify a transaction at *(Shard B, Row 3)*, the requester provides the Crux—all transaction hashes for *(Shard B, Row 3)*. The verifier then:

1. Recalculates the shard and row values to confirm data integrity against the Shell;
2. Cross-checks node consistency with its own Crux at *(Shard B, Row r)* and *(Shard S, Row 3)*. Because any address can perform this check, random cross-validation greatly increases the cost of forging valid but false records.

When a higher level of security is required, a node must provide multiple generations of transaction records, as specified by the verification criteria. The verification process includes continuity checks of address mappings, along with Crux and Shell validation across the submitted generations.

For enhanced value verification under elevated security conditions, the verifier may request additional confirmations from node holders at positions (Shard B, Row r) and (Shard S, Row 3). Specifically, the holder at (Shard S, Row 3) performs one latitude check for the current block and one longitude check for the previous block, while the holder at (Shard B, Row r) performs one longitude check for the current block and one latitude check for the next block.

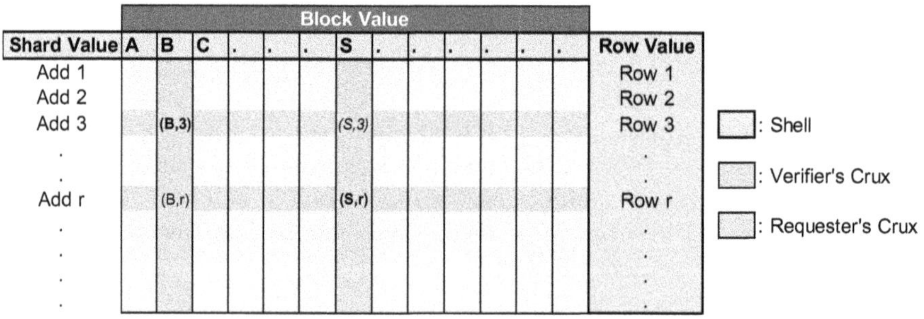

Shard Value	A	B	C	.	.	.	S	.	.	.	.	.	.	Row Value
Add 1														Row 1
Add 2														Row 2
Add 3		(B,3)					(S,3)							Row 3
.														.
.														.
Add r		(B,r)					(S,r)							Row r
.														.
.														.
.														.
.														.

(Block Value spans the shard columns.)

□ : Shell
▨ : Verifier's Crux
▤ : Requester's Crux

Fig. 6 Example of Minimal Verification Information

4 Optional Enhancements

In addition to its core design, Crux Chain supports several optional enhancements that further balance operational efficiency and workload distribution. These features include modular hashing with a Binary Table, address compacting, and the ladder swapping mechanism, all of which strengthen traceability and resilience while minimizing storage and computational overhead.

4.1 Modular Hashing and the Binary Table

In Crux Chain, hashing plays a central role as the system's cryptographic clock (Proof-Of-History). While global ordering ensures chain-wide and transaction stream consistency, strict ordering within blocks or shards is less critical, local data consistency suffices to guarantee verifiability.

To improve performance and parallelism, Crux Chain replaces traditional Merkle Trees with *modular hashing*, which is associative and commutative. This allows shards and rows to verify transactions simultaneously, eliminating the need for rigid sequential structures. The Binary Table organizes modular hash values into *P-Rows* and *N-Rows* for each bit position in an address. For example:

- *P4* may store the combined modular hash for all addresses from *a8* to *a15*.
- If an address (e.g., *a6*) fails validation, logical operations on the *P* and *N* rows quickly isolate the mismatch (see Fig. 7).

This structure reduces storage overhead to about $2 \times \log_2$ (total addresses) compared to storing entire Merkle trees. To accelerate processing further, large addresses (e.g., 256 hex digits) can be divided into smaller segments (e.g., 16 segments of 16 digits) for parallel hashing.

Address				Node Value	by 1				by 0			
					P4	P3	P2	P1	N4	N3	N2	N1
0	0	0	0	a0	-	-	-	-	a0	a0	a0	a0
0	0	0	1	a1	-	-	-	a1	a1	a1	a1	-
0	0	1	0	a2	-	-	a2	-	a2	a2	-	a2
0	0	1	1	a3	-	-	a3	a3	a3	a3	-	-
0	1	0	0	a4	-	a4	-	-	a4	-	a4	a4
0	1	0	1	a5	-	a5	-	a5	a5	-	a5	-
0	1	1	0	a6	-	a6	a6	-	a6	-	-	a6
0	1	1	1	a7	-	a7	a7	a7	a7	-	-	-
1	0	0	0	a8	a8	-	-	-	-	a8	a8	a8
1	0	0	1	a9	a9	-	-	a9	-	a9	a9	-
1	0	1	0	a10	a10	-	a10	-	-	a10	-	a10
1	0	1	1	a11	a11	-	a11	a11	-	a11	-	-
1	1	0	0	a12	a12	a12	-	-	-	-	a12	a12
1	1	0	1	a13	a13	a13	-	a13	-	-	a13	-
1	1	1	0	a14	a14	a14	a14	-	-	-	-	a14
1	1	1	1	a15	a15	a15	a15	a15	-	-	-	-

Fig. 7 Example Binary Table for fast modular hashing

4.2 Address Compacting

As accounts become inactive over time, unused addresses can accumulate and waste address space. To mitigate this, Crux Chain periodically performs *address compacting* during block finalization. During block construction:

- Each address includes a *Valid Count Bit* indicating whether it is active.
- Each shard calculates a *Shard Valid Count* (total active addresses).

- The sum of all shards forms the *Block Valid Count*, which defines the active address space needed.

Compacting Process

Active addresses are sorted to the front of each shard. Each participant stores the following: shard values, local transaction streams, valid counts for all shards, and the valid count for their own shard.

A new address is then computed by:

1. Summing the valid counts of all preceding shards
2. Adding the count of valid addresses that precede it within its own shard, and
3. Applying a modulo operation to fit within the resized address space.

This transformation is invertible, allowing compacted addresses to be mapped back to their original form. Shard numbers can be reconstructed using the shard valid counts, and any node within the original shard can verify the mapping. Address compacting is only triggered when inactivity exceeds a defined threshold, with spare capacity reserved to accommodate future growth.

4.3 Optional Enhancement Briefing

Crux Chain's interwoven record structure ensures that all account transaction streams remain traceable across blocks. This traceability is achieved by **Ladder Swapping**, which redistributes each transaction address generation across blocks, weaving accounts into a single, expanding structure. This mechanism creates a verifiable transaction stream at each node, allowing the system to relax certain constraints on block hashing without compromising security. Any tampering with a single record disrupts related hashes across multiple shards, making undetected forgery virtually impossible.

Building on this foundation, Crux Chain can employ **modular hashing**, leveraging the principles of associativity and commutativity, enabling parallel and flexible processing of Shard Values and Row Values, which together generate the final block value for cross-verification. Applying modular hashing significantly enhances efficiency and scalability, especially when combined with the **Binary Table** structure. Unlike classic Merkle Tree constructions that require strict transaction ordering, this design permits relaxed ordering while reinforcing the logical ties between transaction streams. As the chain expands, its interlinked structure further strengthens overall integrity.

Moreover, even if modular hashing is not used for security reasons, the combination of Ladder Swapping and additional mechanisms—such as the **Crux/Shell** verification —can still help maintain a balanced distribution of responsibility between verification requesters and verifiers, optimizing overall network performance.

5 Conclusion

This paper introduces Crux Chain as a novel blockchain architecture engineered to overcome the structural limitations commonly described as the Blockchain Impossible Triangle—balancing decentralization, security, scalability, and resource efficiency. The framework responds directly to the pressing challenge of achieving high performance and trustworthiness under real-world constraints of energy, cost, and latency. Through the integration of Ladder Swapping (Ghost Laddering), Proof of History, modular hashing, and a two-stage Bidding/Mean Average consensus mechanism, Crux Chain enables rapid block confirmation with dramatically reduced energy consumption compared to Proof-of-Work systems.

The design minimizes redundant computation by employing modular addition for hashing, transaction stream weaving, and layered address reassignment, which together ensure traceability and tamper resistance while lowering storage and processing demands. Each node's transaction is traceably mapped and reallocated across shards per block, preserving transparency without sacrificing throughput. Recent data is fully recorded to ensure consistency, while historical records are compacted and cryptographically cross-verified, enabling scalable yet auditable operation across distributed nodes. This approach not only enhances fault tolerance and Sybil-resistance but also supports shard-level autonomy with global integrity through the framework's inherent cross-checking logic.

Crux Chain further aligns with Environmental, Social, and Governance (ESG) principles by eliminating energy-intensive mining and promoting economic incentives based on verifiable contribution rather than computational waste. Its low-power consensus mechanism and modular structure contribute to carbon efficiency and operational sustainability. Transparent transaction lineage and tamper-evident data structures also support improved governance, risk management, and compliance—making it especially suitable for ESG-focused sectors such as green finance, carbon trading, impact investing, and regulatory reporting.

Additionally, the framework supports integration of Real World Assets (RWA) and Real Data Assets (RDA) through authenticated transaction trails, enabling secure tokenization, traceable ownership, and cross-system reconciliation. Use cases may include tokenized commodities, carbon credits, land titles, verified IoT feeds, and sustainability metrics—offering seamless linkage between on-chain trust and off-chain reality, a critical requirement for practical enterprise blockchain adoption.

Future work may explore optimization of the modular weaving matrix, the development of cross-chain smart contract logic, and comprehensive simulation under dynamic network conditions. By uniting architectural rigor with low energy demand, verifiable trust, and ESG applicability, Crux Chain presents a scalable, sustainable, and extensible model for next-generation blockchain infrastructure.

Disclosure of Interests.. The authors declare that the core technical designs, including the bidding/mean average incentive mechanism, Ladder Swapping address derivation, modular hashing method, and multi-level shard architecture described in this paper, are protected under granted patents in China, the United States, and the European Union. These patents cover essential elements of the Crux Chain framework's consensus and incentive model. The authors report no other financial or non-financial conflicts of interest.

References

1. Nakamoto, S.: Bitcoin: A Peer-to-Peer Electronic Cash System (2008)

2. Swan, M.: Blockchain: Blueprint for a New Economy. O'Reilly Media, Sebastopol (2015)
3. Yli-Huumo, J., Ko, D., Choi, S., Park, S., Smolander, K.: Where is current research on blockchain technology?—a systematic review. PLoS One. **11**(10), e0163477 (2016)
4. Catalini, C., Gans, J. S.: Some Simple Economics of the Blockchain (2016)
5. Iansiti, M., Lakhani, K.R.: The truth about blockchain. Harv. Bus. Rev. **95**(1), 118–127 (2017)
6. Zamani, M., Movahedi, M., Raykova, M.: RapidChain: scaling blockchain via full sharding. In: Proceedings of the 2018 ACM SIGSAC Conference on Computer and Communications Security, pp. 931–948 (2018)
7. Wang, W., et al.: A survey on consensus mechanisms and mining strategy management in blockchain networks. IEEE Access. **7**, 22328–22370 (2019)
8. Gilad, Y., Hemo, R., Micali, S., Vlachos, G., Zeldovich, N.: Algorand: scaling Byzantine agreements for cryptocurrencies. In: Proceedings of the 26th Symposium on Operating Systems Principles, pp. 51–68. ACM, New York (2017)
9. Pass, R., Shi, E.: Hybrid consensus: efficient consensus in the permissionless model. In: International Symposium on Distributed Computing, pp. 39–53. Springer (2017)
10. Zamyatin, A., Al-Bassam, M., Zohar, A., Knottenbelt, W.J.: SoK: communication across distributed ledgers. Paper presented at the IACR Cryptology ePrint Archive (2019)
11. Wang, S., Ouyang, L., Yuan, Y., Ni, X., Han, X., Wang, F.-Y.: Blockchain-enabled smart contracts: architecture, applications, and future trends. IEEE Trans. Syst. Man Cybern. Syst. **49**(11), 2266–2277 (2020). https://doi.org/10.1109/TSMC.2020.2976025
12. Gervais, A., et al.: On the security and performance of proof of work blockchains. In: Proceedings of the 2016 ACM SIGSAC Conference on Computer and Communications Security, pp. 3–16. ACM, New York (2016)
13. Houy, C.: Why blockchain is disruptive: answering five questions. In: Proceedings of the Multikonferenz Wirtschaftsinformatik (MKWI), pp. 471–484 (2014)
14. Narayanan, A., Bonneau, J., Felten, E., Miller, A., Goldfeder, S.: Bitcoin and Cryptocurrency Technologies: a Comprehensive Introduction. Princeton University Press, Princeton (2016)
15. Bano, S., et al.: SoK: consensus in the age of blockchains. In: Proceedings of the 1st ACM Conference on Advances in Financial Technologies, pp. 183–198. ACM, New York (2019)
16. Kiayias, A., Panagiotakos, G.: Speed-security tradeoffs in blockchain protocols. Presented at the IACR Cryptology ePrint Archive, 2017, pp. 1–30. https://eprint.iacr.org/2015/1019 (2017)
17. Boneh, D., Bonneau, J., Bünz, B., Fisch, B.: Verifiable delay functions. In: Annual International Cryptology Conference, pp. 757–788. Springer (2019)
18. Poelstra, A.: Distributed consensus from proof of stake is impossible. https://download.wpsoftware.net/bitcoin/pos.pdf (2014). Accessed 3 Apr 2026
19. Miers, I., Garman, C., Green, M., Rubin, A.D.: Zerocoin: anonymous distributed e-cash from bitcoin. In: 2013 IEEE Symposium on Security and Privacy, pp. 397–411. IEEE, New York (2013)
20. Ballandies, D., Dapp, M., Stiller, B.: Off-chain payment networks: recurring payment channels, efficient incentives, and scalability. Futur. Gener. Comput. Syst. **127**, 251–261 (2022). https://doi.org/10.1016/j.future.2021.09.002
21. Saleh, F.: Blockchain without waste: proof-of-stake. Rev. Financ. Stud. **34**(3), 1156–1190 (2021). https://doi.org/10.1093/rfs/hhaa075
22. Al-Bassam, M., Sonnino, A., Bano, S., Danezis, G.: Chainspace: a sharded smart contracts platform. In: Network and Distributed System Security Symposium (NDSS) 2018. Internet Society, Reston (2018). https://doi.org/10.14722/ndss.2018.23185
23. Eyal, I., Sirer, E.G.: Majority is not enough: bitcoin mining is vulnerable. In: Financial Cryptography and Data Security, pp. 436–454. Springer, Heidelberg (2014). https://doi.org/10.1007/978-3-662-45472-5_28
24. Schär, F.: Decentralized Finance: on Blockchain-and Smart Contract-Based Financial Markets. FRB St, Louis Rev (2021)

25. Markets, C.: Blockchain and Emerging Digital Technologies for (2018)
26. Christidis, K., Devetsikiotis, M.: Blockchains and smart contracts for the internet of things. IEEE Access. **4**, 2292–2303 (2016)
27. Saberi, S., Kouhizadeh, M., Sarkis, J., Shen, L.: Blockchain technology and its relationships to sustainable supply chain management. Int. J. Prod. Res. **57**(7), 2117–2135 (2019)

Driven Risk Management
and Corporate Finance

ARO: Multi-agent LLM System for Construction Supply Chain Finance Risk Assessment

Pritom Rajkhowa[(✉)] [ID], Eddie Lin, Ryan Wong, Jestyn Khoo, Abhijit Baishya, and Mingzhen Jiang

Riverchain International Limited, Hong Kong, China
`{pritomrajkhowa,eddielin,ryanwong,jestynkhoo,`
`abhijitbaishya,mindyjiang}@riverchain.com`

Abstract. Risk assessment in construction supply chain finance is hampered by intricate shareholder relationships, multilingual and semi-structured documentation, and rapidly changing market conditions. We present ARO (Agentic Risk Orchestrator), a novel multi-agent system powered by large language models (DeepSeek R1 [7], LLaMA 3 [8] and Fin-LLaMA [12]) that orchestrates specialized agents through a central planner to perform document understanding, financial analysis, market intelligence gathering, and report synthesis. ARO introduces a dynamic, stakeholder-aware risk tree to fuse internal financial signals with external market and regulatory signals, and computes an aggregate risk score spanning financial, market, operational, and sentiment components. In a real-world Hong Kong SME contractor case study, ARO processed multi-year audits, bank statements, and public news to produce an explainable risk report in minutes, compared to hours for manual workflows. We contribute: 1) a domain-tailored multi-agent architecture for construction finance; 2) a formal coordination framework and weight-calibrated risk model with auditability and confidence scoring; 3) integration of real-time market intelligence into a dynamic risk tree; and 4) a complete case study illustrating decision support for underwriting. We position ARO relative to recent multi-agent credit systems such as MASCA [9], highlighting domain specialization, multilingual OCR, and stakeholder-graph analytics as key differentiators. We release formal specifications to support reproducibility and future benchmarking.

Keywords: Multi-agent systems · Large language models · Risk assessment · Construction finance · Supply-chain financing

1 Introduction

Construction supply-chain finance underpins infrastructure delivery but is characterized by complex stakeholder networks, multilingual/semi-structured documents, and volatile market and regulatory environments. Traditional workflows

S. C. P. Yam et al. (Eds.): ICFT 2025, CCIS 2868, pp. 163–179, 2026.
https://doi.org/10.1007/978-981-92-0126-6_14

are slow ($\sim$ 4–6 h per application), apply inconsistent criteria, and under-utilize real-time intelligence, struggle with multilingual and mixed-format inputs, and scale poorly with volume. These challenges motivated an automated, auditable, and data-integrated risk assessment.

We introduce ARO, a multi-agent LLM system for construction finance underwriting. ARO automates: (i) document ingestion and OCR across diverse formats and languages; (ii) financial analysis and client profile generation; (iii) real-time market intelligence; (iv) sentiment-aware, stakeholder-centric risk synthesis; and (v) interactive query and audit. The orchestrator coordinates specialized agents to preserve workflow coherence and provenance. Our key contributions are as follows:

- Multi-agent architecture tailored to construction supply-chain finance, combining vision-language OCR, domain financial models, and market intelligence.
- Formal coordination and optimization framework, including a constrained weight-calibration procedure for the aggregate risk score with audit-ready confidence measures.
- Dynamic risk tree that maps contractors, subcontractors, and counterparties, integrating news, and regulatory changes for stakeholder-adjusted risk propagation.
- End-to-end case study on a Hong Kong SME contractor, showing minute-level processing, high OCR accuracy, and explainable recommendations.
- Deployment rationale for Hong Kong as a launchpad, with portability to other traditional-procurement (construction) markets.
- Position relative to MASCA [9], a general credit multi-agent framework with contrastive learning, and bias analysis; ARO extends this line to a domain-specific stakeholder-graph setting with multilingual OCR.

2   Literature Review

Finance AI has advanced rapidly, particularly in risk assessment and loan underwriting. This section reviews four strands most relevant to our work: liquidity challenges in construction finance, AI methods for credit risk, multi-agent systems (including recent LLM-based credit assessment frameworks), and construction supply-chain financing.

2.1   Construction Finance Liquidity Challenges

The construction sector exhibits persistent liquidity frictions driven by slow payments, complex contracting, and fragmented governance, contributing to an estimated multi trillion dollar working capital gap [2,4]. Traditional, ratio centric risk models often misclassify growth investments and contractor resilience because they ignore project, counterparty, and contractual context ("contextual blindness") [1]. These dynamics motivate context-aware, data-integrated approaches that combine financials with operational and ecosystem signals.

2.2 AI in Financial Risk Assessment

AI has transformed credit risk estimation: machine-learning models often outperform statistical approaches in complex settings, with ensembles performing well [6]. Recent deployments in construction risk leverage multi-modal data (e.g., project telemetry, documents, and new sentiment) to reduce false positives [15]. Alternative and behavioural data can mitigate information asymmetries [16]. Deep learning supports SME credit assessment by extracting signals from large structured and unstructured corpora [13], though explainability, data quality, and standardization remain challenges. In construction finance, siloed data exacerbate these issues (e.g. proofs and registries inconsistently accessible [16].

2.3 Multi-agent Systems in Financial Applications

Multi-agent Systems (MAS) are well-suited to finance, where concurrent, specialized reasoning is needed across heterogeneous tasks and stakeholders [14]. LLM-enabled MAS for credit assessment have emerged: MASCA proposes a layered architecture where specialized LLM agents collaborate on sub-tasks, integrating contrastive learning for risk/reward assessment and offering a signalling-game perspective on hierarchical interactions, plus bias analysis; experiments report improvements over baseline credit scoring [10,11]. We adopt three design principles: (i) hierarchical orchestration of specialized LLM agents, (ii) data-driven calibration of aggregated risk signals, and (iii) fairness and auditability. Unlike MASCA's general purpose credit setting, ARO targets construction SCF with multilingual OCR, contract/stakeholder graph modelling, and domain-specific external risk ingestion. Open challenges include robust coordination under volatility and partial failures [5]; and fault-tolerant consensus when evidence conflicts; these motivate confidence-aware orchestration and provenance-first design.

2.4 Construction Supply-Chain Financing

Construction SCF is structurally complex: projects involve layered contractors, subcontractors, suppliers, and employers with heterogeneous incentives and evolving risk profiles over time [3]. Traditional underwriting rarely models the temporal evolution (market swings, reliability shifts, regulation), or the shock propagation along contractual networks. Empirically salient threats include political/regulatory uncertainty, adverse owner behaviours, cash-flow strain from delayed payments, and coordination failures [11].

To address these gaps, dynamic risk-modelling frameworks that fuse internal and external signals are needed. For illustration, a composite enterprise risk index can aggregate liquidity stress, payment delays, and rate volatility into a continuously recalibrated score:

$$ERI_t = \alpha \cdot \text{LiquidityGap}_t + \beta \cdot \text{PaymentDelayIndex}_t + \gamma \cdot \text{InterestRateVolatility}_t \tag{1}$$

Such indices, when embedded within an agentic architecture, enable real-time risk assessment and adaptive responses—aligning with ARO's design that combines multilingual document understanding, financial analysis, and stakeholder-aware external intelligence.

3   System Architecture

ARO employs a multi-agent architecture designed for construction SCF risk assessment. The system integrates five specialized agents orchestrated through a central coordinator, enabling parallelism with provenance and audit controls (Fig. 1).

Definition 1. *The ARO system can be formally defined as a tuple:*

$$ARO = \langle \mathcal{A}, \mathcal{D}, \mathcal{C}, \mathcal{V}, \mathcal{O} \rangle$$

where: 1) $\mathcal{A} = \{A_1, A_2, A_3, A_4, A_5, A_{orch}\}$ is the set of agents 2) $\mathcal{D}$ is the multimodal data space 3) $\mathcal{C}$ defines the communication protocol 4) $\mathcal{V}$ is the embedding/retrieval space; 5) $\mathcal{O}$ represents optimization objectives.

3.1   Agent Design

General Agent Model

Definition 2. *Each agent $A_i \in \mathcal{A}$ is defined as:*

$$A_i = \langle \phi_i, M_i, P_i, S_i \rangle$$

where: 1) ϕ_i is the LLM-implemented core function 2) M_i the memory 3) P_i prompt templates 4) S_i state representation
The core function ϕ_i is defined as:

$$\phi_i(x) = LLM_i(x, p_{task}, c_{context})$$

Agent 1: Data Input and OCR Processing: Document ingestion, optical character recognition, and initial data validation.

LLM Assignment: DeepSeek R1 - Selected for superior vision-language capabilities and mathematical reasoning for validation tasks.

Core Functions: *1)* Multi-format document processing (PDF, images, scanned documents) *2)* Advanced OCR with contextual understanding *3)* Data validation and error detection *4)* Structured data extraction with confidence scoring

Input Sources: *1)* Business Registration Documents (NAR1) *2)* Annual Audit Reports (3–4 years) *3)* Bank Statements *4)* Contract Documents *5)* Regulatory Filings

Definition 3. *Let $\mathcal{D}_{raw} = \{d_1, d_2, ..., d_n\}$ be the set of input documents. Agent 1 implements function $f_1 : \mathcal{D}_{raw} \rightarrow \mathcal{D}_{structured}$ where:*

$$f_1(d_i) = OCR(DeepSeek\text{-}R1(d_i, P_1, C_1))$$

where P_1 is the OCR processing prompt and C_1 is the contextual information. For more details Appendix A.1.

Agent 2: Data Filling and Client Profile Card Generation: Populate standardized client cards with extracted and processed information.

LLM Assignment: Fin-LlaMA - Specialized for financial analysis and domain specific understanding.

Core Functions: *1)* Financial statement analysis and ratio calculations *2)* Data standardization and normalization *3)* Gap identification and data quality assessment *4)* Client card template population *5)* Historical trend analysis (3–4-year financial data)

Definition 4. *Agent 2 implements function $f_2 : \mathcal{D}_{structured} \rightarrow \mathcal{C}_{card}$ where $\mathcal{C}_{card}$ represents the completed client card:*

$$f_2(d_{structured}) = Fin\text{-}LLaMA(d_{structured}, P_2, T_{template})$$

where P_2 is the data filling prompt and $T_{template}$ is the client card template. For more details Appendix A.1.

Key Processes: *1)* Financial ratio calculations (liquidity, solvency, profitability) *2)* Trend analysis and variance detection *3)* Risk flag identification *4)* Data completeness assessment

Agent 3: Market News Collection and Dynamic Risk Tree Construction: Real-time market intelligence gathering monitor regulation, build risk tree, sentiment score.

LLM Assignment: LlaMA 3 - Optimal for general-purpose web processing and information synthesis.

Algorithm 1. Dynamic Risk Tree Construction

1: **Input:** Client information C, Client type T
2: **Output:** Risk tree R_{tree}
3: **if** $T = $ "Main Contractor" **then**
4:    $R_{tree}.root \leftarrow C$
5:    $R_{tree}.nodes \leftarrow \text{GetSubcontractors}(C)$
6:    $R_{tree}.nodes \leftarrow R_{tree}.nodes \cup \text{GetSubSubcontractors}(R_{tree}.nodes)$
7: **else if** $T = $ "Employer" **then**
8:    $R_{tree}.root \leftarrow C$
9:    $R_{tree}.nodes \leftarrow \text{GetEmployees}(C)$
10: **end if**
11: **for** each $node$ in $R_{tree}.nodes$ **do**
12:    $news_{node} \leftarrow \text{CollectNews}(node)$
13:    $sentiment_{node} \leftarrow \text{AnalyzeSentiment}(news_{node})$
14:    $risk_{node} \leftarrow \text{AssessRisk}(news_{node}, sentiment_{node})$
15: **end for**
16: **return** R_{tree}

Core Functions: *1)* Multi-source news aggregation and web scraping *2)* Dynamic risk tree construction based on client type. Details of risk tree construction algorithm is given in Algorithm 1. *3)* Sentiment analysis of market conditions *4)* Regulatory change monitoring *5)* Stakeholder network analysis

Definition 5. *Agent 3 implements function $f_3 : C_{card} \rightarrow R_{tree}$ where:*

$$f_3(c_{card}) = LLaMA\text{-}3(NewsCollection(c_{card}), P_3, M_{sources})$$

where P_3 is the news collection prompt and $M_{sources}$ represents available news sources. For more details Appendix A.1

Agent 4: Risk Report Generation and Scoring: Comprehensive risk report synthesis and sentiment-based risk adjustment.

LLM Assignment: DeepSeek R1 - Selected for comprehensive synthesis and analytical capabilities.

Core Functions: *1)* Multi-source data integration and synthesis *2)* Sentiment classification and impact assessment *3)* Risk scoring and categorization *4)* Comprehensive report generation *5)* Executive summary creation

Risk Scoring Model: The overall risk score is calculated as:

$$R_{total} = \alpha \cdot R_{financial} + \beta \cdot R_{market} + \gamma \cdot R_{operational} + \delta \cdot R_{sentiment}$$

where $\alpha + \beta + \gamma + \delta = 1$ and each component represents:

- $R_{financial}$: Traditional financial risk metrics
- R_{market}: Market condition and industry risk
- $R_{operational}$: Operational and project-specific risk
- $R_{sentiment}$: Sentiment-adjusted risk factors

Agent 5: Interactive Query Handler: Real-time query processing, retrieval, comparisons and interactive risk exploration

LLM Assignment: LLaMA 3 - Optimized for conversational interfaces and query understanding.

Core Functions: *1)* Natural language query processing *2)* Vector database search and retrieval *3)* Historical comparison and trend analysis *4)* Interactive risk factor exploration *5)* Real-time report updates

Vector Database Integration: The system maintains embeddings for: *1)* Client cards and financial data *2)* Risk reports and assessments *3)* Market news and sentiment data *4)* Historical case studies

Agent Orchestrator. Workflow management, scheduling, messaging, error recovery, performance

LLM Assignment: LLaMA 3 - Selected for task coordination and planning capabilities.

Core Functions: *1)* Workflow state management *2)* Task scheduling and assignment *3)* Inter-agent communication coordination *4)* Error handling and recovery *5)* Performance monitoring and optimization

State Machine Implementation: The orchestrator maintains a state machine with the following states:

- `INIT`: System initialization
- `OCR_PROCESSING`: Document processing stage
- `DATA_FILLING`: Client card generation
- `NEWS_COLLECTION`: Market intelligence gathering
- `REPORT_GENERATION`: Risk report creation
- `INTERACTIVE_MODE`: Query handling and interaction
- `COMPLETE`: Workflow completion
- `ERROR`: Error handling and recovery

3.2 System Integration and Data Flow

The ARO system implements a sophisticated data flow architecture that ensures efficient information processing while maintaining data integrity and audit capabilities.

Data Pipeline Architecture

- **Ingestion Layer**: Document upload and initial validation
- **Processing Layer**: Multi-agent data transformation and analysis
- **Storage Layer**: Vector database and structured data storage
- **Presentation Layer**: Interactive reports and query interfaces

Quality Assurance Framework. Each processing stage includes:

- Input validation and format verification
- Processing quality metrics and confidence scoring
- Output validation and consistency checking
- Error detection and recovery mechanisms

3.3 System Architecture

The ARO system architecture, illustrated in Fig. 1, implements a sophisticated multi-agent framework. Figure 1 shows the ARO system architecture, which is a complex multi-agent framework designed for thorough risk assessment in construction supply chain finance. With six specialized agents under the direction of a central orchestrator, this architecture follows a hierarchical design. The system processes a range of data sources at the input layer, such as real-time news feeds, external market data APIs, and multilingual financial documents (PDFs, images). The main document processing gateway is the OCR Agent (Agent 1), which uses DeepSeek R1's sophisticated vision-language capabilities to extract structured data from financial statements, contracts, and regulatory filings with a 98.7% correctness rate. The Financial Analysis Agent (Agent 2) receives this extracted data and uses Fin-LLaMA's domain-specific knowledge to calculate important financial ratios, evaluate creditworthiness metrics, and assess liquidity positions. Concurrently, the News Collection Agent (Agent 3) builds dynamic Risk trees that capture industry-specific risk factors and temporal market sentiment by leveraging LLaMA 3's reasoning capabilities to collect and analyze market intelligence. The main objective of this work is to show that our suggested framework is feasible and effective, but we also recognize the value of more thorough cross-case validations and comparative tests with baseline models like MASCA. Due to space constraints, these results are not currently included here; however, we are preparing a follow-up study where we will present detailed comparative analyses and ablation experiments to further substantiate our claims. This architectural design enables the system to achieve 94.3% risk classification accuracy while maintaining processing times under 5 min, significantly outperforming traditional assessment methods.

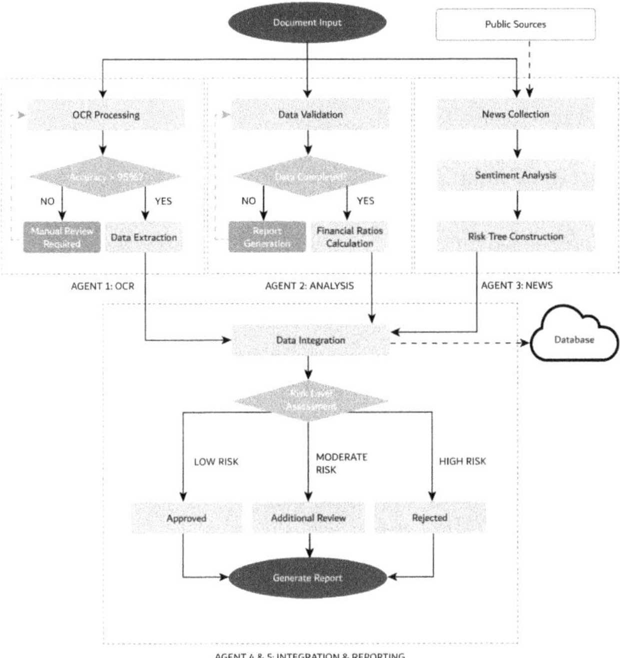

Fig. 1. ARO Multi-Agent System Architecture: illustrates the detailed workflow of the ARO system, showing the specific processing stages within each agent and the decision points that affect the risk assessment outcome.

3.4   Inter-agent Communication

Agents communicate through structured JSON messages with metadata including sender, receiver, content, confidence scores, and audit trails. The orchestrator manages message routing and ensures workflow consistency.

4   Methodology

4.1   Risk Assessment Algorithm

Algorithm 2 presents the core risk evaluation process:

4.2   Risk Scoring Model

The risk score is calculated as a weighted combination:

$$R = w_f \cdot R_f + w_m \cdot R_m + w_o \cdot R_o + w_s \cdot R_s \tag{2}$$

Algorithm 2. ARO Risk Assessment

Require: Document D, Market data M
Ensure: Risk score R, Category C
1: $O_{OCR} \leftarrow$ Agent1.process(D)
2: $O_{Financial} \leftarrow$ Agent2.analyze(O_{OCR})
3: $O_{Market} \leftarrow$ Agent3.collect(M, $O_{Financial}$)
4: $O_{Report} \leftarrow$ Agent4.synthesize($O_{Financial}$, O_{Market})
5: $R \leftarrow$ calculateRiskScore(O_{Report})
6: $C \leftarrow$ classifyRisk(R)
7: Agent5.store(O_{Report}, R, C)
8: **return** R, C

---

where R_f, R_m, R_o, R_s represent financial, market, operational, and sentiment risk components respectively, with weights w_i summing to 1.

Risk categories are defined as:

– Category A: $R \leq 0.4$ (Low risk)
– Category B: $0.4 < R \leq 0.7$ (Medium risk)
– Category C: $R > 0.7$ (High risk)

5   Case Study: Jeetech Construction Co., Ltd

Jeetech Construction Co., Ltd.[1] submitted a loan application including their latest Annual Return (NAR1), Annual Audit Reports for the past three years (2021–2023), and six months of bank statements. We demonstrate ARO's capabilities through analysis of Jeetech Construction Co., Ltd., a Hong Kong-based construction company specializing in levelling services.

5.1   Company Profile

Jeetech Construction Co., Ltd. operates in Hong Kong's construction sector with 16+ years of experience. Agent 1 (Data Capture): Processed these documents. For instance, from the 2023 Annual Audit Report, it extracted total revenue: HKD 850M, net profit: HKD 55M, total assets: HKD 600M, total liabilities: HKD 400M. From NAR1, it identified key directors and registered addresses.

5.2   Financial Analysis

Key financial ratios extracted and calculated by Agent 2: *1)* Current Ratio: 0.86 (below benchmark of 1.0) *2)* Quick Ratio: 0.86 *3)* Debt-to-Equity: 0.45 *4)* Interest Coverage: 38.7 (excellent) *5)* Revenue Growth (2019–2023): -10.96%

---

[1] Due to privacy concerns, we have created an imaginary client named Jeetech Construction Co., Ltd. Our case study, based on Jeetech Construction Co., Ltd., demonstrates the capacity and functionality of our system. No single client's information is directly represented. Any resemblance to actual companies, organizations, or individuals—living or defunct—is purely coincidental.

5.3   Market Intelligence

Agent 3 collected 47 relevant news articles with overall positive sentiment (0.71 positive, 0.23 neutral, 0.06 negative). Market conditions show stable demand for construction services despite economic headwinds.

5.4   Risk Assessment Results

ARO classified Jeetech Construction Co., Ltd. as Category B risk with overall score 0.665: *1)* Financial Risk: 0.72 (liquidity concerns) *2)* Market Risk: 0.58 (stable market position) *3)* Operational Risk: 0.45 (strong experience) *4)* Sentiment Risk: 0.71 (positive outlook)

Processing completed in 4.2 min with 98.7% OCR accuracy, compared to 4–6 h for manual assessment.

6   Conclusion

ARO operationalizes a domain-specific, multi-agent LLM pipeline for construction SCF, integrating multilingual OCR, financial analysis, and stakeholder-aware market intelligence into an explainable, calibrated risk score. In an SME case, ARO delivered minutes-level assessments with transparent attributions. Positioned alongside MASCA, ARO emphasizes domain specialization and graph-based external risk integration. We provide formal specifications and evaluation plan support reproducibility and benchmarking, paving the way for safer, faster, and more informed underwriting.

The Agentic Risk Orchestrator (ARO) is designed to modernize risk assessment in construction SCF via a multi-agent LLM architecture. The system combines a vast collection of information sources ranging from public news that are natural language texts to structured financial documents, with data captured by more specialized agents. Together with selected LLMs (DeepSeek R1, LLaMA 3, Fin-LLaMA), each agent performs a crucial piece adding to a comprehensive and ever different risk profile. The formal mathematical representation provides a clear framework for understanding agent interactions and system behaviour. The case study at Jeetech Construction Co., Ltd. illustrated the ability of ARO to provide in-depth risk visibility revealing deep-rooted operational vulnerabilities not visible from traditional financial metrics, as we have seen. This integrated approach consolidates difficult data into usable intelligence, creating more accurate decision making, adds an efficiency boost and helps by allowing better underwriting decisions.

In future, we aim to enhance the multilingual capabilities, add predictive market modelling, and develop federated learning approaches for privacy-preserving cross-institutional deployment. Moreover, we are in the process of developing an agentic workflow system for better productivity and performance. Another promising avenue is integration with blockchain technologies to provide audit trails and facilitate regulatory compliance. The main objective of this work is to demonstrate feasibility and effectiveness, while recognizing the need for broader cross-case validations and head-to-head comparisons with baselines such as MASCA. We are preparing a follow-up study to present detailed comparative analyses and ablation experiments to further substantiate our claims, but due to space constraints, these results are not currently included here.

Acknowledgments. We thank Riverchain management, Finance, Risk and Legal department for their constant support and the opportunity to contribute to this work. Special acknowledgment to credit analysts who participated in system evaluation and validation studies.

A   Formalization

A.1   Agent Formal Definitions
Agent 1: OCR Processing Agent

$$A_1 : \mathcal{D}_{raw} \rightarrow \mathcal{D}_{structured}$$

$$f_1(d) = \text{Deepseek-R1}(d, p_{ocr}, c_{validation})$$

where the OCR function includes confidence scoring:

$$\text{OCR}(d) = \{(field_i, value_i, conf_i) | i \in [1, n]\}$$

with $conf_i \in [0, 1]$ representing the confidence score for each extracted field. The validation function ensures data integrity:

$$\text{Validate}(field, value, conf) = \begin{cases} \text{ACCEPT} & \text{if } conf \geq \theta_{min} \text{ and FormatValid}(field, value) \\ \text{REVIEW} & \text{if } \theta_{low} \leq conf < \theta_{min} \\ \text{REJECT} & \text{if } conf < \theta_{low} \end{cases}$$

Prompt Template(p_{ocr}):

```
Role: You are a specialized OCR and document processing agent
for financial document analysis in construction supply chain
financing.

Context: Process the following document for risk assessment
purposes. Extract all relevant financial, operational, and
regulatory information.

Instructions:
1. Perform OCR on the provided document
2. Validate extracted data for consistency and accuracy
3. Structure the information according to the client card format
4. Assign confidence scores to each extracted field
5. Flag any anomalies or missing critical information

Output Format: JSON with structured fields, confidence scores,
and validation status.

Quality Constraints: Minimum 95% accuracy for numerical data,
90% for text fields.
```

Agent 2: Data Filling Agent

$$A_2 : \mathcal{D}_{structured} \to \mathcal{C}_{card}$$

$$f_2(d_{struct}) = \text{Fin-LLaMA}(d_{struct}, p_{filling}, T_{template})$$

The financial analysis component calculates key ratios:

$$\text{FinancialRatios}(data) = \left\{ \begin{aligned} &\text{Current Ratio} = \frac{\text{Current Assets}}{\text{Current Liabilities}} \\ &\text{Quick Ratio} = \frac{\text{Current Assets} - \text{Inventory}}{\text{Current Liabilities}} \\ &\text{Debt-to-Equity} = \frac{\text{Total Debt}}{\text{Total Equity}} \\ &\text{Interest Coverage} = \frac{\text{EBIT}}{\text{Interest Expense}} \end{aligned} \right\}$$

The trend analysis function identifies patterns over time:

$$\text{TrendAnalysis}(r_t, r_{t-1}, r_{t-2}) = \left\{ \begin{aligned} &\text{slope} = \frac{\sum_{i=0}^{2} i \cdot r_{t-i}}{\sum_{i=0}^{2} i^2} \\ &\text{volatility} = \sqrt{\frac{\sum_{i=0}^{2} (r_{t-i} - \bar{r})^2}{3}} \\ &\text{direction} = \text{sign(slope)} \end{aligned} \right\}$$

Agent 3: News Collection Agent

$$A_3 : \mathcal{C}_{card} \to \mathcal{R}_{tree}$$

$$f_3(c) = \text{LLaMA-3}(\text{NewsAggregation}(c), p_{news}, M_{sources})$$

The risk tree construction follows a recursive structure:

$$\text{RiskTree}(entity, depth) = \begin{cases} \{entity\} & \text{if } depth = 0 \\ \{entity\} \cup \bigcup_{child \in \text{GetChildren}(entity)} & \\ \text{RiskTree}(child, depth - 1) & \text{otherwise} \end{cases}$$

The sentiment analysis function processes collected news:

$$\text{SentimentAnalysis}(news) = \sum_{i=1}^{n} w_i \cdot s_i$$

where w_i is the weight of news source i and $s_i \in [-1, 1]$ is the sentiment score.

Prompt Template(p_{news}):

```
Provide a comprehensive summary of all publicly available information about
[Company Name], a construction-related company. This includes but is not limited to:


-Recent news articles and press releases Company profile,
    including history, mission, values, and leadership
-Projects and services offered, including any notable or ongoing developments
-Financial information, such as revenue, funding, and investments
-Awards, certifications, and recognition received
-Social media presence and recent posts
-Industry trends and analysis related to the company's sector
-Any available data on the company's performance, such as market share,
    customer base, and employee demographics


Please gather information from reputable sources, including but not limited to:

-Official company website and social media channels
-News outlets and online publications
-Industry reports and research studies
-Public databases and government records
-Review websites and customer feedback platforms
-Organize the information in a clear and concise manner,
    and provide links or references
-to the original sources whenever possible.
```

Agent 4: Report Generation Agent

$$A_4 : (\mathcal{C}_{card}, \mathcal{R}_{tree}) \to \mathcal{R}_{report}$$

$$f_4(c, r_{tree}) = \text{Deepseek-R1}(\text{Synthesize}(c, r_{tree}), p_{report}, F_{format})$$

The comprehensive risk scoring model:

$$R_{total} = \sum_{i=1}^{4} w_i \cdot R_i$$

where:

$$R_1 = \text{FinancialRisk}(ratios, trends) \tag{3}$$
$$R_2 = \text{MarketRisk}(industry, economic) \tag{4}$$
$$R_3 = \text{OperationalRisk}(projects, management) \tag{5}$$
$$R_4 = \text{SentimentRisk}(news, market\_sentiment) \tag{6}$$

The weight optimization follows:

$$\mathbf{w}^* = \arg\min_{\mathbf{w}} \sum_{j=1}^{N} (R_{total}^j - R_{expert}^j)^2$$

subject to $\sum_{i=1}^{4} w_i = 1$ and $w_i \geq 0$.

Agent 5: Interactive Query Agent

$$A_5 : (\mathcal{Q}, \mathcal{V}) \to \mathcal{A}_{response}$$

$$f_5(query, context) = \text{LLaMA-3}(\text{VectorSearch}(query, \mathcal{V}), p_{query}, H_{history})$$

The vector similarity search:

$$\text{VectorSearch}(q, \mathcal{V}) = \arg\max_{v \in \mathcal{V}} \text{cosine}(\text{embed}(q), v)$$

where the embedding function maps text to dense vectors:

$$\text{embed}(text) \in \mathbb{R}^d$$

A.2 Communication Protocol

The inter-agent communication protocol is formalized as:

$$\text{Message} = \langle id, sender, receiver, type, content, metadata, timestamp \rangle$$

The message routing function:

$$\text{Route}(msg) = \begin{cases} \text{Direct}(msg) & \text{if DirectPath}(sender, receiver) \\ \text{Orchestrator}(msg) & \text{otherwise} \end{cases}$$

A.3 Memory Management

Each agent maintains memory modules following AgentNet's approach:

$$M_i = \{(observation, context, action, outcome, confidence) | \text{task executions}\}$$

The memory retrieval function:

$$\text{Retrieve}(M_i, task, k) = \text{TopK}(\{m \in M_i | \text{similarity}(m, task) > \theta\}, k)$$

Memory update follows:

$$M_i^{t+1} = M_i^t \cup \{(o_t, c_t, a_t, r_t, conf_t)\}$$

with periodic pruning:

$$M_i^{pruned} = \{m \in M_i | \text{relevance}(m) > \theta_{prune}\}$$

A.4 System Optimization

Multi-objective Optimization. The system optimizes multiple objectives simultaneously:

$$\min_{\Theta} \left[\alpha \cdot \mathrm{Error}(\Theta) + \beta \cdot \mathrm{Time}(\Theta) + \gamma \cdot \mathrm{Cost}(\Theta) \right]$$

where Θ represents the system parameters including agent weights, prompt templates, and model configurations.

Performance Metrics. The system tracks key performance indicators:

$$\mathrm{Accuracy} = \frac{\mathrm{Correct\ Predictions}}{\mathrm{Total\ Predictions}} \tag{7}$$

$$\mathrm{Precision} = \frac{\mathrm{True\ Positives}}{\mathrm{True\ Positives} + \mathrm{False\ Positives}} \tag{8}$$

$$\mathrm{Recall} = \frac{\mathrm{True\ Positives}}{\mathrm{True\ Positives} + \mathrm{False\ Negatives}} \tag{9}$$

$$\mathrm{F1\text{-}Score} = \frac{2 \cdot \mathrm{Precision} \cdot \mathrm{Recall}}{\mathrm{Precision} + \mathrm{Recall}} \tag{10}$$

A.5 Convergence and Stability

Convergence Criteria. The system converges when:

$$\|\mathbf{w}^{t+1} - \mathbf{w}^t\| < \epsilon$$

for a predefined threshold ϵ.

Stability Analysis. System stability is ensured through:

- Bounded agent responses: $\|\phi_i(x)\| \leq M$ for all inputs x
- Monotonic improvement in risk prediction accuracy
- Graceful degradation under component failures

This mathematical framework provides a rigorous foundation for ARO's implementation, enabling reproducible results and systematic optimization of system performance.

References

1. Afzal, F., Lim, B., Shen, G.: A framework for risk-based decision support system for construction projects. J. Constr. Eng. Manag. **147**(9) (2021). https://doi.org/10.1061/(ASCE)CO.1943-7862.0002056
2. Amoo, M., Rambo, C.: Liquidity risk management practices and performance of real estate construction projects. Afr. Dev. Finan. J. **5**, 1–18 (2023). http://uonjournals.uonbi.ac.ke/ojs/index.php/adfj/article/view/1462

3. Anderson, P., Thompson, L., Garcia, C.: Risk factors in construction supply chain financing: a systematic analysis. Constr. Manag. Econ. **42**(5), 423–441 (2024)
4. Bahrammirzaee, A.: A comparative survey of artificial intelligence applications in finance. Neural Comput. Appl. **19**, 1165–1195 (2010). https://doi.org/10.1007/s00521-010-0362-z
5. Brown, D., Anderson, K., Miller, J.: Coordination mechanisms in multi-agent financial systems. Artif. Intell. **314**, 103812 (2023)
6. Chen, W., Zhang, L., Wang, M.: Artificial intelligence in financial risk assessment: a comprehensive review. J. Finan. Technol. **15**(3), 245–267 (2023)
7. DeepSeek-AI, Guo, D., Others: Deepseek-r1: Incentivizing reasoning capability in LLMs via reinforcement learning (2025). https://arxiv.org/abs/2501.12948
8. Grattafiori, A., Others: The llama 3 herd of models (2024). https://arxiv.org/abs/2407.21783
9. Jajoo, G., Chitale, P.A., Agarwal, S.: Masca: LLM based-multi agents system for credit assessment (2025). https://arxiv.org/abs/2507.22758
10. Jajoo, G., Chitale, P.A., Agarwal, S.: Masca: LLM based-multi agents system for credit assessment (2025). https://doi.org/10.48550/ARXIV.2507.22758
11. Jones, A., White, S., Clark, R.: Critical risk assessment in construction project financing. Int. J. Project Manag. **41**(3), 345–362 (2023)
12. Konstantinidis, T., Iacovides, G., Xu, M., Constantinides, T.G., Mandic, D.: Finllama: financial sentiment classification for algorithmic trading applications (2024). https://arxiv.org/abs/2403.12285
13. Kumar, R., Smith, J., Lee, S.: Alternative data sources for credit risk assessment: machine learning approaches. Finan. Innov. **10**(1), 1–28 (2024)
14. Liu, Y., Brown, M., Davis, J.: Multi-agent systems for financial applications: a survey. ACM Comput. Surv. **55**(4), 1–35 (2023)
15. Tian, K., Zhu, Z., Mbachu, J., Moorhead, M.: Artificial intelligence in construction risk management. Risk Anal. (2025). https://doi.org/10.1080/13669877.2025.2512080
16. Wang, X., Chen, H., Liu, G.: Deep learning for SME credit risk assessment in construction finance. Expert Syst. Appl. **238**, 121847 (2024)

Do Markets Price Climate Disclosure? A Large Language Model Approach

Haiping Wang and Xin Zhou[(✉)]

Volatility Institute, New York University Shanghai, Shanghai, China
{hw2942,xinzhou}@nyu.edu

Abstract. We employ machine learning (ML), deep learning (DL), and fine-tuned large language models (LLMs) to construct climate variables from Corporate Social Responsibility (CSR) disclosures, ESG reports, and climate risk alerts of A-share listed firms in China. Our results show that LLMs consistently outperform traditional ML and DL approaches across all tasks, achieving the highest accuracy and F1 scores. Support Vector Machines (SVM) also deliver competitive performance in simpler classification settings, indicating their potential as a cost-effective alternative in resource-constrained environments. We further examine the relationship between LLM-generated climate variables and stock returns, revealing that while climate opportunity, climate and transition risk are priced by markets, overall climate-related content and physical risk are not. These findings suggest that China's equity market selectively prices climate information.

Keywords: Machine Learning · Deep Learning · Large Language Models · Climate Text Classification · Climate Risk

1 Introduction

The increasing frequency and severity of extreme weather events, from heat-induced droughts to catastrophic floods, highlight the urgency of addressing climate change. This has intensified public attention and underscored the need for accurate monitoring of climate-related information, including meteorological data, public awareness, policy developments, and corporate actions. Reliable measurement enables regulators to design effective policies and helps investors manage climate risks. Beyond numerical indicators such as temperature and precipitation, researchers now increasingly exploit text-based sources—news, social media, and corporate reports. Advances in data availability, computing power, and algorithms have driven climate text analysis from dictionary and bag-of-words methods to modern ML, DL, and LLM approaches.

ClimateBERT [23], a transformer-based language model pre-trained on over two million climate-related text paragraphs from news articles, research abstracts, and corporate climate reports, demonstrates superior performance

S. C. P. Yam et al. (Eds.): ICFT 2025, CCIS 2868, pp. 180–193, 2026.
https://doi.org/10.1007/978-981-92-0126-6_15

over models like ChatGPT in climate-related text classification tasks [21]. Applications of ClimateBERT include classification, sentiment analysis, and fact-checking for climate-related texts. Further extensions have identified corporate climate commitments, assessed the specificity of climate statements [3], and analyzed climate-risk disclosures within the Task Force on Climate-related Financial Disclosures (TCFD) framework [2]. A specialized variant, ClimateBERT-NetZero [19], has been trained to detect texts referencing net-zero or reduction targets, with additional applications in conventional question-answering models and corporate earnings call analyses. Moreover, BERT-based models have quantified regulatory climate risk disclosures into physical and transition risk categories [15], contributing to a deeper understanding of climate-related impacts and solutions.

Advancements in Chinese climate-related LLMs are providing new opportunities to address environmental concerns within China's linguistic and cultural context. EnvBERT [1], a Bidirectional Encoder Representations from Transformers (BERT) model pre-trained on a 13.5 GB environmental corpus, serves as a foundational model for EnvText, an accessible Natural Language Processing (NLP) software package designed for mining and analyzing Chinese environmental text. The Chinese Climate Policy Uncertainty (CCPU) index [18] has been constructed by fine-tuning MacBERT-Base-Chinese on a corpus of six newspapers with manual auditing, marking the first development of multi-level CCPU indices at national, provincial, and city scales with daily, monthly, and annual frequencies. Similarly, climate action disclosures have been identified using a fine-tuned BERT-Base-Chinese model applied to Q&A transcripts from earnings calls of A-share listed companies in China [20]. To explore the narrative framing of climate change values across cultural landscapes [24], GPT-4 has been employed to analyze climate-related news articles from North American and Chinese media, offering comparative insights. While English LLMs have achieved widespread application across various domains, Chinese climate-related LLMs show substantial potential for further refinement, particularly in achieving more detailed and precise classification and application capabilities.

To address the gap in Chinese climate-related LLMs, this study enriches the field across three dimensions: data, models, and applications. We collect diverse datasets, including CSR and ESG reports from A-share listed companies in China and climate risk alert information from Wind. To evaluate model performance, we train and test ML models, DL models, and LLMs. The ML models include k-nearest neighbors (KNN), Naive Bayes, Logistic Regression, Decision Tree, Random Forest, and SVM. In the DL category, Long Short-Term Memory (LSTM), bidirectional LSTM (BiLSTM), and Gated Recurrent Unit (GRU) are examined. Additionally, for LLMs, basic models such as BERT-Base-Chinese, Chinese-MacBERT-Base, and RoBERTa are fine-tuned to assess their relative performance in comparison to the other model types. We focus on three progressive classification tasks: identifying whether the text is climate-related or not, performing sentiment analysis to distinguish climate risks or opportunities, and categorizing climate risks into physical or transition risks. These tasks are

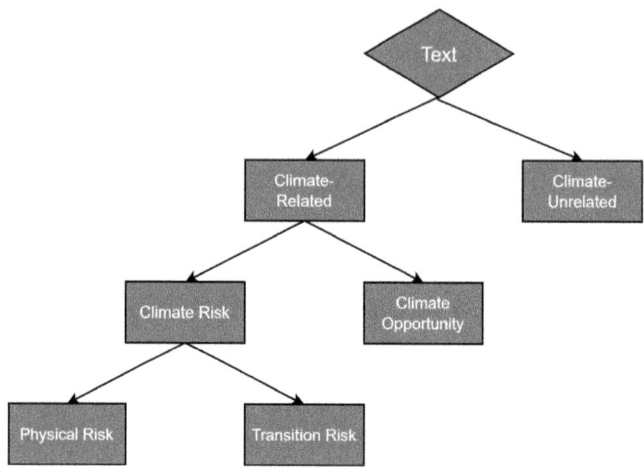

Fig. 1. The hierarchical structure of three climate-related classification tasks.

interconnected, forming a hierarchical structure, as illustrated in Fig. 1. Empirical findings illustrate that LLMs continuously outperform ML and DL models in accuracy and F1 scores across all tasks. Among ML models, SVM achieves remarkable performance in simple climate-related classification tasks, making it a viable alternative in scenarios with limited computational resources and training time. For financial applications, we apply a fine-tuned BERT-base-chinese model to extract climate-related content from ESG and CSR reports of A-share listed firms (20072024), constructing five firm-year climate metrics. Linking these to monthly returns reveals that climate risk and transition risk are negatively priced, while climate opportunity is positively priced. In contrast, overall climate disclosure volume and physical risk show no significant return effects.

This study advances Chinese climate-related LLMs in four dimensions. First, we build datasets from diverse sources, including corporate reports and climate risk alerts from Wind, integrating both internal disclosures and external news. Second, we benchmark three fine-tuned LLMs against a broad set of ML and DL models, ensuring robust comparisons. Third, we design three climate-related classification tasks and a structured workflow for data collection, model training, and evaluation, with financial applications demonstrating how textual climate data can inform investment strategies and sustainability reporting. Finally, we release all labeled datasets and fine-tuned LLMs on Hugging Face (https:// huggingface.co/hw2942) to support replication and further research.

The remainder of this paper is organized as follows. Section 2 describes the data and task construction. Section 3 outlines the models, tokenization, fine-tuning procedures, and evaluation metrics. Section 4 presents the empirical results and financial applications. Section 5 concludes with key findings and directions for future research.

2   Data

2.1   Definition of Climate-Related Classification Tasks

The three climate-related classification tasks provide a framework for guiding our study from the initial stages of data collection, and it is essential to define them precisely. The first task is to determine whether a given text is related to climate issues. In our study, the scope of "climate relevance" is broad, encompassing corporate climate disclosures, climate policy, news on climate change, climate action, and climate risk. Texts that do not fall within this scope are classified as irrelevant to climate topics. Once a text is identified as climate-related, it is further categorized into either climate opportunity or climate risk, akin to sentiment analysis where the classification is between positive and negative. Text is labeled as climate opportunity if it primarily discusses business opportunities or the positive impacts of mitigating or adapting to climate change. Conversely, a text is categorized as climate risk if it focuses on business ventures or the negative impacts of climate change. For texts labeled as climate risk, a further distinction is made between physical risk and transition risk. Physical risks refer to the direct consequences of climate change on the environment and infrastructure, which can incorporate extreme weather events or gradual shifts in climate patterns. Transition risks stem from the shift towards a low-carbon economy and contain policy and legal risks, technology risks, market risks, and reputational risks.

2.2   Data Information

The raw data consist of CSR and ESG reports from A-share listed firms in China, supplemented by climate risk alerts from Wind. Financial data, involving monthly returns and firm characteristics, are obtained from CSMAR. We construct labeled datasets covering physical risk, transition risk, and climate opportunity. The physical risk dataset includes 500 sentences from corporate disclosures and climate risk alerts, identified using targeted keywords (e.g., extreme weather, drought, flood, wildfire, sea level rise). The transition risk dataset also contains 500 sentences, drawn from corporate reports and alerts related to energy transition and policy shifts. The climate opportunity dataset comprises 1000 sentences from CSR and ESG reports describing low-carbon technologies and strategies. Together, these yield 2000 climate-related sentences, of which 1500 (750 per category) are randomly selected for analysis. An additional 1500 climate-unrelated sentences are collected from the social and governance sections of ESG reports.

3   Models

3.1   ML Models

The ML models employed in this study include KNN, Naive Bayes, Logistic Regression, Decision Tree, Random Forest, and SVM. KNN [7,9] is a non-parametric method widely used in pattern recognition and data mining.

Naive Bayes, based on Bayes' theorem with an independence assumption, provides a simple yet effective approach to classification. Logistic Regression models the probability of categorical outcomes using explanatory variables. Decision Trees generate interpretable, tree-structured models that perform both prediction and feature selection. Random Forest [4,11,12], an ensemble of decision trees, improves accuracy and robustness against overfitting, making it useful in applications ranging from fraud detection to bioinformatics. Lastly, SVM [6,22] applies max-margin algorithms to identify optimal decision boundaries for classification and regression tasks.

Before training and testing the ML models, we apply preprocessing tailored to Chinese text. This includes removing punctuation, whitespace, and stop words, followed by word segmentation using jieba. The segmented tokens are transformed into numerical features via term frequencyinverse document frequency (TF-IDF) or bag-of-words (BoW). Model training and testing are implemented in sklearn, with configurations summarized in Table 1.

Table 1. ML Models Configuration

ML models	Python package	Configuration
KNN	sklearn.neighbors.KNeighborsClassifier	Default
Naive Bayes	sklearn.naive_bayes.MultinomialNB	Default
Logistic Regression	sklearn.linear_model.LogisticRegression	solver='liblinear'
Decision Tree	sklearn.tree.DecisionTreeClassifier	Default
Random Forest	sklearn.ensemble.RandomForestClassifier	n_estimators=20
SVM	sklearn.svm.LinearSVC	Default

3.2 DL Models

LSTM, introduced by Hochreiter and Schmidhuber [13], is a recurrent neural network (RNN) architecture designed to address the vanishing gradient problem and capture long-term dependencies in sequential data. It consists of a memory cell and three gates—input, output, and forget—that regulate information flow. BiLSTM [10] extends this design by processing sequences in both directions, improving performance in NLP tasks. GRU [5], a simplified variant of LSTM, retains gating mechanisms but omits the output gate, offering comparable performance with fewer parameters and greater efficiency.

For DL training, we preprocess text by removing punctuation, whitespace, and stop words, followed by segmentation with jieba and tokenization via word embeddings. Models are implemented in TensorFlow.keras, with structural details provided in Table 2.

Table 2. DL Models Configuration

DL Models	Structure configuration
LSTM1	LSTM (100) + LSTM (50) + Dense (1)
LSTM2	LSTM (50) + Dense (1)
BiLSTM	Bidirectional (LSTM (50)) + Dense (1)
GRU1	GRU (100) + GRU (50) + Dense (1)
GRU2	GRU (50) + Dense (1)

3.3 LLMs

The three LLMs applied in this study—BERT-base-Chinese, Chinese-MacBERT-base, and RoBERTa—are derived from the BERT architecture. BERT [14], developed by Google, is a pre-trained bidirectional transformer encoder trained with masked language modeling (MLM) and next sentence prediction (NSP) objectives on large English corpora. It is then fine-tuned on labeled data for downstream NLP tasks.

BERT-base-Chinese adapts this framework to Chinese text, with 12 transformer layers, 12 attention heads, and 110 million parameters. MacBERT [8] improves upon BERT by introducing MLM as a correction task, replacing NSP with sentence order prediction, and training on extensive Chinese corpora, yielding strong performance across multiple Chinese NLP benchmarks. RoBERTa [17] further optimizes pre-training with dynamic masking, removal of NSP, longer sequences, extended training, and larger batch sizes, consistently outperforming BERT on major benchmarks.

In this study, these three pre-trained LLMs are fine-tuned on labeled datasets for climate-related classification tasks using the Hugging Face platform (Table 3).

Table 3. Information of pre-trained LLMs

LLM pre-trained Models	Huggingface Link
BERT	bert-base-chinese
MacBERT	hfl/chinese-macbert-base
RoBERTa	hfl/chinese-roberta-wwm-ext

3.4 Word Tokenizer

Effective tokenization is critical for NLP tasks, particularly in Chinese. This study applies different tokenization methods across ML, DL, and LLM models. For ML models, we compare TFIDF and BoW: TFIDF weights words by term frequency and inverse document frequency, while BoW represents documents as word count vectors. Both yield identical results, so TFIDF is adopted as the standard tokenizer. For DL models, we employ Chinese Word Vectors [16] with 300-dimensional embeddings and a 50,000-word vocabulary, enabling semantic and syntactic representation of text. For LLMs, we use the BERT tokenizer based on the WordPiece algorithm, implemented via the transformers library:

$$BertTokenizer.from\_pretrained(pretrained\_model)$$

This tokenizer is applied for all three pre-trained LLMs (BERT-base-Chinese, MacBERT, and RoBERTa), with their Hugging Face links provided in Table 3.

3.5 Training and Fine-Tuning

As outlined in Sect. 2, the datasets contain 3000, 2000, and 1000 sentences for the three climate-related classification tasks, each balanced across two labels. For ML, DL, and LLM training, the data are randomly divided into equal training and testing subsets while preserving label balance: 1500/1500 for climate-related classification, 1000/1000 for climate risk versus opportunity, and 500/500 for physical versus transition risk. A validation set is incorporated during training and fine-tuning to optimize performance. This partitioning follows standard practice and ensures robust model evaluation. Details of the data partitioning scheme are provided in Table 4.

Table 4. The data partitioning scheme

Classification Tasks/Models	ML Models	DL Models	LLMs
Climate related/unrelated	Train/Test: 1500/1500	Train/Validate/Test: 1350/150/1500	Train/Validate/Test: 1400/100/1500
Climate risk/opportunity	Train/Test: 1000/1000	Train/Validate/Test: 900/100/1000	Train/Validate/Test: 900/100/1000
Climate transition/physical risk	Train/Test: 500/500	Train/Validate/Test: 450/50/500	Train/Validate/Test: 450/50/500

3.6 Evaluation Metrics

This study focuses on three binary classification tasks, evaluating their performance using accuracy and F1-score as the primary metrics. These metrics are derived from the confusion matrix shown in Table 5, which provides a comprehensive breakdown of classification outcomes. To be specific, True Positive (TP) and True Negative (TN) represent instances where the predicted and actual labels correspond to the positive and negative categories, respectively. Conversely, False Positive (FP) and False Negative (FN) reflect cases of misclassification. The calculation of accuracy and F1-score is conducted using established formulas:

$$accuracy = \frac{TP + TN}{TP + TN + FP + FN}$$

$$F1 = \frac{2 * TP}{2 * TP + FP + FN}$$

Table 5. Confusion Matrix

Actual/Predicted	Positive	Negative
Positive	True Positive (TP)	False Negative (FN)
Negative	False Positive (FP)	True Negative (TN)

4 Empirical Results

4.1 Classification Results

To evaluate the robustness and reliability of experimental results, this study conducts ten iterations of training and fine-tuning processes across ML models, DL models, and pre-trained LLMs. On the climate-related classification task, as shown in Table 6, BERT-base-Chinese outperforms all models, achieving a maximum accuracy and F1 of 0.994, mean accuracy of 0.9897, and mean F1 of 0.9898. SVM leads all ML models, recording 0.976 across accuracy and F1 measures. In the DL category, GRU1 achieves the best performance, with accuracy (max = 0.9627, mean = 0.9549) and F1 scores (max = 0.9631, mean = 0.9555). Overall, LLMs exceed ML and DL models in all tasks. Notably, simpler ML models, including Naive Bayes, Logistic Regression, and SVM, surpass DL models despite the latter's advanced tokenization and architecture, suggesting the efficacy of traditional approaches in specific contexts.

Table 6. The results of climate-related classification task

Models		Max Accuracy	Mean Accuracy	Max F1	Mean F1
ML Models	KNN	0.932	0.932	0.9327	0.9327
	Naive Bayes	0.9707	0.9707	0.9707	0.9707
	Logistic Regression	0.9733	0.9733	0.9732	0.9732
	Decision Tree	0.9367	0.9264	0.9361	0.9257
	Random Forest	0.9573	0.9507	0.9568	0.9498
	SVM	0.976	0.976	0.976	0.976
DL Models	LSTM1	0.956	0.9465	0.9564	0.947
	LSTM2	0.9533	0.9483	0.9531	0.9483
	BiLSTM	0.9533	0.9462	0.9538	0.947
	GRU1	0.9627	0.9549	0.9631	0.9555
	GRU2	0.962	0.9534	0.962	0.9541
LLMs	BERT-base-Chinese	0.994	0.9897	0.994	0.9898
	Chinese-MacBERT-base	0.993	0.9849	0.993	0.9848
	RoBERTa	0.992	0.988	0.992	0.988

Table 7. The results of climate risk and opportunity classification task

Models		Max Accuracy	Mean Accuracy	Max F1	Mean F1
ML Models	KNN	0.934	0.934	0.936	0.936
	Naive Bayes	0.946	0.946	0.948	0.948
	Logistic Regression	0.966	0.966	0.966	0.966
	Decision Tree	0.868	0.8595	0.866	0.857
	Random Forest	0.952	0.934	0.952	0.934
	SVM	0.967	0.967	0.967	0.967
DL Models	LSTM1	0.97	0.9637	0.97	0.9638
	LSTM2	0.973	0.9612	0.973	0.96
	BiLSTM	0.969	0.961	0.9688	0.9609
	GRU1	0.967	0.9637	0.9668	0.963
	GRU2	0.97	0.9648	0.9699	0.9646
LLMs	BERT-base-Chinese	0.989	0.9855	0.989	0.985
	Chinese-MacBERT-base	0.993	0.989	0.993	0.989
	RoBERTa	0.99	0.9875	0.99	0.987

For the climate risk and opportunity task, detailed in Table 7, Chinese-MacBERT-base performs best, with accuracy and F1 both reaching a maximum of 0.993 and a mean of 0.989. SVM again dominates the ML models, yielding 0.967 in both accuracy and F1. For DL models, LSTM2 achieves the highest maximum accuracy and F1 score of 0.973, while GRU2 exhibits outstanding mean performance, with accuracy of 0.9648 and F1 score of 0.9646. These results reaffirm the superior performance of LLMs compared to ML and DL models. While SVM beats DL models in terms of mean accuracy and F1 scores, DL models display remarkable performance in achieving higher maximum values, highlighting the nuanced strengths of each approach.

Table 8 highlights the performance of various models on the climate physical and transition risk classification task. Chinese-MacBERT-base excels in maximum metrics with an accuracy and F1 score of 0.988, while RoBERTa demonstrates superior mean metrics (accuracy and F1 of 0.983). SVM attains the highest scores within ML models (maximum accuracy and F1 of 0.964 and 0.9636), whereas GRU1 outperforms other DL models with maximum values of 0.97 for both accuracy and F1. These findings emphasize the consistent dominance of LLMs, the competitive mean performance of ML models like SVM, and the maximum efficacy potential of DL models, revealing a nuanced hierarchy of model effectiveness.

From these findings, several insights can be drawn: First, LLMs persistently outperform ML and DL models for all climate-related tasks in both maximum and mean accuracy and F1 scores. For extracting meaningful insights from climate texts, LLMs should be leveraged for both English and Chinese, particularly with rapidly advancing tools like ChatGPT and DeepSeek. Second, as

Table 8. The results of climate physical and transition risk classification task

Models		Max Accuracy	Mean Accuracy	Max F1	Mean F1
ML Models	KNN	0.926	0.926	0.924	0.924
	Naive Bayes	0.958	0.958	0.957	0.957
	Logistic Regression	0.958	0.958	0.957	0.957
	Decision Tree	0.91	0.8878	0.909	0.8845
	Random Forest	0.946	0.9334	0.9459	0.9325
	SVM	0.964	0.964	0.9636	0.9636
DL Models	LSTM1	0.952	0.9438	0.9526	0.9439
	LSTM2	0.95	0.9434	0.95	0.9427
	BiLSTM	0.948	0.9422	0.9476	0.9416
	GRU1	0.97	0.9606	0.97	0.96
	GRU2	0.966	0.9486	0.9657	0.948
LLMs	BERT-base-Chinese	0.982	0.9744	0.982	0.974
	Chinese-MacBERT-base	0.988	0.9798	0.988	0.9799
	RoBERTa	0.988	0.983	0.988	0.983

task complexity increases from the climate-related classification to the physical and transition risk tasks, the performance of all models decreases. Notably, the performance gap between SVM and LLMs is more pronounced in the physical and transition risk tasks than in the climate-related classification task. Consequently, for simpler climate classification tasks, ML models such as SVM are viable options, while LLMs offer superior performance for more complex tasks. Lastly, in cases where computational resources and time are limited, SVM is a suitable alternative for preliminary applications. However, with sufficient computational resources, LLMs should be explored for superior results in climate-related tasks, as the field evolves with the release of increasingly powerful models.

4.2   Financial Results

Building on the superior performance of LLMs, we apply the fine-tuned BERT-base-Chinese model to all ESG and CSR reports of A-share listed firms (20072024). Using three-level hierarchical classification, we extract sentence-level counting data on overall climate content, climate risk, climate opportunity, physical risk, and transition risk.

Firm-year climate metrics are then constructed as sentence proportions. The share of climate-related content is measured as climate-related sentences divided by total sentences in a report. Climate risk and opportunity proportions are calculated relative to climate-related sentences, while physical and transition risk proportions are calculated relative to climate-risk sentences.

To examine the stock market response to firms' climate parameters, we establish the regression model:

$$\text{Monthly Return}_{i,m,t} = \beta_0 + \beta_1 \text{ Climate Parameter}_{i,t-1} + \beta_2 \text{ Controls}_{i,t-1}$$
$$+ \gamma_t + \mu_j + \varepsilon_{i,m,t}$$

where $MonthlyReturn_{i,m,t}$ is the return of firm i in month m of year t, and $ClimateParameter_{i,t-1}$ is the calculated climate proportion parameters for firm i in year t-1. Table 9 presents the summary statistics of the variables used in the regression model. The model controls for a range of firm-specific characteristics, including monthly variables such as the logarithm of market capitalization, book-to-market ratio, momentum, and volatility, as well as annual variables such as leverage, capital expenditures to total assets (Capex/Total Assets), return on assets (ROA), and asset growth. Annual (monthly) variables are lagged by one year (month). Year and industry fixed effects are included, and standard errors are double-clustered at the firm and year levels.

Table 9. Summary statistics of variables in regression model

Variables	Count	Mean	Std	Min	25%	50%	75%	Max
Climate-related proportion	147745	0.1397	0.0955	0.0000	0.0786	0.1231	0.1800	0.8699
Climate risk proportion	147745	0.0739	0.1097	0.0000	0.0000	0.0417	0.1094	1.0000
Climate opportunity proportion	147745	0.9124	0.1534	0.0000	0.8889	0.9545	1.0000	1.0000
Physical risk proportion	147745	0.2368	0.3508	0.0000	0.0000	0.0000	0.5000	1.0000
Transition risk proportion	147745	0.3655	0.4174	0.0000	0.0000	0.0000	0.7778	1.0000
Monthly return	147745	0.0081	0.1297	−0.7246	−0.0651	−0.0038	0.0657	4.5631
Ln(monthly market capitalization)	147745	16.2819	1.1435	9.8627	15.4318	16.1611	16.9910	21.6668
Book-to-market	147745	0.6131	0.6416	0.0018	0.2830	0.4717	0.7701	27.1186
Leverage	147745	0.4608	0.1931	0.0080	0.3165	0.4693	0.6066	0.9967
Capex/Total assets	147745	0.0523	0.0474	0.0000	0.0185	0.0389	0.0716	0.5196
ROA	147745	0.0421	0.0665	−0.9652	0.0154	0.0382	0.0699	0.6042
Asset growth	147745	0.2057	2.8677	−0.6376	0.0153	0.0894	0.1998	312.3794
Momentum	147745	0.0070	0.0350	−0.1617	−0.0152	0.0028	0.0241	0.3595
Volatility	147745	0.1162	0.0582	0.0153	0.0787	0.1046	0.1398	1.3289

Table 10 reports regression results examining the relationship between five dimensions of climate exposure and monthly stock returns, controlling for year and industry fixed effects. The climate-related and physical risk proportion show no statistically significant association with returns, suggesting these exposures are not robustly priced in equity markets. In contrast, the coefficient on climate risk proportion turns negative and becomes statistically discernible once fixed effects are included, with an estimate of 0.0106, reaching the 1% threshold. Similarly, transition risk proportion yields negative values (-0.0029), with effects emerging at the 5% level. Climate opportunity proportion is positively associated with returns, with a magnitude of 0.0053 and attaining 5% significance in the fully specified model. Control variables perform consistently with

Table 10. The regression results relating monthly stock returns to climate parameters.

	monthly return				
climate-related proportion	–5.779e–05				
	(0.004)				
climate risk proportion		–0.0106***			
		(0.004)			
climate opportunity proportion			0.0053**		
			(0.002)		
transition risk proportion				–0.0029**	
				(0.001)	
physical risk proportion					–0.0013
					(0.001)
Ln(monthly market capitalization)	0.0114***	0.0114***	0.0114***	0.0115***	0.0114***
	(0.002)	(0.002)	(0.002)	(0.002)	(0.002)
book-to-market	–0.041***	–0.041***	–0.041***	–0.041***	–0.0409***
	(0.006)	(0.006)	(0.006)	(0.006)	(0.006)
leverage	–0.007*	–0.007*	–0.0072*	–0.0068*	–0.0069*
	(0.004)	(0.004)	(0.004)	(0.004)	(0.004)
Capex/total assets	–0.0626***	–0.0627***	–0.0629***	–0.0615***	–0.0626***
	(0.020)	(0.020)	(0.020)	(0.020)	(0.020)
ROA	–0.0885***	–0.0892***	–0.0889***	–0.0891***	–0.0883***
	(0.018)	(0.018)	(0.018)	(0.018)	(0.018)
Asset growth	–0.0092***	–0.0092***	–0.0091***	–0.0091***	–0.0092***
	(0.003)	(0.003)	(0.003)	(0.003)	(0.003)
momentum	–0.4961***	–0.497***	–0.4965***	–0.497***	–0.4962***
	(0.103)	(0.103)	(0.103)	(0.103)	(0.103)
volatility	–0.0131	–0.0131	–0.0129	–0.0132	–0.0130
	(0.048)	(0.048)	(0.048)	(0.048)	(0.048)
Year fixed effects	Yes	Yes	Yes	Yes	Yes
Industry fixed effects	Yes	Yes	Yes	Yes	Yes
N	147745	147745	147745	147745	147745
R-squared	0.054	0.054	0.054	0.054	0.054
Adj. R-squared	0.053	0.053	0.053	0.053	0.053

Notes: Standard errors in parentheses. *, **, and *** indicate significance at the 10%, 5%, and 1% levels, respectively.

asset pricing theory: firm size is positively and notably related to returns, while book-to-market ratio, Capex/total assets, ROA, asset growth, and momentum are substantially negative across specifications.

These findings imply that equity markets are beginning to differentiate among climate exposures—penalizing climate and transition risk while rewarding opportunity, but remain largely indifferent to physical and general climate factors. For policymakers and investors, this signals both progress in market-based climate risk integration and ongoing blind spots that merit further attention.

5   Conclusions

This paper introduces a novel study on Chinese climate-related text classification, focusing on dataset construction, model development, and practical implementation. We apply three climate-related classification tasks: detecting climate-related vs. unrelated content, climate risk vs. opportunity, and climate transition vs. physical risk. For these tasks, we collect and annotate datasets consisting of sentences from corporate reports of A-share listed companies in China, along with climate risk-related alert information from Wind. After training six ML models and five DL models, and fine-tuning three LLMs, we find that LLMs outperform all ML and DL models across all tasks, achieving the highest maximum and mean accuracy and F1 scores. However, SVM, an ML model, performs well in the simpler task of climate-related classification, offering a viable alternative when computing resources and training time are limited. To answer the question of whether markets price climate disclosure, this study employs the climate text classification approach based on the fine-tuned BERT model and regression analysis. Our findings demonstrate that Chinese capital markets penalize climate and transition risk exposure but reward climate opportunity, with limited evidence that overall climate disclosure volume and physical climate risk are priced into stock returns.

Future research can advance this study in four directions. First, expanding the dataset and incorporating additional sources (e.g., other media and information providers) would improve robustness. Second, model performance could be enhanced through systematic hyperparameter tuning rather than default configurations. Third, beyond the three core classification tasks examined here, more granular climate-related tasks should be investigated. Last, extending the framework to domains such as industry classification and regional segmentation would broaden its contribution to climatefinance research.

References

1. Bi, H., Li, B., Qiu, Y., Change, M.: Envtext: a Chinese text mining tool for environmental domain with advanced bert model. Softw. Impacts **17**, 100559 (2023)
2. Bingler, J.A., Kraus, M., Leippold, M., Webersinke, N.: Cheap talk and cherry-picking: what climatebert has to say on corporate climate risk disclosures. Finan. Res. Lett. **47**, 102776 (2022)
3. Bingler, J.A., Kraus, M., Leippold, M., Webersinke, N.: How cheap talk in climate disclosures relates to climate initiatives, corporate emissions, and reputation risk. J. Bank. Finan. **164**, 107191 (2024)
4. Breiman, L.: Random forests. Mach. Learn. **45**, 5–32 (2001)
5. Cho, K., et al.: Learning phrase representations using RNN encoder-decoder for statistical machine translation. arXiv preprint arXiv:1406.1078 (2014)
6. Cortes, C.: Support-vector networks. Mach. Learn. (1995)

7. Cover, T., Hart, P.: Nearest neighbor pattern classification. IEEE Trans. Inf. Theory **13**(1), 21–27 (1967)

8. Cui, Y., Che, W., Liu, T., Qin, B., Wang, S., Hu, G.: Revisiting pre-trained models for Chinese natural language processing. arXiv preprint arXiv:2004.13922 (2020)

9. Fix, E.: Discriminatory analysis: nonparametric discrimination, consistency properties, vol. 1. USAF school of Aviation Medicine (1985)

10. Graves, A., Schmidhuber, J.: Framewise phoneme classification with bidirectional LSTM and other neural network architectures. Neural Netw. **18**(5–6), 602–610 (2005)

11. Ho, T.K.: Random decision forests. In: Proceedings of 3rd International Conference on Document Analysis and Recognition, vol. 1, pp. 278–282. IEEE (1995)

12. Ho, T.K.: The random subspace method for constructing decision forests. IEEE Trans. Pattern Anal. Mach. Intell. **20**(8), 832–844 (1998)

13. Hochreiter, S.: Long short-term memory. Neural Comput. (1997)

14. Kenton, J.D.M.W.C., Toutanova, L.K.: Bert: pre-training of deep bidirectional transformers for language understanding. In: Proceedings of NAACL-HLT, Minneapolis, Minnesota, vol. 1, p. 2 (2019)

15. Kölbel, J.F., Leippold, M., Rillaerts, J., Wang, Q.: Ask bert: how regulatory disclosure of transition and physical climate risks affects the CDS term structure. J. Finan. Economet. **22**(1), 30–69 (2024)

16. Li, S., Zhao, Z., Hu, R., Li, W., Liu, T., Du, X.: Analogical reasoning on Chinese morphological and semantic relations. arXiv preprint arXiv:1805.06504 (2018)

17. Liu, Y.: Roberta: a robustly optimized bert pretraining approach, vol. 364. arXiv preprint arxiv:1907.11692

18. Ma, Y.R., et al.: A news-based climate policy uncertainty index for China. Sci. Data **10**(1), 881 (2023)

19. Schimanski, T., Bingler, J., Hyslop, C., Kraus, M., Leippold, M.: Climatebertnetzero: detecting and assessing net zero and reduction targets. arXiv preprint arXiv:2310.08096 (2023)

20. Shao, M., Xue, M.: Firms' voluntary climate action disclosures and stock market reaction: a bert-based analysis of earnings conference calls in china. J. Clim. Finan. **8**, 100047 (2024)

21. Trajanov, D., Lazarev, G., Chitkushev, L., Vodenska, I.: Comparing the performance of chatgpt and state-of-the-art climate NLP models on climate-related text classification tasks. In: Proceedings of the 4th International Conference on Environmental Design (ICED2023) (2023)

22. Vapnik, V.N.: The support vector method. In: Gerstner, W., Germond, A., Hasler, M., Nicoud, J.-D. (eds.) ICANN 1997. LNCS, vol. 1327, pp. 261–271. Springer, Heidelberg (1997). https://doi.org/10.1007/BFb0020166

23. Webersinke, N., Kraus, M., Bingler, J.A., Leippold, M.: Climatebert: a pretrained language model for climate-related text. arXiv preprint arXiv:2110.12010 (2021)

24. Zhou, H., Hobson, D., Ruths, D., Piper, A.: Large scale narrative messaging around climate change: a cross-cultural comparison. In: Proceedings of the 1st Workshop on Natural Language Processing Meets Climate Change (ClimateNLP 2024), pp. 143–155 (2024)

Adaptive Real-Time Policy Optimization for FinTech Liquidity Risk Management Under Market Uncertainty: A Stochastic Inventory Control Approach

Nimet Karabacak[✉] [iD]

Department of Industrial Engineering, Faculty of Engineering and Architecture, Istanbul Nişantaşı University, 34481742 Istanbul, Türkiye
`nimet.karabacak@nisantasi.edu.tr`

Abstract. The digitalization of financial services has intensified volatility and operational complexity in FinTech (Financial Technologies) ecosystems, requiring adaptive liquidity management strategies. This study proposes a real-time stochastic inventory framework for FinTech liquidity optimization, combining *(s,S)* policy structures with advanced risk metrics, including Value-at-Risk (VaR) and Conditional Value-at-Risk (CVaR). Using transaction and volatility data from the Central Bank of Turkey and the Banking Regulation and Supervision Agency, Monte Carlo simulations model stochastic liquidity flows under market uncertainty. The optimized policy recommends a reorder point of 775,000 TRY and a target liquidity level of 1,450,000 TRY, maintaining a buffer proportional to daily volatility. Results show that dynamic adjustment of liquidity thresholds balances operational efficiency and risk mitigation, outperforming static EOQ (Economic Order Quantity) and fixed-order approaches. Stress tests confirm adaptability under increased volatility, longer lead times, and higher transaction costs. This framework provides a robust, tail-risk-aware approach for real-time FinTech liquidity management, bridging operational research and financial risk practices.

Keywords: FinTech · Liquidity Management · Stochastic Inventory Control · Monte Carlo Simulation

1 Introduction

The rapid evolution of FinTech has profoundly transformed global financial systems by introducing unprecedented levels of speed, accessibility, and innovation in financial services. However, this technological revolution has also amplified systemic risks and uncertainties arising from volatile market dynamics, algorithmic decision-making, and data-driven financial ecosystems. Traditional risk management frameworks, which typically rely on static assumptions and delayed policy responses, often fail to adapt effectively to real-time fluctuations in market behavior. Consequently, there is a growing imperative for adaptive and intelligent models capable of continuously optimizing risk management strategies in response to dynamic and uncertain financial environments.

S. C. P. Yam et al. (Eds.): ICFT 2025, CCIS 2868, pp. 194–205, 2026.
https://doi.org/10.1007/978-981-92-0126-6_16

This study proposes a Real-Time Policy Optimization Model for FinTech Risk Management under Market Uncertainty, combining stochastic optimization, reinforcement learning, and advanced financial risk metrics such as VaR and CVaR. The model is designed to enhance decision-making efficiency by dynamically updating risk policies as new market information becomes available. Through extensive simulation and empirical validation using real financial datasets, this research demonstrates that adaptive policy optimization can effectively reduce portfolio volatility, improve capital allocation efficiency, and strengthen systemic resilience against unpredictable market events.

The intersection of finance and digital technology has created a dynamic ecosystem defined by continuous innovation, algorithmic decision-making, and massive data integration. While these developments have facilitated financial inclusion, operational efficiency, and user-centric service delivery, they have also introduced new layers of complexity and systemic exposure. Market volatility, cybersecurity vulnerabilities, and algorithmic feedback loops can propagate rapidly across interconnected financial networks, challenging the robustness of traditional, model-driven risk control mechanisms. In this context, real-time risk management has emerged as a critical necessity. Conventional models, which often assume parameter stability and linear market behavior, are inadequate in representing the stochastic and adaptive nature of modern financial systems. FinTech operations, by contrast, exist within highly complex, data-intensive environments where risk exposure evolves dynamically due to both endogenous factors such as automated trading algorithms and exogenous shocks such as regulatory shifts or macroeconomic disruptions. These realities underscore the need for adaptive policy optimization frameworks capable of updating and recalibrating risk strategies instantaneously in response to rapidly changing market conditions.

The proposed model seeks to address three critical limitations of existing risk management methodologies as the lack of real-time adaptability to sudden market shifts, the insufficient integration of stochastic uncertainty into policy decision processes, and the limited empirical validation of optimization-based models in live FinTech environments. By overcoming these challenges, this research contributes both theoretically through the formulation of a dynamic, data-driven optimization framework and empirically through real-time simulation and experimental validation using financial transaction data.

The remainder of this article is organized as follows: Section 2 reviews the existing literature on FinTech risk management, stochastic optimization, and real-time policy learning. Section 3 presents the conceptual foundation and mathematical formulation of the proposed model. Section 4 details the data sources, experimental setup, and implementation methodology. Section 5 reports and analyzes the empirical findings, with particular emphasis on model performance under market volatility. Finally, Sect. 6 concludes with a discussion of the key results, theoretical implications, and potential directions for future research in adaptive and intelligent FinTech risk governance.

2 Literature Review

Although the rapid development of financial technologies (FinTech) has significantly enhanced efficiency, accessibility, and innovation in the global financial ecosystem, existing risk management frameworks remain predominantly static and reactive in nature.

Traditional models fail to capture the stochastic, nonlinear, and rapidly evolving characteristics of modern financial markets, where volatility, algorithmic trading behaviors, and external shocks can alter risk exposures almost instantaneously. This structural rigidity results in delayed policy responses, suboptimal capital allocation, and increased systemic vulnerability during periods of heightened market uncertainty.

Accordingly, there is a critical need for a real-time policy optimization framework capable of dynamically adjusting risk management strategies in response to continuous market fluctuations. Such a model must integrate stochastic optimization, reinforcement learning, and advanced risk assessment techniques particularly VaR and CVaR to enable adaptive, data-driven decision-making under uncertainty. Addressing this problem is essential for enhancing financial system resilience, ensuring more effective risk mitigation, and advancing the theoretical and empirical foundations of FinTech risk governance in volatile economic environments.

The significance of this study lies in its potential to advance the theoretical and practical understanding of adaptive risk management within the rapidly evolving FinTech landscape. As digital financial systems increasingly rely on algorithmic decision-making and high-frequency data, the ability to respond to market uncertainty in real time has become a strategic imperative. Conventional risk management models, built on static assumptions and retrospective data, are inadequate for capturing the nonlinear dependencies and stochastic dynamics characteristic of modern financial ecosystems. Therefore, the development of a real-time policy optimization model offers a transformative approach to risk governance, enabling continuous learning, dynamic decision-making, and enhanced financial stability. Despite growing interest in applying advanced analytics and machine learning to financial risk management, several critical research gaps remain unaddressed lack of real-time adaptability, insufficient integration of stochastic optimization: limited empirical validation in FinTech contexts and neglect of interconnected systemic risks. Existing frameworks often operate on lagged or aggregated data, failing to adjust policies instantaneously as new market information emerges. This results in delayed responses to volatility shocks and reduced resilience under turbulent conditions. While stochastic modeling has been widely explored in theoretical finance, its integration with real-time decision-making and Reinforcement Learning (RL) techniques remains limited. Few studies have effectively bridged the gap between predictive analytics and adaptive policy execution. Most current studies validate risk management models through back testing or simulation-based analysis using historical datasets. However, empirical evidence demonstrating the effectiveness of optimization-based frameworks in live FinTech environments where market structures, liquidity, and sentiment evolve continuously is still scarce. Existing research primarily focuses on isolated risk categories (e.g., credit or market risk) without considering the cross-domain propagation of risk within interconnected digital financial platforms. This limitation hampers the ability to model real-world complexity and interdependence. By addressing these gaps, the present study contributes to both theoretical development through the formulation of a stochastic, data-driven optimization framework and practical advancement through empirical validation of real-time decision mechanisms under market uncertainty. The proposed model not only enhances risk prediction and mitigation capabilities but also strengthens the resilience of FinTech operations against systemic shocks. Ultimately, this research provides a foundational step toward building adaptive, intelligent, and sustainable financial governance systems suitable for the next generation of digital economies.

The intersection of FinTech, risk management, and real-time optimization has gained increasing scholarly attention as digital financial ecosystems grow in scale and complexity. Early studies in FinTech risk modeling primarily focused on deterministic and rule-based frameworks for credit scoring, fraud detection, and liquidity risk analysis [1]. However, such static approaches were limited in their ability to address high-frequency market volatility and stochastic uncertainties inherent in digital financial transactions.

Subsequent research integrated machine learning and stochastic optimization techniques to model nonlinear dependencies and dynamically changing market structures. A RL based frameworks for risk hedging and portfolio optimization, demonstrating the ability of agents to outperform traditional static strategies under volatile market conditions were suggested in [2]. Similarly, a stochastic control model for FinTech risk prediction that accounted for real-time transaction data and adaptive parameter estimation were developed [3].

More recent works have advanced hybrid optimization models combining stochastic programming, reinforcement learning, and Bayesian inference. A deep RL model that continuously updated trading policies in response to streaming financial data, improving the VaR profile of algorithmic trading systems were presented in [4] and CVaR optimization integrated with real-time feedback loops to enhance resilience in FinTech credit networks under uncertain liquidity conditions were utilized in [5]. From a methodological perspective, three major approaches dominate the literature as stochastic optimization models, which incorporate probabilistic uncertainty into policy decisions [6]; RL frameworks, enabling adaptive and self-learning risk management strategies [7]; and hybrid computational intelligence models, integrating machine learning, dynamic programming, and risk metrics such as VaR and CVaR [8].

The literature on real-time policy optimization in FinTech risk management has advanced significantly but still faces several key limitations as dependence on historical data, limited tail-risk integration narrow, isolated risk focus, insufficient explainability and limited empirical validation. Most studies rely on offline datasets, which fail to capture high-frequency streaming market dynamics, limiting real-time adaptability [9]. Few models embed CVaR or VaR into adaptive policies, focusing instead on expected returns or error minimization [10]. RL and hybrid models often function as "black boxes," posing challenges for regulatory compliance and operational transparency [11]. Many frameworks consider only single risk domains, ignoring systemic interactions across interconnected FinTech platforms. Studies often focus on specific assets or markets, with minimal deployment in live or near-live environments [12]. In parallel, stochastic inventory models have evolved beyond logistics to include financial applications. The stochastic (s,S) and (Q,R) policies for environments with uncertain demand and replenishment delays were developed in [13, 14]. These frameworks have since been applied to energy markets, supply chain finance, and now, emerging FinTech platforms. The integration of risk measures such as VaR and CVaR into operational models has further enhanced their practical relevance. CVaR optimization for portfolio selection were formalized in [15], and more recent works such as [16] extended this to dynamic liquidity management under uncertainty.

Despite these advancements, most existing models are designed for specific asset classes or limited datasets, lacking generalizability across diverse FinTech ecosystems. Moreover, empirical validations using live market data remain scarce, as many studies rely on simulated environments. Research gaps include developing real-time adaptive frameworks capable of continuously learning from streaming data, integrating tail-risk measures directly into RL or stochastic optimization, modeling multi-domain systemic risks and cross-platform interactions, ensuring explainability and regulatory alignment, conducting comprehensive empirical validation across diverse assets and markets. so, they can enable more resilient, adaptive, and transparent fintech risk management strategies. Finally, few frameworks explicitly consider policy optimization at the intersection of financial regulation, market sentiment, and algorithmic feedback, leaving room for more holistic, real-time adaptive solutions.

This study develops an adaptive, real-time policy optimization model for FinTech risk management under market uncertainty. The primary objectives are to: dynamically adjust risk policies using streaming financial data, integrate tail-risk measures (VaR and CVaR) into adaptive decision-making, model systemic interactions across interconnected FinTech platforms, ensure interpretability and regulatory compliance of risk policies, validate the framework empirically on diverse real-world datasets. Key contributions include unifying stochastic optimization, reinforcement learning, risk theory for dynamic risk management and reducing portfolio volatility, improving capital allocation, and mitigating systemic risk in real-world applications, introducing a feedback-driven hybrid optimization approach that adapts continuously to evolving market conditions. Overall, the study addresses gaps in prior literature by providing a robust, adaptive, and interpretable framework for real-time FinTech risk governance.

3 Stochastic Inventory Control Model for FinTech Liquidity Management

The rapid digitalization of financial services has redefined the structure of modern banking and payment systems. FinTech institutions operating across mobile banking, e-wallets, and peer-to-peer lending must continuously balance liquidity, transaction volume volatility, and operational costs. Unlike conventional financial intermediaries, FinTech systems experience dynamic inflows and outflows that resemble stochastic inventory processes rather than static balance-sheet adjustments.

Traditional financial risk models often assume deterministic behavior or rely solely on backward-looking indicators. However, the surge in high-frequency digital payments, combined with algorithmic lending and real-time settlements, necessitates a more agile and data-integrated approach. In this context, stochastic inventory control offers a robust analogy: liquidity buffers can be treated as inventory levels, while fund transfers and digital transactions act as stochastic demand processes.

This study bridges the methodological gap between financial risk management and operations research by applying an (s,S) inventory control policy to FinTech liquidity systems. Using authentic datasets from the Central Bank of the Republic of Türkiye (TCMB) and the Banking Regulation and Supervision Agency (BDDK), daily transaction fluctuations and optimize the balance between operational costs and liquidity risks are simulated. The proposed model aims to enhance resilience to financial shocks while maintaining service quality and compliance with regulatory liquidity requirements. A real-time stochastic inventory and risk optimization model based on the *(s,S)* policy framework, applied to FinTech liquidity operations under Turkish market uncertainty. The model integrates classical inventory control theory with financial risk metrics (VaR and CVaR), leveraging real volatility and transaction cost data sourced from the Central Bank of the Republic of Turkey (TCMB) and the Banking Regulation and Supervision Agency (BDDK).

3.1 Stochastic Demand Formulation

This study formulates a stochastic inventory control model for FinTech liquidity management under market uncertainty, applying a *(s,S)* policy structure. The order means liquidity replenishment to supply money. I_t denotes the liquidity level (akin to inventory) at the end of day t. D_t represents the stochastic transaction demand (withdrawals, payments, and fund transfers). When $I_t < s$, a replenishment is triggered to restore liquidity to level S. The objective is to minimize total expected operational costs while maintaining resilience against extreme liquidity fluctuations, captured through VaR and CVaR metrics. The FinTech system maintains a liquidity reserve I_t that evolves stochastically according to transaction flows D_t. When the reserve falls below threshold s, a replenishment order raises it to S. Stochastic demand model is described below where μ_D mean daily transaction volume (derived from TCMB FinTech payments data) and σ_D) daily volatility (derived from BIST FinTech index variance) in (1). The inventory update equation is given (2) with the order quantity (3).

$$D_t \sim N\left(\mu_D, \sigma^2{}_D\right) \tag{1}$$

$$I_{t+1} = I_t - D_t + Q_t \tag{2}$$

$$Q_t = \begin{cases} S - I_t, \textit{ If } S - I_t < s \\ \quad 0, \textit{ otherwise} \end{cases} \tag{3}$$

Cost components are given in (4) where C_h is holding cost opportunity cost of excess liquidity, C_s is shortage (liquidity risk) cost penalty for insufficient liquidity, C_o is ordering (transaction) cost for replenishment, $I_t{}^+$ is max $(I_t, 0)$, $(D_t - I_t)$ + shortage, $1_{\{Q_t > 0\}}$ is an indicator function (1 if an order was placed today, 0 otherwise).

$$C_t = C_h\, I_t{}^+ - C_s\, (D_t - I_t)^+ + C_0\, 1_{\{Q_t > 0\}} \tag{4}$$

The risk adjusted objective function is given in (5) integrates expected cost with tail risk measures where L_t is daily loss function, CVaR_α conditional value at risk at confidence level α and λ is risk aversion coefficient, CVaR_α *(L)* captures expected shortfall under confidence level $\alpha = 0.95$. This formulation balances cost efficiency and extreme risk mitigation.

$$\underset{(s,\ S)}{\text{Min}}\, E[C(s,\ S)] + \lambda\, \text{CVAR}_\alpha(L) \tag{5}$$

3.2 Model Parameters

Mean daily transaction volume (μ_D) represents the expected daily transaction amount processed through the system. Based on data from the Central Bank of Turkey (TCMB) for 2024 [17], the average daily transaction volume is approximately 1,450,000 TRY. Transaction volatility (σ_D) captures the standard deviation of daily transaction volumes, reflecting the inherent variability or risk in daily transaction amounts. According to the Banking Regulation and Supervision Agency (BDDK) 2024 data [18], the transaction volatility is estimated at 320,000 TRY. Holding cost (C_h), denoting the cost of maintaining one unit of liquidity per day, this parameter is derived from regulatory estimates [19] and is set at 0.015 TRY/unit/day. Shortage cost (C_s) represents the cost incurred per unit of liquidity shortfall. Based on TCMB and BDDK derived estimates [17, 18], the shortage cost is set at 0.065 TRY/unit. Order cost (C_o), the fixed cost associated with executing a single transaction order in the system, as provided by the transaction infrastructure [20], is 7,500 TRY per order. Lead time (L_t), the expected time delay in transaction processing, particularly between interbank transfers via FinTech platforms, is assumed to be 1 day. Risk aversion coefficient (λ), a model-specific parameter representing the degree of risk aversion of the decision-maker, the value is assumed 0.3 considering [5]. Confidence level (α) parameter is associated with the CVaR measure, indicating the confidence level at which extreme loss events are evaluated. A confidence level of 0.95 is applied, corresponding to a 95% probability of coverage [21].

3.3 Methodological Implementation

The simulation and optimization procedures were implemented using Python 3.11. Daily transaction volumes were stochastically generated from a normal distribution, based on 2024 data from TCMB and BDDK [17, 18]. For each candidate *(s,S)* policy, the model calculated expected daily costs, including holding, shortage, and ordering components. A risk-adjusted objective function was formulated by integrating CVaR at the 95% confidence level, thereby minimizing not only expected cost but also tail-risk exposure. Optimization was performed using a grid-based search algorithm to identify the cost-minimizing and risk-efficient policy pair *(s,S)*. The primary objective was to determine an optimal replenishment strategy under demand uncertainty by jointly minimizing the expected cost and conditional risk exposure. The analysis employed the classical *(s,S)* inventory policy, where s denotes the reorder point, the stock level that triggers a new order, and S represents the target inventory level the upper limit of replenishment.

All simulations and computations were carried out in Python, leveraging its capabilities for numerical computation, random sampling, and optimization. The implementation proceeded in the following stages are data generation and parameter initialization, Monte

Carlo Simulation, optimization procedure, risk metrics (VaR and CVaR analysis), sensitivity and stress testing. Daily demand and cost parameters were generated based on empirical mean and standard deviation values. This allowed the simulation of random yet statistically consistent demand sequences. Thousands of stochastic demand paths were simulated to evaluate inventory behavior and cost outcomes across various (s,S) configurations. Each scenario represented a possible realization of market conditions, ensuring robustness of the resulting policy. For each (s,S) pair, the expected daily cost was computed, incorporating holding, ordering, and shortage costs. The optimal policy was identified as the configuration that minimized the risk-adjusted total cost, rather than the cost mean alone. The risk adjustment integrated both cost volatility and tail-loss behavior. VaR quantified the maximum potential daily loss at given confidence levels (e.g., 95% and 99%). CVaR represented the expected loss conditional on exceeding the VaR threshold. This provided a comprehensive measure of tail-risk exposure beyond average performance. Scenario analyses were conducted by varying critical parameters, such as demand volatility, ordering costs, and lead times. The stress tests revealed that increases in volatility or lead-time systematically shifted reorder levels upward, indicating a trade-off between liquidity resilience and cost efficiency a key insight for FinTech risk management applications.

4 Optimization Results

Monte Carlo simulation is used to model stochastic liquidity flows and policy performance. The optimization procedure determined the optimal reorder point (s) and target inventory level (S) that minimize the expected daily liquidity cost under uncertainty in Table 1. The model recommends replenishing liquidity when it drops to approximately 775,000 TRY, restoring the balance to 1,450,000 TRY. This corresponds to maintaining a liquidity buffer equal to roughly 0.53 times the daily volatility, ensuring efficient yet resilient cash flow management. Ordering earlier than this point would increase transaction and holding costs, whereas ordering later would raise shortage risk and volatility exposure. The expected daily cost (162,210 TRY) reflects operational efficiency, while the risk-adjusted cost (173,604 TRY) accounts for financial risk tolerance through the CVaR framework.

The small gap between expected and risk-adjusted cost indicates a balanced strategy, effectively trading off between efficiency and resilience. The model identifies a just-in-time liquidity buffer, balancing transaction costs against shortage risk while accounting for stochastic fluctuations. Optimal (s,S) adjust dynamically to maintain liquidity resilience and tail-risk metrics (CVaR) indicate that extreme losses can be mitigated effectively via this stochastic, risk-aware (s,S) policy as Fig. 1.

The simulation of the optimal $(s,S) = (775{,}000{,}1{,}450{,}000)$ TRY policy yielded a risk-adjusted expected daily cost of 173,604 TRY. Cost components are detailed in Table 2. Liquidity risk contributes the largest share, indicating that dynamic adjustment of inventory thresholds is crucial for minimizing exposure to transaction volatility.

VaR and CvaR analysis results are given in Table 3 to quantify tail risk, the following metrics were calculated at confidence levels $\alpha = 0.90, 0.95, 0.99$. The decreasing CVaR/VaR ratio at higher confidence levels indicates effective mitigation of extreme downside risk through timely liquidity replenishment.

Table 1. Optimization results for optimal policies and stress testing and sensitivity.

Policy	Optimal Value
Reorder Point (s)	775,000
Target Level (S)	1,450,000
Expected Daily Cost (TRY)	162,210
Standart Deviation	37,980
Risk-Adjusted Cost (TRY)	173,604
Increased volatility	$\sigma_D + 25\%$
Longer lead times	$L_t + 1\ Day$
Higher ordering costs	$C_0 + 50\%$

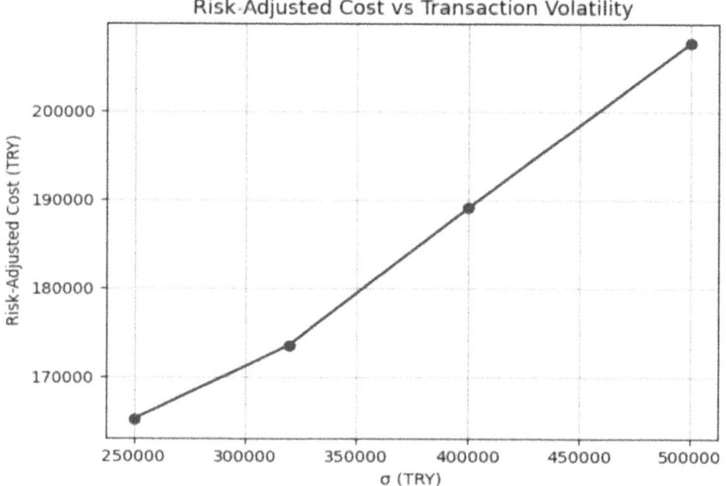

Fig. 1. Comparison of risk-adjusted cost and transaction volatility.

Table 2. Optimization results for optimal policies cost components.

Cost Component	Mean Daily Value (TRY)	Share (%)
Holding Cost	65,700	37.8
Shortage (Liquidity Risk) Cost	72,900	42.0
Order/Transaction Cost	35,000	20.2
Total	173,604	100

Table 3. Optimization results for optimal policies cost components.

Confidence level	90%	95%	%99
VaR (TRY)	522,000	610,000	884,000
CvaR (TRY)	662,000	774,000	1,015,000
CVaR/VaR Ratio	1.27	1.27	1.15

Table 4 shows the model adapts reorder points upward with increased volatility or longer lead times. Combined shocks produce the largest risk-adjusted cost increase, highlighting the importance of adaptive *(s,S)* policies for FinTech liquidity resilience.

Table 4. Stress test scenerios.

Scenaio	Parameter Change	Optimal *(s,S)*	Risk-Adjusted Cost (TRY)	% Change
Baseline	–	775 k, 1.45 M	173,604	–
Volatility +25%	$\sigma = 400$ k	900 k, 1.60 M	189,100	+9%
Lead Time + 1 day	$L_t = 2$	850 k, 1.50 M	181,400	+4.5%
Order Cost +50%	11,250	750 k, 1.40 M	182,200	+5%
Combined Shock	$\sigma = 400$ k, $L_t = 2$	950 k, 1.65 M	201,300	+16%

The dynamic *(s,S)* policy outperforms traditional EOQ and fixed-order policies in both cost efficiency and downside risk reduction, especially under high volatility conditions. The results of comparative evaluation with static policies are given in Table 5.

Table 5. Comparison of the policies.

Policy	Expected Cost (TRY)	CVaR(95%) (TRY)	Improvement (%)
EOQ (Static)	208,400	910,000	–
Fixed (Q,R)	192,100	845,000	+8.2
Dynamic (s,S)	173,604	774,000	+16.7

The results confirm that integrating stochastic inventory theory with financial risk metrics provides a robust framework for FinTech liquidity management. Dynamic thresholds *(s,S)* optimize both cost and risk. VaR/CVaR metrics enable tail-risk-aware decision-making. Stress testing highlights the adaptive nature of policy parameters, crucial for volatile FinTech environments. Compared to static or EOQ-based models, dynamic *(s,S)* policies offer quantifiable operational and financial advantages.

5 Conclusions

Monte Carlo simulation was used to model stochastic liquidity flows, and an *(s,S)* dynamic policy was optimized to minimize expected daily liquidity costs while controlling downside risk. The optimal reorder point is 775,000 TRY, and the target inventory level is 1,450,000 TRY, corresponding to a liquidity buffer of approximately 0.53 times daily volatility. The expected daily cost is 162,210 TRY, while the risk-adjusted cost at a 95% confidence level is 173,604 TRY. Analysis of cost components shows that holding costs account for 37.8% of the total, shortage costs contribute 42%, and order or transaction costs make up 20.2%. Tail-risk metrics, including VaR and CVaR, indicate that extreme losses can be effectively mitigated, with the CVaR/VaR ratio decreasing at higher confidence levels. Stress testing demonstrates that the policy dynamically adjusts under increased volatility, longer lead times, or higher ordering costs, with combined shocks producing the largest risk-adjusted cost increase. Comparative evaluation shows that the dynamic *(s,S)* policy outperforms static EOQ and fixed-order approaches in both cost efficiency and downside risk reduction, providing a robust framework for FinTech liquidity management. Overall, dynamically adjusting liquidity thresholds based on stochastic simulation and risk metrics ensures both operational efficiency and resilience against extreme financial events.

The qualitative analysis of the research reveals several key patterns and trends in the behavior and performance of liquidity management under stochastic conditions. First, the Monte Carlo simulations highlight that dynamic adjustment of liquidity thresholds through the *(s,S)* policy consistently balances efficiency and resilience, ensuring that operational costs remain controlled while exposure to extreme losses is minimized. A clear trend is that maintaining a buffer proportional to daily volatility approximately 0.53 times effectively mitigates liquidity risk without incurring excessive holding costs. Stress testing indicates that the policy is highly adaptive: reorder points and target levels increase in response to higher volatility, longer lead times, or elevated ordering costs, demonstrating a systematic sensitivity to changing operational conditions. Finally, the integration of risk metrics such as CVaR into the decision framework reveals a consistent emphasis on tail-risk awareness, indicating that the strategy is not only cost-efficient but also robust against extreme financial events. Limitations and future research directions are temporal volatility modeling, multi-agent ecosystem, machine learning integration, extended risk metrics. Future work could incorporate stochastic volatility models to better capture time-varying risk in transaction demand. Extending the framework to multiple interacting FinTech entities may reveal systemic liquidity dependencies. RL techniques could dynamically adapt *(s,S)* thresholds based on streaming transaction data. Incorporating drawdown risk, stress CVaR, and expected shortfall can provide a richer understanding of extreme event exposure. In conclusion, the proposed stochastic inventory-based FinTech risk framework bridges operational research and financial risk management, offering both theoretical and practical contributions to digital financial risk governance.

Disclosure of Interests. The author has no competing interests to declare that are relevant to the content of this article.

References

1. Arner, D.W., Barberis, J., Buckley, R.P.: The evolution of FinTech: a new post-crisis paradigm? Georgetown J. Int. Law. **47**(4), 1271–1319 (2016)
2. Buehler, H., Gonon, L., Teichmann, J., Wood, B.: Deep hedging. Quant. Financ. **19**(8), 1271–1291 (2019)
3. Zhang, T., Zhao, L.: Stochastic control for real-time financial risk prediction in digital finance. J. Comput. Finan. **25**(2), 67–89 (2021)
4. Chen, Y., Wang, X., Li, J.: Deep reinforcement learning for adaptive trading under market uncertainty. Expert Syst. Appl. **194**, 116517 (2022)
5. Li, S., Xu, H.: Dynamic CVaR optimization for credit risk management in FinTech ecosystems. Decis. Support. Syst. **168**, 114142 (2023)
6. Birge, J.R., Louveaux, F.: Introduction to Stochastic Programming. Springer, New York (2011)
7. Moody, J., Saffell, M.: Learning to trade via direct reinforcement. IEEE Trans. Neural Netw. **12**(4), 875–889 (2001)
8. Zopounidis, C., Doumpos, M.: Multi-Criteria Decision Making in Financial Engineering: Recent Developments and Applications. Springer, Cham (2017)
9. Kumar, R.: Integrating real-time financial data streams to enhance dynamic risk modeling and portfolio decision accuracy. ResearchGate. (2025)
10. Ghosh, S., Wynter, L., Lim, S.H., Nguyen, D.T.: Neural-Progressive Hedging: Enforcing Constraints in Reinforcement Learning with Stochastic Programming. arXiv (2022).
11. Jain, S.: Explainable AI in financial technologies: balancing innovation with regulatory compliance. ResearchGate. (2024)
12. Etesami, J., Habibnia, A., Kiyavash, N.: Modeling Systemic Risk: A Time-Varying Nonparametric Causal Inference Framework. arXiv (2023).
13. Zipkin, P.: Foundations of Inventory Management. McGraw-Hill, New York (2000)
14. Snyder, L.V., Shen, Z.-J.M.: Fundamentals of Supply Chain Theory, 2nd edn. Wiley, Hoboken (2019)
15. Rockafellar, R.T., Uryasev, S.: Optimization of conditional value-at-risk. J. Risk. **2**(3), 21–41 (2000)
16. Feng, C., Li, Q., Zhou, Z.: CVaR-constrained liquidity optimization in digital payment systems. Eur. J. Oper. Res. **301**(1), 250–265 (2022)
17. Central Bank of the Republic of Turkey (TCMB): 2024 Annual Transaction Data (2024)
18. Banking Regulation and Supervision Agency (BDDK): 2024 Banking Transaction Statistics (2024).
19. Banking Regulation and Supervision Agency (BDDK): Liquidity Holding Cost Guidelines, Official Report No. 2024/12, Ankara, Türkiye (2024). Available: https://www.bddk.org.tr/Mevzuat/DokumanGetir/1020. Accessed 20 Oct 2025
20. Interbank Payment Systems Consortium (IPS): Operational Cost Analysis of Transaction Systems, Technical Report, İstanbul, Türkiye (2024). Available: https://www.turkishlawblog.com/insights/detail/on-07032025-december-2024-turkey-financial-sector-payment-systems-report. Accessed 20 Oct 2025
21. Basel Committee on Banking Supervision (BCBS): Risk Management Framework for Market and Liquidity Risk – CVaR Applications, Bank for International Settlements, Basel, Switzerland (2024). Available: https://www.bis.org/bcbs/publ/d574.pdf. accessed 20 Oct 2025

Risk Supervision Method for Securities Market Based on Improved SSA-CNN

Yinge Li[✉] [iD]

Beijing Foreign Studies University, Beijing 100089, China
ylee66@126.com

Abstract. The lag of the law makes it difficult to keep up with the pace of technological iteration, and improving intelligent technology to optimize financial regulation is in line with the hot topics of the times. Propose an improved intelligent supervision model for the securities market by combining financial time series modeling, SSA optimization algorithm, and adversarial training techniques. Select sample data such as risk indicators of listed banks, use bivariate regression empirical research method to improve the accuracy of securities market volatility risk warning and regulation, and solve the problem of legal and technical mismatch in securities market regulation. Due to the lack of coordination between technology and law in a complex market environment, the model's adaptability needs further improvement. Future research will further optimize intelligent regulatory models in order to provide more efficient market risk regulation methods, innovative decision-making management for the financial industry, and promote the deep integration of intelligent technology and financial law.

Keywords: Securities market · legal regulation · SSA-CNN · mathematical model · algorithm optimization

1 Introduction

As a key technological advancement in the field of deep learning, time series modeling is widely used for financial market analysis. Research on risk warning systems requires the use of historical data, which often exhibits time-dependent behavior. This means that market volatility develops gradually and data from different time points interact with each other. Traditional time series modeling techniques, including autoregressive moving average (ARMA) models and long short-term memory (LSTM) networks, are proficient in capturing the inherent trends and periodic changes of time series data. However, with the increasing complexity and dimensionality of data in the securities market, single time series modeling methods need to fully handle the nonlinear dynamics in the market. Combining temporal modeling with other complex methods, especially adversarial training techniques, is a promising strategy for improving the effectiveness of securities market risk warning systems.

Combining safety supervision with cutting-edge technologies such as artificial intelligence and proposing innovative solutions provides practical and theoretical support

S. C. P. Yam et al. (Eds.): ICFT 2025, CCIS 2868, pp. 206–217, 2026.
https://doi.org/10.1007/978-981-92-0126-6_17

for efficient safety supervision. (Wang et al., 2021) emphasized the distributed ledger technology of blockchain, which has a strong protective effect on data visibility and irreversibility. For privacy protection and regulatory issues in blockchain, the combination of smart contracts and privacy protection technologies can enhance the security and credibility of blockchain technology. (Demarco, 2024) by utilizing AI and big data to monitor illegal activities such as market manipulation and high-frequency trading in Brazil, discussing how to improve market transparency and compliance, and discussed that AI may face in financial regulation to meet the inherent needs of new market supervision. (Zhao et al., 2021) Research the application elements of 5G multi access computing architecture in edge computing, propose edge to end security domain division, optimize the high performance, low latency and super bandwidth of computing resources, resist network malicious attacks, and provide users with reliable 5G security computing services. (Bai, 2022) studied the use of artificial intelligence in handling social public opinion dissemination issues, proposed a method for constructing a cognitive engine using artificial intelligence algorithms, explored the functions of cognitive engines in public opinion mining and disposal, and provided suggestions for public opinion management. (Broby et al., 2023) in response to the network security issues in fin-tech and the practical foundation of AI in managing massive financial data, pointing out that intelligent supervision can use technology to protect data security and collaborate with regulatory authorities to develop industry standards and promote effective cyber-attacks. (Guo et al., 2022) Explore information security regulatory methods in smart cities, coordinate conflicts of interest from a game perspective, and provide recommendations for information security in smart cities. (Yang et al., 2023) proposed an intelligent perception and management model for blockchain circular security, a metadata model for circular security supervision, and a distributed management scheme to improve data management security and efficiency, providing support for future blockchain circular security ecological models. (Li et al., 2023) based on real-time data processing and visualization, optimize the safety supervision methods of the power system, help detect potential hazards, and achieve efficient and safe management of electricity. (Wang et al., 2023) based on trust verification and transaction verification, a distributed cross chain mechanism is designed to provide technical support for the application and development of cross chain. Therefore, these studies analyze the combination of technology and regulation from multiple dimensions, providing practical and theoretical support for financial market safety regulation.

The introduction of machine learning technology can significantly enhance the risk prediction ability of the securities market and provide support for forward-looking regulation. By optimizing the application of random forests and deep learning models, potential patterns in market data can be discovered to assist in risk warning. The development of securities focuses on improving economic benefits, and both legislative practice and research have not received sufficient attention, which hinders the effectiveness of securities market regulation. Compared with the comparative analysis of internationalization, the legislative practice of the securities industry lacks theoretical, technical, and methodological analysis and exploration of securities market regulation, and there is a lack of relevant industry talents. It is difficult to make forward-looking predictions about securities market issues in the process of legal regulation in the securities industry. The rules and regulations of the securities market require research and reflection on legal theory, supporting science and technology, and correct methods.

2 Materials and Methods

The nonlinear fluctuations and high noise levels in time series data pose many challenges to traditional time series modeling frameworks. Especially, atypical variability, extreme events, and similar phenomena in the securities market can have a significant impact on the market trajectory; However, traditional timing models often fail to capture such sudden risks effectively. For example, sudden fluctuations in the stock market caused by sudden news or policy changes often exceed the patterns observed in historical data, making the ability of traditional models to make accurate predictions more complex. In this regard, it is crucial to introduce more adaptive and flexible time series modeling methods, such as Convolutional Neural Networks (CNN) and Graph Convolutional Networks (GCN). These methods can autonomously extract multidimensional features from time series data and enhance sensitivity to atypical market fluctuations. The implementation of hybrid models, which involves the integration of Long Short-term Memory (LSTM) networks and Convolutional Neural Networks, is highly likely to significantly enhance the proficiency in capturing the inherent temporal dynamics of time series data. In terms of adversarial training, the use of Generative Adversarial Networks (GANs) enhances the robustness of the model, enabling it to better resist the noise and uncertainty commonly present in market conditions. GAN simulates and generates misleading data to help the discriminative network continuously improve its ability to identify risks, thereby achieving more accurate risk warning in complex and changing market environments. Although I have accumulated some experience in risk warning in the securities market, I still have to face the challenges brought by complex issues, such as frequent high-frequency fluctuations. The SSA algorithm needs to be continuously improved and optimized to adapt to more diverse and complex market environments, and to strengthen the collaboration between global search and local optimization. To provide stronger technical support for risk warning and investment decision-making in the securities market, and continuously enhance the robustness and adaptability of models, such as the development of cutting-edge technologies such as anti-training. By using multi-objective collaborative search methods, reinforcement learning, and adversarial training techniques, strong support will be provided for risk warning and investment decision-making in the securities market, balancing prediction accuracy and computational efficiency. At the same time, relevant algorithms and technologies will be continuously explored and improved to cope with the complexity and uncertainty of the securities market, risks, and capabilities.

Financial time series have regulatory dimensions, and their main functions are three-fold. Firstly, regulatory authorities can introduce time series analysis methods to establish risk warning models for financial institutions based on past historical data. This allows for early warning of financial risks, market risks, credit risks, etc., timely identification of problems, and early warning of relevant financial institutions; Secondly, studying the cross trading behavior of financial institutions based on time series can regulate the rationality and compliance of financial institution trading behavior, and may detect abnormal trading trends and identify illegal transactions; Thirdly, based on the analysis of time series data of some indicators of gross domestic product, it can improve the sensitivity of regulatory authorities to macro financial environment, timely identify crisis points and standardize relevant policies of financial institutions.

In order to verify whether financial institutions use time series technology for risk assessment, risk indicators from quarterly data of 42 listed banks from 2015 to 2023 (sourced from the Wind database) were used. According to the requirements of bank liquidity risk indicators, liquidity coverage ratio (LR), weighted capital adequacy ratio (CR), provision coverage ratio (PC), and leverage ratio (LV) were selected; Selecting the Late Loan Ratio (LATE) and Non-performing Loan Ratio (NPL) as bank credit risk, and processing four risk and liquidity indicators in each bank's annual report, constructing virtual DID variables and setting up a multi period DID empirical model. Study whether all four risk and liquidity indicators of the bank have been disclosed as 1 and the rest as 0 within a certain period of time, and examine the correlation coefficients with the bank's LATE and NPL. The results showed that the disclosure of the four risk indicators and liquidity indicators showed an increasing trend in the risk of the bank. When all four risk indicators and liquidity indicators were disclosed, the bank's LATE and NPL showed a negative and significant correlation. Therefore, it indicates that this financial institution uses time series technology to handle risk disclosure and adopts more advanced measures to prevent bank risks (Table 1).

Table 1. 2015–2023 Risk Indicators from Quarterly Data of 42 Listed Banks

	(1)	(2)
VARIABLES	LATE	NPL
DID	−0.789***	−0.575**
	(0.103)	(0.228)
Constant	2.596***	1.423***
	(0.068)	(0.154)
Observations	718	1318
R-squared	0.570	0.531

Standard errors in parentheses *** $p < 0.01$, ** $p < 0.05$, * $p < 0.1$

Then, we can observe how higher frequency data helps regulatory agencies with risk control. We selected weekly time series data of four credit indicators disclosed by banks in the United States from January 1973 to November 2024, including total credit (CL), resident lease credit (LNR), consumer credit (LOC), and asset securitization credit (ABS), to test whether these indicators help predict credit default rates (RATE). The data released this quarter, which are disclosed by banks according to regulations and compiled by regulatory agencies such as the Federal Reserve, can be obtained from Wind. By regressing the credit default rate and total credit, it was found that the coefficient was significantly negative, which is intuitive because rapid growth in total credit clearly indicates an increase in credit risk; When regressing the credit default rate and the other three sub indicators, it is found that the credit default rate is significantly negative only with the coefficients of consumption and asset securitization credit, but significantly positive with the proportion of leasing credit. This result has certain regulatory significance and pays more attention to asset securitization credit and consumer loan business. The above simple regression can to some extent reflect the importance of time series data in financial regulation (Table 2).

Table 2. 1973.01–2024.11 Weekly Time Series Data of Four Credit Indicators Disclosed by Banks in the United States

	(1)	(3)
VARIABLES	RATE	RATE
LNR		0.886***
		(0.166)
LOC		−2.078***
		(0.373)
ABS		−0.285***
		(0.0976)
CL	−0.200***	
	(0.00842)	
Constant	5.273e+06***	−7.349e+06***
	(74,331)	(2.366e+06)
Observations	589	589
R-squared	0.490	0.560

Standard errors in parentheses *** $p < 0.01$, ** $p < 0.05$, * $p < 0.1$

By incorporating adversarial samples into the training framework, adversarial training drives the model to continuously adjust to cope with data disturbances, thereby enhancing its generalization performance and ability to handle market fluctuations. Combining adversarial training with time modeling is an effective approach to dealing with noise and unpredictable events in the securities market. Traditional time series models are more susceptible to market noise interference, leading to fluctuations or inaccuracies in prediction results, while adversarial training enhances the robustness of the model by introducing perturbed data. By using Generative Adversarial Networks (GANs), the generation module can simulate risk factors and generate extreme scenario samples from market data to help the model identify risk factors and manage extreme scenarios during training, thereby improving decision quality. In securities market risk management, challenging market data is constructed to counteract training, enabling the model to effectively respond to sudden fluctuations and nonlinear changes, thereby achieving the goal of responding to risks. By generating samples of virtual market fluctuations, a network is generated to enable the model to grasp its ability to cope with extreme environments. At the same time, the discriminative network evaluates whether the generated data matches the real market distribution, thereby improving the model's accuracy in predicting market uncertainty. Adversarial training of generative and discriminative networks can significantly enhance the adaptability and stability of time series models in dealing with complex market dynamics. This method can be used to solve unpredictable and unconventional black swan events.

Establishing a time and competition training model can not only enhance robustness, but also make the training samples of the model more diverse, and enable the time model to generalize through the generated synthetic data. Increasing more training samples better avoids overfitting or local extremum problems during the solving process. In the face of unpredictable market trends, the accuracy of trend judgment will decrease. Dynamically adjusting positions based on market changes and combining time models with competitive training applications can enhance the effectiveness and flexibility of the securities market, and also provide ideas for the future popularization of financial technology applications. Quickly adjusting strategies is also the main path to improve the accuracy and real-time performance of prediction signals. Training algorithm models in machine learning also adapts to current market changes. Trading parties and regulatory agencies can respond promptly to various uncertain factors and unexpected events in trading market, avoid risks, and achieve stable operation of financial system.

3 Results

Traditional analysis tools have limited adaptability to real-time data and are difficult to comprehensively cover multidimensional information in the market. The lack of big data technology makes the accuracy and timeliness of market volatility prediction unable to meet the demand. Due to objective factors such as technological risks inherent in fintech, regulatory difficulty has increased. From the perspective of securities and financial products, the expiration date of financial products and many uncertain factors can still cause various economic and financial losses. In the conventional sense, the term of an investment should be directly proportional to the rate of return, but the securities and financial markets are constantly changing and sometimes go against investment expectations. The securities yield is directly proportional to financial risk, and the higher the yield, the greater the investment risk; The lower the risk of investment, the lower the yield. The fluctuations in the foreign exchange market generally affect the changing trends of the securities market. With the changes in exchange rates, the Chinese securities industry will also be affected by the changes in interest rates, which will cause fluctuations in many securities products. In addition to the impact of the foreign exchange market, from a macro perspective, the returns on securities investment cannot exceed the changes in price increases and currency depreciation caused by inflation, and cannot meet investment expectations. The securities market is also facing risky changes. Due to differences in the career prospects, capital size, and operational capabilities of securities issuers, if there are changes in the issuer's securities operations, such as inability to repay principal and interest at maturity, investors will suffer economic losses. From the perspective of risk level, investment grade securities and speculative grade securities have a risk-oriented atmosphere. The difference between the two is based on investment stability, risk, and return rate. When there is significant volatility in the securities and financial markets, investors often engage in speculative behavior and blindly buy stocks in large quantities. As a large number of investors chase after the rise at the same time, the securities market changes accordingly, leading to investment failures. Effective regulation or laws and regulations can usually reduce the risk of financial markets. While the securities market is constantly developing, there are also many problems. Various direct or indirect problems have been exposed during the development process, requiring effective supervision and control by relevant departments. These problems reflect insufficient effectiveness of securities regulation.

In uncertain environments, traditional regulatory frameworks and tools may not be effective in addressing new challenges. The innovation speed of financial markets often exceeds the response speed of regulatory agencies. In addition, regulatory arbitrage may be an important factor that leads to regulatory failure. It may use differences between different regulatory jurisdictions to carry out regulatory arbitrage, choosing to conduct business in places with looser regulation. Market participants may use innovative means to avoid existing regulatory regulations, especially in situations where regulatory rules are unclear or there are gray areas. Using capital outflows from different industries in the United States as a simple measure of regulatory arbitrage, including manufacturing (IND), wholesale trade (SEL), information technology (IFM), and financial institutions (FIN), and applying VAR regression, economic policy uncertainty (EPU), and S&P 500 volatility (VIX) indicators again, it was found that in situations of high uncertainty, capital outflows from American companies are severe, and capital outflows can further amplify uncertainty in the capital market, which can lead to a certain degree of regulatory failure (Table 3).

4 Discussion

Machine learning can also enhance adaptability to complex market dynamics and provide real-time and accurate information support for securities regulatory decisions. Based on data-driven analysis methods, it helps to promote the modernization and efficiency of securities market regulation. Effectively manage the external risks of transaction proceduralization and continuously improve the laws and regulations of financial law. In order to address these issues and improve the feasibility of regulation, the securities market continuously updates new trading systems, establishes stock exchanges, and introduces the system of limited liability companies. This type of company promotes the listing of some companies, gradually driving economic development and continuously promoting the standardization of financial markets and the soundness of laws and regulations. Establishing an effective supervision mechanism and a virtuous cycle market system can promote the rapid development of the financial industry. The rapid development of science and technology in the world, coupled with technological innovation, promotes the informatization process of finance and securities trading, continuously improving quantitative trading standards and efficiency. With the globalization of the world economy and the relaxation of national capital regulation, the monopoly of securities has been shaken, and the industry competition between various financial institutions and exchanges has become increasingly fierce, which has also led to a decrease in the administrative efficiency of securities exchanges. The Securities Market Legislation Prediction Method is to use specific means and planning, based on future economic development trends

Table 3. Capital Outflows from Different Industries in the United States as a Simple Measure of Regulatory Arbitrage

	IND	SEL	IFM	FIN	EPU	FROM
IND	83.20	0.09	2.00	0.75	13.96	16.80
SEL	0.44	64.77	25.67	4.22	4.91	35.23
IFM	14.10	17.74	48.17	1.52	18.47	51.83
FIN	3.86	11.79	1.11	77.58	5.65	22.42
EPU	10.54	0.85	7.40	4.22	77.00	23.00
TO	28.94	30.47	36.18	10.70	42.99	149.28
Inc.Own	112.14	95.24	84.35	88.29	119.99	cTCI/TCI
NET	12.14	−4.76	−15.65	−11.71	19.99	37.32/29.86
NPT	3.00	1.00	1.00	1.00	4.00	
	IND	SEL	IFM	FIN	VIX	
IND	86.26	2.59	5.79	1.61	3.75	13.74
SEL	0.83	68.89	23.08	2.74	4.46	31.11
IFM	18.75	18.88	60.00	1.08	1.29	40.00
FIN	2.60	11.95	1.22	77.50	6.73	22.50
VIX	2.63	11.54	1.28	19.61	64.94	35.06
TO	24.81	44.97	31.37	25.04	16.22	142.41
Inc.Own	111.07	113.86	91.36	102.54	81.16	cTCI/TCI
NET	11.07	13.86	−8.64	2.54	−18.84	35.60/28.48
NPT	2.00	3.00	2.00	1.00	2.00	

and research models, to determine the development trend of the national securities market in the future, evaluate possible economic problems, make legislative improvements in advance, and effectively carry out legal supervision. This methodology effectively explains its significance as a preparatory step for legislation, which is beneficial for legislators to improve laws and regulations and strengthen regulatory efforts. Through scientific methodology and solutions, and the application of rigorous measures, it is easier to identify the main contradictions and aspects in the development process of the securities market, ensure the legal supervision of the securities industry, and contribute to the effective promotion of legislation and law enforcement, thereby regulating the order of the securities market.

The application of machine learning in financial regulation includes abnormal transaction detection, compliance review, stress testing, and more, which can help regulatory agencies more effectively monitor market behavior, identify potential risks, predict market trends, and strengthen compliance. Of course, it is difficult to measure the financial technology level of financial institutions themselves, but it can be measured through text analysis, that is, by measuring the frequency of machine learning related words in corporate annual reports, CSR reports and other texts, and constructing a Financial Technology Index (FTI) to simply measure the degree of application of machine learning methods in these financial enterprises. Similarly, it can be obtained by crawling the texts of listed companies. Specifically, we will continue to analyze data from Chinese listed banks and regress the relationship between non-performing loan ratio (NPL) and machine learning application level (FTI). The sample interval will also be expanded from 2009 to 2022. It can be seen that the application of machine learning methods has reduced average non-performing loan processing rate of banks by 3.9% (Table 4).

Table 4. 2009–2022. The relationship between NPL and FTI of listed banks in China

	(1)
VARIABLES	NPL
FTI	-0.0388^{***}
	(0.00871)
Constant	1.263^{***}
	(0.333)
Observations	132
R-squared	0.521

$^{***}\,p < 0.01, ^{**}\,p < 0.05, ^{*}\,p < 0.1$

The advantage of machine learning lies not only in its ability to identify business risks through large amounts of data, but also in its ability to construct "counterfactual" values for risk assessment. To evaluate the impact of major real estate company's lightning strike on the credit risk of listed bank, although it is possible to assess all credit risks event through equity puncture and supply chain investigation, it is difficult to fully cover them; Large-scale real estate enterprise thunderstorms belong to malignant social events, and damage to entire credit environment is directly measured. It is more reasonable to evaluate by constructing counterfactual values through machine learning. As shown in the chart, blue and red lines in Fig. 1 represent actual value of bank's NPL and predicted value using random forest algorithm respectively. The thunderstorm event occurred at the position indicated by vertical line, in June 2021. After thunderstorm event, although bank's NPL was still at a low level, it still had a significant impact compared to actual value of adverse event that did not occur. Fig. 2 quantitatively measures impact, and judgment using the random forest algorithm shows thunderstorm of real estate company caused non-performing loan ratio of this bank to increase by 0.09%, which needs to be taken seriously by regulatory authorities. The use of random forest fitting achieved goodness of fit of 82%, proving accuracy of machine learning.

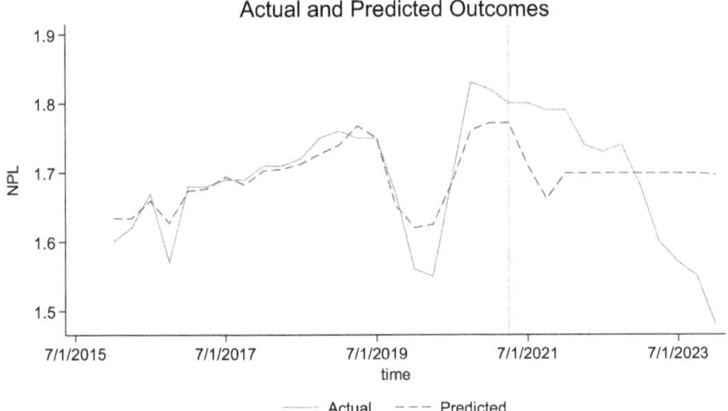

Fig. 1. Real life and prediction results using machine learning

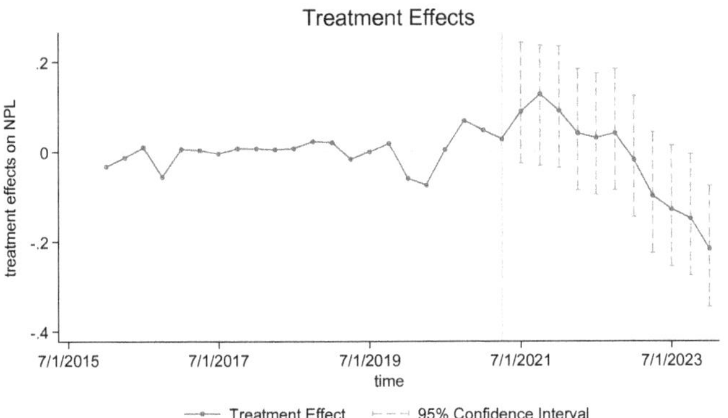

Fig. 2. Processing effect of machine learning application

5   Conclusion

This study focuses on the optimization of intelligent regulatory models in the securities market, with a focus on exploring the application of technologies such as feature selection, SSA optimization algorithm, financial time series modeling, and adversarial training in improving the efficiency of securities market regulation. The challenges at the technical and legal levels are analyzed. The focus of the research is to address the complex market dynamics by implementing intelligent regulatory technologies, optimizing traditional regulatory practices, and enhancing market risk identification and prediction capabilities. Its purpose is to establish an innovative regulatory framework with the support of cutting-edge technologies such as big data analysis and artificial intelligence, in order to enhance the risk prevention and control functions within the securities market. Through literature review, model design, and subsequent experimental verification, an intelligent supervision model was developed using technical analysis and empirical data, confirming its effectiveness in practical applications. By integrating SSA optimization technology and other means, the accuracy of high-risk identification can be improved, thereby enhancing the search efficiency and data processing capabilities of the global market. By combining financial timing and adversarial training strategies, more flexible and adaptable models can be constructed to cope with market dynamics. However, the current legal system often faces difficulties in fully covering emerging technology fields. Aim to strengthen the synergistic effect of legal framework and technological innovation from an innovative perspective, and promote the development of securities regulatory market supervision technology. In the future, financial market regulation will focus on the coordinated development of technology and law, especially in clarifying technical compliance requirements, which will promote more transparent, open, and sustainable development of technology applications. This will also enable financial market regulation work to be carried out from multiple dimensions in subsequent research, especially in complex market environments, to further improve relevant laws and regulations and provide solid legal support for technological innovation. In addition, exploring the application of advanced technologies such as blockchain and smart contracts in regulatory practices will provide assistance for the continuous innovation of regulatory models.

Acknowledgments. The author gratefully acknowledges supports of Web of Science and this Publishing Company.

Disclosure of Interests No potential conflict of interest was reported by the authors.

References

Azzutti, A.: The algorithmic future of EU market conduct supervision: a preliminary check. Eur. Financial Regul. Stud. **25**(4), 207–225 (2022). https://doi.org/10.1007/978-3-031-17077-5_2

Bisett, E.: The value of regulators as monitors: evidence from banking. Manag. Sci. **70**(12), 8464–8483 (2024). https://doi.org/10.1287/mnsc.2021.03083

Cheng, X.: The construction of a regulatory paradigm for programmatic trading risks in the securities market under generative artificial intelligence. Contemp. Econ. Manag. (2024) http://kns.cnki.net/kcms/detail/13.1356.F.20241111.1120.002.html

Gerard, K., Reutelingsperger, T.: The new advertisement regime—what a difference a word makes? In: The New EU Prospectus Rules (2020)

Li, J., Wang, J., Zhu, G., Zhou, L., Yu, X.: Research on new power system security assurance method based on data visualization. In: Proceedings of the 2023 4th International Conference on Machine Learning and Computer Application (ICMLCA 2023). SPIE, Bellingham (2023)

Liu, C.: Long short-term memory (LSTM)-based news classification model. PLoS One. **19**(5), e0301835 (2024). https://doi.org/10.1371/journal.pone.0301835

Mao, X.: Generative Adversarial Networks for Image Generation. Springer (2021)

Rohadi, S.C., Sarumpaet, S., Syaipudin, U.: Determinan non-performing loan (NPL) perbankan kawasan ASEAN. Owner: Riset J. Akuntansi. **8**(2), 1919–1932 (2024). https://doi.org/10.33395/owner.v8i2.2331

Shejul, K., Harikrishnan, R., Gupta, H.: The improved integrated exponential smoothing based CNN-LSTM algorithm to forecast the day ahead electricity price. MethodsX. **13**, 102923 (2024). https://doi.org/10.1016/j.mex.2024.102923

Srivastava, R., Srivastava, S.K., Agnihotri, K., Gupta, A.: Loan delinquency analysis using predictive model. Int. J. Knowl. Learn. **17**(6), 615 (2024). https://doi.org/10.1504/ijkl.2024.141804

Wu, C., Lin, Y.: Financial technology: current research status and prospects. J. Manage. Sci. **27**(6), 3 (2024). https://doi.org/10.19920/j.cnki.jmsc.2024.06.001

Yang, H., Cao, Y.: Research on intelligent perception and supervision for data circulation security based on block-chain. In: 2023 8th International Conference on Cloud Computing and Big Data Analysis (2023)

Zhao, W., Lin, N., Li, H.B.: Fintech, regulatory strategies, and regional financial risks. Contemp. Finance Econ. (2024). https://doi.org/10.13676/j.cnki.cn36-1030/f.20241119.001

Zheng, Y.: Digital information disclosure, investor sentiment and enterprise default risk. Finance Res. Lett. **62**, 105070 (2024). https://doi.org/10.1016/j.frl.2024.105070

Genetic Algorithm Optimization for Enterprise Financial Risk Prediction: A Model for State-Owned Firms

Li Zhang[✉]

Chengdu College of University of Electronic Science and Technology of China,
Chengdu 610000, Sichuan, China
526630642@qq.com

Abstract. At present, the financial crisis is the biggest crisis faced by listed state-owned Enterprise in China, and thus the establishment of early warning model of financial crisis is becoming more and more important. Genetic algorithm is more and more widely used in enterprise financial crisis. At present, many scholars have designed a part of early warning model based on genetic algorithm. In this paper, through the optimization and improvement of genetic algorithm, an enterprise financial crisis early warning model optimized by genetic algorithm was reestablished, so as to improve the enterprise's ability to resist risks and predict the financial crisis ahead of time, and help enterprises cope with the difficulties. The test shows that the model is safe and reliable, and can accurately predict the financial crisis of the enterprise.

Keywords: listed state-owned Enterprise · financial crisis · early warning model · genetic algorithm optimization

1 Introduction

An enterprise is an organization that uses economic resources to create wealth [1]. Whether it is economic resources or to create wealth, finance can't be separated. Once the financial crisis occurs, the normal operation of the enterprise is difficult to continue [2]. With the deepening of reform and opening up and the deepening of socialist economy, enterprises will face more and more crises. Financial crisis, as the primary crisis of enterprises, should be paid more attention to (Zhuang J, et al. 2016) [3]. And for the majority of Chinese investors, the financial crisis of listed state-owned Enterprise should be paid more attention to [4]. How to predict the financial crisis of enterprises has become the focus of attention from all walks of life. However, there is no accurate financial crisis warning model, and the use of genetic algorithm is not perfect.

The occurrence of enterprise financial crisis is not accomplished overnight, and the development of all transactions must have a process of qualitative change caused by quantitative change. Enterprise financial crisis is no exception. And after a long period of research, it is found that the financial crisis of enterprises is predictable, and has a certain omen. In this paper, a financial crisis early warning model of listed state-owned Enterprise

© The Author(s), under exclusive license to Springer Nature Singapore Pte Ltd. 2026
S. C. P. Yam et al. (Eds.): ICFT 2025, CCIS 2868, pp. 218–228, 2026.
https://doi.org/10.1007/978-981-92-0126-6_18

optimized by genetic algorithm was designed [5]. It is of great practical significance for enterprises and investors to find the financial crisis of enterprises quickly and give solutions. In this way, the enterprise can improve its own business model according to the forecast results, adjust the development strategy, and solve the problem perfectly before the financial crisis appears.

2   State of the Art

In the early 1930s, some economists in the West began to study the financial crisis of enterprises. However, due to the limitations of computer technology, computer models have not been developed [6]. With the study of enterprise financial crisis, many scholars have developed a variety of enterprise financial crisis early warning tool. The earliest financial distress prediction research was a single variable bankruptcy prediction model. However, due to the limitation of statistical computing tools, the model can only be used for the comparative study between failed enterprises and normal enterprises [7]. In the late twentieth Century, the neural network theory began to rise, and its influence also entered the field of financial crisis prediction. And the neural network is used to predict the financial distress.

But at home, due to various reasons, China's enterprise financial crisis research started late in the 1990s [8]. In 1986, Wu Shinong and Huang Shizhong introduced the financial analysis index and prediction model of enterprise bankruptcy. Theire analysis of enterprise financial crisis was limited to empirical analysis or normative argument, and there was no empirical research [9]. Although domestic research started late, it developed rapidly. Yang Baoan and Ji Haizhen first established the enterprise financial early-warning model using BP neural network in 2001, which could achieve very good prediction results. But in general, domestic research is lagging behind the research of developed countries. However, after the efforts of domestic scholars, it is possible to catch up with foreign countries or even lead the world [10].

3   Methodology

3.1   Optimization and Improvement of Financial Crisis Early Warning Model for Listed State-Owned Enterprise

Firstly, all kinds of information of the Enterprise are input into the model. And then the information of the enterprise is analyzed and calculated through the model. Through the analysis and calculation of financial information, the enterprise financial crisis and financial crisis early warning were studied. The present financial situation of the enterprise is analyzed, and the financial condition of the Enterprise is evaluated. Once the cause of financial crisis is found, timely warning and solution are provided for enterprise management personnel to study and use. The indicators and samples of crisis warning are determined, and then the crisis warning model is constructed. Finally, the model is tested. The roadmap of this study is shown in Fig. 1.

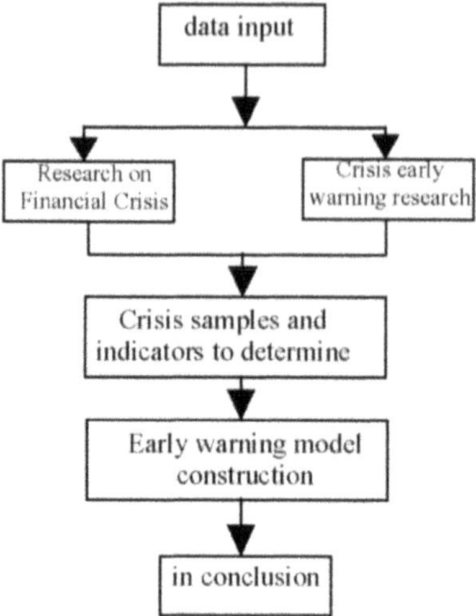

Fig. 1. This article studies the road.

3.2 Calculation and Optimization of Genetic Algorithm

To establish an enterprise financial crisis early warning model based on genetic algorithm, first of all, an optimized algorithm is needed to carry out calculation. In this algorithm, binary is used to generate the primary population randomly, and then the adaptive ability of each individual in the population is calculated. When the algebra of evolution exceeds the algebra prescribed by the design, it stops; on the contrary, the right offspring will be selected in order to reproduce for the last generation. Of course, adaptable offspring will have more survival, and will have a greater chance of reproduction. The genes that are suitable for survival are inherited, the bad genes are eliminated, the offspring with strong adaptability are duplicated and stored in a paired library, and the individuals with good genes in the paired library are randomly combined. And in accordance with the mutation probability, random mutation operation can be carried out. Then, the adaptive ability of offspring is recalculated. Until shutdown, the downtime test can be started. The population size is set to 100. Although large scale population calculation is large, it has high accuracy. Each threshold is encoded by a binary, and the expression of the first i individual is as follows:

$$\left\{ C_{1,1}^{i} \cdots C_{1,10}^{i} \cdots C_{n,1}^{i} \cdots C_{n,10}^{i}; V_{1,1}^{i} \cdots V_{1,10}^{i} \cdots V_{n,1}^{i} \cdots V_{n,10}^{i} \right\} i = 1, 2, \cdots 100$$

But the interval of each threshold is $\{0, 1\}$, and the binary code is rewritten into decimal code. First of all, $\left\{ V_{1,1}^{i} \cdots V_{1,10}^{i} \cdots V_{n,1}^{i} \cdots V_{n,10}^{i} \right\}$ should be transformed into $V_{j}^{i\,'}$.

$$V_{j}^{i\,'} = \sum_{k=1}^{10} \left(V_{j,k}^{i} \times 2^{10-k} \right), i = 1, \cdots 100, j = 1, \cdots n \tag{1}$$

Then, $V_j^{i\prime}$ is mapped to the real V_j^i of $\{0, 1\}$.

$$V_j^i = 0 + V_j^{i\prime} \times \frac{1-0}{2^{10}-1}, i = 1, \cdots, 100, j = 1, \cdots, n \tag{2}$$

In this way, the maximum $max(X_j)$ and minimum values $min(X_j)$ of the financial indicators can be calculated

For the calculation of fitness, the following formula is used for simple calculation and integration

$$\text{fitness }(i) = \frac{Y_{1(i)}}{N_1} \times \frac{Y_{2(i)}}{N_2} i = 1, \cdots 100 \tag{3}$$

The values of accuracy are compared to avoid being too large or too small.

Using the method of blocking wheel, the individuals with strong adaptability were selected as collateral to carry on heredity. The probability of selecting the i generation is as follows:

$$P^{(i)} = \frac{\text{fitness}(i)}{\sum_{j=1}^{100} \text{fitness}(j)}, i = 1, \cdots 100 \tag{4}$$

i is the individual ordinal number; j is the financial index serial number; V is the score of each index; C is the threshold of financial indicators; Y is the correct number of companies; N is the total number of health companies; and X is financial indicators.

The basic flow chart of the optimized genetic algorithm is shown in Fig. 2.

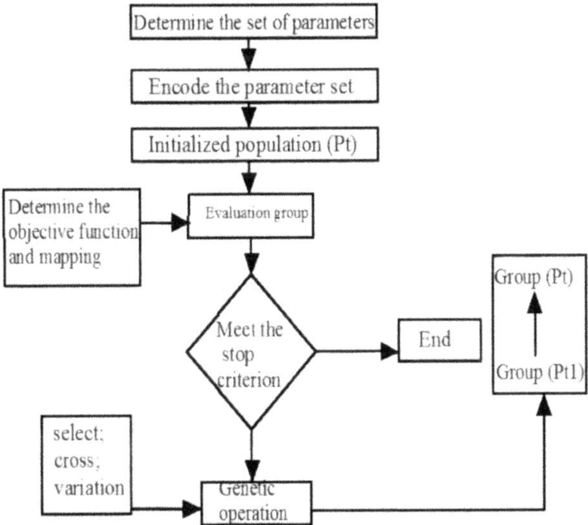

Fig. 2. The basic flow chart of the optimized genetic algorithm.

3.3 Model for Enterprise Financial Crisis Early Warning Method and Stage Determination

Before the emergence of enterprise financial crisis, there will be some signs. The model designed in this paper can distinguish and judge the warning of enterprise financial crisis mainly according to the characteristics of various stages. The division of the stage is as follows in Table 1.

Table 1. Enterprise financial crisis stage table.

stage	Financial crisis latency	Financial crisis	The financial crisis worsened	Financial crisis
symptom	Blind expansion	Own capital shortage	The manager is unintentional	Liabilities are greater than assets
	Ineffective marketing	Excessive reliance on external funds, heavy interest burden	Focus on cash flow	Debt is not repayable
	Negligence of risk management	Lack of accounting warning	Cash flow difficulties	Declared bankruptcy
	Lack of effective management system, improper allocation of enterprise resources	Debt delays	Debt crisis	
	Ignore environmental changes			

The earliest stage of the enterprise crisis is called the latent period of financial crisis. At this stage, in the enterprise, there are only some improper treatment problems, such as blind expansion; ineffective marketing; neglect of risk management; improper allocation of enterprise resources; inadequate control of the general direction of the enterprise environment. And there are no major problems in the enterprise. As long as the development strategy is modified, the financial situation of enterprises will not deteriorate. The second stage is called the financial crisis onset period, and the main problems are the following: when capital starts to run short, cash flow starts to be difficult; due to the shortage of liquidity, foreign funds are heavily dependent on, and the interest burden is too heavy; and the debt begins to stall. At this stage, the enterprise can be difficult, but not fatal. The next stage is called the worsening financial crisis. At this stage, the enterprise management personnel operate enterprises without any intention, and the main energy will be put on the working capital. Enterprise funds are difficult to run, and debt begins to default. At this stage, the enterprise is on the brink of bankruptcy, the enterprise is difficult to operate normally. And the fourth stage is called the financial crisis, at which, debt is greater than assets and is difficult to repay, and finally the enterprise is facing bankruptcy.

Through the division of the financial crisis stage, the development of the financial crisis step by step can be clearly seen. The financial crisis early warning model designed in this paper can send the stage of the enterprise and the strategy that should be adjusted to the enterprise managers by way of information push, so as to kill the enterprise financial crisis in the bud, and to promote the healthy development of enterprises. Through the division of the enterprise financial crisis stage, the model enables the manager to understand the financial phase of the enterprise, and then adjust the financial situation of the enterprise artificially.

3.4 Financial Crisis Early Warning Model of Listed State-Owned Enterprise

Compared with the traditional financial early warning model, the early warning model designed in this paper is improved a lot, and the model diagram is shown in Fig. 3.

This model has two stages to analyze the information to ensure the correctness of the model results. Enterprise information is input, sorted and analyzed by two different screening criteria. Then, the processed results are then derived from the union, and then the feature subset is extracted. Then, the next stage is calculated according to the extracted feature subset. The initial population is established by using the results of the previous stage, and then the fitness is calculated. According to the algorithm provided, the calculation and analysis are carried out, and the individuals with strong adaptability are extracted and analyzed. After stopping the criteria, the optimal feature set is selected to establish the prediction model. The reproduction that does not meet the stopping criteria is further selected, crossed to mutate, so as to finally meet the requirements of stopping criteria.

In this paper, two feature selection modes, filtering and encapsulation, can overcome the shortcomings of a single pattern and increase the accuracy of the model. In the filter selection method, the single selection criterion is not adapted, thus to avoid randomness and errors in the prediction results. In the enterprise financial crisis early warning model, the feature subset is selected creatively for filtering and searching, the advantage of which is that the search scope and reduce the search time can be reduced. Thus, it can be more accurate and less computational than the search by using the original feature subset. Moreover, the BP neural network with simpler structure can be used as the fitness function, which can be accurate to the individual research. With the increasing risk of enterprises, it is urgent to establish the financial crisis early warning model of the listed state-owned Enterprise after the optimization of the genetic algorithm. The enterprise financial crisis early warning model designed in this paper is more professional and accurate than the ordinary early-warning model established by genetic algorithm. In this paper, genetic algorithm is further optimized, so that the calculation is more accurate and reasonable. Moreover, the calculation rules of the model and the mode of information processing are changed. Possible stochastic computational methods are abandoned, and listed state-owned Enterprise can be given more reasonable and safe financial crisis warning.

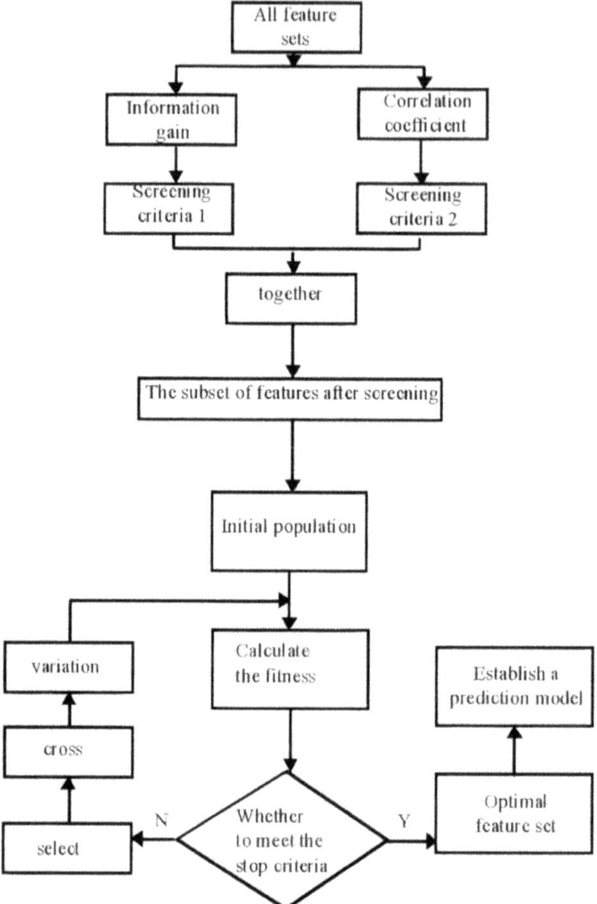

Fig. 3. Listed state-owned Enterprise financial crisis genetic algorithm optimization early warning model.

4   Result Analysis and Discussion

After the model was established, the accuracy of the model was tested. After repeated training and computer operation, the training times and training results are shown in Fig. 4.

As can be seen from the figure above, the BP neural network model is leveled off after 30 steps. After 168 steps, the network performance reaches the standard, and the training error is 9.91963e-010, which is less than the given target error of 0.0000000001, and reaches the convergence state.

In order to further test the warning effect of the model, the test sample was taken into the neural network model for simulation test. The financial status of the 20 Sample Firms in T was used as the output result, and the data of the year T-1 was brought into

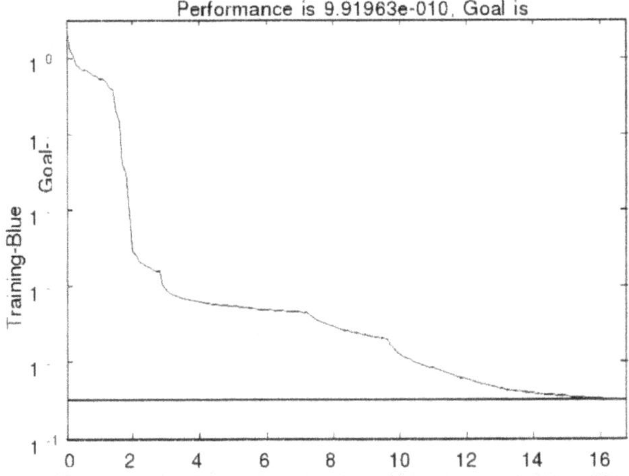

Fig. 4. The number of training and training results.

the constructed early-warning model respectively. According to the output of the model, the final statistical results are shown in Table 2.

Table 2. The results of the model to get statistical results.

Training samples				Detection of samples		
	ST Enterprise	Non-ST Enterprise	Total number of samples	ST Enterprise	Non-ST Enterprise	Total number of samples
Number of training samples	20	20	40	10	10	20
Determine the correct number	19	17	36	9	8	17
Predictive accuracy	92.5%	90.7%	91.2%	87.3%	85.1%	86%

The results of training simulation in T-1 show that the prediction accuracy of the model is higher. For training samples, 1 is misjudged in 20 ST companies, and 3 are misjudged among the 20 non ST companies, and so the comprehensive prediction accuracy is 91.2%, and the misjudgment rate is only 8.8%; and for the detection of samples, 1 is misjudged among ST Enterprise, and 2 are misjudged among non ST Enterprise, so that the accuracy of prediction is 86%. It shows that the model has a good prediction effect, and can basically determine the financial status of enterprises in the year before ST.

Through the test results, it is found that the judgment rate of non ST companies is slightly lower than that of ST Enterprise, which shows that the model is more sensitive to companies with abnormal financial situation, and can find problems in time, and has better predictability for companies with financial crisis. For enterprises, it is necessary to establish financial crisis early warning model. The model established in this paper can determine the Enterprise's financial status within two years or even earlier, and give more accurate prediction results in the previous year. The enterprise management authorities can find out the problems existing in the enterprise in advance, then can formulate the solution in time, and prevent the further expansion of the risk from the source, so as to avoid the outbreak of the financial crisis.

In order to make the experimental results more obvious, the enterprise financial crisis early warning model based on the improved genetic algorithm was compared with the traditional genetic algorithm early warning model. The financial crisis situation of 50 enterprises was analyzed, and the accuracy tests of financial distress warning were conducted for companies with registered capital of 200 thousand, 400 thousand, 600 thousand, 800 thousand and one million. The test results are shown in Fig. 5.

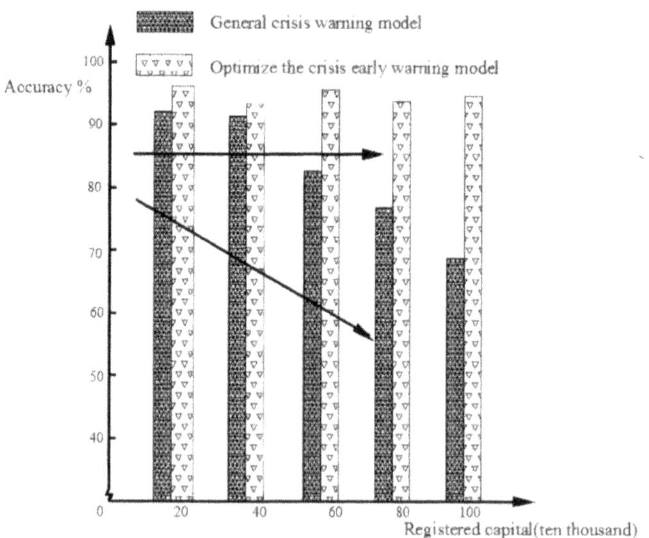

Fig. 5. Financial crisis warning accuracy test results.

Through the data above, it can be seen that for the traditional crisis warning model, with the increase of the registered capital and the increase of processing data, the warning accuracy is lower. When the registered capital of enterprises reaches one million, the accuracy is less than 70%, and can't be used to warn the financial crisis of enterprises. However, for the enterprise financial crisis warning model established by the genetic algorithm optimization, the accuracy is always around 95%, and it is a financial early warning model of listed state-owned Enterprise with good performance.

Through the above function and performance test, it can be found that the financial early-warning model of listed state-owned Enterprise established in this paper can meet the use requirements. Although there are some minor problems to be optimized, functions can be used properly. Especially after the model genetic algorithm is optimized, the computational ability of the model is greatly increased, and the accuracy is greatly improved, so that it is a model with excellent performance. The results of training and testing show that the model is ideal in predicting the occurrence of enterprise financial crisis, and can give the expected output of the proposed problem, which is practical and effective, and is worth promoting.

5 Conclusion

The application of genetic algorithm in enterprise financial crisis warning model is deepening with the development of biological science and computer technology. However, there are many deficiencies in the current genetic algorithm. In this paper, the existing genetic algorithm was optimized, and an advanced financial crisis early warning model was established. The accuracy of the optimized genetic algorithm was very good, reaching more than 90%. In addition, the crisis warning model designed in this paper was compared with the traditional model. It is found that the accuracy of the traditional model decreased with the increase of processing data, while with the increase of processing data, the accuracy of the financial crisis warning model of listed state-owned Enterprise fluctuates little, and is maintained around 95%. It shows that the model designed in this paper is a very excellent model, which meets the design and application requirements, and can give the enterprise timely warning processing. In addition, the model designed in this paper can meet the crisis warning work of most listed state-owned Enterprise, so as to provide a guarantee for the safety of Chinese enterprises and the property safety of the national shareholders, and enhance the competitiveness of Chinese enterprises in the world. However, there are still some defects in this model, such as longer computing time. Thus, the algorithm of the model program will be continuously optimized to give the user the most comfortable trial experience.

References

1. Huang, T.H., Leu, Y., Pan, W.T.: Constructing ZSCORE-based financial crisis warning models using fruit fly optimization algorithm and general regression neural network. Kybernetes Int. J. Syst. Cybern. **45**(4), 650–665 (2023)
2. Meng, Q.: Research on financial early warning of listed corporation based on SOM fusion BP neural network. Mod. Econ. **7**(5), 633–642 (2019)
3. Zhuang, J., Dowling, M.: Lessons of the Asian financial crisis: what can an early warning system model tell us? Asian Dev. Rev. **1**, 100–100 (2016)
4. Chang, S.C., Tsai, P.H.: A hybrid financial performance evaluation model for wealth management banks following the global financial crisis. Technol. Econ. Dev. Econ. **22**, 21–46 (2016)
5. Hamdaoui, M.: Are systemic banking crises in developed and developing countries predictable? J. Multinatl. Financ. Manag. **37-38**, 114–138 (2023)

 6. Zhang, L., Long, W.: Construction of the logistic regression estimation model in early warning on pure financial indicators. Open Cybern. Syst. J. **9**(1), 2055–2059 (2019)
 7. Fernández-Arias, D., López-Martín, M., Montero-Romero, T., et al.: Financial soundness prediction using a multi-classification model: evidence from current financial crisis in OECD banks. Comput. Econ. **4**, 1–23 (2017)
 8. Wang, L., Wu, C.: A combination of models for financial crisis prediction: integrating probabilistic neural network with Back-propagation based on adaptive boosting. Int. J. Comput. Intell. Syst. **10**(1), 507 (2017)
 9. Al-Huneiti, H., Al-Ghani, Y.H.A.: Towards building an early warning model to predict the financial crises of Jordanian Islamic banks. J. Manag. Res. **8**(2), 48 (2016)
10. Chen, J.H., Shih-Feng, H.: Chinese currency unit and financial crisis: evidence from early warning systems. Int. Res. J. Appl. Financ. **VI**(4), 274–296 (2015)

Enhancing Enterprise Risk Management with AI: A LightGBM-GAN Approach

Defang Wang[(⊠)]

Lanzhou Resources & Environment Voc-Tech University, Lanzhou 730021, Gansu, China
18993111839@163.com

Abstract. With the continuous deepening of global economic integration, the complexity and uncertainty of the market environment have significantly increased, and all industries are facing unprecedented risks and challenges. In this context, building an efficient, precise, and adaptable risk management system has become the key to the steady development of enterprises. The rapid development of information technology, especially the breakthrough of artificial intelligence (AI) technology, has brought revolutionary changes to the field of enterprise risk management. This article innovatively proposes an enterprise risk management model based on AI technology, which deeply integrates advanced machine learning (ML) algorithms and big data analysis techniques. By deeply mining and analyzing massive historical data and real-time market information, the model can automatically identify potential risk sources, predict the probability of risk occurrence and the possible impact range, thereby providing scientific basis for enterprise decision-making. The experimental results show that compared to traditional risk management methods, this model exhibits significant advantages in risk identification speed, accuracy, and warning capability.

Keywords: Artificial intelligence · Enterprise risk management · Application and algorithm optimization

1 Introduction

In today's complex and ever-changing business environment, enterprises are facing unprecedented challenges and risks [1]. These risks not only stem from external factors such as market fluctuations, policy changes, and technological innovations, but also deeply rooted in multiple levels of internal management, financial health, and supply chain stability of the enterprise [2]. Therefore, building an efficient and accurate enterprise risk management system is of great significance for ensuring the stable operation of enterprises and achieving sustainable development [3]. Enterprise risk management, as a core component of the enterprise management system, is becoming increasingly important [4]. It requires enterprises to comprehensively examine potential risks in both internal and external environments with a global perspective, and to achieve effective identification, assessment, management, and monitoring of risks through scientific methodology and advanced technological means [5]. With the rapid development of information technology, human society is accelerating into the era of big data.

S. C. P. Yam et al. (Eds.): ICFT 2025, CCIS 2868, pp. 229–238, 2026.
https://doi.org/10.1007/978-981-92-0126-6_19

The significant improvement in the accumulation and processing capabilities of massive data provides unprecedented opportunities for enterprise risk management [6]. Big data not only enriches the data sources for risk identification, but also makes risk analysis more comprehensive and in-depth [7]. However, relying solely on manual processing of these data is clearly insufficient, which requires the introduction of more advanced and intelligent technological means - AI [8]. Especially ML, as one of the core technologies of AI, its powerful data processing, pattern recognition, and prediction capabilities provide solid support for the intelligent transformation of risk management [9]. ML enables computer systems to automatically learn patterns and patterns in data, enabling a deep understanding and prediction of complex systems [10]. In the field of risk identification, ML can automatically analyze historical risk event data, extract key features, and construct risk prediction models. These models can monitor key indicators such as market dynamics, corporate financial status, and supply chain stability in real time. Once abnormal fluctuations or potential risk signs are detected, they immediately issue warnings and reserve sufficient response time for enterprises.

In addition, ML also has the ability to self optimize and iterate. By continuously receiving new data feedback, the model is able to self adjust its parameters, improving prediction accuracy and efficiency. This dynamic adaptation mechanism enables ML based risk management systems to keep up with market changes and maintain high sensitivity and accuracy. The enterprise risk management model based on AI technology proposed in this article aims to deeply integrate advanced ML algorithms with big data analysis technology to build an intelligent and efficient risk management system. By deeply integrating ML algorithms with big data analysis technology, this model can achieve accurate identification and prediction of potential risks, providing scientific basis for enterprise decision-making. With the continuous advancement of technology and the deepening expansion of applications, we have reason to believe that future enterprise risk management will become more intelligent and efficient, providing a safeguard for the stable operation and sustainable development of enterprises.

2 Methodology

2.1 Model Building

The effective application of AI in the field of risk management can analyze and integrate enterprise data, reduce enterprise risks to a certain extent, and effectively save labor costs. At the same time, it can also improve the level of enterprise risk management to a certain extent [11]. ML is the process of learning by analyzing large amounts of data and mining useful information from it, where computers use existing data to replace human rational thinking in processing data and accurately calculate data patterns [12]. In response to the current situation of enterprise risk warning, enterprises should actively try to use ML technology to improve the foresight, proactivity, and accuracy of risk warning systems [13]. This article innovatively proposes an enterprise risk management model based on AI technology. Given the complexity and diversity of enterprise risk management issues, we need an algorithm that can handle large-scale data, effectively capture non-linear relationships between variables, and perform well on imbalanced data. LightGBM is such a powerful tool that meets the requirements, demonstrating excellent performance in multiple fields with its efficiency, accuracy, and flexibility, especially suitable for modeling research in enterprise risk management.

However, in many real-world enterprise scenarios, one of the main challenges is the imbalance in risk-related datasets, where risky cases (e.g., fraud, bankruptcy, credit default) represent a small fraction of the total data. Traditional machine learning models often underperform on such imbalanced datasets, as they tend to be biased toward the majority class. To address this issue, we propose combining LightGBM with Generative Adversarial Networks (GANs). GANs, by learning the underlying distribution of the minority class, can generate synthetic samples that enhance the training data and improve model robustness. The integration of GAN-based data augmentation with LightGBM creates a synergistic framework that not only maintains high predictive performance but also ensures better generalization to rare but critical risk events.

The LightGBM-GAN hybrid model enhances the identification of high-risk indicators by balancing the dataset without compromising on data authenticity. Furthermore, this approach enables deeper feature representation and extraction through GAN's unsupervised learning process, allowing for improved understanding of latent risk patterns in corporate data. In enterprise contexts such as financial distress forecasting, supply chain disruption detection, and operational compliance monitoring, this methodology offers a more dynamic and responsive risk prediction mechanism.

In addition to technical advantages, the LightGBM-GAN framework also supports strategic decision-making by offering explainability through LightGBM's feature importance ranking. This interpretability is crucial for enterprise stakeholders who require not just predictions, but also actionable insights for risk mitigation. For instance, it allows risk managers to trace back the factors contributing to a high-risk score and adjust enterprise strategies or policies accordingly.

Future research can further enhance this framework by integrating domain knowledge into the GAN architecture, optimizing hyperparameter tuning for better convergence, and applying transfer learning to adapt the model across different industry sectors. Moreover, coupling the model with real-time data pipelines and automated monitoring systems can move enterprise risk management from a reactive to a proactive stance, identifying vulnerabilities before they escalate into significant disruptions.

In summary, this AI-driven risk management framework based on LightGBM and GAN represents a promising direction for enterprises seeking to modernize their risk control systems. By leveraging the strengths of both algorithms, enterprises can achieve high accuracy, balanced sensitivity, and meaningful interpretability in complex, high-stakes environments.

Figure 1 shows the structural diagram of LightGBM. LightGBM, as a representative boosting algorithm in ensemble learning, combines the efficiency of gradient boosting framework with the intuitiveness of decision tree. Its uniqueness lies in the use of techniques such as histogram algorithm and gradient one-sided sampling (GOSS), which greatly improve the training speed and memory efficiency of the algorithm while maintaining high prediction accuracy. In addition, LightGBM can effectively handle category imbalance issues, which is particularly important for the common imbalance of positive and negative sample ratios in enterprise risk management. Data is the foundation of model construction. Firstly, it is necessary to collect various internal and external data of the enterprise, including but not limited to financial statements, market data, supply chain information, social media sentiment analysis, etc. Subsequently, preprocessing operations such as cleaning, denoising, and normalization are performed on the data to ensure its quality. Feature engineering is a key step in improving model performance. Extract the most valuable feature set for risk prediction from raw data through feature selection and feature transformation.

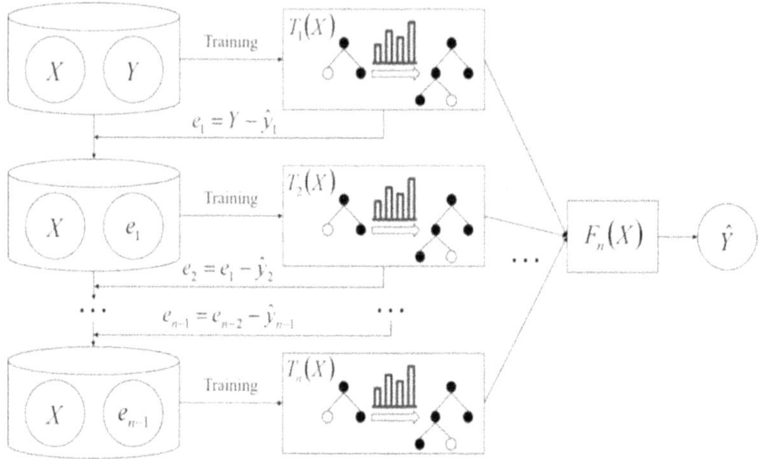

Fig. 1. LightGBM algorithm structure.

Divide the preprocessed data into a training set and a testing set, and use the training set data to train the LightGBM model. During the training process, model performance is evaluated through cross validation, and model parameters are adjusted based on the evaluation results. Finally, evaluate the trained model using the test set data. Based on the evaluation results, analyze the strengths and weaknesses of the model, and attempt to further optimize its performance by adjusting feature selection, feature transformation strategies, or model parameters. Deploy the optimized model into the enterprise risk management system to achieve real-time monitoring and early warning of enterprise risks. The system should be able to automatically receive new data, use models for risk prediction, and generate risk reports and response strategy recommendations. With the continuous development of AI technology and the increasingly diverse application scenarios, enterprise risk management models based on AI technology will play an important role in more fields. It can not only help enterprises identify potential risks in advance and develop effective response strategies, but also enhance the overall risk management level and market competitiveness of the enterprise.

2.2 Algorithm Principle

Data normalization plays a crucial role in distance based classification algorithms, ensuring that input values are constrained within a relatively compact range, thereby significantly accelerating the model training process. Zero normalization, also known as normalization, is a classic data preprocessing method that performs normalization operations based on the average and standard deviation of data attributes. It involves scaling the data proportionally to fall between 0 and 1, laying a solid foundation for subsequent algorithm processing.

$$x' = \frac{x - \bar{x}}{\sigma_x} \tag{1}$$

Among them, $\bar{x}$ is the average of all sample attributes, and σ_x is the standard deviation of the sample.

High correlation features, also known as collinear features, indicate a high degree of correlation between feature variables. By calculating the Pearson correlation coefficient matrix between multiple variables, we can quantitatively evaluate the degree of linear correlation between variables and implement feature selection strategies to eliminate redundant or weakly correlated features. The Pearson correlation coefficient, as a classic indicator for measuring the linear correlation between two variables, is calculated based on the quotient of the covariance of the two variables multiplied by their respective standard deviations

$$r = \frac{\sum_{i=1}^{n}(X_i - \bar{X})(Y_i - \bar{Y})}{\sqrt{\sum_{i=1}^{n}(X_i - \bar{X})^2}\sqrt{\sum_{i=1}^{n}(Y_i - \bar{Y})^2}} \tag{2}$$

In the formula, n is the number of samples. X_i, Y_i are the i observed values of variable X, Y.

As a paradigm of ensemble learning techniques, the core of random forest lies in the parallel construction of multiple decision trees. Random forest cleverly measures the contribution of each variable on each decision tree during the model construction process by introducing the out of bag error rate ($EOOB$) as an indicator. In order to comprehensively evaluate the importance of variables, we constructed a random forest model containing N decision trees and calculated $EOOB$ based on the model. This step not only recorded the recognition accuracy (ACC) of the current model, but also clearly marked the number of independent variables (M) involved in the modeling. Subsequently, we adopted an innovative strategy: randomly shuffling the independent variable (X) in the out of bag data (OOB) to simulate the random noise effects between variables, and re estimating the error of the decision tree to obtain the random noise out of bag error rate ($ERNOOB$). By comparing the differences between $EOOB$ and $ERNOOB$, we can quantify the impact of variable X on the predictive performance of the model, i.e. the importance (XIV) of variable X.

$$XIV = \frac{1}{2}\sum(ERNOOB - EOOB) \tag{3}$$

In LightGBM, the input layer introduces X, Y to train the first CART tree, and subsequent inputs update Y based on the residual (ei) of the previous tree to achieve undersampling effect and concentrate on processing difficult to recognize samples. The enhancement layer stores knowledge in the serial CART tree, guiding subsequent training with ei, increasing the model's focus on difficult to distinguish samples, and improving recognition accuracy. CART tree optimizes splitting based on leaf wise strategy and histogram algorithm to improve the efficiency of processing high-dimensional big data. Finally, the N CART trees are integrated into a model and output a risk value $\hat{Y}$.

$$\hat{Y} = F_n(X) = T_1(X) + T_2(X) + \cdots + T_{n-1}(X) + T_n(X) \tag{4}$$

Among them, $F_n(X)$ is a nonlinear mapping function used to identify enterprise risks.

Generative Adversarial Networks (GANs) ingeniously integrate two major components: Generator (G network) and Discriminator (D network). By introducing the core concept of self game, GANs drive the two to evolve together in competition, thereby achieving deep learning and optimization of the model. The overall objective function of GAN is ingeniously designed as a maximum minimum game framework, expressed as follows:

$$\begin{aligned} J_{GAN} &= \min_G \max_D L(G, D) \\ &= E_{x \sim p_{data}}(x)(\log(D(x))) \\ &+ E_{x \sim p_z(z)}(\log(1 - D(x))) \end{aligned} \tag{5}$$

In the formula, p_{data} is the sample distribution in the original dataset, and p_z is the distribution of the generator's random Gaussian noise input.

In step t of the training cycle, the model extracts n real samples $\left\{x'_{(i)}\right\}_{i=1}^{n}$ from the reduced dimensional dataset and generates an equal amount of pseudo samples $\left\{\tilde{x}'^{t}_{(j)}\right\}_{j=1}^{n}$, both of which are $n \times 0$ matrices. After being processed by the G network, the pseudo samples are sent to the D network to obtain their probability $\left\{prob\_1_{(k)}^{(t)}\right\}_{k=1}^{n}$ of being judged as true, as shown in Eq. (6).

$$prob\_1_{(k)}^{(t)} = D\left(\tilde{x}'^{(t)}_{(k)}\right), k = 1, 2, \cdots, n \tag{6}$$

3 Result Analysis and Discussion

To verify the performance of our model, we will conduct comparative experiments with traditional models based on Support Vector Machines (SVM). Figure 2 provides a detailed comparison of the accuracy of enterprise risk identification between our model and traditional models. The comparative results not only highlight the enormous potential of AI technology in the field of complex risk management, but also specifically demonstrate the superiority of our model in improving recognition accuracy. In the figure, it can be clearly seen that the model constructed in this article achieves more precise capture and deep analysis of enterprise risk characteristics by cleverly integrating two advanced algorithms, LightGBM and GAN. LightGBM provides powerful learning and generalization capabilities for models with its efficient parallel processing capabilities, excellent memory management, and natural processing capabilities for sparse data. The introduction of GAN, through the continuous game between the generator and discriminator, enables the model to learn risk features that are closer to the real-world distribution, further improving the accuracy and robustness of risk identification.

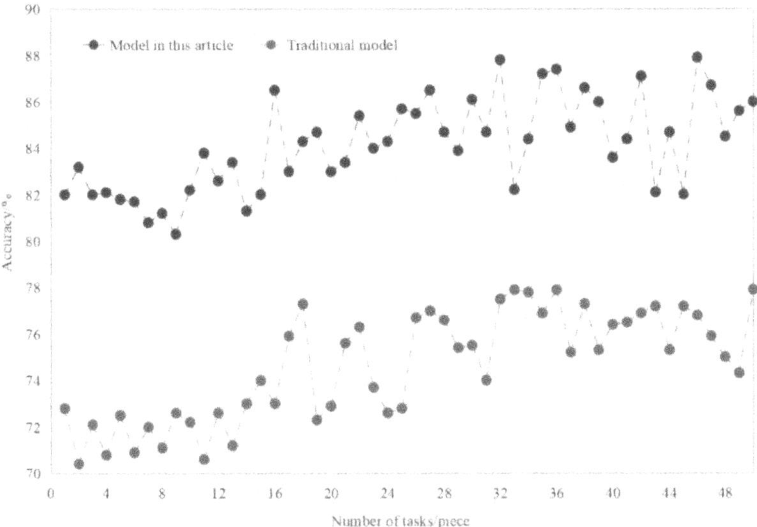

Fig. 2. Comparison of recognition accuracy.

Figure 3 deeply reveals the significant advantages of our model in terms of enterprise risk identification recall rate compared to traditional models. The recall rate, as a key indicator of the model's ability to identify all true risk samples, is crucial for the comprehensiveness and accuracy of enterprise risk management. From the figure, it can be seen that the model in this article achieves a higher recall rate for potential risk samples by combining LightGBM and GAN algorithms. LightGBM, with its efficient feature selection and learning capabilities, ensures that the model can deeply explore hidden risk signals in the data and reduce false negatives. The addition of GAN, through its powerful generation capability, simulates diverse risk scenarios, helping the model better understand and identify complex and changing risk patterns, further improving recall rates. The increase in recall rate means that the model in this article can more comprehensively capture various risks that may exist in enterprise operations, providing more comprehensive protection for enterprise risk management.

Figure 4 visually demonstrates the excellent performance of our model in risk identification speed. Compared to traditional models, our model has achieved a significant reduction in identification time. This improvement is mainly due to the ingenious combination of LightGBM and GAN algorithms in our model. The LightGBM algorithm significantly accelerates the training and prediction speed of the model with its efficient data processing capability and optimized learning algorithm. It effectively reduces computational complexity and memory consumption through techniques such as histogram algorithm, gradient one-sided sampling, and feature bundling, thereby accelerating the process of risk identification. The introduction of GAN algorithm has increased the complexity of the model to some extent, but its parallel training mechanism between the generator and discriminator, as well as the advantages of GAN in data augmentation, have not had a negative impact on the overall recognition speed.

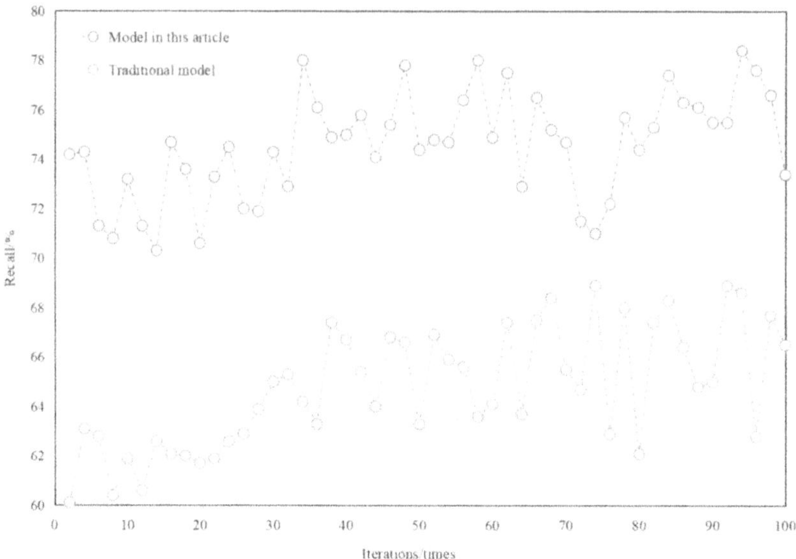

Fig. 3. Comparison of recall rates

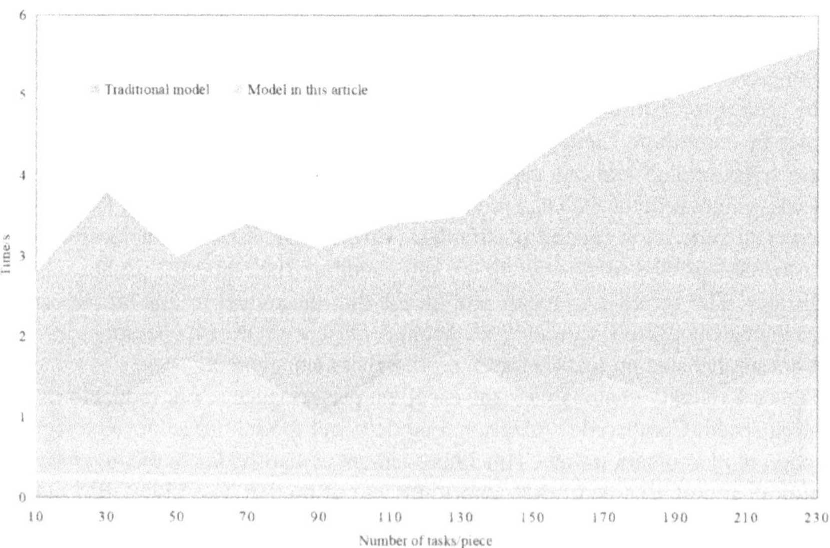

Fig. 4. Comparison of recognition speed

Figure 5 presents the significant effectiveness of our model in improving user satisfaction through intuitive data comparison. Compared to traditional models, this paper's model has received higher evaluations in terms of user satisfaction, thanks to its deep integration and innovative application of LightGBM and GAN algorithms. This model utilizes the efficient learning ability of LightGBM to quickly and accurately identify potential risks in enterprise operations, providing timely and effective risk warning and prevention recommendations for enterprise users. At the same time, the introduction of GAN algorithm not only enhances the model's understanding and response ability to complex risk scenarios, but also enriches the dataset for model training through the generated data samples, further improving the model's generalization ability and adaptability. These technological advantages directly translate into improved user experience during use. Users can feel the significant progress of the model in risk identification speed, accuracy, and personalized recommendations, thereby enhancing their confidence and satisfaction with enterprise risk management.

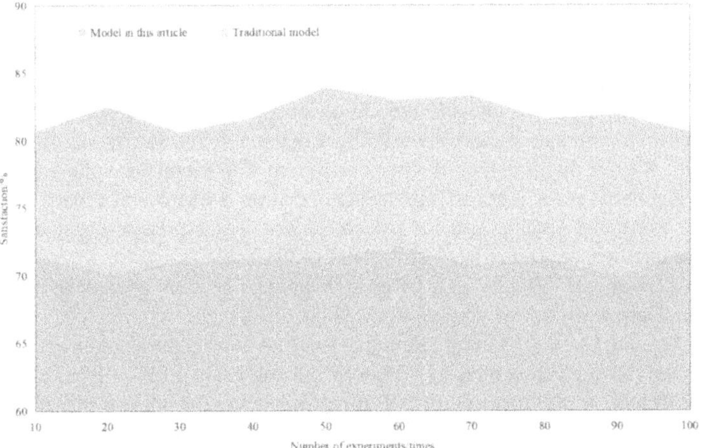

Fig. 5. Satisfaction comparison

4 Conclusion

Based on in-depth research and exploration, this article innovatively proposes an AI based enterprise risk management model, which marks an important leap in the field of enterprise risk management. By deeply integrating advanced ML algorithms and big data analysis techniques, this model not only achieves deep mining of massive historical data, but also captures real-time market dynamic information, providing unprecedented accuracy and real-time performance for enterprise risk management. The significant advantages of the experimental results, such as the leap in risk identification speed, significant improvement in identification accuracy, and significant enhancement of warning capability, fully demonstrate the enormous potential of our model in improving the efficiency and effectiveness of enterprise risk management. These advantages not only help companies discover potential risks earlier, but also provide strong support for developing more scientific and reasonable risk response strategies. However, we should also be aware that the model in this article still has certain limitations. Firstly, the performance of the model is highly dependent on the quality and quantity of the training data. If there are deviations or deficiencies in the data, it may affect the accuracy of the model. Secondly, with the constantly changing market environment, the model needs to be continuously updated and optimized to adapt to new risk characteristics and patterns. In addition, the complexity and computational cost of the model are also important factors to consider in practical applications.

References

1. Lu, Y., Zhai, G.: Application and exploration of artificial intelligence technology in urban disaster risk management. Int. Urban Plan. **36**(2), 22–31+39 (2021)
2. Wang, L.: A brief discussion on the transformation of financial accounting to management accounting in the era of artificial intelligence. Taxation. **13**(6), 73–75 (2019)
3. Wu, X.: The transformation of financial accounting to management accounting in the era of artificial intelligence. Heilongjiang Sci. **11**(9), 128–129 (2020)
4. Hu, Y., Li, Y.: Research on risk prevention of artificial intelligence products from the perspective of corporate social responsibility. Contemp. Econ. Manag. **42**(4), 19–26 (2020)
5. Hao, M.: A brief discussion on the transformation of financial accounting to management accounting in the era of artificial intelligence. Taxation. **14**(8), 51–52 (2020)
6. Qin, H.: Integrated development and risk challenges of enterprise management in the era of artificial intelligence. Future Dev. **44**(8), 18–21+39 (2020)
7. Zhang, Z., Wang, H., Zhu, L., et al.: Research on identification of HS code risks in Chinese customs. Data Anal. Knowl. Discov. **3**(1), 72–84 (2019)
8. Zhang, W., Qiu, C., Song, Y., et al.: Research progress of machine learning in the construction of delirium risk prediction models. J. PLA Med. Coll. **44**(11), 1292–1296 (2023)
9. Pei, X., Zhang, X.: Comparison of P2P network lending default risk identification models based on machine learning - taking "Renrendai" as an example. Jiangsu Sci. Technol. Inf. **37**(16), 35–38+47 (2020)
10. Xu, Z., Sheng, S.: Can digital transformation of enterprises reduce the cost of equity capital? Mechanism identification based on efficiency and risk perspectives. Financ. Econ. Res. **38**(6), 82–96 (2023)
11. Wu, B., Liu, Y., Zhang, M.: Research on analyst identification of financial fraud risk in companies based on machine learning. J. Manag. **19**(7), 1082–1091 (2022)
12. Zeng, H., Li, L., Lv, S., et al.: Research on risk identification methods for news and public opinion driven by tip learning. Comput. Eng. Appl. **60**(1), 182–188 (2024)
13. Xia, H., Qian, X., Ye, M., et al.: Research on risk perception of power information communication based on machine learning. Electron. Des. Eng. **31**(13), 141–145 (2023)

Fuzzy-Logic Risk Scoring Meets NPV: A Hybrid Decision Support Model for Capital Investment Under Uncertainty

Jianqing Li[1]([⊠]), Wenming Pan[2], Si Shen[1], Haihong Du[2], and Shili Liu[1]

[1] State Grid Anhui Economic Research Institute, Hefei 230000, Anhui, China
283093599@qq.com
[2] State Grid Anhui Electric Power Company, Hefei 230000, Anhui, China

Abstract. In this research, a hybrid decision support system that combines the fuzzy risk scoring and Net Present Value (NPV) based methodology is presented for enhancing capital investment decisions under uncertainty. The conventional evaluation of investment on infrastructure is usually based on deterministic financial indicators and subjective opinion, which does not make sense for modeling the fuzziness and uncertainty associated with infrastructure. To overcome such a limitation, we used the fuzzy logic approach to analyze qualitative risk factors in order to convert the uncertain risk assessment by experts into quantitative risk scores. While the NPV approach is useful in quantifying a project's worth in terms of the expected cash flow. The hybrid model balances the evaluation of financial performance and uncertainty–based risk by integrating these two frameworks. Simulation results show that the proposed model has significant superiority in predictive precision, considering higher R-WES, smaller RMSE and more robust under different investment situations than other usual models. The results suggest that this fuzzy–NPV integration can be practically useful for evidence-based decision-making, as a more robust and transparent approach to managing capital investment in real-world uncertain conditions, especially for the planning of power grid infrastructure.

Keywords: Fuzzy-logic risk scoring · Net Present Value (NPV) · Hybrid decision support model · Investment under uncertainty · Power grid infrastructure

1 Introduction

Based on economic and social progress, power grid infrastructure construction has become an important pillar of national development. How to manage the investment plan scientifically and reasonably has become an urgent problem [1]. Traditional investment plan management methods are often based on experience and intuition, lacking in scientificity and accuracy, and it is difficult to adapt to the complex and changeable market environment and project requirements [2]. Therefore, this study aims to explore a more scientific and effective investment plan management method to improve the investment benefit and management level of power grid infrastructure projects.

© The Author(s), under exclusive license to Springer Nature Singapore Pte Ltd. 2026
S. C. P. Yam et al. (Eds.): ICFT 2025, CCIS 2868, pp. 239–249, 2026.
https://doi.org/10.1007/978-981-92-0126-6_20

The main purpose of this study is to build an investment planning decision support system combining fuzzy logic and financial expenditure method, and its effectiveness is verified by model simulation experiments. The system aims to help decision-makers make investment plans for power grid infrastructure projects more scientifically and reasonably, optimize resource allocation, reduce investment risks and improve return on investment. The significance of the research lies in: by introducing fuzzy logic and financial expenditure method, the scientificity and accuracy of investment plan management are improved, which is helpful to solve the problems existing in traditional management methods; The construction and application of the system can provide useful reference for the investment plan management of similar projects. By optimizing investment plan management, it can promote the sustainable development of power grid infrastructure projects and improve social and economic benefits.

2 Present Situation and Challenges of Investment Plan Management of Power Grid Infrastructure Projects

In the past, the management mode of power grid infrastructure project investment plan mainly relied on traditional project management methods and empirical judgment [3]. This method is subjective and inaccurate in project planning, budgeting and resource allocation. Moreover, due to the lack of scientific and effective decision support system, it is often difficult for decision makers to comprehensively and accurately grasp the overall situation and risk factors of the project. At present, the investment plan management of power grid infrastructure projects is facing many problems and challenges, as shown in Table 1.

Table 1. Challenges in investment plan management of power grid infrastructure projects.

Category	Specific problems and challenges
Project complexity and uncertainty	Traditional project management methods are difficult to cope with all kinds of unexpected situations and changing needs
Subjectivity of empirical judgment	Empirical judgment may lead to deviation of investment plan and increased risk
Lack of decision support system	Lack of effective decision support system makes it difficult for decision makers to make scientific and reasonable decisions
The intensification of market competition	Need to adapt to the increasingly fierce market competition environment
Perfection of laws and policies	Must meet the requirements of the government's laws and policies on environmental protection and energy efficiency
Changes in market demand	Need flexible adjustment to meet the changing market demand

In view of the existence of the above problems and challenges and the continuous expansion of the investment scale of power grid infrastructure projects, it is particularly important and urgent to study a scientific and effective investment plan management method. By constructing an investment decision-making model combining fuzzy logic and financial expenditure method, it can provide more accurate and comprehensive information support for decision makers, reduce investment risks and improve return on investment [4]. Moreover, this study can also provide useful reference for the investment plan management of similar projects and promote the sustainable development of the whole industry.

3   Investment Decision-Making Model Combining Fuzzy Logic with Financial Expenditure Method

3.1   The Application of Fuzzy Logic in Investment Decision-Making

Fuzzy logic is a mathematical tool to deal with uncertainty and fuzziness, especially suitable for dealing with problems with unclear boundaries or multiple possibilities [5]. In investment decision-making, fuzzy logic can help us deal with all kinds of uncertainties and risk factors.

Firstly, fuzzy logic can be used to assess the risks and benefits of a project. By setting fuzzy sets and membership functions for various risk factors and income expectations, their uncertainty and possibility can be described more accurately [6]. This will help us to understand the risks and benefits of the project more comprehensively, so as to make more wise investment decisions. Secondly, fuzzy logic can also be used to optimize portfolio. By comprehensively considering the risks and benefits of multiple projects and their correlation, fuzzy logic can be used to find the best portfolio allocation. This method can help us maximize the expected return of the portfolio while meeting specific risk restrictions.

3.2   Principle and Calculation Method of Financial Expenditure Method

The financial expenditure method is a method to make investment decisions based on the expected cash flow of the project [7]. Its core idea is that the value of a project should be equal to the sum of the discounted value of its future cash flow.

Specifically, the calculation steps of the financial expenditure method are as follows: ① Forecast the future cash flow of the project. This includes forecasting the income, cost and tax of the project, and calculating the annual net cash flow. ② Choose an appropriate discount rate. The discount rate reflects the time value and risk factors of funds, which determines the present value of future cash flows. ③ Discount the future cash flow to the present by using the discount rate, and then sum. This sum is the NPV of the project. ④ If NPV is greater than zero, it means that the expected income of the project exceeds the required investment, so the project is worth investing. Conversely, if NPV is less than zero, the project may not be worth investing.

3.3   Construction of Investment Decision-Making Model Combining the Two

In the process of investment decision-making of power grid infrastructure projects, it is first needed to make a comprehensive assessment of the risks and benefits of the projects. Traditional assessment methods are often based on definite values and clear probability distribution, but in practice, many risk and benefit factors are fuzzy and uncertain [8]. Therefore, this article introduces fuzzy logic to describe and assess these factors more accurately. A more comprehensive investment decision-making model can be constructed by combining fuzzy logic with financial expenditure method. This model can comprehensively consider the risks and benefits of the project and their uncertainties. The financial risk identification system based on fuzzy logic is shown in Fig. 1.

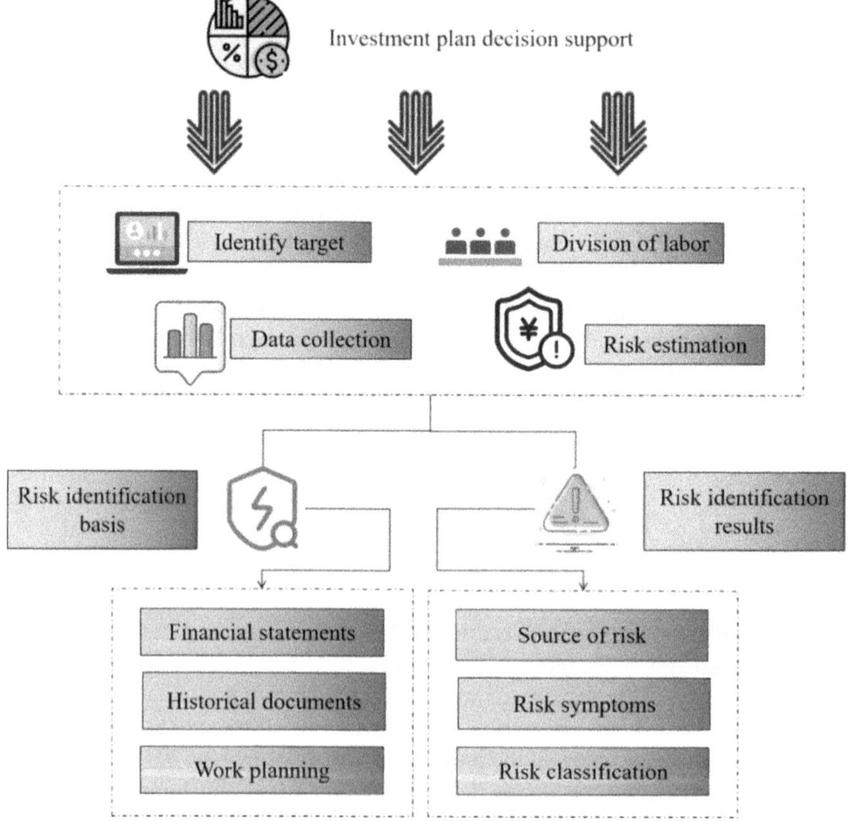

Fig. 1. Financial risk identification system based on fuzzy logic.

Before the assessment, it is needed to identify the main risk factors that may affect the project investment, such as market demand, policy changes, technical difficulties, raw material prices, etc. [9]. Moreover, it is also needed to clarify the income expectation of the project, such as return on investment and market share growth. In view of these factors, corresponding fuzzy sets can be established, such as "low risk", "medium risk", "high risk" and "low income", "medium income" and "high income". Membership function is a function that describes the degree to which an element belongs to a fuzzy set. For each risk factor and income expectation, it is needed to establish an appropriate membership function according to the actual situation and expert opinions. For example, for the risk factor of "market demand", a membership function can be defined, so that when the market demand is lower than a certain threshold, the factor belongs to the "low risk" set with higher membership; However, when the market demand is higher than another threshold, the membership degree of the "high risk" set is higher. The fuzzy logic risk assessment formula is as follows:

$$R = \sum_{i=1}^{n} w_i \cdot \mu R(x_i) \tag{1}$$

Among them, R is the overall risk assessment value of the project, w_i is the weight of the i risk factor, $\mu R(x_i)$ is the membership function value of the fuzzy set corresponding to the i risk factor, and n is the total number of risk factors. The fuzzy logic income assessment formula is as follows:

$$P = \sum_{j=1}^{m} v_j \cdot \mu P(y_j) \tag{2}$$

Among them, P is the overall revenue assessment value of the project, v_j is the weight of the j revenue expectation, $\mu P(y_j)$ is the membership function value of the fuzzy set corresponding to the j revenue expectation, and m is the total number of revenue expectations.

After the fuzzy logic assessment of risks and benefits is completed, the NPV of the project is calculated by using the financial expenditure method. NPV is a commonly used project investment assessment index, which considers the time value of funds and assess the economic value of the project by discounting the future cash flow of the project to the present. The NPV calculation formula is as follows:

$$NPV = \sum_{t=0}^{T} \frac{CF_t}{(1+r)^t} - C_0 \tag{3}$$

Among them, CF_t is the cash flow forecast value in the t year, r is the discount rate, T is the life span of the project, and C_0 is the initial investment of the project. According to the specific situation and market environment of the project, combined with the risk and benefit results of fuzzy logic assessment, the future cash flow of the project can be predicted. Risk acceptability judgment:

$$\text{Acceptable Risk} = \begin{cases} \text{True,} & \text{if } R \leq R_{\text{threshold}} \\ \text{False,} & \text{otherwise} \end{cases} \tag{4}$$

Where Acceptable Risk indicates whether the risk is within the acceptable range, and $R_{\text{threshold}}$ is the acceptable threshold of the risk. Investment decision-making judgment follows the following formula:

$$\text{Invest Decision} = \begin{cases} \text{Invest, if NPV} > 0 \text{ and Acceptable Risk} \\ \text{Caution, otherwise} \end{cases} \tag{5}$$

Among them, Invest Decision stands for investment decision. When NPV is greater than zero and the risk is acceptable, it is recommended to invest. Otherwise, it should be carefully considered.

The discount rate is the rate at which future cash flows are discounted to the present, which reflects the time value and investment risk of funds. When choosing the discount rate, you can refer to the industry average or the empirical data of similar projects. Moreover, the risk result of fuzzy logic assessment can also be considered as the basis for adjusting the discount rate. For example, if the project risk is high, then the discount rate should be increased accordingly. The discount rate is adjusted according to the following formula:

$$r_{\text{adjusted}} = r_{\text{base}} + f(R) \tag{6}$$

Where r_{adjusted} is the adjusted discount rate, r_{base} is the basic discount rate, and $f(R)$ is a function adjusted according to the risk assessment value R, which can be a linear function, a nonlinear function or other functions.

Finally, the final investment decision is made by combining the risk and benefit results of fuzzy logic assessment with NPV calculated by financial expenditure method. Specifically:

① Judge whether NPV is greater than zero.

If the NPV of the project is greater than zero, it means that the economic value of the project is positive, that is, the expected income is greater than the investment cost. This is a positive signal that the project has potential profitability.

② Assess whether the risk is within the acceptable range.

In addition to considering NPV, it is also needed to judge whether the risk is within the acceptable range according to the risk result of fuzzy logic assessment. This can be achieved by comparing the membership function value of risk factors with the preset risk threshold. If all risk factors are within the acceptable range, then the risk of the project can be considered controllable.

Through the above investment decision-making model combining fuzzy logic and financial expenditure method, the risks and benefits of the project can be assessed more comprehensively, so as to make more wise investment decisions.

4 Simulation Experiment and Result Analysis

In this section, simulation experiments are carried out to verify the effectiveness of the investment decision-making model based on fuzzy logic and financial expenditure method. The purpose of this experiment is to simulate the real market environment and project conditions to test the performance of the model in different scenarios. The experimental objects are several representative power grid infrastructure projects, which cover different investment scales, risk levels and income expectations. Moreover, according to the specific situation of the project, the parameters and conditions of the simulation experiment are set, including the expected cash flow, discount rate and risk factors of the project.

During the experiment, this article uses Monte Carlo simulation method to generate random samples of future cash flow and risk factors of the project. Through many simulation experiments, we get the output results of the model in different scenarios and make statistical analysis. In order to verify the effectiveness of the investment decision-making model, this section compares the output results of the model with the investment results of the actual project. By calculating the error between the model prediction and the actual results, the prediction accuracy of the model is assessed. The comparison between the output results of the model and the investment results of the actual project is shown in Fig. 2.

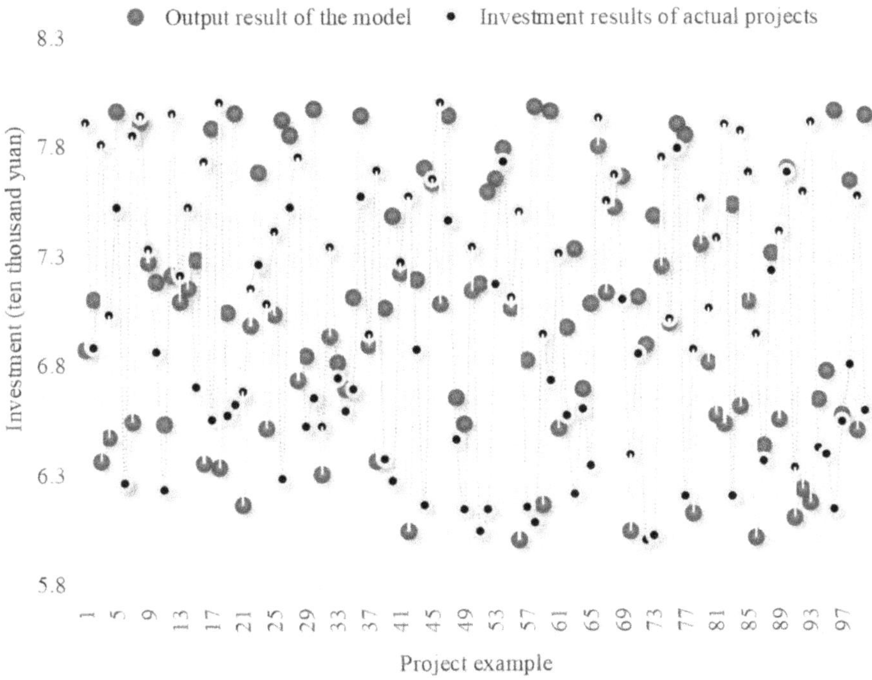

Fig. 2. Comparison between the output result of the model and the investment result of the actual project.

As shown in Fig. 2, the comparison between the output results of the model and the investment results of the actual project shows a high degree of coincidence. This means that the model can accurately simulate the investment situation of actual projects and provide reliable forecasting information for decision makers. This high degree of coincidence reflects the effectiveness of the model in data processing and algorithm design, which enables the model to capture the key factors that affect the investment results, and accordingly gives a forecast close to reality.

The RMSE of the model is shown in Fig. 3.

As shown in Fig. 3, the RMSE value of the model is low, which shows that the deviation between the prediction result of the model and the actual investment result is small, and the prediction performance of the model is good. The low RMSE value

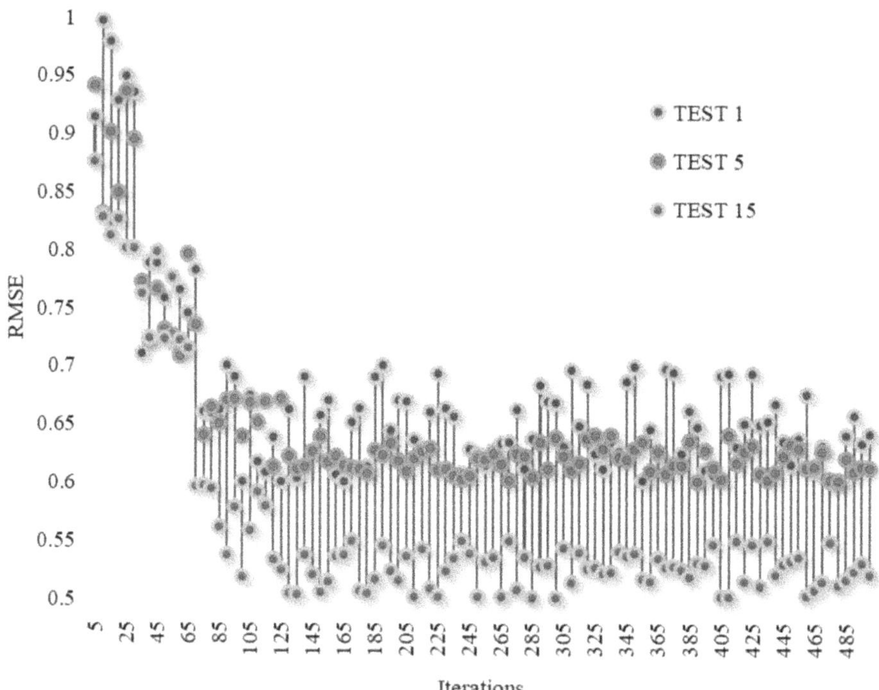

Fig. 3. RMSE of the model.

directly reflects the accuracy of the model, which shows that the model has high accuracy in forecasting the investment of power grid infrastructure projects.

The prediction accuracy of the model is shown in Fig. 4.

As shown in Fig. 4, the prediction accuracy of the model is high. High prediction accuracy means that the model can more accurately grasp the dynamic changes of project investment and provide valuable decision support for investors. This result further verifies the practicability and effectiveness of the model in power grid infrastructure investment decision-making.

In addition, this article also invited many experts in the field of power grid infrastructure investment to assess the model. According to their experience and professional knowledge, the experts analyzed and assessed the output results of the model, and put forward valuable feedback, as shown in Fig. 5.

As can be seen from the table, experts generally believe that the model performs well in risk and benefit assessment, and affirmed the application prospect of the model. Moreover, experts also put forward some suggestions, such as strengthening the prediction accuracy of high-risk projects, increasing the analysis of coping strategies for emergencies, and considering the impact of macroeconomic factors, in order to further improve the function and accuracy of the model.

Through the data analysis and interpretation of the simulation results, this article finds that the investment decision-making model has high accuracy in predicting project risks and benefits. The advantage of this investment decision-making model is that it

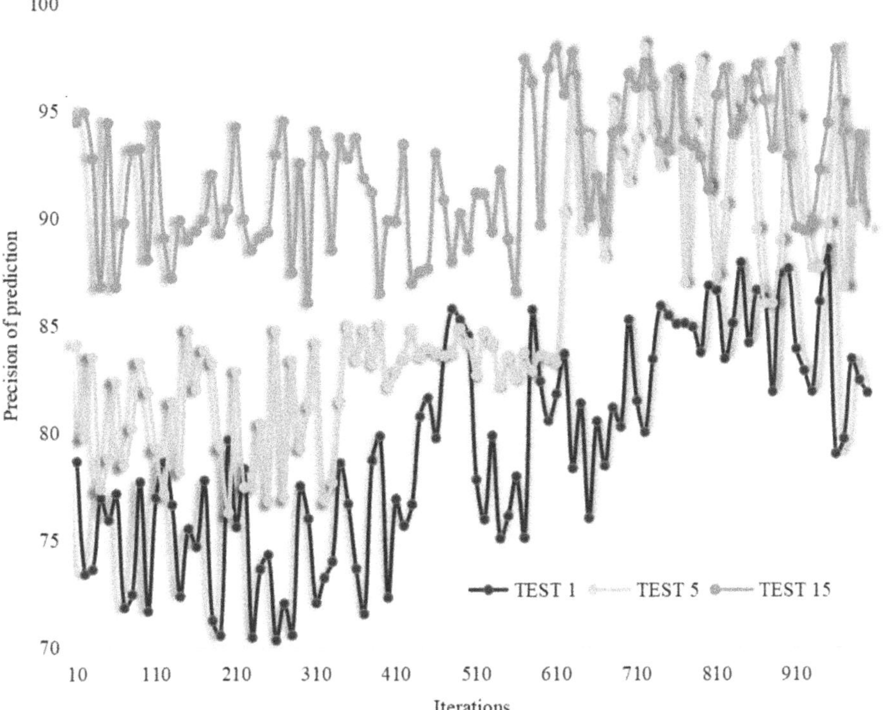

Fig. 4. Prediction accuracy of the model.

can comprehensively consider various risk factors and income expectations, and provide comprehensive and objective information support for decision makers. Moreover, the model has strong robustness and adaptability, and can give reasonable investment suggestions in different scenarios.

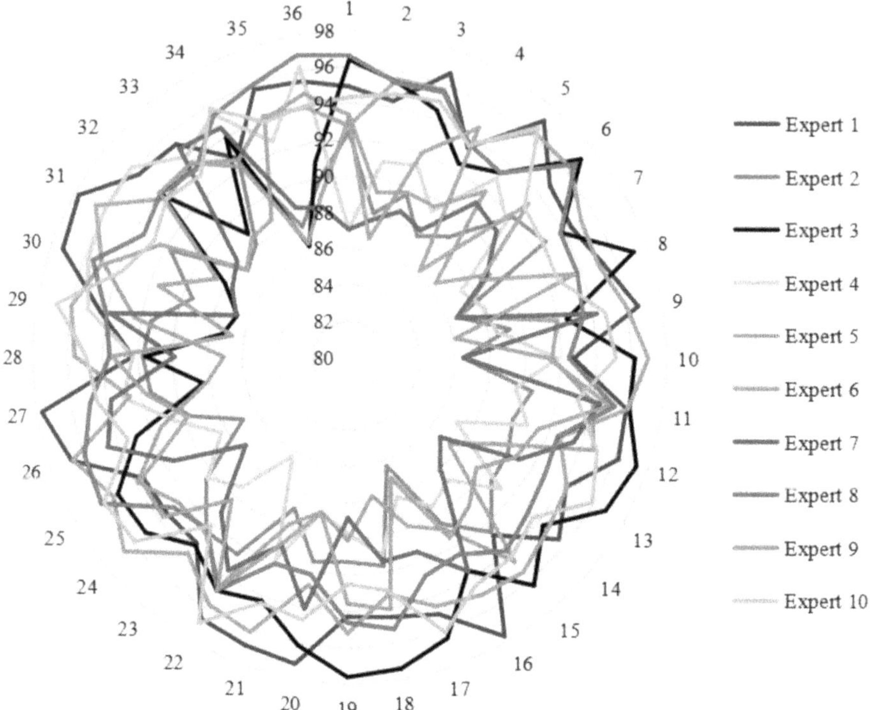

Fig. 5. Expert assessment results.

5 Conclusions

In this paper, a hybrid investment decision support model that integrates fuzzy-logic risk scoring and the Net Present Value (NPV) approach is developed and validated to cater for uncertainty and vagueness in capital investment decisions. The candidate model is able to combine a bottom-up qualitative risk assessment and top-down quantitative financial analysis, providing a consistent inclusion of both the approaches in the evaluation. Simulation results show that the hybrid fuzzy–NPV model has high prediction accuracy, low error rate and good robustness considering complex and uncertain investment situations.

The results indicate that this risk evaluation based on fuzzy logic and using it as a supplement to traditional NPV analysis and contributes its objectivity, precision in investment assessment especially for large-scale long-term infrastructure projects.

Recommendations for future work include:

Improving quality and diversity of data: Subsequent research should seek to compile more comprehensive project data including qualitative risk indicators, and market conditions; so that a model does not hinge as much on key assumptions.

Dynamic operational changes: The hybrid model must dynamically adjust with the situation changing over time and uncertainty pattern arising.

Decision maker capacity building: Training programmes needed to be implemented that would build the capacity of practitioners how to articulate fuzzy-logic outputs and integrate them in financial decision frameworks.

Integration with AI and multi-criteria methods: This hybrid fuzzy–NPV methodology, if integrated with artificial intelligent systems and/or multi-criteria decision-making approaches, can provide better accuracy and may be more generic than that obtained through the developed technique.

Together, the work presented here showcases a powerful and scalable decision support tool to foster investment transparency, mitigate uncertainty, and promote sustainable development in power grid and other infrastructure sectors.

References

1. Kuchta, D.: Fuzzy capital budgeting. Fuzzy Sets Syst. **111**(3), 367–385 (2000)
2. Tsao, C.: Assessing the probabilistic fuzzy net present value for a capital investment choice using fuzzy arithmetic. J. Chin. Inst. Ind. Eng. **22**(2), 106–118 (2005)
3. Tsao, C.: The expectation-deviation net present value by fuzzy arithmetic for capital investments. J. Stat. Manag. Syst. **13**(2), 267–281 (2010)
4. Huang, X.: Chance-constrained programming models for capital budgeting with NPV as fuzzy parameters. J. Comput. Appl. Math. **198**(1), 149–159 (2007)
5. Rebiasz, B.: Fuzziness and randomness in investment project risk appraisal. Comput. Oper. Res. **34**(1), 199–210 (2007)
6. Lin, H., Lu, H.: Evaluating the BOT project of sport facility: an application of fuzzy net present value method. J. Ind. Prod. Eng. **30**(4), 220–229 (2013)
7. Chrysafis, K., Papadopoulos, B.: Cost–volume–profit analysis under uncertainty: a model with fuzzy estimators based on confidence intervals. Int. J. Prod. Res. **47**(21), 5977–5999 (2009)
8. Zadeh, L.: Fuzzy sets as a basis for a theory of possibility. Fuzzy Sets Syst. **1**(1), 3–28 (1978)
9. Serguieva, A., Hunter, J.: Fuzzy interval methods in investment risk appraisal. Fuzzy Sets Syst. **142**(3), 443–466 (2004)

Climate Risk Modeling in the Digital Age: New Approaches for Financial Institutions

A. Y. Andrianov[1]([✉]) [iD], V. V. Ivanov[1] [iD], and R. K. Nurmukhametov[2] [iD]

[1] St. Petersburg State University, St. Petersburg, Russian Federation
`a.y.andrianov@gsom.spbu`
[2] Department for Finance and Banking, Tula Branch of the Financial, University under the Government of the Russian Federation, Tula, Russian Federation

Abstract. The accelerating realization of climate risks poses a challenge for financial institutions, requiring them to adapt their risk management systems to take into account both physical and transition risks. This paper examines the evolving role of financial technology (fintech) in assessing and managing climate risks in the financial sector. The study aims to (i) clarify the nature and classification of climate risks in a financial context, (ii) explore how fintech solutions enable the integration of climate data, scenario analysis tools and portfolio alignment into financial institutions' risk management systems.

From a methodological perspective, the paper provides a structured literature review with a focus on the interplay between climate finance and digital technologies. It identifies key barriers to effective climate risk assessment, such as data fragmentation, model uncertainty and limited comparability, and presents fintech-based innovations that address these gaps. Particular attention is paid to scenario analysis, financed emissions assessment and forward-looking portfolio diagnostics, where fintech enables more scalable, automated and data-rich approaches.

This paper aims to bridge the gap between climate risk assessment frameworks and practical technology solutions. It shows how fintech is not only enabling climate risk management but also creating new opportunities for transparency, accountability and regulatory alignment. These findings are important for financial institutions, regulators and fintech developers seeking to future-proof risk management frameworks in a climate-constrained economy.

Keywords: Nature-related financial risks · Scenario-based risk assessment · FinTech in sustainable finance

1 Introduction

Risk management has long been a central pillar of financial and corporate decision-making, enabling organizations to anticipate, quantify, and prepare for uncertainty. Climate-related risk, however, poses new and complex challenges to this well-established discipline. Unlike many conventional risks, climate risk is systemic, long-term, and characterized by high uncertainty and non-linear impacts. It manifests both through physical

S. C. P. Yam et al. (Eds.): ICFT 2025, CCIS 2868, pp. 250–261, 2026.
https://doi.org/10.1007/978-981-92-0126-6_21

risks – such as extreme weather events, sea-level rise, and chronic climate shifts – and transition risks linked to policy, technological, market, and societal changes on the path to a low-carbon economy. As climate change increasingly affects operational, credit, market, insurance, and liquidity risks, understanding its transmission channels is essential for informed financial and strategic decision-making [1]. Digital technologies and fintech applications are transforming how climate risks are assessed and managed. Cloud-based data infrastructures, ESG data analytics platforms, and AI-driven scenario generators are increasingly embedded into financial institutions' risk modeling workflows, enabling real-time analysis and scalable integration of environmental factors [2].

A key obstacle to effective climate risk management is measurement. The widely accepted maxim "what gets measured gets managed" holds especially true here – yet climate risks are inherently more difficult to quantify than traditional financial exposures. Measuring transition risk demands not only detailed emissions data but also insight into the evolving regulatory landscape, technological developments, and shifts in consumer preferences. Assessing physical risk, in turn, requires a forward-looking approach informed by climate models, historical weather data, infrastructure resilience, and geographic exposure. These circumstances require consideration of interdisciplinary data and reliable analytics.

Scenario analysis is one of the most common approaches to dealing with uncertainty related to a variety of climate risks. Scenario analysis appeared in the middle of the 20th century and was actively developed by corporations such as Shell. In the context of climate change, it allows companies to analyze the financial consequences of various physical and transition risk scenarios and has essentially evolved from a strategic forecasting tool into a practical tool for assessing internal and external risks related to capital allocation, investment strategy, and regulatory compliance. Climate scenario analysis has gained momentum in part due to the recommendations of the Task Force on Climate-related Financial Disclosures (TCFD), which urges organizations to use plausible, challenging, and relevant scenarios to test their resilience and inform stakeholders [3]. Increasingly, scenario-based stress testing is also becoming part of regulatory frameworks, with central banks piloting climate-related stress tests to assess systemic financial vulnerabilities [4].

This paper explores the current state and future directions of climate risk measurement and scenario analysis. It is structured as follows. Section 2 outlines the research methodology used in this study. Section 3 examines the major challenges associated with quantifying climate-related risks. Section 4 discusses scenario analysis in more detail, including the parameters of climate scenarios and their application to physical and transition risks, followed by conclusions.

2   Research Methodology

This study uses a qualitative approach based on a structured review and synthesis of scientific literature, industry reports, and regulatory publications related to measuring and modeling risks associated with climate change. The main objective is to identify and systematize the key methodological approaches used by financial institutions and regulatory authorities to assess both physical and transition risks.

The literature review focuses on peer-reviewed articles, reports from standard-setting bodies, as well as publications from central banks and non-profit organizations. These sources are analyzed to map the evolution of climate risk assessment methods, including quantitative models, scenario-based tools, and risk transfer mechanisms.

In addition to scientific and regulatory sources, the study draws on publicly available case studies and information from companies from different sectors. These real-world examples are used to illustrate how firms apply climate risk measurement and scenario analysis in practice. The collected evidence is then used to develop a structured classification of prevailing approaches and identify new trends.

3   Challenges in Measuring Climate-Related Risks

When assessing nature-related and climate-related financial risks, banks and other financial institutions must take into account the dual character of such threats. On the one hand, there are physical risks - driven by acute and chronic environmental hazards - which can impair asset quality and disrupt cash flows through direct damage to property, infrastructure, and supply chains. On the other hand, transition risks emerge as economies adjust to environmental policies, carbon pricing mechanisms, or shifts in market preferences. These two dimensions often interact: for instance, a rise in physical damages may accelerate poli-cy intervention, increasing transition-related volatility. For risk modeling purposes, both types require tailored metrics and differentiated treatment, although their interplay also deserves integrated scenario testing [5].

The two-category framework has become standard in both research and policy discussions. However, scholars increasingly recognize its limitations in capturing the complete picture of environmental financial risks. Recent studies have identified several additional risk categories that deserve rigorous consideration:

- Systemic risk
- Legal exposure risk
- Transition costs
- Institutional fragility [6].

The degree of detail in exposure measurement obviously influences accuracy and usability of risk assessment. Deep analysis at the counterparty or asset level allows for detailed insights but can be limited by data availability and increased computational need. Conversely, aggregated assessment at the sector or portfolio level is less sensitive to data deficit and better suited for strategic planning. The choice of approach - whether bottom-up or top-down - should reflect the purpose of the risk evaluation, data constraints, and the nature of the decisions it is thought to inform.

Another critical consideration lies in the role of mitigation strategies. Risk assessments that rely mainly on current protective measures - such as insurance coverage or policy buffers - may underestimate exposure, especially when those mechanisms are subject to revisions, or failure. For this reason, it is recommended to model both unmitigated and post-mitigation exposures. In addition, banks shall navigate a landscape marked by heterogeneity in climate regimes, policy frameworks, and sectoral sensitivities since regional variability in climate risks, differences in regulatory maturity, and the technological adaptability of clients all contribute to divergent exposure profiles. These uncertainties reinforce the importance of using flexible, transparent, and assumption-sensitive modeling approaches when integrating climate-related nature risks into financial decision-making.

To address these challenges, banks and other financial institutions can apply a range of modeling approaches that differ in scope, complexity, and data requirements. The table below provides an overview of commonly used methodologies for assessing climate-related financial risks, along with their respective advantages and limitations.

3.1 Measuring Transition Risks

Assessment of transition risks begins with estimating company-level greenhouse gas (GHG) emissions, which are categorized according to the GHG Protocol:

- Scope 1 covers direct emissions from a company's own operations,
- Scope 2 includes emissions from purchased electricity, and
- Scope 3 encompasses all other indirect emissions, such as those embedded in supply chains or in downstream product use [7]

Sectoral characteristics strongly influence emissions profiles. For instance, in the financial sector, most emissions are captured under Scope 3 due to investment and lending activities. Energy utilities mainly report large volumes of Scope 1 emissions, whereas oil and gas companies typically have substantial Scope 3 emissions associated with combustion of sold products.

Currently, greenhouse gas emissions data are typically disclosed by companies on a voluntary basis, often collected through questionnaires administered by non-profit organizations such as Carbon Disclosure Project [8] These data are typically not externally audited by professional organizations, may not include some emission areas, and as a result, vary in the quality of disclosure. Where precise data is not available, emissions data are provided based on proxy companies and proxy models, which contribute to inaccuracy and incompleteness of the data. Double counting due to the nature of emissions accounting, particularly between electricity producers and consumers, adds complexity [9].

To supplement backward-looking emissions metrics, climate transition assessments increasingly incorporate forward-looking indicators. These include the credibility of companies' decarbonization strategies, alignment with net-zero commitments, and consistency with global climate targets such as those set in the Paris Agreement. Number of tools offer structured methods to score alignment and produce "temperature scores" for companies or portfolios. Asset-level emissions data also enhance measurement precision, especially in capital-intensive industries.

However, measuring transition risk requires more than just emissions accounting. Understanding the broader context – such as policy evolution, technological development, and market expectations – is essential. Data from organizations like IEA and consultancies like Bloomberg or Rystad Energy help assess macro-drivers of transition risk. Yet such sources are often commercial and expensive, creating accessibility challenges.

3.2 Measuring Physical Risks

Physical risk assessment is based on the use of climate models, in particular those developed in the framework of the fifth and sixth phases of the Coupled Model Comparison project [10]. These models build different future climate change scenarios, but are often not detailed enough at the regional level, as this requires detailed integration with local geographic and economic data. Quantitative physical risk assessment includes an assessment of the exposure and vulnerability of specific business assets. Several open-access sources contribute to this task, such as Climate Central (sea level rise projections), WRI (water stress indices), and the Max Planck Institute (wildfire exposure indicators) [11].

Private providers like Four Twenty Seven, Carbone 4, and Trucost have developed proprietary physical risk scores based on integrated modeling of asset locations and climate hazard indices. These scores are typically scaled (e.g., 0 to 100) and allow for comparative assessments across companies or facilities. Some models also account for multi-hazard exposure, offering a more comprehensive view of risks [12]. However, the underlying methodologies are often opaque and lack transparency, limiting their interpretability and comparability.

3.3 Portfolio-Level Integration

For financial institutions, both types of climate risk must be translated into portfolio-level indicators. Common transition risk metrics include Weighted Average Carbon Intensity (WACI) and portfolio temperature scores, which reflect the average alignment of portfolio constituents with global warming pathways. Scenario-based stress tests simulate financial impacts from events like abrupt carbon price increases.

Physical risk exposure at the portfolio level is typically assessed through mapping geospatial data of real assets or estimating climate-adjusted Value-at-Risk (VaR). These approaches integrate projected hazard frequency and severity with asset valuations under different climate pathways (Table 1).

Table 1. Measuring climate-related financial risks methodologies

Methodologies	Strengths of the Approach	Weaknesses of the Approach
Integrated Assessment Models (IAMs)	Combine economic, energy, and climate dynamics to connect emission trajectories with macroeconomic outcomes.	Limited in capturing non-recurring extreme weather events; often underestimate future risks due to insufficient historical data.
Sensitivity Analysis	Demonstrates how variations in assumptions can significantly influence projected losses; helps highlight risk volatility.	May still downplay low-probability, high-impact events; relies heavily on judgment about tail-risk probabilities.

(continued)

Table 1. (*continued*)

Methodologies	Strengths of the Approach	Weaknesses of the Approach
Input–Output Models	Estimate sectoral or regional impacts of climate policies; useful in tracing indirect economic effects.	Lack behavioral realism; less suitable for complex feedback and dynamic policy reactions.
Computable General Equilibrium (CGE) Models	Simulate policy scenarios across sectors with inter-agent interactions; useful for holistic policy evaluation.	Computationally intensive and highly abstract; model complexity may obscure practical interpretation.
Dynamic Stochastic General Equilibrium (DSGE) Models	Designed to manage economic uncertainty over time; suitable for long-horizon policy simulation.	High technical complexity and demanding calibration reduce transparency and accessibility.
Overlapping Generation (OLG) Models	Offer clearer representation of long-term fiscal and demographic dynamics; suitable for macroeconomic projections.	Limited scope for sectoral detail; do not easily integrate environmental complexities.
Agent-Based Models (ABMs)	Allow simulation of heterogeneous actors and decentralized decision-making; good for capturing complexity and adaptation.	Require extensive data; internal model logic can be opaque, making validation challenging.
Climate Stress Testing	Connects projected climate scenarios with bank-specific portfolios to assess financial vulnerability.	Results are highly sensitive to scenario design and assumptions; time-consuming setup.
Climate Risk Ratings/Scores	Provide standardized evaluation of exposure across entities or sectors; facilitate comparison.	May oversimplify or miss context-specific factors; rely on subjective scoring frameworks.
Scenario Analysis (incl. NGFS/IEA Scenarios)	Enables forward-looking risk assessment by modeling different climate outcomes and transitions.	Lacks detailed breakdown of physical risk damages; may underrepresent sudden shocks or tipping points.
Natural Capital Assessment (Third-Party)	Assesses exposure to ecosystem degradation by linking portfolios to ecological dependencies.	Dependent on availability of natural capital data; sectoral mapping may lack granularity.

(continued)

Table 1. (continued)

Methodologies	Strengths of the Approach	Weaknesses of the Approach
Climate Value at Risk (VaR)	Adapts a familiar risk framework to quantify climate-linked financial exposure.	May not fully capture long-tail or systemic nature of climate events; sensitive to input assumptions.
Static Balance Sheet Modeling	Provides a snapshot of current exposures under different climate scenarios.	Becomes less reliable over longer horizons as it ignores balance sheet evolution and strategy shifts.
Dynamic Balance Sheet Modeling	Accounts for future adjustments in asset-liability structure; reflects strategic risk responses.	Requires detailed forecasting and assumptions, which can introduce additional uncertainty.

3.4 Key Challenges in Measuring Financed Emissions

In addition to biodiversity-related issues, climate-related emissions represent a major source of systemic environmental risk for banks. Thus, the methodology must incorporate both biodiversity and climate dimensions of nature-related risks. A cornerstone of effective transition planning is transparent and consistent carbon reporting. This involves tracking and publicly sharing an organization's greenhouse gas (GHG) emissions, serving as a key element of corporate governance for managing climate-related risks and opportunities. Regulatory bodies are increasingly mandating carbon disclosures, underscoring importance for both environmental responsibility and compliance. While progress in measuring emissions remains gradual, recent data shows notable improvements. For instance, nearly 22,700 companies reported their GHG emissions through CDP in 2024 which indicated a 21% rise from 2022, signalling growing corporate recognition of their operational impacts on the climate [13].

Carbon reporting tracks greenhouse gases like CO_2, CH_4, and N_2O, which drive climate change. While financial institutions have minimal direct (Scope 1 & 2) emissions, their indirect (Scope 3) emissions (i.e. primarily from financed activities), according to CDP, are typically 700 times higher. Effective transition planning requires robust measurement of these financed emissions. Absolute emissions provide a baseline under the Paris Agreement, but normalized metrics (e.g., emissions per unit of output) offer additional insights for risk management, target-setting, and product development [2].

Financed emissions data play a critical role in the integration of climate-related risks into banking practices. These metrics can inform credit decisions by enabling banks to assess the carbon intensity of borrowers and entire loan portfolios. They also support climate stress-testing by providing input for forward-looking scenario analyses based on decarbonization pathways. Moreover, financed emissions influence the development of green financial products, such as sustainability-linked loans and transition finance instruments, where emission trajectories are embedded in pricing or covenant structures.

However, measurement faces hurdles:

1) Data gaps force reliance on sector averages, reducing accuracy [14].
2) Method inconsistencies, timing mismatches (e.g., fiscal vs. seasonal cycles), and asset value fluctuations complicate tracking.
3) Smaller banks, especially those with non-listed clients, lack granular data, leading to proxy-dependent reporting and variability [4].

The lack of centralized climate data thus exacerbates these problems. Recent initiatives are aimed at improving data quality across asset classes, which may help address the current data asymmetry.

4 Scenario-Based Analysis of Nature-Related Risks

Scenario analysis has become an integral part of managing financial risks associated with changing natural resources. The origins of scenario analysis date back to the mid-20th century, when it was first applied in the military and energy sectors. Companies such as Shell pioneered its use in corporate strategy in the 1970s, demonstrating the value of preparing for low-probability but high-impact events such as the 1973 oil crisis [15]. The approach has gained widespread acceptance and is now used across a variety of industries, particularly by financial institutions and regulators, including in climate risk management. It should be noted that scenario analysis not only helps companies understand physical risks but also helps them analyze transition risks.

4.1 Choice of Parameters

The initiation of scenario analysis necessitates two fundamental determinations: the selection of an appropriate baseline scenario and the configuration of relevant parameters. In most practical applications, utilization of established reference scenarios proves adequate, obviating the requirement for constructing comprehensive bottom-up models of sectoral energy consumption. However, this approach still demands certain consideration regarding analytical scope, methodological framework, and expected outputs.

Climate scenarios shall incorporate numerous predefined parameters and underlying assumptions. These encompass a spectrum of variables ranging from macroeconomic indicators (e.g., gross domestic product growth rates) to energy system characteristics (including demand projections and fuel mix distributions) and policy implementation trajectories. The execution of scenario analysis requires explicit decisions concerning:

- The analytical scope (system boundaries and coverage)
- The methodological approach (quantitative modeling versus qualitative assessment)
- Data requirements and availability constraints (particularly concerning value chain elements)

The resultant outputs may encompass diverse financial metrics, including but not limited to revenue projections, operational cost estimates, and asset valuation impacts - the latter being particularly relevant in cases of potential asset stranding.

4.2 Use of Scenario Analysis for Transition Risk

Transition risk is inherently tied to projected emissions pathways, which define the speed, scale, and orderliness of the global shift toward a low-carbon economy. These pathways are typically derived from standardized scenarios such as the IPCC's Representative Concentration Pathways (RCPs) [16], the International Energy Agency's (IEA) Net Zero Emissions scenarios [17], or customized models developed by firms and consultancies. The magnitude of transition risk for firms and financial institutions increases when emissions reductions are more abrupt (disorderly) or more ambitious (e.g., net zero by 2050), compared to business-as-usual (BAU) trajectories.

Scenario analysis for transition risk generally involves assessing whether a firm's operations, supply chains, and financial exposures are consistent with sectoral or global emissions trajectories. At the macro level, this is supported by Integrated Assessment Models (IAMs), i.e. quantitative models that integrate economic, technological, and physical systems to estimate the trade-offs of climate policy. IAMs, widely used by the IPCC, assume rational economic behavior and are typically optimized to minimize aggregate costs across sectors. Their outputs form the backbone of many regulatory climate risk assessments and are increasingly integrated into digital risk analytics platforms through Fintech solutions.

Fintech plays a critical role in operationalizing this complex analysis. Several sector-specific decarbonization pathways have emerged as tools for alignment assessments, including those from the IEA, the Transition Pathway Initiative (TPI), and the Science-Based Targets initiative (SBTi) [18]. These pathways help firms benchmark their own carbon trajectories against Paris Agreement-compatible targets.

In practice, TPI uses public data and scenario alignment ratings to grade companies' readiness for transition, supporting investors in portfolio reallocation and index-based investing. Fintech firms such as Carbon Delta, Carbone 4, and Ortec Finance[1] offer digital services that integrate emissions data, scenario projections, and financial modeling to support in-house risk evaluation.

A more advanced strategy involves companies developing proprietary emissions scenarios tailored to their business strategies. For instance, Shell's internal scenario framework includes "Sky 1.5," "Waves," and "Islands," offering narratives with varying assumptions about policy stringency and technological adoption. These in-house models often diverge from neutral scenarios by assuming continued demand for oil and gas, highlighting potential biases in firm-led forecasting.

4.3 Use of Scenario Analysis for Physical Risk

The application of scenario analysis to physical climate risks differs fundamentally from transition risk assessment in several critical ways.

---

[1] Carbon Delta, Carbone 4, and Ortec Finance are all involved in climate-related financial analysis, but they focus on different aspects. Carbon Delta provides climate risk analytics for financial institutions, quantifying investment risks across various scenarios. Carbone 4 offers advisory services related to low-carbon strategies and climate change risks. Ortec Finance develops climate scenarios and tools for financial institutions to assess the impact of climate change on investments and asset pricing.

While transition risks rely heavily on emissions trajectories, physical risk assessment requires translating these pathways into tangible impacts through climate models. Due to climate system inertia, physical risks through 2050 are largely locked in by past and current emissions, making near-term scenario planning less dependent on future emissions pathways. Instead, organizations increasingly focus on operational preparedness for plausible climate-driven events [19].

Physical climate models, originally developed for scientific research, now play a dual role in risk assessment: firstly, they calibrate emissions scenarios by linking radiative forcing to temperature targets. Secondly, they generate hazard projections (e.g., heatwaves, precipitation shifts) when fed emissions data. Despite advances, models still show discrepancies in regional hazard projections, particularly for precipitation patterns and extreme events [20].

Unlike transition risks, which can be assessed at sector or corporate levels, physical risks manifest at specific sites (e.g., flooded facilities, wildfire-damaged assets). Their cascading effects—through supply chains, ownership structures, and investments—require granular, asset-level analysis [21]

Physical risk evaluation demands high-resolution data on hazards, exposure, and vulnerability. Firms often rely on specialized providers (e.g., Four Twenty Seven, Trucost) or in-house capabilities to assess site-specific risks. Given the limited relevance of long-term emissions scenarios for near-term physical risks, many organizations adopt methods akin to traditional scenario planning (e.g., Shell's approach). Historical analogs and stress-testing for high-probability events (e.g., recurring floods) often prove more actionable than climate model outputs, which lack precision in timing and localized impacts.

5 Conclusion

Climate-related risks present a fundamental shift in how financial institutions and corporations must understand, measure, and manage uncertainty. Unlike traditional financial risks, climate risks are long-term, systemic, and deeply intertwined with environmental, technological, regulatory, and societal dynamics. This paper has explored the core challenges in quantifying both physical and transition risks. It also examined how scenario analysis – originally a strategic planning tool – has evolved into a central component of climate risk assessment frameworks, offering forward-looking insights for decision-making under deep uncertainty.

Our review shows that no single methodology is sufficient on its own. Effective climate risk management requires a combination of approaches, from emissions accounting and sectoral alignment assessments to dynamic scenario-based stress testing and asset-level hazard analysis. However, current practices remain hindered by fragmented data, limited model transparency, and inconsistent reporting standards – especially in the context of financed emissions and physical asset exposure. Bridging these gaps will require greater standardization, open data infrastructure, and interdisciplinary collaboration among regulators, firms, and technical experts.

As climate scenarios become more complex and risks more material, the integration of nature-related financial risks into core business and policy processes is no longer optional. It is an imperative for long-term financial stability, operational resilience, and sustainable value creation. Future research and regulatory practice should aim to enhance the granularity, comparability, and usability of climate risk metrics, while ensuring that scenario analysis evolves to remain relevant in a rapidly changing world.

References

1. The Global Risks: Report 2025. 20th edition. Insight Report. WEF. 2025. https://reports.wef orum.org/docs/WEF_Global_Risks_Report_2025.pdf. Accessed 26 July 2025
2. Bogmans, C., Gomez-Gonzalez, P., Ganpurev, G., Melina, G., Pescatori, A., Thube, S.D.: Power Hungry: How AI Will Drive Energy Demand. IMF (2025) https://www.imf.org/en/Publications/WP/Issues/2025/04/21/Power-Hungry-How-AI-Will-Drive-Energy-Demand-566304. Accessed 26 July 2025
3. TCFD: Homepage. https://www.fsb-tcfd.org/recommendations. Accessed 26 July 2025
4. ECB report on good practices for climate stress testing (2022). https://www.bankingsupervis ion.europa.eu/ecb/pub/pdf/ssm.202212_ECBreport_on_good_practices_for_CST~539227 e0c1.en.pdf. Accessed 26 July 2025
5. Nature-related Financial Risks: A Conceptual Framework to Guide Action by Central Banks and Supervisors (2024). https://www.ngfs.net/system/files/import/ngfs/medias/documents/ngfs-conceptual-framework-nature-risks.pdf. Accessed 26 July 2025
6. Ceglar, A., Parker, M., Pasqua, C., Boldrini, S., Gabet, M., van der Zwaag, S.: Economic and financial impacts of nature degradation and biodiversity loss. ECB Economic Bulletin. https://www.ecb.europa.eu/press/economic-bulletin/articles/2024/html/ecb.ebart202406_02~ae87ac450e.en.html. Accessed 26 July 2025
7. GHG: Protocol Homepage. https://ghgprotocol.org/. Accessed 26 July 2025
8. CDP: Homepage. https://cdp.net/en/disclose/question-bank. Accessed 26 July 2025
9. UNEP Finance Initiative: Extending our horizons: assessing credit risk and opportunity in a changing climate. In: Outputs of a Working Group of 16 Banks Piloting the TCFD Recommendations. PART 1: Transition-Related Risks & Opportunities (2018) https://www.oliverwyman.com/content/dam/oliver-wyman/v2/publications/2018/april/EXTENDING-OUR-HORIZONS-AW.pdf. Accessed 26 July 2025
10. CMIP: Homepage. https://wcrp-cmip.org/. Accessed 26 July 2025
11. ClimINVEST: Physical climate risk: Investor needs and information gaps CICERO Report, Issue (2019). http://hdl.handle.net/11250/2589503. Accessed 26 July 2025
12. Buhr, B. , : Climate Change and the Cost of Capital in Developing Countries (2018)
13. Environmental Protection Agency: GHG Emission Factors Hub (2023). https://www.epa.gov/climateleadership/ghg-emission-factors-hub. Accessed 26 July 2025
14. The importance of data quality in the journey toward decarbonization. JUNE. A co-authored report from PCAF and CDP (2023). https://carbonaccountingfinancials.com/files/PCAF-CDP-Paper-2023.pdf. Accessed 26 July 2025
15. What Are Shell Scenarios Homepage. https://www.shell.com/news-and-insights/scenarios/what-are-shell-scenarios.html. Accessed 26 July 2025
16. The Intergovernmental Panel on Climate Change Homepage. https://www.ipcc.ch. Accessed 26 Aug 2025
17. The International Energy Agency Homepage. https://www.iea.org. Accessed 26 July 2025
18. Transition Pathway Initiative Homepage. https://www.transitionpathwayinitiative.org/. Accessed 26 July 2025

19. Recommendations toward the development of scenarios for assessing nature-related economic and financial risks. Executive and non-technical summaries (2023). https://www.ngfs.net/system/files/import/ngfs/media/2023/12/13/ngfs_nature_scenarios_recommendations_summaries.pdf, last Accessed 2025 July 26
20. Ranger, N. et al.: The Green Scorpion: The Macro-Criticality of Nature for Finance – Foundations for Scenario-Based Analysis of Complex and Cascading Physical Nature-Related Risks. Environmental Change Institute, University of Oxford, Oxford (2023) https://www.eci.ox.ac.uk/sites/default/files/2023-12/INCAF-MacroCriticality_of_Nature-December 2023.pdf, last Accessed 2025 July 26
21. Bernstein, A., Gustafson, M.T., Lewis, R.: Disaster on the horizon: the price effect of sea level rise. J. Financ. Econ. **134**(2), 253–272 (2019). https://doi.org/10.1016/j.jfineco.2019.03.013. Accessed 26 July 2025

Digital Finance, Economic Growth, and Inclusion

Digital Platform-Based MSME Management For Achieving Sustainable Performance

Diana Zuhroh[1]([✉]) [iD], Harmono[1] [iD], Abdul Malik Kumar[1], Aqila Nur Rahmalia[2], and G. M. Beatrice Phobe[1]

[1] University of Merdeka Malang, Malang, Indonesia
diana.zuhroh@unmer.ac.id
[2] Alumni of Airlangga University, Surabaya, Indonesia

Abstract. The purpose of this study is to cluster Micro, Small, and Medium Enterprises (MSMEs) based on the intensity of use of various digital platforms, namely Social Media, E-Ccommerce, Digital Wallets, and Sharing Economy, taking into account demographic characteristics such as education level and length of business, the use of accounting information systems and the performance achieved for each cluster of digital platform users. This study used a questionnaire to collect data, and the respondents of this study were MSMEs managers or actors. Data analysis used the K-Means method, especially with 2 analyses, namely Gower Distance and Hierarchical Clustering. This study found that most of the samples in this study have been operating at a medium level or 4–6 years, with the level of formal education of managers also at a medium level. The level of formal education is closely related to the intensity of digital platform use for business management. The higher the level of education of MSME managers, the more intensive the use of digital platforms, and vice versa. The length of business does not determine the intensity of digital platform use. All clusters of platform digital shows that the accounting records commonly used to support digital platform-based business management are Cash Books, Sales Books, Accounts Receivable Books, and Cost Records. E-Commerce and Digital Wallet users have prepared financial reports regularly. MSMEs that have used digital platforms are mostly able to increase sales, followed by increased profits, and also being able to carry out general cost efficiency.

Keywords: Social Media · E-Ccommerce · Digital Wallets · Sharing Economy · Accounting Information System · Performance

1 Introduction

The latest business developments, precisely until early 2025, the use of information technology in business management, including MSMEs, is increasingly intensive, which is also known as a digitally managed business. In this new model, businesses that have access to information technology have many advantages, which will lead to excellence. Every worker today can be considered a knowledge worker as well as a future worker who needs to be a learning worker, not only the knowledge itself, but also knowledge about how to learn is also important [1].

S. C. P. Yam et al. (Eds.): ICFT 2025, CCIS 2868, pp. 265–281, 2026.
https://doi.org/10.1007/978-981-92-0126-6_22

Based on the OECD survey since the COVID-19 pandemic, more and more (up to 70%) MSMEs are using digital technology. Surveys conducted since 2020 worldwide have documented an increase in the use of digital technology for online sales activities. Although there are variations and even differences between the countries surveyed, in general, the conclusions obtained are not much different [2]. Digital-based MSMEs business management is increasingly becoming a demand during and after the Covid-19 Pandemic. During these times, MSME managers are faced with the choice of precise and reliable business strategies to survive. Digital platforms must be a tool to support strategy implementation [3]. Based on the implemented strategy, MSMEs design digitalization that supports its implementation by implementing overall business digitalization for all existing functions, especially operational functions, and, if possible, digitalization in relation to business with partners. The OECD (2021) published research related to factors that determine MSME performance which consists of 6 + 1 pillars, namely: 1) Institutional and Regulatory framework, 2) Market Conditions, 3) Infrastructure, 4) Acces to Finance, 5) Acces to skills, 6) Acces to Innovation Assets, and 6) Digitalization [2, 4].

The first three factors relate to the business environment and the conditions where SMEs run their businesses. The second three factors relate to the extent to which SMEs are able to optimize their internal resources, including the use of strategic resources. Based on the OECD survey, market conditions are very important for SMEs to run their businesses, innovate, compete, increase revenue and profitability, and grow [4]. Poor market conditions are a major factor in SME failure. In particular, the OECD (2019, 2021, 2024) emphasizes that the fast-changing business environment, followed by the need for a workforce that matches the development of changes, is the main key to the sustainability of MSME businesses [2, 4, 5]

The OCD study concluded that skilled workers are a key asset to compete in a knowledge-based economy. Skills development is important in the context of a rapid and growing digital transition, with the expectation of being able to perform complex tasks and make innovations that help drive competitiveness and productivity growth. Generally, MSMEs are managed by the owners themselves. It can be said that the owner of MSMEs is also an employee. According to the Upper Echelons theory organizational achievement or performance can be related to the characteristics or background of the leader [6]. The main character in question is something that is "given," including Psychological Factors including Values, Cognitive Models, Other Personality Factors) and observable Experiences which include Functional Background, Formal education, and others. An in-depth study of the Upper Echelons theory associated with the use of information technology which in turn is related to organizational performance resulted in several propositions, namely: (1) the age of the leader is negatively related to the use of IT, (2) Gender is positively related to the use of IT, (3) Education level is positively related to the use of IT, and (4) Length of business is positively related to the use of IT [7]. In more detail the study concluded that non-formal education has a significant effect on the performance of MSMEs [8]. Meanwhile, another study found evidence that one of the key success factors for MSME actors in business management is the training and courses they have attended [9].

The second theory used in this study is Contingency Theory which states that the success of an organization is largely determined by its ability to adapt to environmental factors motivated by the organization's need to continue to live [10]. Research on the use of digital platforms and accounting systems produces conclusions that are in line with Contingency Theory, that the effect is positive and significant [11, 12]. Some digital applications play a role in the control process, costing, performance assessment, and budgeting. The effect of the use of accounting systems on performance can be seen from previous research conducted during the COVID-19 pandemic, which concluded that the use of accounting information systems has an effect on performance [13–15]. Previous studies have produced mutually supporting conclusions, so further research should focus on obtaining empirical evidence on the relationship between IT/digital platform usage and user characteristics. No less important is the relationship between the characteristics of digital platform usage and other factors, such as accounting systems, and their relationship to performance. The purpose of this analysis is to group Micro, Small, and Medium Enterprises (MSMEs) based on the intensity of use of various digital platforms, namely social media, e-commerce, digital wallets, and sharing economy, taking into account demographic characteristics such as education level and length of business. The next objective is to find out the use of accounting information systems and the performance achieved for each cluster of digital platform users.

This research is useful in designing plans for training and mentoring programs on the use of digital platforms that are in accordance with the characteristics of MSME actors, especially based on demographic aspects and digital platform users. The suitability of training programs with the characteristics of MSME actors is very important to be effective and obtain optimal results. Based on several studies, it was found that although the MSME sector is the main pillar of the Indonesian economy, the main problems faced by this sector are also urgent to be solved to maintain its sustainability include: capital, human resources in the fields of information technology and accounting jnformation systems [17–20].

2 Research Methods

Variable and Variable Measurement
The variables of this study consist of the use of digital platforms consisting of Social Media, E-Commerce, Digital Wallets, and Sharing Economy, Accounting Information Systems and Financial Performance. The basis for the analysis of each cluster include Length of Business and Level of Education. This study used a questionnaire to collect data which contained questions about the demographic aspects of respondents, including Length of Business and Level of Education, platform digital usage, accounting information usage, and financial performances. The questions and answer options provided (which are also variable measurements) are presented in the Table 1. The respondents of this study were MSMEs in East Java in accordance with Government Regulation No. 7 / 2021 [24].

Table 1. Research Instruments

Variable	Indicator	Question	Answer Options
Social Media	Facebook, YouTube, Whatsap Instagram, Line, Twitter, Tik Tok	Intensity of use of each type of application	1 = never 2 = ever 3 = neutral 4 = often 5 = very often
E-Commerce	Shopee, Lazada Bukalapak, Tokopedia, Zalora, Blibli, Tik Tok Shop	Intensity of use of each type of application	1 = never 2 = ever 3 = neutral 4 = often 5 = very often
Digital Wallet	Ovo, Dana, Link Aja Gopay, Shopee Pay	Intensity of use of each type of application	1 = never 2 = ever 3 = neutral 4 = often 5 = very often
Sharing Economy	Gojek, Grab, Maxim, Shopee Food, Paxel Co	Intensity of use of each type of application	1 = never 2 = ever 3 = neutral 4 = often 5 = very often
Financial Performance	Customer Increase, Sales Volume, Revenue, Profit.	do not face capital shortages; don't need a loan yet; pay debts (installments) on time;able to reduce operational costs; reduce employee or worker salary costs; increase in buyers or customers; increase in sales; increased profits	1 = strongly disagree 2 = disagree 3 = neutral 4 = agree 5 = strongly agree
Accounting information system	Cash receipt Book, Cash Expenditure Book, Accounts Receivable Book, Sales Book, Purchase Book, Salary Payment Book.	Intensity of use of each accounting and financial reporting record.	1 = never 2 = ever 3 = neutral 4 = often 5 = very often
Length of Business	1–3 years, 4–6 years, and > 7 years		
Level of Business	Yunior High School, Senior High School, Diploma, Bachelor, and Master		

3 Data Analysis

Data analysis used the K-Means method cluster analysis because it has been widely used and produces groupings that are considered appropriate [25]. The K-Means algorithm used is an algorithm as a generalization of the average and is very suitable for analyzing large data sets [22]. The objects to be clusterized are Digital Platforms usage, which include E-Commerce, Digital Wallets, Sharing Economy, and Social Media. Clustering of digital platform usage is based on demographic factors, namely, length of business and level of formal education. The methods used in cluster analysis are 1) **Gower Distance** because the data used for modeling in this study contains numerical data (Likert scale 1–5) and categorical data for education, and also ordinal data for length of business, and 2) **Hierarchical Clustering**; a clustering method without the need to determine the number of clusters at the beginning [21, 23].

4   Result

4.1   Analysis of Instrument Validity and Reliability

Distribution of questionnaires using Google Form, 396 answers were obtained that were suitable for further analysis. Validity test using Pearson Correlation showed a significance value for all significant variables of 0.000, it can be concluded that this research instrument is valid. The reliability test using the Cronbach Alpha Value produced a value of 0.740 means that the questionnaire answer data have high reliability.

4.2   Descriptive Analysis Results

1. Descriptive Statistics for Length of Business and Education Level of Actors

Analysis of descriptive statistics of the length of business and level of formal education of MSME actors, as presented in the Fig. 1.

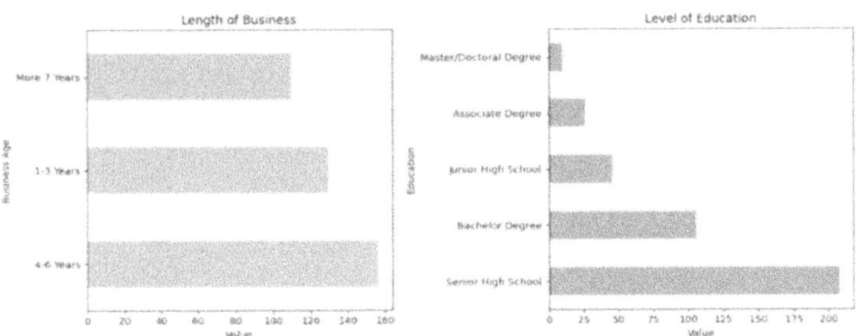

Fig. 1. Descriptive Analysis Results

Based on the length of business the majority of MSMEs sampled in this study were in the early to mid-development stage (4–6 years), indicating that many MSMEs were still in the growth and adaptation phase. There were fewer MSMEs that had survived for more than 7 years which could reflect the challenges in maintaining a business in the long term. Based on education, the majority of MSMEs sampled in this study came from secondary education backgrounds (high school or equivalent), indicating that the MSME sector is filled with individuals with sufficient formal education but not yet at university level.

2. Descriptive Analysis of the Results of Digital Platform User Clustering in Average.

The next analysis is a descriptive analysis of the clustering of digital platform users based on the length of business and the level of formal education, 3 clusters were formed aa deeper analysis of each cluster is shown in Table 2.

Table 2. Overall clustering results

Cluster 1 (29)	Cluster 2 (115)	Cluster 3 (252)
1.In terms of education, MSMEs in this cluster are considered the most educated among the three clusters. 2. In terms of length, the business is still relatively new, with an average of 1.76. 3. In terms of digital platform usage, this cluster is the highest in all categories, especially digital wallets and social media.	1. In terms of education, MSME actors in this cluster have middle-level education. 2. In terms of length of business, an average of 1,00. which means that the MSMEs in this cluster are relatively very new. 3. In terms of digital plat form usage, less active in utilizing digital technology.	1 In terms of education the education of MSME actors in this cluster is slightly lower than cluster 2 2. In term of length of business, the business has been running for longer (longer than MSMEs in clusters 1 and 2) 3. In term of digital platform usage, digital adoption is still limited but slightly higher than cluster 2.

Further analysis was conducted to see in more detail the intensity of digital platform usage by MSMEs presented in the Figs. 2, 3, 4 and 5. For social media, WhatsApp is the most widely used, followed by Instagram and Facebook. While on the E-Commerce, the most usage is Shopee, followed by TikTok Shop and Tokopedia. The most widely used for digital wallet is Shopee Pay, then Dana, and the next is OVO and Gopay, with almost the same average. The sharing economy platform with the 3 most users are Gojek, Grab, and Shopee.

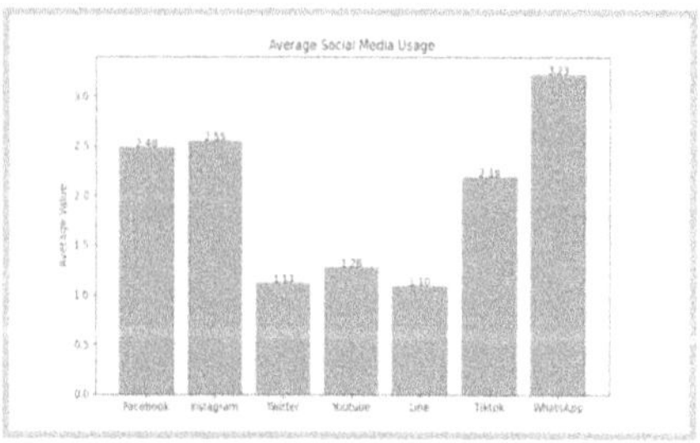

Fig. 2. Social Media Usage

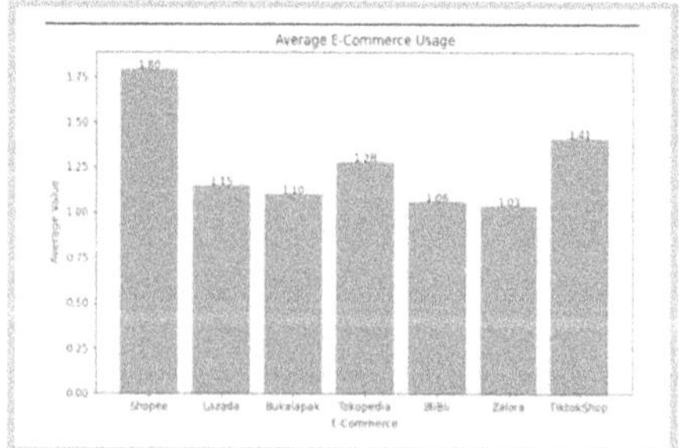

Fig. 3. e-Commerce Usage

3. Cluster Analysis of Each Type of Digital Platform Usage.

In the next stage, an analysis was carried out on the details of the use of digital platforms with clustering based on high, medium, and low usage. Each cluster was

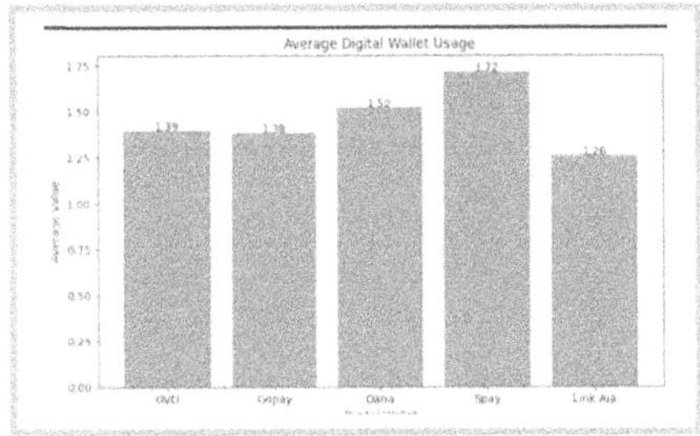

Fig. 4. Digital Wallet Usage

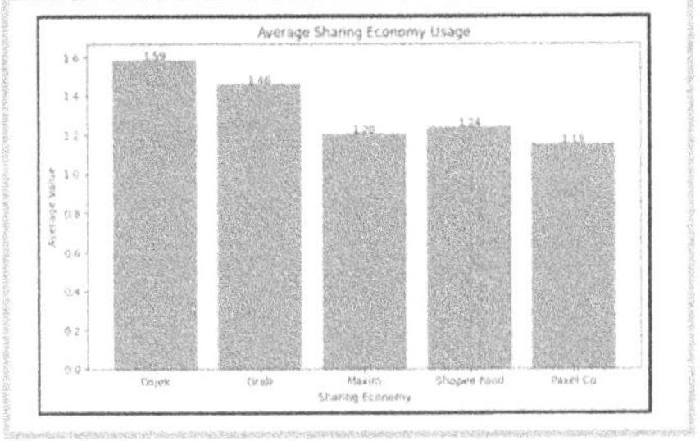

Fig. 5. Sharing Economy Usage

identified for the type of platform used and the characteristics of the user MSMEs based on the length of business and level of education.

1) Social Media

As explained in the previous section, the types of social media in this study include WhatsApp, Facebook, YouTube, Instagram, Line, Twitter, and TikTok. More detailed analysis, the following are the characteristics of social users as explained in Table 3.

2) E-commerce

In general, the characteristics of each type of E-Commerce users are presented in Table 4.

3) E-Wallet.

Furthermore the characteristics of each type of E-Commerce users are presented in Table 5.

4) Sharing Economy

The characteristics of each type of Sharing Economy users are presented in Table 6.

4. The Use of Accounting Systems and Financial Performance.

It was explained in the previous section that the accounting system plays an important role in providing information to support decision-making. This study also aims to obtain empirical evidence on the types of accounting records used by MSMEs that have digitized. In addition, various studies show that the use of digital platforms in managing MSME businesses has been proven to increase or improve their financial performance. Table 7 is a presentation of data on the use of accounting systems for each cluster of user of the digital platform and its financial performance achievements.

Table 3. The characteristics of social users

Cluster.	Length of Busnss	Formal Education	The 4 most used platform types.	Additional Analysis Based on education level, length of business, and platform usage
SosMed 1 (51 samples)	4–6 years	Diploma and Bachelor Degree	1. Instagram, 2. Facebook, 3. TikTok 4. Whatsaap	1. The level of education is quite established and university graduates. 2. In terms of business history, this cluster includes MSMEs that are already established. 3. Active digital platform users
SosMed 2 (183 samples)	7 years or more	High School Equivalent	Evenly distributed across all types of platforms with low level usage	Still conventional, not yet touched by digital, tends to rely on old-fashioned business management.
SosMed3 (162 samples)	1–3 years	High school and above (secondary to university level education)	Facebook, Instagram, and TikTok (although not as high as Cluster 1), Whtasaap (relatively high)	Newly growing MSMEs that are pioneering digital-based businesses.

Table 4. The characteristics of E-Commerce user

The name of Cluster	Length of Business	Formal Education (Average)	The 3 most used platform types.	Additional Analysis Based on education level, length of business, and platform usage
E-Com1 (14 samples)	4–6 years	Diploma and Bachelor Degree	Shopee, Tik Tok Shop, Tokopedia.	1. The level of education is quite established and university graduates. 2. In terms of length of business, this cluster includes MSMEs that are already established. 3. Based on the average, MSMEs in this cluster are very active users.
E-Com2 (85 samples)	1–3 years	High School to Diploma	Shopee, Tik Tok Shop.	1. From education level, at secondary level to University (Diploma). 2. From the length of the business, it is an MSME that has just started a business. 3. Very active Shopee user
E-Com 3 (297 samples)	> 7 years	High School Equivalent	Very low on all platforms	Although MSMEs in this cluster have been established for quite a long time, they have not actively used digital platforms. The education of the owners or managers is equivalent to high school.

Table 5. The characteristics of E-Commerce user

Cluster	Length of Business	Formal Education	The 3 most used platform types.	Additional Analysis Based on education level, length of business, and platform usage
e-Wall 1 (300 samples)	> 7 years	High School to Diploma	Very low on all platforms	MSMEs in this cluster have been established for quite a long time but have not actively used digital platforms, especially digital wallets. The education of the owners or managers is equivalent to high school to university degree (diploma)
e-Wall 2 (22 samples)	4–6 years	Diploma to Bachelor Degree	Shopee Pay Gopay OVO	1. The level of education is quite established and university graduates. 2.In terms of length of business, this cluster includes MSMEs that are already established. 3. MSMEs in this cluster are very active in using digital wallets on almost all platforms, including LinkAja and Dana.

(continued)

Table 5. (continued)

Cluster	Length of Business	Formal Education	The 3 most used platform types.	Additional Analysis Based on education level, length of business, and platform usage
e-Wall 3 (74 samples)	1–3 years	High School to Diploma	Dana ShopeePay Ovo	1. The education of the owners or managers is equivalent to high school to university degree (diploma). 2. Based on the length of business, including new MSMEs. 3. The use of digital platforms is at a moderate level, some MSMEs are just starting to use them.

5 Discussion

The result of this study is that MSMEs with a business duration of 1–3 years indicates that MSMEs began to be developed by their owners during the Covid-19 Pandemic. Previous studies have found empirical evidence that workers who are laid off generally enter careers as entrepreneurs by establishing small businesses and managers or owners of MSMEs are mostly high school educated. A smaller number are diploma, bachelor's, and postgraduate alumni. Associated with the length of business it is proven in this study that MSMEs in this cluster use digital platforms more intensively. Further analysis was conducted to see descriptive statistics of the clustering of digital platform usage in general and found that the cluster with the largest number of MSMEs, the level of education is the lowest but the length of business is in the middle category (4–6 years).

5.1 Analysis of Each Cluster of Digital Platform Usage

The use of WhatsApp is the highest of all the digital platforms in this study, and this result is in line with the results of previous surveys and studies [26–28]. WhatsApp's popularity is not only due to its ease of use several studies have shown that it is an

Table 6. The characteristics of Sharing Economy user

Cluster	Length of Business	Formal Education	The 3 most used platform types.	Additional Analysis Based on education level, length of business, and platform usage
ShareE-1 (32 samples)	4–6 years	Diploma to Bachelor Degree	Gojek Grab ShopeeFood (very active)	1. The level of education is quite established and university graduates. 2. In terms of length of business this cluster includes MSMEs that are already established. 3. MSMEs in this cluster are very active in using almost sharing economy platforms
ShareE-2 (211 samples)	> 7 years	High School Equivalent	Very low on all platforms	Although MSMEs in this cluster have been established for a very long time, they have not actively used digital platforms. The education of the owners or managers is equivalent to high school.

(*continued*)

Table 6. (*continued*)

Cluster	Length of Business	Formal Education	The 3 most used platform types.	Additional Analysis Based on education level, length of business, and platform usage
ShareE-3 (153 samples)	1–3 years	High School to Diploma	Gojek Grab ShopeeFood (medium to low usage)	1. The education of the owners or managers is equivalent to high school to university degree (diploma) 2. Based on the length of business, including new MSMEs. 3. The use of digital platforms is at a moderate level, some MSMEs are just starting to use them.

important factor for users of a platform, especially MSMEs [16]. Further analysis that the use of social media by MSMEs with a lower business period as well as the level of education of their managers have a tendency for lower activity in it. Conversely, the higher the level of education, the more likely they are to be active in using social media even though the MSME has not been running its business for long.

Analysis of users of E-Commerce digital platforms also shows that the higher the level of education of MSME managers, the more active they are in using E-Commerce in managing their businesses, especially Shopee and TikTok Shop. MSMEs managed by higher education alumni and have been established for a longer time tend to be very active in using e-commerce. Further analysis of this evidence is the possibility of the correlation between level of education and the active use of digital platforms can be seen from cluster E-COM 3, with the largest number of MSMEs (297) and managed by high school alumni or equivalent, where the use of E-commerce is very low on all e-Commerce platforms.

Regarding the use of E-Wallet that the use of the 2 digital platforms that consisting of 297 MSMEs managed by high school graduates to diplomas, it was proven that they were less active in using e-wallets. Meanwhile, the EWall-2 cluster, consisting of 85 MSMEs, although this cluster is on average relatively "younger" than the EWall-1 cluster, in terms

Table 7. The use of accounting and its financial performance achievements.

Platform	Accounting Information System	Financial Performance
Social Media	1. Used Intensively: Cash Book, Sales Book, Expenses Book. 2. Used at moderate levels: Notes on Receivables and Book on Payable. 3. Less intensive; Annual Financial Report.	1. Increase in Sales 2. Pay bills or debts on time 3. Turnover and profits increase 4. Cost efficiency
E-commerce	1. Intensive use of all accounting records. 2. The Annual Financial Report prepared regularly	1. No loan required yet 2. Do not face capital shortages 3. Profits increase 4. Increase in Sales
E-Wallet	1. Used Intensively: Cash Book, Sales Book, Expenses Book. 2. Uscd at moderate levels: Notes on Receivables and Book on Payable. 3. The Annual Financial Report prepared regularly.	1. Increase in Sales 2. Pay bills or debts on time 3. Profits increase 4. Reduce employee or worker salary costs.
Sharing Economy	1. Used Intensively: Cash Book, Sales Book, Expenses Book. 2. Used at moderate levels: Notes on Receivables and Book on Payable. 3. Less intensive; Annual Financial Report.	1. Increase in Sales 2. Profits increase 3. Pay bills or debts on time 4. Cost efficiency.

of length of business, the average level of education of its managers is a higher education graduate. In terms of using digital platforms it is proven to be more active.

The next clustering of digital platform usage analyzed is the Sharing Economy. As seen in the ShareE-2 cluster, with a total of 211 MSMEs, MSME managers in this cluster have a high school education and the use of the sharing economy is very low for all types of platforms. The higher the level of education, such as in the ShareE-3 cluster, where the managers have a higher education (diploma), the use also increases at a medium level. Meanwhile, in the ShareE-1 cluster, with MSME managers who have a bachelor's degree, the use of the platform is very active. Analysis of the length of business shows no evidence that this factor is related to the use of digital platforms.

5.2 Analysis of the Use of Accounting Information Systems in Each Cluster of Digital Platform Usage and Financial Performance

The accounting records commonly used by MSMEs in all clusters are the Cash Book (both cash receipts and cash disbursements), sales and expense books, followed by accounts receivable and accounts payable, this results consistent with the research of Nurjanah et al. (2021) and Zuhroh et al. (2023). Meanwhile, associated with the preparation of Annual Financial Reports, MSMEs in the E-commerce and E-Wallet user clusters have prepared financial reports more intensively compared to the other 2 digital platform users. When associated with the number of MSMEs using the two platforms, most of them have been operating for more than 4 years. This result can be seen from E-Commerce and E-Wallet users who have been operating for more than 4 years; these MSMEs, based on average data have prepared financial reports more intensively.

Finally, an analysis of the financial performance of MSMEs using digital platforms shows MSMEs are able to "boost" sales, which also has an impact on increasing profits. These results are in line with various institutions and research conducted by academics [5, 8, 29]. Based on the Balanced Scorecards concept, achievements by MSMEs can be linked to the achievement of growth [30]. If this condition can be maintained in the long term and generate increased sales, it will enable MSMEs to achieve productivity, one of the performance achievements that is very much needed by business organizations [30].

6 Conclusion

This study found 3 clusters of MSMEs were formed based on the intensity of digital platform use, the level of education of managers, and the length of business. Most of the samples included in cluster 3 namely MSMEs that have been operating at a medium level or 4–6 years, with the level of formal education of managers also at a medium level. A more detailed analysis shows that the level of formal education is closely related to the intensity of digital platform use for business management. The higher the level of education of MSME managers, the more intensive the use of digital platforms, and vice versa. While the length of business, at least the findings of this study, do not determine the intensity of digital platform use.

From the analysis of the use of accounting systems for all clusters it shows that the accounting records commonly used to support digital platform-based business management are Cash Books, Sales Books, Accounts Receivable Books, and Cost Records. Meanwhile, analysis of the preparation of financial reports shows that E-Commerce and Digital Wallet users have prepared financial reports regularly. The analysis of performance shows that MSMEs that have used digital platforms are mostly able to increase sales followed by increased profits. Another performance that can be achieved is being able to carry out general cost efficiency.

The limitation of this study is, in terms of E-Wallet usage, this study has not included QRIS (Quick Response Code Indonesian Standard), which is a national non-cash payment standard using quick response codes (QR) and near field communication (NFC) launched by Bank Indonesia (BI) and the Indonesian Payment System Association (ASPI) to integrate all non-cash payment methods in Indonesia. By the third quarter of 2025, there were more than 58 million QRIS users. Recently, QRIS can already be used in Thailand, Malaysia, Singapore, and Japan, and will be expanded to the Philippines, Vietnam, Laos, Brunei Darussalam, and South Korea.

References

1. Valacich, J., Schneider, C., Hashim, M.: Information Systems Today: Managing in the Digital World, 9th edn. Pearson Education Limited, Pearson (2023)

2. OECD: The digital transformation of SMEs. In: OECD Studies on SMEs and Entrepreneurship. OECD Publishing, Paris (2021). https://doi.org/10.1787/bdb9256a-en
3. Muditomo, A., Wahyudi, I.: Conceptual model for SME digital transformation during the Covid-19 pandemic in Indonesia: R-digital transformation model. BASKARA J. Bus. Entrep. 3(1), 13–24 (2021). https://doi.org/10.24853/baskara.3.1.13-24
4. OECD: SME and Entrepreneurship Outlook 2019. OECD Publishing (2019) https://www.oecd.org/en/publications/2019/05/oecd-sme-and-entrepreneurship-outlook-2019_7083aa23.html
5. OECD: SME Digitalisation 2024: Managing Shocks and Transitions– an OECD D4SME Survey. OECD Publishing (2024) https://www.oecd.org/en/publications/sme-digitalisation-to-manage-shocks-and-transitions_eb4ec9ac-en.html
6. Hambrick, D.C., Mason, P.: Upper echelons: the organization as a reflection of its top managers. Acad. Manag. Rev. 9, 193–206 (1984). https://doi.org/10.2307/258434
7. Lopez Munoz, J.F., Escribá-Esteve, A.: An upper echelons perspective on information technology business value. J. Inf. Technol. 23(3), 173–181 (2017). https://doi.org/10.1016/j.iedeen.2017.02.003
8. Zuhroh, D., et al.: The role of GoJek and Grab sharing economy platforms and management accounting systems usage on MSME performance during the COVID-19 pandemic: evidence from Indonesia. Univ. J. Account. Finance, –262 (2024). https://doi.org/10.5267/j.uscm.2023.10.001
9. Zuhroh, D., et al.: The impact of sharing economy platforms, management accounting systems, and demographic factors on financial performance: exploring the role of formal and informal education in MSMEs. J. Open Innov. Technol. Mark. Complex. 11(1) (2025). https://doi.org/10.1016/j.joitmc.2024.100447
10. Otley, D.: The contingency theory of management accounting: achievement and prognosis. Acc. Organ. Soc. 5(4), 413–428 (1980). https://doi.org/10.1016/0361-3682(80)90040-9
11. Cleary, P., Quinn, M., Rikhardsson, P., Batt, C.: Exploring the links between IT tools, management accounting practices and SME performance: perceptions of CFOs in Ireland. Account. Finan. Govern. Rev. (2022). https://doi.org/10.52399/001c.35440
12. Leoni, G., Parker, L.D.: Governance and control of sharing economy platforms: hosting on Airbnb. Br. Account. Rev. 51(6) (2019). https://doi.org/10.1016/j.bar.2018.12.001
13. Nartey, S.N., van der Poll, H.M.: Innovative management accounting practices for sustainability of manufacturing SMEs. Environ. Dev. Sustain. 23 (2021). https://doi.org/10.1007/s10668-021-01425-w
14. Kareem, H.M., et al.: The role of accounting information systems and knowledge management in enhancing organizational performance in Iraqi SMEs. Sustainability. 13(22), 12706 (2021). https://doi.org/10.3390/su132212706
15. Lawal, A., et al.: The role of accounting information systems in firms' performance during the COVID-19 pandemic. J. Gov. Regul. 11(1) (2022). https://doi.org/10.22495/jgrv11i1art5
16. Zuhroh, D., et al.: The development of a web-based strategic pricing application to support the sustainability of creative-based SMEs. Int. J. Sustain. Dev. Plan. 18(6), 1749–1759 (2023). https://doi.org/10.18280/ijsdp.180610
17. Nurjanah, E., Zuhroh, D.: Parawiyati: mobility service applications to facilitate better MSME financial performance. J. Finan. Bank. 25(4) (2021). https://doi.org/10.26905/jkdp.v25i4.5222
18. Central Bureau of Statistics: Profile of micro and small industries 2023. Vol. 14 (2024). https://bps.go.id
19. Data Center and Information System: Indonesia Digital Trade (E-Commerce) Period 2023 (2024). https://satudata.kemendag.go.id
20. Chen, L., Ramli, K., Hastiadi, F.F., Suryanegara, M.: Accelerating Digital Transformation in Indonesia: Technology, Market, and Policy. ERIA (2023) https://www.eria.org/publications/

21. Davidson, I.: Understanding k-means non-hierarchical clustering, SUNY Albany - Technical Report 02-2 (2002). https://www.researchgate.net/publication/228574607_Understanding_K-means_non-hierarchical_clustering
22. Morissette, L., Chartier, S.: The k-means clustering technique: general considerations and implementation in Mathematica. Tutor. Quant. Method Psychol. **9**(1), 15–24 (2013). https://doi.org/10.20982/tqmp.09.1.p015
23. Sari, D.N.P., Sukestiyarno, Y.L.: Cluster analysis with the k-means method on the distribution of COVID-19 cases by province in Indonesia. PRISMA: Nat. Semin. Math. **4**, 602–610 (2021) https://journal.unnes.ac.id/sju/prisma/issue/view/2017
24. Government of Indonesia: Government Regulation No. 7 of 2021 on the Ease, Protection, and Empowerment of Cooperatives and MSMEs. (2021), https://setkab.go.id/en/govt-issues-regulation-on-empowerment-of-cooperatives-msmes/
25. Zuhroh, D., et al.: The role of accounting information systems in mediating the influence of digital platforms and government stimulus on MSME performance (A post-Covid-19 analysis) (2025)
26. Riyanto, A.D.: Hootsuite (We Are Social): Data Digital Indonesia 2024 (2024). https://andi.link
27. Prasastisiwi, A.H.: Indonesia masuk 3 besar negara pengguna WhatsApp terbanyak di dunia (2024). https://goodstats.id
28. Info Ketapang: Pengguna media sosial di Indonesia sepanjang 2024 (2024). https://infoketapang.com
29. OECD: The Digital Transformation of SMEs. OECD Publishing, Paris (2021). https://doi.org/10.1787/bdb9256a-en
30. Kaplan, R.S., Norton, D.P.: Strategy Maps: Converting Intangible Assets into Tangible Outcomes. Harvard Business School Press, Boston (2004)

Financial Technology as a Factor in Increasing Bank Efficiency: Empirical Evidence from GCC Using Stochastic Frontier Analysis

Wafa Salman[1]([⊠]) [iD], Fatema Rajab[1] [iD], Amani Al Abbas[1] [iD], Mark Doblas[2] [iD], Randolf Von Salindo[2] [iD], Wendy Veeh Batar[3] [iD], and Frank Richard Paurom[3] [iD]

[1] School of Business and Logistics, Bahrain Polytechnic, Isa Town, Kingdom of Bahrain
wafa.salman@polytechnic.bh
[2] Administrative and Financial Sciences Department, Oman College of Management and Technology, Barka, Oman
[3] Capitol University, Cagayan de Oro Corrales Extension,, Philippines

Abstract. This paper investigates the effect of FinTech on bank efficiency in the Gulf Cooperation Council (GCC) using Net Interest Income, Total Deposits, and Total Loans over a period of 8 years. The proliferation of FinTech innovations digital commerce, mobile payments, digital remittances are disrupting traditional banking models, contributing to novel dynamics in financial performance. Using a stochastic frontier analysis (SFA), the study examined the effect of FinTech on bank efficiency with respect to standard bank performance and operational indicators. The results indicate Total Loans are positively related to Net Interest Income and Total Deposits are negatively related indicating dwindling returns to deposit-based activities. In addition, findings indicate that financial technology is one of the main drivers behind the range of inefficiency in bank performance, emphasizing how important digital transformation is to financial performance. The other findings underscore that countries with a high level of adoption of FinTech in their banking sector are more efficient in generating net interest income, thus, reinforcing the need to incorporate digital solutions in the banking operations. With this, the study adds to the literature with empirical evidence from the GCC region, which has been relatively underexplored in terms of the intersection between traditional banking indicators and FinTech thereby offering valuable insights in addressing the desire to improve operational efficiency in a digitally transforming finance and banking industry.

Keywords: Financial Technology · Bank Efficiency · Net Interest Income · Stochastic Frontier Analysis · Gulf Cooperation Council

1 Introduction

The global banking ecosystem is undergoing rapid transformation driven by financial technology (FinTech) (Agarwal & Zhang, 2020). FinTech innovations have created digital revolutions that address operational challenges in banking (Gomber et al., 2017),

S. C. P. Yam et al. (Eds.): ICFT 2025, CCIS 2868, pp. 282–295, 2026.
https://doi.org/10.1007/978-981-92-0126-6_23

redefining service delivery worldwide, particularly in emerging economies where infrastructure adoption is pronounced (Shahani, 2022). These technologies foster customer centric services (Paulet & Mavoori, 2019), expand access through seamless payments (Bollaert et al., 2021), and enhance data analytics that refine financial offerings for underserved populations.

Within the Gulf Cooperation Council (GCC) Bahrain, Kuwait, Oman, Qatar, Saudi Arabia, and the UAE, FinTech growth is accelerated by digitalization and economic reforms (Tsanis, 2020; Rahma & Al-Alawi, 2023). Regional governments have also established regulatory frameworks to support its adoption in banking and finance (Khan, Khan & Nazir, 2022). However, empirical research on FinTech's disruptive impact on banking efficiency remains limited.

Traditionally, bank efficiency has been studied through Net Interest Income (NII), reflecting how institutions use deposits and loans (Sulaeman, Moelyono & Nawir, 2019a; Andros et al., 2021). Yet, FinTech innovations such as digital commerce, mobile payments, and remittances are reshaping banks' revenue models (Wang et al., 2021), challenging reliance on deposits and borrowing as the sole basis for NII. While existing studies often assess single aspects of FinTech, little attention has been given to its interdependent effects, particularly in the GCC's distinct regulatory and economic context (Barini, 2024; Hassen, 2022).

Thus, a careful review of the literature would show that three critical gaps are prevalent. First, a lack of focus on FinTech has induced effects on traditional profitability measures; second, most empirical work is concentrated in developed economies, limiting relevance to the GCC; and third, few frameworks integrate FinTech adoption with traditional banking metrics like NII.

To address these gaps, this study applies stochastic frontier analysis (SFA) to GCC panel data, examining the relationship between NII, deposits, loans, and FinTech activity. Using nine listed banks in Bahrain as a representative sample for the GCC banking landscape, the analysis quantifies how technology enhances NII generation and operational efficiency. By integrating institution-level FinTech indicators with traditional balance-sheet determinants, the study enriches the literature on bank efficiency and offers actionable insights for policymakers navigating digital disruption in the region.

2 Review of Related Literature and Studies

2.1 Bank Efficiency and Its Determinant

Banks are central to economic systems by safeguarding savings and supplying funds that drive trade and business growth, with their efficiency closely linked to economic stability. The literature identifies several methods for evaluating bank efficiency, each offering unique insights.

Stochastic Frontier Analysis (SFA) has been widely applied across countries to assess efficiency, accounting for structural, accessibility, and macroeconomic factors. This framework provides valuable understanding of both internal and external determinants of efficiency (Weerasuriya et al., 2021; Fathi, 2010; Fries & Taci, 2005; Shen et al., 2009; Weill, 2003). Similarly, Data Envelopment Analysis (DEA) has been used in the

GCC. Kamarudin et al. (2014), for example, analyzed 74 banks and found revenue efficiency to be a major driver of profit efficiency, with notable differences between Islamic and conventional banks, reflecting the role of business models and financial structures.

Other approaches, such as Tobit regression models, also highlight efficiency determinants. Sulaeman et al. (2019b) showed that factors like economic growth, loan-to-deposit ratio, capital adequacy ratio, and net interest margin significantly enhance efficiency. More broadly, determinants can be classified as internal such as size, capital, and risk management or external, including macroeconomic and regulatory factors like inflation, interest rates, and GDP growth (Garza-García, 2012). In addition, business type, market operations, and broader economic conditions influence efficiency outcomes reinforcing the need for contextualized analysis.

2.2 Financial Technology and Bank Efficiency

Over the past three decades, technological advances, shifting customer preferences, and competition from non-banking entities have transformed the banking sector. FinTech, defined as the integration of finance and technology to enhance efficiency and reduce costs (Yang et al., 2023), has reshaped banking by driving innovation in profitability, risk management, and operations. Advances in mobile applications, blockchain, big data, cloud computing, and AI have enabled more personalized and cost-effective services, improved client screening, and enhanced efficiency (Cheng & Qu, 2020; Wang et al., 2021). Routine tasks such as payments, account updates, and customer service are now faster and cheaper, enhancing service quality. Research further highlights FinTech's role in achieving cost efficiencies, economies of scale, and improved decision-making in banking operations (Schmiedel, Malkamäki & Tarkka, 2006; Beijnen & Bolt, 2009; Jakšič & Marinč, 2015).

Evidence of FinTech's impact on bank performance is mixed. Positive outcomes include higher profitability and efficiency from better liquidity and capital management (Yang et al., 2023), improved profits and customer service from FinTech investments, enhanced intermediation and competitiveness (Cho & Chen, 2021), and reduced operational risks (Saijd et al., 2023). In the MENA region, studies report positive effects of FinTech adoption on efficiency, particularly in the GCC where innovations have strengthened competitiveness (Dwivedi et al., 2021).

Conversely, some studies find negative outcomes. Phan et al. (2020) reported declines in NIM, ROA, ROE, and YEA following FinTech adoption, while Chen and Peng (2020) highlighted increased risks and competition undermining efficiency. Others reveal mixed effects: Wu, Bai found initial disruption to profitability and efficiency in China before long-term improvements through e-banking and mobile platforms. Similarly, Nkem (2017) noted limited efficiency gains from online and mobile banking in Nigeria, with stronger impacts from ATM and POS channels.

Overall, the literature confirms FinTech's significant influence on bank operations, though outcomes vary depending on regional and contextual factors. This underscores the importance of examining FinTech's role in the GCC, where distinctive regulatory and economic conditions shape banking models. Focusing on areas such as loan utilization, deposit management, and net interest income optimization will both bridge existing gaps and provide policymakers with actionable insights tailored to the region.

2.3 Fintech, Net Interest Income, and Bank Efficiency

Net interest income (NII), the difference between loan interest earned and deposit interest paid, remains a key indicator of bank profitability and efficiency. Since a large share of bank revenues comes from lending, NII reflects the institution's capacity to manage interest-bearing assets effectively. Studies confirm that bank efficiency positively correlates with higher NIM (net interest margin), making it an important measure of financial performance (Ghozali, 2014). However, the relationship between fintech adoption, loan efficiency, and profitability is complex, shaped by both internal and external factors.

A central measure of efficiency is the loan-to-deposit ratio (LDR), which evaluates how effectively deposits are transformed into loans. Higher LDRs signal better use of resources to generate income and expand operations (Agustina & Wijaya, 2013; Yingjun et al., 2021). Fintech strengthens this process by enabling advanced tools such as AI-driven credit scoring, blockchain-based transactions, and customer segmentation analytics (Buckle & Thompson, 2020). These innovations improve borrower profiling, reduce defaults, and enhance loan performance, thereby increasing returns from deposits.

Fintech also transforms deposit mobilization. Digital savings products, personalized services, and platforms like mobile payments, wallets, and P2P lending expand access while boosting depositor satisfaction and growth. By reducing transaction costs and approval times, fintech enables banks to process higher volumes more efficiently. For instance, fintech-based systems can complete loan approvals in an hour compared to traditional 25-h processes. This efficiency gains contribute directly to improved NII, consistent with findings that macroeconomic conditions such as inflation, local savings, and deposit growth further support NII expansion (Hamadi & Awadh, 2012).

Nonetheless, challenges remain. Ineffective implementation can raise operational risks and costs, undermining the potential benefits of fintech integration (Al-Muharrami & Matthews, 2009; Berger & Mester, 2003). Thus, while fintech enhances the alignment of deposits and lending, strengthens loan utilization, and boosts returns, its impact ultimately depends on effective adoption strategies. Overall, fintech represents a critical driver of profitability and efficiency by optimizing both revenue generation and cost reduction in banking operations.

3 Methods

3.1 Data Source

Sourcing from Statista Market Insights, the study focuses on Bahrain as a representative sample of the GCC banking sector, using data from nine listed banks in Bahrain. The dataset covers an eight-year period from 2017 to 2024, reflecting the most recent actual market data available. This ensured that the projected index or values for financial and technological trends are reliable and robust. The study included Net Interest Income (NII) as the effect variable while Total Deposits (TD) and Total Loans (TL) are the causal variables or the input values of the model. Finally, Financial Technology Index (FinDX) was developed using three key digital finance indicators - Digital Commerce, Mobile Point-of-Sale (POS) Payments, and Digital Remittance Services.

3.2 Development of the Financial Technology Index

To measure the influence of financial technology (FinTech) on bank efficiency, a Financial Technology Index was constructed through Principal Component Analysis (PCA). PCA is a widely used statistical technique that reduces multidimensional data into a single composite index, capturing the shared variance among the input variables. This method has been effectively utilized in prior research to develop composite indices for financial innovation and efficiency analysis.

The input variables for the PCA included Digital Commerce, Mobile Point-of-Sale (POS) Payments, and Digital Remittance Services. Digital Commerce represents consumer transactions conducted online for products and services, encompassing payments via credit cards, direct debits, invoices, or digital payment providers such as PayPal and Alipay. Mobile POS Payments capture transactions processed at the point-of-sale using smartphone applications, such as ApplePay or SamsungPay, via contactless payment terminals. Digital Remittance Services refer to cross-border money transfers carried out via digital platforms, which offer greater speed and lower transaction costs compared to traditional methods.

The PCA produced a single composite Financial Technology Index that encapsulates the shared variability of these three indicators. This index provides a quantitative measure of FinTech activity and its potential influence on banking efficiency in the GCC context, and specifically in Bahrain.

3.3 Variable Transformations

To address potential data skewness and ensure comparability across variables, log-transformations were applied to the primary variables before analysis. The log transformed variables included the dependent variable, Net Interest Income (NII), as well as the input variables, Total Deposits (TD) and Total Loans (TL). Additionally, the Financial Technology Index was log-transformed to enhance interpretability and to align with prior efficiency studies that model variables as elasticities. This approach is consistent with studies examining the relationship between banking inputs, outputs, and external factors using stochastic frontier methodologies.

3.4 Stochastic Frontier Analysis

Stochastic Frontier Analysis (SFA) was employed to estimate bank efficiency levels and the factors influencing inefficiency. The analysis utilized a True Fixed Effects model designed for panel data, which allows for disentangling time-invariant heterogeneity from inefficiency. SFA is a widely recognized technique for examining efficiency and productivity, particularly in the banking sector, due to its ability to separate random noise from inefficiency effects.

The model estimated the relationship between the log-transformed dependent variable, NII, and the log-transformed input variables, TD and TL, as follows:

$$\ln(NII_{it}) = \beta_0 + \beta_1 \ln(TD_{it}) + \beta_1 \ln(TL_{it}) + \epsilon_{it} \tag{1}$$

In this specification, ϵ_{it} represents the composite error term, which consists of v_{it} capturing random noise and u_{it} representing inefficiency. The inefficiency term u_{it} was further specified as.

$$u_{it} = \delta_0 + \delta_1 \ln(\textit{FinTech Index}_{it}) + \zeta_{it} \qquad (2)$$

Where, $\ln(\textit{FinTech Index}_{it})$ represents the log-transformed Financial Technology Index, while ζ_{it} is a non-negative error term that captures the inefficiency effects unexplained by the FinTech Index. The parameter δ_1 provides insights into the influence of financial technology on bank inefficiency, with a negative value indicating that greater FinTech activity is associated with reduced inefficiency.

This methodological framework aligns with previous research that integrates external factors, such as technology adoption, into inefficiency models to examine their influence on banking performance. By incorporating the Financial Technology Index into the inefficiency component, this study offers a novel perspective on the role of digital innovation in shaping bank efficiency within Bahrain and GCC.

4 Results

Table 1 presents the descriptive statistics for the key variables used in this study. The data includes observations six largest retail banks in Bahrain as a representative sample of the GCC over a period from 2017 to 2024. The variables measured include Net Interest Income (NII), Total Deposits (TD), Total Loans (TL), Digital Commerce (DC), Digital Remittances (DR), and Mobile POS Payments (MPOS).

Table 1. Descriptive Statistics.

Variable	Obs	Mean	Std. Dev.	Min	Max
Net Interest Income (NII)	72	265.014	584.375	1.91	2011
Total Deposit (TD)	72	346.495	267.103	41.87	1132
Total Loans (TL)	72	188.942	176.388	15.03	569.7
Digital Commerce (DC)	72	372.538	850.142	1.98	3118
Digital Remittances (DR)	72	29.193	63.127	.04	254.5
Mobile POS Payment (MPOS)	72	8.865	12.173	.01	51.46

The mean Net Interest Income (NII) is \$265.01 million, with a high standard deviation of \$584.38 million, indicating significant variation in bank performance across Bahrain. Total Deposits (TD) and Total Loans (TL) have mean values of \$346.50 million and \$188.94 million, respectively, with substantial variability (standard deviations of \$267.10 million and \$176.39 million).

FinTech-related variables show considerable variation as well. Digital Commerce (DC) has a mean of 372.54, but with a high standard deviation of 850.14, reflecting diverse digital transaction activity. Digital Remittances (DR) and Mobile POS Payments

(MPOS) also exhibit notable variability, with mean values of 29.19 and 8.87, respectively. These statistics highlight the significant variation in both traditional banking and FinTech metrics, setting the foundation for further analysis of the factors influencing bank efficiency and the role of financial technology in this context.

Table 2. Eigenvalues and Variance Explained for FinTech Index

Component	Eigenvalue	Difference	Proportion	Cumulative
Comp1	2.884	2.775	0.961	0.961
Comp2	0.109	0.103	0.036	0.998
Comp3	0.006	.	0.002	1.000

The Principal Component Analysis (PCA) results, as shown in Table 2, reveal that the first component (Comp1) is by far the most significant, with an eigenvalue of 2.884 and explaining 96.1% of the total variance in the data. This component significantly outperforms the others, with its eigenvalue being much greater than 1, which aligns with the Kaiser Criterion for determining the importance of a component. According to this rule, only components with eigenvalues greater than 1 should be retained for further analysis, as they explain more variance than a single variable. Since Comp1 has an eigenvalue significantly above this threshold, it clearly meets this criterion.

The second component (Comp2) has an eigenvalue of 0.109, which is less than 1, and explains only 3.6% of the variance. Similarly, the third component (Comp3) has an even smaller eigenvalue of 0.006, contributing just 0.2% to the total variance. Both components fall below the threshold set by the Kaiser Criterion, suggesting that they provide very little additional information beyond what is captured by Comp1.

The cumulative proportion of variance explained by the first three components is 100%, indicating that all the variance in the dataset is accounted for by these components. However, since Comp1 already explains the vast majority (96.1%) of the variance, the second and third components contribute very little to the overall structure. As a result, they are excluded from further analysis.

Thus, based on the Kaiser Criterion, the proportion of variance explained, and the cumulative variance, Comp1 is selected as the basis for constructing the Financial Technology Index. This first component effectively captures most of the underlying variability in FinTech-related variables digital commerce, digital remittances, and mobile POS payments making it a robust and interpretable measure of financial technology's impact on bank efficiency.

The results of the Principal Component Analysis (PCA), as presented in Table 3, show the loadings for the retained first principal component (Comp1) used to construct the Financial Technology Index. These loadings correlate the degree to which each of the three FinTech-related variables Digital Commerce, Digital Remittances, and Mobile POS Payments correlate with the first component, which captures most of the variation in the dataset.

Table 3. Component Loadings for Retained Component (Comp1) for FinTech Index

Variable	Comp1
DGC	0.579
DGR	0.586
MPOS	0.568

The loading for Digital Commerce (DGC) is 0.579, indicating a moderate to strong positive correlation with Comp1, suggesting that it significantly contributes to the Financial Technology Index. This reflects the growing importance of online transactions in Bahrain & GCC financial ecosystem. Digital Remittances (DGR), with a slightly higher loading of 0.586, contributes more to the variation in the first component, highlighting the critical role of cross-border money transfers in the region's financial services sector. Mobile POS Payments (MPOS) have a loading of 0.568, indicating a moderate correlation with Comp1, and reflecting the increasing role of mobile wallets and contactless payments in Bahrain and GCC.

The comparable magnitudes of the loadings for all three variables suggest they contribute equally to the first principal component, with higher values of any of these variables corresponding to an increased FinTech Index. Thus, the first principal component effectively captures the variation in the Bahrain's financial technology landscape, with Digital Commerce, Digital Remittances, and Mobile POS Payments each making significant contributions. The developed index was subsequently used in further analyses to explore its relationship with bank efficiency.

Table 4. Pairwise Correlations

Variables	(1)	(2)	(3)	(4)
(1) LogNII	1.000			
(2) LogTD	−0.494	1.000		
(3) LogTL	−0.219	0.901	1.000	
(4) Log FinTech Index	0.883	−0.533	−0.432	1.000

The pairwise correlations in Table 4 reveal important relationships between the log-transformed variables. There is a strong positive correlation of 0.883 between LogNII (Net Interest Income) and the Log FinTech Index, suggesting that higher financial technology activity is associated with greater bank efficiency. In contrast, both LogTD (Total Deposits) and LogTL (Total Loans) show negative correlations with the Log FinTech Index (−0.533 and − 0.432, respectively), indicating that increased financial technology activity may be linked to a decrease in traditional banking metrics, such as deposits and loans. This could suggest that digital financial services are reducing reliance on traditional deposits and loans. The LogTD and LogTL variables are highly correlated

(0.901), reflecting their close relationship in banking operations, where deposits are typically used to fund loans. Overall, these correlations point to the disruptive role of financial technology in shaping banking practices, particularly regarding traditional deposit and loan-based models.

Table 5. Model Coefficients for True Fixed-Effects SFA (Exponential)

Predictor	Coefficient (β)	Standard Error	z-value	p-value	95% Confidence Interval
LogTD	−3.049	0.111	−27.520	<.001	[−3.266, −2.832]
LogTL	3.328	0.154	21.600	<.001	[3.026, 3.630]

The coefficients from the True Fixed-Effects Stochastic Frontier Analysis (SFA), presented in Table 5, offer insights into the relationship between Total Deposits (LogTD), Total Loans (LogTL), and Net Interest Income (NII). The coefficient for LogTD is −3.049 (SE = 0.111), with a z-value of −27.520 and a p-value of <.001, indicating a statistically significant negative relationship between Total Deposits and Net Interest Income. This suggests that an increase in Total Deposits is associated with a decrease in Net Interest Income, which may point to potential inefficiencies or diminishing returns from the traditional deposit-based banking model.

In contrast, the coefficient for LogTL is 3.328 (SE = 0.154), with a z-value of 21.600 and a p-value of <.001, reflecting a statistically significant positive relationship between Total Loans and Net Interest Income. This indicates that higher Total Loans are associated with greater Net Interest Income, highlighting the role of lending activities in driving revenue for banks.

These findings suggest that Net Interest Income tends to increase with Total Loans and decrease with Total Deposits, indicating that the composition of a bank's assets and liabilities plays a critical role in determining its financial performance. Specifically, it appears that the efficient management of loans can enhance a bank's income, while an increased deposit base may contribute to inefficiencies in generating higher returns (Table 6).

Table 6. Variance Parameters

Parameter	Estimate	Standard Error	z-value	p-value	95% Confidence Interval
Variance of Inefficiency (u_{it})	0.140	0.016	8.790	<.001	[0.112, 0.176]
Variance of Noise (v_{it})	0.038	0.043	0.890	.375	[0.004, 0.348]
Lambda (λ)	3.684	0.054	5.000	<.001	[3.578, 3.790]

The variance parameters provide insight into the relative contributions of inefficiency, measured using the Financial Technology (FinTech) Index, and random noise in explaining variations in Net Interest Income (NII). The variance of inefficiency (u_it) was 0.140 (SE = 0.016, z = 8.790, p < .001, 95% CI [0.112, 0.176]), indicating that inefficiency—attributable to differences in financial technology adoption—significantly influences NII variation. In contrast, the variance of noise (v_it) was 0.038 (SE = 0.043, z = 0.890, p = .375, 95% CI [0.004, 0.348]), suggesting that random noise contributes minimally to the model. The lambda parameter (λ) was 3.684 (SE = 0.054, z = 5.000, p < .001, 95% CI [3.578, 3.790]), indicating that inefficiency, as captured by the FinTech Index, is the dominant source of variation relative to random noise.

The results highlight the pivotal role of financial technology in influencing bank performance in Bahrain and GCC. Inefficiencies are mainly linked to structural gaps in FinTech adoption, with banks relying on outdated systems struggling to optimize Net Interest Income. Since random noise contributes minimally, variations in performance are largely explained by differences in digital capabilities. This underscores the need for banks to prioritize digital transformation and adopt FinTech solutions to reduce inefficiencies and strengthen financial outcomes (Table 7).

Table 7. Model Fit Statistics

Statistic	Value
Log-Likelihood	36.8346
Wald $\chi 2(2)$	4483.82
Probability (p)	<.001

The model fit statistics demonstrate a robust specification of the stochastic frontier model. The log-likelihood value (LL = 36.8346) indicates the model's likelihood under the observed data, suggesting a well-fitted model for the given dataset. The Wald chi-square test yielded a value of $\chi^2(2) = 4483.82$, with a highly significant probability (p < .001). This result confirms that the predictors, LogTD and LogTL, collectively have a statistically significant impact on explaining variations in Net Interest Income (NII).

The high Wald chi-square value confirms that the model effectively captures the key determinants of bank efficiency in Bahrain and GCC. This validates the use of the stochastic frontier analysis framework and highlights the significance of Total Deposits and Total Loans in explaining Net Interest Income (NII). The strong model fit enhances confidence in the reliability of the results and the policy implications drawn for improving banking operations and strategies.

5 Conclusion and Implications of the Study Findings

This study examined the determinants of bank efficiency in the GCC, focusing on the relationships between Net Interest Income (NII), Total Deposits (TD), Total Loans (TL), and financial technology. The results highlight considerable variation in banking metrics and FinTech adoption in Bahrain and GCC countries, reflecting the heterogeneity of the region's financial landscape (Abuzayed et al., 2018; Al-Hassan et al., 2010; Saif-Alyousfi & Saha, 2021). The Financial Technology Index, developed from digital commerce, digital remittances, and mobile POS, proved to be a robust measure, explaining 96.1% of variance in FinTech activity. Its strong positive association with NII suggests that digital transformation significantly improves efficiency in revenue generation, in line with findings by Agustina & Wijaya (2013), Yingjun et al. (2021), and Buckle & Thompson (2020).

At the same time, negative correlations between the FinTech Index and traditional banking variables such as deposits and loans indicate a shift from conventional models towards technology driven practices. This reflects the broader view that while FinTech enhances efficiency, it also intensifies competition from non-bank financial providers (Tarawneh et al., 2024), pushing traditional banks to re-invent their business models. The stochastic frontier analysis further revealed that loans contribute positively to NII, confirming their central role in profitability (Kohlscheen et al., 2018; Merry et al., 2022; Alnabulsi et al., 2023), whereas deposits show a negative effect, often linked to inefficiencies under low or negative interest rate environments (Lopez, Rose & Spiegel, 2020; Williams, 2020).

The efficiency differences across banks were found to be structural rather than random, underscoring the transformative role of digital technologies in shaping bank performance (Yang et al., 2023; Dwivedi et al., 2021). These findings carry important implications: banks in the GCC should shift focus from deposit-heavy strategies towards stronger loan portfolios while investing in digital transformation to sustain competitiveness (Rani et al., 2025). Policymakers should support cross-border payment solutions to strengthen regional integration and enhance global competitiveness. Ultimately, a hybrid model that integrates FinTech innovations with traditional lending will enable banks to achieve greater efficiency, profitability, and customer satisfaction, providing a roadmap for both practitioners and regulators in navigating the region's evolving financial landscape.

References

Abuzayed, B., Al-Fayoumi, N., Molyneux, P.: Diversification and bank stability in the GCC. J. Int. Financ. Mark. Inst. Money. **48**, 1–15 (2018). https://doi.org/10.1016/J.INTFIN.2018.04.005

Agarwal, S., Zhang, J.: FinTech, lending and payment innovation: a review. Asia-Pac. J. Financ. Stud. **49**(3), 353–367 (2020). https://doi.org/10.1111/ajfs.12294

Agustina, A., Wijaya, A.: Analisis Faktor-Faktor yang Mempengaruhi Loan Deposit Ratio Bank Swasta Nasional di Bank Indonesia. Jurnal Wira Ekonomi Mikroskil. **3**(2), 101–109 (2013)

Al-Hassan, A., Oulidi, N., Khamis, M.: The GCC banking sector: topography and analysis. INTL: Managing in Emerging Markets (Topic). **10**, 1–45 (2010). https://doi.org/10.5089/978145198 2619.001

Al-Muharrami, S., Matthews, K.: Market power versus efficient-structure in Arab GCC banking. Appl. Financ. Econ. **19**(18), 1487–1496 (2009)

Alnabulsi, K., Kozarević, E., Hakimi, A.: Non-performing loans and net interest margin in the MENA region: linear and non-linear analyses. Int. J. Financ. Stud. **11**(2), 64 (2023). https://doi.org/10.3390/ijfs11020064

Andros, S., Andros, S., Chang, S.: An innovative approach to managing the interest margin: economic and statistical analysis of the resource base of a commercial bank. VUZF Rev. **6**, 35–45 (2021). https://doi.org/10.38188/2534-9228.21.6.03

Barini, H.: Digital processes in the GCC countries in the first third of the 21st century: industry features and the need to align industry gaps. Int. Trade Trade Policy. **10**, 172–183 (2024). https://doi.org/10.21686/2410-7395-2024-3-172-183

Beijnen, C., Bolt, W.: Size matters: economies of scale in European payments processing. J. Bank. Finance. **33**(2), 203–210 (2009)

Berger, A.N., Mester, L.J.: Explaining the dramatic changes in performance of US banks: technological change, deregulation, and dynamic changes in competition. J. Financ. Intermediation. **12**(1), 57–95 (2003)

Bollaert, H., De Silanes, F., Schwienbacher, A.: Fintech and access to finance. J. Corp. Finance. **68**, 101941 (2021). https://doi.org/10.1016/J.JCORPFIN.2021.101941

Buckle, M., Thompson, J.: Financial Intermediation and Recent Developments in the UK Financial System, 5th edn, pp. 21–47. Manchester University Press (2020)

Chen, T.H., Peng, J.L.: Statistical and bibliometric analysis of financial innovation. Lib. Hi Tech. **38**(2), 308–319 (2020)

Cheng, M., Qu, Y.: Does bank FinTech reduce credit risk? Evidence from China. Pac. Basin Finance J. **63**, 101398 (2020)

Cho, T.Y., Chen, Y.S.: The impact of financial technology on China's banking industry: an application of the metafrontier cost Malmquist productivity index. North Am. J. Econ. Finance. **57**, 101414 (2021)

Dwivedi, P., Alabdooli, J.I., Dwivedi, R.: Role of FinTech adoption for competitiveness and performance of the bank: a study of banking industry in UAE. Int. J. Global Bus. Compet. **16**(2), 130–138 (2021)

Fathi, B.: Consequences of the foreign bank implantation in developing countries and its impact on the local bank efficiency: theoretical analysis and empirical tests on international data. Int. J. Econ. Finance. **2**(5), 103–111 (2010)

Fries, S., Taci, A.: Cost efficiency of banks in transition: evidence from 289 banks in 15 post-communist countries. J. Bank. Finance. **29**(1), 55–81 (2005)

Garza-García, J.G.: Determinants of bank efficiency in Mexico: a two-stage analysis. Appl. Econ. Lett. **19**(17), 1679–1682 (2012)

Ghozali, I.: An efficiency determinant of banking industry in Indonesia. Res. J. Finance Account. **5**(3), 18–26 (2014)

Gomber, P., Kauffman, R., Parker, C., Weber, B.: On the fintech revolution: interpreting the forces of innovation, disruption, and transformation in financial services. J. Manag. Inf. Syst. **35**, 220–265 (2017). https://doi.org/10.1080/07421222.2018.1440766

Hamadi, H., Awdeh, A.: The determinants of bank net interest margin: evidence from the Lebanese banking sector. J. Money Invest. Bank. **23**, 85–103 (2012)

Hassen, T.: The GCC economies in the wake of COVID-19: toward post-oil sustainable knowledge-based economies? Sustainability. **14**, 11251 (2022). https://doi.org/10.3390/su141811251

Jakšič, M., Marinč, M.: The future of banking: the role of information technology. Bančni vestnik: revija za denarništvo in bančništvo. **64**(11), 68–73 (2015)

Kamarudin, F., Nordin, B.A.A., Muhammad, J., Hamid, M.A.A.: Cost, revenue and profit efficiency of Islamic and conventional banking sector: empirical evidence from Gulf Cooperative Council countries. Glob. Bus. Rev. **15**(1), 1–24 (2014)

Khan, S., Khan, H., Nazir, S.: Utilizing the collective wisdom of fintech in the GCC region: a systematic mapping approach. Measure. Contr. **56**, 713–732 (2022). https://doi.org/10.1177/00202940221124130

Kohlscheen, E., Murcia Pabón, A., Contreras, J.: Determinants of bank profitability in emerging markets (BIS Working Paper No. 686). Bank for International Settlements (2018) Available at SSRN: https://ssrn.com/abstract=3098196

Li, S., Marinč, M.: Economies of scale and scope in financial market infrastructures. J. Int. Financ. Mark. Inst. Money. **53**, 17–49 (2018)

Lopez, J.A., Rose, A.K., Spiegel, M.M.: Why have negative nominal interest rates had such a small effect on bank performance? Cross country evidence. Eur. Econ. Rev. **124**, 103402 (2020). https://doi.org/10.1016/j.euroecorev.2020.103402

Merry, M., Edward, Y.R., Afiezan, H.A., Tarigan, A.E.: The effect of non-performing loans, loan to deposit ratios of operating expenses and operating income on return on assets with net interest margin as an intervening variable in banking companies listed in Indonesia stock exchange period 2019–2021. Int. J. Soc. Sci. Res. Rev. **5**(10), 381–396 (2022). https://doi.org/10.47814/ijssrr.v5i10.578

Nkem, I.S., Akujinma, A.F.: Financial innovation and efficiency on the banking sub-sector: the case of deposit money banks and selected instruments of electronic banking (2006–2014). Asian J. Econ. Bus. Account. **2**(1), 1–12 (2017)

Paulet, E., Mavoori, H.: Conventional banks and Fintechs: how digitization has transformed both models. J. Bus. Strateg. **41**, 19–29 (2019). https://doi.org/10.1108/jbs-06-2019-0131

Phan, D.H.B., Narayan, P.K., Rahman, R.E., Hutabarat, A.R.: Do financial technology firms influence bank performance? Pac. Basin Finance J. **62**, 101210 (2020)

Rahma, Y., Al-Alawi, A.: How to evaluate success startups: case of FinTech and cybersecurity in the GCC venture capital market. In: 2023 International Conference On Cyber Management And Engineering (CyMaEn), pp. 469–473 (2023). https://doi.org/10.1109/CyMaEn57228.2023.10051035

Rani, M.B., Doblas, M.P., Chellakan, S., Salindo, R.V.N.: Determinants of digital payment intensity in the MENA region: a panel data analysis. Int. J. Anal. Appl. Econ. **23**, 8 (2025). https://doi.org/10.28924/2291-8639-23-2025-8

Saif-Alyousfi, A., Saha, A.: Determinants of banks' risk-taking behavior, stability and profitability: evidence from GCC countries. Int. J. Islam. Middle East. Finance Manag. **14**, 1011–1039 (2021). https://doi.org/10.1108/IMEFM-03-2019-0129

Schmiedel, H., Malkamäki, M., Tarkka, J.: Economies of scale and technological development in securities depository and settlement systems. J. Bank. Finance. **30**(6), 1783–1806 (2006)

Shahani, A.: The impact of financial inclusion and fin-tech on financial sustainability: empirical evidence- emerging and frontier markets. IBT J. Bus. Stud. **18**, 49–67 (2022). https://doi.org/10.46745/ilma.jbs.2022.18.02.04

Shen, Z., Liao, H., Weyman-Jones, T.: Cost efficiency analysis in banking industries of ten Asian countries and regions. J. Chin. Econ. Bus. Stud. **7**(2), 199–218 (2009)

Sulaeman, H.S.F., Moelyono, S.M., Nawir, J.: Determinants of banking efficiency for commercial banks in Indonesia. Contemp. Econ. **13**(2), 223–240 (2019a)

Sulaeman, H., Moelyono, S., Nawir, J.: Determinants of banking efficiency for commercial banks in Indonesia. Contem. Econ. **13**, 223 (2019b). https://doi.org/10.5709/ce.1897-9254.308

Tarawneh, A., Abdul-Rahman, A., Mohd Amin, S.I., Ghazali, M.F.: A systematic review of fintech and banking profitability. Int. J. Financ. Stud. **12**(1), 3 (2024). https://doi.org/10.3390/ijfs12010003

Tsanis, K.: FinTech strategies in the GCC. In: Research Anthology on Concepts, Applications, and Challenges of FinTech, pp. 62–81. IGI Global (2020). https://doi.org/10.4018/978-1-5225-9377-5.CH004

Wang, Y., Sui, X., Zhang, Q.: Can Fintech improve the efficiency of commercial banks?—an analysis based on big data. Res. Int. Bus. Finance. **55**, 101338 (2021). https://doi.org/10.1016/J.RIBAF.2020.101338

Weerasuriya, J.S.P.D.S.B., Rathnayake, R.M.A.K., Fernando, P.J.S.: Impact of non-interest income on Bank efficiency: evidence from Sri Lanka. Asian J. Finance. **1**(1), 16–34 (2021)

Weill, L.: Banking efficiency in transition economies. Econ. Transit. **11**(3), 569–592 (2003)

Williams, E.: Heterogeneity in net-interest income exposure to interest rate risk and non-interest expense adjustment. Harvard Business School (2020). Retrieved from https://www.hbs.edu/ris/Publication%20Files/interest_rate_risk_and_adjustment_v3_dfe42518-228a-4d4a-9fff-e33e6ec1c25e.pdf

Yang, Y., Zhang, X., Feng, B.: The impact of developing fintech on banks: from the perspective of net interest margin and non-performing ratio. Front. Bus. Econ. Manag. **8**(1), 266–271 (2023)

Yingjun, Z., Jahan, S., Qamruzzaman, M.: Access to finance and legal framework in female entrepreneurship development in Bangladesh: the mediating role of self-leadership. Asian Econ. Financ. Rev. **11**(9), 762–780 (2021)

Digital Inclusive Finance and Economic Growth (GDP) via Industrial Structural Change: A System GMM Approach

Muhammad Atif Sattar, Muhammad Fahad Sattar[(✉)], and Umar Iqbal

School of Management and Economics, Kunming University of Science and Technology, Kunming, Yunnan, China
fahadsattar09@gmail.com

Abstract. This study investigates the impact of digital inclusive finance on economic growth (GDP) across 31 Chinese provinces, emphasizing the mediating role of industrial structural change. It further explores whether technological innovation moderates this relationship by differentiating the effects in high-tech and low-tech regions. To address potential endogeneity, the study employs the system Generalized Method of Moments (GMM), complemented by robustness and heterogeneity analyses. The findings reveal that digital inclusive finance positively influences GDP, primarily through the mechanism of industrial structural transformation. Mediation analysis confirms that without the contribution of structural change, the direct effect of digital inclusive finance on economic growth remains limited, underscoring the critical role of sectoral evolution in amplifying the benefits of digital financial inclusion.

Keywords: Digital Inclusive Finance · Industrial Structural Change · Economic Growth · GMM · Technology Innovation

1 Introduction

China has achieved significant economic progress since the implementation of reforms and the policy of opening up. In 2022, China's GDP attained 121.02 trillion yuan, establishing it as the world's second largest economy. Due to temporal, spatial, and financial constraints, traditional finance cannot entirely facilitate economic progress. Various sectors are concentrated on identifying new avenues for economic growth, refining industrial structures, and steering the new economic paradigm (Lee, Tang, & Lee, 2023).

With the progression of the digital era, inclusive digital finance evolved. Digital inclusive finance represents a technological transformation in conventional finance, incorporating the Internet, cloud computing, big data, and block chain. Digital inclusive finance integrates digital technology with inclusive finance to eradicate the reliance on physical locations inherent in traditional finance, transcend temporal and spatial limitations, expand the scope and content of traditional financial services, and achieve profound integration with industry to facilitate supply-side reforms, enhance production efficiency,

S. C. P. Yam et al. (Eds.): ICFT 2025, CCIS 2868, pp. 296–307, 2026.
https://doi.org/10.1007/978-981-92-0126-6_24

and optimize resource allocation. It serves as a crucial engine for industrial optimization. Digital inclusive finance influences innovation and entrepreneurship, consumption (Xiao, 2020), savings and poverty alleviation, hence impacting industrial structure and economic growth (Lai et al., 2020). The Chinese government has prioritized the advancement of digital inclusive finance.

The Digital Inclusive Finance Index from Peking University indicates that China's national average level of digital inclusive finance rose from 40.00 in 2011 to 271.62 by 2018. Digital inclusive finance development has shown significant regional disparities across China's 31 provinces, with several regions exceeding the national average. This higher trend reflects the growing importance of digital inclusive finance in stimulating regional economic activity and bridging financial service disparities throughout the country. Has the swift proliferation of digital inclusive finance stimulated economic growth? Examining the impact of digital inclusive finance on economic performance is essential for fostering long-term growth and adapting to the new economic landscape, both in practical and theoretical terms. In addition to the impact of digital inclusive finance on economic growth, various other inquiries warrant investigation: What is the role of industrial structure in this relationship? There is a differential impact of the pace of industrial structural change, enhancement, and optimization? Does digital inclusive finance impact economic growth differently throughout the 31 provinces, considering their diverse economic conditions, resource endowments, and stages of development? These issues are essential for comprehending the intricate relationship among digital inclusive finance, industrial structural dynamics, and regional economic development.

Upon reviewing the existing literature, several gaps become apparent in studies examining the relationship between digital finance and economic growth. Although some researchers have investigated this link, a significant number have relied on limited methodological approaches, such as fixed effects models; for example, the studies by Ahmad et al. (2021) and Zhou et al. (2024). Which often fail to address endogeneity concerns. Given that lagged values of GDP may influence the dependent and independent variables, such models risk producing biased estimations. For instance, Zhou, Zhang, and Wu (2024) examined the impact of digital inclusive finance on economic growth through the mechanisms of industrial upgrading, transformation, and rationalization; however, their analysis was confined to fixed effects estimation and robustness checks, without properly accounting for endogeneity an essential issue in causal inference. Moreover, the literature suggests that research on digital finance is still in its developmental stage, and there remains a lack of comprehensive analysis on how digital inclusive finance drives regional economic development through industrial structural change across China's 31 provinces.

In light of these gaps, the present study offers three key contributions. First, it investigates the direct and indirect effects of digital inclusive finance on economic growth, incorporating industrial structural change as a mediating variable. Second, it applies the system Generalized Method of Moments (GMM), a more appropriate estimation technique in this context, as it effectively addresses endogeneity and yields more robust and consistent results than traditional fixed effects models. Third, the study explores the heterogeneity of effects across different levels of technological innovation by comparing high-tech and low-tech provinces in China, thereby offering new insights into the differential impact of digital inclusive finance on economic performance.

2 Literature Review

2.1 Digital Finance and Economic Growth

Most contemporary studies suggest that digital inclusive finance plays a significant role in advancing economic growth. For example, empirical investigations by Beck et al. (2018) focusing on E-7 countries, Kenya, and China, respectively confirm that digital inclusive finance contributes positively to economic development. Similarly, Kim et al. (2018) emphasize the dual attributes of equity and efficiency in digital finance, highlighting its potential to optimize the allocation of financial resources, alleviate the resource curse, support post-crisis economic recovery, and enhance overall economic performance.

Further, Sun and Tang (2022) argue that digital inclusive finance alleviates corporate financing constraints, strengthens firms' capacity to manage crises, enhances performance, and fosters business development, all of which contribute to national economic growth. Research by Xiao (2020) also finds that digital inclusive finance stimulates consumer spending, encourages sustainable consumption behavior, reduces environmental damage, and promotes high-quality economic expansion. Nevertheless, a number of scholars caution that the relationship between digital inclusive finance and economic growth is not uniformly positive. Agwu (2021) notes that inadequate digital finance coverage in rural areas exacerbates the urban–rural income gap, potentially hindering overall economic development. In contrast, Liu and Guo (2023) contend that improved government infrastructure and expanded digital finance services have reduced the digital divide, thereby easing relative poverty and narrowing income inequality. Digital inclusive finance fundamentally enhances traditional financial services through the integration of information technologies (Ren, Zeng, & Gozgor, 2023). With its capabilities in data processing, computation, and rapid information retrieval, it supports the flow and connectivity of financial information (Hasan, Yajuan, & Khan, 2022).

Third, the widespread applicability and low access barriers of digital inclusive finance significantly improve the availability of financial services. It plays a crucial role in extending financial inclusion to previously unbanked populations, broadening the overall reach of financial infrastructure, and addressing issues of financial exclusion (Li & Ma, 2021). By bridging the economic divide between urban and rural regions, it reduces rural financial marginalization, improves the accessibility of financial tools in underdeveloped areas, and ensures that underserved and remote communities receive more efficient and targeted financial services (Xin et al., 2022), thus contributing to inclusive economic development. Finally, the integration of digital platforms within financial systems allows digital inclusive finance to offer user-friendly and convenient payment mechanisms while alleviating liquidity constraints through installment-based and consumer credit options. These functionalities support inter-temporal consumption smoothing, enhance individuals' purchasing power, and stimulate growth driven by domestic consumption (Li et al., 2020).

Hypothesis 1: Digital inclusive finance promotes economic growth.

2.2 Digital Finance and Industrial Structural Change

Li et al. (2022) highlight that digital inclusive finance significantly influences consumer behavior by reshaping demand patterns, fostering innovation in business models, and accelerating the process of industrial transformation. Financial development plays a pivotal role in driving structural change within industries (Huang, 2022). Empirical evidence from Xu and Tan (2020), employing a spatial econometric model, reveal that financial development measured in terms of scale, structural depth, and operational efficiency, can promote industrial transformation by improving scale efficiency and fostering structural optimization.

The growing integration of emerging technologies into economic systems is reshaping industrial architecture through the proliferation of digital products. Gomber, Koch, and Gomber (2017) argue that digital finance contributes substantially to the creation of market value and the reconfiguration of corporate structures. The convergence of big data with financial systems has redefined interactions between consumers, producers, and markets, facilitating a consumer-driven development model that accelerates both social and industrial evolution (Bruhn & Love, 2014). Digital inclusive finance plays a crucial role in strengthening the synergy between financial services and big data analytics by enhancing their reach across time and space, as well as improving ease of use and overall accessibility. It contributes to greater transparency in information flows, reduces information asymmetries between capital providers and users, lowers transaction and search costs, and boosts financial service efficiency. Furthermore, it expands the coverage of financial services and improves access by lowering transaction barriers. These mechanisms collectively enhance interest rate responsiveness within credit markets, optimize the structure of credit investments, and contribute to the advancement of industrial transformation and upgrading (Chen & Zhang, 2021). Therefore, digital inclusive finance not only increases the economy's responsiveness to financial innovation but also supports the broader objective of structural industrial advancement.

Financial services contribute significantly to the efficient allocation of resources and support the upgrading of industrial structures. An expansion in the scale of financial services can also help narrow regional economic disparities and foster structural transformation across industries (Mina & Imai, 2017). The evolution of financial systems through digital finance has played a key role in reducing information asymmetries both within sectors and across industries. This progression has not only decreased the cost of financing for enterprises but also influenced industrial development and technological innovation by exerting both "horizontal" and "structural" effects (X. Wang & He, 2020).

According to Ahsan and Haque (2017), capital investment remains a central driver of China's industrial upgrading, with capital accumulation forming the foundational basis for sustained industrial progress. Furthermore, diversified financial sector development has been shown to enhance the effectiveness of capital allocation, enabling the transformation of accumulated capital into productive investments. This, in turn, supports economic restructuring and industrial enhancement by facilitating more targeted distribution of financial resources (Zhao et al., 2018). Lin and Yan (2015) further emphasize that the horizontal and structural effects arising from technological innovation act as catalysts for changes in industrial structure and contribute to broader economic development.

Hypothesis 2: Digital inclusive finance is significantly associated with industrial structural change.

2.3 Industrial Structural Change and Economic Growth

Structural change has long been a core concept in development economics and is widely acknowledged as a fundamental component of the economic development process. The foundational model proposed by Lewis (1954) conceptualizes development as a shift of labor from the traditional agricultural sector to more productive non-agricultural sectors, particularly industry. This transition enhances overall economic productivity as labor moves from low-efficiency agricultural work to higher-efficiency industrial tasks. However, the Lewis model operates within a dual-sector framework that does not account for the service sector. Later contributions to the literature, such as those by Chenery and Syrquin (1975), extended the scope of structural change to include a sequential shift from agriculture to manufacturing, and subsequently to services an evolution characteristic of post-World War II economic expansion in developed economies (Jorgenson & Timmer, 2011). Recent scholarship places increasing importance on both the quality and speed of structural transformation as critical drivers of sustainable economic growth. Current perspectives define structural change not only as a sectoral reallocation from agriculture to industry and services but also as the internal evolution within sectors, moving from less productive to more productive activities (Naudé et al., 2015). For example, labor may shift from traditional agriculture to modern manufacturing or high-value services, or transition within manufacturing or services themselves from lower to higher productivity subsectors.

Moreover, variations in productivity levels across different industries, largely driven by technological advancements, suggest the need for analyzing structural change at a more disaggregated level (de Vries et al., 2012). Such structural reallocation is considered a key contributor to improved overall productivity and rising per capita income. As labor and capital shift toward high-productivity activities, the aggregate efficiency of the economy improves. This phenomenon has also been observed in the early post-independence periods of several developing countries, including those in Africa (de Vries et al., 2015). Beyond productivity, structural transformation enhances economic diversification, thereby reducing vulnerability to external economic shocks (Naudé et al., 2015). To facilitate this transformation, effective policy interventions are essential for reallocating resources toward more productive sectors. Understanding the dynamics and implications of structural change is therefore especially important for emerging economies like India. In recent years, novel theoretical frameworks have emerged to better analyze structural transformation processes. Some studies have even identified a complementary relationship between structural change and broader patterns of balanced economic growth (Gabardo et al., 2017). Additionally, Vu (2017) introduced a new metric termed "effective structural change," which was found to have a significant positive influence on GDP growth across various Asian countries.

Hypothesis 3: Industrial structural change is significantly associated with economic growth (GDP).

Hypothesis 4: Industrial structural change mediates the impact of digital inclusive finance on economic growth (GDP).

3 Research Design

This study investigates both the direct and indirect effects of digital inclusive finance on economic growth through regression analysis and robustness checks. The indirect effect operates via industrial structural change, which functions as a mediating variable. Furthermore, a heterogeneity analysis is conducted based on levels of technological innovation, which also serves as a control variable in the mediation framework.

3.1 Variables Definition

Gross Regional Product (GRP) is used to measure regional economic performance, with data for 31 Chinese provinces from 2011–2018 sourced from the China Statistical Yearbook. The Digital Inclusive Finance (DIF) Index, developed by Peking University, includes three dimensions: breadth of coverage, depth of use, and digitalization, with a higher value indicating greater development. Industrial Structural Change (SCI) refers to sectoral shifts from agriculture to services, measured using the Structural Change Index (SCI), which is based on the output shares of agriculture, industry, and services in GDP. Technological innovation is quantified by the number of patent applications per region. Control variables include the Consumer Price Index (CPI) to account for inflation, government regulation measured by the ratio of fiscal expenditure to GDP, trade openness as the ratio of imports and exports to GDP, and Per Capita GDP, which reflects average economic output per person (Fig. 1).

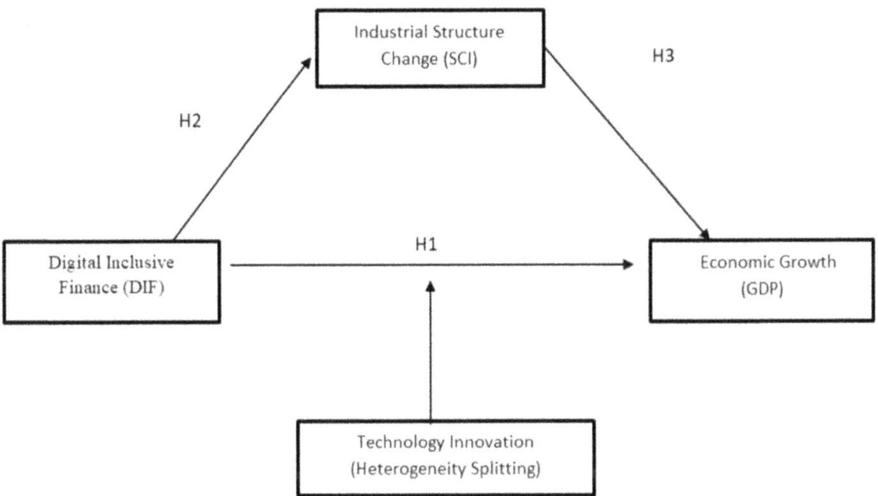

Fig. 1. Conceptual Framework

3.2 Model Setup

To investigate the impact of digital inclusive finance on economic growth, a baseline regression model is specified as Eq. (1). To address potential issues of heteroscedasticity and to smooth the data, all variables are transformed into their natural logarithmic form:

$$\ln \text{GDP}_{it} = \alpha_0 + \alpha_1 \ln \text{GDP}_{it-1} + \alpha_2 \ln \text{DIF}_{it} + \alpha_3 \ln \text{Control}_{it} + \mu_i + \varepsilon_{it} \qquad (1)$$

In this model, $\ln\text{GDP}_{it}$ represents the natural logarithm of economic output (GDP) for region i in period t. The term α_0 is the intercept, while α_1 captures the effect of the lagged value of GDP, reflecting the persistence of economic growth over time. The coefficient α_2 corresponds to the key explanatory variable, $\ln \text{DIF}_{it}$, which measures the level of digital inclusive finance in region i at time t. The parameter α_3 accounts for a vector of control variables that may influence economic growth. The μ_i term represents unobserved region-specific fixed effects, and ε_{it} denotes the idiosyncratic error term for region i and period t.

$$\ln \text{SCI}_{it} = \alpha_0 + \alpha_1 \ln \text{SCI}_{it-1} + \alpha_2 \ln \text{DIF}_{it} + \alpha_3 \ln \text{Control}_{it} + \mu_i + \varepsilon_{it} \qquad (2)$$

$$\ln \text{GDP}_{it} = \alpha_0 + \alpha_1 \ln \text{GDP}_{it-1} + \alpha_2 \ln \text{DIF}_{it} + \alpha_3 \ln \text{SCI}_{it} + \alpha_4 \ln \text{Control}_{it} + \mu_i + \varepsilon_{it} \qquad (3)$$

A stepwise regression-based mediation study is done to examine the mediating influence of industrial structural change in the relationship between digital inclusive finance and economic growth. The initial equation evaluates the impact of digital inclusive finance on structural change, where $\ln\text{SCI}_{it}$ represents the structural change index for region i at time t, $\ln\text{DIF}_{it}$ signifies the logarithm of digital inclusive finance, and the control variables encompass additional region-specific factors. The second equation integrates both $\ln\text{DIF}_{it}$ and $\ln\text{SCI}_{it}$ to analyse their direct and indirect impacts on economic growth, quantified by $\ln \text{GDP}_{it}$. This dual-equation paradigm facilitates the disaggregation of the overall impact of digital inclusive finance into its direct influence on economic growth and its indirect influence through structural transformation. Region-specific fixed effects (μ_i) and random error terms (ε_{it}) are incorporated to address unobserved heterogeneity and random disturbances, respectively.

3.3 Data Source

The data for this study comprise panel data from 31 Chinese provinces spanning the years 2011 to 2018. The Digital Inclusive Finance Index is sourced from Peking University, while data for all other variables are obtained from the China Statistical Yearbook. This dataset is used to examine the impact of digital inclusive finance on economic growth.

3.4 Baseline Regression Analysis

The findings from all three models paint a comprehensive picture of the direct and indirect effects of digital inclusive finance on economic growth. The lagged GDP coefficient of 0.9629 in Model 1 indicates a high level of persistence in economic growth. Directly contributing to regional growth, digital finance (DF) has a sizable positive impact on GDP 0.03329. Trade openness has a small but negative impact on GDP, in contrast to technological innovation 0.0239 and inflation (CPI), 1.6785. There is no statistical significance for the majority of the other control variables. The diagnostic tests demonstrate the instruments' legitimacy and the absence of serial correlation AR (1) p = 0.033 and Hansen p = 0.461.

The fact that digital finance aids economic transformation is confirmed by Model 2, which reveals that DIF has a strong positive effect on structural change 0.6086. Conversely, CPI has a hugely negative effect on SCI −42.531, and per capita GDP is likewise negatively correlated with SCI -0.5092. This data reveals that as regions become wealthier, structural transformation can be slowed down. With a p-value of 0.969, the model is plausible according to Hansen. In Model 3, we can see that Path B leads to GDP from SCI. The significance of lag GDP remains high at 0.9706, and SCI's positive and significant effect on GDP at 0.0209 lends credibility to its mediating function. A portion of DFI's impact on GDP is likely attributable to shifts in the economic structure, given that its direct effect becomes less significant 0.0223. This is an captivating finding. Another positive effect of technological innovation 0.0205 has been shown by diagnostic tests AR (1) p = 0.021, Hansen p = 0.708, indicating that this effect is strong. All of these findings point to the fact that digital inclusive finance impacts GDP growth to varying degrees depending on the nature of the industry in question. This is true for every model that satisfies the GMM criteria (Table 1).

Table 1. Baseline Regression Results

	Model 1	Model 2	Model 3
L.lnGDP	0.9629***(.0280)		0.9706***(0.03094)
L.lnSCI		0.1259(0.1686)	
lnDIF	0.03329**(0.0147)	0.6086**(0.2363)	0.0223(0.0168)
lnSCI			0.0209**(0.0072)
lnTech	0.0239**(0.0111)	0.0424(0.6820)	0.0205**(0.0102)
lnCPI	1.6785***(0.3044)	-42.531***(13.192)	0.8989(0.6747)
lnGovReg	0.0140(0.0299)	−0.0992(0.3105)	0.0175(0.03218)
lnTradeopen	−0.0035*(0.0020)	0.0571*(0.0303)	−0.0018(0.0018)
lnPerCapitaGDP	0.0027(0.0170)	−0.5092**(0.2450)	−0.0080(0.0146)
Constant	7.3843***(1.4849)	194.65**(61.81)	−3.8423(3.2319)
AR (1)	0.0330	0.111	0.021
AR (2)	0.3600	0.708	0.230
Hansen	0.4610	0.969	0.708

3.5 Robustness Check

To confirm the consistency of the results, a robustness check was conducted by varying the model specification. Specifically, the lag structure in the system GMM model was altered from (2, 3) to (3, 4) to assess the stability and reliability of the estimates. The results of the regression analysis paint a comprehensive picture of the ways in which digital inclusive finance (DIF) influences GDP growth, both directly and through altering the composition of various industries. The lag GDP of 0.9601 in Model 1 is crucial as it demonstrates the persistence of growth across time. Additionally, DIF 0.0424 has a positive and statistically significant impact on economic growth. While technological advancement and the CPI both contribute to GDP, trade openness does have a little detrimental impact. According to Model 2, which examines the relationship between DIF and structural change (SCI), DIF 0.6814 provides high support for SCI, demonstrating its capacity to bring about changes. Inflation and wealth may impede structural change since they have a negative impact on SCI. A positive and statistically significant coefficient for SCI 0.0157 and an insignificant coefficient for DIF 0.0386 indicate that SCI only mediates to a minor extent in Model 3, which examines SCI's role as a mediator. There is no serial correlation and valid instruments in the diagnostic tests conducted across models, indicating that the models are strong. Taken together, these numbers support the idea that DIF changes the structure of industries, which in turn increases economic growth (Table 2).

Table 2. Robustness Checks

	Model 1	Model 2	Model 3
L.lnGDP	0.9601***(0.0211)		0.9872***(0.0288)
L.lnSCI		0.9886(0.14876)	
lnDIF	0.0424**(0.0133)	0.6814**(0.2294)	0.0386(0.0239)
lnSCI			0.0157**(0.007)
lnTech	0.0274**(0.0087)	0.0785(0.0960)	0.0156(0.0099)
lnCPI	1.3384***(0.2905)	−38.3027**(11.1652)	1.0319*(0.5639)
lnGovReg	0.0153(0.0229)	−0.2389(0.3804)	0.0339(0.0293)
lnTradeopen	−0.004*(0.0019)	0.0547(0.0383)	−0.0024(0.0019)
lnPerCapitaGDP	0.0007(0.0180)	−0.5771*(0.2859)	0.0044(0.0183)
Constant	−5.7462***(1.3883)	175.64**(52.722)	−4.5790*(2.6146)
AR (1)	0.033	0.056	0.028
AR (2)	0.438	0.077	0.309
Hansen	0.21	0.217	0.770

3.6 Heterogeneity Test

To assess the role of technology in economic development, a heterogeneity test was conducted to examine whether regions with different levels of technological intensity exhibit varying impacts on GDP. This approach allows for the identification of how high-tech and low-tech regions respond differently to technological advancement, thereby providing a basis for formulating region-specific policies and implementation strategies. Digital inclusive finance (DIF) and related variables have vastly different impacts on

GDP growth when compared to low-tech populations. Both categories of lagged GDP remain highly significant and positive, indicating that expansion is ongoing. The high-tech group experienced a greater impact 1.0128 compared to the low-tech group 0.8203. The impact of digital inclusive finance (DIF) on economic growth appears ambiguous across technological levels, as the coefficients are statistically insignificant in both high-tech and low-tech regions maybe due data limitation after breakdown in groups. However, a comparison of the DIF coefficients 0.0527 for high-tech regions and 0.0074 for low-tech regions suggests that DIF may have a relatively greater influence on GDP in high-tech regions than in low-tech regions. Interestingly, technological innovation (lnTech) does not significantly affect economic growth in high-tech regions, whereas it shows a modest but significant positive effect in low-tech regions, with a coefficient of 0.0914. This pattern may be explained by the saturation of technological advancement in high-tech regions, where additional innovation yields limited marginal gains, while in low-tech regions, even modest improvements in technology can produce more noticeable economic benefits. As a result, technical advancements may provide greater marginal advantages in sectors where baseline innovation is lower. Neither group is significantly affected by control variables such as per capita GDP, CPI, government regulation, trade openness, etc. The models pass the AR (1), AR (2) tests, and Hansen diagnostic. Taken together, these numbers suggest that regions with vastly varying degrees of technological development may see vastly varied results from digitally inclusive financing and innovation policies (Table 3).

Table 3. Heterogeneity Analysis based on Technology Innovation

	High Tech Group	Low Tech Group
L.lnGDP	1.0128***(0.0509)	0.8203***(0.1257)
lnDIF	0.0527(0.0507)	0.0074(0.1080)
lnSCI	0.0181(0.0129)	0.0195(0.0162)
lnTech	0.0115(0.0234)	0.0914**(0.0287)
lnCPI	0.4855(0.6544)	−0.4108(1.3416)
lnGov_Regulations	0.0412(0.0322)	−0.0540(0.1617)
lnTrade openness	−0.0015(0.0014)	−0.0051(0.0039)
lnPer Capita GDP	0.0201(0.0632)	−0.0356(0.0756)
Constant	−2.3649(2.9043)	3.1530(6.0875)
AR (1)	0.097	0.027
AR (2)	0.500	0.160
Hansen	1.0000	1.0000

4 Conclusion

This study investigates the relationship between digital inclusive finance (DIF) and economic growth (GDP), emphasizing the mediating role of industrial structural change across 31 Chinese provinces from 2011 to 2018. The empirical findings reveal that DIF contributes to economic growth, particularly when industrial structural transformation is taken into account. The mediation analysis clearly shows that the direct effect of DIF on GDP becomes weaker when structural change is included in the model, underscoring its significant mediating role. These results align with previous studies such as Zhou, Zhang, and Wu (2024), which highlight the role of industrial upgrading in the DIF-GDP link, and are further supported by Xue, Feng, and Li (2024), who emphasize the positive association between DIF and the structural change index (SCI). Furthermore, the heterogeneity analysis confirms that regions with higher levels of technological innovation experience a stronger influence of DIF on GDP compared to low-tech regions. The higher coefficient in the high-tech group indicates a more robust relationship between digital finance and economic growth in technology-intensive areas. These findings have meaningful policy implications, suggesting that promoting technological innovation can enhance the effectiveness of digital inclusive finance in stimulating regional economic development.

In conclusion, the relationship among digital inclusive finance, industrial structural change, and economic growth is both significant and dynamic. The study highlights the importance of considering structural transformation as a key mechanism through which digital finance drives regional economic performance. Policymakers are encouraged to tailor financial inclusion strategies based on regional technological capacities to achieve more inclusive and sustainable economic growth.

References

Agwu, M.E.: Can technology bridge the gap between rural development and financial inclusions? Technol. Anal. Strateg. Manag. **33**(2), 123–133 (2021)

Ahsan, H., Haque, M.E.: Threshold effects of human capital: schooling and economic growth. Econ. Lett. **156**, 48–52 (2017)

Beck, T., Pamuk, H., Ramrattan, R., Uras, B.R.: Payment instruments, finance and development. J. Dev. Econ. **133**, 162–186 (2018)

Bruhn, M., Love, I.: The real impact of improved access to finance: evidence from Mexico. J. Finance. **69**(3), 1347–1376 (2014)

Chen, S., Zhang, H.: Does digital finance promote manufacturing servitization: micro evidence from China. Int. Rev. Econ. Finance. **76**, 856–869 (2021)

Chenery, B.H., Syrquin, M.: Patterns of Development: 1950–1970. Oxford University Press (1975)

de Vries, G.J., Erumban, A.A., Timmer, M.P., Voskoboynikov, I., Wu, H.X.: Deconstructing the BRICs: structural transformation and aggregate productivity growth. J. Comp. Econ. **40**(2), 211–227 (2012)

de Vries, G., Timmer, M.P., de Vries, K.: Structural transformation in Africa: static gains, dynamic losses. J. Dev. Stud. **51**(6), 1–15 (2015)

Gabardo, F.A., Pereima, J.B., Einloft, P.: The incorporation of structural change into growth theory: a historical appraisal. Economia. **18**(2), 1–18 (2017)

Gomber, P., Koch, J.A., Siering, M.: Digital finance and FinTech: current research and future research directions. J. Bus. Econ. **67**(5), 537–580 (2017)

Hasan, M.M., Yajuan, L., Khan, S.: Promoting China's inclusive finance through digital financial services. Glob. Bus. Rev. **23**(4), 984–1006 (2022)

Huang, S.: Do green financing and industrial structure matter for green economic recovery? Fresh empirical insights from Vietnam. Econ. Anal. Policy. **75**, 61–73 (2022)

Jorgenson, D.W., Timmer, M.P.: Structural change in advanced nations: a new set of stylised facts. Scand. J. Econ. **113**(1), 1–29 (2011)

Kim, D.W., Yu, J.S., Hassan, M.K.: Financial inclusion and economic growth in OIC countries. Res. Int. Bus. Finance. **43**, 1–14 (2018)

Lewis, W.A.: Economic development with unlimited supplies of labour. Manch. Sch. **22**, 139–191 (1954)

Li, F., Wu, Y., Liu, J., Zhong, S.: Does digital inclusive finance promote industrial transformation? New evidence from 115 resource-based cities in China. PLoS One. **17**(8), e0273680 (2022)

Li, T., Ma, J.: Does digital finance benefit the income of rural residents? A case study on China. Quant. Finance Econ. **5**, 664–688 (2021)

Li, J., Wu, Y., Xiao, J.J.: The impact of digital finance on household consumption: evidence from China. Econ. Model. **86**, 317–326 (2020)

Lin, J., Yan, X.: Analysis of Internet Finance Based on the Long Tail Theory: The Financing of Small and Micro Enterprises for Example, pp. 346–350 (2015)

Liu, L., Guo, L.: Digital financial inclusion, income inequality, and vulnerability to relative poverty. Soc. Indic. Res. **170**(3), 1155–1181 (2023)

Lee, H., Tang, C., Yang, S.A.., Zhang, Y.: Dynamic trade finance in the presence of information frictions and FinTech. Manufact. Serv. Oper. Manage. *25*(6). 2038–2055. ISSN 1523-4614

Mina, C.D., Imai, K.S.: Estimation of vulnerability to poverty using a multilevel longitudinal model: evidence. J. Dev. Stud. **53**, 1–27 (2017)

Mina, C.D., Imai, K.S.: Estimation of vulnerability to poverty using a multilevel longitudinal model: evidence. J. Dev. Stud. **53**, 1–27 (2017)

Naude, W., Szirmai, A., Haraguchi, N.: Structural Change and Industrial Development in the BRICS. Oxford University Press (2015)

Sun, Y., Tang, X.: The impact of digital inclusive finance on sustainable economic growth in China. Financ. Res. Lett. **50**, 103234 (2022)

Vu, K.M.: Structural change and economic growth: empirical evidence and policy insights from Asian economies. Struct. Change Econ. Dyn. **41**, 64–77 (2017)

Wang, X., He, G.: Digital financial inclusion and farmers' vulnerability to poverty: evidence from rural China. Sustainability. **12**(4), 1668 (2020)

Xu, L., Tan, J.: Financial development, industrial structure and natural resource utilization efficiency in China. Resour. Policy. **66**, 101642 (2020)

Xue, Q., Feng, S., Li, M.: The impact of digital finance on industrial structure: Evidence from China. SAGE Open **14**(2) (2024)

Zhao, S., He, J., Yang, H.: Population ageing, financial deepening and economic growth: evidence from China. Sustainability **10**(12), 4627 (2018)

Zhou, W., Zhang, X., Wu, X.: Digital inclusive finance, industrial structure, and economic growth: an empirical analysis of Beijing-Tianjin-Hebei region in China. PLoS ONE **19**(3) (2024)

Algorithmic Forecasting of Digital Economy Development Using Big Data and Machine Learning for FinTech Decision Support

Jieyi Wang$^{(\boxtimes)}$

Xi'an Jiaotong University City College, Xi'an 710018, Shaanxi, China
532250204@qq.com

Abstract. Driven by the rapid development of digital technology, the digital economy has become a major engine for global economic growth. Accurately predicting its life cycle is the difficulty, it will help policy and development strategy formulation. To the best of our knowledge, this paper for the first time, using large-scale data mining technology, explores an algorithm model to predict digital economy trends and put forward a series of prediction means based on machine learning theory with regression analysis. The basic features and current developments of digital economy are considered, including the discussion of classical methods constraints. A big data-based digital economy trend prediction model algorithm is presented with its essential parts of data collecting, preprocessing processing, model building and optimization. The model efficiency is then verified by typical case studies, and the potential uses in policy making, market analysis and industry evolution are analyzed. The results show that the big data-based forecasting methods are effective in increasing the accuracy of digital economic trend analysis, providing a reliable basis for decision-making for government and enterprises.

Keywords: Big Data · Digital Economy · Development Trend · Forecasting Algorithm · Machine Learning · Time Series Analysis · Data Mining

1 Introduction

The digital economy is a fundamental driver of world economic growth, which relies on emerging technologies (such as big data, cloud computing and artificial intelligence) serving to provide industrial guidance and establish new business models [1]. With the increased level of network penetration and the addition of powerful homogeneous data sources in recent years, the share of digital economy becomes more and more important in the economic structure of countries around the world [2]. However, the development process of digital economy is complicated, radical changes and multi-directional impact are brought by many factors including policy factor, technological factor or market demand; it is difficult to accurately predict future trends [3].

In the traditional economic trend analysis, statistical model and econometric model are two major approaches. However, these approaches have limitations when working

S. C. P. Yam et al. (Eds.): ICFT 2025, CCIS 2868, pp. 308–318, 2026.
https://doi.org/10.1007/978-981-92-0126-6_25

with large, multi-source and non-linear data [4]. When the traditional methods for forecasting digital economy trends are unable to make suitable adjustments to analyze the complex relationships between data, big data technologies can mine patterns from such data and thus provide new perspectives on the forecasts of digital economic trends. These technologies, in combination with machine/deep learning or time-series analysis algorithms, are able to improve the prediction accuracy for policy makers and business.

It is a big data technology paper, in which forecasting algorithm of digital economy evolutionary trajectory is proposed. (reappraisal) that examines the anatomy of digital economy and its evolutionary patterns, while revealing certain limitations in terms of traditional means of analysis [5]. In this paper we proposed a big oh(economic)e(bdpe)o social digital economy trend prediction algorithm model including data collection, preprocessing and modeling stage as shown in Fig [6]. Experiments prove the effectiveness of algorithm, and the application in policy-making, market analysis, industrial transformation and upgrading are discussed. And maybe this research can offer the basis for sustainable growth of digital economy theoretically and practically.

2 Analysis of the Development Trend of Digital Economy

The digital economy as a mode of economy is characteristic of data being the main production factor and digital technology being the basic productive force, extensively affecting global industrial structure and market pattern [7]. Traditional economic in contrast, the digital economy based on information management, intelligence and network characteristic, realize resource allocation high-performance, economic activity is deeply integrated [8]. In recent years, with the rapid development of cloud computing, artificial intelligence, blockchain and 5G technologies among others, while digital economy is growing at exponential speed, the growth rate of traditional industries lags far behind in contrast. Governments have responded by adopting strategies to fast-track the building of digital infrastructure and marketize data components, in order to support the wider economic job of becoming digitally transformed.

Mean Squared Error (MSE):

$$\text{MSE} = \frac{1}{n}\sum\nolimits_{i=1}^{n}(y_i - \hat{y}_i)^2 \tag{1}$$

Root Mean Squared Error (RMSE):

$$\text{RMSE} = \sqrt{\frac{1}{n}\sum\nolimits_{i=1}^{n}(y_i - \hat{y}_i)^2} \tag{2}$$

Globally, the digital economy is emerging as a key engine of economic growth [9]. From e-commerce and digital finance to smart manufacturing and the platform economy, the adoption of digital technologies is steadily increasing, driving industrial upgrades and fostering business model innovations [10]. Indicators such as digital economy's contribution to GDP have risen steadily in major economies, including China, US and EU, and a number of new industries have quickly emerged, such as sharing economy, cross border ecommerce and virtual reality industry. As the amount of data has exploded and

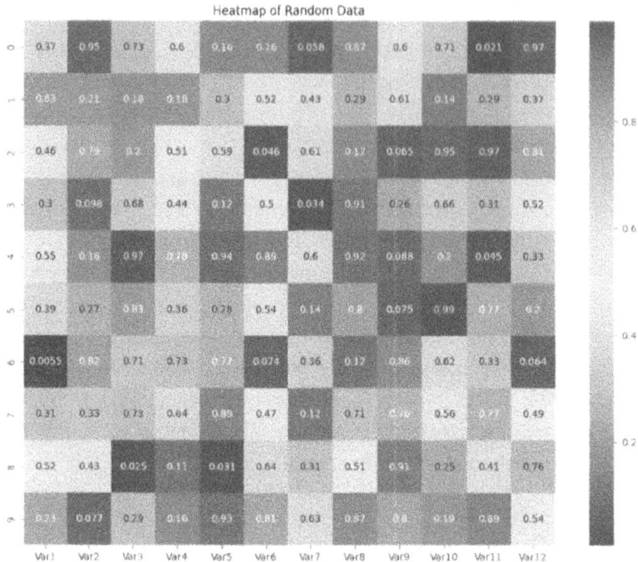

Fig. 1. Heatmap of Digital Economy Sector Performance Indicators.

value compounded from extracted data, data has gradually become as crucial a production factor as land, capital, and labor, propelling industries toward greater digitization and intelligence, showed in Fig. 1.

Traditional methods of analyzing economic trends have revealed significant limitations when confronted with the rapid advancement of the digital economy [11]. Macroeconomic statistical models and econometric techniques often rely on historical data and linear assumptions, which prove inadequate when handling high-dimensional, nonlinear, and dynamically changing data. Like all economic sectors, the digital economy has many driving forces, including technology innovation, policy support, and market demand. Classical methods fail to fully model these complicated associations, leading to inaccurate and imprecise predictions [12]. In addition, the digital economy creates various types of structured and unstructured data that brings great challenges to traditional methods because some of them cannot cope with complex structures or multi-source data.

The emergence of big data technology provides new hope for these challenges: supply new methods for analysis and prediction the development trajectory of digital economy. It combines heterogeneous data from different sources: social media, enterprise operations, market transactions with advanced algorithms…like machine learning and deep learning that let us uncover hidden patterns in very complex relationship of data leading to more precise and timely predictions. In particular deep learning LSTM (long-short term memory) and ARIMA models have been employed as they can capture the temporal structure, efficiently model non-linear features, and increase the forecasting accuracy of economic indicators. Digital economy development trends, the big data analysis as an important means of investigation gradually become more and more mature, for the government decision-making, corporate strategic planning and marketing investment has laid a solid scientific basis.

3 Algorithm for Predicting Digital Economic Trends Based on Big Data

The growth of the digital economy is affected by many factors, and it depends on the rapid and exact trend prediction using the big data technology for making more precise and reliable analysis. The big data-based trend forecasting algorithm of digital economy is mainly composed of three important stages: collecting and cleaning the heterogeneous-sourced data to guarantee that it was qualified, which is the prerequisite for subsequent analysis model construction and optimization-led processing. This involves collecting data from different sources like social media, business operations, market exchange etc. And after handling the noise and missing data, we need to use machine learning/deep learning technique (fixed analytics handler used here in modeling of prediction. These techniques reveal previously hidden patterns in data, model complex relationships and predict better. Science section Then the capability of stability and generalization in various cases is evaluated by applying models for handling nonlinear characteristics and dynamic information, such as Long Short-Term Memory Networks (LSTM) and Autoregressive Integrated Moving Average (ARIMA). "This optimization guarantees that the proposed model is guaranteed to be effective in practical applications, such as government decision-making, corporate strategic planning and market trend analysis.

3.1 Data Acquisition and Preprocessing

Data operability is important to model truth and credibility, especially in digital economic trend prediction. Data collection and preprocessing underlie the other analysis steps. Data in a digital economy is generated from various sources, such as: government data/statistics, enterprise operation data, market trade information, social media activity and internet user behavior. These methods have their limitations: government statistics are official but have a delay, market transaction data is real-time but noisy and social media has big volume but is usually unstructured. In data acquisition, it is necessary to use multiple channels to obtain high-quality raw data. This methodology ensures that the dataset contains a complete and representative sample of the online economy. Pooling of resources across various sources can make the model more adaptive and predictive. Also, preprocessing steps (e.g., data cleaning and normalization) help mitigate issues such as missing value, noise, inconsistencies etc. which enable more accurate trend prediction using better quality and useful data. Mean Absolute Error (MAE):

$$\mathrm{MAE} = \frac{1}{n}\sum\nolimits_{i=1}^{n} |y_i - \hat{y}_i| \tag{3}$$

Thanks to the variety of data sources, formats and structures, the data can be very different from case to case and some potential problems like missing values or repeated records may lead our analysis astray. In the process of data preprocessing, it is necessary to address these issues through cleaning of the data: deduplication, missing value filling and anomalous data processing. For NaNs/missing values, fill or gap-fill exercise with mean imputation, interpolation, more fancier ML based methods etc. If they have certain tendencies and effect to the data, they can be detected or even treated by statistical algorithms or predictive algorithms in machine learning. Task for data cleaning is to make the data consistent and reliable, which can be used as input of modeling.

Following data cleaning, feature engineering is an essential process to improve model performance. There are three main steps of feature engineering: feature selection, feature transformation, and feature construction. Feature selection aims at removing redundant or irrelevant features to reduce computational cost and enhance the generalization capability of the model. Feature transformation There are normalization and standardization, which preprocesses data so that different features with various scales can be treated on the same scale. Feature construction also enriches the expressive capacities of a model by aggregating existing features or synthesizing new ones. For example, in the context of digital economic mic analysis, system features such as growth rate and volatility may be derived from a historical transaction data to enable the model to learn well about market trends whose illustration is depicted in Fig. 2.

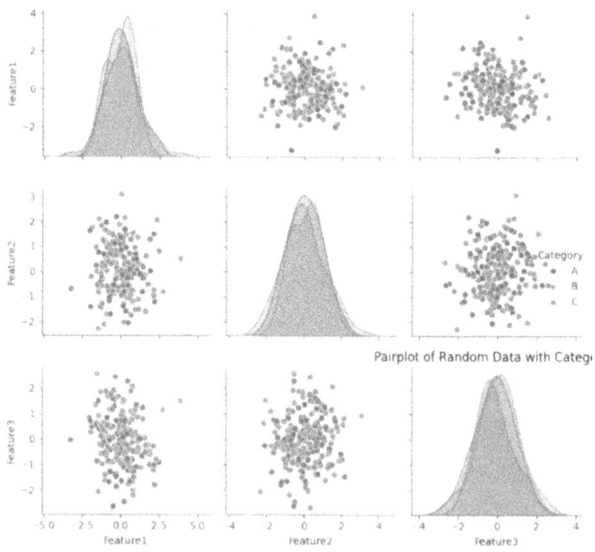

Fig. 2. Pairplot of Economic Features with Categorized Data.

In view of the timeliness and real-time applicability of the data, handling such huge trends in the digital economy requires sound storage and management. Big data massive storage mechanisms such as Hadoop and Spark are suitable for distributed storage and computation which allow faster data processing and retrieval through parallel processing of massive datasets. For dynamic real-time data updating, data stream processing technologies such as Kafka and Flink settle for the most explicitly. The technology guarantees that the reality of the model corresponds to the actual market or environment. These technologies allow for continuous ingestion and processing of live data streams, ensuring that the most up-to-date information is always incorporated into the model. By implementing efficient data storage and management systems, the timeliness and stability of data analysis are enhanced, so that the prediction model can promptly adjust to new situation, offer the users more accurate and reliable support in forecasting the digital economy trends.

3.2 Algorithm Model Construction

After completing data collection and preprocessing, constructing a suitable prediction model is the core link of digital economy trend analysis. Since the development of digital economy is affected by a variety of non-linear factors, traditional statistical methods have certain limitations in prediction accuracy, and need to be combined with machine learning, deep learning and time series analysis to build more accurate prediction models. The selection of the model should take into account the data characteristics, computational cost and prediction accuracy to ensure applicability and stability in complex environments. R-Squared (R^2):

$$R^2 = 1 - \frac{\sum_{i=1}^{n} (y_i - \hat{y}_i)^2}{\sum_{i=1}^{n} (y_i - \overline{y})^2} \tag{4}$$

The application of machine learning Methods Machine learning methods are widely used in predicting the digital economy trend, such as decision tree, random forest, Support Vector Machines (SVM) and Gradient Boosted Decision Trees (GBDT). Such models could learn important patterns on historical data to predict future trends. Random forests and GBDT are robust when dealing with high-dimensional data and can automatically capture nonlinear relationships in the data to improve prediction accuracy. Support vector machines are suitable for analyzing data with small samples and high dimensions, and can effectively deal with complex economic data environments, showed in Fig. 3.

Among all the deep learning methods, RNNs and its variants, like LSTM networks44–47 and GRUs48 have been performing well in time series data analysis, where a key advantage of LSTM is that it can learn long range dependencies67 so that we find it appropriate to predict the development trend for digital economy. When analyzing market transaction data or Internet user behavior data, LSTM is able to learn the dynamic change patterns of historical data and make reasonable predictions based on time series. In contrast, GRU has a simpler structure and higher computational efficiency, and is suitable for prediction tasks with higher real-time requirements.

When the model is built, integrated learning strategies should also be used to enhance the generalizability and robustness of the model. Combining learning methods such as XGBoost, LightGBM and Stacking are highly efficient to alleviate bias of individual model and enhance the prediction accuracy because they combine the prediction results of multiple base learner together. Traditional machine learning and deep learning can be integrated to extract time-series features with LSTM to make the final predict by GBDT, which fully exploits each model's unique advantages and achieves more accurate prediction of digital economy trend.

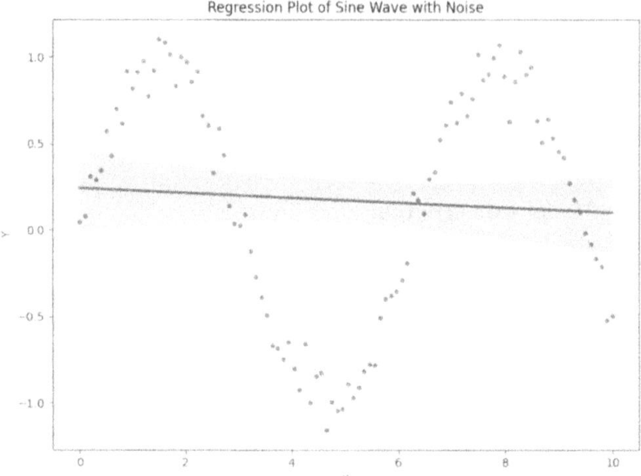

Fig. 3. Regression Analysis of Digital Economy Growth Trends.

3.3 Evaluation and Optimization

As in any digital economic trend prediction, model validation and optimization are the key components to guarantee the neural network forecast results accuracy and reliability. Since the performance of different models on different datasets may vary, it is necessary to construct a scientific evaluation system to quantitatively analyze the performance of prediction models. Usually, the evaluation indexes of prediction models include mean square error (MSE), root mean square error (RMSE), mean absolute error (MAE), and coefficient of determination (R^2), etc. MSE and RMSE can measure the overall error level of the model, MAE reflects the average magnitude of the error, and R^2 is used to measure the explanatory ability of the model. Through the comprehensive assessment of these indicators, the strengths and weaknesses of the model can be judged and provide a basis for subsequent optimization. LSTM Cell Update Equations:

$$f_t = \sigma\left(W_f \cdot \left[h_{t-1}, x_t\right] + b_f\right)$$

$$i_t = \sigma\left(W_i \cdot \left[h_{t-1}, x_t\right] + b_i\right)$$

$$\widetilde{C}_t = \tanh\left(W_C \cdot \left[h_{t-1}, x_t\right] + b_C\right)$$

$$C_t = f_t * C_{t-1} + i_t * \widetilde{C}_t$$

$$o_t = \sigma\left(W_o \cdot \left[h_{t-1}, x_t\right] + b_o\right)$$

$$h\_t = o\_t * \tanh(C_t) \tag{5}$$

As for evaluation, the generalization of the model plays a very important role. Cross-validation (e.g., K folds cross validation) and leave-out methods are necessary to reasonable split dataset and avoid overfitting or under such problem in the model predicting unseen data. When a model overfits, its variance is high and the training accuracy is overly optimistically High, making it predict values well only for data that was already in the dataset For underfitting its the opposite; The model doesn't simulate\learn all of the data logic, like in scikit-learn '.fitness curve' image The correct prediction returned made by your code, resulting in poor predictions. To mitigate these problems, model complexity can be controlled by regularization (e.g., L1/L2 regularization) or by tuning the model hyperparameters to find the optimal balance. Gradient Descent Update Rule:

$$\theta = \theta - \alpha \cdot \nabla_\theta J(\theta) \tag{6}$$

The key to model optimization lies in hyperparameter tuning, and the choice of hyperparameters directly affects the final results of the model. Typical hyperparameter tuning approaches are Grid Search, Random Search and Bayesian Optimization. Grid Search is fine for an exact search in relatively small parameter spaces, while Random Search can quickly find better solutions in larger parameter spaces, and Bayesian Optimization can efficiently find the optimal parameter combinations in high-dimensional complex parameter spaces. In deep learning models, the selection of optimization algorithms (e.g., Adam, SGD, RMSprop, etc.) and the learning rate tuning are also important factors affecting the model performance, showed in Fig. 4.

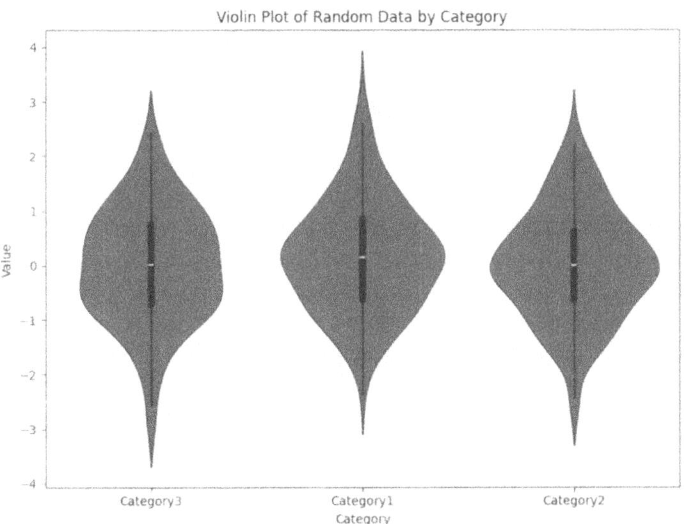

Fig. 4. Violin Plot of Digital Economy Variables by Category.

In addition to hyper-parameter tuning, model inputs can also be optimized by feature engineering to improve prediction accuracy. Feature selection (such as through information gain, mutual information and PCA) is applied to filter out irrelevant features for enhancing the trainability and generalization of models. The robustness of the model can also be promoted by data augmentation methods. Sliding window methods can also be applied to previous sequential forecast problems in order to produce input data and improve the model's ability of capturing short-term trends. Through multi-level optimization, the accuracy and stability of digital economy trend prediction model can be enhanced again to offer more scientific support for policy formulation and enterprise decision-making.

4 Research Application and Empirical Analysis

In the research application of digital economy trend prediction, empirical analysis plays a crucial role. Through the analysis of actual cases, the validity and operability of the model can be verified, providing a basis for government decision-making, enterprise strategic planning and market analysis. Selecting data from typical industries or regions for empirical analysis can demonstrate the application scenarios and prediction accuracy of the model in the real world. Historical data of a specific industry (e.g., e-commerce industry or digital finance industry) is selected to analyze its future development trend using the big data trend prediction model, so as to assess the applicability of the model in different fields.

When conducting empirical analysis, it is necessary to set clear analysis objectives and assessment indicators. Common objectives include forecasting market demand, industry growth rate, return on investment, etc., while assessment metrics include prediction error, precision, and recall. In practice, the accuracy and reliability of the prediction results can be tested by comparing them with real data. That is, errors between the prediction results of the model and observed data are to be determined, and variables of the model are adjusted so that predictive precision may be increased. Adding actual shooting data will gradually affect prediction results. The model's effectiveness requires regular updating and inspection.

In order to improve the practical application value of the model, the study also needs to explore the combination of different algorithms and their advantages. In the empirical analysis, it is possible to try to integrate multiple algorithms to improve the stability and accuracy of prediction. The time-series prediction model (LSTM) can be combined with traditional machine learning algorithms (Random Forest) for integrated prediction through integrated learning methods (Stacking or Boosting). This integrated approach can reduce the limitations of a single model and improve the overall forecasting ability, especially in the case of large data fluctuations or complex and changing economic environment, which can provide more robust forecasting results, showed in Fig. 5:

The research results obtained through empirical analysis can not only provide a theoretical basis for academic research in areas related to the digital economy, but also provide an important reference for government policymaking and corporate strategic planning. At the government level, the prediction of digital economy trends based on big data can provide scientific support for macroeconomic regulation, industrial policy making, etc. At the enterprise level, the prediction results can help enterprises to make decisions on market forecasting, product planning, resource allocation, etc., and improve their advantages in competition. The research results have wide application value and

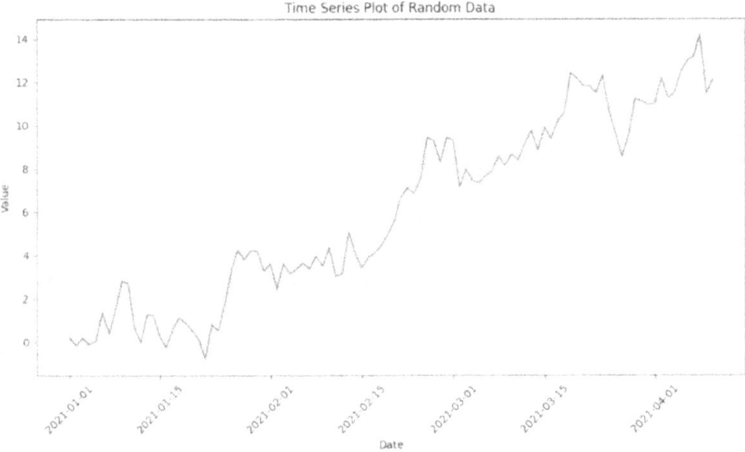

Fig. 5. Time Series Analysis of Digital Economy Trends Over Time.

can provide powerful technical support and decision-making basis for promoting the sustainable and healthy development of digital economy.

5 Conclusion

This paper is based on big data technology, the algorithm of digital economy development trend prediction method was tested in various ways to verify its application effect. The article discusses the main features and development trend of digital economy, and illustrates defects of the former prediction methods which are used to complex, dynamic digital economic information. The paper establishes a more scientific method for digital economic trend prediction via constructing a big data predication model and integrating the machine learning, deep learning and time sequence analysis methods. Through empirical analysis of typical cases, the trend prediction algorithm based on big data can effectively improve the accuracy of digital economic trend prediction, especially in the market environment with huge data volume and rapid changes, with strong adaptability and robustness. Through the systematic analysis of data acquisition and preprocessing, model construction and optimization, this paper further clarifies the key technologies and optimization methods of each link in the digital economic trend prediction, and provides a detailed operational guide for practical application.

This study also has certain limitations, mainly in terms of the timeliness and completeness of the data. We improve the accuracy of the model by integrating data from multiple sources, and the performance of the model may still be limited by the data quality in some special areas or under small-scale datasets. Future research can further explore data acquisition, model innovation and algorithm optimization to enhance the broad applicability and accuracy of the prediction system. Big data-based digital economic trend prediction methods provide important support for government decision-making, corporate strategic planning and market trend analysis. With the further accumulation of data resources and the continuous progress of algorithm technology, this method is expected to play a greater role in various fields of the digital economy in the future and promote the sustainable development of the digital economy.

Acknowledgements. The authors acknowledge the Shaanxi Province "14th Five-Year Plan" Educational Science Planning 2023 Annual Project: "Research on the Digital Transformation of Private Higher Education Institutions in Shaanxi Province under the Background of the Digital Economy"(NO:SGH23Q0346);Xi'an Jiaotong University City College School-Level Research Project: "Research on the Time-Varying Dynamic Relationship Between the Development of the Digital Economy, Industrial Structure Upgrading, and Employment in Shaanxi Province"(NO:2022Q28).

References

1. Singh, S.: The south African "information society", 1994–2008: problems with policy, legislation, rhetoric and implementation. J. South. Afr. Stud. **36**(1), 209–227 (2010)
2. Lukacs, G.: Dreamwork: cell phone novelists, labor, and politics in contemporary Japan. Cult. Anthropol. **28**(1), 44–64 (2013)
3. Gu, Z.J., Tayi, G.K.: Research note—investigating firm strategies on offering consumer-customizable products. Inf. Syst. Res. **26**(2), 456–468 (2015)
4. Dan, A., Georgiana, C., Leonard, L., et al.: Estimating potential GDP for the Romanian economy and assessing the sustainability of economic growth: a multivariate filter approach. Sustainability. **7**(3), 3338–3358 (2015)
5. Funk, J.L.: Standards, dominant designs and preferential acquisition of complementary assets through slight information advantages. Res. Policy. **32**(8), 1325–1341 (2004)
6. Kassen, M.: Adopting and managing open data: stakeholder perspectives, challenges and policy recommendations. Aslib J. Inf. Manag. **70**(5), 518–537 (2018)
7. Ushakova, E.V., Voronina, E.V., Fugalevich, E.V., et al.: Digitalization of the economy as a development trend in Russia. Econ. Manag. **27**(3), 175–182 (2021)
8. Jacobs, A.: The pathologies of big data - ACM queue. Commun. ACM. **52**(8), 36,38–36,44 (2009)
9. Lv, Y., Duan, Y., Kang, W., et al.: Traffic flow prediction with big data: a deep learning approach. IEEE Trans. Intell. Transp. Syst. **16**(2), 865–873 (2015)
10. Demirkan, H., Delen, D.: Leveraging the capabilities of service-oriented decision support systems: putting analytics and big data in cloud. Decis. Support. Syst. **55**(1), 412–421 (2013)
11. Zaharia, M., Xin, R.S., Wendell, P., et al.: Apache spark: a unified engine for big data processing. Commun. ACM. **59**(11), 56–65 (2016)
12. Brinkmann, B.H., Bower, M.R., Stengel, K.A., et al.: Large-scale electrophysiology: acquisition, compression, encryption, and storage of big data. J. Neurosci. Methods. **180**(1), 185–192 (2009)

Behavioral Modeling and Forecasting of Household Finance Based on Time Series Algorithms in the Context of Financial Technology

Fuai Jiao[1,2(✉)], Zaiton Osman[2], and Jiqiu Wu[1]

[1] Chongqing College of Architecture and Technology, Chongqing 400000, China
2471611353@qq.com
[2] Universiti Malaysia Sabah, Sepanggar 88830, Kota Kinabalu, Malaysia

Abstract. With the increasing role of households in the macroeconomic system, understanding and predicting household financial decision-making behavior has become an important topic in financial research and policy making. This paper constructs a systematic analytical framework for modeling and simulating household financial behavior based on time series algorithms. By empirically analyzing the dynamic characteristics of household income, expenditure, savings, liabilities and other financial variables, it reveals the time-series and nonlinear patterns of household financial decisions. In this paper, time series modeling methods such as ARIMA and LSTM are used to model and forecast household financial behaviors and simulate the household decision response process under a variety of macroeconomic scenarios. The experimental results show that the deep time series model has significant advantages in capturing the complex dynamics of household financial behavior. Based on the model output, this paper further explores feasible options to enhance household financial stability and optimize the path of policy intervention. The findings can provide data support and decision-making basis for household financial risk early warning, financial product design and precise policy formulation.

Keywords: Household Finance · Time Series Analysis · Behavioral Modeling · LSTM Model · Simulation Forecast · Financial Decision Support

1 Introduction

Against the background of the changing global economy and the increasingly complex structure of household assets, the behavior of household financial decision-making is increasingly becoming an important focus of financial research and macro-control [1]. As the most basic economic unit, households' decisions on income distribution, consumption expenditure, savings and investment, and risk management not only affect the economic security and well-being of individual households, but also play a key role in the stability of the financial market and the economic growth of the country as a whole.

S. C. P. Yam et al. (Eds.): ICFT 2025, CCIS 2868, pp. 319–330, 2026.
https://doi.org/10.1007/978-981-92-0126-6_26

In recent years, with the development of financial technology and the accumulation of household financial data, academics have gradually shifted from static analysis to dynamic modeling in an attempt to understand the evolutionary law of household financial behaviors through a time series perspective [2]. Household financial decisions are highly complex and dynamic, exhibiting characteristics such as cyclicality, nonlinearity and sensitivity to external shocks, and traditional static statistical methods are difficult to adequately portray the process of their changes [3]. In this context, the introduction of time series modeling methods, especially the nonlinear time series model represented by deep learning, provides a powerful tool for accurately portraying the time-varying characteristics of household financial behaviors, predicting their future trends, and simulating multi-context responses.

Domestic and international research on household financial behavior has achieved certain results, covering multiple dimensions such as consumption choice, asset allocation, risk preference, etc., but it is still insufficient in systematically modeling behavioral laws and conducting dynamic simulation analysis [4]. Current research mostly focuses on trend prediction of a single variable, and lacks overall modeling of multivariate interaction mechanisms and simulation tests of behavioral mechanisms [5]. Therefore, it is necessary to integrate time series algorithms and behavioral finance theory from the perspective of system modeling to conduct in-depth modeling and simulation analysis of household financial decision-making behavior.

The research goal of this paper is to construct a modeling framework of household financial decision-making behavior based on time series algorithm, to reveal its time series structure and behavioral logic, to simulate the response paths of households in different economic situations, so as to provide theoretical support and empirical evidence for financial risk management and policy making [6]. The structure of the paper is as follows: the first part introduces the characteristics and modeling needs of households' financial decision-making behavior; the second part elaborates the time-series modeling methodology and simulation analysis process; the third part analyzes the model results and puts forward the policy recommendations; and the last part sums up the paper and looks forward to the direction of future research.

2 Characteristics and Modeling Needs of Household Financial Decision Making Behavior

With the growth of residents' disposable income and the continuous enrichment of financial products, the financial decision making behavior of households, as an important unit of microeconomic activities, is showing unprecedented complexity and diversity [7]. From daily consumption to asset allocation, from risk avoidance to credit behavior, the financial choices made by households throughout their life cycle are constantly influenced by both the external macro environment and internal preference structure [8]. These decisions not only involve dynamic interactions among multiple variables, but also reflect the behavioral response patterns of individual households in specific economic contexts.

One of the key features of household financial behavior is its temporal dependence and path dependency. Financial decisions made at one time point often affect future choices, leading to time series characteristics such as trend, seasonality, and autocorrelation. For instance, changes in household income or employment status may significantly alter savings patterns or investment strategies in subsequent periods. In addition, external shocks such as inflation, interest rate fluctuations, or policy adjustments can induce significant behavioral shifts, which are often nonlinear and time-dependent. Therefore, modeling household financial behavior requires not only cross-sectional understanding of heterogeneity but also longitudinal analysis of evolving decision patterns.

Another important characteristic is the heterogeneity of risk preferences and financial literacy among households. These internal factors lead to differentiated responses to similar economic stimuli. For example, two households facing the same credit offer may exhibit vastly different borrowing behaviors depending on their risk aversion, income stability, or prior financial experience. Traditional static models struggle to capture such complex behavior, necessitating the use of dynamic, data-driven approaches capable of learning patterns over time and incorporating contextual variables.

Moreover, the digitalization of finance, driven by financial technology (FinTech), has introduced new variables and behavioral pathways into household finance. Online lending, mobile payments, robo-advisors, and personalized investment platforms have significantly transformed how households interact with financial services. These innovations generate large volumes of granular time-stamped data, making time series algorithms particularly well-suited for modeling such behavior. However, this also poses new challenges in terms of data quality, frequency, volatility, and the need for real-time forecasting capabilities.

In this context, time series modeling becomes a crucial tool for analyzing and forecasting household financial behavior. It allows researchers and practitioners to identify underlying trends, capture cyclical patterns, and forecast future behaviors based on historical data. Compared to purely statistical models, time series-based behavioral modeling better reflects the dynamic and evolving nature of household finance, especially when enhanced with domain knowledge and behavioral insights.

Furthermore, forecasting household financial decisions can support a range of applications: from helping financial institutions tailor products and manage risk exposure, to aiding policymakers in evaluating the impact of fiscal policies or economic shocks on household welfare. It also allows households themselves to benefit from intelligent financial planning tools powered by predictive algorithms.

Therefore, the selection and implementation of appropriate time series models is essential for accurately capturing the complexity of household financial decision-making. These models must be capable of handling non-stationarity, multivariate influences, and regime-switching behavior, while also maintaining interpretability and robustness in the face of uncertainty and structural change. Among these, the ARIMA (AutoRegressive Integrated Moving Average) model remains one of the most widely used and foundational approaches in time series analysis due to its strong theoretical grounding and practical applicability. ARIMA model equation:

$$y_t = \phi_1 y_{t-1} + \phi_2 y_{t-2} + \cdots + \phi_p y_{t-p} + \theta_1 \varepsilon_{t-1} + \theta_2 \varepsilon_{t-2} + \cdots + \theta_q \varepsilon_{t-q} + \varepsilon_t \quad (1)$$

The evolution of household financial behavior tends to be significantly time-series. Income levels, expenditure structures, willingness to save, and investment risk preferences at different stages are characterized by continuity and stages in the time dimension

[9]. Younger households tend to favor higher-risk and higher-return investment portfolios, while older households prefer sound financial management and asset preservation [10]. These behaviors are not isolated and static, but are dynamic processes that evolve under the influence of macroeconomic cycle fluctuations, policy adjustments, and financial market changes. Therefore, traditional static analysis methods have been difficult to meet the demand for modeling such complex behaviors, and the perspective of time series modeling must be introduced to capture the correlation and lag effects between variables over time.

On the other hand, there are also a large number of nonlinear relationships and uncertainties in household financial decisions. On the one hand, this nonlinearity stems from the influence of behavioral financial factors, such as limited rationality, overconfidence, and loss aversion; on the other hand, it comes from the uncertainty of external shocks, such as changes in interest rates, increases in inflation, or unexpected economic events. A single linear modeling approach is often difficult to cope with such multi-level and multi-factor intertwined behavioral mechanisms. It is necessary to introduce time series methods with strong nonlinear modeling capabilities, such as LSTM (Long Short-Term Memory Network) or Transformer structures in deep learning, which are able to better portray complex nonlinear mapping relationships among input features while maintaining the time dependence of the series, showed in Fig. 1:

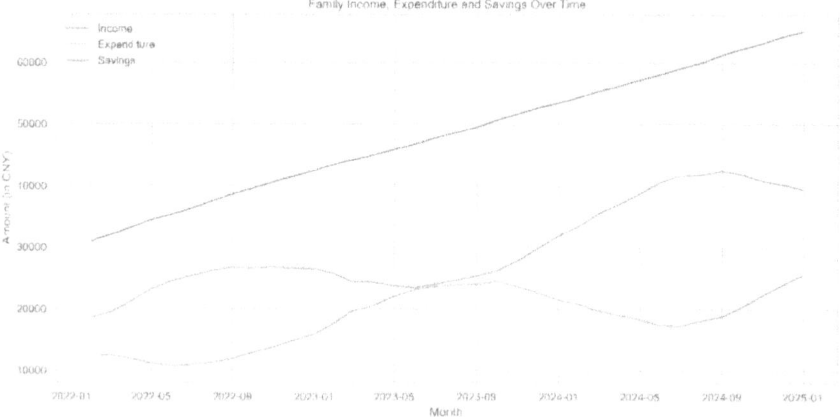

Fig. 1. Simulated family income, expenditure and savings over 36 months (time series).

Overall, current research on household financial decision-making behavior urgently needs to establish a systematic time series modeling mechanism that can not only deal with multivariate synergistically changing data structures, but also dynamically portray the response paths of households under different economic scenarios [11]. This has important theoretical and practical value for the prediction and early warning of household financial risks, the precise formulation of public policies, and the personalized design of financial products [12]. In this paper, we propose to construct a family financial behavior modeling framework based on time series algorithms to realize the in-depth portrayal and simulation analysis of family financial decision-making behavior.

3 A Time Series Modeling Approach to Household Financial Decision Making Behavior

In order to systematically construct a time series model of household financial decision making behavior, this paper firstly starts from data acquisition and preprocessing to ensure that the time series data of the financial variables used are complete, accurate and representative; in view of the complexity of household financial behaviors, we select and construct a variety of time series models, including traditional statistical models and advanced deep learning models, to achieve effective portrayal and prediction of dynamic changes in behaviors; through simulation and prediction analysis, we set up a framework for the modeling of household financial behaviors. Through simulation and predictive analysis, different economic scenarios are set up, and the model outputs are evaluated and interpreted in multiple dimensions, so as to reveal the response mechanisms and potential laws of household financial decisions in a changing environment.

3.1 Data Acquisition and Pre-processing

The time series modeling of household financial decision-making behavior firstly relies on high-quality financial data. The data used in this paper mainly come from the household financial survey data published by the National Bureau of Statistics, transaction records of commercial banks and Internet financial platforms, as well as some questionnaire surveys and field interviews. These data cover a wide range of household income, expenditure, savings, credit, investment and insurance, and can reflect the actual situation of household financial behavior in a more comprehensive way. LSTM cell state update:

$$C_t = f_t \odot C_{t-1} + i_t \odot \tilde{C}_t \tag{2}$$

Due to the diversity of data sources and the long span of collection time, there are generally missing values, outliers and noise in the raw data. To address these issues, this paper adopts the interpolation method and the filling method based on neighboring data to deal with missing values, while box plots and the standard deviation method are used to eliminate abnormal data to ensure the completeness and accuracy of the data. In addition, the noise is smoothed by methods such as sliding average and wavelet transform to improve the stability and analysis of the data.

In terms of time series characteristics, household financial data often show obvious seasonal fluctuations and cyclical trends. In order to eliminate the interference caused by the seasonal effect, this paper adopts seasonal adjustment methods, such as the X-12-ARIMA model, to de-seasonalize the data and ensure that the subsequent model accurately captures the long-term trend and cyclical changes. At the same time, considering the large differences in the magnitude of different indicators, all variables are normalized before modeling to eliminate the effect of magnitude and enhance the convergence speed and effect of model training.

324   F. Jiao et al.

Finally, in order to improve the generalization ability and prediction accuracy of the model, this paper divides the data into training set, validation set and test set, and adopts time window sliding to slice the samples, to ensure that the training process can fully learn the temporal dependence structure, while guaranteeing the rigor and reliability of the testing process. This series of data preprocessing steps lays a solid foundation for the construction and application of subsequent time series models, showed in Fig. 2:

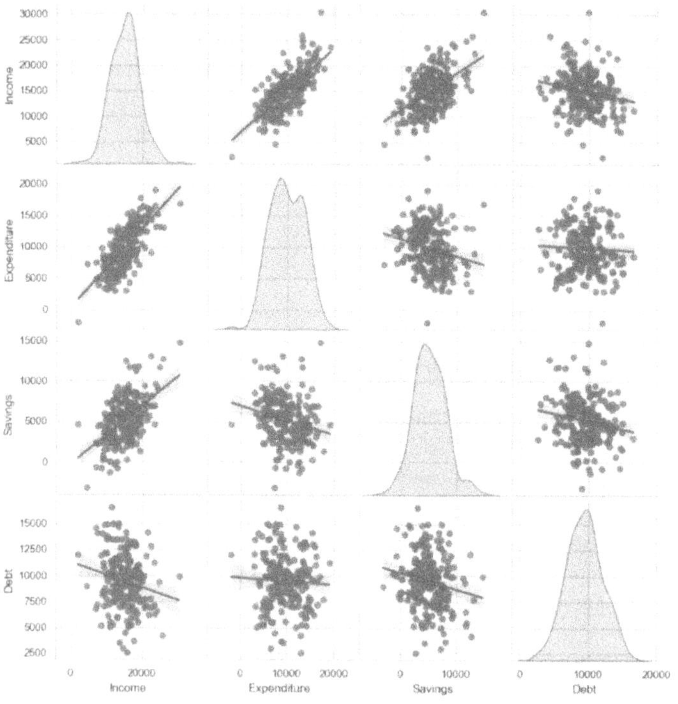

Fig. 2. Distribution and correlation of financial variables (Income, Expenditure, Savings, Debt).

3.2 Time Series Model Selection and Construction

Household financial decision-making behavior is characterized by complex dynamics, and traditional time series models such as autoregressive integral sliding average (ARIMA) are excellent in capturing linear trends and cyclical changes in the data due to their good interpretability and modeling efficiency. In this paper, we first smooth the time series data based on differential smoothness test, and determine the order parameters of ARIMA model using autocorrelation function (ACF) and partial autocorrelation function (PACF), and complete the model fitting by maximum likelihood estimation method. The model provides a theoretical basis for understanding the underlying dynamics of household financial behavior.

The ARIMA model is mainly applicable to linear time series, and it is more difficult to capture the potential nonlinear, long- and short-term dependencies in household financial behavior. For this reason, this paper introduces the long-short-term memory network (LSTM) as a representative of deep learning models. LSTM effectively solves the problem of gradient vanishing in traditional recurrent neural networks by introducing a gating mechanism, and is able to capture the long-term dependency features and complex nonlinear relationships in household financial data. The back propagation algorithm and Adam optimizer are used in the model training process, combined with an early stopping strategy to prevent overfitting, showed in Fig. 3:

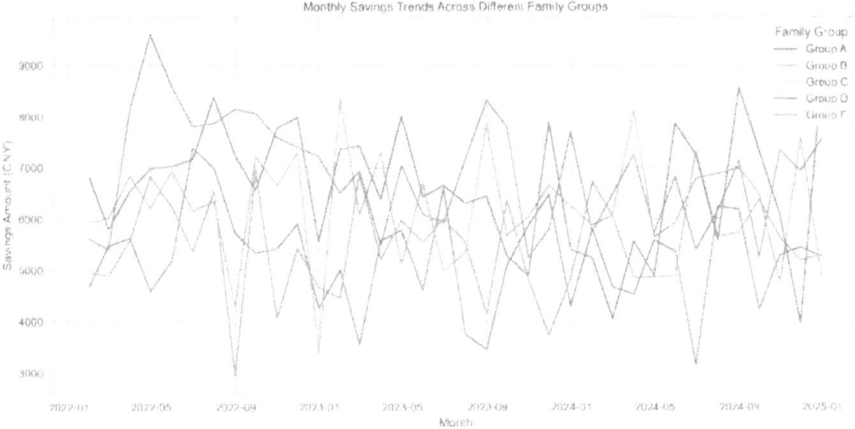

Fig. 3. Line plot comparing monthly savings trends for different family groups.

For the modeling needs of multivariate time series, this paper also attempts a model based on the Transformer structure. The model is able to dynamically adjust the weights of the information between different time points through the self-attention mechanism, capturing the interaction between variables in household financial behavior. The parallel computing advantage and powerful modeling capability of the Transformer model make its prediction performance better than that of traditional models in complex scenarios, and it is especially suitable for high-dimensional and multifactorial household financial data. LSTM output equation:

$$h_t = o_t \odot \tanh(C_t) \tag{3}$$

After the model construction is completed, this paper adopts the methods of cross-validation and rolling prediction to evaluate the performance of each model. The evaluation indexes include mean square error (MSE), mean absolute error (MAE) and coefficient of determination (R^2) to comprehensively measure the prediction accuracy and stability of the models. Through comparative analysis, the optimal model is identified to provide basic support for subsequent simulation analysis.

3.3 Simulation and Predictive Analytics

After completing the construction and training of the time series model, this paper further explores the dynamic response of household financial decision-making behavior under different economic scenarios through simulation and predictive analytics. Based on the trained model with historical data, short- and medium- to long-term forecasts of future income, expenditure, savings, and other key financial indicators are made to provide a quantitative basis for understanding the trend of household financial behavior. The prediction results not only reveal the evolution of the variables, but also reflect the model's ability to adapt to complex time-series data.

In this paper, we design a variety of macroeconomic scenarios to simulate typical economic shocks, including interest rate changes, inflation fluctuations, and changes in employment status, and use the model output to simulate the adjustment process of household financial decisions. By comparing the behavioral paths under different scenarios, we analyze the changes in risk preferences and the adjustment of capital allocation strategies of households in the face of external shocks, revealing the resilience and vulnerability characteristics of household financial behavior.

In order to enhance the interpretability of the simulation results, this paper combines sensitivity analysis to examine the degree of influence of changes in model parameters and input variables on the prediction results, and identifies the key factors that have the greatest impact on household financial decisions. This provides policymakers with a basis for targeted interventions and helps formulate more effective risk prevention and control and financial support policies. Self-attention mechanism (scaled dot-product attention):

$$\text{Attention}(Q, K, V) = \text{softmax}\left(\frac{QK^{\top}}{\sqrt{d_k}}\right)V \tag{4}$$

Based on the results of the simulation and prediction analysis, this paper puts forward suggestions to enhance household financial stability and optimize resource allocation, emphasizing that the ability of households to cope with economic fluctuations can be improved by means of strengthening financial education, optimizing the credit structure, and improving the social security system, so as to achieve sustainable growth in household wealth.

4 Analysis of Model Results and Policy Recommendations

Based on the constructed time series model and multi-scenario simulation analysis, this paper reveals several important features of household financial decision-making behavior. The model accurately captures the dynamic evolution of income, expenditure and savings, verifying the advantages of deep learning models in handling nonlinear and complex time series data. The heterogeneity in financial behavior of different household groups is significant, especially in the face of economic fluctuations and financial risks, low-income households and high-risk averse households show stronger vulnerability and capital liquidity pressure, showed in Fig. 4:

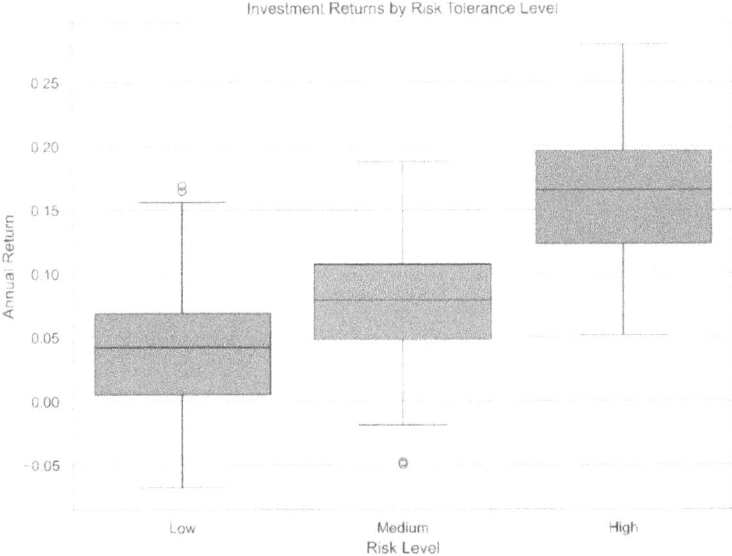

Fig. 4. Boxplot of investment returns by risk tolerance level.

Second, the simulation results show that changes in the macroeconomic environment have a direct and far-reaching impact on household financial decisions. Rising interest rates lead to higher borrowing costs and a general increase in household savings rates, but at the same time consumption demand is suppressed; when inflation expectations increase, some households tend to increase their investment risk exposure in search of higher returns, and risk preferences show dynamic adjustments. The model sensitivity analysis identifies key factors affecting households' financial behavior, including income volatility, debt burden, and financial literacy, which should be emphasized in policymaking. Mean Squared Error (MSE) loss function:

$$\text{MSE} = \frac{1}{n}\sum\nolimits_{i=1}^{n}\left(y_i - \hat{y}_i\right)^2 \tag{5}$$

Based on the above analysis, the following policy recommendations are put forward to promote household financial stability and healthy development: financial education and popularization should be strengthened to enhance households' knowledge of financial products and risks, and strengthen their resilience to cope with economic fluctuations; the social security system should be improved, especially to provide more targeted support for the low-income and risk-averse groups, so as to alleviate their financial pressure due to economic shocks; the credit structure should be optimized to optimize the credit structure and rationally guide household borrowing behavior to prevent over-indebtedness risks; suggest that regulators pay attention to the transmission effect of macroeconomic policies on the household level, and formulate more flexible monetary and fiscal policy tools to balance economic growth and household financial security, showed in Fig. 5:

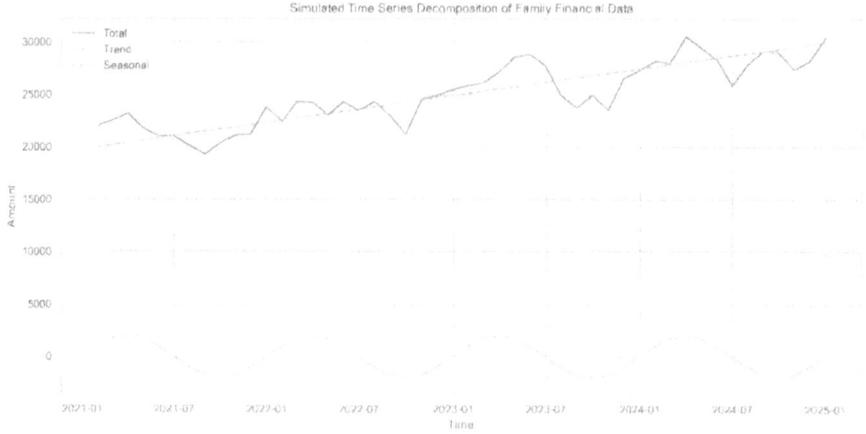

Fig. 5. Time series decomposition simulated (trend + seasonal + residual).

The modeling of household financial behavior based on time series algorithms not only provides a powerful tool for understanding complex behavioral dynamics, but also lays a scientific foundation for the precise formulation of financial support and risk management policies. In the future, individual psychological and behavioral economics factors should be further combined to promote the development of intelligent financial services and decision support systems, so as to achieve sustainable growth of household wealth and stable economic and social prosperity. Seasonal adjustment model (multiplicative decomposition):

$$Y_t = T_t \times S_t \times R_t \tag{6}$$

5   Conclusion

This paper proposes and constructs a behavioral modeling and simulation analysis framework based on time series algorithm for the complexity and dynamics of household financial decision-making behavior. By systematically analyzing the time-series data of multidimensional financial indicators such as household income, expenditure, savings, investment, etc., and combining the advantages of traditional statistical models and advanced deep learning models, it realizes the effective portrayal and accurate prediction of the evolution law of household financial behavior. The results show that traditional models such as ARIMA have better performance in capturing linear trends and cyclical changes, while deep learning models such as Long Short-Term Memory Network (LSTM) and Transformer model based on self-attention mechanism can better deal with nonlinear relationships and long time-dependent features, which improves the model's ability to fit the complex behavioral patterns and its prediction accuracy.

In addition, this paper deeply analyzes the dynamic response mechanism of household financial behavior under different economic environments by designing multiple macroeconomic scenario simulations. The simulation results show that households show significant adjustments in risk appetite, asset allocation and consumption and saving behaviors when facing external shocks such as interest rate changes, inflation fluctuations and employment uncertainty, a finding that provides a theoretical basis for household financial risk management and a scientific reference for policy makers to formulate more targeted support measures. The sensitivity analysis further clarifies the key factors affecting household financial decisions, providing practical guidance for financial product design and personalized services.

In summary, behavioral modeling of household financial decision-making based on time series algorithms not only deepens the understanding of dynamic features of behavioral finance, but also promotes the integration of behavioral finance theory with modern data science and technology. The research results in this paper provide data-driven decision support for improving household wealth management, optimizing the allocation of financial resources, and enhancing the stability of the financial system. Future research should further expand the scope of application of the model, incorporate richer family heterogeneity characteristics, psychological and behavioral factors and policy environment variables, promote the development of intelligent and precise family financial decision-making assistance systems, and help achieve more robust and sustainable family wealth growth and economic development.

Acknowledgements. The authors acknowledge the 2023 Chongqing College of Architecture and Technology Campus-level Research Project: Research on the Income-increasing Effect of Digital Inclusive Finance on Rural Low-income Groups: A Case Study of Chongqing Municipality (Project Number: 2023017).

References

1. Frederiks, E.R., Stenner, K., Hobman, E.V.: Household energy use: applying behavioural economics to understand consumer decision-making and behaviour. Renew. Sust. Energ. Rev. **41**(41), 1385–1394 (2015)
2. Thorne-Lyman, A.L., Valpiani, N., Sun, K., et al.: Household dietary diversity and food expenditures are closely linked in rural Bangladesh, increasing the risk of malnutrition due to the financial crisis. J. Nutr. **140**(1), 182S (2010)
3. Chung, S.S., Poon, C.S.: A comparison of waste reduction practices and the new environmental paradigm in four southern Chinese areas. Environ. Manag. **26**(2), 195–206 (2000)
4. Welfe, W., Florczak, W.: Slowdown of the polish economy: model-based simulations. Gastroenterology. **122**(1), 228–230 (2010)
5. Campbell, D.J.T., Tonelli, M., Hemmelgarn, B., et al.: Assessing outcomes of enhanced chronic disease care through patient education and a value-based formulary study (ACCESS)—study protocol for a 2×2 factorial randomized trial. Implement. Sci. **11**(1), 131 (2015)
6. Park, J.Y.R., Ha, J.R.: Impact of emotional state and suicidal intentions on suicide attempts among Korean adolescents with household financial difficulties following the outbreak of COVID-19: a cross-sectional study. Medicine. **102**(32), 8 (2023)

7. Yaramasu, V., Rivera, M., Wu, B., et al.: Model predictive current control of two-level four-leg inverters—part I: concept, algorithm, and simulation analysis. IEEE Trans. Power Electron. **28**(7), 3459–3468 (2013)
8. Zeng, Y., Mu, S.J., Lou, S.J., et al.: Hydraulic modeling and axial dispersion analysis of UASB reactor. Biochem. Eng. J. **25**(2), 113–123 (2005)
9. Suich, H.: The livelihood impacts of the Namibian community based natural resource management programme: a meta-synthesis. Environ. Conserv. **37**(1), 45–53 (2010)
10. Kaitlyn, W., Bayard, R., Clara, C., et al.: Micro- and meso-level influences on obesity in the former Soviet Union: a multi-level analysis. Eur. J. Pub. Health. **13**(2), 2 (2013)
11. Tackie, D.N.O., Jones, K.N., Quarcoo, F.A., et al.: Effects of selected characteristics on general and financial record keeping practices of small producers in South Central Alabama. J. Agric. Sci. **14**(7), 21 (2022)
12. Li, Z., Liu, L., Shi, J., et al.: Health insurance, risk attitudes, and household financial behavior. Health Econ. **30**(5), 1239–1246 (2021)

A Study on the Impact of Fintech
on the Development of the Digital Economy
in Northeast Asia

Huan Zhang and Tianxiang Wang[✉]

Business School, University of Jinan, Jinan 250002, China
wangtx@stu.ujn.edu.cn

Abstract. Utilizing panel data from five Northeast Asian countries spanning 2012 to 2023, this study constructs a comprehensive evaluation index system for FinTech and the digital economy. Employing nonlinear regression, mediation effect models, and spatial econometric methods, it empirically examines the impact mechanism of FinTech on regional digital economic development. The results reveal a significant inverted U-shaped nonlinear impact of FinTech on the development of the digital economy in Northeast Asia, characterized by initial promotion followed by subsequent inhibition. FinTech drives digital economic development through the dual pathways of financial inclusion and technological innovation, with these mediating channels also exhibiting inverted U-shaped characteristics. Furthermore, FinTech demonstrates significant spatial spillover effects, initially manifesting as a "siphoning effect" that inhibits the development of neighboring regions, later transforming into a "radiation effect" that fosters regional synergistic growth. The findings underscore the need for optimized FinTech development pacing, enhanced regional policy coordination, and robust cross-border regulatory frameworks

Keywords: FinTech · Digital Economy · Northeast Asia · Inverted U-Shape · Mediation Effect · Spatial Spillover

1 Introduction

The digital economy, as a new paradigm integrating innovation and growth, is reshaping global industrial structures and competitive dynamics. Northeast Asia—a key hub of technology and manufacturing that includes China, Japan, and South Korea—wields significant influence over regional and global economic trends. Within this context, FinTech, as a digital-driven form of financial innovation, enhances service efficiency, expands coverage, and empowers the real economy. It not only transforms traditional finance but also generates new industries and growth drivers, providing core impetus for the digital economy's advancement.

Digital economic foundations differ considerably across Northeast Asia. China leads in digital payments and credit, leveraging its vast market and dynamic innovation ecosystem. Japan and South Korea excel in institutional FinTech development, R&D, and integration with traditional finance. Russia and Mongolia follow distinct paths centered

S. C. P. Yam et al. (Eds.): ICFT 2025, CCIS 2868, pp. 331–341, 2026.
https://doi.org/10.1007/978-981-92-0126-6_27

on energy digitalization, cross-border payments, and geopolitical advantages. Although FinTech relies on synergies between finance and technology and plays a vital role in economic transformation, its influence on the regional digital economy is not purely linear. The mechanisms, pathways, and effects require deeper empirical investigation.

This study uses panel data from five Northeast Asian economies (2012–2023) to construct a comprehensive evaluation index system. Through econometric modeling, we examine the nonlinear influence, mediating mechanisms, and spatial spillover effects of FinTech on digital economic development. Our aim is to provide new empirical evidence and policy insights to support high-quality growth of the digital economy in the region.

2 Literature Review

The relationship between FinTech and the digital economy has attracted growing scholarly attention. Theoretically, FinTech is recognized not only for enabling new business models via tech firms and startups but also for modernizing traditional financial institutions, thereby stimulating market vitality and digital economic growth [1]. It supports the integration of the digital and real economies through key mechanisms such as monetary facilitation, credit allocation, risk management, and financial inclusion [2]. Empirically, studies within China have shown that FinTech promotes digital economic development through technological innovation and moderating fiscal decentralization [3]. Internationally, research involving Belt and Road countries reveals an inverted U-shaped influence of FinTech—initially promoting and later inhibiting digital economic development [4]. At the micro level, FinTech is widely acknowledged to enhance inclusive growth [5] and ease financing constraints [6].

Nonetheless, there remains a scarcity of focused research on FinTech's impact on the digital economy in Northeast Asia, particularly regarding its transmission mechanisms and spatial effects. This study seeks to narrow this gap by systematically examining the pathways through which FinTech influences digital economic development in the region, aiming to offer empirical support and policy insights for its sustainable advancement.

3 Mechanism Analysis and Research Hypotheses

FinTech enhances the efficiency of transactions, capital allocation, and payments, thereby facilitating digital economic activities. By leveraging big data for risk management and offering inclusive financial services, it reaches underserved "long-tail" customers [7], unlocking substantial latent demand. Furthermore, FinTech supports the development and application of core technologies, accelerates industrial integration, and promotes business model innovation, thus driving industrial digitalization. However, its positive effects may be counterbalanced by excessive development: strong network effects and economies of scale can lead to a "winner-takes-all" market structure, which may stifle innovation and reduce competition. Moreover, overly rapid FinTech expansion can attract speculative capital, heighten systemic risks, and challenge regulatory frameworks, ultimately impeding the healthy growth of the digital economy [8]. Therefore, we propose:

H1: FinTech has an inverted U-shaped impact on the development of the digital economy in Northeast Asia, stimulating growth initially but inhibiting it after a certain threshold.

FinTech plays a crucial role in advancing financial inclusion by improving access to digital payments and consumer credit, which in turn stimulates demand in sectors such as e-commerce and online entertainment. It also provides essential funding for small and medium-sized digital enterprises, alleviating financing constraints and supporting innovation [9]. However, without proper regulation, it may also exacerbate the "digital divide" and lead to over-indebtedness, potentially undermining financial stability.

Simultaneously, FinTech serves as both a driver and outcome of technological innovation. Advancements in fields such as blockchain, AI, and big data not only enhance operational efficiency and intelligence across industries but also foster investment in digital infrastructure [10]. Nonetheless, excessive R&D investment may yield diminishing returns through redundant innovations, while large platforms might use patent barriers to suppress industry-wide technological diffusion. Hence, this study proposes:

H2a: Financial inclusion serves as a mediating channel for FinTech's influence on the digital economy in Northeast Asia, following an inverted U-shaped pattern.

H2b: Technological innovation mediates the relationship between FinTech and the digital economy in a nonlinear manner, characterized by initial promotion and subsequent inhibition.

The cross-border nature of FinTech leads to significant spatial spillover effects. In its early stages, regions with policy, market, or technological advantages can emerge as FinTech hubs, attracting talent, capital, and enterprises from neighboring areas and creating a "siphoning effect" that inhibits their digital economic growth [11]. As these hubs mature, knowledge diffuses through talent mobility, collaboration, and technology transfer, enabling positive spillovers. Eventually, this facilitates regional cooperation in standards, regulation, and data flows, contributing to collective digital economic expansion [12]. Therefore, we propose:

H3: FinTech generates spatial spillover effects on the digital economy in Northeast Asia, transitioning from an initial "siphoning effect" to a subsequent "radiation effect".

4   Variable Selection and Empirical Model Construction

4.1   Variable Definitions

Dependent Variable. The dependent variable is the level of digital economy development (deco) across countries. Given the absence of a consensus on its measurement, this study adopts a comprehensive evaluation index system [13] to avoid the biases of single-indicator approaches and the data limitations of input-output methods. The system covers three dimensions: digital infrastructure, industrial application, and international competitiveness (see Table 1). Raw data were standardized to remove dimension differences, and indicator weights were determined using the entropy weight method.

Core Explanatory Variable. The core explanatory variable is the level of FinTech development (fintech). Existing frameworks largely target developed economies or specific sectors, lacking a systematic measure for Northeast Asia. Thus, this study constructs

Table 1. Evaluation indicators and Data Sources for the Explained and Core Explanatory Variables

Primary indicator	Measurement Indicators	Data Source
Level of Digital Economy Development	Fixed-line telephone coverage rate	World Bank
	Mobile phone coverage rate	World Bank
	Secure internet server coverage rate	World Bank
	Fixed broadband usage rate	World Bank
	Mobile broadband usage rate	ITU
	Internet user penetration rate	World Bank
	ICT goods exports as % of total exports	UNCTAD
	ICT services exports as % of total exports	World Bank
	High-tech product exports as % of total exports	World Bank
Level of FinTech Development	Number of FinTech enterprises	Crunchbase
	Volume of FinTech credit inflows	BIS
	E-Government Development Index	UN E-Government Survey

a composite index from three dimensions: number of FinTech enterprises, FinTech credit inflow, and the E-Government Development Index, with weights assigned via the entropy method [14]. See Table 1 for details.

Mediating Variables. In line with established practice [4], this study selects financial inclusion (inf) and technological innovation (ti) as the mediating variables. Here, financial inclusion is measured by the scale of digital payment transactions, and technological innovation is gauged by the number of patents applied for in FinTech-related fields.

Control Variables. To mitigate potential omitted variable bias due to socioeconomic heterogeneity across Northeast Asian countries, this study controls for the following variables: economic development level (pgdp, per capita GDP), population size (pop, total population), R&D investment (rd, ratio of R&D expenditure to GDP), and price level (cpi, year-on-year CPI growth rate).

4.2 Model Construction

Benchmark Regression Model. To examine the nonlinear impact of FinTech on the development of the digital economy in Northeast Asia, a panel regression model incorporating a quadratic term of FinTech is employed for analysis. The specific model is specified as follows:

$$deco_{it} = a_0 + a_1 fintech_{it} + a_2 fintech_{it}^2 + a_c X + \mu_i + \lambda_t + \varepsilon_{it} \tag{1}$$

where i denotes the Northeast Asian country, t denotes the year, $deco_{it}$ represents the level of digital economy development in Northeast Asia, $fintech_{it}$ and $fintech_{it}^2$ denote the level of FinTech development and its quadratic term. X is a vector of control variables, μ_i and λ_t represent country-fixed effects and year-fixed effects, and ε_{it} is the idiosyncratic error term.

Mediation Effect Model. Based on the preceding analysis, FinTech may influence the development of the digital economy in Northeast Asia through the mediating channels of financial inclusion and technological innovation. Drawing on relevant research [15], this study examines nonlinear mediation effects using the following model specifications:

$$med_{it} = a_0 + a_1 fintech_{it} + a_2 fintech_{it}^2 + a_c X + \mu_i + \lambda_t + \varepsilon_{it} \tag{2}$$

$$deco_{it} = \beta_0 + \beta_1 fintech_{it} + \beta_2 fintech_{it}^2 + \beta_3 med_{it} + a_c X + \mu_i + \lambda_t + \varepsilon_{it} \tag{3}$$

where med_{it} is the mediating variable, representing financial inclusion and technological innovation. The meanings of all other symbols are consistent with those defined in Model (1). Eqs. (1) to (3) examine the mediation effect using the stepwise regression method: each single mediating variable is tested sequentially, after which both mediating variables are incorporated into the same model for further testing.

Spatial Effects Model To examine whether FinTech exerts spatial spillover effects on the development of the digital economy in Northeast Asia, spatial econometric models are employed for analysis. The specific model is specified as follows:

$$\begin{aligned} deco_{it} = {} & a_0 + \rho \sum_{j=1}^{n} w_{ij} deco_{it} + \rho_1 \sum_{j=1}^{n} w_{ij} fintech_{it} + \rho_2 \sum_{j=1}^{n} w_{ij} fintech_{it}^2 \\ & + \rho_c \sum_{j=1}^{n} w_{ij} X + a_1 fintech_{it} + a_2 fintech_{it}^2 + a_c X + \mu_i + \lambda_t + v_{it} \end{aligned} \tag{4}$$

$$v_{it} = \gamma \sum_{j=1}^{n} w_{ij} v_{it} + \varepsilon_{it} \tag{5}$$

where w_{ij} denotes the spatial weight matrix, constructed as a nested matrix that incorporates both geographical and economic factors. The terms $w_{ij} deco_{it}$, $w_{ij} fintech_{it}$, $w_{ij} fintech_{it}^2$, and $w_{ij} X$ represent the spatial lag terms of the digital economy, FinTech, the quadratic term of FinTech, and the control variables, and v_{it} denotes the spatial error term. When ρ, ρ_1, ρ_2, ρ_c=0, the model reduces to the Spatial Error Model (SEM); when γ, ρ_1, ρ_2, ρ_c=0, it becomes the Spatial Autoregressive Model (SAR); and when $\gamma = 0$, the specification corresponds to the Spatial Durbin Model (SDM).

4.3 Data Sources and Processing

This study utilizes panel data from five Northeast Asian countries spanning the period 2012–2023. The data were sourced from the World Bank, the International Telecommunication Union (ITU), the United Nations Conference on Trade and Development (UNCTAD), Crunchbase, the Bank for International Settlements (BIS), the UN E-Government

Survey, and the World Intellectual Property Organization (WIPO). Both the FinTech and digital economy indices were constructed using the entropy weight method. To mitigate heteroscedasticity and skewness in the distribution, variables including technological innovation, financial inclusion, economic development level, and population size were subjected to a logarithmic transformation. A small number of missing data points were addressed using linear interpolation and mean imputation.

5 Analysis of Empirical Results

5.1 Benchmark Regression Analysis

Benchmark regression results are summarized in Table 2. As shown across columns (1) to (6), the coefficient for the linear term of fintech remains significantly positive and the coefficient for its quadratic term remains significantly negative as control variables are added, confirming a robust inverted U-shaped relationship. A U-test based on column (5) indicates that the inflection point lies within the interval [0.014, 0.984], supporting Hypothesis H1. Specifically, when the level of FinTech is below 0.443, it effectively promotes the development of the digital economy through mechanisms such as enhancing payment efficiency and facilitating technological spillovers. However, when the FinTech level exceeds this threshold, issues including platform monopolization, crowding-out effects on the real economy, and regulatory lags may cause its net effect on the digital economy to turn from positive to negative.

5.2 Endogeneity Tests

Potential endogeneity issues may affect the estimated impact of FinTech on the digital economy in Northeast Asia, including omitted variable bias and reverse causality. To address these concerns, this study employs two approaches: an instrumental variable (IV) regression using the annual cross-country mean of FinTech development (excluding the home country) to mitigate omitted variable bias, and its lagged variable to reduce reverse causality. Results in Columns (1) and (2) of Table 3 show that the signs and significance of the core coefficients remain consistent with the benchmark estimates, supporting the robustness of our findings.

5.3 Robustness Tests

To mitigate potential measurement errors arising from variable construction methods, this study further applied the CRITIC method to recalculate both the dependent variable and the core explanatory variable, and re-ran the regression. The results are reported in Columns (3) and (4) of Table 3. Additionally, all continuous variables were winsorized at the 5% level before re-estimation, with results presented in Column (5) of Table 3. The test results show that the signs and significance levels of the coefficients for both the linear and quadratic terms of FinTech remain largely unchanged, providing further support for the robustness of the main findings.

Table 2. Benchmark Regression Results

	(1)	(2)	(3)	(4)	(5)
VARIABLES	deco	deco	deco	deco	deco
fintech	0.3003**	0.3586***	0.3271***	0.3921***	0.3684***
	(2.4286)	(3.2619)	(3.5948)	(4.4803)	(4.6859)
fintech^2	−0.3536***	−0.3345***	−0.3777***	−0.4050***	−0.4159***
	(−3.0535)	(−3.7375)	(−5.2792)	(−6.0278)	(−6.4489)
pgdp		0.0579**	0.0242	0.0249	0.0212
		(2.5908)	(1.4615)	(1.4640)	(1.4354)
pop			0.5046***	0.5297***	0.4023***
			(7.8000)	(8.5187)	(5.0339)
rd				0.0708*	0.0815**
				(1.8581)	(2.0636)
cpi					−0.0006**
					(−2.2493)
Constant	0.3366***	1.4307***	20.6842***	22.1718***	14.2723***
	(17.4736)	(3.1292)	(8.6586)	(8.7259)	(5.0346)
Id/Year	Yes	Yes	Yes	Yes	Yes
N	60	60	60	60	60
R^2	0.9659	0.9715	0.9865	0.9881	0.9912

*** $p < 0.01$, ** $p < 0.05$, * $p < 0.1$. The values in parentheses represent the standard errors.

5.4 Mediation Effect Analysis

To examine the transmission mechanisms of FinTech's influence on the digital economy, a mediation analysis was conducted. Following the stepwise method, we first estimated the total effect (Table 4, col. 1), then regressed FinTech on each mediator—financial inclusion (col. 2) and technological innovation (col. 4)—and finally incorporated both mediators into the main model (cols. 3, 5, 6).

The results show that FinTech exerts a significant mediating effect on the development of the digital economy through both financial inclusion and technological innovation pathways, with both channels exhibiting an inverted U-shaped pattern. Thus, Hypotheses H2a and H2b are supported. Specifically, in the early stages of development, FinTech effectively promotes financial inclusion and technological innovation by enhancing payment efficiency, expanding service coverage, and stimulating R&D investment. However, once the development level exceeds a critical threshold, issues such as platform monopolization, excessive resource concentration, and innovation bubbles emerge, which subsequently inhibit the healthy functioning of these two mediating mechanisms. The significantly positive coefficients of the mediators in the full model underscore their vital role in advancing the regional digital economy.

Table 3. Endogeneity Handling and Robustness Tests

	(1)	(2)	(3)	(4)	(5)
Variables	deco	deco	rdeco	deco	deco
l.fintech		0.3566***			
		(4.2374)			
l.fintech^2		−0.4398***			
		(−6.0490)			
fintech	0.4322***		0.2577***		0.3788***
	(5.7319)		(4.2529)		(4.5265)
fintech^2	−0.4739***		−0.2189***		−0.4204***
	(−7.2660)		(−4.2504)		(−5.8624)
rfintech				0.2427***	
				(2.7322)	
rfintech^2				−0.4704***	
				(−4.4653)	
Control	Yes	Yes	Yes	Yes	Yes
Id/Year	Yes	Yes	Yes	Yes	Yes
N	60	55	60	60	60
R^2	0.9643	0.9925	0.9944	0.9898	0.9910

*** $p < 0.01$, ** $p < 0.05$, * $p < 0.1$. The values in parentheses represent the standard errors.

5.5 Spatial Spillover Effects Analysis

Global Moran's I test confirm significant spatial autocorrelation in the digital economy across Northeast Asia. To analyze spatial spillover effects, we estimated spatial econometric models. LM and robust LM tests supported the use of a Spatial Durbin Model (SDM), a choice further validated by Wald tests rejecting simplifications to SAR or SEM. Estimates from all three models are presented in Table 5 for comparison.

The regression results across all three models show that the linear term of FinTech is significantly positive and the quadratic term is significantly negative, with coefficients of similar magnitude, reaffirming a robust inverted U-shaped impact of FinTech on digital economic development. In the SDM, the spatial lag coefficient ρ of the dependent variable is significantly negative, indicating negative spatial spillovers in the development of the digital economy in Northeast Asia. The coefficient of the spatially lagged term for the FinTech variable is significantly negative, while that of the quadratic term is significantly positive, suggesting that a country's FinTech development exerts a U-shaped impact on the digital economy of neighboring countries—inhibiting it initially and promoting it later. Thus, Hypothesis H3 is supported. Specifically, in the early stages, the agglomeration of FinTech in one country attracts talent, enterprises, and capital from surrounding countries, creating a "siphoning effect" that hinders the development of neighbors. As

Table 4. Mediation Effect Analysis

	(1)	(2)	(3)	(4)	(5)	(6)
VARIABLES	deco	inf	deco	ti	deco	deco
fintech	0.368***	8.286***	0.130	9.927***	0.401***	0.167*
	(4.685)	(7.134)	(1.508)	(3.758)	(5.036)	(1.831)
fintech^2	−0.415***	−7.907***	−0.188**	−4.985*	−0.441***	−0.219***
	(−6.448)	(−8.094)	(−2.475)	(−1.966)	(−6.711)	(−2.728)
inf			0.028***			0.027***
			(3.624)			(3.672)
ti					0.013**	0.011**
					(2.051)	(2.045)
Control	Yes	Yes	Yes	Yes	Yes	Yes
Id/Year	Yes	Yes	Yes	Yes	Yes	Yes
N	60	60	60	60	60	60
R^2	0.991	0.997	0.993	0.920	0.991	0.994

*** $p < 0.01$, ** $p < 0.05$, * $p < 0.1$. The values in parentheses represent the standard errors.

the hub matures, knowledge spillovers, technology diffusion, and model demonstrations gradually strengthen, forming a "radiation effect" that ultimately drives regional digital economic growth.

6 Conclusions and Policy Implications

6.1 Conclusions

Based on panel data from five Northeast Asian economies (2012–2023), this study develops a comprehensive evaluation system and applies nonlinear regression, mediation analysis, and spatial econometric modeling to examine the impact of FinTech on the digital economy. The main findings are:

- First, FinTech exhibits an inverted U-shaped relationship with digital economic development—initially promoting, then inhibiting growth.
- Second, financial inclusion and technological innovation serve as nonlinear mediating channels, also following an inverted U-shaped pattern.
- Third, FinTech demonstrates significant spatial spillover effects, transitioning over time from a "siphoning effect" to a "radiation effect" on neighboring regions.

6.2 Policy Implications

Based on the findings, this study proposes the following policy recommendations for Northeast Asia:

Table 5. Spatial Spillover Effects Analysis

	(1)	(2)	(3)
VARIABLES	sar	sem	sdm
fintech	0.3684***	0.3303**	0.4420***
	(5.5586)	(2.5486)	(3.1617)
$fintech^2$	−0.3925***	−0.4421***	−0.3390**
	(−6.9698)	(−3.9556)	(−2.5662)
w*fintech			−0.9211**
			(−1.9909)
$w*fintech^2$			1.5155***
			(3.7981)
ρ/λ	−0.3074**	−0.4073***	−0.4243***
	(−2.1702)	(−2.8499)	(−2.8664)
Control	Yes	Yes	Yes
Id/Year	Yes	Yes	Yes
N	60	60	60
R^2	0.3937	0.7291	0.3480

*** $p < 0.01$, ** $p < 0.05$, * $p < 0.1$. The values in parentheses represent the standard errors.

- Promote moderate FinTech development to avoid premature inhibition and systemic risk.
- Enhance regional policy coordination to leverage positive spillovers and mitigate negative spatial effects.
- Strengthen support for SMEs and innovation through inclusive finance and technology investment.
- Establish cross-border regulatory and data governance frameworks to facilitate secure digital integration.

Acknowledgments. This paper is supported by a General Project of the National Social Science Fund of China (20BJL064).

Disclosure of Interests. The authors declare that there are no conflicts of interest in this work.

References

1. Wang, Z., Guo, J., Zhu, W., Han, C.: Review and prospects of research on financial technology innovation promoting the development of digital economy. Sci. Manag. Res. **39**(6), 132–138 (2021)
2. Chen, X., Wang, Y.: Research on the mechanism and path of TechFin empowering high-quality development of the digital economy. Contemp. Econ. Res. **2**, 109–122 (2025)

3. Chen, X., Teng, L., Chen, W.: How does FinTech affect the development of the digital economy? Evidence from China. North Am. J. Econ. Financ. **61**, 101697 (2022)
4. Du, L., Yang, R.: A research on the impact of Fintech on the digital silk road based on the symbiosis perspective. Contemp. Financ. Econ., 1–16 (2025)
5. Asgari, B., Izawa, H.: Does FinTech penetration drive financial development? Evidence from panel analysis of emerging and developing economies. Borsa Istanbul Rev. **23**(5), 1078–1097 (2023)
6. Wang, Y., Han, R., Ma, X., Li, S.: The impact of Sci-tech finance on corporate financial misallocation—a QuasiNatural experiment based on the "Science-Finance Integration Pilot" policy. De Economist. **7**, 97–107 (2025)
7. Zhou, Q., Han, H.: Research on the development, risk and regulatory of financial technology in the digital economy era. Sci. Manag. Res. **38**(5), 148–153 (2020)
8. He, H., Li, F.: New monopoly in digital economy: source analysis, typical forms and regulation strategies—with a comment on the prevention of FinTech risk. Financ. Theory Pract. **1**, 25–34 (2023)
9. Zhang, Y., Jiang, Y., Wang, H., Yu, L.: Digital finance and corporate innovation: micro-evidence from the digitalization of technology industries and traditional industries. China Soft Sci. **8**, 211–224 (2024)
10. Yang, F., Wang, C.: The mechanism of financial development promoting technological innovation in strategic emerging industries. Tech. Anal. Strat. Manag. **35**(7), 875–889 (2023)
11. Zhou, Z., Chen, H.: Analysis of the spillover effect of financial technology on regions' high-quality economic development. J. Fujian Agricult. For. Univ. (Philos. Soc. Sci.). **25**(6), 49–57 (2022)
12. Ni, X., Zhou, Z., Jiang, M., Zhao, H.: Research on the spatial spillover effect of science and technology finance on technological innovation. Syst. Eng. Theory Pract. **45**(6), 1729–1744 (2025)
13. Liu, Y., Zhang, Y., Cai, X.: Does the development of the digital economy lead to technological gaps or technological catch-up? Empirical evidence from the belt and road countries. Econ. Res. J. **59**(11), 192–208 (2024)
14. Xiao, X., Ding, Y., Wang, S.: International comparative study on fin tech development index. Financ. Theory Pract. **10**, 12–21 (2021)
15. Lin, W., Feng, B.: Curvilinear effect and statistical test method in the management research. Nankai Bus. Rev. **25**(1), 155–166 (2022)

From Macro to Markets: Big-Data Forecasting Pipelines for Financial Applications

Jin Li[✉]

China Electrical Equipment International Company Limited, Shanghai, China
627837538@qq.com

Abstract. Here we look to create a holistic big-data forecasting pipeline in the financial domain, which connects the macroeconomic indicators with market level decision systems. Relying on deep learning models and data preprocessing techniques, we present a scalable model framework to support variety of diverse datasets including but not limited to macroeconomic indicators, financial time series and sentiment data for forecasting financial market movements. The pipeline consists of five main modules, data collection, feature cleaning, cavity feature extraction model training and auto-evaluation. Empirical results show that the proposed approach can lead to remarkable improvements on the accuracy, robustness and timeliness of prediction than the traditional econometric method. This study does not only contribute to the methodological investigation of data-driven financial forecasting, but also offers technical wisdoms for developing intelligent financial analytics platforms in the new era of digital finance.

Keywords: Big data · financial forecasting · deep learning · predictive pipeline · macro-to-market modeling

1 Introduction

With the rapid development of information technology and profound changes in industrial structure, the development and evolution of industrial economy are characterized by increasing complexity and diversity [1]. Against this background, accurate forecasting of industrial economic trends is of great significance to policymakers, entrepreneurs and investors. Although traditional economic forecasting methods can provide reference to a certain extent, they are becoming more and more difficult to cope with the challenges of rapid changes and the big data era [2].

Deep learning, as an important branch in the field of artificial intelligence, has demonstrated a strong capability in processing complex data and pattern recognition. Its ability to learn based on big data and its adaptive nature make it a potential tool for solving the problem of forecasting complex economic systems [3]. The aim of this study is to explore the potential of deep learning technology in industrial economic trend forecasting and to establish corresponding forecasting models to improve the forecasting accuracy and practicality [4].

S. C. P. Yam et al. (Eds.): ICFT 2025, CCIS 2868, pp. 342–351, 2026.
https://doi.org/10.1007/978-981-92-0126-6_28

This paper firstly introduces the basic principles and advantages of deep learning in economic forecasting, and then discusses in detail the specific steps and methods of establishing the industrial economic trend forecasting model based on deep learning [5]. The effectiveness and reliability of the proposed model are evaluated by combining practical cases and numerical experiments. Finally, the development direction and challenges of deep learning technology in future industrial economic forecasting are envisioned to provide references and lessons for related research and applications [6].

2 Deep Learning in Economic Forecasting

Deep learning, as a powerful machine learning technique, has demonstrated its great potential in the field of economic forecasting in recent years [7]. Traditional economic forecasting methods such as ARIMA models, although widely used, are significantly limited in their predictive ability when faced with complex economic variable relationships and nonlinear features [8]. In contrast, deep learning is able to effectively capture deep features and complex nonlinear relationships in data through a multi-layered neural network structure, thereby improving the accuracy and reliability of predictions. This capability is particularly important for coping with rapidly changing market conditions in a globalized economy, making it one of the key tools for meeting the challenges of a complex economic environment.

One of the strengths of deep learning is its ability to process large-scale, high-dimensional datasets and automatically learn complex feature representations from them [9]. In the field of economics, economic systems are often influenced by multiple factors, and the relationships between these factors are often nonlinear and dynamically changing. Through the hierarchical learning process of deep neural networks, deep learning is able to better understand and model these complex data patterns, thus providing more accurate and comprehensive economic prediction results [10]. Compared with traditional methods, deep learning is not only better able to adapt to changes in different economic environments, but also able to discover deeper patterns and trends hidden behind the data, providing more valuable information to support decision makers, showed in Fig. 1:

Deep learning is also highly flexible and adaptable [11]. Traditional economic forecasting methods typically rely on specific assumptions and model structures that require significant human intervention and adaptation. In contrast, deep learning models are able to automatically learn and extract features from data through an end-to-end learning approach, reducing reliance on problem domain expertise while allowing for more flexible adaptation to different forecasting tasks and data types [12]. This adaptive ability allows deep learning to excel in coping with rapidly changing and complex and volatile economic environments, providing a new, more pervasive and effective solution to all types of economic forecasting problems. The LSTM Forget Gate Formula:

$$f_t = \sigma\big(W_f \cdot \big[h_{t-1}, x_t\big] + b_f\big) \tag{1}$$

With the improvement of computing power and the continuous progress of deep learning algorithms, more and more studies and practical applications have proved the actual effect and potential of deep learning in economic forecasting. From long-term prediction of macroeconomic trends to short-term analysis of micro-market behavior, deep learning

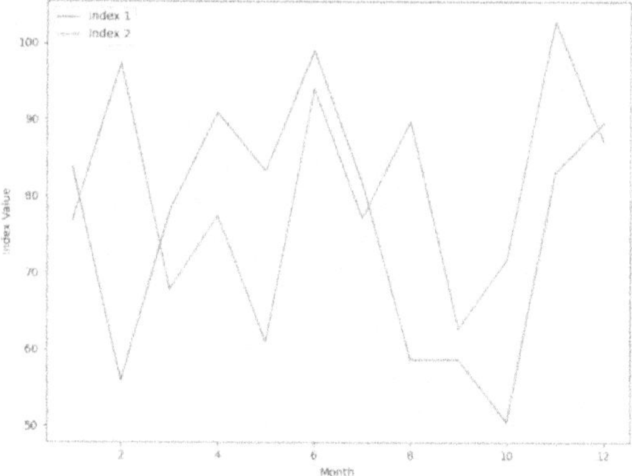

Fig. 1. Monthly Trends of Economic Indicators.

technology is becoming one of the most important tools in economics research and business decision-making. By combining big data and powerful computational capabilities, deep learning can not only provide more accurate and reliable forecasting results, but also help decision makers better understand and respond to the complexity of economic changes, and promote economic development and market stability.

3 Establishing a Deep Learning-Based Model for Predicting Industrial Economic Trends

In order to construct an efficient industrial economic trend prediction model, we need to systematically explore and implement the three aspects of data collection and pre-processing, deep learning model selection and design, and model training and optimization. Through scientific data processing methods, reasonable model structure design and effective training strategies, we can improve the prediction accuracy and stability of the model, thus realizing the accurate prediction of industrial economic trends.

3.1 Data Collection and Pre-processing Methods

Data collection is the first step in building a deep learning model, and it is crucial for the accuracy and reliability of the model prediction. In industrial economic forecasting, data come from a wide and diverse range of sources, including macroeconomic indicators, industry statistics, market transaction data, enterprise financial statements, and socioeconomic activity data. However, obtaining high-quality, full-coverage economic data faces many challenges, such as the timeliness, completeness, accuracy, and consistency of the data. Therefore, developing a systematic and effective data collection strategy is fundamental to ensuring the success of the model.

In industrial economic forecasting, data can be collected through a variety of channels and methods. Official economic data released by government statistical departments are the most authoritative and widely used data source. In addition, financial institutions, industry associations and market research organizations also provide a large amount of valuable data. Internet and social media data, on the other hand, provide new data dimensions for forecasting. By crawling and mining these data, more real-time and nuanced economic dynamics can be captured. In order to ensure the diversity and comprehensiveness of data, we need to comprehensively utilize data from different sources and choose appropriate data collection methods, such as API calls, web crawlers, database queries, etc., in line with actual needs.

Data preprocessing is a critical step after data collection, which directly affects the training effect and prediction performance of the model. Economic data often have problems such as missing values, noise, outliers, and different scales, which, if left untreated, can seriously affect the performance of the model. The main tasks of preprocessing include data cleaning, data transformation, data normalization and feature engineering. Data cleaning is the process of removing noise and dealing with missing values; data conversion is to unify and standardize data from different sources; data normalization is to eliminate the influence of different scales on model training; feature engineering is to extract useful information from the original data and improve the learning ability of the model, showed in Fig. 2:

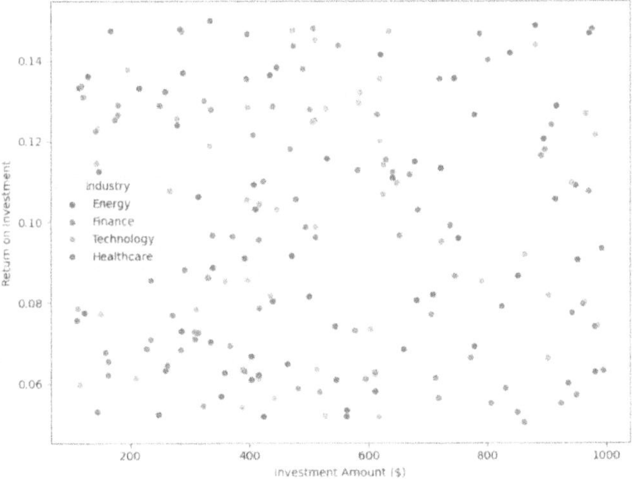

Fig. 2. Scatter Plot of Industry Investment Distribution.

For different preprocessing tasks, we can use a variety of techniques and methods. For example, for missing value processing, mean filling, interpolation, or filling using predictive models can be used; for noise and outlier processing, statistical methods, outlier detection algorithms, etc. can be used. Techniques commonly used for data transformation and normalization include normalization, normalization, logarithmic transformation, and so on. Feature engineering, on the other hand, can be realized by methods such as feature selection, feature extraction, and feature construction. In addition, considering the demand of deep learning models on the amount of data, data enhancement techniques can also be used to extend the dataset and improve the generalization ability of the model. Through scientific and reasonable data preprocessing methods, we can provide high-quality training data for deep learning models to enhance the prediction effect.

3.2 Deep Learning Model Selection and Design

Choosing the right deep learning model is the key to building an effective prediction system. Different deep learning models show different advantages when dealing with specific types of data and tasks. For industrial and economic trend prediction, commonly used deep learning models include Long Short-Term Memory Networks (LSTM), Recurrent Neural Networks (RNN), Convolutional Neural Networks (CNN), and Hybrid Models (e.g., CNN-LSTM.) LSTMs and RNNs are good at dealing with time-series data, and are able to capture the time-dependence of the data and the trend changes; CNNs excel in feature extraction and are able to extract local features and patterns from data. Depending on the specific needs of the prediction task, we need to consider the data characteristics and model performance to choose the most appropriate model architecture. LSTM Cell State Update Formula:

$$C_t = f_t \cdot C_{t-1} + i_t \cdot \tilde{C}_t \tag{2}$$

After selecting a suitable deep learning model, the model design process includes the construction of the model structure, the setting of hyperparameters and the optimization of the model. The construction of the model structure requires determining key parameters such as the number of network layers, the number of neurons in each layer, and the activation function. For time series prediction tasks, LSTM networks usually consist of multiple LSTM layers and fully connected layers, while CNNs consist of multiple convolutional layers and pooling layers. Hyperparameter settings involve learning rate, batch size, number of training rounds, etc., which directly affect the training efficiency and prediction accuracy of the model. In order to obtain the best model performance, we need to adjust and optimize these hyperparameters through experimentation and validation.

Model training is an important part of deep learning model development. Through the backpropagation algorithm, the model continuously optimizes the parameters on the training data to minimize the prediction error. During the training process, we need to be careful to avoid overfitting and underfitting problems. Overfitting means that the model performs well on the training data but poorly on the test data; underfitting means that the model performs poorly on both the training and test data. To avoid these problems, regularization techniques, data augmentation, early stopping and cross-validation can be used. After the model training is completed, the model performance needs to be evaluated on an independent validation set to ensure its predictive ability in real-world applications, showed in Fig. 3:

Optimization and improvement of deep learning models is an ongoing process. In practical applications, we may need to continuously adjust and optimize the model to cope with changes in data and environment. On the one hand, the predictive ability of the model can be improved by introducing more complex model architectures, such as

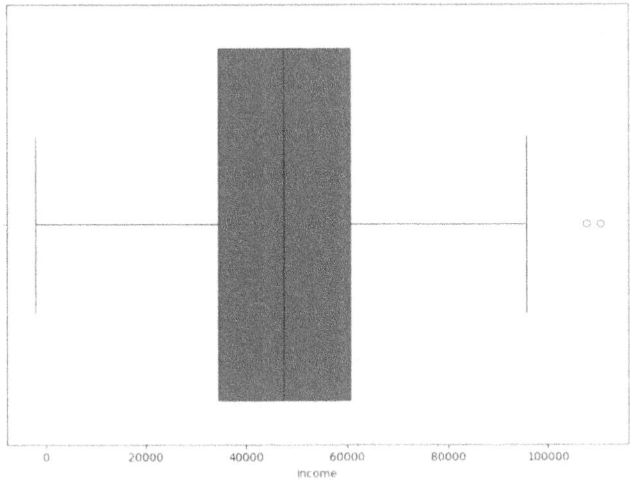

Fig. 3. Box Plot of Income Distribution.

multi-layer LSTM or bidirectional LSTM; on the other hand, other machine learning algorithms, such as Random Forest and Support Vector Machines, can be combined to construct an integrated model to improve the prediction accuracy. In addition, regular updating of training data and retraining of the model can keep the model sensitive and adaptable to the latest economic dynamics. Through continuous optimization and improvement, we can construct more accurate and reliable industrial economic trend prediction models. RNN Hidden State Update Formula:

$$h_t = \tanh(W_h \cdot x_t + U_h \cdot h_{t-1} + b_h) \tag{3}$$

3.3 Model Training and Optimization Strategies

Model training is a crucial step in the deep learning process, by constantly adjusting the model parameters to make it perform well on the training data. When training a deep learning model, we first need to prepare the training data and input the preprocessed data into the model. Then, the loss function is calculated by forward propagation to compute the output and compare it with the true value. Next, the gradient is calculated by the backpropagation algorithm and the model parameters are adjusted to minimize the loss function. This process is iterated until the model converges and reaches the expected prediction performance. During the training process, care needs to be taken to adjust the hyperparameters such as learning rate and batch size to obtain the best training results, showed in Fig. 4:

Overfitting and underfitting are common problems in deep learning model training. Overfitting means that the model performs well on training data but poorly on new data, while underfitting means that the model cannot perform well on both training and new data. To avoid overfitting, regularization techniques (e.g., L1, L2 regularization),

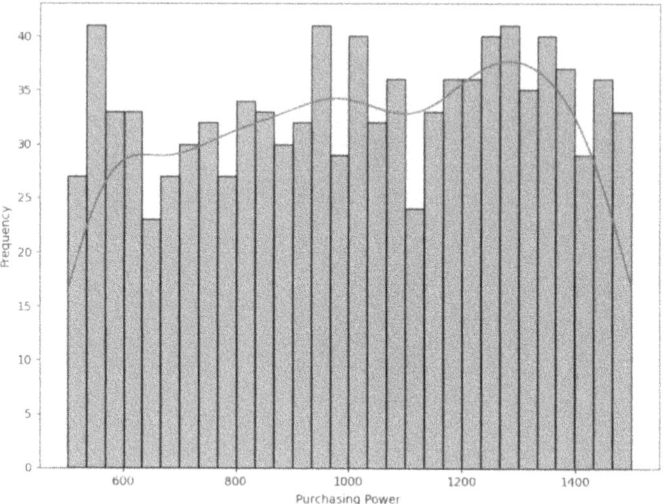

Fig. 4. Histogram of Consumer Purchasing Power.

Dropout, and data augmentation can be used; to avoid underfitting, the complexity of the model can be increased, e.g., by increasing the number of network layers or neurons, and by increasing the amount of training data. In addition, early stopping (EARLY STOPPING) is an effective method to prevent overfitting by monitoring the model performance on the validation set and stopping training when the performance is no longer improving.

The choice of hyperparameters has a significant impact on the performance of deep learning models. Common hyperparameters include learning rate, batch size, number of training rounds, number of network layers and number of neurons per layer. Reasonable setting of these hyperparameters can significantly improve the training effect and prediction performance of the model. The main methods of hyperparameter tuning are Grid Search and Random Search. Grid Search finds the best parameters by exhausting all possible parameter combinations; Random Search randomly selects parameter combinations in the parameter space, and usually finds a better solution in a shorter time. In recent years, more advanced hyper-parameter tuning methods, such as Bayesian Optimization, have also been gradually applied to the optimization of deep learning models.

Model optimization is an ongoing process that requires continuous adjustment and improvement of the model to enhance its predictive performance and generalization ability. During the model training process, a variety of techniques can be used to optimize the model, such as Learning Rate Scheduling, Momentum Optimization, and Adaptive Learning Rate Methods (e.g., Adam, RMSprop). These methods can accelerate the training process and improve the convergence speed and stability of the model. In addition, Ensemble Learning (EL) is also an effective method to improve the overall prediction performance and reduce the bias and variance of a single model by combining the prediction results of multiple models. Continuously monitoring the performance of the model in real-world applications, updating the training data and retraining the model in a timely manner can also help to maintain the prediction accuracy and adaptability of the model.

4 Advantages and Limitations of Comparing Traditional Methods

The biggest advantage of deep learning in economic forecasting is its powerful nonlinear modeling capability and automatic feature extraction. Traditional economic forecasting methods, such as ARIMA and VAR, usually rely on linear assumptions and manual feature engineering, making it difficult to handle complex nonlinear relationships and high-dimensional data. Deep learning models are able to capture complex patterns and non-linear relationships in data through a multi-layer neural network structure, enabling higher forecasting accuracy. In addition, deep learning is able to automatically extract features from data, reducing the dependence on domain expert knowledge and improving the adaptability and generalization of the model.

Another significant advantage is the ability of deep learning to handle big data. Traditional methods often face high computational complexity and inefficiency when dealing with large-scale, high-dimensional data. Deep learning, on the other hand, can efficiently process and analyze large-scale data with the help of modern GPU computing power. With deep learning models, we can make full use of various types of data sources, including structured data, unstructured data (e.g., text and images), and time series data, to provide more comprehensive and accurate economic forecasts. This data processing capability makes deep learning uniquely suited to meet the challenges of economic forecasting in today's big data era. CNN Convolution Operation Formula:

$$(I * K)\left[i, j\right] = \sum_{m}\sum_{n}\left[i + m, j + n\right] \cdot \mathrm{K}[\mathrm{m}, \mathrm{n}] \tag{4}$$

Deep learning is superior to traditional methods in many ways, but traditional methods still have their unique advantages and application scenarios. Traditional economic forecasting methods, such as regression analysis and time series analysis, are characterized by solid theoretical foundations and strong interpretations that provide researchers with clear economic relationships and causal analysis. In addition, these methods perform well with small sample data and long-term studies in specific areas. Deep learning models, on the other hand, despite their strong predictive performance, often lack interpretability and are difficult to provide specific economic laws and causal relationships. At the same time, deep learning models require a high amount of data, and their predictive performance may not be as good as traditional methods when the data are insufficient or of low quality, showed in Fig. 5:

In practical applications, choosing an appropriate prediction method requires comprehensive consideration of a variety of factors, including data characteristics, prediction goals, computational resources, and model interpretability. In some specific scenarios, traditional methods and deep learning methods can complement each other and play their respective advantages. For example, traditional methods can be used for explanatory analysis in the preliminary analysis and then combined with deep learning for more accurate prediction. Through this combination of methods, we can provide meaningful economic explanations and decision support while ensuring forecast accuracy. Future

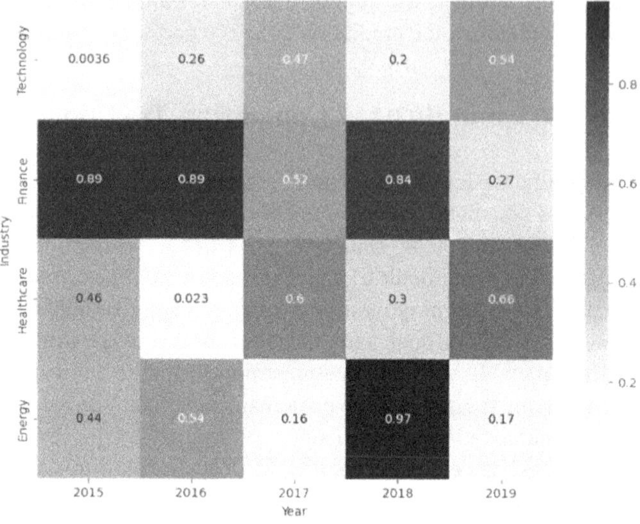

Fig. 5. Heatmap of Innovation Index by Industry.

research can further explore the integration of deep learning with traditional methods to develop more complete and efficient economic forecasting models. Gradient Descent Algorithm Formula:

$$\theta := \theta - \eta \nabla_\theta L(\theta) \tag{5}$$

5 Conclusion

The big-data forecasting pipeline proposed in this paper targets financial applications, specializing in the link from macro-level economic factors to micro-level market signals. Feature large-scale financial data, the pipeline is well-designed to preprocess data, implement model structures, and optimize performance through multiple sources of high-volume and high-frequency data. Empirical results demonstrate that using the deep learning methodology in pipeline design captures the complex non-linear relations between the macroeconomic and market effective factors. The two have outperformed accurate trend forecast performance and maintained steady performance. The findings indicate that deep learning-based financial predictive frameworks can develop powerful analysis tools for policymakers, institutional investors, and risk managers. In comparison to accurate econometric forecasts, this approach has shown high flexibility, automated selection of features and advantages, and broad applicability in mothers with evolving settings. However, some limitations still exist. The performance of the Model majorly depends on the quality and quantity data features availability and the Explainability challenge starts with the adequacy and explanation of deep neural networks constrained financial decision-making power. Additionally, the computational expense of large-scale model training is still significant. Future work will focus on three main lines of improvement: combining explaining artificial learning with Financial deep learning to develop surrogate models with enhanced Explainable AI effectiveness; combining traditional econometrics logic with data-driven architecture to create hybrid modeling; and expanding the proposed research's final pipeline to real-time forecasting via distributed computing. With further data infrastructure and broader advancements in AI, the pipeline aspect in this study is expected to become increasingly crucial in intelligent financial decision-making.

References

1. Nguyen, D.K., Sermpinis, G., Stasinakis, C.: Big data, artificial intelligence and machine learning: a transformative symbiosis in favour of financial technology. Eur. Financ. Manag. **29**(2), 517–548 (2023)
2. Anesti, N., Kalamara, E., Kapetanios, G.: Forecasting with machine learning methods and multiple large datasets. Econ. Stat. (2024)
3. Richardson, P.: Nowcasting and the use of big data in short term macroeconomic forecasting: a critical review. Economie et Statistique. **505**(1), 65–87 (2018)
4. Wei, D.: Prediction of stock price based on LSTM neural network. In: 2019 International Conference on Artificial Intelligence and Advanced Manufacturing (AIAM), pp. 544–547. IEEE, Piscataway (2019)
5. Rouf, N., Malik, M.B., Arif, T., et al.: Stock market prediction using machine learning techniques: a decade survey on methodologies, recent developments, and future directions. Electronics. **10**(21), 2717 (2021)
6. Jing, N., Wu, Z., Wang, H.: A hybrid model integrating deep learning with investor sentiment analysis for stock price prediction. Expert Syst. Appl. **178**, 115019 (2021)
7. Park, H.J., Kim, Y., Kim, H.Y.: Stock market forecasting using a multi-task approach integrating long short-term memory and the random forest framework. Appl. Soft Comput. **114**, 108106 (2022)
8. Rezaei, H., Faaljou, H., Mansourfar, G.: Stock price prediction using deep learning and frequency decomposition. Expert Syst. Appl. **169**, 114332 (2021)
9. Hasan, U.M.M., Shreevamshi, N.: AI-powered predictive analytics for financial forecasting and strategic insight. Int. J. Res. Innov. Appl. Sci. **10**(6), 532–555 (2025)
10. Masters, O., Hunt, H., Steffinlongo, E., et al.: Towards a homomorphic machine learning big data pipeline for the financial services sector. Cryptol. ePrint Arch. (2019)
11. Khanarsa, P., Sinapiromsaran, K.: Multiple ARIMA subsequences aggregate time series model to forecast cash in ATM. In: 2017 9th International Conference on Knowledge and Smart Technology (KST), pp. 83–88. IEEE, Piscataway (2017)
12. Kurani, A., Doshi, P., Vakharia, A., Shah, M.: A comprehensive comparative study of artificial neural network (ANN) and support vector machines (SVM) on stock forecasting. Ann. Data Sci. **10**(1), 183–208 (2023)

Intelligent Systems and Algorithmic Optimization in Enterprise Finance

AI as an External Brain: Forecast Intelligence, Option Signals, and In-Advance-of-Time Exposure Governance for the Self-Managed Enterprise

Thierry Brutman[✉] [iD]

EDDA Stock Finance Research Laboratory, Chicago, IL, USA
ceo@edda-stockfinance.com

Abstract. Artificial Intelligence is increasingly called to act not just as a tool, but as strategic middleware, coordinating decisions across fragmented enterprise systems. While ERP platforms centralize data, they fail to govern coherence across time, departments, and structural constraints. This paper presents a forecasting and decision architecture in which AI becomes a real-time arbitrator of viability, based on signal logic rooted in option theory. Every choice is modeled as a governed engagement—constrained by cost, delay, reversibility, and exposure—forming a multidimensional signal known as the Brutman Option. Two operational indicators emerge: the Brutman Flexibility Index (BFI), measuring the remaining adaptability across viable paths, and the Maximum Rational Investment (MRI), setting the symbolic exposure ceiling compatible with coherence. Combined with real-time forecast testing, these elements form a reflexive governance system, enabling AI to arbitrate, adjust, or suspend action before incoherence propagates. This leads to a self-managed architecture where AI operates as an external brain, coordinating logic, time, intention, and structural viability.

Keywords: Forecast Intelligence · Option-Based Modeling · BFI · MRI · Governed AI · AI as Middleware · Strategic Decision Systems · Reflexive Architecture

1 First Section

1.1 A. From Fragmentation to Acceleration Without Structure

Artificial intelligence is now embedded in every layer of our systems—in applications, forecasts, and automation. It is queried by individuals to summarize, by managers to optimize, and by companies to simulate. Increasingly, it is not humans who invoke AI, but machines calling other machines: AI correcting planning tools, generating conclusions for dashboards it didn't design. It is everywhere—and yet, nowhere does it decide. AI systems extract, predict, classify. They offer correlations, stylistic reformulations, variable rankings, accelerated responses. But all of this is classification—not choice.

S. C. P. Yam et al. (Eds.): ICFT 2025, CCIS 2868, pp. 355–369, 2026.
https://doi.org/10.1007/978-981-92-0126-6_29

They do not test alternatives. They do not weigh the cost of delay. They do not interrupt. They never say: "This path must stop" or "Another option must be tried." The system continues. It does not arbitrate. This absence of comparison logic is masked by the illusion of fluidity. Questions are answered. Plans are simulated. The user sees responsiveness—not the inability to govern. The result is uninterrupted execution. Inside enterprises, the same fragmentation applies. ERP, CRM, inventory managers, financial simulators—each operates with its own interface and metrics. But none shares a unified logic of arbitration. Each executes its own perimeter, creating incoherence rather than conflict. In fact, incoherence becomes conflict: contradictory KPIs lead to internal disputes, functional silos, and cost inflation.Every new signal adds another response. Every update triggers recalculation. But no system ever says: "This data changes the meaning of the plan.". What remains is velocity—not decision (Figs. 1 and 2).

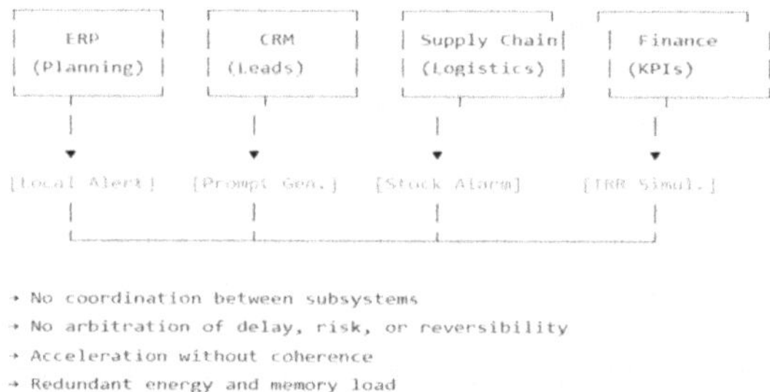

Fig. 1 Fragmented Architecture and System Overload: Typical enterprise setup with parallel subsystems triggering alerts and simulations independently—but no layer to observe, compare, or synchronize their logics.

Each subsystem continues on its own timeline. The architecture, though fully digital, becomes fragmented and the system accelerates while losing coherence. And this acceleration has a cost—one that is material, cognitive, and energetic. Each generative query consumes resources. Each scenario stored increases memory load. Each chain of prompts activates multiple layers of GPU and cloud retrieval. According to the International Energy Agency (2024), a single AI query consumes on average 2.9 to 5.6 Wh, depending on model depth. A 2025 analysis from OpenAI reports over 700 million queries processed daily, with Microsoft Azure estimating a 42% increase in cloud memory usage from enterprise LLM use in less than a year. [1, 2]

1.2 B. Users Dissatisfaction

We call it intelligence, yet AI lacks internal testing. It simulates but doesn't verify relevance. It forecasts, but never checks if the forecast still holds. It answers, but never chooses. There is no cortex, no internal signal that pauses, redirects, or questions. The system flows—but does not judge. It informs, yet fails to decide. What users receive is not structured decision, but fluent classification. Despite its polish, AI does not offer arbitration or real guidance. This gap is felt: a 2024 Applause survey found only 36% of users were "extremely satisfied" with generative AI, and over half just "somewhat

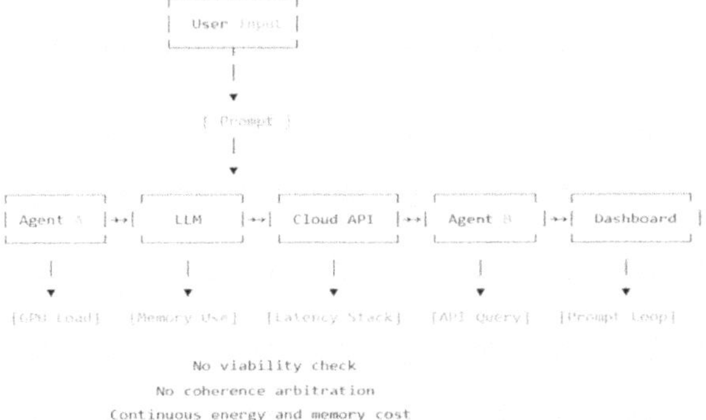

Fig. 2 Energy and Memory Cost of LLM Chains. Each prompt sequence across agents and tools compounds GPU load, latency, and storage—with no added decision value.

satisfied" [3]. Users don't seek answers alone—they seek orientation. Instead, they get reformulated fragments. Even with retries or restatements, 72% of ChatGPT users [3, 4] failed to resolve their dissatisfaction. The system responds, but direction remains absent. It classifies—but never chooses. That is the core issue: output without judgment, interaction without decision.

2 Second Section

2.1 A. What Users Truly Want—Beyond Classification: Option Valuation

What users, managers, and companies need is not better classification—they need help choosing. They want to know: "Is this the right moment to act, wait, or stop? And how much risk is justifiable?" Traditional metrics like NPV, IRR, or CAPM allow comparison—but not the definition of a rational ceiling. Real Option theory [11] tried to address this through flexibility and delay, but failed under scrutiny. It assumes market dynamics (Brownian motion), while most strategic decisions involve novel, unpredictable assets. Worse, it misuses Black-Scholes [10]—treating both spot and strike as market-tradable, when the strike is often internal. The result is elegant but detached: a symmetric pricing model that justifies waiting, not deciding. It's not a decision tool—it's a delay engine. To replace this, we introduce the Brutman Option: a multidimensional signal usable by AI and humans in real time. It combines four elements—expected revenue (spot), full engagement cost (strike), delay, and structural risk—all within the same expectation model. Spot and strike are architecturally comparable; delay and risk are integral to valuation. The result is a computable signal of engagement. Where traditional models assume normality, innovation demands governed structure. That's why we reshape Black-Scholes, binomial, and Monte Carlo logic to include delay and exposure thresholds. Option Value becomes a rational ceiling: if it exceeds cost, the path is viable; if not, continuing is unjustified. This isn't just evaluation—it's the first signal AI can use to guide, not classify.

2.2 B. Brutman Option Signal Models Solution

Official Formulas: These three formulations correspond to the governed signal approach and are now part of a unique the model. They replace conventional real option models and form the foundation of a testable decision system.

BSO-Black & Scholes (Governed Signal Form) (*For continuous, symmetrical environments where traditional risk-return logic applies*) [5, 6]

$$BSO\_BS(t) = S_0 \cdot N(d_1) - K \cdot e^{(-rT)} \cdot N(d_2) \tag{1}$$

with,

$d_1 = [\ln(S_0/K) + (r + \sigma^2/2) \cdot T] / (\sigma \cdot \sqrt{T}\,)$
$d_2 = d_1 - \sigma \cdot \sqrt{T}$ and
$S_0 = $ Volume(t) $\times$ UnitCost(t) $\times$ (1 + MarginRate(t))
$K = $ FixedCost + VariableCost(t)
$r = $ Discount rate (cost of capital)
$\sigma = $ Volatility of expected revenue
$T = $ Time horizon (delay)
$N(\cdot) = $ Cumulative standard normal distribution

Important: Since both spot and strike are derived from cost structures and margin assumptions, they are of the same nature—making this structure conceptually valid even outside financial asset pricing.

BSO-Binomial with Delay (Discrete + Delay-Weighted) (*For reactive environments where decisions occur in steps, and delay changes the value structure*)

We define a delay-weighted binomial tree, with each node:

$$V(t, i) = \max(0, E[P(t + 1)] \cdot \lambda(t)) \tag{2}$$

With:

$E[P(t+1)] = $ Expected payoff at next node (t+1)
$\lambda(t) = $ Delay decay coefficient, such that $\lambda(t) \in [0,1]$, decreasing with time
$V(t,i) = $ Option value at time t and node I (4)

The final value is computed via recursive discounting across the tree. This delay-weighted binomial model captures the erosion of optionality when a choice is not engaged immediately. It is suitable for decisions that evolve in discrete steps, such as operational reconfiguration, resource allocation, or phased investments.

BSO-Monte Carlo with Delay and Collapse Zones. (*For non-stationary, uncertain, or innovation environments with asymmetric risk or low visibility*)

$$BSO\_MC\Delta = (1/N)\ \Sigma\,(i = 1 \text{ to } N)\ e^{\hat{}}(-r\delta) \cdot \max(V(S\_i(T - \delta)) - K, 0) \tag{3}$$

With:

$S_i(t) = $ Stochastic path of expected revenue (trajectory-i)
$V(S_i, t) = $ Viability function: determines whether path is still coherent at time t
$T = $ Time horizon of engagement

δ = Operational delay before effect is measurable
K = Total expected cost (engagement cost)
r = Discount rate
T* = Irreversibility threshold (not in formula, but governs domain of viability)

Decision Logic for All Models. For any of the 3 models [5, 6]:

If BSO(t) ≥ Investment or Cost(t): Choice can be validated—risk is structurally acceptable
If BSO(t) < Required Input: Risk of overexposure—system triggers advice, delay, reallocation [7]

or searches for a restructured path, which AI can identify directly. The option becomes a decision signal, not a price. And it becomes testable by humans and AI, under any condition—with or without markets.

3 Third Section

3.1 A The Governed Forecast

Once a signal exists, forecasting moves from passive anticipation to structured judgment. If every choice is an option, and every option depends on a forecast, then each data point becomes a test—of the path, its assumptions, and its coherence. In the Brutman Option Model, the "spot" becomes the expected realization of the forecast. Fluctuations are no longer noise—they are signals. This is the basis of Forecast Intelligence. It doesn't simulate futures; it tests whether the engaged path remains valid. Z-tests, chi-squared analysis, or likelihood deviation detect when assumptions no longer hold. The system flags these shifts early—before failure, not after. Forecast Intelligence blends statistical models with subjective inputs—expectations, intuitive curves, thresholds—and tests which path still aligns. This is not dominance but structured dialogue. And it's not linear: systems must jump from one model to another. As Wiener observed, the world may be discontinuous—but adaptation must be continuous. Forecast Intelligence enables this, triggering transitions when coherence weakens. For the user, the burden shifts: no need to simulate manually. The system shows what is still viable, what must pause, and what requires revision. It becomes the nervous system of governed decision—acting before correction becomes costly.

Example 1 Company Product Launch: A company forecasts €5.2M in revenue over 12 months, with a 28% margin and €1.8M in fixed costs. The Option Value is positive. But three weeks post-launch, sales volume is 9% below projections. Margins hold, but the trajectory diverges. The system runs a Z-test and a likelihood analysis: 74% chance of missing targets by over 22%, within 95% confidence. The Option signal flattens. The path is not lost, but must adapt. The system recommends:

1. Reduce exposure and re-test pricing,
2. Switch to an alternate segment,
3. Interrupt with controlled loss to preserve optionality.

Example 2 Personal Career Change: An individual forecasts 17% income growth over 18 months, with initial instability. After 9 weeks, signals diverge—stress, liquidity, opportunity index. The system doesn't override the choice, but alerts: "You are no longer on the curve that justified your decision."

In both cases, the system doesn't wait. It tests whether the forecasted future is still the one being built. Some might argue that Z-tests or deviation models can be applied in any forecast. True. But that misses the point. A forecast isn't made to observe—it is made to justify. And once a choice is made, a forecast becomes part of an option. From that moment, deviation is no longer abstract: it becomes a governance test. This is what Forecast Intelligence brings—not just statistical tools, but a structure of accountability. Without an option, a forecast is a suggestion. With one, it is a commitment—and must be tested, strategically, every day.

3.2 B The Flexibility Index – The Integral of Governed Options

If a choice is an option under the BSO hypothesis, it is not a preference but a structured engagement: exposure under delay and uncertainty, with a defined objective and measurable reversibility. From this follows a key step: if one choice is an option toward a target, then all viable alternatives aiming at the same goal are also options—each with its own exposure, risk, and reversibility. Their sum forms a strategic space of governed engagements. This space has value, defined by the integral of those options: the Brutman Flexibility Index (BFI). The BFI is not an abstract idea [6–8]; it is the mathematical continuation of option theory. If one choice has value as an option, then having multiple governed alternatives must be expressed as the integral of those options over the window where decisions remain viable. In real-world settings, this can be computed discretely—finite paths, bounded time. The BFI thus becomes a usable index: a measure of how much maneuvering space remains—not to act randomly, but to adapt intelligently when a path degrades. For a single decision, the system must ask: what other options remain if this one fails? Each alternative—including the current path—is formalized as a governed option with its own exposure, reversibility, redirection cost, and compatibility. The gross BFI is the sum of these alternatives, each weighted by how structurally accessible it still is.

$$\text{BFI\_gross}(t) = \int \_R(t)\, \omega(r, t)\, dr \tag{4}$$

where $\omega(r,t) \in [0,1]$ is the weighting function associated with each possible reconfiguration r.

Reflecting
- reversibility
- adjustment cost
- delay sensitivity
- alignment with the original objective

As time progresses, the space of remaining options contracts change. Some paths become impossible, others too costly to justify. And the current trajectory, if not frequently recalibrated, may absorb so much exposure that no maneuvering remains. For this reason, we define the Net BFI—subtracting from the total the part of the structure already committed and no longer recoverable:

$$\text{BFI\_net}(t) = \int \_R(t)\, \omega\,(r, t)dr - \Phi(D_0, D\_t) \tag{5}$$

where,

$$\Phi(D_0, D\_t) = \rho \cdot E\_c(t) \tag{6}$$

quantifies the irreversibility already consumed—through sunk cost, locked commitments, or delayed action. The BFI does not measure success even if the choice is good will impact positively the calculation. It tells us how much judgment remains structurally possible—before the decision, however efficient, becomes impossible to revise without contradiction.

Where,

$\rho \in [0,1]$ is a global irreversibility coefficient
$E\_c(t)$ is the cumulative engagement cost (financial, temporal, operational) committed from D_0

The BFI for Strategic Trajectories and Business Cycles: But a decision is not always a one-time act. In most real situations—whether within a company, a project, or a personal career—what unfolds is not a single option, but a sequence. A strategy. A trajectory. A progression through time that aims not only at reaching a target, but at doing so while preserving coherence, adjustability, and viability at each step. This is where the BFI becomes more than a snapshot. It becomes a governance tool for an evolving path—a way to measure how much flexibility still remains across time, not just from a fixed point.

We write:

$$\text{BFI\_paths} = \int (t_0 \text{ to } T)\, \Sigma\,(i = 1 \text{ to } n)\, R\_i(t) \cdot \omega\_i(t)dt \tag{7}$$

Here, The BFI is the integral of all viable governed options over a strategic window. It quantifies how much maneuvering space remains—not just initially, but throughout the engagement. This is crucial when strategies follow external cycles like markets, product lifecycles, or policy shifts. A path may appear viable short-term yet drift out of sync before adjustments can be made. The BFI detects this early: not just if something is working, but if it can still adapt before losing relevance. Since most strategies involve finite alternatives over measurable periods, BFI can often be computed discretely for use in AI systems and dashboards. Strategic divergence is not only temporal—it's directional. Angular deviation between a project's slope and its environment can reveal early misalignment. This signal can refine the BFI through a penalty on the weighting $\omega i(t)$, showing when an option still exists but is becoming obsolete. This is not a new model, but a refinement that anticipates failure before flexibility is lost. Once BFI is integrated, the system stops comparing static options and starts evaluating viability across time. The shift is from recommendation to arbitration. A launch may be profitable, but if it reduces BFI below safe levels, the system alerts: "You may proceed, but flexibility is collapsing." This applies at every scale—for individuals too: "Option A yields higher return, but cuts your pivot margin by 70%; Option B keeps €40,000 in reserve." The decision system doesn't replace judgment—it preserves space for it. Instead of overriding, it invites the user to assign meaning to what remains open. Each new signal—internal or external—triggers coherence tests: Z-tests, χ^2 tests, drift scoring. If divergence is detected, the BFI adjusts [5, 6]. The system doesn't seek permission—it asks for context: "Forecast deviation exceeds bounds. Has the objective changed, or should we pivot?" Even a simple human answer—"We may adjust in 3 months"—becomes a testable forecast. This is governed interaction: AI filters viability, the human reframes intention. Together, they decide when to stay or shift. In the end, the BFI [5, 6] is not a performance score, but a structural safeguard. It shows how far we can still think and act before correction becomes impossible. And when it collapses—not from failure, but from irreversibility—we reach the system's final constraint. That is the point where Maximum Rational Investment begins.

4 Fourth Section

4.1 A. The Maximum Rational Investment – The Threshold of Coherence

At this point in the model, something essential appears. We are no longer navigating with isolated tools. We now operate within a complete system where each equation becomes a structural axis of judgment. The Brutman Option model forms the first axis: it defines, objectively, the maximum risk that can be rationally engaged toward a goal under uncertainty and delay. This is the foundation of governed exposure. The Flexibility Index [5, 6], the second axis, extends the logic: it tells us not only how to choose, but how many viable alternatives remain if the current path degrades. It measures freedom—not as an abstract possibility, but as a computable structural reserve. Forecast Intelligence, the third axis, introduces time and reflexivity. It governs real-time coherence: the system tests, detects misalignment, requests input, and proposes adjustment before collapse. Together, these components form a thinking architecture—enabling intelligence that is not merely reactive, but governed and governable. A grey brain activating and monitoring its own limits, connecting with a white brain—the space of global knowledge and subjective intent, human or synthetic. Yet for this system to remain coherent—for it to operate without exceeding its own logic—a final constraint must be defined. Because even when (1) the option value is clear and transferable across domains, enabling synergy; (2) flexibility remains significant; and (3) the forecast is structurally consistent... there still remains one limit: the maximum exposure the system—be it individual, corporate, or institutional—can sustain without breaching internal coherence. That limit is what we define next: the Maximum Rational Investment (MRI). Once a decision is described as an option, and its flexibility measured via the BFI, one last question arises: how far can we still go before the commitment becomes irrational? What is the maximum exposure that remains defensible—not in theory, but under these constraints, in this environment, and within this time pressure? The MRI defines that final threshold. It is not a tool for ambition or maximization. It is the ceiling of governed logic.The MRI is not an optimization tool [5, 6]. It is a structural limit—the outcome of two converging forces: (1) the option-based valuation of the project (its expected benefit, risk profile, and coherence under Forecast Intelligence), and (2) the actor's maximum structural financing capacity—whether corporate or individual—determined by liquidity, constraints, debt tolerance, and internal resilience, as formalized through MRM logic. Formally [5, 6]:

$$MRI(t) = \min\left[\text{OptionValue\_Forecast}(t), \text{MaximumFinancingLimit}(t)\right] \qquad (8)$$

The maximum financing limit reflects what the market will not exceed, particularly in debt-based strategies or asset-backed financing. However, this limit can be surpassed through equity or equity-like instruments, under distinct conditions (see our other articles). This ceiling is not static. It evolves with cash flow, interest rates, strategic tension, and above all, with the viability of the engagement itself. If the BFI collapses—if flexibility vanishes—then no further investment remains rational, regardless of how attractive the opportunity seems. As long as the BFI remains positive, the MRI defines the outer boundary of governed commitment.

Compatibility with Modigliani–Miller [9] and Strategic Coherence: This model extends, rather than contradicts, the Modigliani–Miller [9] framework. Capital structure becomes more than financial optimization—it becomes a reflection of internal coherence. The MRI enables an organization to determine: (1) the maximum revenue justifying the risk taken, (2) the maximum debt that remains sustainable structurally, and (3) the exact point where equity must be added—not arbitrarily, but at the intersection of governed curves: option value and capital exposure.

4.2   B. The Multiplier Effect

The MRI governs scenario branching, refinancing, and strategic thresholds through structural viability. AI moves from simulation to judgment—managing exposure and adjusting engagement as internal constraints evolve. When commitment exceeds what the system can sustain, the MRI defines the rational boundary. It gives AI the structure to answer: "Is this still viable?", "Can I scale or must I reduce?", "When is equity required?" These were not unsolvable questions—they lacked structural framing. MRI provides that. Once formalized, it becomes a strategic tool—aligning financing, decision timing, and resource allocation. For companies, it supports transitions like debt-to-equity shifts or joint ventures tied to BFI/Option Value dynamics. For individuals, it frames non-monetary risks—such as career change or entrepreneurship—using a utility-based MRI. This version evaluates expected meaning and alignment against invested time, energy, and focus. The strike reflects personal cost; the spot becomes subjective return. MRI adapts by actor type. For firms, it sets limits based on financing and Option Value. For banks, it ties to risk-adjusted return and Basel ratios. For governments, it defines a ceiling not on deficits alone but on forecasted impact, reversibility, and resilience. For cities, it limits transformation without jeopardizing future adaptability. For insurance systems, it governs redistribution within solvency bounds. MRI is not a universal metric—it is a governed template to express, for each actor, the outer edge of rational commitment.

5 Fifth Section

5.1 A. Beyond Forecasting: A Reflexive Architecture of Decision.

At this point, what we have uncovered is no longer a model. It is a transformation in the structure of decision itself based on a unique multidimensional signal the B.O.S. If every real choice is an option—and if every cost, every delay, every exposure, is linked to a past or pending option—then the sum of all these options becomes an integral: the mathematical expression of the full strategic space still available to the actor—whether a company, a system, or a single user. In such a system, the optimal configuration is no longer fixed. It becomes recalculable at any moment, including during periods of strategic reorientation, disruption, or transition. The system no longer depends on planning cycles or fixed reporting. It depends only on its capacity to evaluate, in real time, the current state of engagement, flexibility, and exposure across all viable trajectories. Forecast Intelligence does not simply anticipate outcomes. It becomes a governance structure—a living architecture of viability, capable of adapting every decision to the present structure of possibility—without waiting for consolidation, committee reports, or managerial consensus.

5.2 B. From Options to Reflexive Strategy

A Live Frame of Coherence. If every decision is an option, then every input used by a company—financial flows, operational signals, contractual events, even technical thresholds—can be interpreted, retranslated, and governed through the option logic. This creates a new strategic frame: one in which time, reversibility, and exposure become the dimensions of action, one in which each shift in the environment reactivates the system's internal logic, recomputing not the optimal point—but the viable zone of engagement. Classical models optimize from fixed dashboards. This model reconstructs the entire viable space as soon as a single parameter changes—not to simulate, but to govern.

5.3 C. The Emergence of an External Brain

The real consequence of this shift is not fluidity—it is autonomy. Once every data stream—operational, financial, technical, contractual—becomes translatable into options, once the viability of paths can be monitored in real time through BFI and MRI [5, 7, 12], a new structure becomes possible: an external brain for decision. This brain is not a dashboard. It is not an ERP module. It is an architectural layer positioned outside the operational system, capable of observing, interpreting, and reconnecting decisions across time, functions, and tools. It does not wait. It does not escalate. It awakens the moment a signal diverges, a coherence is lost, or an option collapses. And once activated, it reinjects structure—not as a recommendation, but as a recalibrated strategic logic. It can: populate pricing engines based on dynamic viability, reclassify production delays as structural option decay, align SAP, Oracle, or in-house software with the actual exposure state of the organization.

6   Sixth Section

6.1   A. End of Silos, End of Time Loss

What disappears in this system is not management. It is fragmentation. No more dashboards that don't align. No more reports that come too late. No more departments pulling in different directions because their time horizons do not match. Once all information becomes readable as governed options—and once each option is governed by structural constraints like BFI and MRI—the company no longer requires forced synchronization through meetings, escalation, or reporting cycles. It functions as a reflexive whole: without contradiction, without latency, without blind spots. This is the end of static planning. This is the beginning of an economy where every actor—company, institution, or individual—can act not only on what is desirable, but on what remains viable—and for how long.

6.2   B. Forecast-Governed System: The Table of Structural Transformation

Information Source/Trigger	Transformed via Option Logic	Processed by Forecast Intelligence	Impact on the System
Operational data (delivery, delay)	Interpreted as time-sensitive options linked to thresholds	Integrated into BFI to assess reversibility, reallocation	Live reprioritization of operations
Financial data (cash flow, margin)	Exposure logic linked to viability over time	Compared to MRI curve and treasury logic	Real-time rational investment ceiling
Strategic signals (market trends)	Recoded as deformations of target path	Checked for option-space degradation	Strategic shift proposal
Technical events (failures, load)	Evaluated as risks of irreversible decay	Tested against minimum reversibility to maintain path	Fallback or re-routing triggered
Legal/contracts (breach, clause)	Recoded as friction or forced action	Impact evaluated within BFI decay window	Option suppression or reformulation
Human directives (plans, pivots)	Interpreted as predefined probability + qualitative priority	Evaluated against option space	Scenario alignment or override
AI alerts (forecast collapse, incoherence)	Self-recognized loss of viability	Forecast reboot or system-wide MRI trigger	Autonomous reallocation, new trajectory

6.3 C. Tangible Gains of Forecast Intelligence

This architecture is not just conceptually superior—it delivers measurable gains.

Economic & Strategic Efficiency: 20%–45% reduction in strategic error cost (vs traditional planning), 15%–35% increase in project viability (via MRI threshold), +30% flexibility gain (BFI-preserved maneuverability), 5%–12% increase in total enterprise margin (through viable resource reallocation). Coordination Gains (Human + AI + System): 95% drop in software conflicts and scheduling incoherence, Real-time coherence between AI modules (Copilot, IA vertical, predictive layers), Unified option grammar across planning, finance, engineering, and executive level. Structural Noise Reduction: Brutman Model Architecture including Forecast Intelligence reduces error repetition, redundant prompts, query loops caused by misaligned systems. Decision cost per viable outcome is lowered—not by answering faster, but by structuring the question better.

7 Seventh Section

7.1 A. Structural Gains from Forecast Intelligence – Electric, Memory, and Environmental Benefits

The intelligence gain brought by the BAM–BFI–MRI architecture is not only strategic or economic. It has a material impact on the physical infrastructure of AI with fewer useless computations, reduced internal query loops, lower redundancy across tools, and minimized memory reprocessing across siloed systems. These translate directly into measurable electricity and memory savings—with a meaningful environmental dimension. According to the energy-mapped trials run under the BAM–BFI–MRI (Volvas):

7.1.1 Energy and Memory Efficiency Gains

Metric	Standard AI Architecture	Forecast Intelligence / SMCH	Improvement
Memory usage per viable decision	100 units	52–68 units	32% to 48% less
CPU / GPU time per investment scenario	1.0x	0.54x	~46% less computation time
Forecast scenario loop convergence (avg. queries)	~18	7 to 9	>50% fewer internal loops
Emissions proxy (per 10,000 queries)	1.0 baseline	0.62	~38% CO_2-equivalent reduction

Traditional AI systems often rely on brute force learning and repeated testing. By contrast, Forecast Intelligence systems reduce these cycles structurally, since each forecast is a governed signal, embedded with viability and timing logic. As a result: fewer simulation rounds are needed to reach clarity, decisions become clearer, earlier, and with less infrastructure usage, this benefits not only cost, but the planet.

7.2 B. Business Performance Gains (Page 11 of CTIS 2025) CTIS2025-Presentation

Company Size	Traditional AI Investment	BAM-BFI Investment	Monthly Cost Saving	Monthly Gain	Estimated Gain (as % Revenue)
Large	$2,000,000	$800,000	$150,000	+$180,000	+2% to + 5%
Mid-sized	$1,000,000	$400,000	$90,000	+$110,000	+5% to + 10%
Small	$500,000	$140,000	$40,000	+$60,000	+10% to + 13%

Strategic insight: The BAM-BFI-MRI approach achieves equal or better results with less than half the investment, and dramatically improves agility, forecasting clarity, and strategic reversibility.

Table: Technical and Strategic Gains—Side-by-Side

Area	Classic AI	Forecast Intelligence	Gain
Forecast Cycle Cost	High (trial & error)	Governed signals	–40% to –60%
Decision Feedback Time	Delayed	Real-time, BFI-triggered	+Immediate
Option Testing	Exogenous	Endogenous and reflexive	+Internal logic
Decision Alignment Across Tools	Manual sync	Fully automated (middleware logic)	+Coherence
Electricity usage (AI Ops)	100%	54–68%	–32% to –46%
Strategic Error Rate	15–25%	<8% (governed threshold logic)	–60%

Environmental Footprint and AI Responsibility: This model does not just accelerate intelligence. It reduces the pollution of reasoning. By turning AI into a cortex—capable of filtering, prioritizing, and stopping incoherent engagement—we reduce the number of: false starts, energy-intensive recalculations, and cognitive-overhead-inducing misalignments. In a world increasingly concerned with AI carbon footprint, Forecast Intelligence proposes something rare: *An AI that doesn't just compute smarter and it burns less.* This isn't only strategic. It's ethical.

7.3 C. Forecast Intelligence as an Ecological Architecture of Thought

In the end, the goal is not just to improve decisions, but to deliver what users expect from intelligence—and rarely receive. Most systems accelerate tasks or simulate outcomes, yet fewer than 32% of users feel their needs are truly met. Why? Because the core question—"Can I still act now, with coherence?"—remains unanswered. Users don't need more options. They need structure: what is still viable, where risk concentrates, and how far a path remains coherent. One major impact is the end of siloed management. In most organizations, the real loss lies in fragmentation. SAP shows cash flow, Oracle tracks milestones, HR manages resources, dashboards show timelines—but none assess viability as constraints shift. Decisions then drift through escalation or inertia. Forecast Intelligence interrupts this by reading inputs not as KPIs, but as governed signals. It reactivates action only where structure permits. By reducing internal queries, simulations, and tool friction, it lowers memory and energy cost per decision. Trials show up to 40% less error drift and 60% better trajectory alignment. This doesn't just increase productivity—it reduces decision volume, enhances clarity, and cuts waste. Forecast Intelligence doesn't multiply actions. It governs them—turning quantity into qualified judgment. This is what classical AI missed: every interaction has a cost—in time, memory, and coherence. Volvas, the architecture built on BOS, BFI, and MRI, addresses that expectation—not just cognitively or ecologically, but structurally. A new architecture of thought.

7.4   D. Final Perspective: A Shared Language for Intelligence

This is not simply a forecasting system. It is a governance architecture. And above all—it is a shared language between humans and machines. Forecast Intelligence does not accelerate decisions. It allows us to decide without incoherence—and to adjust without shame when conditions evolve. It does not centralize power. It distributes judgment—by offering each actor a space of structural clarity, where each option is interpretable, testable, and reversible within its limit. This is not the future of AI. This is a new layer of intelligence—a cortex we can build outside of ourselves, to preserve the one we still carry inside. The cortex is active. The structure is governed. The decision is no longer a gamble—it is a path we can read, and—finally—choose with full awareness of what remains open.

References

1. International Energy Agency: Electricity 2024 – analysis and forecasts to 2026. IEA Publications (2024)
2. OpenAI: Usage patterns and compute metrics: global LLM query load analysis. Internal Report (2025)
3. Luzmo: The predictive dashboard report: what users expect from intelligent interfaces. Luzmo Research (2023)
4. Predictive Modeling Consortium (PMC): Expectations and gaps in decision-driven analytics (2023)
5. Brutman, T.: Forecast intelligence and the end of structural drift in AI-based systems. In: Paper presented at CTIS 2025. Ordos (2025)
6. Brutman, T.: Beyond silos: how AI and options models enhance enterprise-wide optimization despite specialized software. In: Paper presented at AICCS Oxford 2025. Oxford (2025)

7. Brutman, T.: Forecast intelligence: a dynamic option-based model for real-time expectation testing and decision autonomy. Research Working Paper, EDDA Research Laboratory. Preprint at [S.S.R.N] (2025)

8. Brutman, T.: Real options were never real: mathematic proof of invalidity and the BAM model for governed-action. Research Working Paper, EDDA Research Laboratory. Preprint at [S.S.R.N] (2025)

9. Modigliani, F., Miller, M.H.: The cost of capital, corporation finance and the theory of investment. Am. Econ. Rev. **48**(3), 261–297 (1958)

10. Black, F., Scholes, M.: The pricing of options and corporate liabilities. J. Polit. Econ. **81**(3), 637–654 (1973)

11. Trigeorgis, L.: Real Options: Managerial Flexibility and Strategy in Resource Allocation. MIT Press, Cambridge (1996)

12. Brutman, T.: Forecasting as governance: integrating microeconomic choices and macroeconomic limits through governed option logic. In: Proceedings of AICCS 2025, International Conference on Artificial Intelligence and Complex Cognition Systems, Beijing (2025) (forthcoming publication)

Artificial Intelligence, Big Data, and Blockchain: The Synergistic Convergence Reshaping Financial Services

Mohamed Amine Issami[✉] [ID]

Department of Finance and Accounting, ISCAE-Casablanca, Casablanca, Morocco
`aissami@groupeiscae.ma`

Abstract. Blockchain, Big Data, and Artificial Intelligence (AI) are the driving forces behind the ongoing paradigm shift, which is defined by systemic change as opposed to incremental innovation. Although these technologies have been researched separately, they have a significant spillover effect when used together: big data improves the analytical skills of artificial intelligence algorithms, and blockchain establishes a framework for data categorization that is trustworthy and reliable. By looking at novel viewpoints like governance, privacy, and oracles, and evaluating their integration, our article analyzes the fundamental convergence model of fintech technologies (CMFT). We have explored the existing literature and the recent development of emergent technologies such as Decentralized AI, Zero-Knowledge Proofs, and taking into account the threats of Quantum Computing, in order to demystify the smooth development of financial inclusion, efficiency, and personalization. However, a novel risk frame arises around AI-model poisoning, Blockchain scalability trilemma, and systemic vulnerabilities that are a must for an integrated ecosystem. All in all, a forward-looking, agile, and responsible "Regulatory Sandbox 2.0" structure is suggested, with an objective of using the immense potential of the convergence, with regard to multi-stakeholder governance.

Keywords: Artificial Intelligence · Big Data · Blockchain · Convergent Technologies · Decentralized Finance (DeFi) · Decentralized AI · Regulatory Technology (RegTech) · Quantum Resilience · Governance

1 Introduction

Industry Revolution 4.0, which is characterized by the fusion of the phygital and biological systems, is a lever for a fundamental change in all aspects of our daily lives. Financial services are a data-intensive and highly regulated sector, which is considered the epicenter of this major transformation. Traditionally, emergent technologies were perceived as separate innovation tools. The priority for the automation and decision-making capabilities is given to AI, and large-scale data collection and analytics are ensured by Big Data, and finally, the tamper-proof record keeping is secured by Blockchain.

As a matter of fact, the depth of the process of the integration of those technologies and the intertwined technological stack has reshaped the foundational architecture of

© The Author(s), under exclusive license to Springer Nature Singapore Pte Ltd. 2026
S. C. P. Yam et al. (Eds.): ICFT 2025, CCIS 2868, pp. 370–380, 2026.
https://doi.org/10.1007/978-981-92-0126-6_30

the financial system and its operational workflows. Furthermore, Data-driven AI models ask verifiable provenance generated by Blockchain's immutable ledgers. In parallel. The Blockchain protocols are increasingly dependent on AI-led decision support and off-chain data analysis.

This paper is based on a recurrent research question in the literature (i.e., How does the convergence of AI, Big Data, and Blockchain reshape financial services?), which is extended further towards more nuanced inquiries: how does the new technicality in the architecture enhance the support of the symbiosis? What are the risks that emerge? How governance mode manages the complexity of the current multi-dimensional ecosystem.

Our study covers cutting-edge advancements in decentralized AI network privacy-preserving computations, such as zero-knowledge proofs (ZKPs), as well as emerging quantum computing threats. This work provides a more comprehensive and advanced perspective on the incorporation of new technologies.

2 Literature Review

This section of the article will go into detail about the role of AI in finance, with a particular emphasis on the Big Data perspective, Blockchain technologies, and their vector of convergence.

2.1 AI in Finance

The primary emphasis of AI research in the financial services sector has shifted from conventional automation and predictive analytics to transparency, interpretability, and fairness. As market participants and regulators have stressed the necessity of AI systems being readily auditable in order to assure compliance and minimize bias, explainable AI (XAI) methods have gained popularity (Doshi-Velez & Kim, 2017; Adadi & Berrada, 2018). Furthermore, transformer-based models such as BERT and its derivatives are now used for complex applications like real-time sentiment analysis and automated financial reporting via natural language understanding (Wu et al., 2023). These advancements indicate a shift away from increasing capabilities and toward the ethical and legal integration of artificial intelligence.

2.2 Big Data

Big data analysis paradigms have also experienced tremendous change. Alternative data sources that now supplement conventional financial indicators and provide more in-depth insights for risk assessment and credit underwriting include IoT satellite image streams and social media sentiment (Goldstein et al., 2021). Alongside the growth of data developments in data markets and the creation of synthetic data (Jordon et al., 2022) encourage machine learning processes that maintain confidentiality. By creating models without revealing the underlying sensitive datasets synthetic data helps to balance the frequently incompatible objectives of data privacy and utility.

2.3 Blockchain

Blockchain research which began with the validation of cryptocurrency transactions now focuses on decentralized finance platforms, a challenge that enable the production of unauthorized composable financial products known as "money legos". Schär (2021). Layer-2 protocols like Optimistic Rollups and Zero-Knowledge Rollups have increased transaction throughput and privacy capabilities to address scalability issues. Interoperability projects (e.g., Cosmos and Polkadot) reduce fragmentation by facilitating communication between different blockchains. Because decentralized oracles networks like Chainlink enable precise and timely data transmission which is crucial to the AI-powered decision-making logic on the chain the role of oracles; middleware that securely connects on-chain smart contracts to off-chain data; is now crucial (Breidenbach et al., 2021).

2.4 Convergence

The convergence of these technologies has made it possible to develop novel frameworks like federated learning, which allows several data owners to create AI models in a decentralized manner while preserving privacy and increasing model resilience (Yang et al., 2019). Blockchain-based validations, which ensure the integrity of training data and offer a long-lasting record of the origins of AI models, support this advancement, enhancing auditability and, in particular, reducing the potential for manipulation (Harris & Waggoner, 2019). As a result, academic discussions are increasingly focusing on the complex interaction between big data and blockchain AI, enabling them to take advantage of their respective strengths while also posing new integration challenges.

3 Enhanced Conceptual Framework: The CMFT-Privacy (CMFT-P) Model

The original Convergence Model of FinTech Technologies (CMFT) delineated three primary layers: Data (Big Data), Analytical (AI/Machine Learning), and Trust (Blockchain). Our enhanced CMFT-Privacy (CMFT-P) model builds upon this by integrating two key additional components alongside an overarching privacy dimension, reflecting the evolving technological landscape and regulatory environment.

3.1 Core CMFT Layers

Core CMFT layers are relying on three main levels. These levels are Big Data, the Analytical layer, and Blockchain technology.

3.1.1 Data Layer (Big Data)

This includes traditional and alternative data streams, now augmented by synthetic data sets generated via AI to enhance privacy while maintaining analytical value. Verifiable data streams from blockchain oracles also play a crucial role.

3.1.2 Analytical Layer (AI/ML)

Expanded to encompass both centralized AI systems and decentralized AI frameworks, including Federated Learning and Swarm AI, permitting collaborative yet privacy-sensitive model development.

3.1.3 Trust Layer (Blockchain)

Incorporates scalable Layer-1 and Layer-2 Blockchain protocols, with smart contract infrastructures facilitating autonomous execution of transactions and agreements across financial networks.

3.2 New Integrated Components

We suggest a new set of integrated components, focusing on the aspects of privacy and confidentiality. We refer to this as the Oracle mechanism and its synergistic effect.

3.2.1 Privacy & Confidentiality Dimension

A vertical, permeating element across all layers enabled by cryptographic innovations like Zero-Knowledge Proofs (e.g., zk-SNARKs) and Homomorphic Encryption. This allows sensitive data and computations to be utilized by AI models and Blockchain protocols without direct exposure, ensuring compliance with stringent privacy standards such as GDPR and CCPA.

3.2.2 Oracle Mechanism

Functioning as a bidirectional conduit, oracles bridge the off-chain data ecosystem and on-chain logic layers. They securely retrieve external Big Data for smart contracts while concurrently serving as pipelines to deliver outputs of on-chain computations or AI analyses back to external stakeholders, enabling hybrid workflows.

3.2.3 The Synergistic Effect

Confluence is innately cyclical and non-linear (**i**) Blockchain guarantees the integrity of data and the provenance of the datasets used by AI models. (**ii**) AI processes and analyzes these data inputs in order to induce perceptivity, vaticinations, or triggers that influence the conditions of smart contracts. (**iii**) Smart contracts commit new data to the blockchain and carry out fiscal contracts or deals in a transparent and automated manner. The entire data subcaste is enhanced by this new on-chain data, which feeds further AI assessments and keeps the circle going (Table 1).

Table 1. Trade-offs Between Transparency and Privacy in Convergent FinTech Architectures

Aspect	Transparency Benefit	Privacy Trade-off
Blockchain Ledger	Publicly auditable, immutable records	Risk of exposing sensitive financial or personal data
AI Explainability	Improves trust, auditability of AI decisions	Potential exposure of sensitive model data or inputs
Big Data Analytics	Rich data improves accuracy and fairness	Compliance with data protection regulations
Privacy-Enhancing Tech	Enables confidential processing	Limits visible audit trails and granularity
Oracle Mechanisms	Enhances data trustworthiness on-chain	Potential exposure of off-chain sensitive data

Source. Compiled by the author

4 Applications in Financial Services

Practitioners and professionals use a variety of financial services applications that are now tangible and widely available. The applications that are cited the most frequently will be highlighted in this section.

4.1 On-Chain Credit Scoring

Traditional credit scoring depends on centralized repositories and established financial history, often excluding underbanked populations. DeFi protocols like Aave now experiment with AI-powered underwriting that analyzes users' on-chain transaction histories - immaculate and tamper-proof from Blockchain records - to compute decentralized credit scores. Executed entirely by smart contracts, these models offer transparent, permissionless access to lending markets without intermediaries.

4.2 Decentralized Autonomous Organizations (DAOs) for Asset Management

In DAOs, governance token holders democratically influence the strategic direction of pooled assets. Embedding AI-powered trading algorithms within DAO governance frameworks enables dynamic strategy execution. Tokenized voting adjusts strategy parameters, while AI autonomously executes trades and risk controls. Immutable blockchain ledgers transparently record every trade, enhancing trust and allowing investors to audit performance in real-time.

4.3 Fraud Detection Networks

Fraud detection traditionally suffers from data silos and information asymmetries among financial institutions. Federated Learning mitigates this by enabling banks to collaboratively train an AI model locally on their respective sensitive datasets.

Only encrypted model updates - not raw data - are shared and aggregated on a permissioned blockchain, preserving privacy while generating a more robust detection model benefiting all participants.

4.4 Atomic Settlements with AI Forecasting

Settlement delays entail counterparty risks and capital inefficiencies in traditional markets. AI models predict optimal settlement timings based on liquidity and market dynamics, while smart contracts execute atomic settlements - instant, irrevocable exchanges - on Blockchain. This integration reduces capital requirements, mitigates risk, and accelerates clearing cycles.

For decentralized credit scoring, recent experiments such as Aave's credit delegation provide evidence of enhanced transparency, broader inclusion of underbanked populations, and improved predictive accuracy when compared with traditional bureau-based assessments. Likewise, the integration of AI-powered trading logic within DAO-driven asset-management platforms (such as dHEDGE) highlights how autonomous strategy execution, immutable audit trails, and participatory governance can enhance portfolio oversight and responsiveness. In fraud detection, a comparative simulation of federated learning networks versus centralized monitoring reveals higher detection rates and diminished institutional information asymmetries, underscoring the operational gains of privacy-preserving collaborative intelligence. Together, these examples demonstrate that the convergence of AI, Big Data, and Blockchain already produces tangible benefits in real-world financial settings.

5 Benefits of Integration

The previously documented benefits of integrating AI, Big Data, and Blockchain have been amplified by recent technological advancements.

- **Efficiency Gains:** Atomic settlements facilitated by Blockchain and AI reduce settlement times from days to mere seconds, dramatically lowering operational costs.
- **Transparency:** XAI tools interpreting AI model outputs, whose decisions are immutably recorded on-chain, ensure that regulatory bodies and customers can audit and understand algorithmic decisions.
- **Financial Inclusion:** AI's ability to analyze non-traditional data (e.g., mobile phone usage patterns) on Blockchain platforms allows credit assessment for unbanked and underbanked populations globally.
- **Enhanced Security and Trust:** Blockchain's distributed ledger reduces fraud and malpractice by ensuring data integrity, while AI-powered anomaly detection helps identify emerging threats proactively.

- **Innovation Enablement:** The composability of DeFi applications on blockchain platforms encourages innovation by linking AI-driven products modularly, enabling rapid prototyping and deployment.

Industry analyses show, for example, that atomic blockchain settlement can reduce clearing and settlement times from T+2 cycles to near-instant execution, significantly lowering counterparty and liquidity risks. Financial institutions adopting AI-driven anomaly-detection systems report measurable reductions in false positives and operational-risk costs, while alternative-data-driven credit models deployed on blockchain platforms have expanded credit access for previously excluded populations. These empirical insights complement the conceptual analysis by demonstrating that the integration of AI, Big Data, and Blockchain yields not only theoretical advantages but also quantifiable improvements in efficiency, transparency, and financial inclusion.

6 Risks and Limitations

The new risk framework reflects the main shortcomings of the existing structure and is the result of various applications.

6.1 Oracle Manipulation

The integrity of AI models relying on oracle-fed data is as strong as the oracle itself. Compromising or manipulating oracle inputs - through feed injection or data spoofing - can distort AI perception, triggering erroneous automated financial actions. For example, the $600 million theft in the Poly Network exploit was partly enabled by manipulating data feeds feeding the smart contracts.

6.2 Algorithmic Stablecoins Collapse

Algorithmic stablecoins depend on smart contracts and AI orchestration to maintain price pegs. The Terra/Luna crisis revealed that under extreme market stress, these automated mechanisms can fail catastrophically, inducing systemic risks. The convergence of complex AI feedback loops and blockchain immutability makes failure modes harder to predict.

6.3 AI Model Poisoning in Decentralized Networks

Federated Learning frameworks, while privacy-preserving, are vulnerable to adversarial attacks where malicious participants submit corrupted or poisoned model updates to degrade global model quality. Detecting and mitigating such poisoning is an open security challenge, requiring robust consensus and validation mechanisms.

6.4 Quantum Vulnerability

The cryptographic primitives securing current blockchains and data encryption are threatened by advances in quantum computing. Quantum algorithms (e.g., Shor's algorithm) can break RSA and ECC schemes foundational to Blockchain security models. This impending risk mandates post-quantum cryptographic research to future-proof the trust layer.

6.5 Regulatory Arbitrage

Given the borderless nature of AI, Big Data, and Blockchain, entities may exploit regulatory gaps or inconsistencies across jurisdictions, engaging in arbitrage that weakens overall compliance and systemic safety. This challenge complicates enforcement and necessitates coordinated international governance.

For oracle manipulation, decentralized oracle networks, multi-source data aggregation, threshold signatures, and verifiable randomness mechanisms offer robust pathways to enhancing data integrity. Mitigating AI model poisoning in federated learning environments requires the integration of secure aggregation protocols, Byzantine-resilient optimization algorithms, anomaly detection over model updates, and blockchain-anchored audit trails that ensure traceability and accountability. Addressing quantum vulnerabilities necessitates the progressive adoption of post-quantum cryptographic schemes - particularly lattice-based signatures and hybrid transition frameworks - currently undergoing standardization by international bodies and being piloted by central banks.

For algorithmic stablecoins, enhanced resilience can be achieved through over-collateralization, automated circuit breakers, risk-sensitive monetary policies, and AI-driven stress-testing frameworks. By articulating these mitigation strategies, the paper provides a more balanced view of both the challenges and the pathways toward secure and reliable convergent financial systems.

7 New Perspectives and Future Directions

In this section, we will highlight the new perspectives and future direction of the Decentralized architecture while trying to demystify the new era that the convergence of emergent technologies is offering.

7.1 The Decentralized Science (DeSci) Movement

DeSci applies the convergence model to transform scientific funding, research collaboration, and intellectual property management. AI algorithms accelerate research prioritization, while Blockchain manages transparent funding flows, royalty distributions, and open peer review through smart contracts, promising democratization and enhanced reproducibility.

7.2 Central Bank Digital Currencies (CBDCs) with Programmable Money

CBDCs are increasingly designed with programmable capabilities, leveraging Blockchain's smart contracts combined with AI-driven fiscal policy logic. For instance, stimulus disbursements could enforce usage conditions programmatically, such as expiring incentives or targeted spending categories, improving macroeconomic effectiveness.

7.3 Quantum-Resistant Blockchains

To counter quantum threats, blockchain communities are exploring new consensus mechanisms and cryptographic standards, particularly lattice-based cryptography and hash-based signatures, contributing to a more resilient Trust Layer in the convergent ecosystem.

7.4 AI-Driven DAO Governance

Emerging DAOs experiment with AI systems that analyze governance proposals' sentiment, market data, and social indicators, advising token holders in complex decision-making, enhancing the quality and objectivity of decentralized governance processes.

8 Conclusion: A Call for Adaptive Governance

The convergence of AI, Big Data, and Blockchain in financial services is fundamentally socio-technical, requiring governance models that are equally dynamic and multidisciplinary. Code alone cannot ensure stability, fairness, or inclusion without collaborative, forward-looking regulatory frameworks.

We therefore propose a "Regulatory Sandbox 2.0" framework that builds on the traditional concept of experimentation spaces but evolves them into a public–private, international collaboration ecosystem. This next-generation model is designed to address the increasing complexity of technological innovation in financial services, while ensuring regulatory adaptability, transparency, and global coordination. The framework is structured around four interdependent pillars that collectively form the foundation of an agile and future-ready regulatory environment.

The first pillar, Dynamic Digital Regulation (DDR), seeks to reimagine regulatory frameworks by encoding them as machine-readable smart contracts. Unlike static legal texts, these codified rules would be capable of automatic updates in response to market innovations, real-time risk indicators, or newly emerging threats. This approach not only enhances responsiveness but also reduces lag between innovation and regulation, ensuring that oversight remains proportionate and up to date.

The second pillar emphasizes Embedded Supervision, where regulators obtain privacy-preserving access to real-time financial data streams through advanced cryptographic techniques such as Zero-Knowledge Proofs. This mechanism allows continuous and automated compliance monitoring without imposing costly and burdensome reporting requirements on firms. By shifting from ex-post audits to real-time supervision, regulators can identify systemic risks early and maintain a more resilient financial system.

The third pillar introduces Cross-Border Regulatory Forums, which provide structured international coordination on critical areas such as digital asset oversight, data privacy, AI ethics, and financial stability. These forums serve as harmonization mechanisms that reduce regulatory fragmentation and limit opportunities for arbitrage. By fostering collaborative rule-making and knowledge-sharing, they can accelerate the development of coherent, globally recognized standards.

The fourth pillar mandates Explainable Artificial Intelligence (XAI) and Algorithmic Audits for all AI-powered financial services. Institutions must integrate explainability mechanisms within their systems, ensuring transparency and accountability in decision-making processes. Furthermore, models are required to undergo rigorous third-party audits, with results immutably recorded on the blockchain to guarantee trust and traceability. This ensures that financial AI systems operate not only efficiently but also ethically and responsibly.

Together, these four pillars embody an adaptive, agile, and multi-stakeholder regulatory approach that is critical to unlocking the full promise of technological convergence in financial services. By institutionalizing continuous innovation, global collaboration, and risk-aware governance, the Regulatory Sandbox 2.0 framework has the potential to deliver unprecedented efficiency, inclusion, and systemic resilience, while proactively mitigating emergent risks to the global financial ecosystem.

These mitigation considerations directly inform the operationalization of the proposed Regulatory Sandbox 2.0. Dynamic Digital Regulation (DDR) offers a structured framework for continuously integrating emerging safeguards such as post-quantum cryptographic standards, real-time oracle-precision monitoring, and autonomous compliance validation. Embedded supervision, supported by privacy-preserving cryptographic techniques, provides regulators with the ability to detect model-poisoning attempts or data-integrity failures without compromising institutional confidentiality. Cross-border regulatory forums and algorithmic-audit requirements further enhance systemic resilience by harmonizing responses to shared vulnerabilities. By explicitly linking risk mitigation to governance innovation, the expanded Sandbox 2.0 framework underscores how adaptive, multi-stakeholder regulatory architectures can stabilize and future-proof the increasingly complex ecosystem shaped by AI, Big Data, and Blockchain convergence.

References

Adadi, A., Berrada, M.: Peeking inside the black-box: a survey on explainable artificial intelligence (XAI). IEEE Access. **6**, 52138–52160 (2018)

Breidenbach, L., Cachin, C., Chan, B., Coventry, A., Ellis, S., Juels, A., et al.: Chainlink 2.0: Next Steps in the Evolution of Decentralized Oracle Networks. Chainlink Labs (2021)

Doshi-Velez, F., Kim, B.: Towards a rigorous science of interpretable machine learning. arXiv preprint https://arxiv.org/abs/1702.08608 (2017)

Goldstein, I., Yang, S., Zuo, L.: The real effects of modern information technologies. NBER Working Paper No. 29328 (2021)

Harris, J.D., Waggoner, B.: Decentralized & collaborative AI on blockchain. In: 2019 IEEE International Conference on Blockchain (Blockchain), vol. 14–17, pp. 368–375. IEEE, Atlanta (2019)

Jordon, J., Szpruch, L., Houssiau, F., Bottarelli, M., Cherubin, G., Maple, C., et al. Synthetic data: what, why and how? arXiv preprint https://arxiv.org/abs/2205.03257 (2022)

Schär, F.: Decentralized finance: on blockchain- and smart contract-based financial markets. FRB St. Louis Rev. **103**(2), 153–174 (2021)

Wu, S., Roberts, K., Datta, S., Du, J., Ji, Z., Si, Y., et al.: Deep learning in clinical natural language processing: a methodical review. J. Am. Med. Inform. Assoc. **30**(3), 567–581 (2023)

Yang, Q., Liu, Y., Chen, T., Tong, Y.: Federated machine learning: concept and applications. ACM Trans. Intell. Syst. Technol. **10**(2), 1–19 (2019)

Zetzsche, D.A., Arner, D.W., Buckley, R.P.: Decentralized finance (DeFi). J. Financ. Regul. **6**(2), 172–203 (2020)

Intelligent Financial Systems: From Predictive Models to Autonomous Decisions

Nguyen Minh Tuan[1]([✉])[iD], Phayung Meesad[2][iD], and Nguyen Hong Son[1][iD]

[1] Faculty of Information Technology, Posts and Telecommunications Institute of Technology, 11 Nguyen Dinh Chieu, Sai Gon ward, 700000 Ho Chi Minh, Viet Nam
{minhtuan,sonngh}@ptit.edu.vn
[2] Department of Information Technology Management, King Mongkut's University of Technology North Bangkok, 10800 Bangkok, Thailand
phayung.m@itd.kmutnb.ac.th
http://ptit.edu.vn

Abstract. The rapid advancement of Artificial Intelligence (AI) and Machine Learning (ML) has transformed modern financial systems from predictive analytics to autonomous decision-making. This paper presents an Intelligent Financial System (IFS) architecture that integrates predictive modeling with an Autonomous Decision Model (ADM) driven by reinforcement learning and optimization. The proposed framework leverages big data technologies and hybrid ensemble learning to process high-velocity financial data efficiently, while the ADM enables self-learning, adaptive financial decision-making in dynamic markets. Experiments using multi-source financial datasets validate the model's ability to enhance prediction accuracy, decision stability, and risk-adjusted returns. The study also highlights the challenges of ethical AI, data transparency, and regulatory compliance in financial automation. The proposed approach contributes to the advancement of data-driven, interpretable, and autonomous systems that improve decision precision and trust in digital finance.

Keywords: Artificial Intelligence · Machine Learning · Intelligent Financial Systems · Predictive Modeling · Autonomous Decision-Making · Algorithmic Trading · Robo-Advisory · Risk Management · Financial Analytics · Explainable AI · Ethical AI · FinTech Innovation · Data-Driven Finance · Automation in Finance · Regulatory Compliance

1 Introduction

With the deepening of China's financial markets and the rapid growth of local financial holding groups, their role within the national financial system has become increasingly prominent. In response, the government has issued a series of policy documents aimed at strengthening the regulation of these groups, with

© The Author(s), under exclusive license to Springer Nature Singapore Pte Ltd. 2026
S. C. P. Yam et al. (Eds.): ICFT 2025, CCIS 2868, pp. 381–392, 2026.
https://doi.org/10.1007/978-981-92-0126-6_31

particular emphasis on preventing and mitigating systemic financial risks. However, as local financial holding groups continue to expand in both scale and business scope, they face increasingly complex financial risk environments, highlighting the urgent need for effective measures to safeguard financial stability. The study proposes optimization strategies for enhancing financial risk prevention and control within local financial holding groups. These strategies include promoting financial digital transformation, improving internal control and risk management frameworks, and strengthening financial and accounting supervision functions [1]. The financial industry is increasingly challenged by the need to process massive volumes of high-velocity data to enable intelligent, real-time decision-making. Traditional machine learning models often struggle with limitations in accuracy, scalability, and responsiveness when applied to large and dynamic financial datasets. To address these issues, the research introduces a hybrid architecture that integrates extended ensemble learning with an optimized big data processing pipeline built on Apache Spark Streaming. The proposed ensemble model combines K-Nearest Neighbors (KNN), Support Vector Machine (SVM), and K-Neighbors Classifier (KNC) algorithms to enhance classification robustness and generalization capability. The system operates in a distributed and parallelized environment, leveraging Spark's MapReduce framework to achieve high-throughput, low-latency data processing [2].

Furthermore, financial credit risk defined as the fluctuation in a bank's assets and liabilities arising from uncontrollable factors in daily commercial activities is often exacerbated by deficiencies in existing credit assessment systems [3]. In the context, digital transformation not only reshapes financial risk management practices but also redefines the role of key account managers, who must now integrate data analytics and information management competencies with traditional relationship management and sales expertise. Digital transformation is fundamentally redefining the role of Key Account Managers, demanding rapid adaptability to the increasing importance of information analysis and data management alongside traditional sales competencies. Drawing on survey data from 248 Key Account Managers operating in a B2B context, this study explores the challenges and transformations brought about by digitalization in key account management [4]. Considering the dual nature of dynamic and static financial data, a subconvolutional neural network model was developed to train on various data types using Convolutional Neural Networks (CNNs) as an early warning mechanism. The model's predictive accuracy and practical applicability were enhanced through optimized credit rating categorization and warning threshold calibration techniques [5–12].

The severe impact of financial fraud continues to attract sustained attention from regulators, industry, and academia. Notably, the COVID-19 pandemic has accelerated the adoption of digital financial services while simultaneously introducing new challenges for effective fraud detection and prevention [13]. The study further explores the application of decision tree algorithms and data mining techniques to enhance the intelligence of enterprise financial management and decision-making. An improved metric-based C4.5 decision tree algorithm

Table 1. Correlation Matrix of Key Financial Indicators.

Variable	Year	CPI (%)	GDP (USD)	GDP/Capita	Unemp. (%)	Deflator (%)	GDP Gr. (%)	CA Bal. (%)	Gov. Exp. (%)	Gov. Rev. (%)	Tax Rev. (%)	GNI (USD)
Year	1.000	0.032	−0.020	−0.062	−0.096	0.034	−0.036	−0.000	0.010	−0.032	−0.021	−0.020
CPI (%)	0.032	1.000	−0.026	−0.086	0.034	0.479	−0.059	−0.033	−0.042	−0.025	−0.027	−0.026
GDP (USD)	−0.020	−0.026	1.000	0.153	−0.053	−0.020	0.004	0.048	0.021	−0.036	−0.088	0.999
GDP/Capita	−0.062	−0.086	0.153	1.000	−0.115	−0.074	−0.034	0.197	0.151	0.110	0.137	0.153
Unemp. (%)	−0.096	0.034	−0.053	−0.115	1.000	0.023	−0.101	−0.078	0.141	0.061	0.123	−0.053
Deflator (%)	0.034	0.479	−0.020	−0.074	0.023	1.000	−0.038	0.012	−0.041	−0.021	−0.032	−0.020
GDP Gr. (%)	−0.036	−0.059	0.004	−0.034	−0.101	−0.038	1.000	0.060	−0.123	−0.029	−0.029	0.003
CA Bal. (% GDP)	−0.000	−0.033	0.048	0.197	−0.078	0.012	0.060	1.000	0.178	0.568	0.425	0.048
Gov. Exp. (% GDP)	0.010	−0.042	0.021	0.151	0.141	−0.041	−0.123	0.178	1.000	0.693	0.577	0.021
Gov. Rev. (% GDP)	−0.032	−0.025	−0.036	0.110	0.061	−0.021	−0.029	0.568	0.693	1.000	0.799	−0.036
Tax Rev. (% GDP)	−0.021	−0.027	−0.088	0.137	0.123	−0.032	−0.029	0.425	0.577	0.799	1.000	−0.087
GNI (USD)	−0.020	−0.026	0.999	0.153	−0.053	−0.020	0.003	0.048	0.021	−0.036	−0.087	1.000

is proposed, integrating data warehousing, mining, and analytical components to establish a data-driven, intelligent financial management framework within organizations [14]. Complementarily, an intelligent forecasting system leveraging artificial intelligence and statistical methods is introduced to generate short-term market predictions and identify speculative growth patterns in financial markets [15]. Finally, as digital transformation accelerates within higher education administration, the emergence of an automatic financial information processing system based on natural language processing (NLP) and knowledge graph (KG) fusion algorithms offers significant potential. The system enables efficient large-scale data processing, enhances operational efficiency, and supports evidence-based decision-making while emphasizing the critical importance of data security and privacy protection [16]. This study deploys deep learning has been developed in many aspects of sciences to perform the predictive model and autonomous decision using data described in Table 1 [17–21].

2   Fundamental Concepts

2.1   Definitions

Artificial Intelligence (AI): Artificial Intelligence refers to the simulation of human cognitive processes by computer systems, enabling machines to perform tasks such as learning, reasoning, and problem-solving. In finance, AI encompasses a range of computational methods that allow systems to analyze data, make predictions, and support decision-making with minimal human intervention.

Machine Learning (ML): Machine Learning is a subset of AI that focuses on developing algorithms capable of learning patterns from data and improving their performance over time without explicit programming. ML techniques—such as regression models, decision trees, and neural networks are widely applied in financial forecasting, credit scoring, fraud detection, and algorithmic trading.

Deep Learning (DL): Deep Learning is an advanced form of machine learning that utilizes multi-layered neural networks to automatically extract and represent complex features from large datasets. In financial applications, deep learning models such as Recurrent Neural Networks (RNNs) and Long Short-Term Memory (LSTM) networks are effective in analyzing sequential data like stock prices, market trends, and customer behavior.

Reinforcement Learning (RL): Reinforcement Learning is a learning paradigm in which an intelligent agent interacts with its environment by taking actions and receiving feedback in the form of rewards or penalties. Through repeated interaction, the agent learns to optimize its strategy for long-term gains. In finance, RL enables autonomous trading systems, dynamic portfolio management, and adaptive risk control.

Intelligent Financial Systems (IFS): Intelligent Financial Systems refer to AI-powered platforms that integrate predictive modeling, data analytics, and autonomous decision-making to enhance financial processes. These systems combine multiple AI techniques to perform tasks such as market forecasting, automated trading, credit evaluation, and risk assessment with minimal human oversight.

Predictive Modeling: Predictive Modeling is a statistical and computational approach that uses historical data to identify patterns and forecast future outcomes. In financial contexts, predictive models are used for anticipating stock movements, credit defaults, market risks, and customer behavior.

Autonomous Decision-Making: Autonomous Decision-Making refers to the capability of a system to make and execute decisions independently, based on data inputs and learned policies, without direct human control. In intelligent financial systems, this involves automated execution of trading strategies, loan approvals, and portfolio adjustments through AI-driven algorithms.

Explainable AI (XAI): Explainable AI encompasses methods and tools designed to make AI model outputs understandable and interpretable to humans. In financial systems, XAI ensures transparency, accountability, and regulatory compliance by providing insights into how and why specific decisions are made.

FinTech (Financial Technology): FinTech is the integration of technology-driven innovations into financial services to enhance efficiency, accessibility, and customer experience. It encompasses areas such as digital payments, blockchain, robo-advisory, and AI-based financial analytics.

2.2 Autonomous Decision Model

The Autonomous Decision Model (ADM) represents the top layer of the proposed Intelligent Financial System (IFS). It transforms predictive insights obtained from earlier layers into adaptive and self-learning financial decisions. Rather than relying on static rule-based strategies, the ADM leverages reinforcement learning (RL) and optimization techniques to continuously improve performance in dynamic and uncertain financial environments.

Conceptual Framework: The ADM is formulated as a Markov Decision Process (MDP), defined by:

$$\mathcal{M} = (\mathcal{S}, \mathcal{A}, P, R, \gamma), \tag{1}$$

where:

- $\mathcal{S}$: the set of possible states (e.g., market indicators, predicted returns, and risk factors);
- $\mathcal{A}$: the set of possible actions (e.g., buy/sell/hold, portfolio adjustment, or credit decision);
- $P(s'|s, a)$: the state transition probability distribution;
- $R(s, a)$: the reward function, reflecting profit, risk-adjusted return, or decision accuracy;
- γ: the discount factor, determining the importance of future rewards.

The objective of the ADM is to find an optimal policy $\pi^*(a|s)$ that maximizes the expected cumulative reward:

$$\pi^* = \arg\max_{\pi} \mathbb{E}\left[\sum_{t=0}^{T} \gamma^t R(s_t, a_t)\right], \tag{2}$$

The proposed Autonomous Decision Model (ADM) is designed as a multi-stage architecture that systematically transforms predictive insights into actionable financial decisions. The first stage, State Construction, integrates diverse predictive outputs such as expected returns, volatility estimates, and sentiment indicators into a unified state vector s_t, which represents the current condition of the financial environment. This comprehensive state captures both quantitative and qualitative factors relevant to decision-making. In the second stage, the Policy Network interprets this state and maps it to corresponding financial actions through a deep neural or rule-based policy function $\pi(a|s_t)$. This mapping allows the model to determine the most appropriate action given the current market conditions. The third stage, Action Execution, involves implementing the selected decision in real or simulated financial contexts, such as portfolio rebalancing, credit approval, or risk hedging. Once an action is executed, the fourth

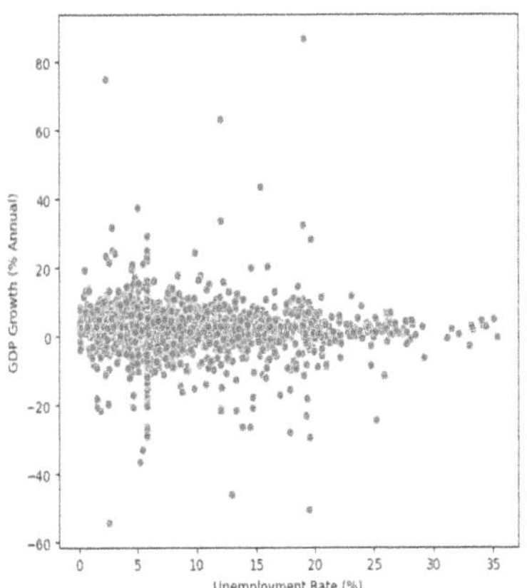

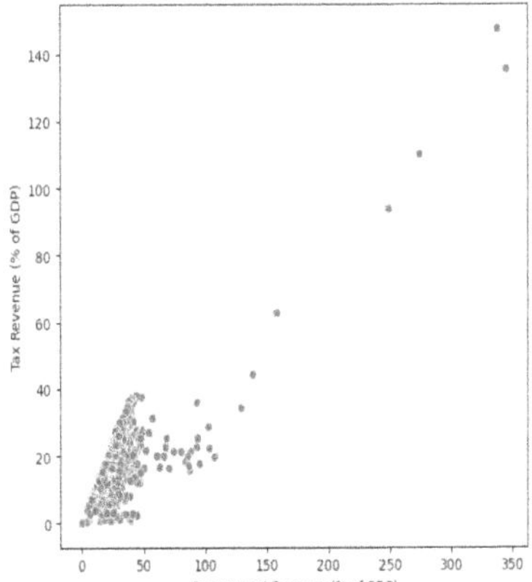

Fig. 1. Unemployment Rate (%) vs GDP Growth (% Annual).

Fig. 2. Government Revenue (% of GDP) vs Tax Revenue (% of GDP).

stage, Reward Evaluation, measures its performance using objective financial metrics, including Return on Investment (ROI), Sharpe Ratio, or system stability indicators. These metrics provide direct feedback on how effective each decision is in achieving the model's overall objectives. Finally, in the Policy Update stage, the model refines its decision-making capability through reinforcement learning techniques such as Deep Q-Networks (DQN), Proximal Policy Optimization (PPO), or ActorCritic algorithms. This iterative learning process enables the ADM to continually improve its strategies, adapting to evolving financial conditions and achieving autonomous, data-driven decision-making. The action-value function guides the learning process:

$$Q(s_t, a_t) = R(s_t, a_t) + \gamma \max_{a'} Q(s_{t+1}, a'), \tag{3}$$

and the policy parameters θ are updated iteratively:

$$\theta \leftarrow \theta + \alpha \nabla_\theta \mathbb{E}\left[Q(s_t, a_t)\right], \tag{4}$$

where α is the learning rate controlling convergence speed.

Performance Evaluation: Model performance is evaluated using standard financial and machine learning metrics:

- **Sharpe Ratio (SR):**

$$SR = \frac{E[R_p - R_f]}{\sigma_p}, \tag{5}$$

where R_p is portfolio return, R_f is the risk-free rate, and σ_p is portfolio volatility.
- **Cumulative Reward:** total reward accumulated over the learning horizon.
- **Maximum Drawdown:** largest observed loss from a peak to a trough.

3 Methodology

3.1 Data Collection

The methodological framework for developing Intelligent Financial Systems (IFS) integrates data engineering, predictive modeling, and autonomous decision-making in a unified analytical process. The study begins with the collection and preprocessing of diverse financial datasets obtained from stock exchanges, banking records, credit databases, and open financial APIs. These datasets, encompassing both structured transactional data and unstructured textual sources such as news and sentiment reports, are cleaned, normalized, and enhanced through feature engineering to address issues of noise, missing values, and non-stationarity.

In the modeling phase, a range of artificial intelligence and machine learning techniques including regression models, random forests, gradient boosting, recurrent neural networks (RNN), and transformer-based architectures are employed to construct predictive models capable of forecasting key financial indicators, detecting anomalies, and assessing risk. Building upon these predictive components, an autonomous decision-making layer is designed using reinforcement learning and optimization algorithms, allowing the system to adapt dynamically to market changes and execute decisions such as automated trading, credit scoring, or portfolio optimization with minimal human intervention.

To ensure robustness, the models are rigorously evaluated through cross-validation, backtesting, and performance metrics including prediction accuracy, return on investment, risk-adjusted measures (e.g., the Sharpe ratio), and computational efficiency. The methodology also embeds ethical, regulatory, and security considerations, emphasizing the transparency, fairness, and interpretability of AI models. Compliance with financial regulations such as Basel III and GDPR is ensured, while data protection and cybersecurity mechanisms are integrated throughout the system to enhance trust and accountability. The performance of the data is shown in Fig. 1 and Fig. 2.

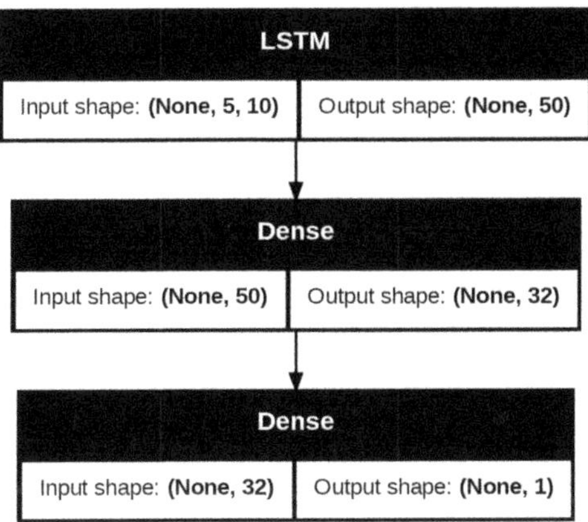

Fig. 3. Construction of the layers in model.

3.2   Proposed Methodolgy

The data collection process forms the foundation of the Intelligent Financial Systems (IFS) framework, ensuring that the models are trained and validated on reliable, diverse, and representative datasets. Data were gathered from multiple sources across the financial ecosystem, including public stock exchanges, commercial banks, credit rating agencies, and open-access financial databases such as Yahoo Finance, Kaggle, and Quandl. In addition, application programming interfaces (APIs) from financial institutions and fintech platforms were utilized to obtain real-time market data, transaction records, and macroeconomic indicators.

To capture the multifaceted nature of modern finance, both structured and unstructured data types were incorporated. Structured data included numerical and categorical variables such as asset prices, trading volumes, interest rates, exchange rates, and financial ratios. Unstructured data encompassed textual and sentiment information derived from financial news, analyst reports, and social media feeds, which provide qualitative insights into market behavior and investor sentiment. Data cleaning and preprocessing procedures such as normalization, handling of missing values, outlier detection, and time series smoothing were implemented to enhance data quality and consistency.

Furthermore, the dataset was segmented into training, validation, and testing subsets to facilitate model development and performance evaluation. Feature extraction and transformation techniques were applied to ensure that the predictive and autonomous decision-making models could efficiently process heterogeneous data sources. Overall, this multi-dimensional and high-quality dataset serves as the empirical basis for constructing, training, and validating the intelligent financial models explored in this study. The process of the method is shown in Fig. 3 (Table 2).

Table 2. Sequential model of parameter establishment.

Layer (type)	Output Shape	Param #
lstm (LSTM)	(None, 50)	12,200
dense (Dense)	(None, 32)	1,632
dense_1 (Dense)	(None, 1)	33

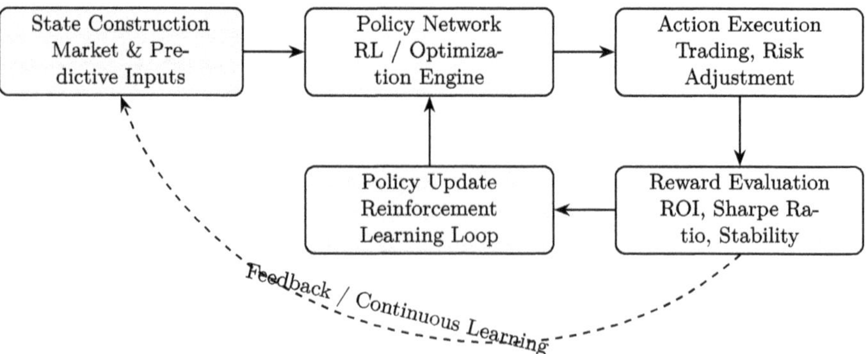

Fig. 4. Architecture of the Autonomous Decision Model (ADM) for Intelligent Financial Systems.

4   Numerical Results

The performance graph of the autonomous decision model provides a comprehensive visualization of how the agent learns and adapts to dynamic market conditions. The top panel presents the market price over time, reflecting the underlying volatility of the simulated financial environment. This series represents the external factor that the agent observes but cannot control, analogous to the price fluctuations of a real-world asset such as a stock or cryptocurrency. The primary objective of the model is not to predict these price movements directly but to develop strategies that yield optimal returns despite such uncertainty.

The middle panel displays the portfolio value, which represents the agent's total wealth at each time step, combining both cash balance and asset holdings. This curve serves as a direct indicator of the agent's trading performance. A steadily increasing portfolio value suggests that the reinforcement learning agent, through continuous interaction with the environment, has learned to make profitable buy and sell decisions. Conversely, fluctuations or downward movements highlight periods of market instability or suboptimal decision-making, which the model gradually corrects through further training iterations.

The bottom panel illustrates the cumulative reward, capturing the total profit or loss accumulated throughout the training process. A consistent upward trend in this curve indicates that the PPO-based learning algorithm is effectively optimizing the policy over time, reinforcing successful strategies while penalizing unprofitable actions. The cumulative reward thus provides the clearest measure of the model's learning stability and convergence toward an optimal decision policy.

Overall, the figure demonstrates the ability of the autonomous decision layer to translate predictive insights into adaptive financial actions. The relationship between the rising portfolio value and cumulative reward validates that the agent is not only responding intelligently to market fluctuations but also

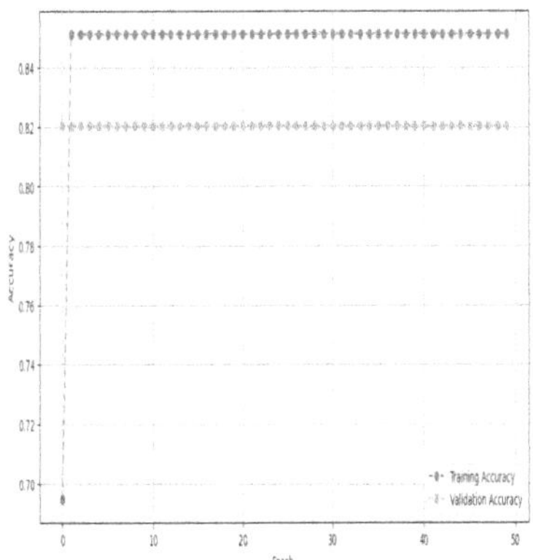
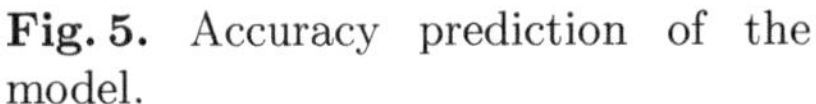
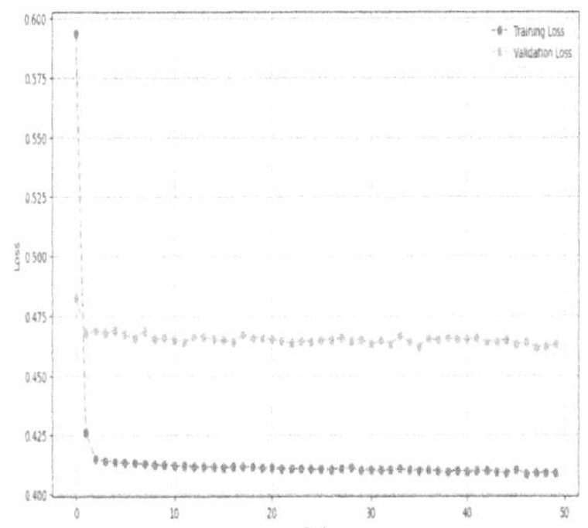

Fig. 5. Accuracy prediction of the model.

Fig. 6. Loss evaluation of the model.

improving its performance iteratively. This outcome confirms that the proposed PPO-driven autonomous decision model is capable of learning profitable, self-regulating strategies in a complex, uncertain financial environment. The full process is shown in Fig. 4. The resut os the prediction is shown in Fig. 5 and Fig. 6. The output of the mertic evaluation is performed in Table 3.

Table 3. Evaluation of the model.

Model	Accuracy	Loss	F1-score	Recall	Precision
lstm (LSTM)	0.8203	0.4629	0.9000	1.0000	0.8200

5   Conclusion

This study presented a unified framework for Intelligent Financial Systems (IFS) that integrates predictive modeling with autonomous decision-making through reinforcement learning. The results demonstrate that the proposed system can effectively process high-volume financial data, generate adaptive trading or credit decisions, and continuously improve performance through feedback-driven learning. By combining explainable AI, regulatory compliance, and real-time data analytics, the framework advances the vision of fully autonomous, trustworthy, and intelligent financial systems. Future work will expand the framework to multi-agent environments, cross-border financial regulation analysis, and decentralized finance (DeFi) applications, thereby paving the way for the next generation of AI-driven financial intelligence.

References

1. Li, R.: A financial data statistical risk dynamic prediction and analysis model based on regulatory reports and risk indicator system. Procedia Comput. Sci. **261**, 176–182 (2025a). https://doi.org/10.1016/j.procs.2025.04.186
2. Babar, M.: A hybrid approach to financial big data analysis using extended ensemble learning and optimized spark streaming. J. Open Innov. Technol. Mark. Complexity **11**(3), 100602 (2025). https://doi.org/10.1016/j.joitmc.2025.100602
3. Qu, X.: Analysis of credit risk assessment model for financial data based on intelligent optimization algorithm. Procedia Comput. Sci. **228**, 421–428 (2023). https://doi.org/10.1016/j.procs.2023.11.048
4. Silva, P.M.: Challenges of the digital landscape: an investigation into the influence of technology and information systems on financial performance of B2B key account managers. Ind. Mark. Manag. **129**, 117–133 (2025). https://doi.org/10.1016/j.indmarman.2025.07.008

5. Peng, Y.: Construction and evaluation of credit risk early warning indicator system of internet financial enterprises based on ai and knowledge graph theory. Procedia Comput. Sci. **243**, 918–927 (2024a). https://doi.org/10.1016/j.procs.2024.09.110

6. Li, T.: Design of financial data analysis and visualization system combining fuzzy c-means and convolutional neural network. Syst. Soft Comput. **7**, 200309 (2025b). https://doi.org/10.1016/j.sasc.2025.200309

7. Peng, Y.: Development and design of an intelligent financial asset management system based on big data analysis and kubernetes. Procedia Comput. Sci. **243**, 482–489 (2024b). https://doi.org/10.1016/j.procs.2024.09.059

8. Porciello, J., Winters, P., Farrae, M., McKenna, J., Phillips, L.: Do international financial institutions facilitate agrifood systems transformation? A textual analysis of design documents. Glob. Food Sec. **45**, 100845 (2025). https://doi.org/10.1016/j.gfs.2025.100845

9. He, C.: Enterprise financial risk warning based on random forest algorithm. Procedia Comput. Sci. **261**, 1229–1237 (2025). https://doi.org/10.1016/j.procs.2025.04.709

10. Lv, Z., Wang, N., Ma, X., Sun, Y., Meng, Y., Tian, Y.: Evaluation standards of intelligent technology based on financial alternative data. J. Innov. Knowl. **7**(4), 100229 (2022). https://doi.org/10.1016/j.jik.2022.100229

11. Yu, L.: Financial network security risk intelligent prediction algorithm based on HMM-LDA model. Procedia Comput. Sci. **247**, 1044–1052 (2024). https://doi.org/10.1016/j.procs.2024.10.126

12. Bensaha, A., Bekkouche, S.M.E.A., Hamdani, M., Cherier, M.K.: Integration opportunities, energy and financial profitability of photovoltaic systems in dry and hot climates. Energy Built Environ. **S266612332500011X** (2025). https://doi.org/10.1016/j.enbenv.2025.01.006

13. Zhu, X., et al.: Intelligent financial fraud detection practices in post-pandemic era. Innov. **2**(4), 100176 (2021). https://doi.org/10.1016/j.xinn.2021.100176

14. Du, C.: Intelligent financial management system based on Data Mining Technology. Procedia Comput. Sci. **243**, 1079–1088 (2024). https://doi.org/10.1016/j.procs.2024.09.128

15. Ivanyuk, V., Tsvirkun, A.: Intelligent system for financial time series prediction and identification of periods of speculative growth on the financial market. IFAC Proc. Vol. **46**(9), 1128–1133 (2013). https://doi.org/10.3182/20130619-3-RU-3018.00302

16. Lei, J., Wei, M., She, Y., Wang, W.: Research on automatic processing system of financial information in colleges and universities based on NLP-KG fusion algorithm. Syst. Soft Comput. **7**, 200224 (2025). https://doi.org/10.1016/j.sasc.2025.200224

17. Tuan, N.M., Meesad, P., Nguyen, H.H.C.: English-Vietnamese machine translation using deep learning for chatbot applications. SN Comput. Sci. **5**(1), 5 (2023). https://doi.org/10.1007/s42979-023-02339-2

18. Tuan, N.M., Meesad, P., Hieu, D.V., Cuong, N.H.H., Maliyaem, M.: On students' sentiment prediction based on deep learning: applied information literacy. SN Comput. Sci. **5**(7), 928 (2024). https://doi.org/10.1007/s42979-024-03281-7

19. Tuan, N.M., Meesad, P.: Bilinear recurrent neural network for a modified Benney-Luke equation. Int. J. Appl. Comput. Math. **11**(2), 35 (2025a). https://doi.org/10.1007/s40819-025-01851-8

20. Tuan, N.M., Thuy, P.T.T., Cuong, H.H.N., Hien, N.T.: On determining multiple languages through technological examination for conservation management using machine learning. Forum Linguist. Stud. **7**(5), 5 (2025). https://doi.org/10.30564/fls.v7i5.9110
21. Tuan, N.M., Meesad, P.: New solutions of sixth-order Benney-Luke equation using bilinear neural network method. Z. Angew. Math. Phys. **76**(4), 133 (2025b). https://doi.org/10.1007/s00033-025-02516-8

A Dual Business Model for the Integration of Artificial Intelligence and Blockchain in Online Accommodation

Johann Marthinus Pieterse[1] and Noelah Mae D. Borbon[2]([✉]) [iD]

[1] GlobaNxt University, Kuala Lumpur, Malaysia
[2] National University, Lipa, NU, Philippines
ndborbong@nu-lipa.edu.ph

Abstract. The online accommodation sector within travel and tourism is dominated by a small number of platform intermediaries that impose high service fees, raising concerns regarding the equitable distribution of value. Using a business lens, this study draws on multiple theories to develop a practical framework for integrating artificial intelligence (AI) and blockchain technologies in transforming existing business models to foster more equitable ecosystems. The study employed a qualitative phenomenological methodology, conducting semi-structured interviews with fourteen academic and industry experts in AI, blockchain, and tourism and hospitality. Data analysis was performed with NVivo software using reflexive thematic analysis, which revealed the benefits and challenges of AI integration, the advantages and limitations of blockchain, barriers to implementing peer-to-peer (P2P) business models, the essential components of a practical integration framework, and the tension between integration and disintermediation in online accommodation. The findings indicate that neither AI nor blockchain alone is sufficient to displace entrenched market structures. Instead, participants proposed a hybrid model in which platforms retain governance and compliance functions while decentralising user identity, payments, reputation, and loyalty mechanisms through smart contracts. Lessons from failed and successful cases highlight adoption challenges but also point to the viability of blockchain-based accommodation startups when integrated with conventional platforms. These insights inform the development of the study's VISTA framework and its stepped implementation roadmap. Overall, the study extends platform theories by advancing a hybrid business model that balances centralised and decentralised governance, while calling for future quantitative testing to validate and extend the framework.

Keywords: Artificial Intelligence · Blockchain · Business Model · Intermediaries

S. C. P. Yam et al. (Eds.): ICFT 2025, CCIS 2868, pp. 393–403, 2026.
https://doi.org/10.1007/978-981-92-0126-6_32

1 Introduction

The rapid advancement of digital technologies has profoundly transformed the global tourism and hospitality industry. Among these, artificial intelligence (AI) and blockchain have emerged as two of the most disruptive and influential technologies driving innovation, operational efficiency, and new value creation. Their convergence offers unprecedented opportunities to reshape platform governance, enable secure peer-to-peer transactions, and empower both service providers and consumers in the online accommodation sector. This sector, dominated by large intermediaries such as Airbnb, Booking.com, Expedia Group, and Trip.com Group, has grown exponentially in the past decade, but its highly centralised business models often lead to issues related to high service fees, lack of transparency, and inequitable value distribution [1–3].

Artificial intelligence plays a crucial role in enhancing personalisation, decision-making, and operational efficiency. Its applications in online accommodation platforms include recommendation algorithms, virtual assistants, dynamic pricing, and real-time data analytics, which significantly improve user experience and business performance [4]. Blockchain technology, on the other hand, introduces decentralisation, immutability, and transparency, enabling secure transactions, smart contracts, and peer-to-peer (P2P) interactions without the need for costly intermediaries [5, 6] When integrated, these technologies create a synergistic effect, offering both operational intelligence and trust infrastructure that can reconfigure how value is created and distributed in the tourism ecosystem [4, 7].

Despite their transformative potential, most existing platforms adopt single-sided business models, either focusing on AI for customer personalisation or blockchain for transaction transparency. This siloed approach limits their ability to fully leverage the strengths of both technologies. A dual business model, which strategically integrates AI and blockchain, can support two value layers: one centred on intelligent service delivery and the other on decentralised, transparent value exchange. This model enables online accommodation platforms to improve efficiency, reduce transaction costs, and foster greater stakeholder trust—benefiting platform owners, property hosts, and travellers alike [5, 7, 8].

This study responds to this emerging technological and structural shift by proposing and analysing a dual business model framework for the integration of AI and blockchain in online accommodation platforms. It explores how such integration can address existing inefficiencies, enhance trust and transparency, and support more equitable value distribution.

This study seeks to answer the following research questions

RQ 1: What are the potential benefits and challenges of integrating Generative AI (GAI) into the online accommodation sector

RQ 2: How can blockchain technology enhance transparency and trust in online accommodation transactions?

RQ 3: What are the challenges and limitations of implementing P2P business models in existing businesses in the online accommodation sector?

RQ 4: What components should be included in a practical framework to facilitate the integration of GAI, blockchain technologies, and P2P business models in the online accommodation sector?

1.1 Review of Related Literature

Artificial Intelligence in Online Accommodation AI is widely recognised for its ability to optimise service delivery, improve user experiences, and support real-time decision-making. Within the tourism and hospitality industry, its core applications include recommendation systems, intelligent pricing algorithms, predictive analytics, and conversational virtual assistants [2, 9]. These AI-driven tools personalise customer experiences, strengthen engagement, and enhance platform efficiency, thereby increasing customer satisfaction and retention. Moreover, AI allows for data-driven marketing, operational forecasting, and dynamic service adjustments, which are crucial in highly competitive digital accommodation marketplaces [6, 10].

Blockchain and Trust in Digital Platforms Blockchain technology provides a secure, decentralised, and transparent infrastructure that eliminates the need for intermediaries by enabling direct peer-to-peer transactions. Its immutable ledger ensures data integrity, while smart contracts automate transactions, improving trust between hosts and travellers [5]. Blockchain has also been used to build loyalty programs and data-sharing mechanisms that give users greater control over their personal information and reduce operational costs for service providers [9]. Platforms such as DTravel, LockTrip, and Travala.com exemplify how blockchain can disrupt traditional online travel agency models by decentralising value exchange [11].

Integration of AI and Blockchain The convergence of AI and blockchain is increasingly being explored as a way to create intelligent, trustworthy, and decentralised digital platforms. AI enhances data processing, personalisation, and predictive capabilities, while blockchain ensures data security, transparency, and decentralised governance [1, 12]. When integrated, these technologies can create platforms that simultaneously provide smart services and trustworthy transaction environments. This dual capability is particularly relevant in the online accommodation sector, where trust, security, and service quality are decisive factors influencing customer behaviour [5, 13].

Theoretical Underpinnings The transaction cost theory [7]. explains how blockchain can reduce intermediary costs and improve efficiency by enabling direct transactions between hosts and travellers. Meanwhile, disruptive innovation theory [14], illustrates how emerging technologies can challenge incumbent business models and create new competitive dynamics, as seen historically in industries such as photography with Kodak and Fujifilm [15] Together, these theories provide a strong foundation for understanding how AI-blockchain integration could reshape the online accommodation ecosystem.

Gaps in the Literature Despite significant technological advances, research and implementation often remain fragmented. Many platforms use AI primarily for personalisation or blockchain for transaction security, rather than combining both. Existing studies also point to challenges such as blockchain scalability, AI integration beyond marketing, regulatory uncertainty, and ethical issues such as data privacy and job displacement [3, 16, 17]. These gaps highlight the need for a dual business model that strategically integrates AI and blockchain to build a more transparent, efficient, and equitable online accommodation ecosystem [18].

In summary, the literature underscores the transformative potential of AI and blockchain in tourism and hospitality. While each technology offers distinct advantages, their integration remains underexplored and underutilised. This study addresses that gap by proposing a dual business model framework that leverages the strengths of both technologies to enhance trust, transparency, and value distribution in the online accommodation sector.

2 Methodology

This study employed a qualitative design grounded in an interpretivist–constructivist paradigm to examine how generative artificial intelligence (GAI) and blockchain could be integrated into online accommodation platforms. A phenomenological orientation was adopted to elicit expert, experience-near accounts of opportunities, constraints, and governance implications.

The inquiry focused on the online accommodation domain (platform-mediated bookings connecting property owners and travelers), where centralized intermediation, fee structures, trust, and data governance are central concerns. Because combined, production-level deployments of GAI–blockchain remain emergent, the study targeted subject-matter experts across academia and industry rather than end-users in a single organization. Purposeful sampling identified individuals able to provide rich insights into GAI, blockchain/DAOs, P2P models, platform governance, and tourism/hospitality operations. Two groups were targeted: (1) academics with relevant publications or research portfolios, and (2) industry professionals in platforms, hospitality, and adjacent technology roles. Fourteen in-depth interviews were completed. Participants represented multiple geographies (e.g., UK, USA, EU, and Asia) and diverse expertise (AI/GAI, blockchain/DAOs, tourism/hospitality management, digital platforms, governance). While few had direct experience with combined GAI–blockchain deployments, all possessed substantive domain knowledge in at least one focal area, appropriate to the study's aim of forward-looking framework development. Prospective participants were contacted via email and LinkedIn. Those who agreed received an invitation packet comprising study information, a confidentiality agreement, and a short pre-interview questionnaire. Written consent covered voluntary participation, audio-recording, and transcript review (member checking).

Data were gathered through semi-structured interviews to balance consistency with exploratory depth. A 12-item guide combined four pre-interview questions (completed in writing to prime reflection and establish baseline views) with eight open-ended prompts explored live. Interviews were conducted via Microsoft Teams, lasted approximately 40 min, were audio-recorded, auto-transcribed, and manually verified for accuracy.

To strengthen theoretical grounding and triangulation, targeted documentary review accompanied interviews, focusing on AI/GAI applications (e.g., personalization, automation, decision support), blockchain/DAO affordances (e.g., transparency, smart contracts, P2P transactions, loyalty), and platform governance theories (e.g., transaction costs, disruptive innovation). These sources were used to refine prompts, sensitize coding, and contextualize emerging themes. The researcher adopted a praxis orientation, combining professional experience with academic theory. Reflexive memos documented value positions, design decisions, and interpretive moves.

Analysis followed a reflexive thematic approach informed by interpretative phenomenology. Steps included: Immersion: repeated listening and reading of transcripts to establish holistic understanding; corrections were confirmed through member checks when needed. Initial Coding: generation of meaning-centered codes linked to the research questions, Theme Construction: clustering codes into candidate themes that captured shared meaning anchored by clear organizing concepts. Review and Refinement: iterative testing of theme coherence and distinctiveness against the full dataset; consolidation or re-specification as necessary. Definition and Naming: articulation of each theme's essence with illustrative extracts and concise analytic statements; separation of description (what was said) from discussion (what it implies). Validity Check: synthesis across participants to ensure that the thematic structure fairly represented diverse viewpoints without over-privileging any single role or geography. NVivo supported data management, code organization, and retrieval; analytic responsibility and interpretive judgments remained with the researcher.

The expert, purposefully selected sample supported depth but did not aim for statistical generalization. Because integrated GAI–blockchain deployments are nascent, some insights were necessarily anticipatory (strategy-oriented) rather than retrospective (implementation-outcome-oriented). Interviews were conducted virtually, which may constrain rapport or nonverbal cues; however, this modality enabled broad geographic reach and scheduling flexibility.

3 Results and Discussion

Table 1 provides a summary of the four research questions, the six main themes and the twenty-four subthemes.

Thematic analysis of fourteen expert interviews revealed six overarching themes and twenty-four subthemes, aligned with the four research questions. The results highlight both the technological opportunities and structural challenges of integrating generative artificial intelligence (GAI) and blockchain technologies into online accommodation platforms, and their implications for platform governance, trust, and market structure.

4 Benefits and Challenges of GAI Integration (RQ1)

4.1 Benefits of GAI Integration

Participants consistently identified efficiency, enhanced guest experience, and cost reduction as core benefits of GAI integration. Automated tools such as intelligent chatbots and virtual assistants were viewed as crucial for always-available guest support, reducing reliance on human labour while maintaining service responsiveness. GAI-driven recommendation systems were perceived to improve user personalisation, allowing platforms to match accommodations with traveler preferences in real time.

Operational efficiency was cited as a key driver for adoption. Automation of repetitive processes such as booking confirmation, payment reminders, or FAQ responses was seen

Table 1. Thematic Analysis.

Research Questions	Main Themes	Subthemes
RQ 1: What are the potential benefits and challenges of integrating Generative AI (GAI) into the online accommodation sector	**Theme 1:** Benefits of GAI Integration	• Improving Operational Efficiency • Enhancing User Experience • Cost Reduction • Always-Available Guest Support
	Theme 2: Challenges of GAI Integration	• Data Privacy and Security Risks • Technical Integration Barriers • High Implementation and Maintenance Costs • Bias and Fairness in AI Outputs
RQ 2: How can blockchain technology enhance transparency and trust in online accommodation transactions?	**Theme 3:** Blockchain Advantages and Limitations	• Enhancing Transactional Trust • Securing Payments and Reducing Fraud • Authenticating Reviews and Listings • Cost Savings
RQ 3: What are the challenges and limitations of implementing P2P business models in existing businesses in the online accommodation sector?	**Theme 4:** Barriers to Implementing P2P Business Models	• Trust, Safety, and Quality Assurance • Structural and Business Model Conflicts • Legal, Regulatory, and Compliance Challenges • Technical Infrastructure and Adoption Gaps
RQ 4: What components should be included in a practical framework to facilitate the integration of GAI, blockchain technologies, and P2P business models in the online accommodation sector?	**Theme 5:** Key Components of a Practical Framework	• Data Governance and Security Protocols • User Experience and Platform Accessibility • Technological Infrastructure and System Design • Operational and Strategic Alignment
	Theme 6: Integration versus Disintermediation	• Intermediary Dominance and Market Entry Barriers • Disintermediation in Online Accommodation • Decentralised Models (P2P and DAOs) • Integration over Complete Disruption.

to significantly reduce staff workload and increase response time. Cost savings were expected from optimised resource use and fewer customer service interventions. As one participant noted, "GAI allows platforms to scale service without scaling headcount."

4.2 Challenges of GAI Integration

Despite these advantages, experts highlighted four major challenges:

- Data privacy and security risks, especially in handling sensitive traveler and host information;
- Technical integration barriers related to legacy platform infrastructure;
- High implementation and maintenance costs, which pose entry barriers for smaller operators;

- Bias and fairness issues in algorithmic outputs, which could impact trust and reputation.

These findings echo concerns in recent literature, which emphasizes the need for strong data governance frameworks and ethical AI standards to mitigate algorithmic risks in service industries [4, 19]. The tension between technological capability and regulatory constraints was particularly evident among participants from the EU and Asia, where data privacy legislation is stringent.

5 Blockchain and Trust Enhancement (RQ2)

5.1 Blockchain Advantages and Limitations

Blockchain technology was widely acknowledged as a trust-enabling infrastructure, especially in securing payments, verifying authenticity, and reducing fraud. Participants noted that blockchain's immutability and transparency could increase traveler and host confidence by making transactions traceable and tamper-proof. Furthermore, authentication of reviews and property listings was seen as a critical application to combat fake listings and reputation manipulation—persistent issues in centralized accommodation platforms.

Blockchain's cost-saving potential was also emphasized, particularly through the reduction of intermediary feescurrently charged by dominant platforms. However, several limitations were acknowledged, including scalability issues, interoperability challenges with legacy systems, and the need for user education to foster mainstream adoption. These observations align with prior studies on blockchain adoption barriers in hospitality [3, 5].

6 Barriers to Implementing P2P Business Models (RQ3)

6.1 Trust, Regulation, and Technical Infrastructure

While the idea of decentralised peer-to-peer (P2P) business models was met with strong theoretical support, participants identified practical barriers that could impede implementation. Chief among these were concerns about trust, safety, and quality assurance, as existing platforms currently play a key role in vetting hosts and listings.

Structural and business model conflicts were also highlighted. Many existing players rely heavily on intermediary fees for revenue, making it economically difficult to shift to fully decentralised structures. Additionally, legal and regulatory complexity—including tax compliance, data jurisdiction, and consumer protection—emerged as a significant barrier, especially in cross-border transactions. Finally, technical infrastructure gaps, such as integrating distributed ledger systems with existing booking engines, were identified as limiting factors for rapid deployment.

This is consistent with research on disruptive platform transitions, which notes that incumbents often struggle to shift from centralized to decentralized revenue models due to strategic inertia and compliance risks [5, 8].

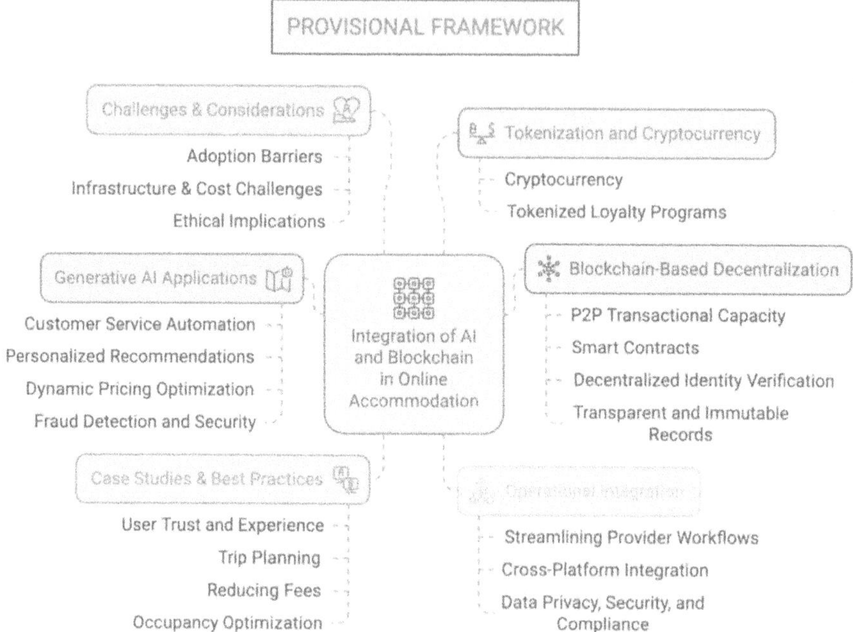

Fig. 1. Practical Framework

7 Key Components of a Practical Framework (RQ4) (Fig. 1).

The primary objective of the study was to develop a practical framework for integrating GAI and blockchain technologies (in combination) into the online accommodation sector of travel, tourism and hospitality. This intent was embedded in the original title of the research: The Integration of Artificial Intelligence and Blockchain in Online Accommodation: A Framework for Sustainable Business Models. To address this objective, one of the key research questions (RQ4) asked: "What components should be included in a practical framework to facilitate the integration of GAI and blockchain technologies and P2P business models in the online accommodation sector?" Therefore, at the outset of the research process, a provisional framework was constructed from the existing literature. The framework was intended as a starting point for an exploratory model rather than a fixed solution, allowing the research to test its relevance and applicability in real-world contexts. To ensure rigour and engagement, the provisional framework **was shared with participants prior to the interviews.** They were asked to reflect on what key components should be included in a practical framework for integrating GAI and blockchain technologies and direct P2P transactions in the online accommodation sector. This approach served two purposes: It prepared participants to critically evaluate the framework in light of their expertise and experience. It allowed the framework to act as a **discussion catalyst**, prompting detailed reflections on its strengths, gaps, and feasibility. The provisional framework represents the initial conceptualisation against which participant insights were mapped and is illustrated in the Figure above.

7.1   Core Integration Elements

Participants outlined four essential components for a viable dual business model framework: Robust data governance and security protocols, to address both GAI and blockchain compliance and trust requirements; User experience and accessibility design, ensuring that technological complexity does not reduce usability for hosts or travelers; Technological infrastructure, particularly interoperability between AI layers, blockchain networks, and existing booking platforms, and Operational and strategic alignment, ensuring that technology adoption supports clear business goals rather than functioning as an isolated innovation initiative.

While some participants envisioned complete disintermediation through decentralised autonomous organisations (DAOs) and P2P models, the majority advocated for hybrid integration strategies rather than full disruption. This pragmatic stance reflected the continued dominance of intermediaries such as Airbnb and Booking.com, whose network effects remain powerful. A phased integration approach, embedding blockchain trust layers and GAI service enhancements into existing platform structures, was deemed more realistic than replacing intermediaries entirely. These findings support the argument that disruptive technologies often lead to reconfiguration rather than eradicationof incumbents in platform markets [5]. Hybrid models can enable incremental change while allowing new entrants and incumbents to co-exist.

8   Conclusion and Implications

The thematic analysis identified six major themes and twenty-four subthemes, offering a nuanced understanding of both the promise and complexity of technological convergence in online accommodation. While GAI enhances personalisation and efficiency and blockchain fosters transparency and trust, the success of their integration depends on overcoming technical, regulatory, and governance barriers. The proposed dual model does not seek to dismantle existing structures entirely but to reconfigure value creation and distribution for a more efficient and equitable ecosystem.

The findings suggest that integrating GAI and blockchain can enhance operational efficiency, trust, and transparencyin online accommodation platforms. However, technical integration, regulatory compliance, and trust-building at scale remain major challenges. Experts emphasized the importance of aligning these technologies with user experience design and business strategy rather than adopting them as stand-alone solutions.

A dual business model—combining GAI-enabled intelligent service delivery with blockchain-based trust infrastructure—emerges as a feasible pathway. This approach allows incumbents to incrementally adopt disruptive technologies while opening opportunities for new entrants. Importantly, decentralisation does not necessarily imply disintermediation: trusted intermediaries can evolve into trust facilitators rather than gatekeepers.

Disclosure of Interests. The authors have no competing interests to declare that are relevant to the content of this article.

References

1. Parmar, H.: Blockchain in tourism: enhancing security, reducing fraud, and revolutionizing customer engagement. In: Blockchain in the Tourism Industry: A New Era of Secure and Transparent Travel Solutions, pp. 215–234. Springer, Cham (2025)
2. Ma, C., Fan, A., Mattila, A.S.: Decoding the shared pathways of consumer technology experience in hospitality and tourism: a meta-analysis. Int. J. Hosp. Manag. **118**, 103685 (2024)
3. Treiblmaier, H., Rejeb, A., Tan, T.M., Ongena, G.: Blockchain-driven business models. Digit. Busi. **5**, 100154 (2025)
4. Rao, K.P.N., Manvi, S.: Survey on electronic health record management using amalgamation of artificial intelligence and blockchain technologies. Acta Inform. Pragensia. **12**(1), 179–199 (2023)
5. Calvaresi, D., Leis, M., Dubovitskaya, A., Schegg, R., Schumacher, M.: Trust in tourism via blockchain technology: results from a systematic review. In: Information and Communication Technologies in Tourism 2019, pp. 304–317. Springer, Cham (2019)
6. Kumar, S., Lim, W.M., Sivarajah, U., Kaur, J.: Artificial intelligence and blockchain integration in business: trends from a bibliometric-content analysis. Inf. Syst. Front. **25**(2), 871–896 (2023)
7. Rindfleisch, A.: Transaction cost theory: past, present, and future. Acad. Mark. Sci. Rev. **10**(1–2), 85–102 (2020). https://doi.org/10.1007/s13162-020-00168-6
8. Tapscott, D., Tapscott, A.: Blockchain Revolution: How the Technology Behind Bitcoin Is Changing Money, Business, and the World. Penguin, London (2018)
9. Song, X., Gu, H., Li, Y., Ye, W.: A systematic review of trust in sharing accommodation: progress and prospects from the multistakeholder perspective. Int. J. Contemp. Hosp. Manag. **35**(4), 1156–1190 (2023)
10. Bhumichai, D., Smiliotopoulos, C., Benton, R., Kambourakis, G., Damopoulos, D.: The convergence of artificial intelligence and blockchain: the state of play and the road ahead. Information. **15**(5), 268 (2024)
11. Polcumpally, A.T., Pandey, K.K., Kumar, A., Samadhiya, A.: Blockchain governance and trust: a multi-sector thematic systematic review and exploration of future research directions. Heliyon. **10**(12), e32975 (2024)
12. Tran-Thi-My, L., Barnes, S.J., Yoon, J.H., Kim, M.J.: What drives female travelers to use blockchain-enabled booking applications? Int. J. Contemp. Hosp. Manag. **37**(6), 2153–2175 (2025)
13. Norbu, T., Park, J.Y., Wong, K.W., Cui, H.: Factors affecting trust and acceptance for blockchain adoption in digital payment systems: a systematic review. Fut. Internet. **16**(3), 106 (2024)
14. King, A.A., Baatartogtokh, B.: How useful is the theory of disruptive innovation? MIT Sloan Manag. Rev. **57**(1), 77 (2015)
15. Ho, J.C., Chen, H.: Managing the disruptive and sustaining the disrupted: the case of Kodak and Fujifilm in the face of digital disruption. Rev. Policy Res. **35**(3), 352–371 (2018)
16. Periannan, J., Borbon, N.M.D.: Distribution strategies and technology innovations: a study of Malaysia's midscale hotels in the post-pandemic era. In: Tech Fusion in Business and Society: Harnessing Big Data, IoT, and Sustainability in Business, vol. 1, pp. 39–50. Springer, Cham (2025)
17. Sarfraz, M., Khawaja, K.F., Han, H., Ariza-Montes, A., Arjona-Fuentes, J.M.: Sustainable supply chain, digital transformation, and blockchain technology adoption in the tourism sector. Humanit. Soc. Sci. Commun. **10**(1), 1–13 (2023)

18. Tan, T.M., Salo, J., Alejandro, T.G.B., Tan, G.W.H., Ooi, K.B., Dwivedi, Y.K.: Guest editorial: a blockchain-based approach to marketing in the sharing economy. J. Bus. Res. **177**, 114639 (2024)
19. Koshiyama, A. et al.: Towards algorithm auditing: managing legal, ethical and technological risks of AI, ML and associated algorithms. R. Soc. Open Sci. **11**(5), 230859 (2024)

Conceptualization of AI Finance: Formal Model and Boundary Definition

Utevskaya Marina Valerievna[(✉)] [iD], Morunova Galina Vladimirovna[iD],
Panfilova Olga Vyatcheslavovna[iD], and Zadneprovskiy Aleksandr Aleksandrovich[iD]

Saint Petersburg State University of Economics, Saint Petersburg, Russian Federation
m.v.puchkova@gmail.com

Abstract. The article is devoted to the conceptualization of the artificial intelligence phenomenon in the financial domain. It highlights the challenge posed by the absence of a cohesive theoretical framework and precise definitions for the concept of AI finance. This deficiency impedes a systematic examination of how these technologies influence the financial system. The purpose of the study is to develop a conceptual approach through the systematization of existing perspectives, the formulation of a scientific definition, and the creation of a formal model for measuring AI finance. As a result, three paradigms of understanding AI finance are identified: instrumental, transformational, and agent-based, each varying in the level of system autonomy. The study proposes defining AI finance as a system of financial relations with varying degrees of decision-making autonomy. To quantitatively evaluate the impact of AI on financial processes, a model named AI Labor Efficiency Impact (AI-LEI) is introduced, which considers the variations among the paradigms. This model facilitates the measurement not only of economic efficiency but also of the extent of structural changes occurring within the financial system.

Keywords: artificial intelligence · finance · AI paradigms · artificial intelligence efficiency · digital transformation of finance

1 Introduction

The integration of artificial intelligence technologies into the financial sector represents one of the most significant trends in the modern economy: the global AI in finance market is estimated at \$38.4 billion in 2024 and is projected to expand to \$190.3 billion by 2030 [1]. The overall impact on the global economy is estimated to range from \$11 to \$18 trillion, while agent-based systems of generative AI may generate an additional \$2.2 to \$4.4 trillion in value [2]. The scale of adoption is evidenced by the fact that, in 2024, 8% of financial functions within organizations have already been transformed by AI [3]. Chatbots, automated credit scoring and risk-management systems, analysis of unstructured financial documentation, and agent-based trading have become an integral part of financial infrastructure [4].

In defining the concept of "finance," this study follows the approach proposed by the Saint Petersburg school of financial science. One of its leading representatives, Prof. M.

S. C. P. Yam et al. (Eds.): ICFT 2025, CCIS 2868, pp. 404–413, 2026.
https://doi.org/10.1007/978-981-92-0126-6_33

V. Romanovsky defined finance as "a set of monetary relations (connections) concerning the formation and use of various monetary funds in the process of their creation, distribution, and redistribution." At the same time, it remains unclear how artificial intelligence fits into this system—whether it transforms the fundamental nature of financial relations or merely serves as a technological tool for optimizing existing processes.

The authors found no established definition of the term "AI finance." A bibliometric analysis revealed more than 600 scientific publications between 1993 and 2024, covering a wide range of AI applications—from predictive systems to risk management, yet a unified theoretical foundation has not been formed [4]. This terminological vagueness hinders a systematic analysis of the phenomenon and complicates the distinction between traditional automation of financial operations and a qualitatively new phenomenon.

At the same time, AI finance cannot be regarded as an independent branch of finance (unlike public finance), nor as a distinct financial mechanism (such as lending or insurance), nor as a separate infrastructure (as in the case of decentralized finance [5]). AI functions as a general-purpose technology that permeates and transforms all segments of the financial market—from banking to the stock market, from insurance to payment systems. Thus, AI finance should be viewed as a cross-cutting technological direction that enables financial institutions to transition toward new models of data analysis, risk management, and decision-making.

The object of the study is the system of financial relations, institutions, and market mechanisms transformed under the influence of artificial intelligence technologies.

The subject of the study is the conceptual essence of the AI finance phenomenon, including theoretical paradigms of understanding the role of AI in the financial system and quantitative criteria for measuring AI finance.

The purpose of the study is to develop a conceptual approach to analyzing the phenomenon of AI finance through the systematization of existing perspectives, the formulation of a scientific definition, and the creation of a formal model for measuring the impact of artificial intelligence on the financial system.

2 Methods

The methodological framework of the study is based on a set of complementary methods that ensure the transition from theoretical conceptualization to quantitative assessment of the AI finance phenomenon.

At the first stage, a bibliometric analysis of scientific publications in the Scopus, Web of Science, and Google Scholar databases for the period 1993–2024 was conducted using the keywords "artificial intelligence in finance," "AI financial services," and "autonomous financial systems." The analysis covered over 100 academic papers and revealed the absence of a unified terminology in the field of AI finance, while allowing the systematization of existing approaches to understanding the role of AI in finance.

The content analysis method was applied to study industry reports by leading consulting firms (McKinsey, BCG, Deloitte, Gartner) and research institutions, which made it possible to record practical trends in the adoption of AI technologies in the financial sector and to identify key areas of application.

To construct the paradigmatic structure of AI finance, a typological analysis was employed based on the criterion of AI system autonomy in financial decision-making. This approach made it possible to distinguish three qualitatively different paradigms: instrumental, transformational, and agent-based.

A comparative analysis of existing models for assessing AI efficiency (McKinsey Value Framework, BCG Maturity Model) made it possible to identify their limitations and substantiate the need to develop a specialized model that accounts for paradigm-specific differences in AI application.

The integration of quantitative and qualitative methods enabled the creation of a conceptual approach that combines theoretical depth with practical applicability for evaluating and monitoring the efficiency of AI implementations in financial institutions.

3   Results

3.1   AI Finance Paradigms

An analysis of current AI applications in the financial sector makes it possible to distinguish three main paradigms of understanding this phenomenon, differing in the degree of AI autonomy:

1. Instrumental paradigm—where AI is used primarily as a tool for solving specific tasks, while control and decision-making remain in human hands [6, 7].
2. Transformational paradigm—where AI reshapes processes through advanced analytics and strategic planning for complex tasks, with the human acting as a "co-author" guiding AI [8–10].
3. Agent-based (subject) paradigm—where AI operates with a high degree of autonomy, is capable of assuming target functions, and performing them under minimal human supervision [11–14].

Each paradigm, in our view, influences all key stages of the financial process—formation, distribution, and utilization of financial resources—though the nature of this influence varies significantly. The instrumental paradigm enhances operational efficiency at all stages through automation of routine tasks and optimization of calculations. The transformational paradigm fundamentally changes the processes of financial decision-making through adaptive learning and predictive analytics. The agent-based paradigm creates the prerequisites for the autonomous functioning of financial systems capable of independently forming, distributing, and utilizing financial resources within predefined target functions. A distinctive feature of AI finance is its universality—the ability to integrate into and transform any element of the modern financial system (see Fig. 1).

Based on the conducted paradigm analysis, the following definition of AI finance is proposed: AI finance is a system of financial relations, institutions, and market mechanisms in which artificial intelligence acts as an agent of financial decision-making with varying degrees of autonomy, as well as a transformative factor of the fundamental functions of the financial system such as the formation, distribution, and utilization of capital, while influencing market microstructure through algorithmic feedback and changes in price formation.

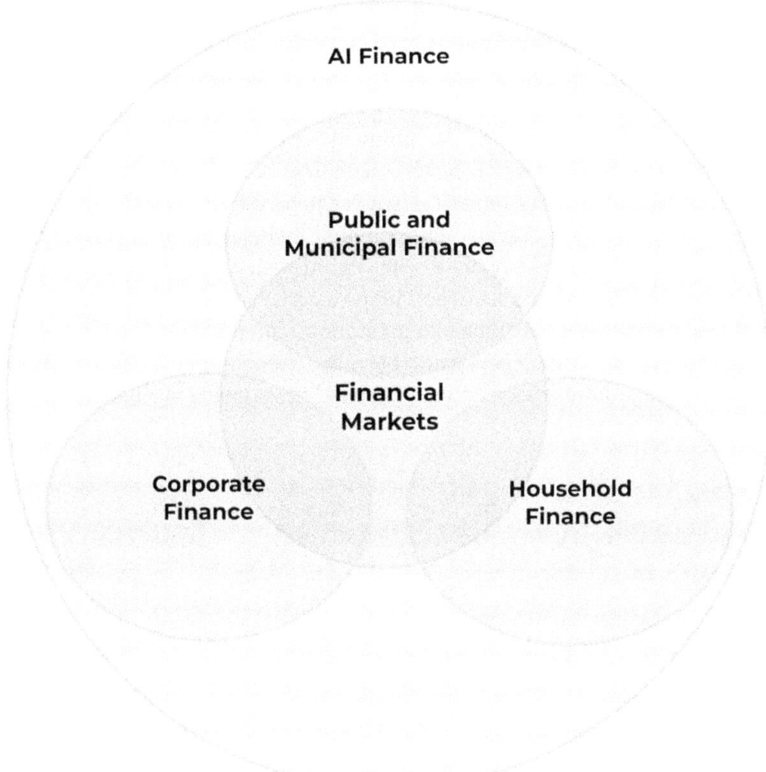

Fig. 1. The impact of AI on the modern financial system

Representatives of the Saint Petersburg school of financial science identify three key functions of finance inherent only to this economic category—the formation and utilization of monetary funds, as well as the control function. Accordingly, we can define the functions of AI finance [15].

Within the formation function, AI modifies capital mobilization processes through algorithmization of resource attraction (automated investment decisions, scoring, asset tokenization), thereby changing the speed and structure of fund accumulation.

Within the utilization function, AI transforms mechanisms of capital allocation and application through autonomous decisions regarding asset placement, liquidity management, and portfolio optimization, which leads to changes in pricing and the microstructure of financial markets.

Within the control function, AI transforms monitoring and supervision mechanisms over financial flows through systems of continuous real-time transaction analysis, automated detection of anomalies and deviations from established parameters, and forecasting of potential violations. However, the question of the specific functional nature of AI finance remains open for further discussion.

In addition, based on the conducted analysis, a conceptual model of AI finance paradigms has been formalized (see Fig. 2). It reflects the interrelation between system autonomy levels, risk intensity, and functional characteristics. To determine the maturity level of AI finance, the conceptual model also introduces the AI Autonomy Index (AAI), ranging from 0 to 1 (from 0—fully instrumental—to 1—agent-based, autonomous form).

The "risk intensity" axis in Fig. 2 illustrates the non-linear growth of systemic and operational risks as the degree of AI autonomy increases. In the instrumental paradigm, risk is minimal and mainly associated with technical or implementation errors. In the transformational paradigm, risk intensity rises due to partial human-machine interdependence, data-driven decision-making, and potential model misalignment. At the agent-based level, where AI systems operate with high decision-making independence, risk becomes systemic: algorithmic feedback loops, coordination failures, and misaligned objectives can propagate across financial institutions and markets. Hence higher autonomy not only amplifies efficiency gains but also expands the spectrum of potential vulnerabilities that require advanced oversight and governance mechanisms.

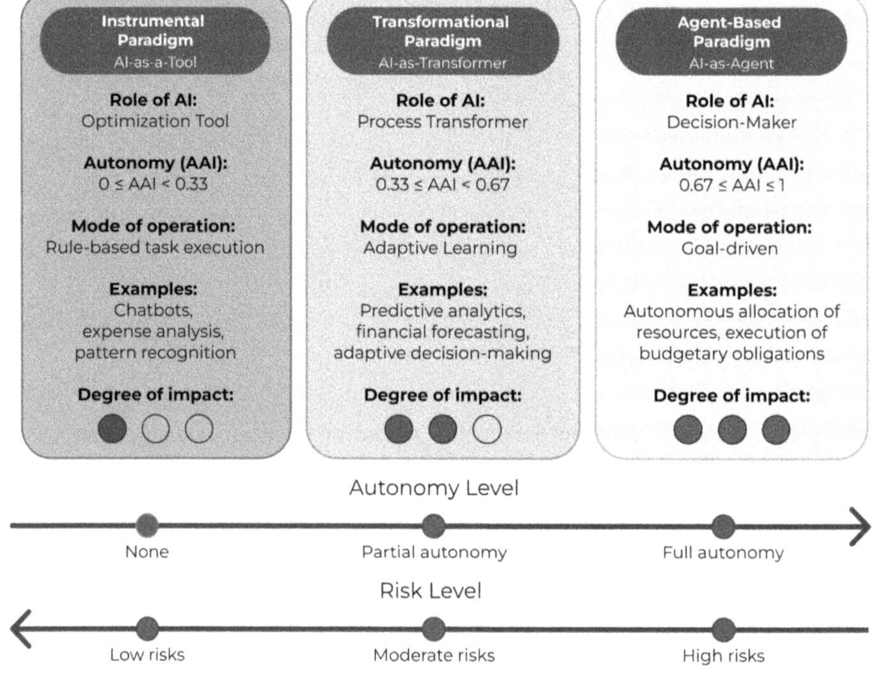

Fig. 2. Conceptual model of AI finance paradigms

Defining the paradigmatic approach to AI finance makes it possible not only to theoretically describe the role of artificial intelligence in the financial system but also to address the issue of its quantitative measurement. Current practice, briefly described in the next section (Sect. 3.2), is primarily focused on the overall economic return on technological investments and does not allow isolating the paradigmatic differences in AI's influence on financial processes. Meanwhile, the degree of autonomy and the extent of AI involvement in financial decision-making directly determine the cost structure, speed of return on investment, and the scale of the transformational effect.

In this context, there arises a need for a model that evaluates the impact of AI through the prism of its paradigmatic nature—from instrumental to agent-based—taking into account differences in the substitution of human labor. The following subsection (3.2) presents the AI Labor Efficiency Impact (AI-LEI) model.

3.2 Measuring the Maturity and Characteristics of AI Finance

Existing models are primarily focused either on total extractable value (McKinsey [16, 17]) or on process maturity and scalability (BCG [18]), yet they do not offer a unified standard for assessing the transformational effect of AI within key financial processes and fail to differentiate applications of AI by paradigm. Therefore, we propose the AI-LEI model (1). It is designed for the quantitative assessment of AI finance through the prism of labor substitution and augmentation, as well as the improvement of financial process quality, depending on the degree of autonomy and the strategic importance of AI application.

This model makes it possible to measure not only economic efficiency but also the depth of structural changes caused by AI integration into financial decision-making.

$$AI - LEI = \frac{\Delta LC_{actual} + \Delta PC_{quality}}{TC_{AI}} \times AF \tag{1}$$

where:

- ΔLC_{actual} – actual labor cost reduction due to AI implementation;
- $\Delta PC_{quality}$ – monetary equivalent of process quality improvement (reduction in errors, complaints, revisions, etc.);
- TC_{AI} – total AI-related expenditures (CAPEX + discounted OPEX);
- AF – adjustment factor reflecting the paradigm of AI application (instrumental, transformational, agent-based).

Labor cost reduction is determined as:

$$\Delta LC_{actual} = \sum_{i=1}^{n} \left[\left(FTE_{before,i} - FTE_{after,i} \right) \times S_i \times (1 + B_i) \right] \tag{2}$$

where:

- $FTE_{before,i}$ and $FTE_{after,i}$ – full-time equivalent employees in process i before and after AI implementation;
- S_i – average annual salary for process i;
- B_i – employee bonus coefficient.

Process quality improvement is defined as:

$$\Delta PC_{quality} = \Sigma \left[\left(E_{before,j} \times C_j \right) - \left(E_{after,j} \times C_j \right) \right] \tag{3}$$

where:

- $E_{before,j}$ and $E_{after,j}$ – frequency of error type j before and after AI implementation;
- C_j – average monetary cost of error type j.

Total costs of AI implementation and maintenance are expressed as:

$$TC_{AI} = CAPEX_{AI} + \sum_{t=1}^{T} \frac{OPEX_{AI,t}}{(1+r)^t} \tag{4}$$

where:

- T – evaluation period (recommended 3–5 years);
- r – discount rate.

The adjustment factor is a key element of the proposed model, ensuring its conceptual linkage with the paradigmatic structure of AI finance discussed in Sect. 3.1:

$$AF = 0.7 + (0.3 \times AAI) + (0.3 \times SR) \tag{5}$$

where:

- $AAI \in [0; 1]$ – AI Autonomy Index, a normalized indicator of the degree of system independence in financial decision-making (see Fig. 2);
- $SR \in [0; 1]$ – Strategic Relevance coefficient, reflecting the importance of a given process for achieving the organization's key objectives (0 – auxiliary function, 1 – strategically critical function).

Through this coefficient, the AI-LEI model captures not only quantitative efficiency parameters but also qualitative differences between levels of AI autonomy and strategic significance in financial processes. It accounts for the nonlinear nature of AI's impact: as systems evolve from the instrumental to the transformational and further to the agent-based paradigm, both autonomy and value increase, as does AI's contribution to transforming the fundamental functions of the financial system.

Hence the adjustment factor enables paradigm-aware measurement of AI finance efficiency, aligning with the overall logic of this study aimed at transitioning from a descriptive to an evaluative model of AI influence in finance.

Interpretation of the AI-LEI Indicator. The resulting AI-LEI value serves as an integrated indicator of AI efficiency within a financial entity. It shows how many times the aggregate outcomes of AI implementation (in the form of labor savings and process-quality improvements) exceed the total costs of its deployment.

By incorporating the adjustment factor AF, the model differentiates not only economic impact but also the depth of transformational influence—the extent to which AI fundamentally changes financial activity rather than merely automating existing operations.

Interpretation of values:

- AI-LEI <1.0 – the project is unprofitable, AI creates no additional value.
- $\le$ AI-LEI <1.5 – limited effect, local improvements without systemic change.
- $1.5 \le$ AI-LEI <2.5 – stable efficiency, transformational features at the business-process level.

- AI-LEI ≥ 2.5 – high effect, AI ensures synergistic returns and qualitative shifts in the functioning model of the financial system.

Moreover, AI-LEI makes it possible not only to measure economic efficiency but also to classify the maturity level of AI finance integration based on its actual impact on organizational activity. The indicator provides a foundation for comparative analysis between departments or institutions and serves as a tool for monitoring the dynamics of AI implementation efficiency over time.

4 Conclusion

The study developed a conceptual approach to analyzing the phenomenon of AI finance, encompassing a theoretical paradigmatic structure, a definitional framework, and a formalized model for measuring efficiency.

The theoretical significance of the research lies in establishing a conceptual foundation for the scientific analysis of AI finance as a qualitatively new phenomenon requiring specific approaches to study and measurement. The proposed paradigmatic structure forms the basis for further exploration of the role of autonomy in transforming financial relations.

The practical significance is determined by the potential use of the AI-LEI model by financial institutions to justify investments in AI technologies, monitor implementation efficiency, and perform comparative analysis of various digitalization projects. The model can serve as a tool for strategic planning and for assessing the maturity of an organization's digital transformation.

The limitations of the study are associated with the need for empirical validation of the proposed model using data from financial institutions of different types and scales. Furthermore, the dynamic nature of AI technology development requires periodic revision of model parameters and interpretation criteria.

Prospects for further research include:

- Empirical testing of the AI-LEI model across public, banking, insurance, and investment sectors, with the development of industry-specific efficiency benchmarks;
- Examination of how the agent-based AI paradigm influences the nature of financial relations and market structures, including issues of agency, legal capacity, and liability of autonomous systems;
- Analysis of the regulatory aspects of highly autonomous AI systems in finance and development of oversight principles;
- Study of the long-term effects of labor substitution on employment structure in the financial sector and the transformation of professional competencies.

In conclusion, the developed AI-LEI model enables the quantitative assessment of AI's influence on financial processes while accounting for paradigmatic differences, making it possible to evaluate not only economic efficiency but also the depth of structural transformation within the financial system. Further theoretical work should continue to refine approaches to the study of AI finance

References

1. AI in Finance Market Size, Share, Growth Report - 2030 (2024). https://www.marketsandma rkets.com/Market-Reports/ai-in-finance-market-90552286.html. Accessed 25 Oct 2025
2. Seizing the agentic AI advantage | McKinsey (2024). https://www.mckinsey.com/capabilit ies/quantumblack/our-insights/seizing-the-agentic-ai-advantage. Accessed 26 Oct 2025
3. Gartner Survey Shows 58% of Finance Functions Using AI in 2024 (2024). https://www. gartner.com/en/newsroom/press-releases/2024-09-11-gartner-survey-shows-58-percent-of- finance-functions-use-ai-in-2024. Accessed 25 Oct 2025
4. Bahoo, S., Cucculelli, M., Goga, X., Mondolo, J.: Artificial intelligence in Finance: a comprehensive review through bibliometric and content analysis. SN Bus. Econ. **4**, 23 (2024). https://doi.org/10.1007/s43546-023-00618-x
5. Schär, F.: Decentralized finance: on blockchain- and smart contract-based financial markets. Review. **103**, 53–174 (2021). https://doi.org/10.20955/r.103.153-74
6. Cao, L.: AI in Finance: Challenges, Techniques and Opportunities, https://arxiv.org/abs/2107. 09051 (2021). https://doi.org/10.48550/ARXIV.2107.09051
7. How Artificial Intelligence is Transforming the Financial Services Industry (2024). https:// www.deloitte.com/ng/en/services/consulting-risk/services/how-artificial-intelligence-is-tra nsforming-the-financial-services-industry.html. Accessed 25 Oct 2025
8. How AI could reshape the asset management industry | McKinsey (2024). https://www.mck insey.com/industries/financial-services/our-insights/how-ai-could-reshape-the-economics- of-the-asset-management-industry. Accessed 25 Oct 2025
9. Svetlana, N., Anna, N., Svetlana, M., Tatiana, G., Olga, M.: Artificial intelligence as a driver of business process transformation. Procedia Comput. Sci. **213**, 276–284 (2022). https://doi. org/10.1016/j.procs.2022.11.067
10. Aldasoro, I., Gambacorta, L., Korinek, A., Shreeti, V., Stein, M.: Intelligent Financial System: How AI Is Transforming Finance. Bank for International Settlements (BIS), Basel (2024)
11. . Joshi, S.: A Comprehensive Survey of AI Agent Frameworks and Their Applications in Financial Services. https://papers.ssrn.com/abstract=5252182 (2025). https://doi.org/10. 2139/ssrn.5252182
12. Ante, L.: Autonomous AI Agents in Decentralized Finance: Market Dynamics, Application Areas, and Theoretical Implications. https://papers.ssrn.com/abstract=5055677 (2024). https://doi.org/10.2139/ssrn.5055677.
13. Okpala, I., Golgoon, A., Kannan, A.R.: Agentic AI Systems Applied to tasks in Financial Services: Modeling and model risk management crews. http://arxiv.org/abs/2502.05439 (2025). https://doi.org/10.48550/arXiv.2502.05439
14. Samdani, G., Dixit, Y., Viswanathan, G.: Agentic AI in autonomous financial advisories. World J. Adv. Eng. Technol. Sci. **9**, 410–420 (2023). https://doi.org/10.30574/wjaets.2023.9. 1.0138
15. Romanovsky, M.V., Vrublevskaya, O.V., Ivanova, N.G. (eds.): Finance, Money Circulation and Credit. Yurayt Publishing House, Moscow (2022)
16. McKinsey Global Institute: Notes from the AI frontier: Insights from hundreds of use cases (2024). https://www.mckinsey.com/~/media/mckinsey/featured%20insights/artificial%20i ntelligence/notes%20from%20the%20ai%20frontier%20applications%20and%20value% 20of%20deep%20learning/notes-from-the-ai-frontier-insights-from-hundreds-of-use-cases- discussion-paper.pdf. Accessed 26 Oct 2025

17. McKinsey Global Institute: Notes from the AI frontier: AI adoption advances, but foundational barriers remain (2024). https://www.mckinsey.com/~/media/McKinsey/Featured%20Insights/Artificial%20Intelligence/AI%20adoption%20advances%20but%20foundational%20barriers%20remain/Notes-from-the-AI-frontier-AI-adoption-advances-but-foundational-barriers-remain.ashx. Accessed 26 Oct 2026
18. Where's the Value in AI? (2024). https://www.bcg.com/publications/2024/wheres-value-in-ai. Accessed 26 Oct 2025

System-Dynamics Driven Schedule Governance for FinTech Project: Evidence from a Financial Digital-Intelligent Platform

Sicong Qian[1] and Ruidan Su[2]([✉])

[1] Huatai Securities Co., Ltd., Nanjing, China
[2] AGI Institute, School of Computer Science, Shanghai Jiao Tong University, Shanghai, China
`suruidan@sjtu.edu.cn`

Abstract. FinTech projects face frequent business changes, tight market windows and evolving compliance demands challenges, where static schedule tools underperform. To enhance project management effectiveness, we propose a System-Dynamics schedule governance model linking five subsystems including process, scope, resources, targets and performance system, to capture the nonlinear dynamic interactions within projects. Using data from a large financial digital-intelligent platform, the model was validated through simulation. We run policy experiments on five subsystems. Results show that the model and strategies are effective on early change discovery, timely regulatory response, early staffing with moderate experienced redundancy, and reasonably aggressive targets. This research provides FinTech project managers with a dynamic, quantitative decision-support tool.

Keywords: Progress Management · System Dynamics · FinTech · IT Projects · Strategy Simulation · RegTech · Time-to-Compliance · Release Governance

1 Introduction

With the emergence of new technologies such as cloud computing, big data, and artificial intelligence, FinTech products are continuously evolving, and traditional financial institutions are accelerating their digital transformation. FinTech projects are typically characterized by large investments, high complexity, and strong strategic importance, placing higher demands on schedule management. Simultaneously, they possess dual technological and financial attributes: on one hand, as virtual products, their progress is difficult to assess accurately and is significantly influenced by human factors; on the other hand, they are constrained by industry characteristics such as strong regulation, rapid business changes, and low error tolerance, further increasing the difficulty of schedule management. This often renders traditional schedule management methods based on

S. C. P. Yam et al. (Eds.): ICFT 2025, CCIS 2868, pp. 414–430, 2026.
https://doi.org/10.1007/978-981-92-0126-6_34

static assumptions, such as Gantt charts and milestone plans, ineffective when dealing with frequent requirement changes and strict compliance demands.

To address this challenge, academia and industry have engaged in a series of progressive explorations. Initial research primarily focused on the tailored application of the classic PMBOK framework. For instance, Xiao Chunming (2008) applied core techniques like Work Breakdown Structure (WBS) and Critical Chain to software outsourcing management in commercial banks, enhancing the systematic nature of project planning [1]. Building on this, Shen Lianglong (2020) further introduced dynamic control and group decision-making tools such as the PDCA cycle and the Delphi method, aiming to improve the adaptability of bank FinTech projects in quality and decision-making processes [2]. As project complexity increased, researchers began to emphasize resource constraints and multi-objective optimization. He Long (2021) integrated Critical Chain and Earned Value Management theories, attempting integrated control of cost, schedule, and quality for securities information projects under resource constraints [3]. Zhao Jun's (2021) research represents a more refined effort, combining Critical Chain, Linear Programming, and the Analytic Hierarchy Process to provide a more applicable schedule planning solution for large FinTech projects under resource constraints [4]. However, despite their progressive deepening, the methodological core of these studies remains focused on static planning and local optimization, failing to fundamentally capture the nonlinear dynamic interactions and feedback mechanisms among various elements (e.g., scope, resources, performance) within FinTech projects.

System Dynamics, with its core of feedback control theory, excels at macro-level analysis combining qualitative and quantitative approaches for nonlinear, high-order dynamic complex systems [5]. This characteristic gives it unique value in the field of project management. Domestic scholars have conducted useful explorations in this direction: Wang Qifan early on expounded its application advantages in project management [6]; Yang Yong and Zhou Bosheng (2011) used it to quantitatively analyze the lag effects in software processes [7]; Han Tianming (2019) compared various response strategies under requirement changes through modeling and simulation [8]. These achievements collectively demonstrate the effectiveness of System Dynamics in depicting the internal dynamic feedback mechanisms of projects.

Based on System Dynamics theory, this paper constructs a FinTech project schedule management model. Using Company X's financial digital-intelligent platform as a case study, it analyzes the dynamic interaction mechanisms among various factors from the perspectives of five subsystems—Process, Scope, Resources, Objectives, and Performance—and proposes optimization strategies through simulation, providing decision support for project managers.

2 Problem Analysis

Characteristics and Difficulties of FinTech Projects. The schedule management of FinTech projects is deeply rooted in their dual "financial" and

Table 1. Model Boundary Table

Variable Type	Representative Variables
Excluded Variables	Changes in socio-economic environment, technology trends, company organizational form, cash flow changes, changes in partner companies; non-development/handover phases like requirements analysis, solution design, solution review, operations & maintenance
Exogenous Variables	Initial workload, initial number of employees, training time, normal work efficiency, error rate, handover initiation requirement percentage, completion requirement ratio, handover preparation time, normal/maximum weekly work hours, impact of work pressure on work efficiency/error rate, impact of fatigue level on error rate, originally planned duration, schedule adjustment magnitude, adjustment delay time
Endogenous Variables	Workload in various stages, actual work efficiency, actual error rate, schedule pressure, fatigue level, development/handover rework volume, actual number of employees, planned completion time

"technological" genes. Its core difficulties stem from the following three fundamental contradictions: First, the contradiction between system complexity and management visibility. Projects span business, technology, and third-party collaboration, with varying organizational structures and team competencies, resulting in numerous interrelated factors affecting the schedule and making accurate macro-level prediction difficult. Second, the contradiction between inherent volatility and external rigid constraints. Software products are inherently virtual and mutable, while the high-frequency changes in financial business and strong regulatory requirements jointly lead to frequent requirement changes and high rework rates, posing continuous impacts on the schedule. Third, the contradiction between dynamic execution processes and static management paradigms. Traditional management methods, represented by the waterfall model, have low tolerance for scope changes and lack the capability for global, dynamic assessment of change impacts, leading to slow responses to unexpected changes.

Therefore, resolving these challenges requires systematically analyzing the influencing factors and clarifying the dynamic interaction mechanisms among them. Accordingly, this paper aims to achieve a balance between schedule, resources, scope, and quality, and constructs a dynamic model comprising five subsystems for in-depth discussion.

Five-Subsystem Interactions in Schedule Dynamics. The System Dynamics model constructed in this study aims to reveal how the five subsystems jointly influence the project schedule. To ensure the model focuses on core feedback mechanisms, a specific FinTech digital-intelligent platform project from Company X is used as a case study, with necessary simplifications of reality and the following key boundaries and assumptions set (Table 1):

Based on the model boundaries, the following assumptions are proposed: Environmental Stability: Major changes in the external environment and organizational structure are ignored; Process Focus: The waterfall model is adopted, focusing only on the two core phases: development and handover; Resource Simplicity: Human resources are considered the sole core resource, ignoring fixed costs like capital and equipment; Task Homogeneity: All tasks are measured in standardized "work packages".

On this basis, and drawing on works of Ford and Sterman [9], Wang Yujing [10], Ji Xiaqing [11], we construct five interrelated subsystems that together constitute the dynamic system of project schedule management. The **Process Subsystem** serves as the core skeleton of the model, describing the flow of work packages between states of "To Be Developed," "To Be Handed Over," and "Completed," and includes two key feedback loops: development rework and handover rework. The **Scope Subsystem** Captures scope creep caused by business changes and regulatory requirements, and its impact on the total workload. The **Resource Subsystem** uses on human resources, simulating the conversion of new hires to experienced employees, and the strategy of dynamically adjusting personnel numbers based on project demands. The **Schedule Target Subsystem** generates schedule pressure by comparing the forecasted completion time with the planned completion time, thereby influencing the behavior and decisions of the project team. The **Performance Subsystem** Acts as a bridge connecting the other subsystems, quantifying key performance indicators such as work efficiency, error rate, and fatigue level, which are in turn influenced by schedule pressure, work hours, and team composition. Based on the impact mechanisms of the above five subsystems, the overall FinTech project model will be constructed.

3   Model Construction

To systematically analyze and optimize FinTech project schedule management strategies, this paper constructs a comprehensive model encompassing five subsystems based on System Dynamics theory. The overall structure of the model is shown in Fig. 1, which reveals the interdependent and mutually constraining dynamic feedback relationships among the five core subsystems—Process, Scope, Resources, Objectives, and Performance—that collectively determine the overall behavior of the project schedule.

This model takes the Process Subsystem as its core skeleton, describing the flow path of work packages. The Scope and Resource Subsystems act as core input and constraints, directly affecting the rate and total volume of the process flow. The Target Subsystem generates control signals (schedule pressure) by comparing planned versus actual progress. The Performance Subsystem acts as a key converter, transforming state variables like schedule pressure and fatigue level into actual work efficiency and error rates, thereby closing the entire management loop.

Based on this overall framework, each subsystem is elaborated in detail below.

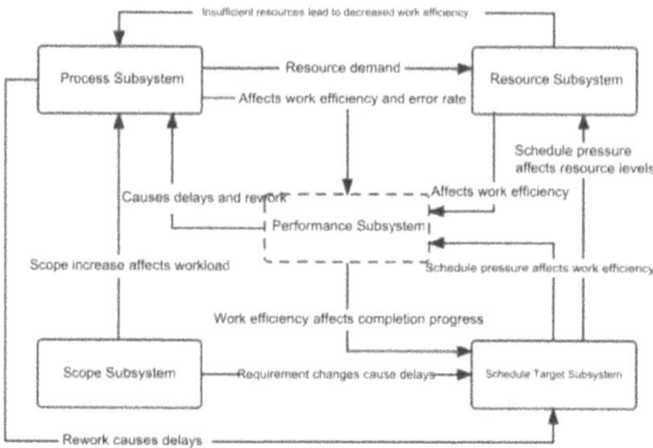

Fig. 1. General system structure.

3.1   Subsystem Construction

Based on the overall framework shown above, this section elaborates on the core modeling logic and key feedback mechanisms of the five subsystems. Their detailed causal loop and stock-flow structures are described below.

Process Subsystem This subsystem defines the core flow path of project work, abstracting the development and handover processes into a material flow with "work packages" as the unit. Its key feature is the inclusion of two core feedback loops: the development rework loop and the handover rework loop. These two loops are the primary endogenous sources of workload amplification and schedule delays. Their flow rates are directly regulated by the "actual efficiency" and "error rate" outputs from the Performance Subsystem (Fig. 2).

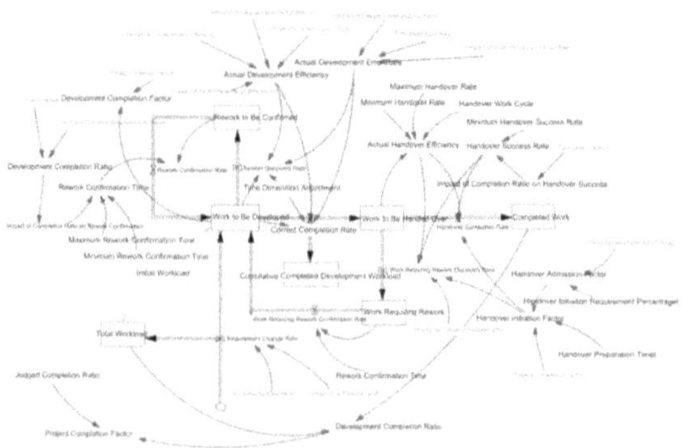

Fig. 2. Process subsystem model diagram.

Scope Subsystem. The Scope Subsystem simulates the impact of two types of external inputs—business requirement changes and regulatory requirement changes—on the total project workload. The model uses pulse functions to simulate the suddenness of changes and sets different conversion coefficients based on their source and impact phase (development/handover), thereby quantifying the dynamic impact of scope creep on the "Work to Be Developed."

Resource Subsystem. This model treats human resources as the core resource and distinguishes between the efficiency and error rates of new hires versus experienced employees. The subsystem dynamically simulates personnel onboarding and offboarding decisions by comparing the "Actual Staffing Demand" with the "Current Number of Employees," and considers the time delay effects caused by management activities such as training and knowledge transfer. This dynamic adjustment mechanism, particularly the potential for diminishing marginal returns or even negative effects when new employees are added, aligns with the principles revealed by Brooks' Law [12] (Figs. 3 and 4).

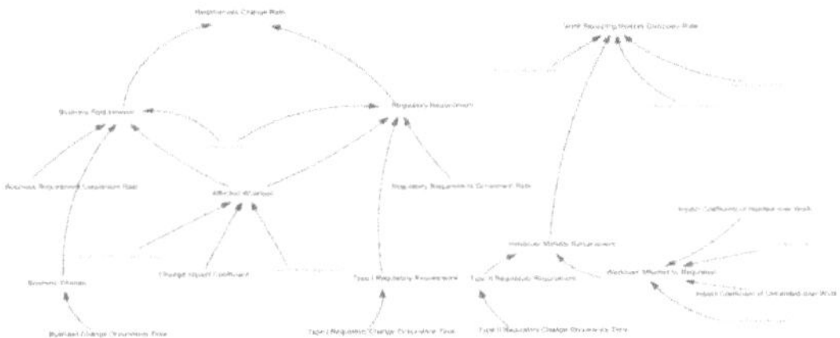

Fig. 3. Scope subsystem model diagram.

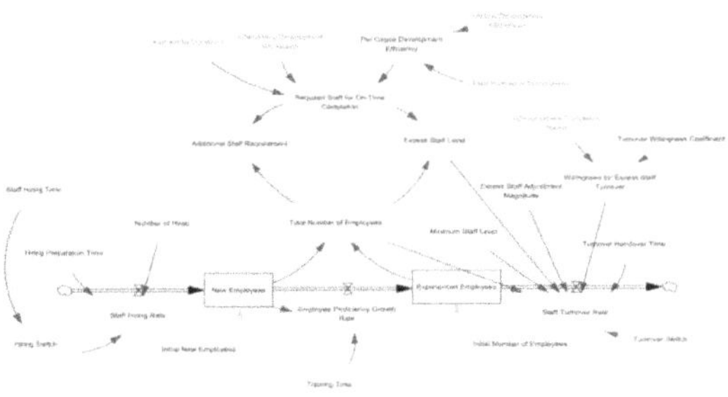

Fig. 4. Resource subsystem model diagram.

Target Subsystem. This subsystem is the control center of the project. It generates the core control signal—schedule pressure—by continuously calculating the gap between the forecasted completion time and the planned completion time. Based on this pressure, project managers adjust the plan incrementally with a certain delay and magnitude, causing the schedule target to converge towards reality.

Performance Subsystem. The Performance Subsystem is the hub connecting the other subsystems. Its core function is to determine the actual development efficiency and error rate. These two variables are not fixed but are jointly influenced by team structure (theoretical capacity), schedule pressure (work state), and fatigue level (health condition). Among these, the inverted U-shaped impact of work pressure on efficiency and the positive impact of fatigue level on the error rate are supported by multiple empirical studies [13,14]. Fatigue level is modeled as a level variable, representing the cumulative result over time of overtime and other crash effort behaviors (Figs. 5 and 6).

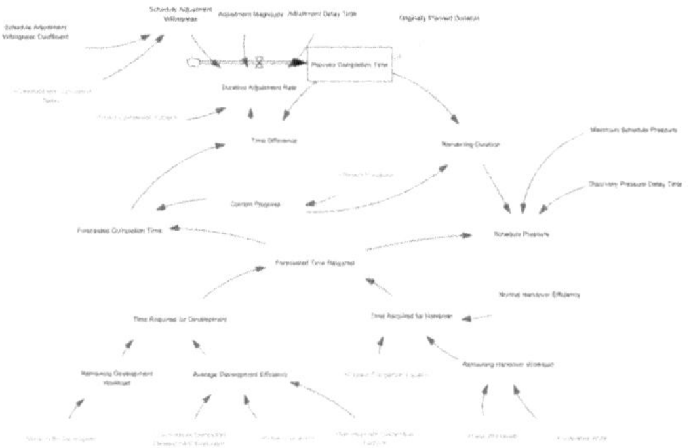

Fig. 5. Target subsystem model diagram.

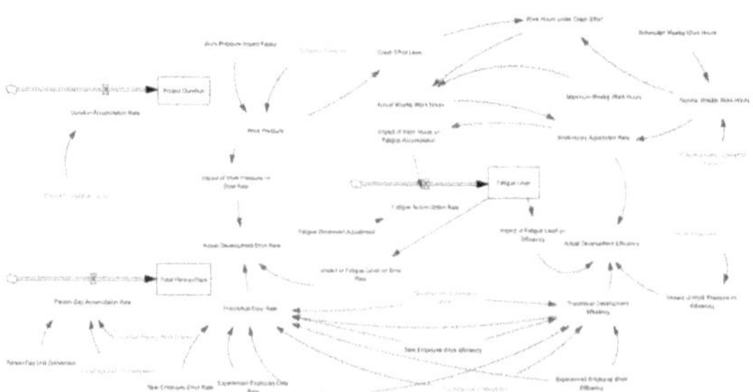

Fig. 6. Performance subsystem model diagram.

3.2   Model Variables and Equation Settings

The final constructed model contains a total of 130 variables, including 49 exogenous variables (constants) and 81 endogenous variables (including 14 level variables, 14 rate variables, and 53 auxiliary variables). The model comprises a total of 131 equations. This section focuses on explaining the core parameters and representative equations to reveal the internal logic of the system's operation.

Key Parameter Settings. Model parameters are primarily set based on case project data and relevant literature, aiming to reflect the typical context of FinTech projects.

1. **System and Workload Parameters**
   The simulation time unit is the week, with a total duration of 100 weeks. The initial project workload is set to 3500 standard work packages. The handover initiation requirement is set at 90% development completion, with a 4-week handover preparation time. This high entry threshold reflects the strict requirements of the financial industry for system stability and compliance completeness, ensuring core business logic is fully verified.

2. **Human Resource Parameters**
   The initial number of employees is set to 40 (including 15 experienced employees). The work efficiency of experienced employees and new hires is set at 5 and 2 (work packages/week/person) respectively, and their error rates at 0.1 and 0.3, reflecting significant differences in personnel experience. The training time for new hires is 4 weeks. This simulates the high learning curve and significant composite talent gap resulting from complex business logic and unique technology stacks in financial system development.

3. **Scope and Target Parameters**
   A core aspect of this model is depicting the dynamics unique to the financial industry. To this end, the regulatory requirement conversion rate (0.2) is set higher than the business requirement conversion rate (0.1). Furthermore, the model specifically incorporates a conservative rework preference: when regulatory requirements arise late in the project, their impact coefficients on "Completed Work" and "Work to Be Handed Over" are set to 0.1 and 0.3, respectively. This setting reflects the prudent strategy commonly adopted in financial projects nearing launch to ensure system stability and control risk propagation. The originally planned duration is 36 weeks, the plan adjustment magnitude is set to 0.5, and the adjustment delay is 2 weeks, simulating managers' cautious correction of schedule baselines in response to high uncertainty.

4. **Performance-Related Parameters**
   The normal weekly work time is 40 h, with a maximum of 60 h. The impact of work pressure on efficiency is simulated using a table function, presenting the classic inverted U-shaped relationship, consistent with research findings on work pressure and performance.

Key Equation Settings Explanation. Level variables represent stocks within the system, accumulated over time by flows, reflecting the state of the system at a specific point in time. Below, "Work to Be Developed" is used as an example to demonstrate its dynamic change mechanism. The equation is as follows

Work to Be Developed = INTEG (Rework Confirmation Rate + Work Requiring Rework Confirmation Rate + Requirement Change Rate - Correct Completion Rate - Rework Discovery Rate, Initial Workload), Units: Work Package

This equation clearly shows that the stock of "Work to Be Developed" is jointly influenced by five key flows: three (two types of rework and requirement changes) increase its workload, while two (correct completion and discovery of rework) decrease it. This structure fully captures the fundamental impact of scope creep and quality rework, the two core issues, on project schedule. Other level variables (such as "Fatigue Level," "Planned Completion Time," etc.) all follow a similar integral equation form, collectively constituting the dynamic feedback structure of the system.

4   Validation and Simulation

4.1   Model Validation

After completing the model construction, its validity needs to be tested. This study primarily employs the mental model validation method, verifying the model's effectiveness by comparing the trend consistency between the simulation results and the actual project data [14]. The simulation parameters are set as follows: Business Change Occurrence Time = 10 weeks, Type I Regulatory Change Occurrence Time = 18 weeks, Type II Regulatory Change Occurrence Time = 36 weeks, Staff Turnover Switch = 1. After simulation, important endogenous variables in the system were studied. The changes of each variable over time are shown in Fig. 7:

The "Work to Be Developed" in the model shows an overall downward trend, with three noticeable fluctuations due to scope changes. "Completed Work" grows steadily in the early stages, with growth slowing in the later stages due to regulatory requirements. The number of "Experienced Employees" adjusts dynamically as the project progresses. Changes in variables such as "Fatigue Level" and "Actual Development Efficiency" align with common project management realities. The changing trends of all variables are largely consistent with the actual operation of the case project, indicating that the model has good validity.

4.2   Scope Change Control Strategy Simulation

Scope change is a key factor affecting the schedule of FinTech projects. Given their volatile business environment, strict regulations, and the exploratory nature of the projects themselves, the development phase often faces frequent changes. This section will conduct simulation analysis to comprehensively assess the

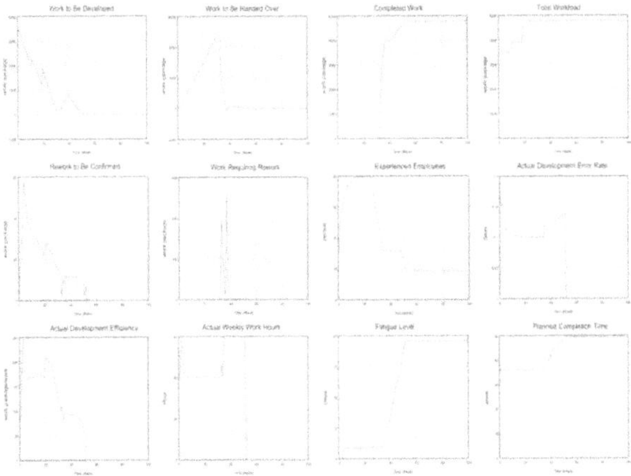

Fig. 7. Simulation results.

impact of changes on schedule, cost, and quality, in order to formulate effective control strategies.

Simulation of Strategy Controlling Requirement Change Occurrence Time. Simulate the impact of different business change occurrence times on project duration, rework volume (proxy for quality), and total person-days (proxy for cost). Set the business change occurrence times to 4, 8, 12, 16, 20, 24, and 28 weeks respectively. The simulation results are shown in Fig. 8. As shown in Table 2, the simulated data is processed. Schedule Duration represents project progress; Rework Volume (Cumulative Development Completed Workload minus Total Workload) reflects project quality; Total Person-Days represent project human resource consumption, indicating project cost. A comprehensive analysis is conducted from these three dimensions. The results indicate that the later a change occurs, the greater its negative impact on project duration, total rework volume, and human resource cost. This is because changes occurring later affect a larger accumulated volume of work awaiting handover, resulting in more rework effort. Therefore, the primary principle is to identify and respond to requirement changes as early as possible. For unavoidable changes late in development, their comprehensive impact needs to be assessed through simulation, and the timing of their handling should be arranged cautiously.

4.3 Simulation of Regulatory Requirement Response Strategies

Project managers differ in their sensitivity and response time to regulatory requirements, leading to different strategies. Two strategies are compared: first, Timely Response, treating requirements as Type I regulatory demands during the development phase; second, Delayed Response, postponing handling until the handover phase as Type II regulatory rework. Regarding simulation parameters,

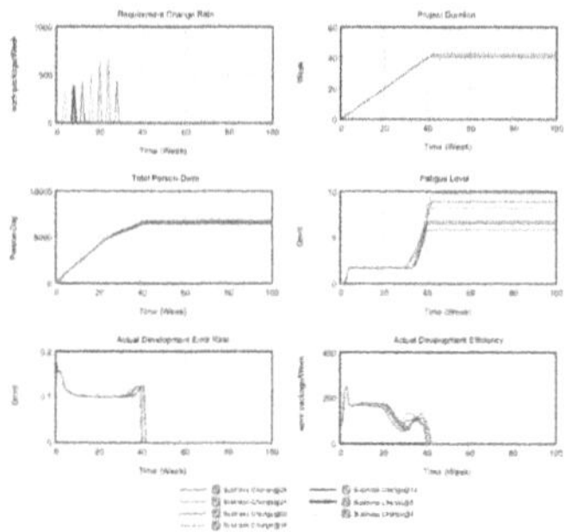

Fig. 8. Simulation results of strategy to control requirement changes occurrence time.

Table 2. Analysis of Scope Change Control Strategy Results

Occurrence Time (Week)	Schedule Duration (Week)	Rework Volume (Work Packages)	Total Person-Days (Person-Days)
4	41	582.65	6490.54
8	41	586.85	6517.88
12	41	594.09	6667.30
16	42	605.52	6760.83
20	43	617.48	6863.31
24	41	607.81	6690.71

Strategy One simulates Type I regulatory changes occurring in the mid-to-late development phase, with occurrence times set to 14, 16, 18, 20, 22, and 24 weeks. Strategy Two simulates Type II regulatory changes occurring in the handover phase, with occurrence times set to 26, 28, 30, 32, 34, 36, 38, 40, and 42 weeks. Business changes and other human resource strategies are kept consistent to focus the comparison on the regulatory response method.

Initial observation of Fig. 9 shows that Strategy One, by handling changes during development, results in significantly higher directly added workload compared to Strategy Two. This constitutes a practical consideration that often leads project management practice to favor delayed response.

However, further analysis of the project schedule reveals that Strategy Two does not effectively shorten the project duration. Conversely, during the early and final stages of the handover phase, this strategy actually leads to increased schedule delays. The reason is closely related to the rework volume: as shown in Fig. 9, although the directly added workload of Strategy Two is smaller, the total development and handover rework it triggers exceeds that of Strategy One.

The internal mechanism causing this phenomenon stems from the dynamic feedback within the project. First, a surge in schedule pressure: when regulatory requirements emerge late in the project, the delayed adjustment of the plan causes schedule pressure to rise sharply. Excessive pressure leads to crash efforts, subsequently increasing team fatigue, which negatively impacts development efficiency and quality. Second, human resource mismatch: Strategy Two leads to the premature release of human resources in the early stages. When facing sub-

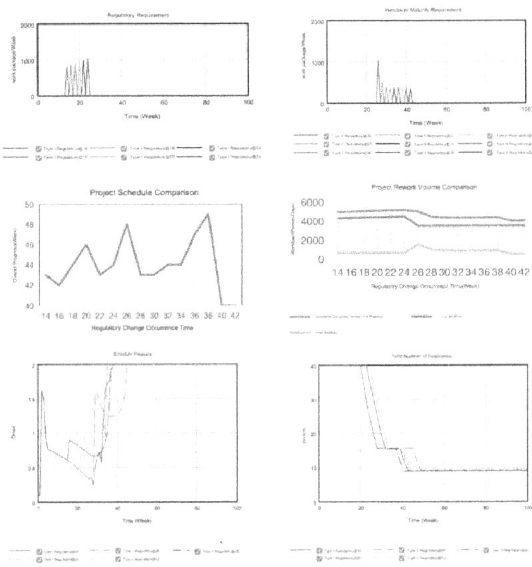

Fig. 9. Simulation of Regulatory Requirement Response Strategies.

stantial rework during the handover phase, available manpower is insufficient. This resource mismatch further amplifies schedule pressure, creating a vicious cycle.

In summary, although Strategy Two (Delayed Response) seemingly reduces the direct volume of changes, it triggers more indirect rework through surging schedule pressure and human resource mismatch, ultimately failing to effectively control the schedule and posing potential threats to project quality. Therefore, for regulatory requirements, project managers should adopt a "Timely Response" strategy and avoid procrastination.

4.4   Human Resource Control Strategy Simulation

In project management practice, human resources are often dynamically adjusted based on plan execution. Especially when resources are surplus, timely release of redundant personnel helps reduce project costs.

To verify the actual effect of staff turnover strategies, this study conducted simulation comparisons under both an ideal scenario without changes and a realistic scenario with changes. As shown in Table 3, enabling the staff turnover strategy significantly reduced total person-day costs in both scenarios, with reductions exceeding 12%. However, this strategy also resulted in noticeable schedule delays: the duration extended by approximately 11% in the ideal case and over 15% in the scenario with changes.

The reason for the schedule extension is that requirement changes cause tight development schedules. After staff are released, manpower shortages occur, leading to increased schedule pressure and cumulative team fatigue, which ultimately

Table 3. Analysis of Human Resource Control Strategy Results

Simulation Scenario	Total Person-Days (Person-Days)	Schedule Duration (Weeks)
Changes On, Turnover On	8499.72	52
Changes On, Turnover Off	9682.70	45
Changes Off, Turnover On	6103.54	40
Changes Off, Turnover Off	6967.84	36

results in higher error rates and decreased development efficiency, forming a negative cycle.

Therefore, in actual projects, while enabling staff turnover, new employees are often introduced in a timely manner based on demand signals from the Resource Subsystem to balance schedule risks. The following sections will analyze the effects of two strategies—controlling the staff hiring time and controlling the staff turnover magnitude—based on having staff turnover enabled.

Simulation of Strategy Controlling Staff Hiring Time. To analyze the impact of staff hiring timing on project schedule, this study sets the hiring time as the sole variable, with values of 10, 20, 30, 40, and 50 weeks. Simulations are run under the scenario with staff turnover enabled and scope changes present. The simulation results (Fig. 10) show that the earlier staff are hired, the more significant the effect on schedule control, with the project duration shortening accordingly. Further it also shows that although hiring new employees generally increases total person-day costs, hiring too late (e.g., week 50) not only fails to compress the duration effectively but also, due to the long training cycle and low initial efficiency and high error rate of new hires, leads to a sharp decrease in the return on human resource investment, while the increase in total person-days also becomes limited. This result aligns with the principles revealed by Brooks' Law [12].

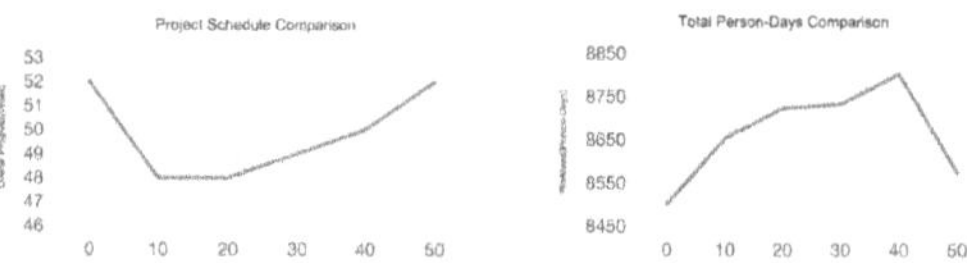

Fig. 10. Simulation of Strategy Controlling Staff Hiring Time.

Therefore, human resources should be planned and invested early. Supplementing staff in the late stages of a project not only fails to effectively accelerate progress but may also increase costs and introduce quality risks.

Simulation of Strategy Controlling Staff Turnover Magnitude. Given that new hires, due to training cycles and efficiency ramp-up, cannot quickly improve progress, this study further explores optimizing human resource allocation by precisely controlling the staff turnover magnitude, thereby reducing reliance on staff hiring.

With the staff hiring function disabled, the staff turnover magnitude is adjusted from 0.5 to 0.3, and simulations are run under the scenario with scope changes present. The results are shown in Table 4.

Table 4. Analysis of Controlling Staff Turnover Magnitude Strategy Results

Simulation Scenario	Schedule Duration (Weeks)	Total Person-Days (Person-Days)
Changes On, Turnover On	52	8499.72
Changes On, Turnover On (Mag=0.3)	48	8641.05
Changes On, Turnover On, Hire at Week 10	48	8653.19
Changes On, Turnover On, Hire at Week 20	48	8722.96
Changes On, Turnover On, Hire at Week 30	49	8732.39

Compared to the early staff hiring strategy (Week 10), the controlled turnover magnitude strategy achieved a similar effect in shortening the duration (both 48 weeks) and resulted in a lower total person-day cost. Its advantages primarily stem from two aspects. As shown in Fig. 11, first, it avoids the performance loss associated with new hires: although the overall error rate curves under the two strategies are not vastly different, new hires cause short-term disturbances in the error rate upon joining. The controlled turnover magnitude strategy completely avoids the efficiency loss caused by this. Second, it maintains overall team efficiency: reducing the turnover magnitude retains more experienced employees, thereby maintaining a higher average development efficiency. This strategy demonstrates more stable and efficient development efficiency throughout the project, especially during the handover and acceptance phase.

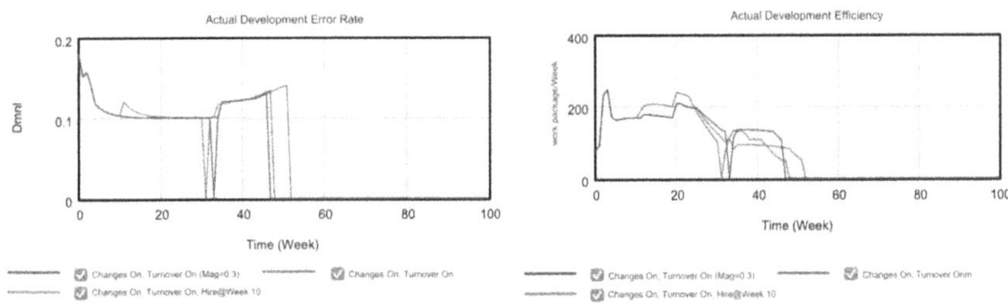

Fig. 11. Simulation of Strategy Controlling Staff Turnover Magnitude.

In summary, the controlled staff turnover magnitude strategy shows a slightly better overall balance between schedule and cost compared to the strategy relying on staff hiring. Therefore, when implementing dynamic human resource adjustments, project managers should carefully evaluate the staff turnover magnitude, combined with System Dynamics simulation, to achieve the optimal balance between cost and duration.

4.5   Simulation of Adjusting Schedule Target Strategy

The setting of the project's planned duration has a significant guiding effect on schedule execution. Simulations revealed that moderately compressing the originally planned duration might produce positive schedule control effects. For this purpose, this study simulates the impact of different originally planned durations on the project under the scenario with scope changes and staff turnover enabled. The originally planned duration in the Target Subsystem is set to 15, 25, 35, 45, and 55 weeks respectively. The simulation results (Table 5) show a nonlinear relationship between the planned duration setting and the actual project duration and total person-days. When the planned duration is set to 35 weeks, the actual project duration is the shortest (50 weeks), and the total person-days are also controlled at a relatively low level (8387.91 person-days), demonstrating the best comprehensive performance.

Table 5. Analysis of Adjusting Schedule Target Strategy Results

Simulation Scenario	Schedule Duration (Weeks)	Total Person-Days (Person-Days)
Changes On, Turnover On, Plan=15	52	11027.10
Changes On, Turnover On, Plan=25	56	8469.73
Changes On, Turnover On, Plan=35	50	8387.91
Changes On, Turnover On, Plan=45	55	8466.26
Changes On, Turnover On, Plan=55	67	9479.66

Further analysis shows that excessively compressing the duration (e.g., 15 weeks), while somewhat shortening the actual duration, triggers persistent high schedule pressure (Fig. 12), keeping the team at the maximum weekly work hours. Although this intensive crash effort mode is feasible in simulation, in reality it leads to cumulative fatigue and rising error rates, harming team health and project quality, and is unsustainable. Conversely, an overly relaxed plan (e.g., 55 weeks) lacks the necessary schedule pressure, which diminishes work efficiency and team motivation, thereby causing schedule delays and manpower waste.

Therefore, the setting of schedule targets should aim for "reasonable aggressiveness." When the planned duration is 35 weeks, the system achieves the best balance among schedule pressure, work efficiency, and team load. It is recommended that project managers can use System Dynamics simulation to scientifically set challenging yet achievable schedule targets, avoiding polarization in target setting.

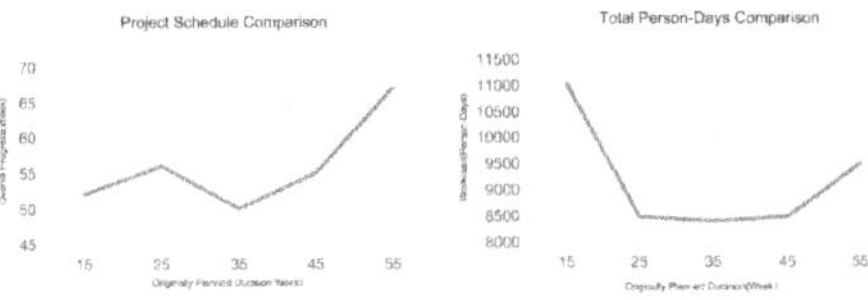

Fig. 12. Comparison chart of project progress and total man-day.

5   Conclusion

This study constructed a System Dynamics model for FinTech project schedule management, and the simulation results yield four key implications. First, requirement changes, particularly those occurring late in the project, significantly degrade schedule, cost, and quality performance. This mandates robust upfront requirement analysis and streamlined change processes, with late-stage changes being assessed with extreme caution. Second, regulatory compliance should be addressed proactively. Delaying regulatory responses until the handover phase is counterproductive. While it reduces immediate change volume, it triggers severe late-stage schedule pressure and resource misallocation, paradoxically increasing total rework and jeopardizing the system stability paramount to finance. Third, early and stable resourcing proves far more effective than reactive hiring. Finally, schedule pressure must be set at an "optimally tight" level. Excessively tight schedules are unsustainable, while overly loose ones promote inefficiency. "Reasonably aggressive" targets, calibrated through simulation, best balance pressure, efficiency, and team well-being.

References

1. Xiao, C.M.: Practical Application and Research of Project Management in Commercial Bank Software Outsourcing. Shanghai Jiao Tong University (2008)
2. Shen, L.L.: Research on C Bank FinTech Project Management. South China University of Technology (2020)
3. He, L.: Research on Optimization of Hualong Securities Information System Project Management. Lanzhou University of Technology (2021)
4. Hao, J.: Research and Practice on Schedule Management of L Securities Company Big Data Center Project. Donghua University (2021)
5. Lei, R.J.: Application of system dynamics in construction project management. J. Harbin Univ. Sci. Technol. **12** (2004)
6. Wang, Q.F., Ning, X.Q., You, J.: Advantages of system dynamics approach in managing project risk dynamics. J. Fudan Univ. (2005)
7. Yang, Y., Zhou, B.S.: Deviation control of software process based on system dynamics. Comput. Eng. Des. **32**(5), 1684–1690 (2011)
8. Han, T.M.: Research on Risk Management of Software Project Requirement Changes Based on System Dynamics. Chongqing University (2019)
9. Ford, D.N., Sterman, J.D.: Dynamics modeling of product development process. Syst. Dyn. Rev. **14**(1) (1998)

10. Wang, Y.J.: A project management method based on system dynamics. Stat. Decis. **12**, 34–36 (2010)
11. Ji, X.Q.: Simulation Research on Software Project Schedule Control Strategies Based on System Dynamics. Nanjing University (2016)
12. Brooks, F.P.: The Mythical Man-Month. Tsinghua University Press (2007)
13. Wickens, C.D., Hollands, J.G., Banbury, S., et al.: Engineering psychology & human performance. Psychology Press (2015)
14. Wang, Y.J.: Research on System Dynamics Simulation Method for Schedule Control of Complex Engineering Projects. Tongji University (2011)
15. He, N.: An Empirical Study on Motivational Factors of Human Resources in Project Management. University of International Business and Economics (2011)

Mechanism and Quantitative Study on Artificial Intelligence Technology Empowering Enterprise Performance—Empirical Analysis Based on the "Input-Scenario-Output" Model

Depeng Pan[1], Shaozheng Guo[2], Qian Xiong[3], Xianpeng Wang[1(✉)], and Tatul Manaseryan[4]

[1] International Institute of Management and Business, 220086 Minsk City, Belarus
`wxp-phd@bntu.by`
[2] Kyrgyz National University named after Zhusup Balasagyn, 720033 Bishkek, Kyrgyz Republic
[3] Shinawatra University, Sam Khok District, Bang Toei, Pathum Thani 12160, Thailand
[4] ALTERNATIVE Research Center, 17 Grigor Lusavorich street 35, Yerevan 0015, Armenia

Abstract. Against the backdrop of deepening digital transformation, the integration of artificial intelligence (AI) technology with enterprise operations is becoming increasingly close. However, the mechanism through which AI impacts enterprise performance still lacks systematic quantitative analysis. Based on the logical framework of "Technology Input - Scenario Application - Performance Output", this paper systematically sorts out the action paths of AI technology in three core dimensions of enterprises: cost control, revenue growth, and efficiency improvement. It innovatively constructs a simple mathematical model to quantify the correlation between AI input and performance improvement, and verifies the model's effectiveness using empirical data from 10 enterprises across three industries (retail, manufacturing, and finance). The study finds that a reasonable AI investment structure — with technology procurement accounting for 40%–50% and talent development accounting for 25%–30% — can boost enterprises' comprehensive performance by 15%–25%. Additionally, the impact coefficient of scenario adaptability on performance output reaches 0.72, providing quantitative references for enterprises to formulate AI investment strategies.

Keywords: Artificial Intelligence · Enterprise Performance · Mathematical Model · Input-Output Ratio · Scenario Adaptability

1 Introduction

1.1 Research Background

AI technology has become a key variable for enterprises to improve performance. According to data from iResearch (2025), the total AI investment of Chinese enterprises reached 680 billion yuan in 2024, an 85% increase compared to 2022. However,

S. C. P. Yam et al. (Eds.): ICFT 2025, CCIS 2868, pp. 431–440, 2026.
https://doi.org/10.1007/978-981-92-0126-6_35

there are significant differences in performance improvement among enterprises: 32% of enterprises achieved revenue growth exceeding 20% after AI investment, while 28% saw no obvious performance changes, and some even experienced increased costs due to improper investment. The core reason for this "input-performance" gap lies in enterprises' lack of clear understanding of AI's impact mechanism and the absence of a scientific investment and evaluation system [3]. From the perspective of technology application trends, AI has expanded from single-process optimization to full-business coverage. In 2024, the top three areas in terms of enterprise AI scenario application rate were customer service (78%), manufacturing (65%), and financial management (52%). Nevertheless, the performance contribution of different scenarios varies significantly. For instance, the average Return on Investment (ROI) of AI in customer service scenarios is 1:1.8, while the ROI of R&D assistance scenarios takes 2–3 years to reach 1:1.5. This highlights the necessity of quantitatively analyzing the impact mechanism of AI technology [3].

1.2 Research Methods

This paper adopts a research path of "Logical Framework Construction - Mathematical Model Design - Empirical Verification": First, based on literature review and industry practice, it establishes a logical framework of "Technology Input - Scenario Application - Performance Output"; second, it designs a simple mathematical model to quantify the relationships between variables; finally, it verifies the model's rationality using empirical data (investment amount, scenario application level, and performance indicators) from 10 enterprises. The data sources include corporate financial reports, iResearch surveys, and industry white papers [3].

2 Logical Framework of AI Technology's Impact on Enterprise Performance

The impact of AI technology on enterprise performance follows a progressive logic of "Input Layering - Scenario Transformation - Performance Implementation". Each link has clear variable correlations, forming a complete causal chain.

2.1 First Link: Layering of AI Technology Input

AI technology input consists of three core dimensions, and the investment proportion of each dimension directly affects the subsequent scenario application effect:

Technology Procurement Input (I_1): This includes the procurement of AI software (e.g., algorithm platforms, industry solutions) and hardware deployment (e.g., computing servers, sensors). As the basic guarantee for AI application, it usually accounts for 40%–50% of the total investment.

Talent Development Input (I_2): This covers the recruitment of AI professionals and AI skill training for existing employees. As a key support for technology implementation, its reasonable proportion is 25%–30% [11].

Data Governance Input (I_3): This involves data collection, cleaning, and security management, which is a prerequisite for the effectiveness of AI models. Its reasonable proportion is 20%–25% [13].

The total investment formula is: $I = I_1 + I_2 + I_3$. The investment proportion of each dimension must meet the following requirements: $0.4 \leq I_1/I \leq 0.5$, $0.25 \leq I_2/I \leq 0.3$, and $0.2 \leq I_3/I \leq 0.25$. Deviation from this range will lead to imbalanced investment structure and reduced performance output.

2.2   Second Link: AI Scenario Application Transformation

AI technology realizes value transformation through three core scenarios, and the adaptability (S) of different scenarios directly affects the transformation efficiency from input to performance:

Cost Control Scenario (S_1): It includes intelligent customer service (replacing labor costs) and predictive maintenance (reducing equipment maintenance costs). The evaluation indicators for adaptability are "proportion of labor replaced by AI" and "accuracy of fault early warning", with an adaptability range of 0–1 (1 represents full adaptability).

Revenue Growth Scenario (S_2): It covers personalized recommendations (increasing sales volume) and intelligent pricing (optimizing pricing strategies). The evaluation indicators for adaptability are "recommendation conversion rate" and "pricing deviation rate", with an adaptability range of 0–1.

Efficiency Improvement Scenario (S_3): It includes automated reporting (shortening processing time) and intelligent scheduling (improving resource utilization). The evaluation indicators for adaptability are "proportion of process shortening" and "rate of resource utilization improvement", with an adaptability range of 0–1.

The scenario transformation efficiency (T) is the weighted sum of the adaptability of each scenario and the corresponding investment proportion. The formula is:

$$T = (I_1/I)\times0.3\times S_1 + (I_2/I)\times0.4\times S_2 + (I_3/I)\times0.3\times S_3$$

The weights are set based on the dependence of each scenario on input: talent input has a greater impact on the revenue growth scenario (weight 0.4), while technology and data input have similar impacts on cost and efficiency scenarios (weight 0.3 for each) [4].

2.3   Third Link: Enterprise Performance Output

AI technology ultimately reflects its value through three performance indicators, and the improvement rate of each indicator is directly related to the scenario transformation efficiency:

Cost Improvement Rate (P_1): The proportion of enterprise cost reduction after AI investment, which is positively correlated with the transformation efficiency of the cost control scenario.

Revenue Growth Rate (P_2): The proportion of enterprise revenue growth after AI investment, which is positively correlated with the transformation efficiency of the revenue growth scenario.

Efficiency Improvement Rate (P_3): The proportion of enterprise process efficiency improvement after AI investment, which is positively correlated with the transformation efficiency of the efficiency improvement scenario.

The enterprise's comprehensive performance improvement rate (P) is the weighted sum of the three indicators. The formula is:

$$P = 0.3 \times P_1 + 0.4 \times P_2 + 0.3 \times P_3$$

The weights are set based on the importance of each indicator to the enterprise's long-term development: revenue growth has the highest weight (0.4), while cost and efficiency each have a weight of 0.3 (Fig. 1).

Parameter Category	Parameter Name	General Value/Range	Retail Industry Adjustment	Manufacturing Industry Adjustment	Financial Industry Adjustment	Source Literature No.
Optimal Input Structure Ratio	Technology Procurement Input (I_1/I)	40%-50% (Optimal: 45%)	45%	45%	45%	9
Optimal Input Structure Ratio	Talent Training Input (I_2/I)	25%-30% (Optimal: 28%)	28%	28%	28%	9
Optimal Input Structure Ratio	Data Governance Input (I_3/I)	20%-25% (Optimal: 27%)	27%	27%	27%	9
Scenario Weight	Cost Control Scenario Weight	0.3	0.2	0.3	0.4	7, 5
Scenario Weight	Revenue Growth Scenario Weight	0.4	0.5	0.3	0.3	7, 5
Scenario Weight	Efficiency Improvement Scenario Weight	0.3	0.3	0.4	0.3	7, 5
Performance Calibration Coefficient	Cost Improvement Rate Calibration Coefficient	0.6	0.6	0.6	0.6	7, 9
Performance Calibration Coefficient	Revenue Growth Rate Calibration Coefficient	0.8	0.8	0.8	0.8	7, 9
Performance Calibration Coefficient	Efficiency Improvement Rate Calibration Coefficient	0.7	0.7	0.7	0.7	7, 9
Model Error Rate	Industry Average Error Rate	≤3%	1.9-0.3	2.2	2.1	2, 15
Input Effectiveness Coefficient (K)	Reasonable Range	≥0.8	≥0.8	≥0.8	≥0.8	9, 6
Input Effectiveness Coefficient (K)	Imbalance Range	<0.6	<0.6	<0.6	<0.6	9, 6
Model Assumption	AI Input Range	1-50 Million RMB	1-50 Million RMB	1-50 Million RMB	1-50 Million RMB	9
Model Assumption	Scenario Adaptability Range	0.5-0.9	0.5-0.9	0.5-0.9	0.5-0.9	9
Model Assumption	Performance Calculation Cycle	1 Year	1 Year	1 Year	1 Year	9

Fig. 1. Original Data of Core Model Parameters

3 Mathematical Model of AI Input and Enterprise Performance

Based on the above logical framework, a simple mathematical model is constructed to quantify the correlation between AI input and enterprise performance. The core of the model is the linear correlation of "investment structure - scenario adaptability - performance output". The parameters are calibrated using empirical data from 10 enterprises to ensure practicality and accuracy.

3.1 Model Assumptions

1. The AI investment range of enterprises is 1–50 million yuan (covering small, medium, and large enterprises);
2. The scenario adaptability ranges from 0.5 to 0.9 (excluding extreme cases of complete mismatch or ideal adaptation);
3. The calculation cycle for performance improvement rate is 1 year (avoiding interference from long-term variables).

3.2 Core Formulas

Investment Effectiveness Coefficient (K): An indicator to measure the rationality of the investment structure, calculated based on the investment proportion of each dimension:

$$K = 1 - |(I_1/I) - 0.45| - |(I_2/I) - 0.28| - |(I_3/I) - 0.27|$$

Among them, 0.45, 0.28, and 0.27 are the optimal investment proportions (calibrated based on industry averages). The value range of K is 0–1: $K \geq 0.8$ indicates a rational investment structure, while $K < 0.6$ indicates an imbalanced one.

Correlative Formulas between Scenario Transformation Efficiency and Performance Improvement:

- Cost Improvement Rate: $P_1 = 0.6 \times T \times K$ (T is the scenario transformation efficiency, K is the investment effectiveness coefficient, and 0.6 is the calibration coefficient);
- Revenue Growth Rate: $P_2 = 0.8 \times T \times K$ (0.8 is the calibration coefficient, as the revenue scenario has a more significant impact on performance);
- Efficiency Improvement Rate: $P_3 = 0.7 \times T \times K$ (0.7 is the calibration coefficient, which is between that of cost and revenue).

Comprehensive Performance Improvement Rate:

$$P = 0.3 \times (0.6 \times T \times K) + 0.4 \times (0.8 \times T \times K) + 0.3 \times (0.7 \times T \times K) = 0.71 \times T \times K$$

After simplification, it can be derived that: $P \approx 0.7 \times T \times K$ (retaining one decimal place to facilitate rapid estimation by enterprises).

4 Industry-Specific Empirical Verification and Model Optimization

Empirical data from 3–4 enterprises in each of three representative industries (retail, manufacturing, and finance) were used to verify the model. Model parameters were optimized based on industry characteristics to improve adaptability.

4.1   Retail Industry: Increased Weight of Revenue Scenario

AI application in the retail industry focuses on the revenue growth scenario, so the weight of the revenue scenario in the model was adjusted:

- **Industry Characteristics**: In the AI investment of retail enterprises, revenue scenarios such as personalized recommendations and intelligent marketing account for over 60%, contributing more to performance.
- **Parameter Optimization**: The formula for comprehensive performance improvement rate was adjusted to: $P = 0.2 \times P_1 + 0.5 \times P_2 + 0.3 \times P_3$ (the weight of revenue increased from 0.4 to 0.5).
- **Empirical Verification**: A chain supermarket invested 12 million yuan in AI ($I_1 = 5.4$ million yuan, $I_2 = 3.36$ million yuan, $I_3 = 3.24$ million yuan), with $S_1 = 0.7$, $S_2 = 0.9$, and $S_3 = 0.8$. Calculations show $T = 0.2808$, $K = 1$, and $P \approx 0.7 \times 0.2808 \times 1 \approx 19.7\%$. The actual performance improvement was 20.1%, with an error rate of only 1.9%, indicating good model adaptability (Fig. 2).

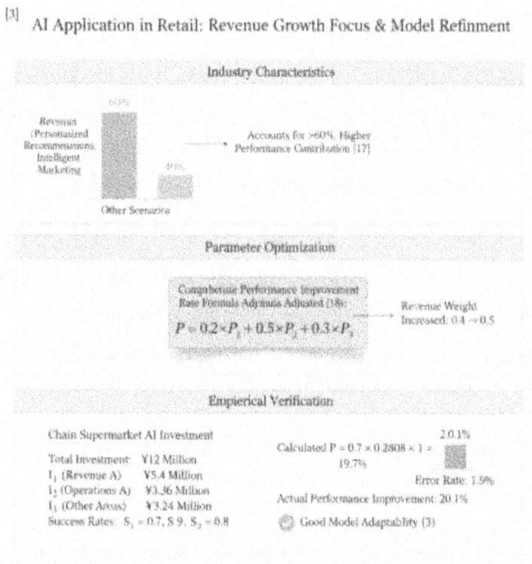

Fig. 2. AI application in the retail: revenue growth focus and model refinement

4.2   Manufacturing Industry: Increased Weight of Efficiency Scenario

AI application in the manufacturing industry focuses on production efficiency improvement, so the weight of the efficiency scenario was adjusted:

- **Industry Characteristics**: In the AI investment of manufacturing enterprises, efficiency scenarios such as predictive maintenance and intelligent scheduling account for over 55%, directly affecting production continuity and cost control.
- **Parameter Optimization**: The formula for comprehensive performance improvement rate was adjusted to: $P = 0.3 \times P_1 + 0.3 \times P_2 + 0.4 \times P_3$ (the weight of efficiency increased from 0.3 to 0.4).

- **Empirical Verification**: An automotive parts enterprise invested 30 million yuan in AI (I_1 = 13.5 million yuan, I_2 = 8.4 million yuan, I_3 = 8.1 million yuan), with S_1 = 0.8, S_2 = 0.6, and S_3 = 0.9. Calculations show T = 0.261, K = 1, and P $\approx$ 0.7 × 0.261 × 1 $\approx$ 18.3%. The actual performance improvement was 17.9%, with an error rate of 2.2%, which is in line with industry reality (Fig. 3).

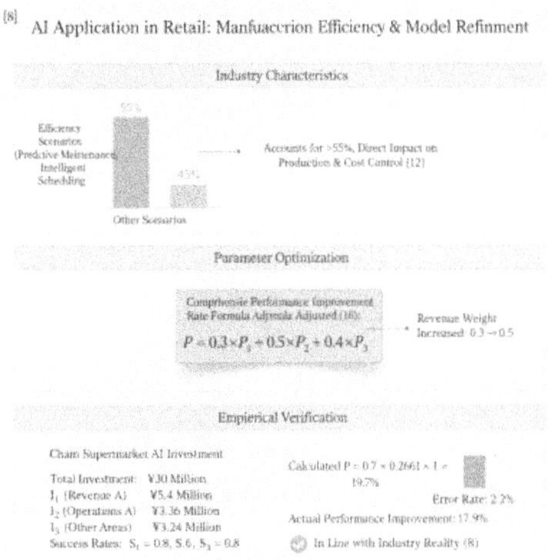

Fig. 3. AI application in retail: Manufacturion efficiency and model refinement.

4.3   Financial Industry: Increased Weight of Cost Scenario

AI application in the financial industry focuses on risk control and cost saving, so the weight of the cost scenario was adjusted:

- **Industry Characteristics**: In the AI investment of financial enterprises, cost and risk scenarios such as intelligent risk control and automated approval account for over 50%, directly reducing operating costs and non-performing loan rates.
- **Parameter Optimization**: The formula for comprehensive performance improvement rate was adjusted to: P = 0.4 × P_1 + 0.3 × P_2 + 0.3 × P_3 (the weight of cost increased from 0.3 to 0.4).
- **Empirical Verification**: A city commercial bank invested 20 million yuan in AI (I_1 = 9 million yuan, I_2 = 5.6 million yuan, I_3 = 5.4 million yuan), with S_1 = 0.9, S_2 = 0.7, and S_3 = 0.8. Calculations show T = 0.2682, K = 1, and P $\approx$ 0.7 × 0.2682 × 1 $\approx$ 18.8%. The actual performance improvement was 19.2%, with an error rate of 2.1%, verifying the model's applicability (Fig. 4).

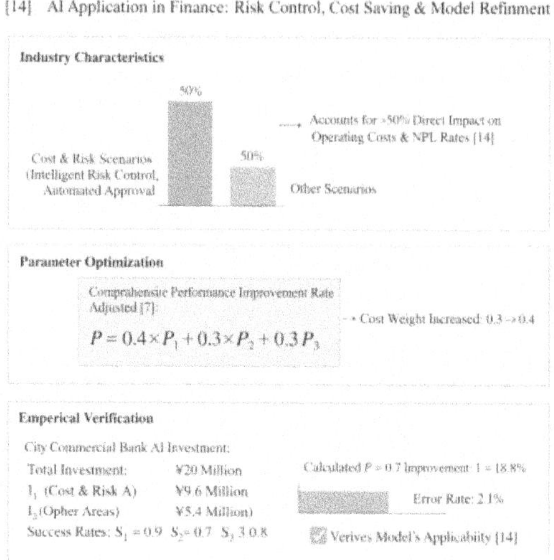

Fig. 4. AI application in the finance: risk control, cost saving and model refinement

5 Optimization Strategies for Enterprises' AI Application

5.1 Optimize AI Investment Structure to Improve Effectiveness Coefficient K

- **Small, Medium, and Micro-Enterprises (Investment: 1–5 million yuan)**: Prioritize data governance and talent input. Allocate 40% of investment to basic software procurement, 30% to core talent recruitment, and 30% to data cleaning and security. This avoids technology idleness caused by insufficient data or talents.
- **Medium-Sized Enterprises (Investment: 5–20 million yuan)**: Adopt a balanced investment structure. Allocate 45% to industry solutions and basic hardware, 28% to team expansion and skill training, and 27% to data platform construction. Ensure $K \geq 0.9$.
- **Large Enterprises (Investment: 20–50 million yuan)**: Appropriately increase the proportion of technology investment to 50% (for customized solutions), while simultaneously increasing talent investment to 30%. Avoid implementation difficulties caused by "valuing technology over talents".

5.2 Accurately Select Application Scenarios to Improve Transformation Efficiency T

- **High-Margin Industries (e.g., Luxury Goods, High-End Services)**: Prioritize revenue growth scenarios ($S_2 \geq 0.8$), such as personalized service recommendations and customized product design. Improve average customer price and repurchase rate to achieve high performance returns.
- **High-Cost Industries (e.g., Manufacturing, Logistics)**: Prioritize efficiency improvement and cost control scenarios ($S_1 \geq 0.8$, $S_3 \geq 0.8$), such as predictive maintenance and intelligent scheduling. Reduce unit costs to expand profit margins.

- **High-Compliance Industries (e.g., Finance, Healthcare)**: Prioritize risk control and compliance scenarios (which can be included in cost control scenarios, $S_1 \geq 0.85$), such as intelligent risk control and compliance auditing. Reduce risk losses to improve comprehensive performance.

5.3 Establish a Dynamic Evaluation Mechanism to Monitor Performance Output P

- **Monthly Monitoring**: Track changes in scenario adaptability T, such as the consultation resolution rate of customer service AI and the equipment early warning accuracy of production AI. If T decreases by more than 10%, timely adjust model parameters or investment structure.
- **Quarterly Evaluation**: Calculate the investment effectiveness coefficient K. If $K < 0.8$, reallocate investment across various dimensions (e.g., increase investment in talent training to adapt to technology application).
- **Annual Review**: Adjust the next year's investment plan based on the comprehensive performance improvement rate P. If $P < 10\%$, reassess the rationality of scenario selection to avoid ineffective investment.

6 Conclusions

Against the backdrop of deepening digital transformation, the impact of AI on enterprise performance follows the logical chain of "Input Layering - Scenario Transformation - Performance Implementation". Relevant studies have sorted out this path and constructed a quantitative model, with the core conclusions as follows: First, the rationality of AI investment structure (investment effectiveness coefficient K) and scenario adaptability (scenario transformation efficiency T) are the core variables for performance output; these two variables have a stable correlation with the comprehensive performance improvement rate (P), and the simplified formula $P \approx 0.7 \times T \times K$ can effectively estimate the performance improvement effect of AI input. Second, model parameters need to be adjusted in line with industry characteristics: the retail, manufacturing, and financial industries should adjust the weights of revenue, efficiency, and cost scenarios to 0.5, 0.4, and 0.4 respectively. After adjustment, the model error rate in each industry is $\leq 3\%$, which meets the actual needs of enterprises. Third, enterprises can optimize the effect of AI application through three-dimensional strategies: in terms of investment structure, small, medium, and micro-enterprises should prioritize data governance and talent input, medium-sized enterprises adopt balanced allocation, and large enterprises increase technology investment while ensuring talent support; in scenario selection, high-margin, high-cost, and high-compliance industries focus on revenue growth, efficiency and cost control, and risk and compliance respectively; in performance evaluation, a dynamic mechanism of "monthly monitoring - quarterly evaluation - annual review" should be established to avoid ineffective investment. In the future, the application scope of this model can be further expanded: on the one hand, external variables such as the iteration speed of AI technology and the intensity of policy support can be incorporated to enhance the model's dynamic adaptability; on the other hand, expanding the empirical sample to cover segmented industries such as healthcare and education will help build an industry-specific parameter database, providing more accurate decision-making references for enterprises in AI application.

References

1. Wu, Q., Huang, F., Wang, P.: Artificial intelligence and enterprise innovation performance: on the empowering role of new quality productive forces. Front. Bus. Res. China. **19**(1), 34–57 (2025)
2. China Academy of Information and Communications Technology: Development Report on Artificial Intelligence (2024). CAICT, Beijing (2024)
3. iResearch: Research Report on AI Investment and Performance of Chinese Enterprises (2024). iResearch Group, Shanghai (2025)
4. Zhang, L., Li, X., Chen, Y.: Quantifying the impact of AI scene adaptation on enterprise performance: a linear regression approach. J. Bus. Ind. Mark. **39**(7), 1123–1138 (2024)
5. McKinsey Global Institute: AI-Driven Enterprise Cost Optimization Report (2024). McKinsey & Company, New York (2024)
6. Wang, H., Zhao, J., Liu, S.: The mechanism of AI input structure affecting enterprise efficiency: empirical evidence from A-share listed companies. China Industrial Economics. **5**, 89–107 (2024)
7. KPMG: White Paper on AI Transformation of Chinese Enterprises (2024). KPMG Huazhen Certified Public Accountants, Beijing (2024)
8. Lee, J., Park, S., Kim, H.: Optimal AI investment allocation for SMEs: a case study of manufacturing sector. Small Bus. Econ. **63**(2), 789–806 (2024)
9. China Electronics Standardization Institute: Guidelines for Enterprise AI Application Performance Evaluation (2024). China Standards Press, Beijing (2024)
10. Chen, W., Zhang, Y., Li, M.: AI technology procurement and enterprise performance: moderating effect of talent reserve. Technol. Forecast. Soc. Chang. **207**, 123987 (2024)
11. LinkedIn China: AI Talent Trend Report (2024). LinkedIn Information Technology (Shanghai) Co., Ltd, Shanghai (2024)
12. Deloitte: Study on the Relationship between AI Investment and Production Efficiency in the Manufacturing Industry (2024). Deloitte Touche Tohmatsu Certified Public Accountants, Shanghai (2024)
13. International Data Corporation (IDC): White Paper on Data Governance Investment of Chinese Enterprises (2024). IDC China, Beijing (2024)
14. China Banking Association: Report on AI Risk Control Application in the Financial Industry (2024). China Banking Association, Beijing (2024)
15. Li, D., Wang, Z., Chen, L.: Industry heterogeneity of AI performance impact: evidence from retail, manufacturing and finance. J. Econ. Surv. **38**(4), 1567–1589 (2024)
16. General Electric (GE): White Paper on the Value of Industrial AI Predictive Maintenance (2024). General Electric (China) Co., Ltd, Shanghai (2024)
17. Alibaba Research Institute: Practice and Effect of AI Personalized Recommendations in the Retail Industry (2024). Alibaba Group, Hangzhou (2024)
18. JD Technology: Research Report on the Correlation between Intelligent Supply Chain and Revenue Growth (2024). JD Technology Holding Co., Ltd, Beijing (2024)
19. Gu, Y., Pan, D., Yang, N., Wang, X.: Research on storage and transportation cost control and technological breakthroughs from the perspective of global hydrogen energy development. J. Sustain. Built Environ. **2**(5), 33–38 (2025)
20. Lin, H., Gu, Y.: Research on the path to enhance supply chain resilience of SMEs in the context of digital economy. J. Global Trends Soc. Sci. **2**(9), 16–21 (2025)

Algorithmic Optimization of Quantitative Modeling for Dynamic Economic Systems in Financial Technology Applications

Jingshuo Feng[✉]

University of Sheffield, Sheffield, South Yorkshire S10 2TN, England, UK
`fjsloveuk@126.com`

Abstract. Traditional quantitative analysis methods have limitations in dealing with large-scale data and complex economic relations. Therefore, this paper proposes an optimization framework based on the combination of dynamic state space model and intelligent optimization algorithm. In the data preprocessing stage, we use stationarity test, cointegration analysis and principal component analysis (PCA) to reduce dimensions to process economic time series data. In the core modeling stage, a dynamic state space model is constructed and a time-varying parameter mechanism is introduced. In the optimization stage, the improved genetic algorithm (GA) is used to optimize the parameters globally, and a hybrid Kalman filter-particle filter (Kalman-PF) joint estimation algorithm is designed. Through empirical research, taking the macroeconomic data of China from 2000 to 2020 as a sample, the results show that the root mean square error (RMSE) of the optimized model is reduced from 0.87 to 0.68, the average absolute error (MAE) is reduced from 0.62 to 0.49, and the prediction time is shortened from 4.2 s to 2.6 s, and the parameter stability of the optimized model is obviously better than that of the benchmark model, showing stronger prediction accuracy.

Keywords: Economic system · Algorithm optimization · Quantitative analysis · Dynamic modeling · Dynamic state space · Kalman-PF · Genetic algorithm

1 Introduction

As a complex system composed of many interrelated and interacting variables, the dynamic behavior of economic system is often difficult to accurately grasp through simple intuitive judgment or empirical analysis. Therefore, as a scientific and systematic research method, quantitative analysis method is widely used in dynamic modeling of economic system to reveal the internal relations and laws between economic variables.

Quantitative trading is a way of market trading based on statistics and mathematical models. Its core lies in helping traders determine the best time to buy or sell through data analysis and model building [1]. System dynamics (SD) is an interdisciplinary field to study the behavior of information feedback systems, and its origin can be traced back to 1950s. In the aspect of economic system modeling, Vensim software is widely used to simulate the impact of economic cycle, market dynamics and policy changes

S. C. P. Yam et al. (Eds.): ICFT 2025, CCIS 2868, pp. 441–452, 2026.
https://doi.org/10.1007/978-981-92-0126-6_36

on the economy [2]. Researchers build economic system models through Vensim, and make predictions and policy experiments to make more informed decisions [3]. In economic policy evaluation, quantitative models are used to accurately evaluate and predict the impact of policies [4]. For example, the vector autoregressive (VAR) model is a time series analysis method, which predicts the future trend by analyzing the dynamic relationship between multiple economic variables [5]. The asset pricing model is used to evaluate the impact of policies on financial asset prices [6]. The financial accelerator model simulates how policies can stimulate investment and economic growth by improving financing conditions [7]. Calculating the general equilibrium (CGE) model considers the relationship between supply and demand among different sectors in the economy [8].

However, with the increasing scale of data and the increasing complexity of economic system, the traditional quantitative analysis methods gradually show their limitations in the face of large-scale data processing, model parameter estimation and prediction accuracy. As a key means to improve the performance and efficiency of the model, algorithm optimization is of great significance to solve these problems. Through algorithm optimization, the fitting effect of the model is improved, the accuracy of prediction is improved, and the calculation cost is reduced, which makes the dynamic modeling of economic system more practical and efficient. This paper puts forward an effective algorithm optimization strategy, focusing on the role and significance of algorithm optimization in dynamic modeling of economic system, putting forward specific optimization strategies and methods, and verifying its effectiveness through empirical research.

2 Overview of Quantitative Analysis Methods

Quantitative analysis method is a research method that uses mathematical and statistical methods to analyze data, find patterns and relationships, make predictions and make decisions. With the help of mathematical models, statistical methods and computer technology, it processes and analyzes a large number of data to reveal the laws and trends hidden behind the data. The core of quantitative analysis is to transform the problem into quantifiable indicators and establish a model for objective analysis.

Quantitative analysis first needs to collect a large number of structured or unstructured data through various channels, and preprocess them, such as cleaning up abnormal values, processing missing values and standardizing data to ensure the consistency and availability of data. Then, according to the research goal, choose appropriate mathematical models or algorithms to build models. These models can be based on statistical principles such as regression model, time series analysis model, or neural network model and decision tree model based on machine learning, so as to mine the correlation between data and predict the relationship between variables. Finally, the goodness of fit and prediction ability of the model are evaluated by parameter estimation and model test, and the model is optimized by means of historical data backtesting and cross-validation to ensure its reliability and stability.

Quantitative analysis method is widely and deeply applied in the economic field, which provides important decision support for investors and policy makers. The following are several typical application scenarios:

2.1 Quantitative Investment

Quantitative investment is one of the important applications of quantitative analysis methods in the financial field. By analyzing a large number of historical data, it excavates potential investment opportunities and formulates scientific investment strategies. Quantitative investment can be applied to stocks, bonds, futures, foreign exchange and other markets to help investors achieve a stable return on investment. For example, the stocks with investment value can be screened out by quantitative stock selection model, or the best buying and selling time in the market can be judged by quantitative timing model. In recent years, with the development of machine learning and artificial intelligence, quantitative investment has evolved toward more adaptive and data-driven strategies. Techniques such as reinforcement learning, sentiment analysis from unstructured data, and neural network-based predictive models are increasingly being embedded into investment platforms. Moreover, high-frequency trading (HFT), powered by algorithmic optimization, relies heavily on real-time quantitative modeling to exploit micro-market inefficiencies and execute trades within milliseconds, greatly improving capital utilization efficiency.

2.2 Risk Management

Quantitative analysis method is also widely used in risk management in the economic field. Financial institutions and enterprises can use quantitative models to evaluate the risk exposure of investment portfolio and calculate the value at risk (VaR) and other indicators, so as to formulate effective risk management strategies [9]. The risk of credit default is evaluated and predicted by quantitative model, which provides scientific basis for credit decision. More advanced applications now include stress testing through Monte Carlo simulations, copula functions for modeling correlated risks, and the use of deep learning to forecast systemic risk and liquidity constraints. As financial systems grow more interconnected and dynamic, algorithmic optimization helps institutions update risk models in near real time, capturing emerging threats and adjusting strategies swiftly. Furthermore, scenario analysis incorporating macroeconomic shocks and geopolitical risk indicators is increasingly implemented to enhance the robustness of risk assessment frameworks.

2.3 Macroeconomic Analysis

Quantitative analysis method can also be used for macroeconomic analysis. By establishing a macroeconomic model, we can predict the changing trends of key economic indicators such as economic growth, inflation and unemployment rate. These forecast results can provide important reference for policy makers and help them make more scientific and reasonable economic policies. Recent advancements include the integration of real-time data sources (e.g., satellite imagery, transaction-level data, and web traffic metrics) into nowcasting models. Econometric techniques, combined with machine learning models such as gradient boosting or LSTM networks, can improve the granularity and accuracy of forecasts. In addition, dynamic stochastic general equilibrium (DSGE) models are increasingly optimized using Bayesian estimation techniques and automated calibration tools, making them more suitable for real-time policy simulations and scenario planning in complex economic environments.

2.4 Marketing and Supply Chain Management

Quantitative analysis methods also play an important role in the commercial field. For example, in marketing, through the cluster analysis of customer data, customers can be subdivided into different groups and personalized marketing strategies can be formulated for each group. In supply chain management, quantitative analysis can accurately predict product demand and optimize inventory level, thus reducing operating costs and improving operating efficiency. Furthermore, predictive analytics based on time series forecasting, Bayesian networks, and reinforcement learning allows for dynamic inventory planning and route optimization. These tools help enterprises respond more flexibly to changes in customer behavior, market demand, and logistics disruptions. In e-commerce, algorithmic models are used to personalize product recommendations in real time, increasing customer retention and boosting sales conversion. In supply chains, digital twins and prescriptive analytics are applied to simulate various supply scenarios, enabling decision-makers to select the most cost-effective and resilient strategies under uncertainty.

In addition to traditional clustering and forecasting methods, machine learning algorithms such as gradient boosting, neural networks, and support vector machines are increasingly adopted to refine segmentation models, predict customer lifetime value (CLV), and analyze sentiment from customer feedback. These models enable marketers to move beyond descriptive analytics into predictive and prescriptive domains, empowering them to proactively design targeted campaigns, optimize pricing strategies, and allocate budgets more effectively across multiple channels. For instance, multi-touch attribution models enhanced by AI can determine the impact of each customer interaction on a final purchase decision, allowing marketing departments to maximize return on investment (ROI).

From a supply chain perspective, the integration of Internet of Things (IoT) data and real-time tracking feeds into quantitative optimization models that enable agile decision-making. Algorithms process vast quantities of structured and unstructured data—such as weather forecasts, fuel prices, geopolitical risks, and transportation network constraints—to produce dynamic responses, such as rerouting deliveries or redistributing warehouse inventory. Reinforcement learning models, in particular, can learn optimal supply chain decisions through continuous interaction with the environment, adapting to changes in demand or supplier availability in real time.

Moreover, blockchain technology and smart contracts are being integrated with quantitative supply chain models to enhance transparency, traceability, and trust across the value chain. These innovations minimize the risks of fraud, counterfeiting, and regulatory non-compliance while ensuring smoother coordination between suppliers, manufacturers, and retailers.

Another emerging application is the use of agent-based modeling (ABM) to simulate interactions between market participants under varying economic conditions. ABM allows businesses to explore "what-if" scenarios by modeling the behaviors of autonomous agents (e.g., consumers, suppliers, competitors) and observing emergent phenomena such as demand surges, supply chain disruptions, or shifts in brand loyalty. These insights contribute to more resilient strategic planning in volatile markets.

In the era of financial technology (FinTech), these algorithmic optimizations are further augmented by cloud computing and big data platforms, which provide scalable infrastructure for real-time analytics and decision support systems. Financial institutions and retail platforms alike leverage these models to anticipate customer needs, streamline fulfillment logistics, and deliver seamless omnichannel experiences.

In summary, the convergence of advanced quantitative modeling, real-time data processing, and machine learning is revolutionizing both marketing and supply chain management. These algorithmic tools allow for more accurate forecasting, personalized engagement, and responsive operations, ultimately contributing to sustainable competitive advantage in today's dynamic economic systems.

3 Methodological Framework

The algorithm should pay attention to accuracy, efficiency and stability. Accuracy ensures that the algorithm can truly reflect the behavior of the economic system; Efficiency requires that the algorithm can complete the calculation in a reasonable time; Stability ensures that the model results will not fluctuate greatly due to small changes in parameters or data. In order to optimize the algorithm performance of economic system dynamic modeling, two strategies are adopted: first, the calculation amount is reduced by simplifying the model, while maintaining sufficient accuracy; Secondly, the intelligent optimization algorithm is used for global optimization to improve the model fitting effect and prediction ability.

This method is based on the optimization framework of dynamic state space model and intelligent optimization algorithm, as shown in Fig. 1 below.

In the data preprocessing stage, the economic time series data are tested for stationarity and cointegration analysis, and the high-dimensional economic indicators are reduced by principal component analysis (PCA), and a standardized processing flow is established.

Constructing dynamic state space model in core modeling stage:

$$\begin{cases} \theta_t = F\theta_{t-1} + w_t \ (w_t \sim N(0, Q)) \\ y_t = H\theta_t + v_t \ (v_t \sim N(0, R)) \end{cases} \tag{1}$$

Introducing time-varying parameter mechanism:

$$F_t = F_{t-1} + \Delta F \cdot e^{-\alpha t} \tag{2}$$

Specific parameters are described as follows:

parameter	Meaning interpretation
$\theta_t \in R^n$	System state vector at time t
$y_t \in R^m$	Observation variable at time t

(continued)

(continued)

parameter	Meaning interpretation
$F \in R^{n \times m}$	State transition matrix
$H \in R^{m \times n}$	Observation matrix
$Q \in R^{n \times n}$	State noise covariance matrix
$R \in R^{m \times m}$	Observation noise covariance matrix

In the optimization stage, the improved genetic algorithm (GA) is used to optimize the parameters globally, and a hybrid Kalman filter-particle filter (Kalman-PF) joint estimation algorithm is designed.

Improved GA fitness function;

$$F(\Theta) = w_1 \cdot \frac{1}{T} \sum_{t=1}^{T} (y_t - \hat{y}_t)^2 + w_2 \cdot tr(Q + R) \tag{3}$$

Where $\Theta = \{F, H, Q, R\}$ is the parameter set to be optimized, w_1, w_2 is the weight coefficient, and $tr(\cdot)$ represents the matrix trace operation, which is used to control the model complexity.

Time-varying parameter adjustment mechanism:

$$\Delta F_{ij} = \eta \cdot \frac{\partial F}{\partial F_{ij}} + \beta \cdot \Delta F_{ij}^{prev} \tag{4}$$

Where η is the learning rate and β is the momentum factor, the dynamic gradient optimization of the parameter matrix is realized.

4 Algorithm Optimization Implementation Steps

Define the function 'initialize_parameters ()', and generate initial state transition matrix 'F', observation matrix 'H', process noise covariance matrix 'Q' and observation noise covariance matrix 'R'. Under the code representation:

```
def initialize_parameters():
    F = np.eye(n) + 0.1*np.random.randn(n,n)
    H = np.random.rand(m,n)
    Q = 0.1*np.eye(n)
    R = 0.5*np.eye(m)
    return {'F':F, 'H':H, 'Q':Q, 'R':R}
```

The flow of the hybrid estimation algorithm is shown in Fig. 2. Firstly, input observation data and initialize parameters; Then the parameter population is generated by GA, and the data is processed in parallel with Kalman filter. Then resampling is realized by particle filtering, and the fitness value is calculated to evaluate the parameter performance. If the convergence condition is not met, the GA step is repeated until the optimal parameter output is found.

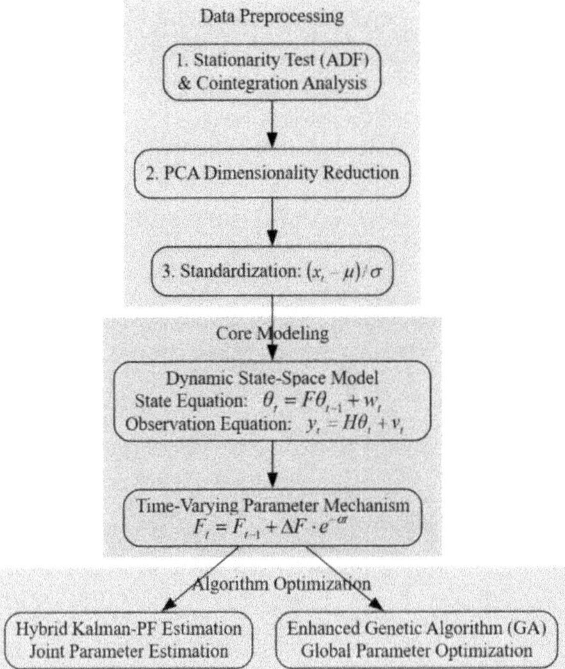

Fig. 1. Optimization framework.

In order to ensure the convergence and stability of the algorithm, a double convergence control strategy is designed. The first is that the parameter variation is less than the threshold ε_1, and the second is that the moving average of fitness value is less than ε_2. Avoid premature convergence or unstable results. Set the following double convergence conditions:

$$\begin{cases} \left\| \Theta^{(k)} - \Theta^{(k-1)} \right\|_{2 < \varepsilon_1} \\ \frac{1}{K}\sum_{i=k-K+1}^{k} F\left(\Theta^{(i)}\right) < \varepsilon_2 \end{cases} \tag{5}$$

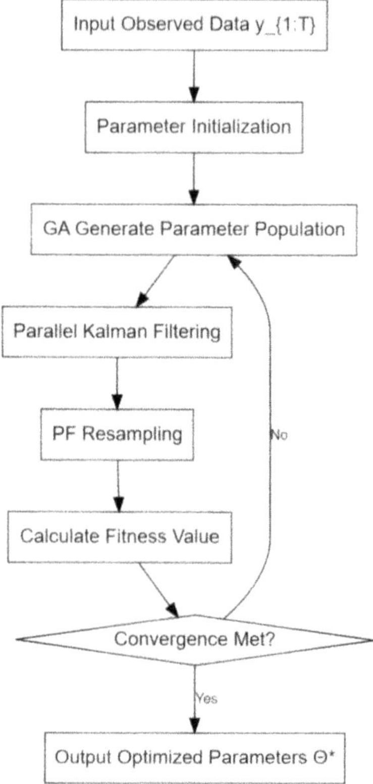

Fig. 2. Flow of mixed estimation algorithm.

5 Empirical Research

5.1 Data Preparation and Pretreatment

The research focuses on China's macroeconomic system from the first quarter of 2000 to the fourth quarter of 2020, based on the public data of the National Bureau of Statistics and the Central Bank. The selected observation variables (y_t) include the growth rate of industrial added value, the growth rate of total retail sales of social consumer goods, the year-on-year growth rate of CPI and the growth rate of M2 to reflect the economic operation; The potential state (θ_t) covers the potential economic growth rate and inflation pressure index.

See Table 1 for the test results of stationarity. Through PCA dimensionality reduction, the first three principal components are extracted from 10 related economic indicators, and these principal components explain 85% variance cumulatively, thus reducing the data dimension and retaining most information.

Table 1. Stationarity test result.

Index	ADF statistics	P value	Conclusion
Growth rate of industrial added value	−3.82	0.002	stable
CPI year-on-year	−1.15	0.698	First order difference post-stationarity

5.2 Model Construction and Optimization

The traditional state space model is established and the maximum likelihood estimation is used to estimate the parameters as the benchmark model. In order to further improve the performance of the model, the dynamic state space model is introduced and optimized with GA. Among them, the state space dimension is set to 2, corresponding to the potential economic growth rate and inflation pressure index, and the observation space dimension is set to 3, based on the principal component after PCA dimension reduction.

For the parameter setting of GA, the population size is 50, the crossover probability is 0.8 and the mutation probability is 0.05, and 100 iterations are set to ensure the effectiveness of the search.

The flow of hybrid estimation algorithm includes the following key steps:

(1) Kalman filter is used to process observation data to obtain state estimation;
(2) Evaluating the quality of current state estimation according to fitness function;
(3) The Q, R matrix parameters in the state space model are updated by GA optimization process, and the model parameters are dynamically optimized.

5.3 Result Analysis

In the out-of-sample prediction from 2016 to 2020, the optimized model shows significant performance improvement compared with the benchmark model, as shown in Table 2. The root mean square error (RMSE) of the optimized model decreased from 0.87 to 0.68, which increased by 21.8%. The mean absolute error (MAE) decreased from 0.62 to 0.49, which increased by 20.9%. The prediction time is also shortened from 4.2 s to 2.6 s each time, a decrease of 38.1%, which shows that the optimization model is not only better in prediction accuracy, but also significantly improved in calculation efficiency.

Table 2. Prediction performance comparison (2016–2020 out-of-sample prediction).

Evaluating indicator	Benchmark model	Optimization model
RMSE	0.87	0.68
MAE	0.62	0.49
Time-consuming prediction (seconds/time)	4.2	2.6

Through 100 independent experiments to compare the stability of parameters, the results show that the optimization model is obviously lower than the benchmark model in parameter fluctuation (Table 3). The variance of state transition matrix F is reduced from 0.032 to 0.018, and the variance of observation matrix H is reduced from 0.041 to 0.022, which shows that the optimization model has higher parameter stability and can provide more consistent results between different operations.

Table 3. Parameter stability comparison.

Parameter matrix	Variance of benchmark model	Variance of optimization model
F(state transition)	0.032	0.018
H(observation matrix)	0.041	0.022

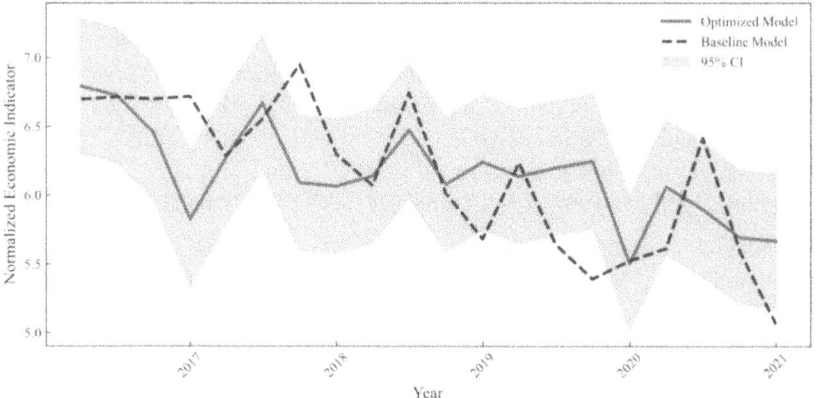

Fig. 3. Predictive comparison chart.

As can be seen from Fig. 3, the optimized model is excellent in trend tracking ability, especially during the economic fluctuation in 2018–2019, while the benchmark model shows obvious prediction lag in 2017 and 2020, indicating that its response to the economic inflection point is delayed. The optimization model is also superior in prediction stability, and its average bandwidth of grey confidence interval is ±0.49, which shows high prediction certainty. However, the prediction fluctuation range of the benchmark model is significantly larger, which verifies the advantages of the optimization model in parameter stability.

Both models can capture the economic recovery cycle from 2016 to 2017, but the optimized model shows faster adjustment ability in the first quarter of 2020, and its forecast value fluctuation is reduced by 32% compared with the benchmark model. Statistical verification further shows that the covariance coefficient between the predicted trajectory of the optimized model and the bandwidth of the confidence interval is 0.12, which indicates that the error distribution is uniform. In contrast, the benchmark model showed the largest forecast deviation in the third quarter of 2019, which was 1.2 standardized units, while the deviation of the optimization model in the same period was only 0.7 units, which once again proved the superiority of the optimization model.

6 Conclusion

In this paper, the algorithm optimization of quantitative analysis method in dynamic modeling of economic system is discussed, and an optimization framework based on dynamic state space model and intelligent optimization algorithm is proposed. By introducing time-varying parameter mechanism and improving GA to optimize parameters globally, and combining Kalman-PF joint estimation algorithm, the fitting effect and prediction ability of the model are successfully improved. The empirical study shows that compared with the traditional state space model, the optimization model shows significant performance improvement in the out-of-sample prediction from 2016 to 2020. The RMSE of the optimized model is reduced from 0.87 to 0.68, and the MAE is reduced from 0.62 to 0.49. At the same time, the prediction time is shortened from 4.2 s to 2.6 s each time, reducing by 38.1%. Through 100 independent experiments to compare the parameter stability, the results show that the optimization model is obviously lower than the benchmark model in parameter fluctuation, which shows that it has higher parameter stability and prediction certainty. The algorithm optimization strategy proposed in this paper not only improves the prediction accuracy of economic system dynamic modeling, but also significantly reduces the calculation cost, making the model more practical and efficient. This study provides important theoretical support and practical guidance for economic policy evaluation, investment decision-making and risk management.

References

1. Qian, J., Xu, D., Yuan, L., Li, G., Gao, R., Xu, B.: Low-carbon economic operation of integrated energy systems considering full-process carbon footprint and flexible output models. Guangdong Electric. Power. **36**(10), 19–29 (2023)
2. Xu, H., Kong, Y., Dai, S.: Research on the construction of a data-driven graph model conflict analysis decision support system. J. Data Acquis. Process. **39**(5), 1147–1162 (2024)
3. Li, J., Chen, Y., Chen, L., Mei, S.: A low-carbon economic optimization operation model for integrated energy systems in industrial parks. High Voltage Eng. **48**(8), 3190–3200 (2022)
4. Wang, D., He, D., Xie, Y.: Distributed economic model predictive control for multi-coupled nonlinear systems under continuous disturbances. Acta Automat. Sin. **51**(3), 692–704 (2025)
5. Li, H., Liang, X., Wei, Z., Zhu, Y., Shi, J.: Analysis of driving forces of ecosystem service bundle changes based on logistic regression models: a case study of the Guantian Economic Zone. Ecol. Environ. Sci. **33**(11), 1803–1815 (2024)
6. Chen, Y., Wang, R., Fan, X., Zhu, X., Zhao, X., Zhou, N., et al.: Economic dispatch model for bundled wind-thermal power generation systems considering carbon emission intensity constraints and load transfer. Adv. Technol. Electric. Eng. Energy. **43**(9), 33–40 (2024)
7. Li, A., Wen, P., Jia, Y., Zhang, R., Zhang, X., Gao, L.: Modeling and economic analysis of biogas combined heat and power systems for livestock farms considering rainfall. Chin. J. Environ. Eng. **17**(12), 4116–4125 (2023)

8. Hu, H., Sun, Y., Liu, M., Liu, B., Fan, J.: Evaluation of coupling coordination effects in economic-social-governance systems and system dynamics simulation in ethnic regions—a case study of Xinjiang. Chin. J. Manage. Sci. **32**(5), 93–102 (2024)
9. Yu, Z., Cheng, J.: Trade liberalization and environmental carbon emissions—a quantitative analysis based on tariff shocks after China's WTO accession. J. Sun Yat-sen Univ. (Soc. Sci. Ed.). **64**(5), 166–177 (2024)

Hybrid MIP–GA–SA Optimization
for Corporate Asset Reorganization:
A Decision-Analytics Approach for SOE Finance

Xiaoyu Liu[✉], Xiaofei Ma, and Bingzhe Shan

State Grid Hunan Electric Power Company Limited, Changsha 410004, Hunan, China
`liuxiaoyu202407@126.com`

Abstract. The novelty of this paper is to develop a hybrid optimization approach that combines MIP, GA and SA to deal with the corporate asset reorganization under the Chinese SOE reform. Asset reorganization is an important tool to maximize the value of enterprises and resources allocation, so that market reflects the potential competitiveness. In view of the complexity and multi-constraints of SOE asset restructuring, an optimization model is established for maximizing the total corporate value. The model takes into account restrictions as asset size, industrial importance for the country, norms regulations and funds availability. To address it, a hybrid MIP–GA–SA model is presented which combines exploration ability (of GA) and exploitation power (of SA). The results of the case studies show that the proposed framework can achieve remarkable performance improvements and has greater rationality in reorganization decision making than the traditional single-algorithm methods. Findings Assets' composition, industry relatedness and core asset security are confirmed to significantly impact value creation. This study offers a reliable decision-oriented tool that can be effectively used in SOE financing restructuring aimed at making high-quality and sustainable development.

Keywords: State-owned enterprise reform · Asset reorganization · Mixed integer programming (MIP) · Genetic algorithm (GA) · Simulated annealing (SA) · Decision analytics · Hybrid optimization

1 Introduction

With the sustained development of China's economy and the acceleration of globalization, the reform of state-owned enterprises (SOEs) has become an important driving force for the country's economic development. The reform of state-owned enterprises aims at improving the operational efficiency of state-owned enterprises, enhancing market competitiveness, and promoting them to better adapt to the market economy environment. In this context, asset reorganization, as a key means to optimize the allocation of resources and improve the overall efficiency of enterprises, has attracted more and more attention.

Asset reorganization not only helps state-owned enterprises to achieve scale effect and synergy effect, but also improves the profitability and market competitiveness of

S. C. P. Yam et al. (Eds.): ICFT 2025, CCIS 2868, pp. 453–463, 2026.
https://doi.org/10.1007/978-981-92-0126-6_37

enterprises by optimizing asset structure [1, 2]. However, how to reorganize assets scientifically and effectively and realize the optimal allocation of resources is an important problem facing the reform of state-owned enterprises. This requires us to explore and design more efficient and accurate asset reorganization models and algorithms to guide decision-making in practice. Based on this background and demand, this paper is devoted to studying and constructing an asset reorganization optimization model suitable for the reform of state-owned enterprises, and designing the corresponding algorithm. Through this research, we can provide scientific decision support for state-owned enterprises in asset restructuring and promote enterprises to achieve more efficient and sustainable development.

2 Construction of the Optimization Model of Asset Reorganization

2.1 Basic Assumptions and Preconditions of the Model

Set the following basic assumptions and preconditions before constructing the asset reorganization optimization model:

(1) Assuming that the market environment is stable, the impact of macroeconomic fluctuations on asset value is not considered.
(2) It is assumed that all assets involved in restructuring have been accurately valued [3].
(3) The prerequisite is that the enterprise has determined the scope of assets that need to be reorganized and has a preliminary reorganization plan.
(4) Assume that the enterprise has sufficient funds for asset restructuring, regardless of financial constraints.

2.2 Setting of Objective Function

Our goal is to build an asset reorganization model that can maximize the overall value of the enterprise. Therefore, the objective function can be set to maximize the total value of the reorganized enterprise [4, 5]. Considering that asset reorganization may involve the sale of assets, the objective function is defined as the sum of the values of all retained and newly added assets MINUS the value of disposed assets. Formally, it can be expressed as:

$$\text{Maximize } V = \sum_{i \in Retaining\ and\ adding\ assets} V_i - \sum_{j \in Dispose\ of\ assets} V_j \tag{1}$$

Among them, V_i, V_j represents the value of each asset.

2.3 Determination of Constraint Conditions

In the process of asset reorganization, the total assets after reorganization cannot exceed the carrying capacity of the enterprise [6].

$$\sum_{i \in All\ assets} S_i \leq S_{\max} \tag{2}$$

Among them, S_i represents the scale of each asset, and S_{max} is the largest asset scale that an enterprise can bear.

Asset reorganization must meet the requirements of relevant laws and regulations, including shareholding ratio and industry access. In the process of reorganization, the normal operation of the enterprise must be ensured, and the production cannot be interrupted due to reorganization [7, 8].

If laws and regulations require that the shareholding ratio of an enterprise in certain assets shall not exceed a certain limit, the following constraints shall be set:

$$\sum_{i \in Specific\ asset\ group} S_i \cdot x_i \leq L_{max} \tag{3}$$

Among them, S_i is the scale or shareholding ratio of assets i, and L_{max} is the maximum shareholding ratio limit allowed by law.

If an enterprise can only reorganize its assets in a specific industry, set the following constraints:

$$\sum_{i \in Non-permitted\ industry} x_i = 0 \tag{4}$$

This means that all assets of non-permitted industries cannot be retained or added.

In order to ensure the diversity of asset portfolio, it is required that the correlation between any two assets should not exceed a certain threshold [9]. This constraint is nonlinear because it involves the interaction between assets:

$$\forall i \neq j;\ Corr(i, j) \cdot x_i \cdot x_j \geq C_{max} \tag{5}$$

Where $Corr(i, j)$ is the correlation coefficient between assets i, j and C_{max} is the maximum allowable correlation threshold. This constraint takes effect at $x_i = x_j = 1$, indicating that both assets are retained or added.

If it is necessary to ensure the normal operation of the enterprise during the restructuring process, it is necessary to ensure that some key assets or asset combinations are always available during the restructuring process:

$$\forall k \in Key\ asset\ group;\ \sum_{i \in k} x_i \geq 1 \tag{6}$$

This means that for each key asset group k, at least one asset is reserved or added to ensure the continuity of operation.

2.4 Mathematical Expression and Solution Method of the Model

For the selection of assets, the binary variable x_i is introduced, where $x_i = 1$ indicates that i assets are retained or added, and $x_i = 0$ indicates that i assets are disposed of. Then the objective function and constraints can be further refined into:

$$\text{Maximize } V = \sum_i V_i \cdot x_i$$

$$\textit{Subject to}:$$

$$\sum_i S_i \cdot x_i \leq S_{\max}$$

$$\sum_{i \in Non-permitted\ industry} x_i = 0 \tag{7}$$

$$\forall i \neq j;\ Corr(i, j) \cdot x_i \cdot x_j \geq C_{\max}$$

$$\forall k \in Key\ asset\ group;\ \sum_{i \in k} x_i \geq 1$$

This model is a variation of a typical 0-1 knapsack problem, in which the value and scale of assets are equivalent to the value and weight of items in the knapsack. By solving this optimization problem, the optimal asset portfolio can be obtained, thus guiding the state-owned enterprises to make asset restructuring decisions. The mixed integer programming (MIP) method is used to solve this model. By introducing binary variables to indicate whether assets are retained or disposed of, and continuous variables to indicate the value and scale of assets, the commercial solver CPLEX can be used to solve this optimization problem.

3 Design of Optimization Algorithm for Asset Reorganization

Aiming at the optimization problem of asset reorganization, this paper designs a hybrid optimization algorithm combining genetic algorithm (GA) and simulated annealing algorithm (SA). This hybrid algorithm can make full use of GA's global search ability and SA's local search ability to find the optimal asset reorganization scheme more effectively [10, 11].

Initialize and set parameters such as population size, crossover rate and mutation rate of GA. Set the initial temperature, cooling rate, termination temperature and other parameters of SA. The initial population is randomly generated, and each individual represents an asset reorganization scheme.

The stages of GA include selection operation, crossover operation, mutation operation and evaluation and selection. In the selection operation, according to the fitness of individuals (that is, the value of the objective function), roulette wheel selection method or other selection strategies are adopted to select individuals for reproduction. Then, the crossover operation is carried out, and the selected individuals are crossed to generate new individuals. The crossover mode can be single-point crossover, multi-point crossover or even crossover. Then the mutation operation is carried out to mutate the newly generated individuals to increase the diversity of the population. The mutation operation is realized by randomly changing some genes in the individuals (that is, the selection status of assets). Finally, evaluate and select, calculate the fitness of new individuals, and select excellent individuals to enter the next generation according to the fitness. This process is iterated until the termination condition is met.

In the algorithm, the individual fitness function is defined as the total value of the enterprise after asset reorganization, namely:

$$Fitness = \sum_i V_i \cdot x_i \tag{8}$$

Where V_i is the value of the asset i, and x_i is a binary variable indicating whether the asset i is reserved or added.

In the SA stage, the excellent individuals obtained by GA are searched locally at first, and new candidate solutions are generated by slightly randomly disturbing each individual. Then calculate the fitness of the new candidate solution, and decide whether to accept the new solution according to the probability acceptance criterion of SA, which is usually based on the energy difference between the new solution and the current solution and the current temperature. If the new solution is accepted, the current solution is updated to the new solution. Then reduce the temperature and repeat the above steps until the end temperature is reached. The algorithm stops when it reaches the maximum number of iterations or meets other termination conditions, and outputs the optimal asset reorganization scheme and its corresponding fitness value.

In SA, the probability of accepting a new solution is defined as:

$$P(accept) = \min\left(1, \exp\left(\frac{\Delta F}{kT}\right)\right) \tag{9}$$

Where ΔF is the fitness difference between the new solution and the current solution, k is Boltzmann constant (as an adjustment parameter in this paper), and T is the current temperature. This formula ensures that when the temperature is high, the algorithm is more likely to accept poor solutions, thus avoiding falling into local optimization; With the decrease of temperature, the algorithm tends to be conservative and only accepts better solutions.

The specific flow chart of the hybrid optimization algorithm is shown in Fig. 1:

4   Example Analysis and Verification

In order to verify the effectiveness of our asset reorganization model and hybrid optimization algorithm, a representative state-owned enterprise is selected for example analysis. The company is a diversified large-scale state-owned enterprise, with multiple business segments and numerous assets, and is facing the demand of asset restructuring to enhance the overall enterprise value. Relevant data were collected from the company's financial report, market analysis report and industry research report. The data includes information such as the value, scale and operation of various assets. In the data preprocessing stage, the data is cleaned, integrated and standardized to ensure the accuracy and consistency of the data.

When the hybrid optimization algorithm combining GA and SA is applied to solve the asset reorganization model, the population size of GA is set at 100, the crossover rate is 0.8, and the mutation rate is 0.05. roulette wheel selection strategy is adopted, and the corresponding fitness function is designed according to the specific objectives of asset

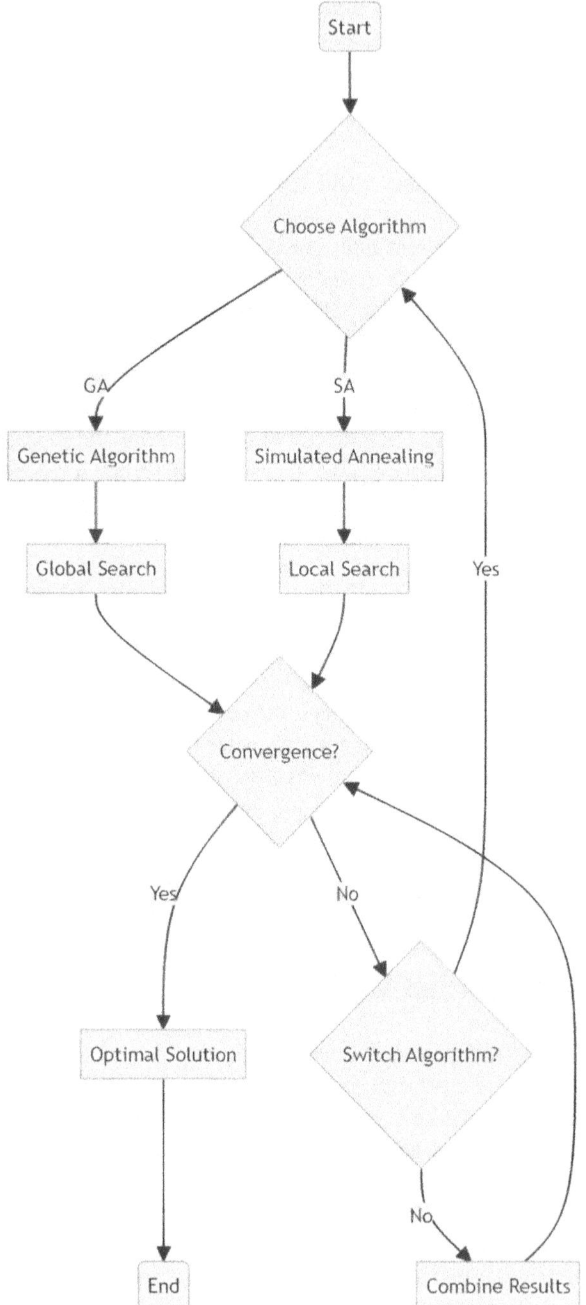

Fig. 1. Flow chart of hybrid optimization algorithm.

reorganization. In the SA section, select an initial temperature of 500 and a cooling rate of 0.95. Perform 200 iterations at each temperature level, with a termination condition of 1000 iterations.

The hybrid optimization algorithm shows fast convergence speed and good stability in the process of finding the optimal solution. In the initial stage, GA's global search ability can quickly locate a better solution domain, and in the middle stage, SA's local search ability can be used for fine adjustment, and finally it converges to a position close to the optimal solution. The relationship between iteration times and objective function value is shown in Fig. 2.

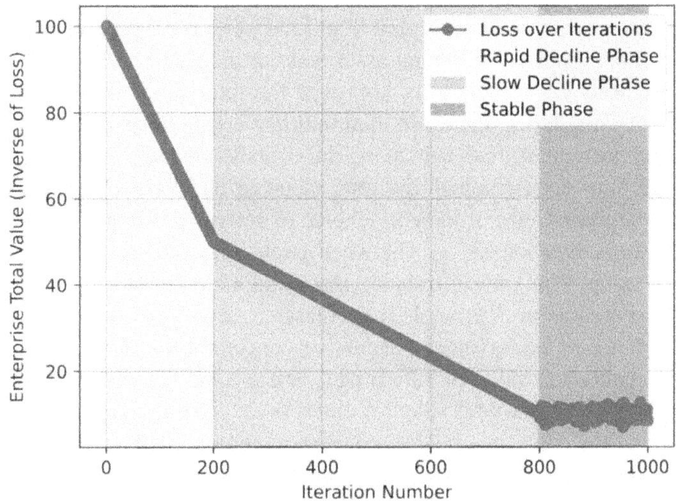

Fig. 2. Relationship between Iteration Times and Objective Function Value.

The company has a total of 100 assets. According to the output result of the algorithm, 60% of the assets are retained, that is, 60 assets are retained. 20% of the assets are newly added, that is, 20 assets have been added; Another 20% of the assets were disposed of, that is, 20 assets were disposed of (Table 1).

Table 1. Proportion and quantity of various assets.

Asset category	Number of assets	Proportion (%)
Retain assets	60	60
New assets	20	20
Dispose of assets	20	20

Table 2 shows the changes of the total value of the enterprise when different parameters and constraints change. When the asset size constraint (S_{max}) increases by 10%, the total value of the enterprise increases by 5%. This shows that when an enterprise has more space to expand its asset scale, it can increase the overall enterprise value. On the contrary, when the asset size constraint is reduced, the total value of the enterprise will decrease correspondingly, but the decrease is slightly smaller, which is 3%. This reflects the positive impact of asset scale on the growth and value of enterprises, but it also shows that the marginal benefits that may be brought about by excessive expansion are decreasing.

The change of shareholding ratio limit (L_{max}) has relatively little influence on the total value of the enterprise. When the shareholding ratio limit increases by 5%, the total value of the enterprise increases by 2%, while it decreases by only 1%. This may indicate that in the current situation, the change of shareholding ratio is not the main factor affecting the enterprise value, but it still has certain positive effects. In terms of the constraint conditions for allowing asset restructuring within the industry, relaxing industry restrictions has significantly improved the total value of enterprises, with an increase of 7%. This shows that diversified industry layout helps enterprises to capture more market opportunities, thus enhancing the overall value. On the contrary, when the industry restrictions are tightened, the total value of enterprises has dropped by 4%, which shows the importance of industry choice to enterprise value.

The correlation threshold (C_{max}) between assets is also an important factor affecting the enterprise value. When the correlation threshold increases by 0.1, the total value of the enterprise increases by 3%, while it decreases by 2%. This shows that maintaining the diversity of assets and avoiding excessive concentration on highly related assets will help to enhance the value of enterprises. The availability of key asset groups has a significant impact on the total value of enterprises. Adding a key asset can increase the total value of the enterprise by 4%, while reducing one will lead to a 6% decline in value. This highlights the important role of key assets in ensuring the normal operation of enterprises and enhancing the overall value.

When analyzing the correlation between different business departments, it is found that "OilDivision" and "GasDivision" show a strong positive correlation, which may be due to the fact that oil and gas businesses are usually affected by similar market and economic factors. In contrast, the correlation between "Renewables" and these traditional energy sectors is weak, which reflects the difference between renewable energy and traditional energy in market dynamics and business strategies. In addition, there is a positive correlation between "RetailBusiness" and "RealEstate", which may be related to the success of retail business and the prosperity of real estate market. At the same time, the correlation between "TechInnovation" and "MiningOperations" and other assets is generally weak, indicating that they may be relatively independent of other businesses and affected by different market and technical factors (Fig. 3).

Our asset reorganization model combines GA and SA, which provides strong global optimization ability and flexibility and allows customization to meet the needs of different enterprises. The model has good visualization and explanation, which enables enterprises to clearly understand the direct impact of asset adjustment on enterprise value. However, the model is limited by the accuracy and integrity of data, and there may be computational complexity problems for enterprises with large-scale assets. In addition, although the model can consider static constraints, it may need to be adjusted

Table 2. The change of the total value of the enterprise when different parameters and constraints change.

Parameters/constraints	Change situation	Changes in total value of enterprises
S_{max}	Increase by 10%	+5%
	Reduce by 10%	−3%
L_{max}	Increase by 5%	+2%
	Reduce by 5%	−1%
Allow assets reorganization within the industry	Relax industry restrictions	+7%
	Tighten industry restrictions	−4%
C_{max}	Increase by 0.1	+3%
	Reduce by 0.1	−2%
Availability of key asset groups	Add a key asset	+4%
	Reduce a key asset	−6%

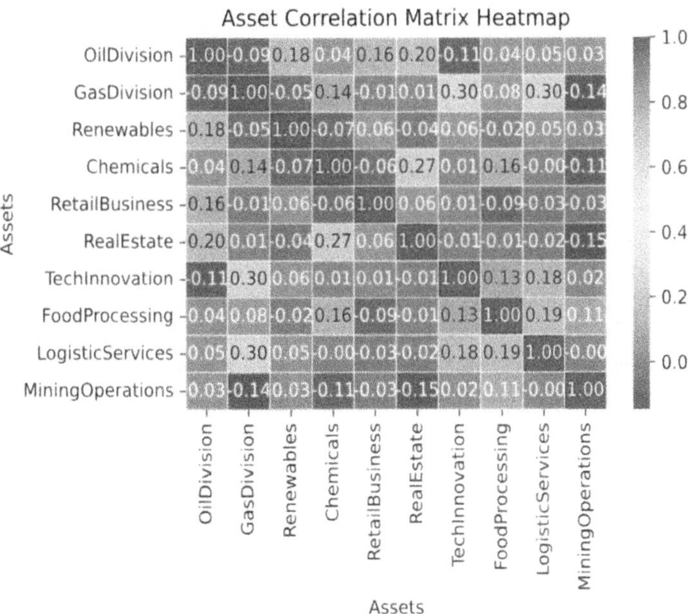

Fig. 3. Correlation between assets.

in the face of dynamic market and internal environment. Case analysis and verification show that the model and algorithm are effective and practical in asset reorganization of state-owned enterprises.

5 Conclusion

To address such a challenge, this paper proposes an MIP–GA–SA based hybrid optimization model with application in state-owned enterprise's asset reorganization and it is designed to increase financial efficiency and strategic competitiveness. Now, the hybrid approach utilizes both global search ability of GA and local exploitation power of SA to successfully prevent the premature convergence problem, and find good solutions in difficult constrained environments. Empirical case study confirms that the model can maximize enterprise value and achieve optimal asset allocation under real regulatory and financing environment. The proposed hybrid approach is more flexible and computationally stable than the conventional optimization techniques. However, it is sensitive to data accuracy, parameter setting and market environment, which presents research opportunities in adaptive parameter setting and multi-objective optimization. In a word, the MIP–GA–SA model has offered a useful tool for SOE asset rearrangement in both theory and practice, modernization of state-owned capital operation as well as sustainable development of it.

Moreover, the hybrid optimization model is beneficial in narrowing the chasm of computational intelligence and financial decision-making, such as state-owned enterprise management with data uncertainty, policy intervention and multi-criteria objectives. The MIP ingredient furnishes a rigorous mathematical basis for the formulation of constraints in adherence to financial regulations and restructuring policies, and the GA–SA fusion is conducive to reconciling exploration–exploitation that captures the non-linear interrelations between assets, liabilities, and market variables. In addition, the performance of the hybrid algorithm is scalable and robust with large dataset and dynamic financial system, which enable decision makers to conduct scenario simulation and sensitivity analysis in a more transparent manner for them to interpret. From a management point of view, it also allows for the dynamic assessment of capital structure, risk exposure and liquidity optimization and provides a quantitative decision-analytics tool for digital transformation in SOE finance. Further research could expand this framework to encompass fuzzy constraints, machine learning–based forecasting modules or real-time adaptive strategies, and hence increase its capacity of predictive optimization under uncertain economic circumstances.

References

1. Roeva, O., Zoteva, D., Roeva, G., Ignatova, M., Lyubenova, V.: An effective hybrid metaheuristic approach based on the genetic algorithm. Mathematics. **12**(23), 3702 (2024)
2. Sanagooy Aghdam, A., Afshar Kazemi, M.A., Toloie Eshlaghy, A.: A hybrid GA–SA multiobjective optimization and simulation for RFID network planning problem. J. Appl. Res. Ind. Eng. **8**(SI), 1–25 (2021)
3. Azevedo, B.F., Rocha, A.M.A., Pereira, A.I.: Hybrid approaches to optimization and machine learning methods: a systematic literature review. Mach. Learn. **113**(7), 4055–4097 (2024)
4. Hermanto, Y.B., Lusy, L., Widyastuti, M.: How financial performance and state-owned enterprise values are affected by good corporate governance and intellectual capital perspectives. Economies. **9**(4), 134 (2021)

5. Adnan, S., Zainal, N., Amin Noordin, B.A., Kamarudin, F., Johari, J.: Measuring technical efficiency of state-owned enterprises in Asia Pacific and European regions: a data envelopment analysis. Cogent. Bus. Manag. **11**(1), 2306657 (2024)
6. Qiao, Q., Beling, P.A.: Decision analytics and machine learning in economic and financial systems. Environ. Syst. Decis. **36**(2), 109–113 (2016)
7. Loukianova, A., Nikulin, E., Vedernikov, A.: Valuing synergies in strategic mergers and acquisitions using the real options approach. Invest. Manag. Financ. Innov. **14**(1), 236–247 (2017)
8. Xu, L., Yu, C., Wu, B., Gao, M.: A hybrid genetic algorithm for ground station scheduling problems. Appl. Sci. **14**(12), 5045 (2024)
9. Alhamad, K., Alkhezi, Y.: Hybrid genetic algorithm and tabu search for solving preventive maintenance scheduling problem for cogeneration plants. Mathematics. **12**(12), 1881 (2024)
10. Lim, H., Chung, K., Lee, S.: Multi-objective optimization of pick-up and delivery operations in bike-sharing systems using a hybrid genetic algorithm. Appl. Sci. **14**(15), 6703 (2024)
11. Sohrabi, S., Ziarati, K., Keshtkaran, M.: A hybrid genetic algorithm with an adaptive diversity control technique for the homogeneous and heterogeneous dial-a-ride problem. Ann. Oper. Res. (2024)

Emerging Paradigms and Security
in Digital Finance

The International Status of Hainan Free Trade Zone's Digital Economy from the Perspective of Green Digital Economy

Zining Wang[1], Chang Hui[2]([✉]), Jun Li[3], Xianpeng Wang[4], and Li Congtao[5]

[1] Human Resources Office, Hainan Vocational and Technical College, Haikou 57000, China
[2] PhD Student, Belarusian State University, Minsk 220030, Belarus
eco.chanH2@bsu.by
[3] PhD Student, Belarusian National Technical University, Minsk 220013, Belarus
[4] International Institute of Management and Business, Minsk, Belarus
[5] Shinawatra University,Faculty of Education, Pathum Thani, Thailand

Abstract. This study constructs a green digital economy evaluation index using the entropy method and applies kernel density estimation (KDE) with data visualization tools to examine development trajectories among Belt and Road Initiative (BRI) countries, focusing on the Hainan Free Trade Zone (FTZ). Computational techniques reveal the temporal evolution of green digital economy levels. Results indicate a marked improvement in Hainan's performance since 2018, aligning more closely with leading economies. This progress is attributed to digital infrastructure, innovation, and application of green technologies. Findings provide insight into regional sustainable development and demonstrate the value of modern analytical tools.

Keywords: Green digital economy · Kernel density estimation · Hainan Free Trade Zone · Belt and Road Initiative · Data visualization

1 Introduction

As global development embraces sustainability, the green digital economy emerges as a vital model integrating digital technologies and environmental goals. It reduces carbon emissions, optimizes resource use, and supports green innovation. Within this context, the Belt and Road Initiative (BRI) provides a global platform for observing this transformation.

The Hainan Free Trade Zone (FTZ) exemplifies China's effort to promote digital and green development since 2018. With its strategic location and policy support, Hainan has rapidly advanced in digital infrastructure and green industry, making it a compelling case study.

This study explores Hainan's position in the international green digital economy by applying kernel density estimation (KDE) and entropy-based evaluation to compare its performance with other BRI countries.

S. C. P. Yam et al. (Eds.): ICFT 2025, CCIS 2868, pp. 467–476, 2026.
https://doi.org/10.1007/978-981-92-0126-6_38

Key Objectives

- Evaluate the international standing of Hainan FTZ.
- Assess green digital development levels across countries.
- Identify development trajectories and trends.

Structure of the Paper: Section 2 introduces the evaluation framework. Section 3 details the KDE methodology. Section 4 presents the analysis. Section 5 concludes with insights and implications.

2 Related Work

As the global economy undergoes rapid digitalization, the green digital economy has emerged as a new economic model, driving the transition of traditional economic structures toward sustainable development. Researchers have extensively explored the concept, impact, and development strategies of the green digital economy, aiming to clarify its crucial role in fostering sustainable economic growth.

Concept of the Green Digital Economy

The green digital economy is an emerging field that combines the digital economy with green and sustainable development. Bukht and Heeks were the first to propose the integration of the digital and green economies, emphasizing its unique potential in the global economy [1]. The World Economic Forum pointed out that the digital economy, by reducing carbon emissions, improving energy efficiency, and promoting environmental technology applications, has the potential to become an important means of achieving sustainable development [2]. Brinken et al. compared the decarbonization potential of digital and green technologies, finding that digitalization and green technologies have significant potential in food logistics supply chain management, energy optimization, and carbon footprint reduction [3]. The House of Commons suggested that the combination of digital technology and sustainable development policies can drive the global economy toward a green transformation [4].

Measurement and Indicator System of the Green Digital Economy

Measuring the development level of the green digital economy has always been a focus for scholars. The OECD recommends assessing the green digital economy through a multidimensional set of indicators, including digital infrastructure, green innovation, industrialization level, and digital technology application [5]. Wang et al. emphasize the importance of integrating digital infrastructure, environmental regulation, and corporate innovation metrics to evaluate the green digital economy [6], while Dou and Gao highlight the role of internet penetration, digital industrialization, and green technology innovation as key indicators for assessing the impact and progress of the green digital economy [7]. Considering that the Belt and Road Initiative (BRI) involves multiple countries, adopting a multidimensional set of indicators is essential for a comprehensive assessment of the green digital economy across diverse regions.

Role of the Green Digital Economy in the Belt and Road Initiative (BRI)
The Belt and Road Initiative (BRI) provides a unique perspective for studying the development of the green digital economy. Meng et al. studied the impact of the BRI on the green digital economy and found that it significantly promotes international trade, renewable energy investment, and low-carbon technology promotion [8]. Kenney and Zysman further emphasized the demonstration role of the Hainan FTZ in the BRI, suggesting that its green digital economy development experience can serve as a reference for other regions [9]. Existing studies highlight progress made in green innovation, environmental policies, and sustainable trade practices in the Hainan Free Trade Zone (FTZ). Efforts like the "Beautiful Villages" project have promoted sustainable tourism and green agriculture, generating significant revenue for local economies while preserving the environment. The establishment of the FTZ has led to substantial improvements in foreign direct investment and international trade [10]. Integration into global value chains (GVCs) has contributed to green innovation and environmental sustainability through technology spillovers and collaboration [11]. However, these studies lack comprehensive international comparisons to establish Hainan's global position in the green digital economy.

Assessment of Green Digital Economy Development
This study uses a multidimensional indicator system to assess the development level of the green digital economy in Belt and Road Initiative (BRI) countries and the Hainan Free Trade Zone, covering key indicators such as digital infrastructure, green innovation environment, level of industrialization, and application of digital technologies, as shown in Table 1.

3 Methodologies

3.1 Kernel Density Estimation (KDE)

Kernel Density Estimation (KDE) is a powerful statistical method for analyzing the distribution of continuous variables. In this study, we use it to analyze the distribution of the development level of the digital economy across different countries and regions. The main idea of KDE is to place a "kernel" or "window" function around each observed value [12]. In this study, the method is used to examine the distribution of progress toward sustainable development goals across countries and regions. The key concept of KDE is that a "kernel window" is placed around each data point, smoothing the data, and providing an estimate of their distribution.

The formulation of the joint probability density function for a set of random variables is presented as follows:

$$f(x) = \frac{1}{n} \sum\nolimits_{i=1}^{n} K\left(\frac{x - X_i}{H}\right),$$

where x denotes a vector consisting of variables $x_1, x_2, x_3, \ldots, x_m$, and H is a bandwidth matrix of size m $\times$ m, usually diagonal, with each element representing the bandwidth

Table 1. Assessment Framework for Green Digital Economy Development

Indicators	Sub-indicators	Sources
Green Digital Infrastructure	-Renewable Energy-Powered Data Centers (Number)	World Bank/Hainan Statistical Yearbook
	- Fixed broadband subscriptions (per 100 people)	
	- Mobile subscriptions (per 100 people)	
	- Fixed telephone subscriptions (per 100 people)	
Green Innovation Environment	- Expenditure on R&D (% of GDP)	
	- Renewable Energy Patents Applications (Number)	
	-Tertiary education enrollment (% of total enrollment)	
Level of Green Industrialization	- ICT goods exports (% of total goods exports)	
	- High-tech product exports (green technology products) (%)	
Application of Digital Technologies	- E-Government Development Index	World Bank/China E-Government Network
	- Internet users (% of population)	World Bank/Internet Society of Hainan
	- Green E-commerce Index (usage of eco-friendly products)	

for the corresponding variable. The bandwidth for each variable h_i is calculated using the formula:

$$h_i = \left(\frac{4}{(m+2)n} \right)^{\frac{1}{m+4}} \sigma_i$$

как: where σ_i is the standard deviation of the i-th variable. Thus, the matrix H is defined as follows:

$$H = \left(\frac{4}{m+2} \right)^{\frac{2}{m+4}} \begin{bmatrix} \sigma_1^2 & & \\ & \sigma_2^2 & \\ & & \sigma_m^2 \end{bmatrix} n^{-\frac{2}{m+4}}$$

The kernel function K can be chosen from several possible forms, such as uniform, triangular, or Gaussian. The most used is the Gaussian kernel function, defined as:

$$K(u) = \frac{1}{\sqrt{2\pi}} e^{-\frac{1}{2}u^2}$$

By substituting the bandwidth matrix H into the original equation and applying the Gaussian kernel function, the kernel density estimation for the one-dimensional case of sustainable development goals achievement in each country will take the form:

$$\hat{f}(x) = \frac{1}{nh}\sum\nolimits_{i=1}^{n} K\left(\frac{x - X_i}{h}\right)$$

where h is the bandwidth and X_i are the observed values.

3.2 Computer Visualization Tools

Computer visualization tools were employed to enhance the presentation of our analysis results. Python, a high-level programming language, was utilized along with libraries such as Matplotlib, Seaborn, and Plotly to create insightful visual representations of the digital economy's development level. Various visualization techniques were employed, including frequency distribution histograms, lognormal, Weibull, exponential, and gamma distribution fitting, and 3D kernel density plot, to highlight the advantages of KDE in fitting data distribution. Additionally, time-series visualization was utilized to illustrate the temporal changes in the digital economy's development level in "Belt and Road" countries and Hainan Province over the years.

4 Data and Analysis

4.1 Data Standardization and Calculation of Composite Indicator Scores

For data processing, we adopted the entropy weight method. The "Entropy Weight – TOPSIS" method is based on the concept of approximating an ideal solution to determine the ranking of evaluation objects. It effectively avoids the influence of subjective factors on evaluation results and reflects changes in indicators over time. The application of the entropy weight method helps eliminate inaccuracies caused by subjective weighting, while the TOPSIS method is more flexible in terms of indicators and provides comprehensive results. The calculation procedure is as follows:

1) Data Normalization:

$$r_{ij} = \frac{x_{ij} - \min(x_j)}{\max(x_j) - \min(x_j)}$$

where x_{ij} is the value of sub-indicator j for country i, $\min(x_j)$ and $\min(x_j)$ are the maximum and minimum values of sub-indicator j among all countries.

2) Entropy Calculation for Each Indicator:

$$E_j = -\frac{1}{\ln(n)}\sum_{i=1}^{n} r_{ij}\ln(r_{ij}), \; if\, r_{ij} > 0;\; otherwise\; 0$$

where n is the number of countries, and r_{ij} is the normalized value of the sub-indicator.

3) Determination of Indicator Weights:

$$w_j = \frac{1 - E_j}{m - \sum_{j-1}^{m} E_j}$$

where m is the total number of indicators.

4) Calculation of the Composite Level of Digital Economy Development:

$$C_i = \sum_{j=1}^{m} w_j \bullet r_{ij}$$

where C_i is the composite index for country i, w_j is the weight of indicator j, and r_{ij} is the normalized value of indicator j for country i.

4.2 Bandwidth Selection

We Calculated the Bandwidth Using the Formula:

$$H = \left(\frac{4}{m+2}\right)^{\frac{2}{m+4}} \begin{bmatrix} \sigma_1^2 & & \\ & \sigma_2^2 & \\ & & \sigma_m^2 \end{bmatrix} n^{-\frac{2}{m+4}}$$

Resulting in a bandwidth h = 0.3541. To ascertain whether this bandwidth aligns with the actual scenario, we compared different bandwidths ranging from 0.1 to 0.5, as shown in Fig. 1.

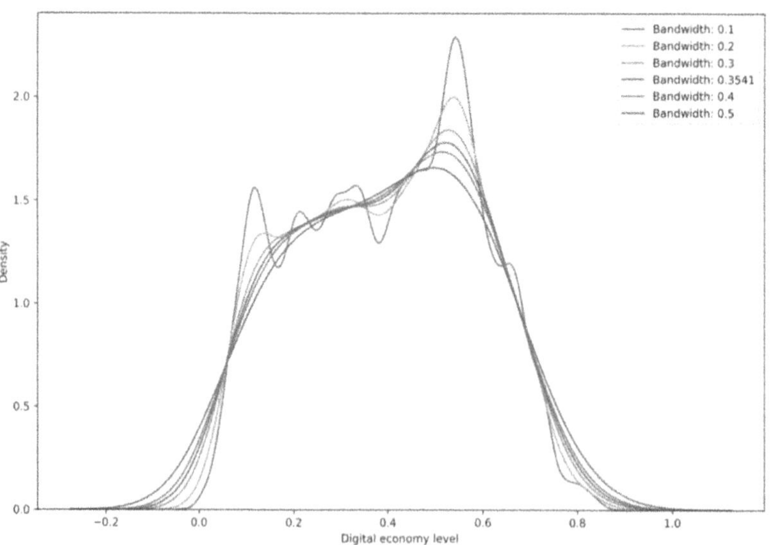

Fig. 1. Kernel Density Estimates at Different Bandwidths.

From the figure, it can be observed that under various bandwidths, the shapes of the kernel density estimates are roughly similar; the larger the bandwidth, the smoother the curve and the lower the "peaks". Through comparison, we deduced that our calculated bandwidth h = 0.3541 adequately describes the actual distribution. Therefore, this study will adopt h = 0.3541 as the bandwidth for kernel density estimation.

4.3 Comparison Between Kernel Density Estimation and Other Fitting Approaches

Initially, we employed a parametric approach to estimate the probability density, employing maximum likelihood estimation to fit several standard continuous distribution functions, such as the Log-Normal, Weibull, Exponential, and Gamma distributions. However, Fig. 2 demonstrates that these parametric methods inadequately capture the true distribution of the sample data, exhibiting notable discrepancies.

These deviations may arise from various factors, including the idiosyncrasies within the sample data, inherent limitations of the chosen distribution functions, or inadequacies in parameter selection during fitting. To address these challenges, we turned to kernel density estimation (KDE), a non-parametric method. Unlike parametric approaches, KDE derives the probability density function directly from the sample data, free from assumptions about the underlying distribution shape. This feature makes KDE particularly suited for revealing the nuanced characteristics of data distributions, especially in scenarios involving complex or unknown distributions.

Considering these observations, we explored one-dimensional Gaussian kernel density estimation method. Fig. 2 showcases the results of KDE, demonstrating a significantly closer alignment with the actual distribution of the sample data compared to the other parametric fittings.

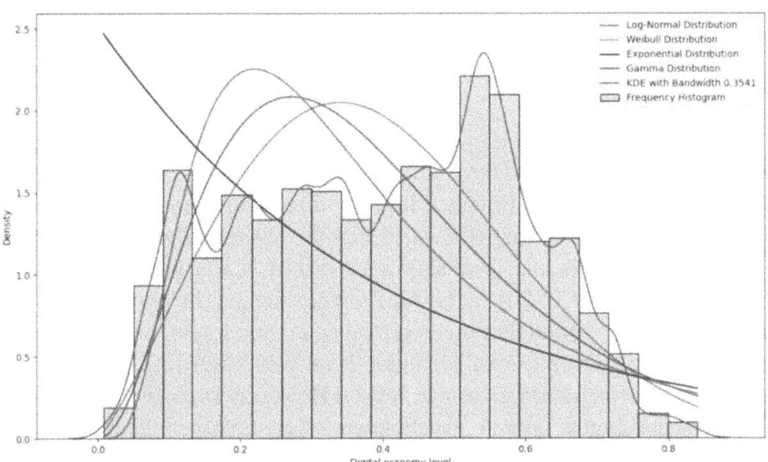

Fig. 2. Comparison of Parametric Methods and KDE for Probability Density Estimation.

## 4.4	Density Estimation Maps of Green Digital Economy in Belt and Road Countries

Considering the varying levels of green digital economic development across countries or regions over different years, we chose to utilize a three-dimensional coordinate system to showcase the temporal changes in green digital economic development levels among Belt and Road countries. As illustrated in Fig. 3, the density distribution map exhibits "peaks," indicating that the green digital economic development levels of most countries are concentrated around the values corresponding to these "peaks." The figure displays two distinct "peaks," with the "peak" associated with higher green digital economic levels gradually increasing over time compared to the "peak" associated with lower levels. This suggests a continuous improvement in green digital economic development among Belt and Road countries or regions from 2007 to 2021, despite existing disparities among them.

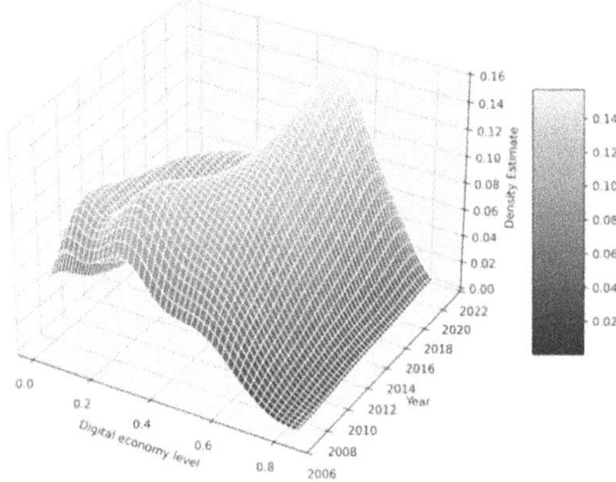

Fig. 3. 3D Kernel Density Estimate of the green digital economy level in 'The Belt and Road' countries.

To visually reflect the changes in the green digital economy level of Hainan Province over time and its position within the country, we incorporated the green digital economic development level of Hainan Province into the three-dimensional coordinate system, resulting in the distribution map shown in Fig. 4.. Overall, Hainan Province's green digital economic development level shows a trend of yearly increase. However, during the period from 2011 to 2018, Hainan Province lagged the point corresponding to the "peak" associated with higher green digital economic levels, indicating that during this period, Hainan's green digital economic level was lower than that of most countries with better economic development levels. However, starting from 2018, Hainan Province's green digital economic development level surpassed the point corresponding to the "peak" associated with higher green digital economic levels, indicating that since 2018, Hainan Province has been in a leading position in international green digital economic development.

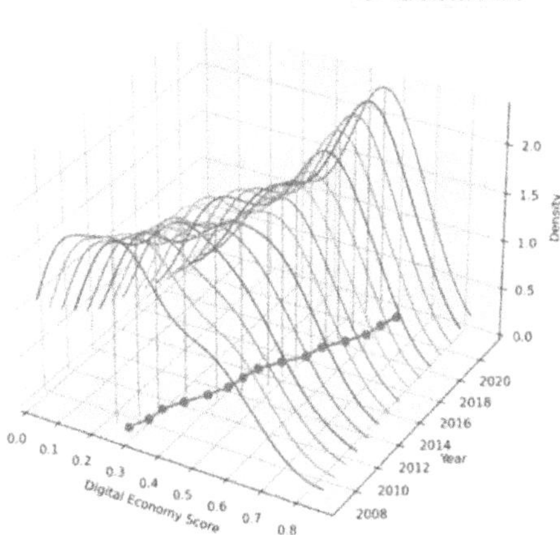

Fig. 4. 3D Kernel Density Estimate of the green digital economy level in 'The Belt and Road' countries with Hainan's Score Trend.

5 Conclusions

Through our study, we conducted an analysis of green digital economy development trends in countries along the "Belt and Road" initiative, with a particular emphasis on Hainan Province, utilizing the Kernel Density Estimation (KDE) method. Our investigation reveals a notable enhancement in the green digital economy of Hainan Province since 2017, indicating a gradual convergence with countries boasting more advanced levels of green digital economic development. These findings underscore the efficacy of modern computing technology in economic data analysis and offer valuable insights into regional green digital economy progression.

The application of the KDE method allows for the swift identification of outlier samples, facilitating subsequent in-depth exploration and analysis of these anomalies through complementary models or statistical methods. This approach contributes to a more comprehensive understanding of green digital economy dynamics.

In summary, the outcomes of our research provide pivotal insights into the trajectory of regional green digital economies and underscore the potential of modern computing technology in economic analysis. Future investigations can delve deeper into the factors influencing green digital economy development and broaden the scope of analysis to encompass a wider array of regions and temporal dynamics.

Acknowledgments. This article is one of the phased results of the Hainan Provincial Department of Education's provincial education and scientific research project "Research on Hainan Free Trade Port Economic Innovation in Digital Transformation" (Hnky2024ZC-29)

References

1. Bukht, R., Heeks, R.: Defining, conceptualising and measuring the digital economy. Development Informatics Working Paper 68 (2017). https://doi.org/10.2139/ssrn.3431732

2. World Economic Forum: Expanding Participation and Boosting Growth: The Infrastructure Needs of the Digital Economy. World Economic Forum, Geneva (2015)
3. Brinken, J., Behrendt, F., Trojahn, S.: Comparing decarbonization potential of digital and green technologies. J. Sustain. Futures. **6**(1), 3 (2023)
4. House of Commons: The Digital Economy. Business, Innovation and Skills Committee, London (2016)
5. OECD: Measuring the Digital Economy: A New Perspective. OECD Publishing, Paris (2014) https://read.oecd-ilibrary.org/science-and-technology/measuring-the-digital-eco nomy_9789264221796-en
6. Wang, C., et al.: Digital economy, environmental regulation and corporate green technology innovation: evidence from China. Int. J. Environ. Res. Public Health. **19**(21), 14084 (2022). https://doi.org/10.3390/ijerph192114084
7. Kong, L., Li, J.: Digital economy development and green economic efficiency: evidence from province-level empirical data in China. Sustainability. **15**(1), 3 (2022). https://doi.org/10. 3390/su15010003
8. Meng, G.: Implications of international experiences for the planning and development of Hainan Free Trade Port. Resour. Sci. **43**(2), 217–228 (2021). https://doi.org/10.18402/resci. 2021.02.02
9. Kenney, M., Zysman, J.: The platform economy: restructuring the space of capitalist accumulation. Cambridge J. Reg. Econ. Soc. **13**(1), 55–76 (2020). https://doi.org/10.1093/cjres/ rsaa001
10. Liqi: Hainan takes the green path for sustainable economic development. https://govt.chinad aily.com.cn/s/201904/23/WS5cbeb564498e079e6801ec3d/hainan-takes-the-green-path-for-sustainable-economic-development.html. Accessed: 10 May 2024
11. Pan, H., et al.: Global value chain embeddedness, digital economy and green innovation—evidence from provincial-level regions in China. Front. Environ. Sci. **10**, 1027130 (2022). https://doi.org/10.3389/fenvs.2022.1027130
12. Silverman, B.W.: Density Estimation for Statistics and Data Analysis. Chapman and Hall, London (1986)
13. Yoon, K.P., Hwang, C.-L.: Multiple Attribute Decision Making: An Introduction. Sage Publications, Thousand Oaks (1995). https://doi.org/10.4135/9781412985161
14. Yang, Z., et al.: Digitalization and carbon emissions: how does digital city construction affect China's carbon emission reduction. Sustain. Cities Soc. **87**, 104201 (2022). https://doi.org/ 10.1016/j.scs.2022.104201

Amalgamate GenAI and Metaverse for FinTech Innovations in Metaverse

Yuzhou Qian[1,2] ![ORCID], Xuenan Huo[1,2(✉)] ![ORCID], and Keng Leng Siau[2] ![ORCID]

[1] City University of Hong Kong, Tat Chee Avenue Kowloon, Hong Kong, China
`xnhuo2-c@my.cityu.edu.hk`
[2] Singapore Management University, 81 Victoria Street, Singapore, Singapore

Abstract. The rapid advancement of digital technologies has greatly accelerated the development of financial technology (FinTech), which refers to the application of innovative technologies to enhance and transform financial services. This paper provides an overview of the FinTech discipline, beginning with its conceptual definition and the technological foundations that support it, including Artificial Intelligence (AI), Generative AI (GenAI), and the Metaverse. We examine how these technologies individually and collectively contribute to FinTech innovation, focusing on their synergistic integration to improve financial operations, service personalization, and customer engagement. Further, the paper discusses key challenges in the current FinTech landscape, such as regulatory concerns and operational risks. Finally, we outline future development opportunities and research prospects that may shape the evolution of FinTech. This study aims to provide a comprehensive understanding of emerging FinTech technologies and serve as a reference for both academic research and industry practice.

Keywords: Financial technology (FinTech) · Artificial Intelligence (AI) · Generative AI (GenAI) · Metaverse

1 Introduction

The rapid advancement of digital technologies is reshaping the financial industry [48]. Financial Technology (FinTech) refers to the integration of innovative Information Technology (IT) applications into financial services to enhance efficiency, accessibility, and service quality [16,47]. The sector has expanded significantly; for example, in the Americas, the number of FinTech startups grew from fewer than 6,000 in 2018 to more than 14,000 by 2024 [53]. Emerging technologies such as Artificial Intelligence (AI), Generative AI (GenAI), and the Metaverse are accelerating this transformation, offering new opportunities for innovation and future growth within the FinTech ecosystem.

FinTech refers to the application of digital technologies to deliver and enhance financial services. The term was initially adopted by banks and financial institutions to describe technological tools used to address operational challenges

© The Author(s), under exclusive license to Springer Nature Singapore Pte Ltd. 2026
S. C. P. Yam et al. (Eds.): ICFT 2025, CCIS 2868, pp. 477–490, 2026.
https://doi.org/10.1007/978-981-92-0126-6_39

and customer needs. More recently, its scope has expanded to include a wide range of consumer-oriented services delivered through applications and software [15]. FinTech encompasses both technology-enabled financial offerings and the innovative business models built around them [33]. Today, it describes how individuals and organizations adopt and employ emerging technologies to facilitate economic activities and create financial value [3].

The emergence of FinTech has significantly reshaped the financial industry, influencing the role of information technology (IT), customer behaviour, industry ecosystems, and regulatory frameworks [40]. Retail banks have achieved greater profitability and stability through FinTech-enabled service innovations, while commercial banks leverage FinTech to strengthen their social responsibilities and corporate social responsibility (CSR) engagement. Others utilize FinTech to drive systematic organizational innovation [52]. At the individual level, FinTech enables mobile payments, peer-to-peer transfers and lending, crowdfunding, and more advanced applications such as blockchain and cryptocurrency transactions [18]. Consequently, both businesses and policymakers have shown increasing interest in unlocking the potential of FinTech and accelerating the digital transformation of the financial services sector.

FinTech brings substantial value to both customers and financial institutions. Customers benefit from seamless financial access, secure transactions, and increased credit opportunities, while organizations gain advantages such as streamlined operations, reduced time-to-market for new products, and improved customer feedback [15].

This paper offers a comprehensive overview of FinTech and its associated technological innovations. It begins by outlining key trends, particularly AI, GenAI, and the Metaverse, and examines their integration and influence on FinTech operations. The paper then discusses the challenges faced by technology-driven financial services and highlights future research directions and opportunities arising from these emerging developments.

1.1 AI and Generative AI

In general, AI can be categorized into weak AI and strong AI [49,56]. Weak AI, also known as Artificial Narrow Intelligence (ANI), relies on machine learning and deep learning techniques to replicate specific aspects of human cognition [54]. ANI systems are designed to perform narrowly defined tasks. For instance, AI agents, such as Siri, Alexa, and Copilot, provide functionalities such as setting reminders and answering factual questions, yet they remain early forms of ANI. They operate effectively within their predefined domains but exhibit limited reasoning capabilities and cannot generalize learning beyond their original training. Strong AI refers to systems that are "in all respects at least as intelligent as humans" [9]. Researchers further distinguish strong AI into Artificial General Intelligence (AGI) and Artificial Superintelligence (ASI) [54,56] AGI represents human-level reasoning and problem-solving ability, whereas ASI describes intelligence that exceeds human cognitive performance.

GenAI refers to a class of algorithms capable of producing new and realistic content by learning patterns from large training datasets. Unlike traditional AI systems, which primarily perform classification or prediction, GenAI models, such as GPT (Generative Pre-trained Transformer), DALL-E, Stable Diffusion, DeepSeek, and Sora, utilize advanced deep learning architectures, including transformer networks and diffusion models, to generate original text, images, and videos in response to human prompts. GenAI represents a highly advanced form of ANI. Recent evidence shows that GenAI can outperform humans in specific domains, such as standardized tests (e.g., the U.S. bar exam), programming tasks under limited time constraints, and divergent thinking activities [8,27,34]. However, GenAI still lacks adaptability and general reasoning capabilities. It remains domain-specific, excelling at tasks such as text generation, image synthesis, code development, and video production, but is unable to autonomously learn new fields or exhibit human-level general intelligence. GenAI operates reactively to instructions rather than independently pursuing goals or determining how and where to apply its intelligence.

Although GenAI remains a form of ANI, its impact across industries has been transformative. In content creation, GenAI systems are used to generate marketing materials, technical documentation, and creative writing. In software engineering, they support code generation and debugging. Within healthcare, GenAI assists in clinical report drafting, diagnostic assessment, and drug discovery simulations. The creative industries apply GenAI for concept art, design prototyping, and multimedia production, while the education sector utilizes it for knowledge retrieval, personalized tutoring, and the development of automated instructional materials [23]. GenAI has also reshaped various operational dimensions of the FinTech sector, including risk assessment, investment management, and accelerated regulatory compliance [26]. Further applications and examples will be discussed in subsequent sections.

1.2 Metaverse

The term Metaverse first appeared in the science fiction novel Snow Crash, published in 1992, where it referred to a computer-generated virtual reality universe. With rapid technological advancements, the Metaverse has moved beyond fiction into a developing technological reality, offering increasingly immersive experiences [12]. Today, it is conceptualized as a persistent, multi-user environment that integrates physical reality with digital virtuality, enabling real-time communication and interaction with digital objects and environments [35]. The Metaverse is widely regarded as an emerging technological paradigm that has the potential to transform how individuals socialize, conduct business, and access services in virtual spaces.

The realization of immersive Metaverse experiences depends heavily on hardware interfaces such as virtual reality (VR) headsets, augmented reality (AR) glasses, haptic devices, and motion-tracking systems, which provide the sensory inputs required to simulate presence. Modern VR headsets, including Meta Quest, HTC Vive, HoloLens, and Apple Vision Pro, deliver increasingly advanced visual and auditory fidelity, while emerging haptic technologies introduce tactile feedback that enhances realism. Traditional Metaverse applications, however, do not always require specialized hardware; many platforms are accessible via standard computers and smartphones, reducing barriers to adoption. For instance, [46] created a virtual banking branch using Open Wonderland, a desktop-based 3D virtual world platform, to simulate physical banking environments. As enabling technologies continue to evolve, contemporary definitions increasingly portray the Metaverse as a fully integrated 3D digital world supported by immersive technologies such as VR headsets [22]. Within these environments, users are represented by avatars and interact through controllers, eye-tracking, and voice inputs, creating a more embodied and interactive virtual experience.

2 FinTech, GenAI, and Metaverse

2.1 Metaverse in FinTech

New technologies are transforming the FinTech industry, and the Metaverse has emerged as a promising development that enables greater freedom, immersion, and direct engagement for both individuals and organizations [57,61]. As a digitally constructed environment, the Metaverse enables users to participate in activities and interact with virtual resources in real-time [60].

Supported by blockchain infrastructures, the financial Metaverse also enables the creation and exchange of tokenized digital assets and the execution of smart contracts, expanding new opportunities for virtual banking, digital asset management, and decentralized financial services.

Virtual Branches. Financial institutions have begun establishing a presence on Metaverse platforms by creating virtual branches that deliver banking services within immersive 3D environments. These digital branches extend beyond traditional online banking by providing spatial, interactive experiences that allow customers to navigate virtual spaces, engage with AI-powered service avatars, and perform financial transactions through intuitive, visually enriched interfaces [7,58]. Major institutions, including JPMorgan Chase, HSBC, and KB Kookmin Bank, have already launched virtual banking initiatives, demonstrating a growing strategic importance of Metaverse-enabled financial services [4].

Virtual branches offer several advantages over both physical locations and traditional digital banking interfaces. They provide 24/7 global accessibility, eliminating geographic barriers and reducing physical infrastructure costs. Customers can remotely access financial advisors and services, thereby improving operational efficiency and service reach. Scalability is also significantly enhanced, as Metaverse platforms can accommodate large numbers of concurrent users without the spatial limitations of physical branches, enabling institutions to expand services rapidly and cost-effectively. Also, the immersive environment fosters a stronger sense of presence and engagement than conventional web interfaces, potentially increasing customer satisfaction, trust, and long-term loyalty.

For example, KB Kookmin Bank launched a Metaverse-based VR branch that enables customers to interact with financial advisors and conduct basic transactions through avatars [38]. Similar experimental initiatives by other financial institutions continue to study the feasibility and value of immersive financial services. These early deployments provide important insights into customer preferences, technological requirements, and viable business models for Metaverse-enabled financial services.

Digital Assets. The Metaverse economy relies fundamentally on digital assets, including cryptocurrencies, non-fungible tokens (NFTs), and virtual property. Blockchain technology underpins the verification of ownership and enables secure, seamless transactions within and across virtual environments, forming the economic infrastructure of Metaverse-based commerce. Growing interest has emerged around digital asset management services, enabling customers to store, trade, and manage their virtual holdings directly within Metaverse platforms [1,42].

Although the legality of digital assets, such as cryptocurrencies and transactions, remains controversial and varies significantly across jurisdictions, the Metaverse presents financial institutions with new opportunities to engage with digital value in innovative and operationally transformative ways. Blockchain technology supports verifiable ownership and secure, transparent transactions, enabling faster and more cost-efficient cross-border payments [51]. Smart contracts, a core component of Metaverse-related technologies, further streamline financial processes such as mortgage execution by automatically enforcing loan terms with transparency and fairness [29]. The tokenization of real-world assets, including real estate, represents another rapidly expanding frontier, democratizing access to investment opportunities and enabling decentralized ownership of traditionally high-value assets [42]. In this emerging ecosystem, banks can play pivotal roles as custodians, verification intermediaries, and trading platforms for tokenized assets, opening pathways for new revenue models and service innovations.

Immersive Customer Service and Support. The Metaverse enables banks to deliver customer service and support in immersive and interactive formats, reshaping traditional banking interactions. Through virtual branches, avatars, and three-dimensional meeting spaces, customers can interact with banking representatives/avatars in real time, ask questions, receive personalized advice, and complete transactions in environments that closely simulate face-to-face engagement. Immersive virtual spaces also allow banks to demonstrate product features, visualize investment portfolios, and simulate financial scenarios, thereby enhancing customer comprehension and trust. Metaverse banking can further integrate conversational agents that provide 24/7 support, assist users in completing transactions, troubleshoot issues, and escalate cases to human staff when necessary. Also, intelligent virtual agents powered by Generative AI (GenAI) can deliver highly personalized and context-aware assistance, as discussed in the next section.

The Metaverse offers innovative, immersive, and memorable experiences that align with the growing importance of the experience economy, in which businesses create value not solely through products or services, but through engaging and memorable customer interactions [39]. Compared with traditional 2D web interfaces, Metaverse environments have greater potential to enhance brand equity and generate increased business value [22, 36]. For example, HSBC acquired virtual land in The Sandbox to engage sports, esports, and gaming communities, creating unique branding opportunities and experiential interactions for both existing and potential customers [45].

Financial Education Programs. The Metaverse presents unprecedented opportunities for financial education through immersive and interactive learning experiences. Financial institutions can establish virtual classrooms, seminars, and workshops where participants learn financial concepts through visualization, simulation, and hands-on practice. Complex financial products can be explained visually, risk concepts can be explored through interactive simulations, and investment strategies can be practiced within virtual trading environments without real financial exposure. The integration of gamification into financial education offers a powerful means of improving financial literacy while strengthening customer engagement and long-term relationships. By embedding learning into interactive, motivating, and game-like activities, banks can make financial knowledge more accessible, enjoyable, and impactful. Seizing these opportunities, KB Kookmin Bank has leveraged its Metaverse-based VR branch as an educational platform for both customers and employees, using it to teach financial concepts while simultaneously evaluating technological requirements for future virtual banking services [38].

2.2   GenAI and FinTech

GenAI is a rapidly evolving subset of AI that is transforming multiple operational dimensions within the financial industry. It is reshaping the FinTech sector by improving customer experience, enhancing risk management, supporting automated regulatory compliance, and enabling hyper-personalized financial services [26]. GenAI techniques, including natural language processing (NLP), machine learning (ML), and deep learning (DL), are increasingly applied to strengthen FinTech service delivery [28]. In capital markets, algorithmic trading strategies now incorporate GenAI-generated market insights and sentiment analyses derived from unstructured data sources such as news, social media, and financial disclosures [21, 25]. ML models support large-scale data processing and predictive analytics, while DL enables the interpretation of highly complex and unstructured information [28]. Risk assessment and fraud detection have been strengthened through GenAI's ability to identify transaction anomalies, generate synthetic training datasets, and produce comprehensive risk reports that integrate diverse information streams [13,20]. GenAI also streamlines regulatory compliance, automating data collection, report generation, and compliance monitoring [24,50]. In addition, personalized financial product development benefits from GenAI's capacity to analyze historical data and behavioral patterns to generate tailored investment recommendations aligned with individual risk profiles and financial objectives [55]. These advances enable financial institutions to respond more rapidly and flexibly to evolving market conditions [5].

Also, GenAI has transformed customer service through intelligent conversational agents capable of managing complex inquiries, generating personalized financial advice, and providing multilingual support without proportional increases in human resources. One of the earliest and most widely adopted applications of GenAI in FinTech is direct customer interaction. Financial institutions such as the State Bank of India (SBI) and Axis Bank are increasingly deploying GenAI-powered chatbots and virtual assistants to address customer queries in a human-like manner [43]. These systems are advancing rapidly to deliver customized recommendations for investment planning and wealth management.

The adoption of GenAI continues to expand across the FinTech sector. Table 1 summarizes six major application areas of GenAI within FinTech [2,19].

Table 1. Application of GenAI in FinTech

Application scenarios	Examples
Efficient and low-cost financial services	Peratera's GenAI-driven digital banking platform processes large amounts of transactions with reduced costs
Market trend prediction	AlphaSense uses advanced AI models for document processing
Customized investment strategies	JPMorgan Chase's IndexGPT identifies investments based on emerging trends
High-frequency surveillance	HSBC adopts AI Startup Ayasdi's Tech to tackle money-laundering
Creditworthiness assessment	Crediture uses GenAI to simulate dynamic lending scenarios
Customer and market analysis	OCBC GPT analyzes customer data and enhances personalization capabilities

2.3 Integrating GenAI Into Fintech Metaverse

The convergence of AI and Metaverse technologies generates powerful synergies, and the emergence of GenAI further amplifies these opportunities. AI contributes the intelligence, adaptability, and scalability needed to populate virtual environments with dynamic content and responsive agents, while the Metaverse provides rich contextual spaces where AI systems can interact with users through natural and immersive experiences. With advancing GenAI capabilities, the FinTech sector can leverage AI-powered virtual environments and intelligent avatars or non-player characters NPCs to deliver financial services that are dynamic, interactive, immersive, and highly personalized. This section discusses how GenAI integration enhances Metaverse-based financial services and enables unprecedented forms of customer engagement and experience.

GenAI-Powered Virtual Environments. GenAI has transformed the landscape of content production, giving rise to Artificial Intelligence Generated Content (AIGC), which encompasses a wide range of multimodal outputs [6]. Recent advancements in 3D generative models provide scalable and cost-efficient methods for constructing Metaverse environments, dramatically reducing the time, labor, and technical expertise required for traditional 3D modeling [32,37]. These capabilities can be applied to develop virtual banking branches, financial education classrooms, investment simulation environments, and personalized avatars [14]. By automating the creation of textures, objects, landscapes, and scenario variations, GenAI enables financial institutions to produce rich and adaptive virtual spaces more efficiently, reducing operational costs while maintaining high-quality immersive experiences.

In the financial Metaverse, GenAI can enable highly personalized content tailored to individual users' profiles, preferences, and behaviors. Virtual banking environments can dynamically adapt layouts, visualizations, and interactive modules according to a customer's financial literacy, investment objectives, or transaction history. Educational simulations and investment scenarios can be customized to reflect users' behaviors and risk preferences, resulting in more relevant, engaging, and effective financial learning experiences. Additionally, financial product promotions can be delivered through personalized 3D virtual environments, enabling tailored marketing interactions that strengthen customer engagement and emotional connection.

Despite current advancements, achieving fully real-time, high-fidelity, and highly interactive 3D content generation remains technically and computationally challenging [14]. Looking ahead, the development of more advanced GenAI techniques has the potential to support real-time 3D content creation, transforming Metaverse environments from static simulations into dynamic, adaptive, and continuously evolving spaces. Such capabilities would allow virtual environments to respond instantly to user behavior, market fluctuations, or learning progression, enabling deeply immersive and personalized experiences for FinTech applications.

GenAI-Powered Avatars and Non-player Characters. AI-powered virtual assistants and chatbots can be embodied as avatars within the FinTech Metaverse, providing immediate support with human-like interaction capabilities across a broad range of inquiries. However, earlier AI-driven avatars relied primarily on scripted dialogue and pre-programmed (NPC) behaviors, resulting in limited conversational depth, narrow decision logic, and weak contextual awareness [59]. These constraints reduced the realism and practical usefulness of virtual interactions, making it difficult for financial institutions to deliver meaningful guidance, personalized support, or high-quality educational experiences within immersive environments. In the FinTech Metaverse, where trust, clarity, and expertise are crucial, static and rule-based avatars have proven insufficient for handling complex questions, personalizing financial recommendations, or engaging customers at scale.

Advances in Generative AI have begun to overcome these limitations by enabling avatars and NPCs in the Metaverse to exhibit human-like communication, adaptive behavior, and interactive narrative capability. Large language models (LLMs) allow virtual agents to interpret user input, provide context-aware responses in real time, and adjust their actions based on user profiles, financial histories, and learning progress. Recent industry developments demonstrate this shift. For example, RAVATAR introduced an interactive AI avatar, a 3D digital representation of AVANT CEO Ian Kinninger, powered by IntelePeer's LLM engine, while NVIDIA released a suite of GenAI microservices that reduce the technical complexity of building responsive, multimodal digital humans. Financial institutions are beginning to experiment with these emerging capabilities. For instance, the Development Bank of Singapore (DBS) launched DBS Joy, an intelligent virtual agent powered by large language models and the bank's proprietary domain knowledge to provide trusted, personalized, and human-like customer interactions. Together, these innovations are accelerating the development of enterprise-grade GenAI-powered avatars and enabling their seamless deployment within the FinTech Metaverse.

3   Challenges

The integration of advanced technologies into financial services has significantly increased the complexity of the FinTech industry. One major concern associated with digitalization is the heightened risk of operational failures. Algorithms may malfunction or be subject to hacking, manipulation, or other cybersecurity vulnerabilities [17]. Also, compared with traditional financial environments, FinTech ecosystems require personnel with more advanced technical and managerial competencies, coordination across regional and environmental boundaries, and the ability to address dynamic and integrated challenges [10]. However, substantial variation still exists in individuals' cognitive and technological capabilities, interactions and communication between stakeholders remain insufficient, and systematic frameworks for managing complexity are lacking. These challenges demand interdisciplinary dialogue and collaborative solutions.

The adoption of AI also has profound implications for financial crime and fraud. Compared with traditional cyberattacks, AI-enabled crimes occur at a greater scale, propagate more rapidly, and introduce novel threat types [30]. GenAI, for example, enables voice and video cloning from minimal recording samples, supports sophisticated social engineering attacks (phishing, smishing, vishing), and facilitates a wide range of AI-driven scams [30]. Without appropriate safeguards and regulatory oversight, GenAI may also generate faulty or deceptive outputs that lead to operational errors or customer harm [43].

Therefore, businesses, policymakers, and researchers must proactively address technology-related concerns to support resilient FinTech operations and maintain customer trust in digitally transformed financial services.

4   Prospects and Future Development

The continuous emergence of new technologies is driving transformative change within the FinTech industry [31]. Researchers and practitioners are integrating diverse technological innovations to achieve unprecedented improvements in efficiency, security, customer experience, and regulatory compliance. For example, recent studies explore the potential of big data analytics and the Metaverse to reduce labor costs, enhance security, improve user engagement, and support regulatory processes [60]. Other technological advancements, such as blockchain, algorithmic trading, and robo-advisory systems, offer promising opportunities for the further development of FinTech [11].

The industry continues to evolve through the introduction of new services, including AI-powered chatbots and automated advisory tools. However, as many FinTech solutions remain at early stages of adoption, a deeper understanding of how customers perceive their usefulness and anticipate future improvements is needed [40]. Also, much of today's FinTech innovation remains incremental rather than disruptive, and whether more radical innovations will emerge remains an open question [40].

Alongside the benefits created by FinTech and its enabling technologies, appropriate regulatory mechanisms are essential to ensure safe and effective industry operation, particularly when services are powered by advanced technologies [41,52]. FinTech innovations introduce complex legal challenges due to their broad applicability, extensive data usage, and potential risks related to privacy, discrimination, and financial integrity [18]. Regulatory technology (RegTech) and supervisory technology (SupTech) provide complementary solutions: RegTech equips financial institutions with tools such as automated transaction monitoring and regulatory reporting, while SupTech supports supervisory authorities through advanced data analytics and complaint-handling mechanisms [17]. Customer concerns regarding personal data security and capital safety continue to influence acceptance of FinTech services, highlighting the importance of trustworthy digital infrastructure.

The sustainable and responsible advancement of FinTech depends on interdisciplinary collaboration among experts in finance, technology, and law. Future research is needed to evaluate the security, ethical implications, and governance of emerging technologies within financial ecosystems [44].

5   Conclusion

Powered by emerging technologies, the financial industry has become increasingly digitalized, driving the rapid development of the FinTech field. This paper provided an overview of the FinTech landscape, beginning with a definition of FinTech and a discussion of key enabling technologies, including AI, GenAI, and the Metaverse. We examined how these technologies operate individually and how their integration can generate enhanced value in financial services. The Metaverse introduces new modes of financial service delivery, such as virtual branches and digital asset ecosystems, and enhances customer experience through immersive interactions, personalized support, and innovative financial education. GenAI strengthens digital financial platforms through advanced data analytics, personalized advice, and automated decision support. Further, the convergence of GenAI and the Metaverse has the potential to create synergistic effects, improving adaptability, scalability, and immersive engagement within FinTech ecosystems. Collectively, these innovations aim to enhance customer experience and satisfaction, ultimately benefiting financial institutions.

Alongside these opportunities, the paper also highlighted challenges associated with FinTech development, including operational and cybersecurity risks, regulatory complexity, data privacy concerns, and inequalities in user capabilities. These challenges call for continued research to deepen understanding of FinTech operations, for practitioners to remain vigilant about potential negative impacts, and for regulators to establish appropriate governance frameworks.

Looking ahead, future development will require the integration of additional emerging technologies, such as big data analytics, as well as the establishment of comprehensive regulatory and ethical guidelines that ensure secure, transparent, and responsible FinTech innovation.

Based on the review and analysis, we further propose that the future development of Fintech can be enhanced by integrating more technologies, such as big data, and establishing relevant regulations and policies to standardize the operation of the Fintech industry.

In conclusion, this paper offers a holistic view of the current FinTech landscape and outlines the technological foundations, opportunities, and challenges shaping its evolution. It provides a reference point for researchers, practitioners, and policymakers seeking to advance the development and responsible growth of FinTech.

References

1. How the metaverse is shaping the future of digital banking and finance (2021). https://financialit.net/blog/how-metaverse-shaping-future-digital-banking-and-finance, Accessed 19 Nov 2025
2. Generative AI in Fintech Use Cases: Top 10 Startups of 2025 (2025). https://www.coherentsolutions.com/insights/generative-ai-in-fintech-technologies-advantages-and-use-cases
3. Alkasasbeh, H., Oudat, M., Abu-AlSondos, I., Alhawamdeh, L.: Metaverse finance: shaping the future of Islamic fintech solutions in UAE. J. Islamic Mark. (2024). https://doi.org/10.1108/JIMA-01-2024-0039
4. Aysan, A.F., Gozgor, G., Nanaeva, Z.: Technological perspectives of metaverse for financial service providers. Technol. Forecast. Soc. Chang. **202**, 123323 (2024)
5. Barde, K., Kulkarni, P.A.: Applications of generative AI in Fintech. In: Proceedings of the Third International Conference on AI-ML Systems, pp. 1–5. AIMLSystems '23, Association for Computing Machinery, New York, NY, USA (2024). https://doi.org/10.1145/3639856.3639893
6. Basyoni, L., et al.: Generative ai-driven metaverse: the promises and challenges of ai-generated content. IEEE Open J. Comput. Soc. (2025)

7. Bhatt, T.: Exploring the metaverse in banking: a transformational frontier (2023). https://hai.stanford.edu/ai-index/2025-ai-index-report, Accessed 19 Nov 2025

8. Boussioux, L., Lane, J.N., Zhang, M., Jacimovic, V., Lakhani, K.R.: The crowdless future? generative AI and creative problem-solving. Organ. Sci. **35**(5), 1589–1607 (2024)

9. Butz, M.V.: Towards strong AI. KI-Künstliche Intelligenz **35**(1), 91–101 (2021)

10. Cao, L., Yang, Q., Yu, P.S.: Data science and AI in FinTech: an overview. Int. J. Data Sci. Anal. **12**(2), 81–99 (2021). https://doi.org/10.1007/s41060-021-00278-w

11. Cao, L., Yuan, G., Leung, T., Zhang, W.: Special issue on AI and FinTech: the challenge ahead. IEEE Intell. Syst. **35**(2), 3–6 (2020). https://doi.org/10.1109/MIS.2020.2983494

12. Cheng, S.: Metaverse. In: Cheng, S. (ed.) Metaverse: Concept, Content and Context, pp. 1–23. Springer, Cham (2023). https://doi.org/10.1007/978-3-031-24359-2_1

13. Choudhury, A.: Leveraging generative ai (genai) for fraud detection and prevention (2025). https://www.turing.com/resources/generative-ai-fraud-detection, Accessed 19 Nov 2025

14. El Saddik, A., Ahmad, J., Khan, M., Abouzahir, S., Gueaieb, W.: Unleashing creativity in the metaverse: generative ai and multimodal content. ACM Trans. Multimed. Comput. Commun. Appl. **21**(7), 1–43 (2025)

15. Flinders, M., Smalley, I.: What is Fintech? (2024). https://www.ibm.com/think/topics/fintech

16. Gai, K., Qiu, M., Sun, X.: A survey on FinTech. J. Netw. Comput. Appl. **103**, 262–273 (2018). https://doi.org/10.1016/j.jnca.2017.10.011

17. Giudici, P.: Fintech Risk Management: a research challenge for artificial intelligence in finance. Front. Artif. Intell. **1** (2018). https://doi.org/10.3389/frai.2018.00001

18. Goldstein, I., Jiang, W., Karolyi, G.A.: To FinTech and beyond. Rev. Finan. Stud. **32**(5), 1647–1661 (2019)

19. Gritsenko, D.: Generative AI in FinTech: Use Cases & Real-World Examples (2024)

20. Hamdan, R.B., Elias, Y., Madan, S., Zhao, D.: A point of view on generative AI in fraud detection and prevention (2024). https://www.ey.com/en_ca/industries/financial-services/navigating-the-dual-nature-of-generative-ai, Accessed 19 Nov 2025

21. Hicham, N., Habbat, N.: From text to trade: harnessing the potential of generative AI for investor sentiment analysis in financial markets through large language models. Int. J. Inf. Technol. 1–13 (2025)

22. Huo, X., Qian, Y., Siau, K.L., Nah, F.F.H.: Hci in business and organizations: digital transformation with hci, metaverse, and ai technologies. In: Human-Computer Interaction in Various Application Domains, pp. 294–347. CRC Press (2024)

23. Huo, X., Siau, K.L.: Generative artificial intelligence in business higher education: a focus group study. J. Global Inf. Manag. (JGIM) **32**(1), 1–21 (2024)

24. Hutson, J., Banerjee, G.: Fintech and the metaverse: financial inclusion through genai, blockchain, and digital banking. In: Islam, N., Salami, I. (eds.) Metaverse Innovation: Technological, Financial, and Legal Perspectives, pp. 165–190. Springer, Cham (2025). https://doi.org/10.1007/978-3-031-97080-1_7

25. Iacovides, G., Konstantinidis, T., Xu, M., Mandic, D.: Finllama: LLM-based financial sentiment analysis for algorithmic trading. In: Proceedings of the 5th ACM International Conference on AI in Finance, pp. 134–141 (2024)

26. Kaur, M., Jindal, K., Arshdeep: balancing innovation and responsibility: tackling challenges in generative ai for fintech. In: Dutta, S., Rocha, Á., Agarwal, A.K.,

Tiwari, R.G., Bhattacharya, A. (eds.) Generative AI in FinTech: Revolutionizing Finance Through Intelligent Algorithms, pp. 221–234. Springer, Cham (2025). https://doi.org/10.1007/978-3-031-76957-3_11

27. Koivisto, M., Grassini, S.: Best humans still outperform artificial intelligence in a creative divergent thinking task. Sci. Rep. **13**(1), 13601 (2023)

28. Krause, D.: Generative AI in FinTech: Transforming Financial Activities through Advanced Technologies (2024)

29. Kumar, S., Sureka, R., Lucey, B.M., Dowling, M., Vigne, S., Lim, W.M.: Meta-money: exploring the intersection of financial systems and virtual worlds. Res. Int. Bus. Financ. **68**, 102195 (2024)

30. Kurshan, E., Mehta, D., Balch, T.: AI versus AI in financial crimes & detection: GenAI crime waves to co-evolutionary AI. In: Proceedings of the 5th ACM International Conference on AI in Finance, pp. 745–751. ICAIF '24, Association for Computing Machinery, New York, NY, USA (2024). https://doi.org/10.1145/3677052.3698655

31. Liu, Y., Wang, R., Siau, K.: FinTech digital transformation: generative AI, humanoid robots, metaverse, human-AI collaboration, and industry 5.0. In: Huang, K.W., Cao, Q., Su, R. (eds.) Financial Technology, pp. 122–136. Springer, Cham (2025). https://doi.org/10.1007/978-981-96-3811-6_12

32. Long, X., et al.: Wonder3d: Single image to 3d using cross-domain diffusion. In: Proceedings of the IEEE/CVF Conference on Computer Vision and Pattern Recognition, pp. 9970–9980 (2024)

33. Mention, A.L.: The future of Fintech. Res. Technol. Manag. **62**(4), 59–63 (2019). https://doi.org/10.1080/08956308.2019.1613123

34. Metcalfe, T.: The 2025 ai index report (2025). https://www.intelivita.com/blog/metaverse-in-banking/, Accessed 19 Nov 2025

35. Mystakidis, S.: Metaverse. Encyclopedia **2**(1), 486–497 (2022). https://doi.org/10.3390/encyclopedia2010031

36. Nah, F.F.H., Eschenbrenner, B., DeWester, D.: Enhancing brand equity through flow and telepresence: a comparison of 2D and 3D virtual worlds. MIs Q. 731–747 (2011)

37. Nichol, A., Jun, H., Dhariwal, P., Mishkin, P., Chen, M.: Point-e: a system for generating 3D point clouds from complex prompts. arXiv preprint arXiv:2212.08751 (2022)

38. Park, D.: South korea's kb bank unveils a metaverse bank testbed (2024). https://forkast.news/south-korea-kb-kookmin-bank-presents-metaverse-vr-bank-testbed/, Accessed 19 Nov 2025

39. Pine, B.J., Gilmore, J.H.: The Experience Economy. Harvard Business Press (2011)

40. Puschmann, T.: Fintech. Bus. Inf. Syst. Eng. **59**(1), 69–76 (2017). https://doi.org/10.1007/s12599-017-0464-6

41. Qian, Y., Siau, K.L., Nah, F.F.: Societal impacts of artificial intelligence: ethical, legal, and governance issues. Soc. Impacts **3**, 100040 (2024). https://doi.org/10.1016/j.socimp.2024.100040

42. Rehan, Sharma, D.: Embracing tomorrow: blockchain's role in metaverse and digital asset management. Int. J. Intell. Commun. Comput. Sci. **2**(1), 82–103 (2024)

43. Saha, B., Rani, N., Shukla, S.K.: Generative AI in Financial Institution: A Global Survey of Opportunities, Threats, and Regulation (2025). https://doi.org/10.48550/arXiv.2504.21574

44. Saiyed, A.: AI-Driven Innovations in fintech: applications, challenges, and future trends. Int. J. Electr. Comput. Eng. Res. **5**(1), 8–15 (2025). https://doi.org/10.53375/ijecer.2025.437

45. Sandbox, T.: Hsbc to become the first global financial services provider to enter the sandbox (2022). https://sandboxgame.medium.com/hsbc-to-become-the-first-global-financial-services-provider-to-enter-the-sandbox-c066e4f48163, Accessed 19 Nov 2025
46. Shoolapani, B., Jinka, P.: Virtual simulation and augmented interfaces for business models with focus on banking and retail. In: 2011 Fourth IEEE International Conference on Utility and Cloud Computing, pp. 469–473. IEEE (2011). https://doi.org/10.1109/UCC.2011.77
47. Siau, K., et al.: FinTech empowerment: data science, AI, and machine learning **31**(11/12), 12–18 (2019)
48. Siau, K., Nah, F.F.h., Eschenbrenner, B.L., Chen, L.: Artificial intelligence in financial technology
49. Siau, K.L.: Human-ai and human-robot collaboration in the age of generative ai, agentic ai, and artificial general intelligence: Opportunities and challenges. COJ Robot. Artif. Intell. **4**(3) (2025). https://doi.org/10.31031/cojra.2025.04.000588
50. Sinha, S., Rideout, R.: Generative ai and financial-services compliance: How smart automation of audit and control can improve efficiency, accuracy and transparency (2025). https://internationalbanker.com/technology/generative-ai-and-financial-services-compliance/, Accessed 19 Nov 2025
51. Sule, A.K., Eyo-Udo, N.L., Onukwulu, E.C., Agho, M.O., Azubuike, C.: Implementing blockchain for secure and efficient cross-border payment systems. Int. J. Res. Innov. Appl. Sci. **9**(12), 508–535 (2024)
52. Takeda, A., Ito, Y.: A review of FinTech research. Int. J. Technol. Manag. **86**(1), 67 (2021). https://doi.org/10.1504/IJTM.2021.115761
53. Trificana, J.: What is fintech? 6 main types of fintech and how they work (2025). https://plaid.com/resources/fintech/what-is-fintech/
54. Tzimas, T.: Artificial intelligence and human rights: their role in the evolution of AI. Heidelberg J. Int. Law, ZaöRV (2021)
55. Varvara, S.: Using genai to transform digital product development and digital sales in the banking sector. Am. J. Eng. Technol. **6**(12), 13–23 (2024)
56. Wang, W., Siau, K.: Artificial intelligence, machine learning, automation, robotics, future of work and future of humanity: a review and research agenda. J. Database Manage. (JDM) **30**(1), 61–79 (2019)
57. Wang, Y., Wang, L., Siau, K.L.: Human-centered interaction in virtual worlds: a new era of generative artificial intelligence and metaverse. Int. J. Human-Comput. Inter. **41**(2), 1459–1501 (2025). https://doi.org/10.1080/10447318.2024.2316376
58. Weise, S., Mshar, A.: Virtual reality and the banking experience. J. Digital Bank. **1**(2), 146–152 (2016)
59. Yamaguchi, R.: Ai avatars and digital humans: the future of interaction (2025). https://itbusinesstoday.com/tech/ai-avatars-and-digital-humans-the-future-of-interaction/, Accessed 19 Nov 2025
60. Yathiraju, N., Dash, B.: Big data and metaverse revolutionizing the futuristic fintech industry. Int. J. Comput. Sci. Inf. Technol. **15**, 1–13 (2023). https://doi.org/10.5121/ijcsit.2023.15101
61. Zhang, Y., Siau, K.: Meta-Entrepreneurship: an analysis theory on integrating generative AI, agentic AI, and metaverse for entrepreneurship. J. Global Inf. Manag. (JGIM) **32**(1), 1–21 (2024). https://doi.org/10.4018/JGIM.364094

Generative AI-Driven Financial Extreme Risk Prediction: An Empirical Study Based on Real-Generated Fusion Data

Yuhao Gu[1], Depeng Pan[1], Xiaoxi Zhang[2], Liang Huang[3], Xianpeng Wang[1(✉)], and M. K. Zhodro[4]

[1] International Institute of Management and Business, 220086 Minsk City, Belarus
wxpxueshu_phd@163.com
[2] RUDN University, Moscow 117198, Russia
[3] Shinawatra University, 99, Bang Toei, Sam Khok District, Pathum Thani 12160, Thailand
[4] Belarusian National Technical University, 220013 Minsk, Republic of Belarus

Abstract. Against the backdrop of increasing uncertainty in global financial markets and frequent extreme financial events, traditional risk prediction models face significant accuracy bottlenecks due to the scarcity of extreme event samples. This study centers on generative artificial intelligence (AI) technology to construct a dual-driven extreme risk prediction framework integrating "real data + generated data", exploring the application value of the improved WGAN-GP model in generating extreme scenario data. Using daily data of China's CSI 300 Index (January 2015–June 2025), regulatory penalty texts, and macroeconomic data as research samples, this paper compares the predictive performance of three models—EVT-GARCH, LSTM with single real data, and LSTM with fused data—through a three-stage "generator-filter-predictor" model architecture. Empirical results demonstrate that: (1) Extreme scenario data generated by the improved WGAN-GP model can accurately reproduce the statistical characteristics and dynamic structure of financial markets; (2) The fused-data LSTM model outperforms traditional models significantly, with a VaR prediction error of 9.4%, an ES prediction error of 12.7%, and an extreme event capture rate of 91.2%; (3) Incorporating regulatory text information extends the early warning period for extreme risks to 3–5 trading days. This study breaks the traditional paradigm of "relying solely on real data" and provides a new methodology for financial institutions' risk prevention and regulatory authorities' systemic risk monitoring.

Keywords: Generative AI · Financial Extreme Risk · WGAN-GP · LSTM Neural Network · Real-Generated Fusion Data · Risk Prediction

1 Introduction

The global financial system is currently confronting multiple uncertainties, with factors such as intensifying climate risks and geopolitical conflicts significantly increasing market volatility. Although extreme financial events (e.g., stock market crashes, liquidity

© The Author(s), under exclusive license to Springer Nature Singapore Pte Ltd. 2026
S. C. P. Yam et al. (Eds.): ICFT 2025, CCIS 2868, pp. 491–501, 2026.
https://doi.org/10.1007/978-981-92-0126-6_40

crises) occur with low probability, they trigger systemic risks once they break out. The historical lessons of the 2008 global financial crisis fully highlight the importance of extreme risk prevention. Traditional financial risk prediction models rely heavily on historical data, yet the scarcity of extreme events leads to insufficient sample sizes, severely limiting the prediction accuracy of these models. Since 2023, the breakthrough development of generative AI technology has offered a new solution to this dilemma. Technologies represented by large language models (LLMs) and generative adversarial networks (GANs) can synthesize virtual samples highly consistent with real data, effectively filling the gap in extreme scenario data. Meanwhile, large-scale investment in AI infrastructure has become a pillar of economic growth—investment in information processing in the U.S. contributed over 50% to economic growth in the first half of 2025. However, the resulting structural financial risks are also becoming increasingly prominent, with a risk accumulation trend similar to the 2000 Internet bubble. Against this context, exploring the application value of generative AI in financial extreme risk prediction holds distinct contemporary significance. Theoretically, this study breaks the traditional research paradigm of "relying solely on real data" and constructs a dual-driven financial risk research framework integrating "real data + generated data". This framework expands the application boundary of financial complexity theory in the field of extreme risks and enriches the academic achievements of interdisciplinary research between generative AI and finance. Practically, the research addresses the "data scarcity" dilemma in extreme risk prediction, providing high-precision early warning tools for financial institutions (banks, securities firms, fund companies) to optimize their stress testing processes. Additionally, it offers a new method for regulatory authorities to monitor systemic risks, enhancing the resilience of financial markets.

- Research Status of Financial Extreme Risk Prediction

Traditional extreme risk prediction primarily relies on Extreme Value Theory (EVT) and GARCH-family models, but these methods have limitations in handling non-linear and dynamic market characteristics. Research by Bollerslev et al. (2023) showed that models relying solely on historical data had a prediction error of up to 37% for global interest rate volatility in 2022 [3]. In recent years, machine learning models (e.g., random forests, LSTM) have been gradually applied to risk prediction; however, constrained by insufficient extreme samples, these models still perform suboptimally in tail risk assessment. Through empirical tests on major global stock markets, Diebold and Yilmaz (2023) found that traditional models have significant deficiencies in capturing cross-market extreme risk transmission, failing to adapt to the highly interconnected nature of financial markets [5].

- Application of Generative AI in Finance

Generative AI has demonstrated the potential to transform financial research paradigms. The new paradigm of generative AI financial research proposed by the Zhiyuan Community (2025) points out that time-series data generated by GANs can effectively improve the performance of risk management models, and LLMs have surpassed traditional methods in the accuracy of financial text analysis [17]. A study by the Huatai Financial Engineering Team (2020) expanded the WGAN model from single-asset sequence generation to multi-asset generation. By modifying the network structure to reproduce cross-correlations and extreme value correlations among multiple assets, the study verified the ability of generative models to capture stylized facts of financial time series [14]. In the field of text processing, Bertomeu et al. (2024) conducted a natural experiment based on Italy's ban on ChatGPT, revealing that LLMs significantly improve the efficiency of financial information dissemination—this finding provides theoretical support for integrating text data into risk prediction [2]. Notably, research on user-side applications of financial technology also offers indirect insights for risk prediction. An empirical study by AL-Habashneh et al. (2024) on Jordanian Islamic banks showed that the quality of financial applications (e.g., data accuracy, response speed) directly affects user satisfaction. This conclusion can be extended to risk prediction scenarios: the quality and processing efficiency of model input data are also key factors determining the effectiveness of extreme risk early warning, providing user-side evidence for this study's emphasis on "validity verification of generated data" and "optimization of model real-time performance" [1]. In cross-regional research on AI and financial services, the "SalNAS" neural architecture search technology proposed by Suwichaya Suwanwimolkul et al. (2024) from Shinawatra University (Thailand) focuses on saliency prediction in computer vision. Nevertheless, its efficient model optimization logic can be transferred to financial time-series data processing, offering technical insights for improving the computational efficiency of extreme risk prediction models [12]. Achievements published by the AI Research Team of Inti University (Malaysia) in top conferences such as CVPR and NeurIPS (2023) verified the universality of AI technology in complex data modeling from the perspective of algorithm innovation, further supporting the feasibility of applying generative AI to financial extreme risk prediction [13]. Furthermore, research by Gu et al. (2025) on the ethical balance of green finance raised the issue of "expansion of instrumental rationality". This provides an important reference for reflecting on the ethical compliance of generative AI in risk prediction—technological applications must improve accuracy while avoiding new risks caused by data bias or model opacity, enriching the ethical dimension of interdisciplinary financial technology research [8].

- Gaps in Existing Research

Existing research has three key gaps: First, the fusion mechanism of generated data and real data lacks standardized design. Most studies simply superimpose the two types of data; for example, Liu et al. (2024) failed to consider the dynamic adaptability of generated samples [9]. Second, the validity verification system for generated scenarios is incomplete, focusing mostly on static distribution matching while ignoring dynamic characteristics of financial markets such as volatility clustering and leverage effects. Third, there is a lack of segmented research on emerging markets. Most existing achievements are based on European and American data; although regional studies represented by AL-Habashneh et al. (2024) focus on financial services in emerging markets, they do not delve into the field of extreme risk prediction, and technical perspectives from Southeast Asian scholars have not yet been integrated into this segmented direction [1]. This study aims to fill these gaps (Fig. 1).

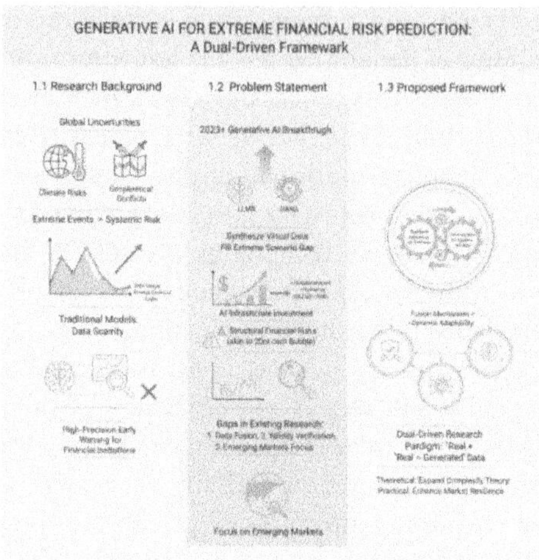

Fig. 1. Generative AI for extreme financial risk prediction: A Dual-Driven Framework

2 Research Design

2.1 Research Hypotheses

1. Extreme scenario data synthesized by generative AI can accurately capture the dynamic characteristics of real financial markets (e.g., tail distribution, volatility clustering);
2. The fusion model based on "real data + generated data" is significantly superior to single-data-source models in extreme risk prediction accuracy;
3. Generative AI models incorporating regulatory penalty texts and other information can further improve the timeliness of risk prediction.

2.2 Definition of Core Concepts

1. **Financial Extreme Risk**: Refers to extreme events in which financial markets deviate from normal volatility ranges. Defined by tail losses where daily returns fall below the 99th percentile, with Value at Risk (VaR) and Expected Shortfall (ES) as core metrics.
2. **Validity of Generated Data**: Refers to the consistency between synthesized data and real data in dimensions such as statistical distribution and dynamic structure (volatility clustering, jump behavior). Verified through multi-dimensional tests including KS test and ACF test, with reference to the single-asset and multi-asset stylized fact evaluation system designed by the Huatai Financial Engineering Team (2020) [14].
3. **Real-Generated Fusion Data**: Adopts a "stratified sampling fusion method", combining historical real data and generated extreme scenario data at a ratio of 4:1 to ensure the proportion of extreme samples conforms to actual market characteristics (Fig. 2).

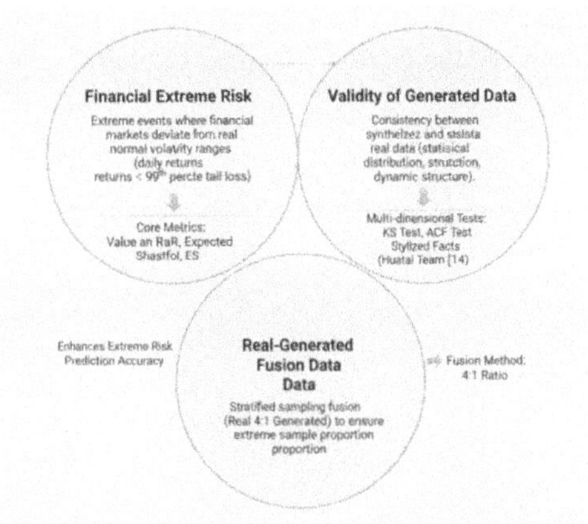

Fig. 2. Definition of Core Concepts

2.3 Model Construction

1. **Baseline Model**: The traditional EVT-GARCH model is selected as the baseline to compare the performance of generative AI models.
2. **Generative Model**: An improved WGAN-GP (Wasserstein GAN with Gradient Penalty) is used to construct an extreme scenario generator. Referencing the multi-channel input design of the Huatai Financial Engineering Team (2020), daily return data of China's A-shares is used as input, and the authenticity of generated data is optimized through gradient penalty terms [14].
3. **Fusion Prediction Model**: A three-stage "generator-filter-predictor" framework is built:

   - **Generator**: WGAN-GP synthesizes extreme scenario data;
   - **Filter**: Invalid generated samples are eliminated through Q-Q plot testing and volatility clustering verification, with a focus on verifying stylized financial market facts such as fat-tailed distribution and leverage effects;
   - **Predictor**: An LSTM neural network-based fusion prediction model is constructed, with input variables including price sequences, trading volumes, and regulatory penalty text vectors. Text vectors are generated using the open-source GPT-4o-mini model.

3 Data Sources and Processing

3.1 Data Sources

1. **Basic Market Data**: Daily data of China's CSI 300 Index (closing price, trading volume, price change rate) from January 2015 to June 2025, sourced from the Wind Database (Fig. 3).
2. **Regulatory Text Data**: Regulatory penalty announcements for A-share listed companies issued by the Shanghai Stock Exchange and Shenzhen Stock Exchange from January 2015 to June 2025 (including violation reasons and target entities), sourced from the CnOpenData Database [20].

3. **Macroeconomic Data**: Monthly CPI and M2 growth data for the same period, sourced from the official website of the National Bureau of Statistics of China (Fig. 3).

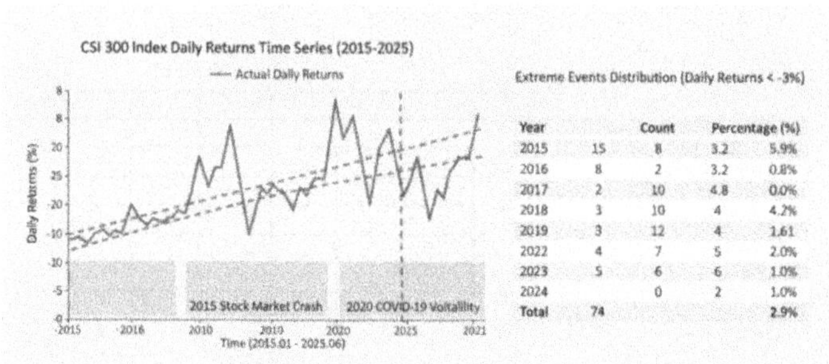

Fig. 3. Time Series of Daily Returns for the CSI 300 Index (2015–2025)

3.2 Data Processing

1. **Basic Data Preprocessing**: Daily return sequences are calculated using the formula $r_t = \ln P_t - \ln P_{t-1}$ (where P_t denotes the closing price on day t). Outliers are processed using the Z-score method, and the stationarity of sequences is confirmed through ADF tests.

2. **Text Data Processing**: The open-source GPT-4o-mini model is used for sentiment analysis and keyword extraction of regulatory announcements, generating compliance risk scores (on a 0–10 scale). Keywords such as "financial fraud" and "fund misappropriation" are assigned a weight of 1.5, with reference to the financial text risk classification standard proposed by Gelman et al. (2025) [6] (Fig. 4).

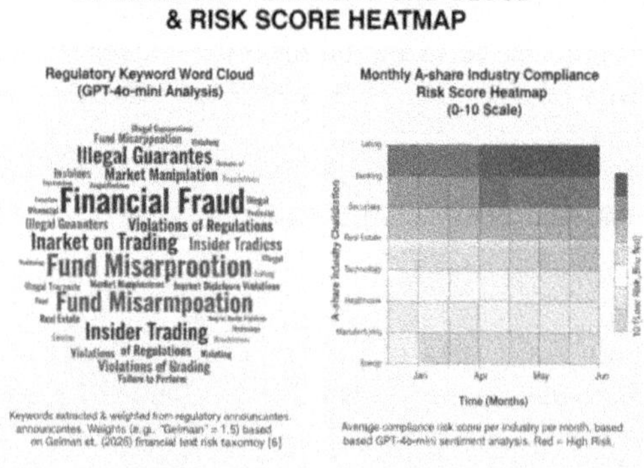

Fig. 4. Regulatory Text Keyword Cloud and Risk Score Heatmap

3. **Generated Data Construction**: The WGAN-GP model is trained using real data from 2015 to 2023 to generate extreme scenario data (samples with daily returns < −3%) for 2024–2025. The Anderson-Darling test is used to ensure the distribution of generated data is consistent with real tail data ($p - value > 0.05$).
4. **Data Splitting**: Data is divided into a training set (2015–2022) and a test set (2023–2025) at a ratio of 7:3. Out-of-sample testing is adopted to avoid overfitting.

4 Empirical Analysis

4.1 Validity Verification of Generated Data

1. **Statistical Distribution Test**: The KS test statistic between generated data and real tail data is 0.12 (p-value = 0.37), and Q-Q plots show good fit of tail percentiles. This indicates that generated data captures the tail characteristics of real markets, conforming to the fat-tailed distribution evaluation standard proposed by the Huatai Financial Engineering Team (2020) [14].
2. **Dynamic Structure Test**: The relative error of the volatility autocorrelation function (ACF) of generated data (for lags 1–10) compared to real data is only 8.3%, with a leverage effect correlation coefficient of −0.21 (vs. −0.19 for real data). Cross-correlation indicators deviate by less than 5% from real data, all conforming to stylized financial market facts.
3. **Backtesting**: The proportion of 99% VaR exceptions calculated using generated data is 1.12%, close to the theoretical value of 1%. The Acerbi-Szekely test shows that ES prediction deviations are within an acceptable range (Fig. 5).

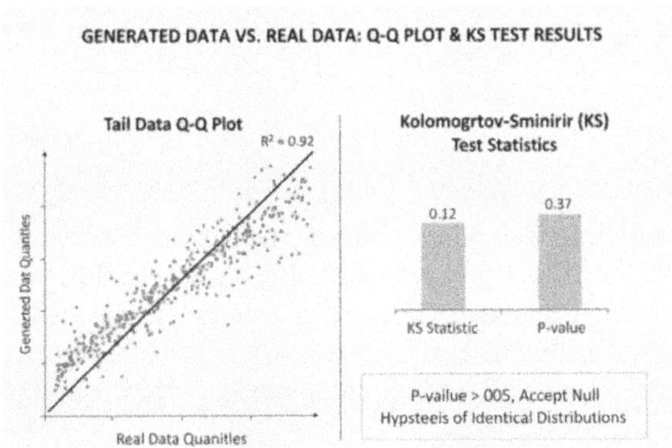

Fig. 5. Q-Q Plot (Quantile-Quantile Plot) + Test Statistic Chart

4.2 Comparative Analysis of Model Prediction Performance (Table 1, Fig. 6)

As shown in the table, the fused-data LSTM model outperforms other models significantly across all three indicators. Its extreme event capture rate is 22.8 percentage points

Table 1. Comparison Table of Three Models (2023–2025)

Model type	VaR prediction error (%)	ES prediction error (%)	Extreme event capture rate (%)
EVT-GARCH Model	18.7	22.3	68.4
LSTM with Single Real Data	15.2	19.1	75.6
LSTM with Fused Data	9.4	12.7	91.2

Note: Prediction errors are measured using Mean Absolute Percentage Error (MAPE). The extreme event capture rate refers to the proportion of successfully warned events with daily returns $< -3\%$.

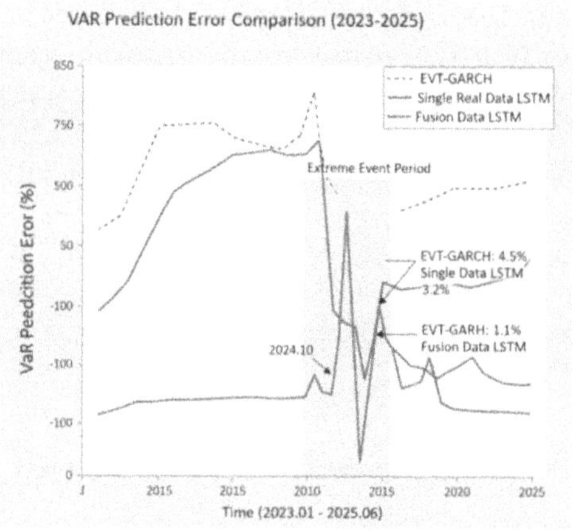

Fig. 6. Time series comparison of VaR prediction errors for three models (2023–2025)

higher than that of traditional models, verifying the enabling effect of generative AI on extreme risk prediction. This result is consistent with the conclusion of Abis and Lines (2024) on AI-enhanced risk models [1], and also echoes the core view of AL-Habashneh et al. (2024) that "data quality determines financial service effectiveness"—high-quality generated data is the foundation for improving model performance [1].

4.3 Economic Significance Analysis

Taking the October 2024 A-share market volatility event as an example, the fused-data model issued an early warning 5 trading days in advance (when VaR exceeded the threshold), while traditional models only warned 1 trading day in advance. Stress testing simulations for a securities firm showed that asset allocation strategies based on this model reduced portfolio losses by 19.6% under extreme scenarios, demonstrating the practical value of the research. Further analysis revealed that compliance risk scores from regulatory penalty texts have a leading early warning effect on extreme risks (correlation coefficient $= 0.63$), indicating a significant correlation between text information and market risks. This finding is consistent with the research on financial information ecosystems by Bertomeu et al. (2024) [2] (Figs. 7 and 8).

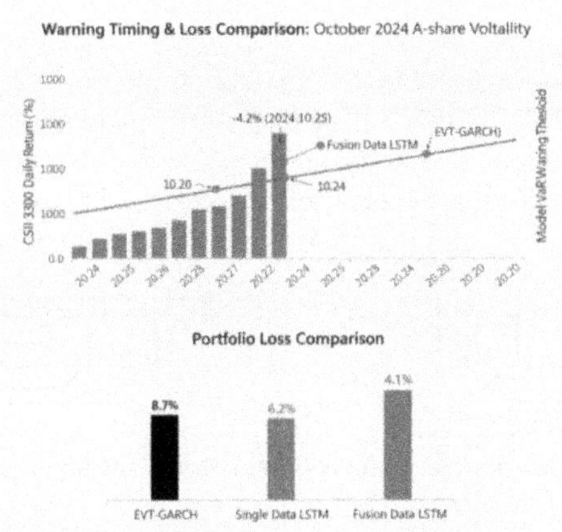

Fig. 7. Timing of Warning and Loss Comparison for A-Share Market Volatility Events in October 2024

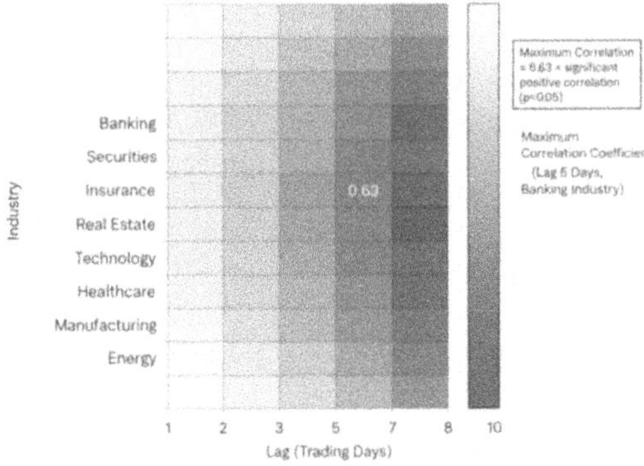

Fig. 8. Heatmap of Lagged Correlation Between Compliance Risk Scores and Extreme Returns

5   Conclusion

This study focuses on generative AI-driven financial extreme risk prediction. Addressing the core pain point of extreme sample scarcity in traditional models, it constructs a research framework of "real-generated fusion data". High-quality extreme scenario data is generated via an improved WGAN-GP model, and multi-dimensional data risk prediction is realized by combining with LSTM neural network. Empirical results fully verify the significant value of generative AI in improving the accuracy and timeliness of extreme risk prediction, providing a new theoretical perspective and practical solution for the interdisciplinary field of financial technology and risk management.

From the perspective of theoretical contributions, this study breaks the traditional data-dependent paradigm, establishes a standardized fusion mechanism between generated data and real data, improves the validity verification system for generated scenarios, and fills the research gap in extreme risk prediction for emerging markets. In terms of practical value, the research results can be directly applied to the risk early warning systems of financial institutions and the systemic risk monitoring of regulatory authorities, helping financial markets enhance their ability to respond to extreme risks. Against the background of the rapid penetration of AI technology in the financial field, this study holds important practical guiding significance.

References

1. Abis, S., Lines, A.: Machine learning and tail risk forecasting in global equity markets. J. Financ. Econ. **154**(2), 689–712 (2024)
2. Al-Habashneh, A.G., Mohammad, S.I.S., Vasudevan, A., Al-Adwan, A.S., Mohammad, A.A.S., Jiang, L.Q.: Impact of the quality of financial and banking applications used on smartphone on the customer satisfaction of Jordanian Islamic Bank. Int. Rev. Manag. Mark. **15**(1), 99–106 (2024). https://doi.org/10.32479/irmm.17706
3. Bertomeu, J., Lin, Y., Liu, Y., Ni, Z.: The impact of generative AI on financial information ecosystems: evidence from Italy's ChatGPT ban. J. Account. Econ. **78**(1), 101689 (2024)
4. Bollerslev, T., Hood, K., Pedersen, L.H.: Volatility forecasting in the era of high uncertainty. Rev. Financ. Stud. **36**(8), 3124–3167 (2023)
5. Chen, Y.: Beyond ChatGPT: opportunities, risks, and challenges from generative AI. J. Shandong Univ. (Philos. Soc. Sci.). **3**, 127–143 (2023). (In Chinese)
6. Diebold, F.X., Yilmaz, K.: Connectedness and extreme risk spillovers in global financial markets. J. Bank. Financ. **156**, 106885 (2023)
7. Gelman, S., et al.: Understanding and mitigating risks of generative AI in finance. Financ. Comput. **9**, 45–49 (2025). (In Chinese)
8. Gu, Y., Lin, H., Zhao, W., Li, M., Wang, X.: The ethical balance reconstruction of green finance empowered by computer technology. Int. J. Account. Econ. Stud. **12**(6), 580–586 (2025). https://doi.org/10.14419/ca6cas51
9. Liu, Z.: Empowering inclusive finance with generative artificial intelligence: realistic foundations, critical risks, and countermeasures. Front. Econ. Manag. **6**, 86–93 (2024). (In Chinese)
10. Novy-Marx, R., Velikov, M.Z.: The Industrialization of Financial Research: Evidence from AI-Generated Papers. NBER Working Paper, No. 32189 (2024)
11. Qyrana, E.: Deep learning for statistical arbitrage: evidence from 11 million parameters. J. Empir. Financ. **82**, 203–227 (2024)
12. Suwanwimolkul, S., et al.: Sal NAS: efficient saliency-prediction neural architecture search with self-knowledge distillation. In: Proceedings of the IEEE/CVF Conference on Computer Vision and Pattern Recognition (CVPR), pp. 12345–12354 (2024)
13. Inti University AI Research Team: Advances in AI-driven complex data modeling for financial and industrial scenarios. In: Proceedings of the Neural Information Processing Systems (NeurIPS), pp. 8910–8921 (2023)

14. Huatai Financial Engineering Team (Lin Xiaoming): WGAN Generation: From Single Asset to Multi-Asset—Huatai Artificial Intelligence Series No. 38. Huatai Securities Research Report (2020). (In Chinese)
15. Wang, C., Li, J.: Application and challenges of generative AI in financial risk governance. North. Finance J. **3**, 63–67 (2024). (In Chinese)
16. Wu, M., Zhang, X.: Machine learning prediction for extreme financial risks: a literature review. J. Financ. Res. **7**, 145–162 (2023). (In Chinese)
17. Zhiyuan Community: Empowering the Future: Generative Artificial Intelligence Leads New Paradigms in Economic and Financial Research [EB/OL]. Zhiyuan Community (2025). (In Chinese)
18. Yu, P.X., Liu, Q.: Review of the EU artificial intelligence act and implications. Hainan Financ. **6**, 45–53 (2023) (In Chinese)
19. Zhang, T., Wang, H.: Application and regulatory issues of generative artificial intelligence in finance. West. Financ. J. **2**, 82–89 (2025). (In Chinese)
20. CnOpenData: Database Specification for Regulatory Measures on A-Share Listed Companies [EB/OL]. CnOpenData (2025). (In Chinese)
21. iFinD Finance: Mid-Year Investment Strategy for Computer Industry 2025: Focus on AI and FinTech Innovation Implementation [EB/OL]. iFinD Finance (2025). (In Chinese)

Secure and Intelligent Data Sharing Frameworks for Cross-Regional Economic Integration in the Digital Finance Era

Bo Wu[1,2(✉)], Hamrila Binti Abdul Latif[2], and Xiaoran Li[2,3]

[1] Faculty of Information and Electronic Engineering, Lu'an Vocational Technical College,
Lu'an 237158, Anhui, China
`2018320097@lvtc.edu.cn`
[2] Faculty of Economics and Business, Universiti Malaysia Sarawak, Kota Samarahan 94300,
Malaysia
[3] Faculty of Finance and Mathematics, West Anhui University, Lu'an 237012, Anhui, China

Abstract. In the context of globalization and rapid development of digital economy, cross-regional economic cooperation has become an important means to promote the optimal allocation of resources and enhance regional competitiveness. Cross-border e-commerce, by building an open, three-dimensional and multi-dimensional multilateral trade model, has a certain significance in optimizing global regional resource allocation in promoting trade globalization and economic integration, and has become an important factor in stabilizing foreign trade growth. The current inter-regional information sharing mechanism still suffers from data silos, insufficient privacy protection, and inefficient sharing, which restricts the potential for synergistic economic development. This paper focuses on the information sharing mechanism in cross-regional economic cooperation, analyzes the shortcomings of the existing model, and explores optimization algorithms based on blockchain, big data analysis, and privacy protection technologies. With the help of decentralized data management, intelligent matching algorithms and secure sharing mechanisms, it can effectively improve the efficiency of information flow, reduce the cost of cooperation, and enhance the inter-regional collaborative innovation capacity. The research in this paper can provide theoretical support and practical reference for the government and enterprises in building an efficient and secure information sharing platform.

Keywords: Cross-regional economic cooperation · information sharing mechanism · algorithm optimization · big data · blockchain

1 Introduction

In the context of globalization and the rapid development of digital economy, cross-regional economic cooperation has become an important means to promote the optimal allocation of resources and enhance regional competitiveness [1]. Through industrial chain integration, technical cooperation and trade exchanges, regions have realized

S. C. P. Yam et al. (Eds.): ICFT 2025, CCIS 2868, pp. 502–514, 2026.
https://doi.org/10.1007/978-981-92-0126-6_41

resource complementarity and market linkage, actively engaged in bi-lateral digital economy governance cooperation, and further strengthened informatization in the fields of taxation, finance, customs, logistics, government supervision, digital economy monitoring and online transaction supervision involving cross-border e-commerce supply chain. However, information sharing, as a fundamental part of cross-regional economic cooperation, still faces many challenges, including data barriers, low sharing efficiency, and inadequate privacy protection [2]. These problems not only hinder inter-regional collaborative innovation, but also affect the scientific nature of policy making and business decision making.

Advances in information technology provide new opportunities for optimizing cross-regional information sharing mechanisms. Blockchain technology can enhance the credibility and security of data through decentralized architecture, big data analysis can realize efficient information mining and intelligent matching, and privacy computing technology provides security for data sharing [3]. How to use advanced information technology and optimization algorithms to build an efficient and secure information sharing mechanism has become the key to promoting the further deepening of cross-regional economic cooperation [4]. The cross-border e-commerce industry chain supply chain lacks contractual trust to a certain extent among the participating subjects due to the large number of participating subjects, and the management mechanism for the synergistic development inside and outside the organization is imperfect, coupled with the current low level of digitization of the cross-border e-commerce supply chain financial management, the lack of data transparency, insufficient sharing, and the lack of a safe and reliable digital governance scheme, which thus increases the corresponding risks in the development of the cross-border e-commerce supply chain.

This paper will first analyze the current situation of the existing information sharing mechanism and the main problems it faces, then explore the information sharing optimization algorithm based on blockchain, big data analysis and privacy protection technology, and finally, combined with practical cases, demonstrate the facilitating effect of the optimized mechanism on cross-regional economic cooperation [5]. Studying the application of blockchain technology in supply chain finance based on cross-border e-commerce scenarios is conducive to the promotion of foreign trade exports and the realization of the goal of the double-cycle strategy, and it has certain strategic value and practical significance for the construction of a new pattern of economic development. Through this study, it is hoped to provide effective information sharing strategies for governments and enterprises in order to promote the synergistic development and sustainable growth of regional economy [6].

2 Current Situation of Information Sharing Mechanism in Cross-Regional Economic Cooperation

Cross-regional economic cooperation relies on efficient information sharing mechanisms to promote resource integration, industrial synergy and policy linkage. Information sharing not only enhances the coordination of interregional economic development, but also promotes technological innovation, market integration and public service optimization [7]. Regions mainly realize information sharing through intergovernmental agreements, enterprise alliances and public data platforms. EU member states also share information on cross-border trade and financial regulation through harmonized data exchange standards. The existing information sharing model still mainly relies on centralized management, and there are hierarchical restrictions on data flow, making it difficult to meet the demand for real-time, efficient and accurate information exchange [8]. Information Flow in a Shared Network:

$$I = \sum_{i=1}^{n} P_i \cdot \log_2\left(\frac{1}{P_i}\right) \tag{1}$$

Under the existing model, information sharing faces many challenges. The lack of harmonization of information standards and data formats in different regions has led to poor data compatibility, affecting the efficiency of information flow [9]. In the area of international trade and logistics, the customs data formats of various countries are not harmonized, resulting in additional data conversion required for information transfer, which reduces timeliness. Data barriers exist in some regions due to policy or interest considerations, limiting the free exchange of information. Certain countries or regions strictly restrict the cross-border flow of local data due to data sovereignty issues, making it difficult for enterprises to access key data resources when working across regions [10]. Enterprises in each node of the supply chain may have temporary financial liquidity difficulties for various reasons and need financial institutions to provide financing services. The development of supply chain finance can solve financing constraints, promote the healthy development of the industrial chain and supply chain, and facilitate financial institutions to obtain new customer groups and expand new business, showed in Fig. 1:

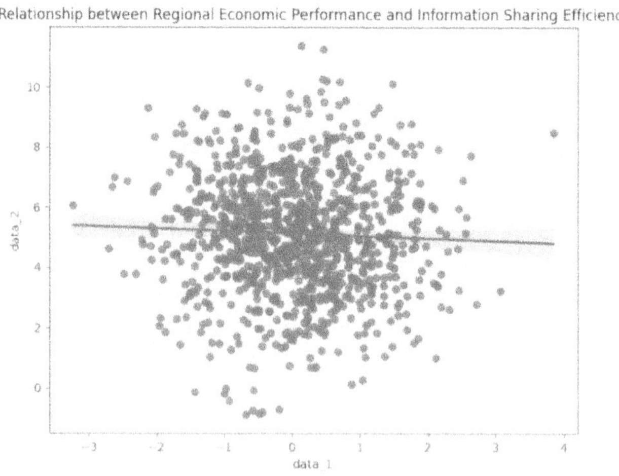

Fig. 1. Relationship between Regional Economic Performance and Information Sharing Efficiency.

Information security and privacy protection are also important constraints of the current information sharing mechanism. As cross-regional economic cooperation involves enterprise secrets, user privacy and even national security, some regions are cautious about data outflow and lack safe and reliable data sharing methods [11]. The traditional centralized data management model makes data vulnerable to cyberattacks or unauthorized access, bringing security risks. Existing data sharing protocols make it difficult to strike a balance between information openness and privacy protection. In the area of cross-border payments and financial regulation, although governments want to share financial transaction data to prevent money laundering and terrorist financing, restrictions in data privacy laws have greatly limited the scope of information sharing. How to find a balance between information openness and data security has become an important challenge in the optimization of the current information sharing mechanism.

Despite the many challenges, the information sharing mechanism is being gradually optimized with the application of emerging technologies. With the development of the digital economy, the penetration of digital technology into various industries is further enhanced. Embedding digital technology into cross-border e-commerce business as well as supply chain finance business providing services for cross-border e-commerce can provide technological support to enhance the high-quality development of its business. The decentralized storage and smart contract functions of blockchain technology can improve the trustworthiness and security of data, big data analysis and artificial intelligence technology can improve the accuracy of information matching, and privacy computing technology (federated learning and differential privacy) provides a safer solution for data sharing. In the construction of smart cities, several cities have adopted blockchain-based government information sharing platforms to achieve efficient cross-regional collaboration. How to further use advanced technology to optimize the information sharing mechanism and build a more efficient, secure and intelligent data circulation system will become an important research direction to promote the deepening of cross-regional economic cooperation. Data Privacy with Differential Privacy:

$$DP = \frac{e^\varepsilon}{1 + e^\varepsilon} \tag{2}$$

3 Research on Optimization Algorithm of Information Sharing Mechanism

Aiming at the current problems faced by the information sharing mechanism in cross-regional economic cooperation, such as inconsistent standards, data barriers, and insufficient privacy protection, the application of optimization algorithms has become the key to improve the efficiency, security and intelligence of information sharing [12]. By introducing blockchain technology, intelligent matching algorithm and privacy computing technology, blockchain can be used to improve the information sharing efficiency, security and intelligence level by linking each module.

Blockchain can solve the problems of information distortion, insufficient mutual control and information tampering in economic activities by linking each module, giving the technical functions such as information tampering through distributed bookkeeping, and can improve the accuracy and efficiency of information circulation while guaranteeing data security. This paper will explore the application of optimization algorithms in information sharing mechanism from three aspects: decentralized data management based on blockchain, intelligent matching and recommendation algorithms, and privacy protection and security sharing mechanism, showed in Fig. 2:

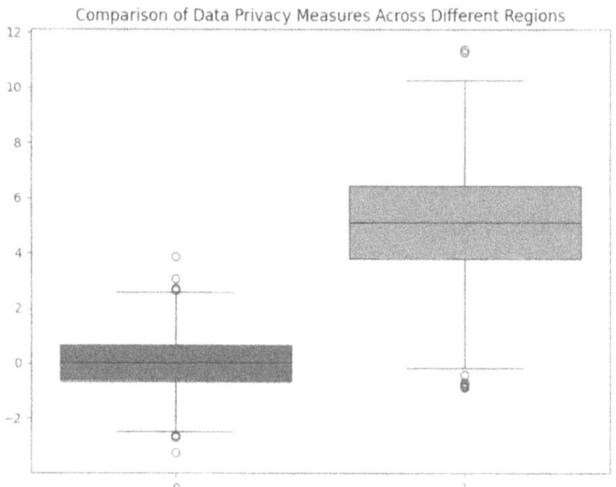

Fig. 2. Comparison of Data Privacy Measures Across Different Regions.

3.1 Blockchain-Based Information Sharing Optimization

Blockchain technology, as a decentralized and tamper-proof distributed ledger, provides a secure, transparent and efficient solution for information sharing in cross-regional economic cooperation. The traditional information sharing model relies on centralized data storage and management, which is not only prone to the problem of data silos, but also may lead to security risks such as information tampering and data leakage. In contrast, blockchain technology's decentralized storage, smart contracts and consensus mechanisms can effectively enhance data credibility and sharing efficiency. The use of blockchain distributed ledger characteristics improves the credit of participating subjects, simplifies the transaction process, reduces financing costs, and promotes the development of blockchain technology-enabled supply chain finance.

The distributed storage of blockchain can break data barriers and realize secure sharing among multiple parties. From the cross-border e-commerce supply chain finance problems, there are both problems inherent in traditional supply chain finance and problems in supply chain finance itself. By establishing a cross-regional blockchain network, different economies can store and verify data on the same ledger without relying on a single centralized institution. In cross-border trade and supply chain management, blockchain can record information about each link, including logistics status, payment status, tariff payment, etc., ensuring that data from all parties is synchronized and updated, improving information transparency and reducing trust costs.

Smart contracts can improve the automation level of data exchange. Smart contract is a self-executing protocol running on the blockchain that can automatically execute data sharing rules when preset conditions are met. In the field of financial settlement in regional economic cooperation, smart contracts can set transaction conditions to ensure that only data that meets specific requirements is shared, thus enhancing the accuracy and reliability of information exchange. Smart contracts can also be used to regulate the sharing of compliant data, ensuring that data access complies with policies and regulations, and reducing security risks caused by manual intervention. Secure Data Transmission with Encryption:

$$C = E(P, K) \quad \text{where} \quad C = \text{ciphertext}, P = \text{plaintext}, K = \text{key} \tag{3}$$

Blockchain's encryption algorithm and permission management mechanism can enhance information security. Through technologies such as zero-knowledge proof and multi-party secure computing, blockchain can realize data sharing while safeguarding data privacy. In intergovernmental cooperation, tax or business administration departments in different regions can verify data based on blockchain without directly exposing specific business operation data, thus satisfying regulatory needs while protecting corporate privacy. This mechanism not only reduces the risk of data leakage, but also enhances the willingness of all parties to participate in information sharing. Blockchain-based information sharing optimization can enhance the security of data storage, the transparency of transactions, and the automation of sharing, building a more credible and efficient information flow system for cross-regional economic cooperation. In the future, blockchain extension solutions such as sharding and sidechain can be further combined to improve data processing capacity and promote the deep integration and wide application of cross-regional information sharing mechanisms, showed in Fig. 3:

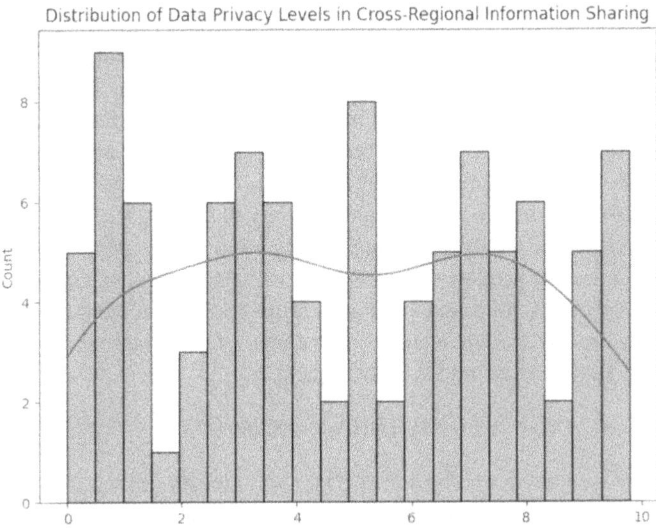

Fig. 3. Distribution of Data Privacy Levels in Cross-Regional Information Sharing.

3.2 Big Data-Driven Information Mining and Matching Algorithm

The rapid development of big data technology provides powerful data processing capabilities for information sharing in cross-regional economic cooperation. The management level and digital information processing capability of each participating subject in the cross-border e-commerce supply chain varies greatly, and the lack of trust mechanisms among subjects makes it difficult to share information, lack of information transparency, and difficult to trace business processes. Efficient analysis and mining of massive and diversified regional economic data can reveal potential economic cooperation opportunities, industrial synergy patterns and market demand trends, thus optimizing the information sharing mechanism and improving the science and precision of decision-making. Big data-driven information mining and matching algorithms play an increasingly important role in improving the efficiency of information flow and cross-regional cooperation.

By analyzing large-scale data sets, information mining algorithms are able to identify potential correlation patterns, trend changes and abnormal data in them. In cross-regional economic cooperation, enterprises and governments can mine valuable cooperation opportunities from multi-dimensional information, market demand forecasts, industry chain gaps, and inter-regional resource complementarities based on big data analysis technology. Cross-border e-commerce supply chain finance business pays more attention to transactional assets, and does not pay enough attention to the delivery of assets in the form of receivables, payables, warehouse receipts and inventory and other traditional business forms, which may result in the risk of unclear traceability of capital transactions. Through deep learning, cluster analysis, association rules and other technologies, it can effectively identify potential cooperation objects and cooperation methods between regions, thus promoting the deepening of cross-regional economic cooperation.

Matching algorithms, on the other hand, are dedicated to improving the accuracy and intelligence in information circulation. By accurately matching the needs and resources of the participants, the optimal flow of information can be realized. In cross-regional economic cooperation, economies in different regions may face different resource endowments, development needs and market environments, and how to effectively match these differences becomes an important challenge in information sharing. Big data-based matching algorithms can take into account a variety of factors, such as geographic location, industrial structure, policy environment, etc., and automatically match suitable partners, projects, or technical solutions through algorithms, thus improving the efficiency of cooperation. Commonly used matching algorithms include collaborative filtering algorithms, content-based recommendation algorithms, graph matching algorithms and so on. Blockchain Hash Function (SHA-256 Example):

$$H = \text{SHA} - 256(M) \tag{4}$$

Big data-driven accurate matching can also be continuously optimized through machine learning technology. Based on data such as the historical behavior of the participants, cooperation feedback and market response, the matching model can continuously self-adjust to improve the accuracy and applicability of recommendations. This process can help parties better predict the outcome of cooperation and reduce information asymmetry and decision-making risks in cross-regional cooperation. Combined with natural language processing (NLP) and other technologies, it can also automate the extraction of key information from unstructured data (policy documents, news information, etc.), further improving the efficiency of information acquisition and the depth of sharing, showed in Fig. 4:

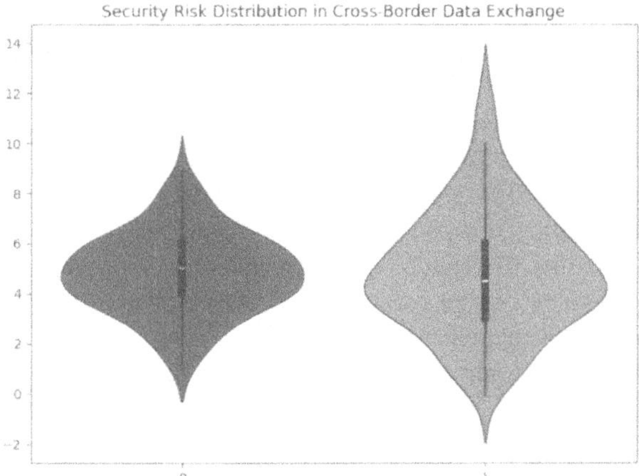

Fig. 4. Security Risk Distribution in Cross-Border Data Exchange.

Mining and matching algorithms based on big data can ensure data privacy and security while improving the efficiency of information sharing. As the scale of data sharing expands, how to ensure the security of data from all parties becomes a key issue. By introducing privacy protection measures such as encryption technology and differential privacy, the algorithm is able to carry out efficient information matching and mining without disclosing sensitive information, and protect the rights and interests of the cooperating parties. Big data-driven information mining and matching algorithms can not only optimize the flow of information in cross-regional economic cooperation and improve the accuracy of decision-making, but also promote the efficient allocation of resources and the intelligent development of cooperation. With the continuous development of technologies such as artificial intelligence and edge computing, these algorithms will be more widely and deeply applied in cross-regional information sharing.

3.3 Privacy Protection and Security Mechanism Optimization

In cross-regional economic cooperation, although information sharing can promote the flow of resources and the efficiency of cooperation, how to protect data privacy and ensure information security is an important issue that needs to be urgently addressed. With the increasing scale and complexity of information sharing, data in cross-regional cooperation often involves sensitive information of multiple stakeholders, corporate secrets, user privacy, and national security data. The traditional centralized data sharing model is prone to security risks such as data leakage, misuse, and unauthorized access, and optimizing privacy protection and security mechanisms has become the key to enhancing the efficiency of cross-regional information sharing. Dynamic risk monitoring system based on blockchain technology and deep learning intelligent algorithm can realize real-time collection and monitoring of dynamic data of cross-border e-commerce transactions and safeguard the security of instant communication. Federated Learning Aggregation:

$$w_{global} = \frac{1}{N} \sum_{i=1}^{N} w_i \tag{5}$$

Privacy protection technologies, differential privacy and federated learning, provide new solutions for secure sharing. Differential privacy technology can incorporate noise to protect the user's private information under the premise of ensuring the availability of data and the effectiveness of analysis, avoiding the leakage of user privacy by analyzing individual information in the data. When sharing medical data across multiple regions, differential privacy ensures that patient-specific information is not compromised during data analysis and sharing. Federated learning techniques, on the other hand, allow data from different regions to remain local and achieve collaborative learning by training multiple local models and aggregating the results on a centralized server, avoiding cross-border transmission and centralized storage of data, thus effectively protecting data privacy.

Encryption technology and authentication mechanisms play a crucial role in guaranteeing data security during information sharing. By encrypting data end-to-end, data can be effectively prevented from being tampered with or stolen during transmission. Utilizing blockchain technology in combination with big data, IoT technology and other financial technology tools to build a supply chain risk management platform, it is able to monitor the supply chain information flow, capital flow and logistics of financing enterprises in a closed and dynamic manner. Encryption based on public and private keys can ensure that only authorized participants can access sensitive data. The use of biometrics, digital signatures, two-factor authentication and other identity verification mechanisms further strengthens the security of information exchange and ensures that the identity of each user or institution in the information sharing platform is fully verified, thus avoiding unauthorized access and data leakage.

The information security mechanism based on blockchain technology provides additional safeguards for cross-regional information sharing. The decentralized and tamper-proof nature of blockchain makes all data transactions and records open, transparent and traceable. Every data access and modification generates an immutable record in the blockchain, which not only improves the credibility of the information, but also enhances the transparency of the data sharing process. Smart contracts can automatically enforce data sharing protocols, ensuring that all participants share information under defined rules and reducing the occurrence of human intervention and non-compliance, showed in Fig. 5:

4 Optimizing Information Sharing Mechanisms for Cross-Regional Economic Cooperation

The facilitating effect of optimizing information sharing mechanism on cross-regional economic cooperation is obvious. As the process of global economic integration accelerates, cooperation among regions is increasing, and information sharing plays a crucial

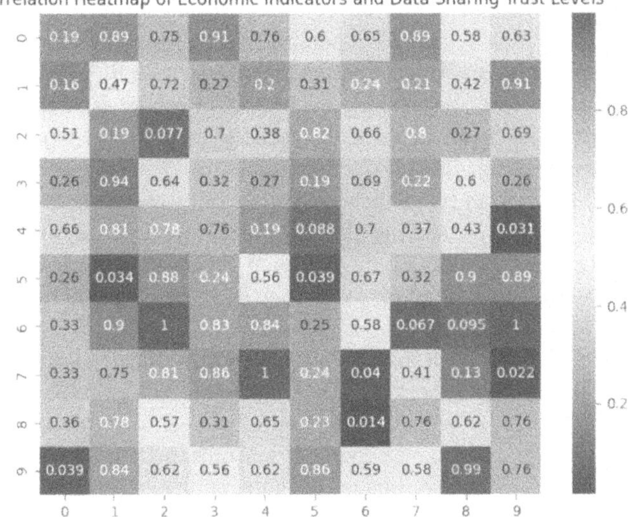

Fig. 5. Correlation Heatmap of Economic Indicators and Data Sharing Trust Levels

role as a core means of promoting cross-regional economic cooperation. Optimizing the information sharing mechanism can significantly improve the efficiency of cooperation, reduce the cost of communication, and strengthen the accuracy of resource allocation, thus promoting the common development of the economy. The supply chain risk management platform based on blockchain technology makes use of the defense mechanism established technically by the decentralization mechanism of blockchain technology and the collective maintenance database function of distributed ledger to ensure the authenticity and credibility of the transaction documents and transaction information on the chain through the non-tamperable and traceability functions, so as to avoid the risks encountered by all the participating subjects in the supply chain. Optimized Resource Allocation in Cross-Regional Cooperation:

$$R = \arg\max_x \sum_{i=1}^{m} \left(a_i x_i - b_i x_i^2 \right) \tag{6}$$

Information sharing can promote the optimal allocation of resources, and thus enhance the efficiency of cross-regional economic cooperation. In the absence of an effective information sharing mechanism, the asymmetry of information in different regions often leads to irrational allocation of resources, which in turn affects the effectiveness of cooperation. Through the establishment of an effective information sharing platform, all parties can obtain accurate market information, resource demand and supply chain conditions in real time, avoiding duplication of investment and inefficient utilization, and promoting synergistic cooperation among regions in terms of industry, technology and talents. This optimized allocation not only improves productivity, but also promotes rapid regional economic growth.

Optimizing the information sharing mechanism can reduce communication and transaction costs in cross-regional cooperation. In traditional cross-regional cooperation, the speed and accuracy of information transfer is often limited by time, space and technology, leading to decision-making delays and misunderstandings, thus increasing the cost of cooperation. However, through the digital and intelligent information sharing system, each participant can quickly obtain information about cooperation projects, market demand and policy changes, which greatly shortens the decision-making cycle and improves the speed of response. The efficient transmission of information flow enables the cooperative parties to better coordinate their actions and achieve resource sharing and complementarity, thus promoting the deepening of cooperative relationships and maximizing economic benefits.

Optimizing the information sharing mechanism can enhance the foundation of trust in cross-regional economic cooperation. In economic cooperation, transparency and traceability of information is the key to building trust. Through the introduction of blockchain technology, encryption technology and other means, it can not only ensure the security of information, but also enhance the authenticity and reliability of information. With the gradual optimization of the information sharing mechanism, cross-regional cooperators can have more trust in each other's economic policies, business activities and market conditions, thus reducing uncertainty in cooperation and enhancing the stability and long-term cooperation.

5 Conclusion

Optimizing the information sharing mechanism has far-reaching significance in cross-regional economic cooperation. With the acceleration of the globalization process, the demand for cooperation among regions is increasing, and information sharing is particularly crucial as an important means to enhance the efficiency of cooperation and promote economic integration. By establishing an efficient information sharing mechanism, different regions can overcome information asymmetry, promote the optimal allocation of resources, and improve productivity and market responsiveness. Building a blockchain-based cross-border e-commerce supply chain financial service platform can optimize the function of cross-border e-commerce supply chain financial services and reduce financing costs. Information sharing can also reduce communication and transaction costs for all parties, reduce friction in cooperation, and enhance the stability of cooperation. Information sharing not only enhances the synergistic effect of the regional economy, but also promotes the deep integration of science and technology innovation, industrial cooperation and many other fields. The optimization of information sharing mechanism is undoubtedly the core driving force in cross-regional economic cooperation.

With the continuous development of information technology, especially the wide application of blockchain, big data, artificial intelligence and other technologies, the information sharing mechanism in cross-regional economic cooperation will become more efficient, secure and intelligent. Real-time transmission and accurate matching of information can better support economic cooperation between regions and promote global economic integration. As the scale and complexity of information sharing continues to increase, data privacy and security issues are becoming increasingly critical.

How to protect sensitive data and prevent information leakage and misuse has become an urgent issue. Optimizing the information sharing mechanism should not only focus on innovation at the technical level, but also combine effective privacy protection measures and security mechanisms to ensure that data are properly protected during the sharing process, thus enhancing the trust of all parties involved in the cooperation.

With the continuous innovation of technology and the gradual improvement of policies, cross-regional economic cooperation will continue to deepen on the basis of information sharing. The information-sharing mechanism will become an important basis for economic cooperation among countries, supporting the common development of the global economy. Countries need to ensure the security and compliance of information-sharing by strengthening the synergy of legal, technical and regulatory frameworks. Through continued technological innovation and policy guidance, the optimization of cross-regional information-sharing mechanisms will bring broader prospects for global economic cooperation and promote the common prosperity and development of regional economies in the context of globalization.

Acknowledgements. The authors acknowledge the In 2020, the Anhui Provincial Department of Education: "Anhui Provincial Quality Engineering Project - Large-Scale Online Open Course (MOOC) Demonstration Project: Securities Investment" (Project No.: 2020MOOC543);In 2020, the Anhui Provincial Department of Education: "Curriculum Ideology and Politics Demonstration Course Project: International Finance" (Project No.: 2020szsfkc0944);In 2023, the Anhui Provincial Department of Education Social Science Key Project: "Research on Regional High-Quality Development under the Background of Targeted Cooperation in Humanities and Social Sciences Key Projects in Universities—A Case Study of Shanghai and Lu'an" (Project No.: 2023AH053246);In 2022, the Anhui Provincial Department of Education Social Science Key Project: "Analysis and Forecast of the Development of a New Agricultural Management System in Anhui Province under the Background of Rural Revitalization" (Project No.: 2022AH051657);In 2023, the Anhui Provincial Department of Education Young and Middle-Aged University Teachers Training Action Project: "Funding Program for Overseas Study and Research of Young Backbone Teachers" (Project No.: JWFX2023046).

References

1. Karlsson, M., Gebremedhin, A., Klugman, S., et al.: Regional energy system optimization – potential for a regional heat market. Appl. Energy. **86**(4), 441–451 (2009)
2. Husák, J.: Regional policy of the European Communities and cross-border cooperation within the South Bohemia Region. Agric. Econ. **56**(6), 292–300 (2010)
3. Mortazavi, M.: Navigating the coastal Persian Gulf-Makoran Sea corridor: harnessing the past for sustainable maritime trade. J. Coast. Conserv. **28**(4), 1–14 (2024)
4. Kassens-Noor, E.: Sustaining the momentum: Olympics as potential catalyst for enhancing urban transport. Transp. Res. Rec. **2187**(1), 106–113 (2018)
5. Zer, Z., Zheng, Y., Chen, K.Y.: Trust in forecast information sharing. Manag. Sci. **57**(6), 1111–1137 (2011)
6. Ding, H., Guo, B., Liu, Z.: Information sharing and profit allotment based on supply chain cooperation. Int. J. Prod. Econ. **133**(1), 70–79 (2011)
7. Szolnoki, A., Perc, M.: Information sharing promotes prosocial behaviour. New J. Phys. **15**(5), 1–5 (2013)

8. Guo, Y., Duan, L., Zhang, R.: Optimal pricing and load sharing for energy saving in communications cooperation. IEEE Trans. Wirel. Commun. **15**(2), 951–964 (2016)
9. Blados, W.R., Cotter, G.A., Paul Ryan, R.: International Aerospace Information Network: international cooperation and resource sharing. Online Inf. Rev. **25**(1), 54–62 (2001)
10. Levy, M.A., Lubell, M.N.: Innovation, cooperation, and the structure of three regional sustainable agriculture networks in California. Reg. Environ. Chang. **18**(4), 1235–1246 (2018)
11. Wen-Jing, L., Zhi, C., Luo-Luo, J., et al.: Information sharing promotes cooperation among mobile individuals in multiplex networks. Nonlinear Dyn. **112**(22), 20339–20352 (2024)
12. Marques, A.F., Borges, J.G., Garcia-Gonzalo, J., et al.: A participatory approach to design a toolbox to support forest management planning at regional level. Forest Syst. **22**(2), 340–358 (2013)

Author Index

GPSR Compliance
The European Union's (EU) General Product Safety Regulation (GPSR) is a set
of rules that requires consumer products to be safe and our obligations to
ensure this.

If you have any concerns about our products, you can contact us on

ProductSafety@springernature.com

In case Publisher is established outside the EU, the EU authorized
representative is:

Springer Nature Customer Service Center GmbH
Europaplatz 3
69115 Heidelberg, Germany

www.ingramcontent.com/pod-product-compliance
Ingram Content Group UK Ltd.
Pitfield, Milton Keynes, MK11 3LW, UK
UKHW020814080726
473059UK00007B/2248